The Coast Guardsman's Manual

SEVENTH EDITION

The Coast Guardsman's Manual

Revised by Captain Robert F. Bennett,
U.S. Coast Guard (Retired)

Naval Institute Press
Annapolis, Maryland

Copyright © 1983
by the United States Naval Institute
Annapolis, Maryland

All rights reserved. No part of this book
may be reproduced without written permission from
the publisher.

Library of Congress Catalog Card Number: 52–61512
ISBN: 0–87021–118–8

All photographs not otherwise credited are official
U.S. Coast Guard photos.

Printed in the United States of America

C. 1

Contents

	Foreword	vii
	Preface	ix
	Acknowledgments	xi
1	History and Missions	3
2	Organization	27
3	Leadership and Discipline	47
4	Personal Standards	61
5	Military Fundamentals	81
6	Uniforms and Awards	119
7	Watches and Routines	141
8	Ship Construction	177
9	Seamanship	197
10	Boathandling	245
11	Communications	269
12	Weapons	293
13	Navigation	309
14	Rules of the Road	337
15	General Drills	353
16	Damage Control and Fire Fighting	373
17	Survival	407
18	Swimming and Lifesaving	441

19	First Aid	465
20	Safety	509
21	Maintenance	539
22	Security	557
23	Ships and Aircraft	573
24	Customs and Ceremony	591
25	Rates and Ratings	617
26	Career Information	629
27	Other Mariners	659
	Appendixes	
A	Ribbons of Decorations and Awards	703
B	Allied Naval Signal Pennants and Flags and International Alphabet Flags	706
C	USCG Buoyage of the United States	709
D	Channel Markers	710
E	Storm Warning Signals	711
F	Beaufort Scale	712
	Notes on Sources and Suggested Reading Material	719
	Index	723

Foreword

The Coast Guardsman's Manual is written for all military members of the Coast Guard: officers and enlisted, regulars and reserves, "boots" and "old salts." It is intended as a practical guide to the work and workings of our proud service. We have a long tradition of being where the action is—in a wide variety of missions. So each of us must be a multi-mission resource. We must learn, teach, perform, and lead *well*, in whatever duties we are assigned. Each and every one of us has an important role to play in fulfilling our common goal of unparalleled professional service to our country and humanity. This manual can help you. Make it your friend. Use it to reinforce your own knowledge and your pride in yourself and the United States Coast Guard.

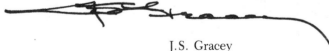

J.S. Gracey
Admiral, U.S. Coast Guard
Commandant

Preface

History, tradition, seamanship, customs, and courtesies are but a few of the many subjects covered in this book. You, the men and women of the Coast Guard, will be required to use the knowledge contained herein throughout your careers.

The Coast Guard men and women who have gone before us in service to our great country have set the course, and we are expected to follow their fine example while we have "the watch." It is every Coast Guard person's responsibility to learn and retain the basic knowledge in this manual, regardless of your rating.

I encourage all of you to "take a round turn" on the skills enumerated in this book so that you can increase your competence, pride, professionalism, and satisfaction while serving in our Coast Guard.

Carl W. Constantine

Carl W. Constantine
Master Chief Petty Officer
of the U.S. Coast Guard

Acknowledgments

The Coast Guard is never without change, and it is this characteristic that has earned the service its reputation and its motto. *The Coast Guardsman's Manual* must be revised from time to time to keep pace with the continuing changes. Undoubtedly, some of the information published in this edition will be out of date by the time it rolls off the presses.

I am especially grateful to a number of persons who helped with this seventh edition. First, I thank the American Red Cross and the National Geographic Society, whose published material on first aid and shark research was of great assistance in updating our manual. In particular, I also wish to thank Lieutenant Phil Glenn and Chief Warrant Officers Dennis George and Chuck Goettsch for their technical assistance, and Sara Jenkins for her help with portions of the manuscript. Deserved thanks also go to the countless other Coast Guard people at Headquarters and other commands who contributed so richly and fully to this effort.

My wife and my daughters provided me with invaluable support both in research and in manuscript preparation. Also, I am singularly grateful to my father, Albert F. Bennett, who taught me to understand and respect the surf. And last, but not least, I wish to express my appreciation to Carol Swartz of the Naval Institute for her patience and outstanding assistance.

The
Coast Guardsman's
Manual

CHAPTER 1

History and Missions

HISTORY—IN PURSUIT OF NATIONAL PURPOSES

Unlike some federal organizations, the United States Coast Guard did not begin at any one time for any single purpose. Instead, today's Coast Guard is a collection of other federal organizations that no longer exist; most of them are long forgotten.

In order to tell the whole organizational history of the Coast Guard properly, it would be necessary to begin with the individual histories of each of those old defunct organizations, which are usually and politely referred to as "predecessor agencies." To write such a history would far exceed the pages available in this manual.

Another way to tell the story of the Coast Guard is to think of the Coast Guard as being the chief agent for the promotion of a whole range of national purposes in the maritime arena. Looking at the service in this way is less complicated and much more attuned to the actual work the Coast Guard now performs. There are many ways to present the national objectives performed by the Coast Guard. Sometimes these duties are called missions, sometimes roles, sometimes programs, and occasionally the word *area* is thrown in to further describe these terms. In an historical sense, however, we might think of the Coast Guard as carrying out the following traditional duties:

promoting safe and efficient marine transportation;
promoting the collection of national revenues;
promoting measures to enhance national security; and

Figure 1–1. A 41-foot boat crewman scans the horizon for a distressed vessel.

promoting the preservation of life and property following maritime incidents.

You will note that the word "promoting" has been used in describing each of these national purposes. This is fitting for the Coast Guard, because the Latin root word for "promote" means "to move forward." In the Preamble to the U.S. Constitution, the authors included the clause "to promote the general welfare." It was this wording that has been used by the U.S. Congress to justify most of the national purposes assigned to the Coast Guard since 1789. While other federal organizations have been created over the ensuing years to "maintain" various things, the Coast Guard predecessors were charged with moving ahead— taking the ball and running with it. Historically, the merging of the predecessor agencies into the Coast Guard took place because, although they were charged with moving forward a national purpose, they took on a "maintain what we have" approach instead.

Coast Guard history can also be viewed as a series of unrelated but important events that can be selectively presented because they establish precedents, reinforce traditions, provide a neat comparison with another military organization, or have some special local interest. The Coast Guard is rich in this kind of history, which encourages pride in our present organization without regard to the identity of the predecessor or the national purpose it was fulfilling.

Leaving a detailed organizational history of the old predecessor agencies to scholars and serious historians, let us view the history of the Coast Guard as being the sum total of the history of itself plus that of its predecessors. Let us see our history as a reflection of national purpose, highlighted by the important events of the past.

One of the first orders of business our founding fathers had to contend with was maritime trade. In those days almost all trade beyond the borders of the United States was done by ships. Different colonies had taken a number of steps to promote safe and efficient marine transportation, but in their new role as states, it was believed that such promotion ought to be national in purpose and be handled by the federal government—at least in so far as building and maintaining the devices that would assist navigation were concerned. The new states may have been anxious to retain control over the pilots who guided vessels into the coastal ports, but the maintenance of expensive structures was something they were happy to pass on to the federal government.

Thus in 1789, the Coast Guard began the business of maintaining lighthouses. Under the supervision of the U.S. Army Corps of Engineers, new lighthouses and beacons were built during the early 1800s with federal funds, and former lighthouses, built by private subscriptions of maritime interests, were taken over by the federal government. The general supervision of this effort to promote safe and efficient marine transportation fell to the Secretary of the Treasury. For many years, this function was performed by the Fifth Auditor of the Treasury, Samuel Pleasanton. In 1852, a special group within the Treasury Department was formed and called The Lighthouse Board. The Board consisted of Army engineers, Navy officers and civilian scientists.

At about the same time that our new nation realized it had a duty to promote safe and efficient marine transportation, it was faced with a greater, more immediate challenge—the successful collection of revenues. In an atmosphere of almost total disregard by some marine interests for the new customs laws, where smuggling of commodities from foreign countries into the U.S. marketplace without paying customs duties was commonplace, this was no mean challenge. The collection of revenues arising from customs fees and tariffs was one of the only ways the new federal government could raise the money required to run the government; there was no income tax in those days! And there were, indeed, costs involved in running the government, particularly if the government was to "provide for the common defense and promote the general welfare," as stated in the Preamble to the Constitution.

In October 1789, Secretary of the Treasury Alexander Hamilton asked the various collectors of customs about the need for boats to protect and ensure revenue collection. Sharp Delany, the collector at Philadelphia, replied that he was already using a vessel for that purpose and fully endorsed the concept. In April of 1790, Hamilton asked Congress to create a Revenue Marine service with a fleet of ten small cutters. As the Continental Navy had been disestablished after the Revolution and would not be reestablished until 1799, there were no armed federal vessels in existence with which a Revenue Marine service could be created.

On 4 August 1790, Congress passed Hamilton's Revenue Cutter Bill, which provided for the construction of the needed boats. The result was the following:

Station	Cutter Name	Rig	Tonnage	Length
New Hampshire	Scammel	Schooner	51	58 ft.
Massachusetts	Massachusetts	Schooner	70	60 ft.
Connecticut	Argus	Schooner	35	48 ft.
New York	Vigilant	Schooner	35	48 ft. Keel
Pennsylvania	General Greene	Sloop	30	Unknown
Maryland	Active	Schooner	50	Unknown
Virginia	Virginia	Schooner	35	40 ft. Keel
North Carolina	Diligence	Schooner	40	Unknown
South Carolina	South Carolina	Schooner	35	Unknown
Georgia	Eagle	Schooner	50	Unknown

The date 4 August 1790 is important to the Coast Guard, because it is celebrated as the Coast Guard's birthday. Even though the nation had announced its intention to promote safe and efficient marine transportation a calendar year earlier in 1789, our national commitment to construct, maintain, and man a fleet of armed vessels for actual law-enforcement operations is of far greater historical significance. It would not be until 1847 that official consideration would be given toward using federal lighthouse people for anything other than maintenance and lamplighting. By that time, the role of Hamilton's armed federal vessels had expanded to meet several other national objectives, including the promotion of safe and efficient marine transportation.

Mr. Hamilton's first ten armed vessels were not large by modern standards. In fact, today we would call them boats, not cutters. Nor were they a single "class" of vessels as the preceding table shows. Despite the absence of uniformity in design, these vessels established the precedent that all ships of the Coast Guard would forever be called cutters.

Scarcely eight years had elapsed from the time that Hamilton first considered using armed federal vessels to promote revenue collection when a new threat emerged. Foreign armed vessels had begun making unprovoked attacks on our merchant marine. On 1 July 1797, Congress authorized the president to "increase the strength of the several Revenue Cutters. . . to defend the sea coast and to repel any hostility. . . ." Thus, the Coast Guard became "multimission," having the two jobs of providing for the common defense as well as collecting revenues. Over the ensuing decades, other national purposes were served by our revenue cutters—specifically, enhancing the preservation of life by rescuing the shipwrecked, and promoting safe transportation by supporting the lighthouse establishment.

In 1838, the Congress responded to a rash of explosions on steamboats. The technology of the steam engine was relatively new, and its application to marine transportation, while economically successful, wasn't always safe when left solely to the steamboat industry. To protect passengers from this risk, Congress enacted a federal steamboat inspection law calling for the enforcement of vessel safety standards. This law and a host of statutes that followed in its wake were enforced by federal inspectors whose job was to prevent maritime disasters and the resulting loss of life. Ultimately, they were very successful. The Coast Guard inspectors also became investigators. The inspector/investigator role expanded to include crew licensing, vessel documentation, protection of ports from dangerous cargoes, the physical security of ports, the safety of waterways, and the preservation of the marine environment. The inspectors, as in the case of other Coast Guardsmen, have also become involved in promoting more than one national purpose. In licensing and documentation, they foster safe and efficient marine transportation, and in port security, they advance measures to enhance national security.

As the middle of the nineteenth century approached, our nation's population swelled from shiploads of European immigrants. New York was their destination, and the coastlines of Long Island, New York, and New Jersey became the final resting places for many of the immigrant packet ships that fell victim to winter storms.

Colonial laws also dealt with the matter of shipwreck as they applied to salvage. Different colonies had different laws, and when the former colonies became states, many of those laws became state laws. Merchants at the principal seaports along our coasts were interested in seeing to it that the goods being carried by ship to and from their ports reached their destinations. Ship owners, on the other hand, did not wish to lose their ships to shipwrecks, and the insurers of those ships had a very great interest in preventing or minimizing the effect of wrecks.

Acting together with the interests of merchants, ship owners, and marine insurers, colonial law combined to create a sort of safety system. Lighthouses were funded and built by local interests. Skilled local navigators, called *pilots,* were required by colonial governments to be employed by masters on board oceangoing vessels. Humane societies were founded to care for shipwreck victims, and in some cases, to engage in rescue operations. Colonies, and later states, established government posts, called variously *wreckmasters, commissioners of vendue, vendue masters,* etc., whose job it was to rally local boat crews, row boats out to the wrecks, rescue the people on board, and save the vessel and cargo if possible. Often the laws provided that the boat crew that rescued the people got the salvage job, too. But the safety system was not very well developed, and there was no lifesaving technology employed other than the use of an experienced and skillful boat crew. If boats could not be launched because of sea conditions, there was little that could be done except to care for the shipwrecked persons who were washed ashore within reach of human hands and to bury the dead.

On 3 August 1848, a physician from New Jersey named Newell, who was also a member of the U.S. Congress, introduced an amendment to a lighthouse appropriation bill to provide $10,000 for "surfboats, rockets, and carronades and other apparatus necessary for the better protection of life and property from shipwreck on the coast of New Jersey, between Sandy Hook and Little Egg Inlet." In an impassioned speech calling for this appropriation, Newell dwelt heavily upon the responsibility of the federal government to promote the general welfare—in other words, to promote the preservation of life and property following a maritime incident. The amendment was passed, and the federal government entered into the search-and-rescue business as a specific objective. A chain of coastal rescue stations, manned by paid crew members, was not begun until 1871; nevertheless, Newell's appropriation did provide the immediate basis for a very effective, volunteer, manned rescue system on the coasts of New Jersey and Long Island, N.Y. In the twenty-two years that the volunteer lifesavers were at work, aided by substantial support from marine insurance interests, about 90 percent of all persons on board vessels shipwrecked in their area reached shore safely. In areas not so protected, and during the years previous to 1848, the existing safety system allowed between 50 percent to 60 percent of those on board wrecks to survive. In the years following the establishment of the full, paid-crew, coastal rescue system, about 99 percent of those on board wrecked vessels made it ashore safely. During those later years, the "lifesavers" (as they were called) of the coastal rescue stations were to expand their role beyond that of solely serving to promote the preservation of life and property following a maritime incident.

The lifesavers were of service to U.S. Customs, being on the lookout for smuggling; hence, they were involved in collecting national revenues. But perhaps the single most important other service they were involved in was that of national security, when they provided over 60 percent of the nation's coastal sentry force during the Spanish-American War.

In discussing the national purposes traditionally assigned to the Coast Guard, law enforcement is not listed. Law enforcement is not listed because virtually everything the Coast Guard does *is* law enforcement! The concept of our moving forward as an organization means that the Coast Guard has actively pursued the will of our citizens as expressed through the Congress in the passage of legislation that became the law of the land. Coast Guard actions have included enforcement operations directed against greedy ship owners whose chief interest was in making money and not in safe and efficient marine transportation, against smugglers who cared little for the national revenue, against saboteurs who would destroy our national security, and against wanton poisoners of our marine environment who would threaten the safety of our lives and property by carelessly or deliberately causing marine pollution incidents. Law enforcement is a way of life for Coast Guardsmen; it is one of the main tools we use in achieving our national objectives. It is a means to an end, but it is not, of itself, an end.

Military Milestones of Coast Guard History

In fulfilling its responsibilities to promote the general welfare, the U.S. Coast Guard was also charged with many duties that were specifically military in nature. Today, these duties are referred to as military operations; they form a very special portion of Coast Guard history and deserve to be treated separately. The record of our military operations can be traced back to the Quasi-War with France and brought forward through the Vietnamese Conflict.

Quasi-War of 1798–1801

The original ten cutters placed into service in 1791 were soon replaced by larger ones. In 1798, the United States was without a navy, the Continental Navy having been disbanded following the Revolutionary War. Aggressive military and naval activity by France resulted in the seizure of several U.S. merchant vessels by armed French vessels on the high seas. The naval response of the United States was to employ the revenue cutters in the defense of our merchant fleet. In these operations, the cutters responded effectively, as they would in future conflicts in support of the nation's naval missions. Especially outstanding were the *Pickering*, Commodore Preble's first command, and the *Eagle*. The latter fought a memorable engagement with the French privateer *Revenge* in 1799, recapturing the American vessels *Nancy* and *Mehitable*.

War of 1812

From 1801 until the war with England in 1812, the cutters were busy enforcing the Embargo and Non-Intercourse Acts. After the War of 1812 began, the cutter *Jefferson* captured the first enemy prize, in June. The cutter *Vigilant* captured the *Dart*. Some cutter actions ended in defeat. The futile defense of the *Surveyor* against the British frigate *Narcissus* impressed Americans and British alike. The most famous action was fought by the cutter *Eagle*. When she was caught by two British ships, her captain ran the ship ashore on Long Island. The crew dragged guns to a cliff top and beat off the enemy. That night they refloated their ship and headed for New Haven, but she could make little speed and the enemy finally captured her.

The end of the war brought no peace for the cutters. For the next quarter century they fought pirates, slavers, smugglers, and Indians. The *Alabama* and the *Louisiana* broke up the notorious La Fitte gang of bandits in the Gulf of Mexico, and the *Dallas* and the *Jackson* fought the Seminole Indians in Florida.

Mexican War

During the war with Mexico (1846–48) cutters performed scout, convoy, towing, and blockade duty, transported troops and supplies, carried mail and dispatches, and put down a mutiny of troops on the *Middlesex*. The cutters *Ewing* and *Legare* delivered rifles to U. S. troops before the battles of Monterey and Buena Vista.

Civil War

During the Civil War, all the military services were torn by officers who "went South" to fight for their native states. To prevent the cutter *McClelland* from being turned over to the Confederates, Secretary Dix issued a dispatch containing the words that became a rallying cry of the North: ". . . If anyone attempts to haul down the American flag, shoot him on the spot."

In May of 1862, President Lincoln and his staff embarked on the *Miami* and cruised down Chesapeake Bay to Norfolk where the Union

Figure 1–2. The side-wheeler *Harriet Lane* was a steam cutter in the Revenue Marine Service. The first warship ordered to sea at the outbreak of the Civil War, she was captured by the Confederates in 1863.

transports, loaded with troops, were anchored. Officers claimed that the water was too shoal for a landing, but that night the *Miami* steamed inshore and landed the President on Confederate soil. Safely back aboard the cutter, Lincoln personally ordered the assault for the next day. It was completely successful.

Spanish-American War

Even before the outbreak of war with Spain, a squadron of cutters patrolled the Straits of Florida to prevent violations of American neutrality. Seven vessels were seized, two filibustering expeditions were broken up, and a dozen gun-runners were chased back into American ports. The new *McCulloch*, on the round-the-world shakedown cruise, joined Dewey's squadron at Hong Kong and participated in the defeat of the Spanish fleet at Manila Bay. Meanwhile, the cutters on the East Coast joined naval forces in actions against Spanish forces in Cuba.

World War I

During World War I, 280 lifeboat stations were active, and 15 cruising cutters patrolled off the U.S. coast. Overseas, six cutters patrolled between Gibraltar and England.

Near the end of the war, the *Tampa*, presumably struck by a torpedo, was lost with all hands. The Coast Guard has had a higher percentage of its personnel killed in action than any other service.

It was in this same period that Coast Guard aviation was born. Lieutenant E. F. Stone, USCG, one of several early Coast Guard flyers, was copilot on the Navy NC-4 flying boat, the first aircraft to cross the Atlantic.

After the war, the job of enforcing the Eighteenth (Prohibition) Amendment by sea was given to the Coast Guard. This antismuggling duty entailed considerable expansion in both ships and aircraft. Prior to World War I, extensive scouting flights had met with such success that Congress had authorized the establishment of ten Coast Guard air stations. The war stopped the development, but under influence of the Prohibition Amendment, the scouting flights were resumed.

On 1 July 1939, the Lighthouse Service was combined with the Coast Guard. This augmented the service by some 8,000 men, who became the nucleus for the tremendous wartime expansion that followed.

World War II

In September 1941, the cutter *Northland* frustrated a German attempt to set up weather stations in Greenland by capturing the *Buskoe*, the first naval capture in World War II.

Immediately after the Japanese attack on Pearl Harbor on 7 December 1941, cutters were ordered to escort duty. One of the first successful attacks on a German submarine was credited to the 165-foot cutter *Icarus*, which forced the submarine to the surface with depth charges and forced her to surrender with a 3-inch "popgun."

Another famous attack was delivered by the *Campbell*. In early 1943 she ran into the center of a wolf pack. One submarine was sunk by ramming after a sharp gun battle. The *Campbell* was badly damaged. The entire crew volunteered to remain aboard, but the captain permitted only 125 to stay. This party kept the ship afloat during a 600-mile tow to port.

Later the same year, the *Spencer* made an attack that involved the difficult feat of tracking a submarine through a convoy. This successful attack was conducted with such skill that the action report became part of the antisubmarine force doctrine.

In World War II, Coast Guardsmen operated escort destroyers, frigates, corvettes, PC boats, and sub-chasers, while planes patrolled the coasts and assisted in the war on submarines. Beach patrols and Port Security Units ensured coastal safety.

In the Pacific war, amphibious operations employed thousands of Coast Guardsmen, where their small-boat experience proved invaluable. Over 180,000 Coast Guardsmen served on combat ships and in the support forces, where they manned naval transports, attack transports, and attack supply vessels. Douglas Munro, a signalman, was posthumously awarded the only Medal of Honor won by a Coast Guardsman. He heads a long list of men who were cited for their courage and skill in action.

As a wartime measure, in 1942 the Bureau of Marine Inspection and Navigation was consolidated with the Coast Guard because of the importance of marine safety laws to the war effort. In 1946 this was made permanent.

The Korean War

In 1946 a Coast Guard team was sent to Seoul, Korea, to "organize, supervise, and train a Korean Coast Guard." That service later became the National Maritime Police.

A shipyard was set up, a supply and communications system was arranged, training facilities were established, and nineteen ships were transferred to Korea from the Japanese and U. S. navies.

With the outbreak of hostilities, marked by the invasion by North Korean Communist forces southward across the 38th parallel into the Republic of South Korea, the United Nations responded with a "police action," usually called the Korean War. The Coast Guard manned a number of Navy destroyer escorts, performing a variety of missions in the Western Pacific. A chain of mobile Loran stations was established in the Far East to support the air and sea navigational needs of U. S. and other U. N. forces. One of those Coast Guard stations was situated at Pusan, Korea.

Coast Guard in Vietnam

In 1964 the Navy was faced with the problem of preventing the movement of enemy forces and supplies by water, in areas where large combatant naval vessels could not operate. Vietnam's long and irregular coastline and the prevalence of fishermen and coastwise commerce in sampans made it difficult to distinguish friend from foe. The Coast Guard's highly maneuverable craft were ideal for operations there, and in April 1965 it sent seventeen of its 82-footers to Vietnam. The cutters were heavily armed, and their crews received extensive training. Later, nine more cutters joined them.

Coast Guardsmen boarded all suspicious-looking craft, searching for weapons, ammunition, and other contraband. In addition, the cutters took part in hundreds of naval gunfire support missions, assisting ground forces with mortar fire on selected enemy targets.

In mid-1967 the Coast Guard sent five larger cutters to operate from Subic Bay, Republic of the Philippines, and patrol off Vietnam.

Coast Guard involvement in South Vietnam also included an extensive aids-to-navigation operation; port safety teams to supervise off-loading of ammunition from ships; and a merchant marine detail. Loran stations were built in Vietnam and Thailand to aid air and sea navigation in the area.

The Coast Guard turned over all of its 82-footers on duty in Vietnam to the Republic of Vietnam Navy in 1969 and 1970, along with four 311-foot, high-endurance cutters.

Humanitarian Milestones of Coast Guard History

Some other milestones in Coast Guard history stand out as specific instances in which the Coast Guard served the nation in other, but nonetheless, vital missions. These other milestones, as with the military operations, deserve special mention.

Coastal Rescue of the Ayrshire

The new federal rescue stations authorized in 1848 had barely been built and outfitted when the sailing ship *Ayrshire* was driven ashore in a blizzard at Chadwicks on the New Jersey coast. On board were 202 persons, mostly Scots-Irish immigrants. The wreckmaster for that part of the coast was John Maxon. He also was in charge of the federal station house and the new equipment stored inside. Maxon called out his volunteer crew as soon as the wreck was discovered. Through the surf and storm and howling gale, the volunteers successfully fired a line out to the ship and pulled 201 persons safely to shore in groups of three and four using a small covered boat called a "surf car." One passenger died when he panicked and tried to ride ashore hanging on to the outside of the surf car. This was the first use of a U.S. lifesaving station and its rescue equipment. The scene was repeated hundreds of times in later years by other volunteers, paid Life-Saving Service crews, and finally by Coast Guardsmen.

Alaskan Operations

Shortly after the purchase of Alaska in July of 1867, the cutter *Lincoln* was sent there "to make local surveys, investigate locations for lighthouses and coaling stations, determine suitable points for custom houses, search out probable haunts for smugglers, locate fishing banks, inquire into the physical characteristics and resources of coastal areas, and collect specimens for the Smithsonian Institution." This comprehensive program soon set the pattern for future Alaskan cruising. Cutters were ordered to enforce the law, to protect whites and natives, and to aid the American whaling fleet. In 1897 eight ships and 300 men were trapped by ice at Point Barrow. Lieutenants Jarvis and Bertholf and Surgeon Call left the *Bear* (figure 1-3) to travel overland, carry supplies, purchase and drive reindeer for food, and to care for the whalermen. They reached Barrow just in time to prevent many deaths from scurvy and starvation. The *Bear* arrived later and rescued everyone. This feat competed with the Spanish-American War for public interest and acclaim.

International Ice Patrol

On 14 April 1912, the SS *Titanic*, the largest ship in the world, struck an iceberg off Newfoundland while making her maiden voyage across

Figure 1–3. The barkentine *Bear* was one of the most colorful ships in Coast Guard history. Built in 1874, she served in Alaska for more than forty years, finally sank in the North Atlantic in 1963.

the Atlantic, and sank with the loss of 1,517 lives. The following year the cutters *Seneca* and *Miami* were ordered to patrol the shipping lanes and issue radio warnings of ice. The results were so impressive that the maritime nations of the North Atlantic agreed to share the cost of the patrol, and the Revenue-Cutter Service took over the operation of the International Ice Patrol (figure 1-4).

Each nation agreed to share the cost of the patrol in proportion to its interest. The area patrolled is east and south of Newfoundland and covers about 300,000 square miles; it has the heaviest shipping traffic in the world. About four hundred icebergs drift into it each year, and during March and early April the northern part is usually covered with field ice, blocking the steamship routes.

The Coast Guard scouts the area with planes and cutters, and broadcasts the location of all ice to ships via the Coast Guard radio station at Argentia, Newfoundland. Since even radar-equipped ships might fail to detect bergs, the warning of the ice patrol provides their only sure protection.

Ocean Search and Rescue

In 1942 the President designated that the Coast Guard furnish search-and-rescue facilities in connection with the International Civil Aviation Organization. Vessels assigned to this duty make weather reports, stand plane guard, and handle communications and assistance along trans-

Figure 1–4. Seventy years after the International Ice Patrol began, the Coast Guard still warns ships of icebergs off the Grand Banks. The *Vigorous* was the first ship of her class assigned to this duty.

oceanic air routes. Since 1946 a large number of cutters, aircraft, and boats have been engaged in this work.

What these ocean station vessels meant for air travel, over and above the weather reports they made, was demonstrated in October 1947 by the cutter *Bibb*. She was on station eight hundred miles east of Newfoundland when the flying boat *Bermuda Sky Queen*, bound from Ireland to Newfoundland, ran low on fuel and ditched near the *Bibb*. Four days later, the *Bibb* reached port with every one of the sixty-nine people who had been aboard the plane.

In 1956 the *Chincoteague* performed a similar rescue when the German freighter *Helga Bolten* was battered by stormy seas. The *Chincoteague* raced through heavy seas and 40-knot winds and rescued thirty-three persons from the storm-lashed ship.

Polar Operations

The icebreaker *Northwind* was on Operation Deepfreeze in 1948, and a *Wind*-class icebreaker has been part of the Antarctic task force ever since. An icebreaker is always part of the Arctic resupply operation. On the Alaskan side, the *Northwind* continues Bering Sea patrols and resupply missions and in 1963 completed an oceanographic survey off the Siberian coast.

In 1957, the *Bramble, Spar,* and *Storis* completed the first deep-draft traverse of the Northwest Passage through the Arctic across the top of North America, and in consequence also became the first American vessels to circumnavigate the North American continent. Twelve years later, the *Northwind* assisted the Canadian icebreaker *John MacDonald* in taking the icebreaking tanker *Manhattan* through the Northwest Passage.

MISSIONS, WHAT WE DO

It is not possible to separate the history of the Coast Guard from its missions. In order to fulfill the objectives that the citizens have set for us through federal laws, we should understand how and why we got started in the first place. For example, it is important that Coast Guardsmen know that the reason we originally carried out certain safety inspections was to protect ships and their passengers and crew members, from ignorant, careless, or greedy ship owners who were not interested in safety. Times change, as do missions, but any Coast Guardsman who understands the basic historical reasons for our safety missions should know that the Coast Guard's job is to protect lives and property from maritime accidents and the results thereof. It surely is not to provide a service to the owner of a vessel; the owner has insurance to protect his investment, and the Coast Guard is not in the insurance business. So history is important to know, because it provides us with background and the reasons *why* we do what we do. Missions, however, are *what* we do; they are the most important and should demand our very best efforts.

Coast Guard missions are the specific groups of activities that carry out the national purposes discussed earlier. Sometimes missions are called *progams* or *operating programs*. Every few years the Coast Guard rearranges these programs, depending upon national emphasis, and renames them. At the time this edition goes to press, there are fourteen operating programs of the Coast Guard:

Bridge Administration (BA)
Commercial Vessel Safety (CVS)
Domestic Ice Operations (DIO)
Enforcement of Laws and Treaties (ELT)
Marine Environmental Response (MER)
Military Operations/Military Preparedness (MO/MP)
Marine Science Activities (MSA)
Port and Environmental Safety (PES)
Polar Ice Operations (PIO)
Radio Navigation Aids (RNA)
Recreational Boating Safety (RBS)
Search and Rescue (SAR)
Short Range Aids (SRA)
Waterways Management (WWM)

In general terms, programs are sometimes lumped together into groups called program areas and labeled "missions." These, too, are subject to some rearrangement, but for a number of years they have been referred to as:

Merchant Marine Safety
Aids to Navigation
Search and Rescue
Maritime Law Enforcement
Military Readiness
Boating Safety
Port Safety

Marine Environmental Protection

This list does not include all the operating programs, but does represent most of the major peacetime operations that have taken place within the Coast Guard over the past fifteen years. The list of missions is not totally representative of today's Coast Guard activities.

Before defining each of the programs, three points should be made: (1) these fourteen programs are operating programs, meaning they are operational in that they relate directly to the Coast Guard's performance of a responsibility to the citizen; (2) there are also "support programs," which have the primary purpose of supporting the operating programs, and (3) when necessary, both operating and support programs can respond across program lines of responsibility to become "multimissions." Sometimes people in the Coast Guard say that something is "operational" as being opposed to "support." Other times, the term *operational* is used to describe something that is not regulatory. Support does not mean regulatory. Support is that which backs up the field operating units. Support can be financial, supply, engineering, research and development, personnel, legal, etc. The Coast Guard has whole shoreside organizations and units that provide support services to operating units. What is confusing is that sometimes support units also are operating shore units. When that happens, the department of the unit that does operations is usually separate from the other departments; it is usualy called *operations*. Most Coast Guard shore units are operational, however, as are all Coast Guard floating units. What makes them different is their missions, or programs. Some operational shore units have a special purpose to enforce safety and pollution laws. Because these laws are so complicated, a number of regulations have been published by the commandant and the Secretary of Transportation so that the public will know the laws and that the laws will be enforced the same way in different regions. Actually, these units are carrying out programs that are law-enforcement responsibilities of the Coast Guard, but because of the special knowledge required of persons at those operating shore units in understanding the regulations that apply, it has been convenient to say that those operating programs are regulatory. Some people conclude, therefore, that the units that perform regulatory programs are not operational. That is not true and is completely opposite to what many of the Commandant's directives say. Any program that meets a Coast Guard responsibility is operational. All Coast Guard programs are maritime in nature, which means that our attention is focused upon the oceans and our inland waters, as well as upon vessels and their passengers and crew. Some operating programs are pretty small and limited in scope, such as bridge administration. Others, such as search and rescue, are large and extensive—involving cutters, aircraft, boats, shore command centers, as well as Coast Guard people whose primary duties are in other programs.

The most interesting aspect of the Coast Guard is that it is multimission. That means that there are very few operating units that perform only one program or mission. This is unlike most federal civilian agencies. Most every Coast Guard operating unit requires the operation of cutters, aircraft, or boats, even if only on occasion, to meet all its mission requirements. Some operating units, of course, are cutters; others are the places from which aircraft, boats, and vehicles operate. When Coast Guard people are under way, they are multimission because they "carry the flag" with them. The longer the Coast Guard person has been in the service, the more training and experience he usually has in a variety of Coast Guard missions. It is Coast Guard people, and their varied capability, that makes us miltimission. Multimission saves the taxpayer money. For example, all Coast Guard people, all the time, are participating in part of the Military Operations/Military Preparedness Program. A cutter on law and treaty enforcement patrol is also a potential search-and-rescue platform. A harbor patrol boat on a port and environmental safety mission may also detect a drug smuggler. All the Coast Guard units at a port will respond during the time of natural or maritime disaster to perform all the missions required, with safety of life as the highest priority. That's multimission!

Programs Briefly Described

The description of most of the operating programs is found in their titles. A more detailed description can be found in the various Coast Guard budget documents. However, a brief description of Coast Guard programs/missions along with the principal Coast Guard operating units involved follows:

Bridge Administration

This program is responsible for administering the laws having to do with the construction, maintenance, and operation of bridges across the navigable waters of the United States to ensure safe navigation under them. This responsibility is performed mostly by career civilian specialists in Coast Guard Headquarters and at the Coast Guard's district offices.

Commercial Vessel Safety

The Coast Guard is charged with administering and enforcing various safety standards for the design, construction, equipment, and maintenance of commercial vessels of the United States and offshore structures on the outer continental shelf. The program includes enforcement of safety standards on foreign vessels subject to U.S. jurisdiction and the administration and enforcement of crew qualification standards.

Investigations, including surveillance operations and boarding, are conducted of reported marine accidents, casualties, violations of law and regulations, misconduct, negligence, and incompetence occurring on commercial vessels subject to U.S. jurisdiction. The program also functions to facilitate marine transportation by admeasuring vessels, supervising the employment and records of employment of merchant marine personnel, and administering the vessel documentation laws.

This program is carried out at the field level by operational shore units called marine safety offices, marine inspection offices, marine inspection detachments, and marine safety detachments. Certain elements of this program are performed at the district offices and Coast Guard Headquarters.

Domestic Ice Operations

The purpose of this program is to facilitate safe and expeditious marine transportation during periods that icing occurs on U.S. navigable waters. Also, this program aids in the prevention of flooding on domestic waters. The principal operating units in this program are Coast Guard icebreakers, ice-capable buoy tenders, and other ice-capable cutters.

Enforcement of Laws and Treaties

This broad program involves the employment of all types of Coast Guard aircraft and vessels, and focuses most of its operations offshore, although some onshore enforcement of U.S. criminal statutes is carried out by this program in U.S. waters. Basically, this program enforces, or assists in the enforcement of, applicable federal laws and treaties and other international agreements to which the United States is party, on and under the high seas and waters subject to the jurisdiction of the United States, and may conduct investigations into suspected violations of such laws and international agreements. The Coast Guard works with other federal agencies in the enforcement of such laws as they pertain to the protection of living and nonliving resources and in the suppression of smuggling and illicit drug trafficking.

Marine Environmental Response

The purpose of this program is to minimize the damage caused by oil and other hazardous substances that are discharged into the marine environment, as well as to contain and ensure the safe removal of pollutants that may potentially damage the marine environment. This program functions in concert with other federal, state, and local agencies as well as with the maritime and chemical industries. It employs primarily the resources of marine safety offices and detachments, other COTP (Captain of the Port) units, aircraft, and the National Strike Force.

Military Operations/Military Preparedness

The purpose of this program is to maintain a state of military readiness to function as a specialized service in the Navy in time of war, or as directed by the president. The Coast Guard Reserve is a vital part of this preparedness mission, providing qualified individuals and trained units for active duty in time of war or national emergency, or at other times as national security requires. Virtually every kind of Coast Guard unit is involved with this program.

Marine Science Activities

This program involves applied oceanography in support of other Coast Guard programs and missions. The Coast Guard administers and operates the international Ice Patrol, which provides an iceberg warning service in the area of the Grand Banks off Newfoundland. Resources employed include fixed wing aircraft and cutters.

Port and Environmental Safety

This program involves the enforcement of rules and regulations governing the safety and security of ports and the anchorage and movement of vessels in U.S. waters. Port safety and security functions include supervising cargo transfer operations, both storage and stowage, boarding of special interest vessels, conducting harbor patrols and waterfront facility inspections, establishing security zones as required, and the control of vessel movement.

In addition, this program is responsible for maintaining or improving the quality of the marine environment. The functions conducted include boarding tankers, monitoring transfer operations, and inspecting liquid bulk facilities to ensure compliance with the laws, executive orders, and agreements that constitute the legal mandate for the marine environmental protection. This program primarily involves COTP units and marine safety offices and detachments. Patrol boats are deployed routinely from those units.

Polar Ice Operations

Similar to its sister program, domestic ice operations, this requires the operation of ice-capable cutters. Icebreakers are principally used, supported by rotary-wing aircraft for ice reconnaissance. The program facilitates polar transportation, supports logistics to U.S. polar installations, and supports scientific research in Arctic and Antarctic waters.

Radio Navigation Aids

The Coast Guard establishes and maintains the United States aids-to-navigation system. Part of this system is the Radio Navigation Aids program, which includes long-range radio navigation aids, marine radio beacons, and racons. Long-range aids, such as Loran, extend beyond the Western Hemisphere to the Arctic, Europe, the Middle East, and the Western Pacific. These aids directly assist navigators in establishing the positions of their vessels. Some radio aids are automatically operated from unmanned stations, others are transmitted from operational shore units in both populated and remote, isolated locations.

Recreational Boating Safety

This marine safety program is aimed at making the operation of small craft in U.S. waters both pleasurable and safe. This is accomplished by establishing uniform safety standards for recreational boats and their associated equipment; encouraging state efforts through a grant-in-aid and liaison program; coordinating public education and information programs; administering the Coast Guard Auxiliary; and enforcing compliance with federal laws and regulations relative to safe use and safety equipment requirements for small boats. The Auxiliary is a nonmilitary volunteer organization of private citizens who own small boats, aircraft, or radio stations. Auxiliary members assist the Coast Guard by conducting boating education programs, search-and-rescue operations, and courtesy marine examinations. Boating safety enforcement is performed by various operating units, including patrol boats from groups, stations, and marine safety offices. Investigations of fatal boating accidents are performed by marine safety and marine inspection units.

Search and Rescue

The search-and-rescue program of the Coast Guard is, perhaps, the one most familiar to most people. The Coast Guard maintains a system of rescue vessels, aircraft, and communications facilities to carry out its function of saving life and property in and over the high seas and the navigable waters of the United States. This function includes flood relief and removing hazards to navigation. Some of the operating units comprising this system were specifically established for the purpose of search and rescue. Other units perform as a part of this system on a multimission basis. Virtually every Coast Guard unit is part of this vital program.

Short-Range Aids

With its sister program of radio navigation aids, this program rounds out the United States aids to navigation system. Short-range aids include lighthouses, lightships, buoys, beacons, racons, and fog signals. Other aids to navigation functions include the origin of marine information radio broadcasts and the publication of *Local Notices to Mariners* and Coast Guard *Light Lists*. Short-range aids are intended to help the navigator determine the position and safe course of his vessel, or to warn him of dangers and obstructions to navigation. Coast Guard operating units primarily performing this mission are buoy tenders, aids to navigation teams, stations, and bases.

Waterways Management

This relatively new Coast Guard program is concerned with the use of the nation's waterways, both inland and those offshore approaches to our ports and waterways. Functions included are developing and establishing nautical rules of the road and administering vessel traffic management systems. Neither of these two elements of the program are new, however, and their application in the field involves district offices and a variety of field units, including vessel traffic management organizations and marine safety, marine inspection, and COTP offices.

CHAPTER 2

Organization

In peacetime the Coast Guard operates under the Department of Transportation, and the Commandant receives orders from the secretary of that department. In time of war or when directed by the President, the Coast Guard operates within the naval establishment and the Commandant reports to the Secretary of the Navy and the Chief of Naval Operations.

COMMAND STRUCTURE

Coast Guard Headquarters, district offices, and individual units in the field follow the basic Coast Guard organization. In most instances, the duties are performed by individual ships and stations, marine safety and inspection offices, training centers, bases, depots, detachments, and repair shops.

The Commandant plans, supervises, and coordinates overall activities of the Coast Guard. He also gives immediate direction to special service units (figure 2-1), which report directly to headquarters even though they are located within the geographical limits of a district.

An area commander acts on an intermediate level of command between the Commandant and the district commanders. As a senior operational commander, he controls designated area units. The district commander of the third district serves as the Atlantic Area Commander, and the district commander of the twelfth district acts as the Pacific Area Commander.

Figure 2-1. The Coast Guard Training Center at Cape May, New Jersey. The West Coast "boot" camp is at Alameda, California.

Area commanders are primarily concerned with search-and-rescue operations, ocean-station programs, oceanographic and ice-breaking efforts, and readiness and mobilization planning. They direct and co-ordinate the performance of duties by field units within their districts.

A commanding officer or officer-in-charge is responsible for a particular unit; his responsibility for his unit is absolute unless competent authority relieves him of his duty. He may delegate authority to his subordinates to carry out details, but this delegation of authority does not relieve him of the responsibility for the safety, efficiency, and well-being of his command.

Chain of Command

The chain of military command, and operational and administrative control, ordinarily runs from the Commandant to the district commander and from the district commander to the commanding officer or officer-in-charge of a particular unit located in his district. In the case of units reporting directly to headquarters (headquarters units), the chain of command runs directly from the Commandant to the commanding officer of the unit.

In a small organization the manager can execute all of his functions. However, as the organization becomes larger, the manager must delegate part of his functions to subordinates. These subordinates as a group comprise his staff. The concept of staff is an essential feature of Coast Guard organization.

Staffs assist the Commandant and district commanders. Their authority comes from the Commandant or their district commander. They can take action on a variety of matters; however, they must take action in behalf of, or in the name of, the appropriate staff officer in charge.

In a staff component of an organization, the chain of command runs from the military chief of the component through the military assistant chief to subordinates within the component. Where civilians serve as the chief or assistant chief of a component, they serve in recognized supervisory roles, but are not in the military chain of command.

In addition to the general levels of organization, several special organizational levels within the Coast Guard have been created to handle special geographical areas not included in the district organization. These special organizations include the section command, group command, and European command.

Headquarters Organization

Headquarters, U.S. Coast Guard, is located in Washington, D.C. From headquarters, the Commandant directs the policy, legislation, and administration of the Coast Guard. He is assisted by a chief of staff and a staff comprised of the following offices:

Office of Marine Environment and Systems
Office of Chief Counsel
Office of Merchant Marine Safety
Office of Engineering
Office of the Comptroller
Office of Operations
Office of Personnel
Office of Reserve
Office of Civil Rights
Office of Research and Development
Office of Boating, Public and Consumer Affairs
Office of Health Services
Office of Navigation
Office of Telecommunications

Each staff office performs specific functions related to a specific area. For example, the Office of Engineering performs functions of an engineering nature such as the design, construction, repair, maintenance, outfitting, and alteration of vessels, aircraft, aids to navigation machinery, electronic equipment, and utilities. The Office of Personnel deals with the procurement, training, assignment, and separation of personnel.

Coast Guard Districts

There are twelve Coast Guard districts, each under the command of a district commander, who is the direct representative of the Commandant in all matters pertaining to the Coast Guard within his district. He is responsible for the proper administration of his district and for the efficient, safe, and economical performance of Coast Guard duties within the district. A staff of administrative and technical personnel assists the district commander. These assistants serve as principal advisors to him for the fields in which they are individually assigned. The teams in which they work are smaller and are called divisions instead of offices.

District Office

A district office consists of the immediate office of the district commander and several staff offices. The Reserve, Personnel, Comptroller, and Engineering Divisions supply the technical skill, material, funds, and personnel for supporting the overall operations of the district. The Operations Division assures the effective performance of some of the operational programs of the district; maintaining the aids to navigation system comes under its direction. The Marine Safety Division assures the effective performance of the marine safety and pollution prevention operational programs of the district ; for example, this division enforces the navigation and vessel inspection laws to prevent accidents to U.S. merchant ships.

The Coast Guard consists of over 1,500 shore units and ships. Each unit is headed by a commanding officer or officer-in-charge and is provided with personnel and material for performing a specific operational mission (figure 2-2). Units are divided into two classes for command purposes: headquarters units (floating and shore) and district units (floating and shore).

Headquarters Units

Certain Coast Guard units, even though physically located within the geographical limits of a district, operate independently of the district commander; they are under the direct control of the Commandant (figure 2-3). These units, known as headquarters units, were established because they satisfy a total service requirement. For instance, the Coast Guard Yard at Curtis Bay, Maryland, is the sole major industrial establishment of the Coast Guard. It is responsible for major ship repairs to Coast Guard vessels. Some headquarters units were established because of their location or because of the nature of their duties. Training centers (figure 2-3) are classified as headquarters units, since their duty or function is to provide training support to a broad segment of the Coast Guard.

Major headquarters shore units include:

Academy
Air Station (Arlington, Virginia)
Aircraft Repair and Supply Center
Electronics Engineering Center
Examiner Offices
Field Testing and Development Center

Figure 2–2. Coast Guardsmen on duty at Governors Island have their own transportation system, the ferries *Coursen* and *Minve,* to take them to Manhattan Island.

Institute
Reserve Training Center (Yorktown, Virginia)
Supply Center
Training Centers
Washington Radio Station
Yard

District Units

A district unit is under the control of the district commander. In some instances, the district commander may exercise control of a particular unit through a group or section commander, discussed later in this section. The various types of district shore units include:

Air facilities
Air stations
Bases

Figure 2–3. Admiral J.S. Gracey, Commandant, U.S. Coast Guard.

Captain of the port offices
Coast Guard stations (lifeboat stations)
Communication stations
Depots
Electronic shops (telephone)
Light stations
Loran monitor stations
Loran transmitting stations
Marine inspection offices
Marine safety offices
Port security stations
Recruiting offices

The Coast Guard has created standard organizational structures for several types of units. For instance, a base is responsible for maintaining, servicing, repairing, and operating certain Coast Guard units and facilities, as follows:

Operate small craft attached to the base;

Furnish mooring facilities for Coast Guard vessels;

Service, tend, and maintain aids to navigation within an assigned area;

Maintain, repair, and modify Coast Guard small boats, vehicles, machinery, engines, aids-to-navigation equipment, and designated shore stations;

Perform minor repairs and modifications to Coast Guard vessels;

Preserve, store, maintain, stock, issue, and ship aids-to-navigation equipment and other equipment.

Coast Guard Stations

The more than 160 Coast Guard stations (lifeboat stations) have no standard pattern of organization. They are manned by nearly 10 percent of the Coast Guard enlisted personnel strength. Their primary functions are to:

Maintain lookouts, communications, patrols, and other watches;

Take immediate, positive action to safeguard and relieve life or property endangered or distressed on the water or along the coasts of a station's operational range;

Enforce federal laws in accordance with Coast Guard regulations and directives;

Service and tend aids to navigation within an assigned area;

Maintain liaison with local public and private agencies.

The personnel allowance is only sufficient to operate all boats assigned to the station and to keep a live communications watch. Because of this small allowance, all hands assist whenever necessary; therefore, standard departmental organization is of little value. Ratings commonly assigned to Coast Guard stations are boatswain's mate (all pay grades), engineman (all pay grades), seaman, fireman, and commissaryman (all pay grades).

If tenant activities are located on the Coast Guard station, additional ratings may be assigned. A tenant activity is created when two or more shore units are located on the same reservation. Each unit retains its own commanding officer or officer in charge. In these situations, the larger command becomes the landlord activity and furnishes support and services to the tenant activities. Examples are Cape May Recruit Training Center and Cape May Station, and Alameda Base and Alameda Recruit Training Center. The tenant activity has control over its own operation, but it follows the orders of the landlord command in nonoperational matters that affect the appearance of the unit and the quality or quantity of support and services.

Intermediate Commands

In addition to these levels of organization, there are intermediate command levels organized to meet special requirements of the service. These requirements arise from the complexity and diversity of Coast Guard operations and from the geographical location of various Coast Guard facilities. The intermediate levels of organizational structure in the Coast Guard are the section command, group command, and European command.

There are four section commands. Normally a section command is located outside the continental United States in areas far removed from district offices, such as the Greater Antilles Section and the Far East Section. Under the direction of the district commander, the section commander exercises operational and administrative control of all units— floating, shore, and aircraft—within the geographical limits of his section.

There are some fifty group commands. Ideally, a group consists of four to six stations and units. For example, Group Boston at one time consisted of the following:

Fort Devens Reserve Training Detachment
Boston Group Office
Boston Harbor Station
Boston Lightship (WLV-539)
The Graves Light Station
Deer Island Light Station
Point Allerton Station
Boston Light Station
Scituate Station
Plymouth Light Station

A group commander has operational and administrative control over the units within his assigned group. Within each group command, a communications center maintains distress frequency watches and communications by landline (telephone and teletype) between the group and its shore units.

Section and group commands are formed because of geographical limitations, similarity of task, or the need to achieve common goals, such as military readiness. Group commanders and section commanders must keep the district commander informed of the activities within their respective units. A section extends over vast expanses of ocean while the group covers a smaller area. Additionally, the units in a group frequently have officers in charge; most of the units in a section, however, have commanding officers assigned.

Coast Guard Activities, Europe, was established as a special command to control all Coast Guard activities in Europe and adjacent territories. The European Commander (also called the Commander, Coast Guard Activities, Europe) serves as the principal agent and representative of the commandant. His command consists of staff offices and individual units such as Loran stations and air facilities.

SHIP ORGANIZATION

When a number of people get together, even if only for a casual game of baseball, they can't accomplish much until they are organized. Aboard ship, organization is even more important; people thrown together in a department or division may individually possess great talent and ability, but until they are organized, nothing happens. Because of the great need for efficiency in all operations, Coast Guard regulations prescribe a standard organization, called the *Organization Manual,* designed to help people work best together.

The *Organization Manual* provides ship's personnel with a ready source of information about their duties, responsibilities, and authority in administering and operating the ship. It contains a complete written and graphic description of the ship's organization.

The commanding officer may modify these regulations to some extent to meet the needs of his ship. For this reason, your first duty when reporting aboard ship is to study the organization and regulations manual—it may be slightly different than in your last ship.

Departmental Duties

Coast Guard ships are organized, under a commanding officer and an executive officer, into at least three departments: operations, engineering, and deck or weapons (figure 2-4). Depending on the size and type of ship, there may also be a supply department and medical

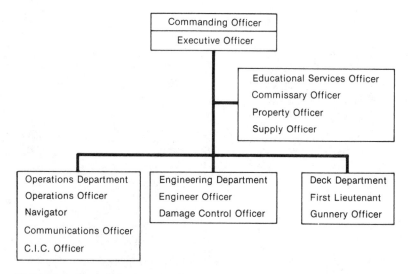

Figure 2–4. Typical departmental organization of a Coast Guard ship.

department. Each department is directed by a commissioned, warrant, or petty officer called the department head.

Departments are subdivided into divisions. The smaller the ship, the fewer the divisions (figure 2-5). Each division is headed by a division officer. In small ships, one officer may hold several positions; for example, he may be a division officer as well as a department head.

Commanding Officer

The officer ordered to command a ship is always called the "captain," no matter what his rank may be. He is responsible for the operation and efficiency of his ship and the conduct and performance of his crew. He enforces all regulations and directives from higher authority. All authority, command direction, and responsibility for the command rest with him. In practice, the commanding officer delegates duties for carrying out the functions of the ship to the executive officer, department heads, other officers, and certain crew members.

Executive Officer

The officer ordered as assistant to the commanding officer is the executive officer (exec or XO). He is next in the chain of command below the captain. The XO is in charge of the personnel, routine, and dis-

Figure 2–5. A shipboard division at Captain's Inspection.

cipline of the ship. Department heads may consult directly with the captain, but the executive officer must be informed of any decisions the captain may make.

Department Heads

The commanding officer assigns officers to head up each department of a ship. In small ships, an officer may have two departments. The department head represents the commanding officer in all matters pertaining to his department and is responsible to the commanding officer for the general condition of his department. All men in a department make requests to the executive officer through their department head.

Operations Department

The officer in charge of this department is the operations officer. He is assigned to such duty by the commanding officer. He is responsible for handling operational and combat intelligence and maybe assisted by the navigator, communications officer, electronics material officer, and combat information center officer.

Navigator

This officer is responsible to the commanding officer for the safe navigation of the ship. He reports first to the commanding officer and then to the operations officer on all matters having to do with navigation. He is responsible for the good condition of all charts and instruments and the steering equipment of the ship.

Communications Officer

This officer is responsible for all exterior communications, including electrical, cryptographic, and visual signals. He keeps a record of all messages handled by the ship and has custody of classified registered publications and coding machines.

The *electronics material officer* is responsible for the material readiness of all electronic equipment on board.

The *combat information center* (CIC) *officer* is responsible for the operation and readiness of the combat information center. The CIC collects, displays, evaluates, and distributes tactical information, such as surface or air radar contacts.

Engineering Department

The officer in charge of the engineering plant of a ship is the engineer officer, who is assigned to that duty by headquarters. He is responsible for the propulsion plant, auxiliary machinery, all related systems, and hull repairs. He is also responsible for damage control; for this he is assisted by the damage control officer.

Deck Department

The officer in charge of the deck department is called the first lieutenant. He is responsible for all deck and ordnance equipment and for upkeep and cleanliness of parts of the ship not assigned to other departments. He handles ground tackle, mooring lines, rigging, towing gear, and all boats. He may be assisted by a weapons officer, who is responsible for armament and ammunition.

Collateral Duties

Some jobs aboard ship are not assigned directly to the executive officer or department heads. These are known as collateral duties and may be assigned to any individual aboard ship, who then acts as an assistant to the executive officer. Collateral duties may include educational services, commissary and crew's mess, property accounting, and supply.

The departments, billet titles, and billet levels will differ among the various types of ships, because each ship must fulfill its particular mission. For example, the WMEC type vessel has only three departments; however, the WHEC- and WAGB-type vessels also have a supply department and a correspondingly larger personnel allowance.

Because of the number of officers assigned to a ship, the billet titles may be different from those discussed here.

Billets

The ship's company is further organized so that each member is assigned to a billet—a set of duties. It would be impossible to place enough men aboard ship so that each man could have a billet assignment for one contingency only. Each man must have an assigned duty for each type of emergency that the ship might encounter. If he is transferred, his successor takes over his duties. Thus, each man has a group of duties to perform, and the total number of groups of duties determine the allowance necessary to man the ship. Soon after reporting aboard ship you will be given a billet slip that assigns you a billet number, bunk number, locker number, and your duties for general drills and emergencies. Learn them as soon as possible.

In making up the lists of duties ("bills") for each emergency, every billet is assigned a number ("billet number"). This number is the same on each bill. A billet number has four digits, or a letter followed by three digits. The first digit or letter represents the division, the second the section, and the third and fourth the individual number. A man whose billet number is 1215 is in the first division, second section, and his individual number is 15. The last digit may also indicate port or starboard watch, odd or even, when two-watch liberty is being granted. On reporting to a new ship, learn all the duties to be performed at emergency drills and related activities.

Watch, Quarter, and Station Bill

All contingencies, as well as those covered by the billet slip, are included in the Watch, Quarter, and Station Bill. The duties of other men in your division are listed, and from this bill you can see how your job fits in with the entire operation.

The Watch, Quartet, and Station Bill will be posted on a bulletin

board for each division. It will usually assign men to billets for the
following drills:

Fire
Collision
Special sea detail
General emergency
Submarine attack
Abandon ship
Man overboard
Rescue and assistance
Plane ditch and rescue
Landing party
Replenishment at sea

Depending on the type of ship and the nature of her operations, other
drills may be listed.

Watch Organization. This depends on the type and size of the ship,
and changes when the ship goes from port routine to underway operations (see figures 2-6 and 2-7).

Officer of the Deck

There is much activity aboard a ship even when it is quietly moored
in a safe harbor. It is impossible for the captain and the executive
officer to stay awake day and night supervising all the details and

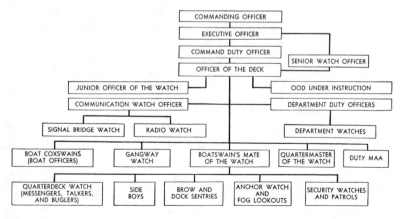

Figure 2–6. Typical watch organization for a ship in port.

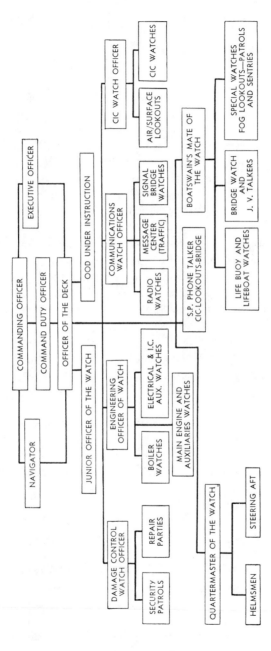

Figure 2-7. Typical watch organization for a ship under way. This may be modified to fit different types of ships.

operations of each watch. Hence it is necessary that there be an officer to act as a central clearing station and keep the daily happenings organized. This officer must have the ability and authority to act immediately in an emergency.

When the ship is under way, it is even more important that all operations be under the control of an officer of the watch. The engine-room watch cannot be expected to know whether the ship should be suddenly stopped, slowed, or speeded up. The lookouts cannot observe an object in the water and then run to the bridge and tell the helmsman which way to turn the rudder. There must be an officer constantly on watch to receive the incoming reports, act on some of them immediately, and decide what others should be referred to the captain, executive officer, or other officer. The officer so in charge of each watch is known as the officer of the deck.

Responsibility and Authority. The officer of the deck is the officer on watch in charge of the ship. He is responsible for the safety of the ship, and every person on board who is subject to the captain's orders, except the executive officer, is likewise subject to the orders of the officer of the deck. Only the captain and the executive officer are superior to the officer of the deck while he is carrying out his duties.

General Duties. The officer of the deck must see that the ship follows the course prescribed by the captain. He must keep the helmsman on his course, the lookouts alert, the engines at proper speed; and he must use such devices and equipment as are available to help conduct the ship safely.

The OOD is responsible for carrying out the ship's routine at sea and in port. He must make such inspections as are necessary to ensure that everything is ready for service and that proper safety precautions are observed. He sees that the boats are properly manned and equipped, that they are operated correctly, and that their crews obey all courtesies and regulations. He sees to it that all honors and ceremonies are properly carried out. He inspects persons coming aboard or leaving the ship and makes sure that no unauthorized articles are brought aboard or taken ashore.

At sea the OOD takes his station on the bridge. In port he is stationed on the quarterdeck or at the main gangway, depending on the construction of the ship and the decision of the commanding officer as to the limits of the quarterdeck.

All the ship's company must cooperate fully with the OOD in the performance of his duties, and his orders must be obeyed quickly and cheerfully.

Engineering Officer of the Watch

The *engineering officer of the watch* is the officer on watch in charge of the ship's main propulsion plant and of the associated auxiliaries. He sees that the engineering log, the engineer's bell book, and the prescribed operating records are properly kept, and that all orders received from the officer of the deck are promptly and properly executed.

He may be directed in the duties of the watch by the engineer officer or the main propulsion assistant, either of whom may assume charge of the watch if they consider such action necessary. The engineering officer of the watch reports to the officer of the deck and to the engineer officer any defects of machinery, boiler, or auxiliaries that may affect the proper operation of the ship. He ensures that frequent inspections of engines and boilers are made and that all safety precautions are observed.

Logs

The *deck log* is a complete daily record, by watches, in which are described every circumstance and occurrence of importance or interest that concern the crew and the operation and safety of the ship, or that may be of historical value. The navigator has general responsibility for preparation and care of the smooth deck log. Each OOD, however, makes out this log in the rough for his watch.

The *quartermaster's bridgebook* is a record of events occurring during the watch. Entries in the quartermaster's bridgebook are made at the time of occurrence or when knowledge of such occurrence is first obtained. The quartermaster's bridgebook is signed by the quartermaster of the watch on being relieved. It is then used in preparing the deck log, also called the smooth log.

Inspections

No man and no organization can be perfect or alert all the time. But plans can be made in advance to prepare for emergencies and for human mistakes or mechanical failures, to minimize them as much as possible, and to overcome their consequences as fast as possible. Likewise, a system of routine inspections has been established by the Coast Guard to prevent emergencies, improve maintenance, and keep things in order.

It is impossible to carry out any operations without the constant daily observation and supervision of people, materials, and equipment. But the Coast Guard has found from experience that certain formal inspections are necessary to keep up its standards over extended periods of time. Inspections required by *Regulations for the United States Coast Guard* include those described here.

Daily Inspections

The first lieutenant is required to make frequent inspections of all spaces not assigned to a specific department. In practice he usually covers the whole ship for its general appearance, cleanliness, and upkeep.

At daily quarters for muster the division officers inspect their men for cleanliness and appearance of uniform and person.

The executive officer prepares a daily *binnacle list*, which informs the commanding officer of the health of the crew.

The officer of the deck makes—or causes to be made—inspections to ensure the security of the ship, its watertight integrity, and degree of closure, the condition of armament, ground tackle, or mooring lines in use, the good order and discipline of the crew, and all other matters that may affect the safety of the ship. He must require the boat coxswains (usually boatswain's mates) to inspect the lifeboats and report their conditions to him at sunset.

The duty officer must sample each meal served in the general mess and report anything that is unsatisfactory.

Weekly Inspections

The commanding officer and executive officer inspect once a week, usually on Friday. Any day except Sunday may be used for these inspections. When a man is in charge of the cleanliness or order of a certain space or compartment or is on watch by certain equipment, he stands by during the inspection. He meets the inspecting party, salutes the commanding officer and sounds off with his name, rate, and the area in his charge, as, "Jones, seaman apprentice, forward crew's compartment ready for inspection, sir." He listens respectfully to any remarks the commanding officer makes, following the commanding officer about the compartment as necessary. When the commanding officer leaves, he salutes again and remains at attention until the inspecting party is out of sight.

Field Day. Field day is clean-up day. Field days are held once a week to prepare for inspection, at which time all hands turn to and thoroughly clean the ship or station.

Formal Inspections of Personnel. The method of forming for inspections of personnel at daily quarters or for commanding officer's inspection aboard ship is described in chapter 6. This section describes some of the other inspections included in the normal routine.

Inspection Before Going on Watch. Before going on watch or sentry duty, each man is inspected by an officer of the watch or of the guard to see that he is properly dressed and equipped for the watch. On smaller ships this is done by the officer of the deck.

Inspection Before Going on Liberty. Enlisted people going on liberty will usually be inspected by the officer of the deck.

Bag or Locker Inspection. Such inspections are held to make certain that clothes are clean, properly marked, and that each man has the required items.

CHAPTER 3

Leadership and Discipline

A complex organization such as the Coast Guard doesn't just "run." It requires people who decide what must be done, how and when it will be done, and who will do it. These people may be petty officers, department heads, or commanding officers, but they all have one common attribute—leadership.

LEADERSHIP

As long as you are a Coast Guardsman, you will be concerned with leadership. This is a quality like courage or intelligence, or being able to concentrate on a job. All men have some leadership skill, and most men can develop more of it. Leadership is important to everyone in the service, from top to bottom. As a recruit, you may be put in charge of two other recruits and told to sweep the messhall. You are now a leader; you must get the work done, and see that your people do it. If one of them fools around and gets no sweeping done, it's up to you to get him squared away and see that he keeps at his work until it's done.

If you all do a good job, you, as the leader, will be given a "well done." If the job is not done well, you, as the leader, will hear about it. Leadership is nothing mysterious; every person in the service is a leader at some time or other, but he also follows other leaders. The commanding officer of your ship or station, for example, has someone

Figure 3–1. Work on a buoy deck is hard and dangerous. Each man has a role—good leadership and discipline are critical.

above him, right on up to the Commandant, who follows the leadership of the Secretary of Transportation, who is responsible to the President of the United States. Even the President must follow the desires of the people as represented by the Congress.

You have a double job to do in the Coast Guard; to be a leader when you are put in a position that requires leadership and to be a follower of the leaders appointed over you, cheerfully doing what you are told to do. As you advance in the Coast Guard, you will do more leading; this is one of the biggest rewards of being promoted.

MORAL RESPONSIBILITY

This is a term you must understand. It has many meanings. It means doing your job honestly, the best you know how. It means living up to the rules and regulations that were made for good reasons, not just to annoy people. It means acting in a responsible manner when you go ashore, and showing pride and self-respect. It means thinking of other people, not just yourself.

There are really only two kinds of people. One kind, the majority, understand moral responsibility. They do their job when on duty and keep out of trouble, on duty and off. The others—and fortunately there are not many—are the ones who haven't got the word. They are the ones who will goof off on the job and get into trouble no matter where they are.

Your behavior ashore is important, and especially so in any foreign port. There, you not only represent your ship and the Coast Guard; you also represent the United States. People recognize you as an American and base their ideas of America on how you act. The least show of rowdiness or drunkenness can bring severe criticism of Americans and the United States, and will provide anti-American propaganda for subversive elements. Always keep this in mind—your behavior ashore in any foreign land must be perfect, because you represent the United States.

DISCIPLINE

Like moral responsibiity, *discipline* is another word with more than one meaning. Sometimes discipline is used to mean punishment. But the real meaning of discipline can best be described by the words, *right attitude*. A well-disciplined group of people have the right attitudes. They are willing to follow orders because they believe in what they are doing, they respect their leaders, and feel they are getting a square deal from them. They behave in a military manner, wear the right uniforms, take pride in their division, their ship or station, and are ready to fight bravely in defense of their country.

When discipline fails—that is, when some people do not have the right attitude—then punishment may be judged necessary for those who fail to observe rules and regulations. In the Coast Guard, as in civilian life, laws, orders, and regulations must be obeyed, and persons who fail to do so are subject to trial by courts-martial, which can punish them according to the laws.

Uniform Code of Military Justice

Discipline in all the military services is based on the Uniform Code of Military Justice, or "UCMJ," which became law on 5 May 1950 under an Act of Congress. UCMJ is the basis for the *Manual for Courts-Martial, 1951.* Before that time, the various services all had different disciplinary systems. The only variations that now exist among the services are those that result from the fact that each governmental department, under which a service operates, issues regulations based upon the differences in the structures of the services. The basic principles are the same for all.

The manual recognizes the military authority of persons of one service over those of another; it even specifies that personnel can be tried by courts-martial composed of members of another service. Thus it is evident that Coast Guardsmen are subject to the orders of Navy shore patrolmen and the Armed Forces Police. Likewise, Coast Guard shore patrols have the duty of enforcing the code upon members of the other armed services.

Necessity for the Disciplinary System

All of the armed services, including the Coast Guard, were established to accomplish objectives that are determined by Congress. The missions of the services, both in war and peace, involve personal risk. A well-trained, closely-knit, disciplined group of people can carry out a mission with a minimum loss of life, but in order to do so, the leaders who direct their operations must have the necessary authority.

Value of the Disciplinary System

The courts and laws of the nation exist to protect all people against criminal acts, and to prevent invasions of, or loss of, the rights of individuals. The disciplinary system of the Coast Guard protects all members of the service. The regulations of the Coast Guard and the Uniform Code of Military Justice protect loyal, law-abiding military personnel from being victimized by criminal or lawless actions.

The disciplinary system also protects conscientious, hard-working members of the service from being unfairly burdened with the work of people who fail to do their share of it. If such people get out of doing assigned work, those with a sense of responsibility must do it. The system sets up penalties for failure to perform assigned duties. It also prohibits compulsory self-incrimination (you cannot be forced to testify against yourself—Article 31); prohibits cruel or unusual punishment (Article 55); specifies that parts of the UCMJ be explained to you (Article 137); and provides for a system to make complaints if you are unfairly treated (Article 138). So it works both ways.

Protection of the Accused

Like the laws of our country, the laws of military justice protect those accused of offenses, even the convicted lawbreakers. An accused has a right to be informed about the charges against him, to make reply to charges, and to confront and question his accuser. He has a right to legal counsel—of his own choosing, if that is possible under the existing military conditions. There are limitations on the questioning of prisoners, and rules requiring humane treatment. Trials must be fairly conducted. Punishments are limited in accordance with the seriousness of the offense; cruel and inhuman punishments are prohibited. Finally, there is an elaborate system of reviews to ensure that all these provisions for protecting the rights of the accused have been observed and that the court's decision is just.

Mistaken Loyalty

A mistaken concept of loyalty to shipmates sometimes causes otherwise well-intentioned persons to refrain from reporting crimes. Tale bearers who constantly run to officers with reports of minor derelictions by other crew members are a nuisance, but you should be able to distinguish between tale bearing and giving information about a serious offense. If an act or a neglect constituting a legal offense has been committed—or you have serious reason to believe one has been committed—it is your duty to report this to someone in authority. If you fail to do so, you are punishable under the Code. In permitting an offender to escape punishment, you are weakening the disciplinary system that protects you and all your shipmates. You owe loyalty to those who keep the laws, not to those who break them.

Offenses Under Military Law

The basic disciplinary laws of the Coast Guard are stated in the *Uniform Code of Military Justice*, in *Regulations for the United States Coast Guard,* and in *Coast Guard Reserve Regulations.* Articles 77 to 134 of UCMJ cover offenses.

It is your responsibility to acquaint yourself with these laws. The oath you took on entering service obligates you to observe them. As in civilian life, ignorance of the law is no excuse for breaking it.

The Code was explained to you when you entered the Coast Guard. Copies of it are posted where you can read it for yourself. You should note especially the listing of offenses and their definitions. To assist you, certain legal terms are discussed here.

Differences Between Military and Civilian Offenses

In general, acts that would constitute offenses against civilian laws are also offenses under military law, but some acts are military offenses that would not be cause for arrest in civilian life.

A civilian who doesn't show up for work, or who walks off the job will probably lose his job, but that is all that will happen. In a military organization, the same act would be unauthorized absence and perhaps neglect of duty or disobedience to an order. The civilian who quarrels violently with his boss will not be arrested as long as he doesn't harm the boss or threaten harm. In the service a man would be charged with insubordination and possibly other offenses. Coming to work late, refusal to obey orders, drinking on the job—all of these would probably be cause for discipline by a civilian employer, but not reasons for arrest. Yet in a military service each can send a man before a court-martial.

The nature of military duty and the conditions of military life account for the difference. Your military duties are necessary for the Coast Guard to carry out its mission—the defense of the nation, the enforcement of national and international law, and the safety of life at sea. You cannot quit your job, be absent or late without permission, or fail to do your work without endangering that mission. The man who rebels against lawful authority and stirs up trouble is a menace to the teamwork that is necessary for his own safety and that of his shipmates, as well as for the accomplishment of his unit's assigned mission.

Principals and Accessories

A person who commits a crime or who aids in its commission is a *principal*. If a person advises, orders, or persuades someone to commit an offense, and that person does commit the crime, both are principals. After a crime has been committed, anyone who knows the person who committed it, and who helps the offender to escape trial or punishment, is an *accessory after the fact*. Principals and accessories are both punished according to the table of maximum punishment.

Lesser Included Offenses

If, during the trial of a man charged with desertion, it develops that he was absent without leave but did not intend to abandon the service permanently, the court may find him guilty of, and punish him for, unauthorized absence. This is a lesser included offense within the more serious one originally charged. Punishment for a lesser included offense may occur under other charges. Housebreaking, for example, might be a lesser offense under a charge of burglary.

Attempt. An attempt to commit an offense is a violation even though the crime is not consummated. An attempt to commit a particular crime is always a potential lesser included offense when a perpetrator is tried for the crime.

Conspiracy. When two or more persons agree to violate the Code by concerted action, and any one of them performs any action seeking to accomplish the agreed objective, all of the parties to the agreement are guilty of conspiracy.

Offenses Related to Orders

Strictly speaking, *orders* tell a man *what* to do, but not *how* to do it. "Paint this bulkhead" would be an order. *Commands* require performance in a specified manner, such as "1. Right, 2. FACE." For the purposes of the disciplinary system the term "order" includes both *orders* and *commands*.

Offenses Related to War

Certain offenses become much more serious if committed when the United States is at war. Others are particularly related to wartime situations. Among those that become more serious are desertion and assaulting or disobeying an officer. For each of the offenses listed below, the death penalty may be imposed in time of war:

Misbehavior before the enemy
Subordinate compelling surrender
Forcing a safeguard
Improper handling of captured or abandoned property
Aiding the enemy
Misconduct as a prisoner of war
Spying

General Article

Article 134, the last of the punitive articles, makes it an offense to commit acts or to neglect duties that result in creating disorders, which are to the prejudice of good order and discipline, or which bring discredit upon the Coast Guard. Such offenses are subject to trial by the appropriate courts-martial.

Liability Under Civil Laws

What about civil laws? For example, suppose you do not pay your personal debts or that you run off with another man's wife. Can you be given military punishment for such nonmilitary offenses? Yes, you can. In the first place, of course, you are liable to civil lawsuits and the actions of the civil courts and police. But military courts can also try you for conduct casting discredit on the Cost Guard, and can award you various types of punishment.

Suppose you are arrested for speeding, for drunkenness, or being criminally involved with drugs, and are held in prison until you are absent over leave. You not only will have to pay your fine and suffer your imprisonment, but you may also be before captain's mast and perhaps a court-martial for your AWOL (Absent Without Leave) time and for any discredit you have cast on the Coast Guard. If you willfully refuse to pay just debts, you will be warned by your commanding officer (CO). Then you may lose advancement, because the Coast Guard does not promote men who are not honest. Finally, if you continue to run up unpaid debts, you will probably receive an undesirable or bad conduct discharge. (On the other hand, if you are being gouged by unscrupulous dealers, see your executive officer or legal officer. They can help you in many ways.)

Purpose of Punishment

The punishment used by the Coast Guard—such as extra duty, loss of liberty, loss of pay, and confinement—has three purposes:

To deter you from breaking the rules;

To encourage you to do your duty;

To provide an example to others.

The smart man learns from the mistakes of others. When he sees other men being punished for being late, out of uniform, or careless in their duties, he makes sure that he himself is on time, in proper uniform, and attentive to duty.

If you ever receive punishment in the Coast Guard remember:

You brought it on yourself by your behavior.

Take it like a man; don't grouse, and don't be sorry for yourself.

Learn your lesson. Avoid the habits, attitudes, and companions that led you to do wrong.

Don't hold any grudges. The men who punished you are simply doing their duty—which they wouldn't have had to do if *you* had done *your* duty.

Courts-Martial

There are three types of military courts. In addition, certain kinds of offenses may be punished by a commanding officer or officer in charge without a court-martial.

Pretrial Procedure

Any Coast Guardsman who knows that an offense has been committed can prefer charges. Ordinarily, he reports the facts to his superior, who relays them to the commanding officer or the officer in charge, who then takes the necessary action.

Apprehension and Restraint. Any officer, petty officer, or other member of the service assigned to guard or police duty may apprehend a suspect. No physical contact is necessary to apprehend, but the man must be clearly notified that he is being taken into custody. *Arrest* is moral restraint limiting the man's liberty pending disposition of charges. If there is reason to believe he will not observe his military obligation to obey the order of arrest, he may be placed in *confinement*. This is forcible detention, but it is not for punishment, and the man must be so advised.

Preliminary Inquiry. The commanding officer has a preliminary investigation held to develop sufficient information to permit intelligent disposition of the case. The accused is informed of the charge and is permitted, but not required, to make a statement. He is advised that any statement he makes may be used against him. After the investigating officer has developed the facts, he makes a full report to the commanding officer; if an offense has been committed, he may sign the charge sheet. If the offense is within the jurisdiction of the commanding officer, he convenes a court-martial or takes other appropriate action. If the offense requires general court-martial, the full report is forwarded to the district commander or other officer exercising general court-martial supervision over the unit. If a general court-martial is to be held, it must be preceded by a formal investigation.

Non-Judicial Punishment (Mast)

If you break a rule or are negligent, careless, or unmilitary in your conduct, you may be *placed on report* by a petty officer or commissioned officer. This means that you must appear before the captain at a specified time for a hearing and possible punishment. That is, you must appear at *captain's mast*.

The captain's mast gets its name from the old sailing days when the setting for this form of naval justice was on the weather deck, at the foot of the ship's mainmast.

The commanding officer is authorized to assign certain punishments for minor offenses. Cases are tried and punishments given at captain's mast. At mast the commanding officer may give the following punishments:

Type of Punishment	CO (LCdr or Above)	CO (Lt or Below)	Officer in Charge
Admonition or reprimand	Yes (written)	Yes (written)	No
Correctional custody (E-5 and below)	30 days	7 days	No
Extra duties	45 days	14 days	14 days
Restriction	60 days	14 days	14 days
Forfeiture of pay	½ of one month's pay for 2 months	7 days pay	3 days pay
Reduction to next inferior grade (E-6 and below)	Yes	Yes	No

Mast is not always held for disciplinary purposes. A *meritorious mast* is held by the captain to give awards or commendations to men who have earned them.

On many ships and stations a certain time of the day is set aside by the executive officer to hear requests from members of the crew. This practice is called *request mast*.

Summary Courts-Martial

An officer who is designated as a commanding officer may convene a summary court-martial. It is composed of one officer, preferably a lieutenant or higher, and has authority to try any noncapital offense. The court has jurisdiction only over enlisted personnel, and such personnel have the right to refuse trial by it; in the latter case, the trial will be held by special or general court-martial.

A summary court is authorized to award punishment up to the maximum allowed under the *Manual For Courts-Martial* except the punishments of death, punitive discharge, confinement over one month, hard labor over 45 days, or forfeiture of pay in excess of two-thirds pay for one month.

The record of the court is prepared on a special form; however, if the finding on any charge is "guilty" where the plea had been "not guilty," a summary of the testimony on that charge must be forwarded with the form.

Special Courts-Martial

An officer who is designated as a commanding officer may convene a special court-martial. It is composed of three or more persons, one third of whom must be enlisted if the accused is enlisted and so requests. It has authority to try any member of the service for any offense not carrying the death penalty. In special cases the district commander may direct a special court to try cases on charges for which the death penalty is allowed. Trial and defense counsels of equal qualifications are appointed by the convening authority.

The court may award any punishment up to the maximum allowed by the *Manual* except death, dishonorable discharge, dismissal, confinement over six months, hard labor over three months, or forfeiture of pay exceeding two-thirds pay per month for longer than six months.

If the trial results in a bad conduct discharge being awarded, a complete verbatim transcript must be prepared. If a lesser sentence is adjudged, or if the trial results in an acquittal, only a summarized report of the testimony is required.

General Courts-Martial

General courts-martial are convened by the Commandant or by a district commander. They are composed of five or more members, one third of whom must be enlisted if the accused is enlisted and so requests. Trial and defense counsels of equal qualifications are appointed by the convening authority.

A general court has the power to try any member of the Coast Guard for any offense, and to award any punishment up to the maximum allowed under the *Manual For Courts-Martial*. Complete verbatim transcripts of the proceedings are prepared in all cases and forwarded for review.

Masters-at-Arms

The masters-at-arms (MAA) are men assigned to maintain order on a ship or station. They are the assistants of the executive officer. Large ships may have a chief master-at-arms (CMAA) with several assistants. Men are assigned to the MAA force for several months or longer, and, while acting as MAAs, they are relieved of most of their normal watches and duties.

Shore Patrol

The *shore patrol* (SP) is the military police patrol of the Navy and Coast Guard. It consists of officers and petty officers assigned to maintain order among naval personnel off the ship or station. They are identified by armbands with the letters SP.

The Army and Marines, have their military police (MP) and the Air Force has its air police (AP). You must obey the MPs and APs as well as the SPs. In some areas a combined or unified Armed Services Police Detachment (ASPD) is organized. It consists of men from all the Services—SP, MP, AP—under one command and wearing the same armbands.

The mission of these military patrols is to:

Give assistance to military personnel.

Protect military personnel from harmful practices on the part of civilian establishments.

Investigate accidents and offenses involving military personnel.

The shore patrol and the military patrol have authority to stop, question, apprehend, or take into custody any member of the Armed

Forces. If stopped by the SP, you must show your I.D. (identification) card, leave papers, or orders, and you must obey any directions given you by the SP.

On the other hand, if you need advice, directions, or help, you should go to or call the nearest SP patrol or headquarters. Their primary job is to help and to protect military personnel.

CHAPTER 4

Personal Standards

The Coast Guard will train you to perform your military and professional duties, but your ability to perform them quickly and efficiently will depend on your physical and mental condition. Good health and a cheerful attitude will make your job easier and improve relations with other people. However, no one can order you to be healthy and keep cheerful; that's entirely up to you. The following pages offer some helpful suggestions.

PERSONAL CARE

As a Coast Guardsman you will live better, and be healthier, than most of the people in many nations of the world. Even the smallest cutter or shore station has facilities to provide nourishing meals, well-ventilated and heated berthing spaces, laundry service, hot and cold running water, and sanitary living conditions. It's almost impossible not to keep clean and healthy, but a few people will always manage.

Exercise and Conditioning

To accomplish your job, you must be physically and mentally fit. Good health is no accident. You can achieve it through careful attention to personal cleanliness, a balanced diet, moderation in the use of alcohol and tobacco, plenty of fresh air and exercise, good posture, and proper rest. Exercise invigorates and stimulates the whole body. Mild exer-

Figure 4–1. Regularly scheduled exercise periods should not terminate with recruit training. No matter what your duty assignment, take time for exercise.

cise, for a few minutes every day, is important (figure 4–1). If an exercise area is not available, or an exercise period is not provided in the daily routine, work out your own system of conditioning exercises and follow them every day. These should include warming up exercises in various positions: standing, kneeling, sitting, and lying prone. Follow with limbering exercises: body stretching, twisting, bending, knee bending, and running in place. Include deep breathing exercises.

Remember that cleanliness and health are very nearly the same. The person with athlete's foot, ringworm, "crotch itch," or "jungle rot" generally is not unlucky; he is just not smart enough to keep clean. Sometimes it's not easy to keep clean where washrooms are crowded, but the effort is worthwhile. Shower daily in warm weather or when you are sweating heavily. In cool weather, once every other day should be enough—but wash your face and hands well with hot water and soap before every meal. Wash your hair at least once a week. Use talcum powder between your toes and, if necessary, around your crotch, to keep free from itching.

Dysentery

Dysentery is common in the tropics, and it can occur in the United States. The major symptom is loose bowels, although nausea, stomach cramps, and vomiting also occur. Water and flies are definite factors, but dysentery is more likely to be spread by food handlers or through vegetables fertilized with human waste. Ashore, in countries where dysentery is known to exist, avoid any uncooked food, particularly lettuce, celery, cabbage, or radishes. If you must eat ashore, eat in reputable restaurants, and avoid "dives." In areas where dysentery might exist, water should be boiled for at least five minutes, and then put into sterile containers. When in doubt, drink bottled water.

Care of Teeth

The three most common dental diseases are these: tooth decay (caries); inflammation of the gum (gingivitis); and disease of the gum and bone surrounding the teeth (pyorrhea). They cause the needless loss of teeth, for they can be prevented or controlled.

Caries

There is no positive way to prevent all tooth decay, but it can be cut down by brushing the teeth correctly and by reducing the amount of sweets each day. At the first sign of tooth decay, see a dentist.

Gingivitis

Normal and healthy gums are pale pink and firm in texture. If they are swollen or puffy, hang loosely about the teeth, and bleed easily, then you have gingivitis.

Pyorrhea

If gingivitis goes untreated you may notice pockets or crevices between the tooth and gum, an indication of pyorrhea (or periodontitis). Surprisingly, more teeth are lost from these two diseases than from tooth decay. Most dental disease results from poor mouth hygiene combined with the *misuse* of the toothbrush.

Toothbrushes

Proper use of a toothbrush is most effective in control or prevention of dental diseases. Keep at least two brushes, so you can always use a dry one. When the bristles become soft, throw the brush away.

Brush your teeth regularly, after each meal if you can. Use dental floss at least once a day. Avoid candy and don't forget to see a dentist twice a year.

The proper toothbrushing technique will clean the teeth and gums, stimulate circulation in the gum tissues, and toughen the gums by the friction of the bristles, but will not injure the teeth or gums. Brush with the mouth barely open, the muscles relaxed, permitting easier access to hard-to-get-at areas.

Diet

The Coast Guard takes great care to serve attractive, well-balanced meals (figure 4–2), but they will do you little good unless you observe certain rules in your diet. Don't concentrate on meat, potatoes, and pie and skip the "rabbit food." Do yourself, your strength and stamina, your general health, and your teeth and gums a favor; balance your diet. The basic foods, with suggested daily amounts of each, are listed below.

Green, leafy, yellow vegetables, and fruits	1 or more servings
Citrus fruits, (orange, grapefruit, lemons) or equivalents (tomatoes, green salads, berries)	1 or more servings

Figure 4–2. Good health depends on proper diet and eating habits. Coast Guard menus are planned for your benefit; take advantage of them.

Other vegetables and fruits	2 or more servings
Milk, ice cream, cheese	2 cups
Meat or fish, shell fish, poultry, eggs, dried beans and peas, nuts	4 ounces or 1 serving
Bread, flour, and cereals	4 to 6 slices or the equivalent
Butter or fortified margarine	5 pats

Don't overload. It's not necessary to eat everything in sight to let the cooks know you like their cooking. Watch your weight, and keep it under control. It's easier to give up seconds than to have to buy new uniforms.

Drug Abuse

Drugs, as used here, refers to barbiturates, narcotics, various hallucinogenic compounds, and other substances taken for nonmedical purposes. People faced with problems they cannot handle—anxiety, discontent, frustration, despair—may try to escape through the use of drugs. Those who have a sense of security, or can find answers to their problems through self-reliance or counseling, have no need for such escape.

Drugs are classified as *hallucinogens, stimulants, depressants* and *tranquilizers, opiates, narcotics,* and—surprise—*petroleum products.* More on that later. The proper medical terms for these drugs sometimes have little relation to what they are called by street freaks making the scene where the action is. Hallucinogens include LSD (acid), STP, PCP, DMT, MDA, and MMDA, mescaline-peyote, THC, psilocybin, marijuana (grass), and hashish (hash). Stimulants (speed) include the amphetamines Benzedrine (bennies), Dexadrine, Methamphetamine, Desoxyn, Drinalfal, D.O.E., Methadrine, Norodin, Syndrox, and cocaine. Depressants include the barbiturates (downers or barbs) such as Amytal, Nembutal, Seconal (reds), Phenobarbital, Tuinal, and—no matter what the ads say—alcohol. Tranquilizers and sleeping pills are also depressants. Petroleum products include gasoline, paint, and model airplane glue.

The effects of the various hallucinogenic drugs vary according to the individual using them. With LSD, the more messed up the mind, the more messed up the trip. In using any drug not produced under controlled laboratory conditions, there is the risk of impurities. Peyote cooked up by someone not knowing what he was about could contain enough strychnine to make the trip your last one. Psilocybin is made from a certain kind of mushroom, and by the time you learn it was made from the wrong kind, it will be too late.

Speed makes the entire body "run fast." A person on speed will have no appetite and won't sleep; his liver and kidneys are overworked and his arteries may "balloon." There will eventually be brain damage, followed by death, but it will not come quickly, or painlessly. Downers work the other way; they slow down the heart and lower the blood pressure, for a lazy, drunken-like high. Brain functions are destroyed by the reduced oxygen supply to the brain cells. Downers are more dangerous than any type of speed; their users will sooner or later die from an overdose, or from withdrawal seizures. "Glue freaks," those who sniff airplane glue or other petroleum products, will never die a spectacular death like cocaine snorters or pill poppers; worse than that, they keep on living, suffering from toxic poisoning and are unable to feed themselves, dress themselves, or get to a head by themselves.

Some drugs are highly addictive; also, if you use a little bit one day, the next day you need a bit more to get the same high. After only a week or so of shooting heroin every day or every other day, the hook is in deep and you are psychologically incapable of staying away from it. Depending on the drug and the market, a fix may cost up to $100 a day. A habit like that can't live on ComRats. The only people who make out on heroin are the pushers who sell it. With cocaine, there is the same need for more and more, plus the easy chance that cocaine snorters can take an overdose that produces convulsions and death. Even Seconal pills, mixed with beer or wine, can be fatal. A side effect from using any drugs intravenously—shooting into the veins with a needle—is that a dirty needle can transmit hepatitis, and that can produce cirrhosis of the liver, and that can kill a person.

There are two ways to approach the drug problem. A person can experiment a bit. He'll ride high for a while, but before he knows it he's hooked. If he doesn't break the habit, the result is always the same. Sooner or later, in street talk, "he's had an over amp and flipped out for good." That's permanent. The best approach is—don't start.

The best deterrent to drug abuse is a well-balanced individual sense of values and understanding of the consequences involved, aside from the health factor. There is also the fact that under the UCMJ "use or possession of drugs or narcotics is a felony," punishable by dishonorable discharge, confinement at hard labor for five years, forfeiture of all pay and allowances, and reduction to the lowest pay grade. The use of drugs can also result in cancellation of any security clearance held.

There is a continuous program on drug education. Recruits are lectured on drugs, and seagoing and shore commands have key personnel trained to discuss drug problems. However, the program can help only those who want to help themselves. It's free, voluntary, and confidential; if you have a problem or question concerning drugs, someone is ready to help you.

Marijuana Use

A very substantial portion of the Coast Guard's operating budget is spent in interdicting traffic in illegal substances. The major substance being interdicted by the Coast Guard is marijuana. It must seem rather silly to the marijuana user that so much money is spent to stop something that "everyone does." And the analogy between "booze" and "pot" is usually thrown in at this point, because it seems relevant to the user's argument.

Marijuana is considered as a controlled substance much the same as narcotics and illegal drugs. Its sale is forbidden by federal and state statutes as is its growth as a plant, its distribution, and its use. In short, marijuana, called "pot," "grass," "mary jane," etc., (as well as the tar-like derivative of the marijuana plant flower, hashish) is flat-out illegal. Certain civilian enforcement jurisdictions have more lenient policies than do others concerning the growth, sale, distribution, and use of marijuana. It is illegal, however, for Coast Guardsmen to do any of the above.

Marijuana became popular during the 1960s among young persons, partly because of the intoxicating effects of its smoke and partly because its illegality made it a faddish way to rebuke "the establishment." Many persons have both regularly used and experimented with marijuana. Because marijuana has not been determined to be physically addictive, its use has not presented the risk to the user posed with "hard drugs," such as heroin. Hence the tendency among some regular users has been to equate the use of marijuana with social drinking. Recent medical reports, however, dispute the contention of the relative harmlessness of marijuana. This information has been made available to each Coast Guard command and can be obtained and read in detail. It might be hard to convince a regular grass user that these different studies aren't just more of the "cigarettes will stunt your growth," stuff that has been used for years by parents to scare their kids away from bad habits. Nevertheless, the evidence is in the record. In summary, regular use of marijuana, for example, a joint or two a day, does three things to your body:

1. The tars in marijuana smoke are far more likely to cause cancer of the lungs than those in tobacco smoke.

2. The THC crystals in the smoke, the substance that gives the high, affect the chromosomes in the female ova and distort the male sperm.

3. The THC crystals collect in the nerve endings in the brain, ultimately affecting memory, physical activity, and learning ability.

So if you want to end up in a few years ignorant and helpless with lung cancer and a deformed kid, just keep on puffing those joints. But make sure you do it where you won't get caught. Its still a felony under the UCMJ.

Alcohol Abuse

Alcoholic beverages are an accepted part of American life, and "social drinking" is considered normal behavior. But while we may not always want to admit it, alcohol abuse is a major problem in our society. Since the Coast Guard is representative of our society as a whole, it also has a "drinking problem." A person doesn't have to be an out-and-out caricature of a Bowery Bum in order to have an alcohol problem. You have an alcohol problem when your drinking creates problem situations; the Coast Guard has a problem when your alcohol problem costs the service time lost through absence, sickness, treatment, administration, and performance. Your hangover, a source of joking by your shipmates and a temporary aggravation to you, can be a serious matter to the service, which needs your 100 percent effort in order to perform its missions.

There are very few social functions sponsored by service-connected organizations where drinking is not encouraged. Service clubs run specials during "Happy Hour," and beer and package goods are sold at discount prices by nonappropriated fund activities. Shipmates brag about how "crocked" they were during a particular party, and people that don't drink are often shunned or put down. If the service was so concerned about its drinking problem, then why doesn't it do something about it?

Well, it tries to. First off, a person drinking sensibly is usually not a problem. What's sensible? Think of the word *sense* . . . use good sense by keeping all your senses alert and limit yourself accordingly. Don't drink on an empty stomach, or when you are fatigued, or when you are taking medication, or when you have to drive or operate machinery. Be considerate of others. If a friend or shipmate isn't drinking, there must be a reason. If you accept the fact that this person is your friend and that he has a right to be at the same gathering as you, why not respect that person's reason not to drink? As a responsible member of your command, help your shipmates who have too much to drink. Don't encourage them to get blasted out of their minds. Too many people have exceeded their limits and wound up dead—not dead drunk, just dead, period. If a man or a woman develops an alcohol problem, that person should be encouraged to get professional help before trouble results. Alcohol abuse training isn't intended for alley drunks, but for people who are having problems that are alcohol related. That's where the Coast Guard comes in and will help. In fact, some Navy training programs offer college credit hours to their participants. Remember getting drunk isn't salty; it merely shows that you didn't use good sense.

Tattoos

A tattoo does not make a sailor salty either; it merely proves he is not very bright. Tattoos are regarded as the "in" thing by certain cults, but at the best they are crude designs, often embarrassing, and once applied, they are permanent. There is no way to remove a tattoo. Tattoo parlors, if not out of bounds, are unsanitary; and a dirty needle can infect you with hepatitis, abscesses, or tetanus. The pigments used may also produce an allergic reaction. The best advice on getting a tattoo is—*don't*.

Venereal Diseases (VD)

Venereal diseases, like alcoholism, were for many years "swept under the rug" and not mentioned in polite society. "Nice people" didn't even know what to call the various types of infection, although that didn't prevent both royalty and riff-raff from getting them. Now VD is no longer a hush-hush subject; it is discussed in newspapers and magazines, and should be a matter of concern for everyone because, despite the use of "wonder drugs" such as penicillin, it is on the increase.

Many contagious diseases can be transmitted from one person to another without the two people coming near each other, by mosquitoes, fleas, flies, sneezing, dirty dishes, improper food handling, contaminated water, or in clothing, but VD is an infectious disease that can be transmitted only by contact between one person and another. The "contact" is not always what might be considered the usual source, such as prostitutes or "bar flies." More and more, VD is infecting young people who have a casual outlook on things—street people, groupies, high school students, and teeny-boppers. And VD is one disease the prevention of which depends nearly 100 percent on the individual—no contact, no VD.

There are five general types of VD: *syphilis* (syph, pox, old Joe); *gonorrhea* (clap, dose, the drip, GC); *chancroid* (bubo, hair cut); *granulema inguinale*; and *lymphogranuloma venereum*. All can be transmitted from an infected person, man or woman, to an uninfected person, woman or man, through sexual intercourse. Syphilis can also be transmitted by a kiss if an infected person has an open sore on the lips. A woman can transmit syphilis to her unborn child, or gonorrhea to a child at birth.

The incubation period—time from contact until first symptoms appear—varies; 10 to 90 days for syphilis; 2 to 14 days for gonorrhea and chancroid; longer times for the others. However, a person who has become infected can transmit the disease to another *before* signs of infection appear; there is *no* way to tell that a person is not infected. The results of VD infection may appear years later. Latent syphilis, the state in which clinical signs and symptoms of infection are absent, may appear "early," four years after infection, or "late," as much as 20 years afterward. Among the infinite variety of results to be expected then are destructive ulcers, disease of the heart or blood vessels, blindness, and insanity. Other kinds of VD have other kinds of results, none of them pleasant.

Venereal disease control is a worldwide effort, but it all depends on the individual. Medical department personnel will emphasize that individual abstinence from sexual intercourse other than marital relations is the one sure way to avoid venereal infection. Medical department personnel will also instruct in the effective use of prophylactics.

In this connection it should be emphasized that a liberal attitude toward sex, made possible by use of "the pill" and readily available abortions, only increases the chance of VD infection.

There is no military punishment for contracting a venereal disease, but it is misconduct to conceal an infection. It is the duty of the individual to avoid casual sexual intercourse, to prevent infection by prompt and proper prophylaxis, and to report for medical attention promptly at the first symptom of any infection. This is necessary for two reasons; to commence treatment to cure the infection, and to make certain that the contact—the person from whom the infection was received—is identified and also given treatment. Remember—VD doesn't just happen. It can be cured, but it can also be prevented. Prevention is a lot less trouble than the cure. Don't go asking for trouble.

Homosexuality

Recent media attention given to homosexual rights activists, as well as open treatment of the subject in films and television drama, have made the matter of homosexuality an issue of importance to military organizations. The Coast Guard is, as we know, a military organization with about the same cross section of kinds of people that comprise the population of our nation. Despite attempts by some gay rights groups to assert that homosexuality is an acceptable, alternate life style, homosexual behavior is, in fact, repugnant to the moral standards of most Americans. It is also considered sodomy by the military and is therefore punishable under the UCMJ as a criminal offense.

The word *sodomy* comes from the name of the biblical city, Sodom. Some scholars believe that the ruins of Sodom are beneath the waters of the Dead Sea, which have risen since the city was destroyed about 1900 B.C. The patriarch Abraham, significant to the Christian, Hebrew, and Islamic religions, had a nephew named Lot who lived in Sodom for a time. The God of Abraham had considered destroying the city and its inhabitants, but at Abraham's pleading sent two male messengers, or angels, to meet Lot and investigate the moral fiber of the city. When the messengers arrived the men of Sodom surrounded Lot's house and attempted to rape them. That's the origin of the word, which now means engaging in unnatural sexual relations.

Since ancient times, civilizations have dealt with homosexuality. Most societies have suppressed it, considering it unnatural, and have imposed drastic and cruel punishments for homosexuals. A few cultures have condoned or advanced it, but they no longer exist. Homosexuals in our modern society are not associated with any particular occupation nor do they generally have any similarities in appearance. Many of these citizens have made, and continue to make, very significant contributions to our society. Most are persons with the same basic values as the heterosexuals who make up the majority—*except* they deviate from the majority in that they prefer sexual relations with members of the same sex, and that's an important difference! While heterosexual behavior is considered natural and homosexual behavior unnatural, any military person engaged in homosexual activity is committing a serious breach of military discipline, regardless of his or her stated sexual preference.

This issue of homosexuality in the military is very sensitive and has been heard in the courts. Homosexuals are considered to be a threat to the discipline and cohesiveness of a military organization. With the augmentation of significant numbers of women in the military, the issue of sexual activity between consenting military adults has obviously arisen. Heterosexuality is a natural situation and no person in or out of the military can rightfully act surprised or shocked that such activity occurs. Whether acceptable or not under the morals of our society, the fact that a military male makes sexual advances to a willing military female does not enrage or seriously threaten the security of the organization. Homosexual advances, on the other hand, do threaten the organization and often result in violent responses, blackmail, breaches of national security, and a very significant administrative, medical, and legal work load. As a result of the problem homosexuals pose, they are not suitable for military service even when society is willing to deal tolerantly with their situation.

ATTITUDE TOWARD OTHERS

The first requirement is to show respect, tolerance, and consideration. Perhaps for the first time you will be mixed up with people from different social backgrounds with various levels of education; they will be different colors and have different religions—in fact, they will be just as different from you as you are from them. Each one has to respect the other's different beliefs, be tolerant of the different ways of saying or doing certains things, and most of all, be considerate. Consideration can be a fairly simple thing; for example, if the man in the bunk next to you has the midwatch, go somewhere else to practice your guitar.

People in the Coast Guard come from every state in the United States. As might be expected, they don't all look alike, believe alike, think alike, or even like the same kinds of food. They may be black, red, white, or yellow, and include members of every recognized political party and religious denomination in the country. Their national origin—the land from which they or their ancestors came—is equally varied; people come from all over. There is only one thing that every one has in common—they are all Coast Guardsmen.

Women in the Coast Guard

The concept of women serving in the Armed Forces is not new. In each war in which the United States has been engaged, women have served their country not only in support roles behind the lines, but in the heat of battle as well. The assignment of Coast Guard women to

Figure 4–3. Sports provide needed exercise and promote good fellowship as well, helping one to get along with all kinds of people.

certain ratings and to duties afloat, however, is relatively recent, and the proportionate numbers of women serving in the Armed Forces have increased considerably. Moreover, the role of working women in American society as a whole has also changed over the past ten years. Where the new working roles of women cause them to compete with men for jobs once considered "male territory only," conflict occasionally arises. This conflict is more deep-rooted than that normally found in competition between men over pay, promotions, and working conditions. Unfortunately, attitudes fostered by years of sexual role modeling often bring about resentment by male workers who can't accept the fact that a female can perform as well as he in a job considered by him to be "masculine." This leads to discriminatory attitudes and practices that are unfair to women and, in the Coast Guard, are contrary to the service's equal opportunity policies. Often this kind of discrimination leads to sexual harassment, another form of discrimination.

Sexual harassment, like the concept of women in the military, is not something new. For the most part, however, it is a new expression that describes an old evil that working women have accepted but resented in the past. Sexual harassment means making unwelcome advances toward a member of the opposite sex in an environment where the person being harassed is subjected to pressures from superiors or peers if that person protests the harassment. Sexual harassment is a matter of perception on the part of the person being bothered.

Natural sexual roles in our society designate the male as the sexual aggressor. In other works, the man is attracted to and pursues an unattached female. She may protest, perhaps, but he may consider her protest only a teasing invitation, so he persists a little more, awaiting a stronger signal indicating her true wishes. A normal mature man usually senses when the woman of his attention is not really interested in him, with the result that he will shrug off the disinterest and move on. Insensitive and immature males are usually interested only in themselves, with the result that their imaginations won't permit them to recognize a "turn off." These guys are probably the source of most bona fide sexual harassment complaints by women. There are only rare instances of sexual harassment complaints by men against women.

Sexual harassment can be sexually oriented communications, comments, gestures, or physical contact. It can also be offers or threats to influence or alter, directly or indirectly, an individual's career or other conditions of service in order to secure sexual favors. It could be repeated requests for dates. Or it could be the promise of an especially good duty assignment by a superior if the subordinate will go along with the boss's sexual plans.

OK then, a reader might ask, "But don't some women use sex to gain special advantages?" Sure, some do. Some men gain special advantages from others by brown nosing, too. But this has nothing to do with sexual harassment. Both men and women in the Coast Guard have an obligation to each other and to their service to respect another person's dignity. That's the basis of civil rights, and it is required conduct for all service people.

In the event of sexual harassment or other perceptions of sexual discrimination, the Commandant of the Coast Guard has provided procedures for a person to follow; see the Commandant Instruction 5350.11 series for details.

Racial Understanding

Because of all the differences of race, creed, religion, or national origin, discrimination may crop up, but with thought and understanding it should be eliminated. There are no bars between people in the Coast Guard; it is a service in which all persons have equal opportunities, minority groups are represented in enlisted and commissioned ranks, bias is eliminated, and racial and interracial understanding and cooperation are thoroughly understood and practiced.

In all discussions of race, you have to define your terms. The following appear frequently.

Race Relations

These are the relationships between groups and members of groups that have been socially defined as races on the basis of *physical* criteria. ("I'm black, you're white.")

Ethnic Groups

These are groups of people with a common cultural tradition, which differs from that of other members of their society; they may have their own language, religion, and customs. Swedes, Germans, and Poles in parts of the U.S. are ethnic groups; so are mountain folk in the Appalachian Mountains and Cubans in Miami.

Minority Group

This can be any group in a community that can be identified by ethnic, racial, or religious differences from the majority of the community. This difference can give rise to prejudice and discrimination against members of the minority group, not because of their behavior as individuals, but merely because they are members of the group. Minority members in the Coast Guard are considered such more for racial than ethnic or religious differences. Virtually any person could be a part of a minority group within the confines of a local situation. In other words, a white, Anglo-Saxon Protestant living in a neighborhood of a nationally identified minority could be the subject of racial prejudice and discrimination. It is important to recognize that the expression of "minority members in uniform" usually means racially different people as compared with the national majority of white people of European descent.

The key to respecting minority members in the Coast Guard is to consider the Coast Guard as being a team made up of players from all ethnic, racial, and religious backgrounds—all with skills, all with human dignity. Taken one person at a time against the background of his or her teammates, no one person is a majority. Each has acquired skills to serve the purpose of the team, and the team needs those skills. The person's ethnic, racial, or religious background is of no importance except that it might incidentally broaden the team's understanding of human values. Human dignity is what motivates one player to praise another for his play, or to feel a oneness with the others because all members are genuinely accepted as equal and important, even if some have to "warm the bench." Respect for another's right to dignity is what civil rights is all about. Anyone can recognize the skill of an athlete, but if team members don't respect a fellow member's right to emotion, to express himself, to be a part of the whole, and to share victory and defeat, they are bigots because they have deprived their fellow teammate of the human dignity necessary for true team membership and oneness.

For a team to be able to function properly requires bringing together, in harmony, all the skills on the team to accomplish a mission. The teams that stand out as winners in collegiate and professional sports are those where the team players play as a single unit, not as a bunch of individuals each looking out for "number one." Team play means respecting one another, both as regards to one's skills as well as to one's dignity. The Coast Guard is no different.

Minority Members in Uniform

These people include American blacks, Chicanos, Puerto Ricans, American Indians, and Oriental Americans. They all have their different attributes and are proud of them. Black men and women do not cease to be black when they wear a uniform; they are still black, and resent having their racial pride taken as evidence that they are black militants or racists. Chicanos and Puerto Ricans grew up under a different life style than white Americans and consider themselves as neither black nor white; they are what they are, and others must accept them as so. The American Indians are the only real Americans; they were here long before Columbus arrived (and thought he was somewhere else), and were considerably ahead of the Spaniards in much of their philosophy and culture; if they appear proud, they have a heritage to be proud of. The Oriental Americans—Chinese, Japanese, and others—all have cultural histories far older than anything in American history, yet they have met opposition, hostility, and ignorance in this country. Many of these people have racial characteristics that make it possible for a prejudiced or ignorant person to say "they don't look American." The point is, they *are* Americans, and entitled to the same treatment and the same opportunity that everyone else is.

It may come as a surprise to the average black man or woman entering military service today, but they are not the first to do so. During World War II more than a million black men and women were in uniform, and more than 6,000 of them were officers. Blacks have been in military service long before there was a United States; black men began training for the militia in Massachusetts in 1652, and the first American killed in the Revolutionary War, shot in the Boston Massacre on 5 March 1770, was a black soldier, Crispus Attucks. Other Revolutionary War heroes who were black were Peter Salem and Salem Poor, who fought at Bunker Hill, and Mark Stalin, who *commanded* the gunboat *Patriot* in the Continental Navy.

More than 5,000 black men served in the Continental Army, and more blacks have served in every war since. In the Civil War, they fought on both sides. They fought Indians in the American West, Spaniards in the Spanish-American War, and Filipino insurrectionists in the Philippines after that war.

In World War I, the first black officer training school was set up in Des Moines, Iowa. Black laborers sent to France unloaded cargo at the rate of 25,000 tons a day, long before forklifts and pallets were invented. The 369th Infantry, black, served under fire in the front lines longer than any other American unit, for 191 days, and never had a man retreat or be captured, while Private Henry Johnson became the first American to receive the prestigious French award, the Croix de Guerre.

The long struggle for equality gained strength when the Selective Service and Training Act of 5 September 1940 barred discrimination against any person because of race or color. There has been a definite change in attitudes regarding race and color in all the services since that time; people now are more concerned in how men and women handle their jobs than in how they look or where they came from. Black men and women now serve in enlisted and officer status in all services, and some officers have advanced to flag rank.

EQUAL OPPORTUNITY

In striving to achieve equal treatment for all, the government has established an Equal Opportunity Policy. This means equal opportunity for all, regardless of race, creed, religion, or national origin. It pertains to educational, recreational, and social programs, and is designed to help those who may be culturally deprived or underprivileged, but who have the talent and capability to compete with others.

The goal of this program is to help all personnel reach the highest possible level of responsibility that their talent and diligence can handle.

RELATIONS WITH THE PUBLIC

When you put on the Coast Guard uniform, you become a representative of the Coast Guard, and civilians will base some of their ideas about the service on the way you look and act. In a foreign country, you also represent the United States, and the people you meet will take your appearance and behavior as being representative of all Americans. Be careful to make a good impression. Remember that at all times, no matter where you may be or what position you hold, you are performing a public relations duty. Do not confuse public relations with public information—the technical term for military work with the press, radio, and other information media. Just try to keep good relations with the public.

FOREIGNERS

As a U.S. citizen, you regard people from other countries as foreigners. Bear in mind that when you visit any other country in the world, *you* are the foreigner. The customs of other people may seem strange to you, but that's their way of doing things, and they like it. Don't make fun of anyone or anything in another country; at best it's impolite, and at the worst such thoughtlessness can result in serious trouble.

CHAPTER 5

Military Fundamentals

The purpose of military drill is fourfold: To teach the fundamentals of military bearing; to provide experience in giving and following commands; to prepare for military operations on land; and to facilitate movements of companies from one place to another (figure 5–1).

DRILL COMMANDS

Preparatory commands are indicated in this chapter by SMALL CAPITAL LETTERS and those of execution by LARGE CAPITAL LETTERS.

There are two parts to a military drill command:

1. The preparatory command, such as HAND, which indicates the movement that is to be executed.

2. The command of execution, such as SALUTE, HALT, or ARMS, which causes the desired movement, or halt, or element of the manual to be executed.

When appropriate, the preparatory command includes the name or title of the group concerned, as, FIRST DIVISION, HAND SALUTE.

In certain commands, the preparatory command and the command of execution are combined, as for example: FALL IN, AT EASE, and REST.

To call back or revoke a command or to begin again a movement that has started wrong, the command AS YOU WERE is given, at which the movement stops and the former position is taken.

Figure 5–1. A smart appearance at ceremonies means that each person must be well grounded in basic military fundamentals.

THE POSITIONS

Position of Attention

Command: AT–TEN-SHUN or FALL-IN. Heels close together, feet turned out to form an angle of 45 degrees, knees straight, hips level, body erect, with the weight resting equally on the heels and balls of the feet. Shoulders squared, chest arched, arms hanging down without stiffness so that thumbs are along the seams of the trousers, palms and fingers relaxed. Head erect, chin drawn in, and eyes straight to the front. In coming to Attention, the heels are brought together smartly and audibly.

The Rests

Commands: FALL OUT; REST; AT EASE; and 1. PARADE, 2. REST.
FALL OUT. Men break rank but remain nearby. Men return to places and come to attention at the command FALL IN.
REST. Right foot is kept in place. Men may talk and move.
AT EASE. Right foot is kept in place. Men keep silent, but may move about.
1. PARADE, 2. REST. Move the left foot smartly 12 inches to the left from the right foot; at the same time, clasp the hands behind the back, palms to the rear, the right hand clasping the left thumb, arms hanging naturally. Keep silent and motionless.
To resume attention from any rest other than FALL OUT the command is, for example: 1. DETAIL, 2. ATTENTION.

Eyes Right or Left

The commands are: 1. EYES, 2. RIGHT (or LEFT); 3. READY, 4. FRONT. At the command RIGHT, each man turns his head and eyes smartly to the right. The men on the extreme right file keep the head and eyes to the front. At the command FRONT, the head and eyes are turned smartly to the front. The opposite is carried out for EYES LEFT.

Hand Salute

Command: 1. HAND, 2. SALUTE, 3. TWO. the command TWO is used only when saluting by command. At the command SALUTE, salute smartly, looking toward the person saluted.
At the command TWO, drop the arm to its normal position by the side in one movement and turn the head and eyes to the front. In

passing in review, execute the hand salute in the same way. The salute is held until six paces beyond the person saluted.

FACINGS

Right or Left Face

Command: 1. RIGHT (LEFT), 2. FACE. At the command FACE, slightly raise the left heel and right toe; face to the right, turning on the right heel, putting pressure on the ball of the left foot. Hold the left leg straight. Then place the left foot smartly beside the right.

Half Right or Left

Command: 1. RIGHT (or LEFT) HALF, 2. FACE. Execute half face as prescribed above, turning only 45 degrees.

About Face

Command: 1. ABOUT, 2. FACE. At the command, place the toe of the right foot about a half-foot length to the rear and slightly to the left of the left heel without moving the left foot. Put the weight of the body mainly on the heel of the left foot, right leg straight. Then turn to the rear, moving to the right on the left heel and on the ball of the right foot. Place the right heel beside the left to complete the movement.

STEPS AND MARCH COMMANDS

All movements executed from the halt, except right step, begin with the left foot. FORWARD, HALF STEP, HALT, and MARK TIME may be executed one from the other in quick or double time.

The following table prescribes the length in inches and the cadence in steps per minute of steps in marching.

Step	Time	Length	Cadence
Full	Quick	30	120
Full	Double	36	180
Full	Slow*	30	—
Half	Quick	15	120
Half	Double	18	180
Side	Quick	12	120
Back	Quick	15	120

*This is a special step executed only as a funeral escort is approaching the place of interment. The cadence, in accordance with that set by the band, varies with different airs that may be played.

All commands of execution are given on the foot, right or left, in the direction the movement is going. For example, if the march is to be to the right, as 1. BY THE RIGHT FLANK, 2. MARCH, the command MARCH is given on the right foot.

Quick Time

All steps and movements are executed in quick time, which is what most people understand as normal marching pace, unless the unit is marching double time, or unless DOUBLE TIME is added to the command. Example: 1. SQUAD RIGHT, DOUBLE TIME, 2. MARCH.

Marching

At halt, to march forward to quick time, the commands are: 1. FOR-WARD, 2. MARCH. At the command FORWARD, shift the weight of the body to the right leg. At the command MARCH, step off smartly with the left foot and continue the march with 30-inch steps taken straight forward without stiffness or exaggeration of movements. Swing the arms easily in their natural arcs about 6 inches straight to the front and 3 inches to the rear of the body.

Double Time

To march in double time, the commands are: 1. DOUBLE TIME, 2. MARCH.

1. If at halt, at the command DOUBLE TIME, shift the weight of the body to the right leg. At the command MARCH, raise the forearms, fingers closed, knuckles out, to a horizontal position along the waistline and take up an easy run with the step and cadence of double time, allowing the arms to take a natural swinging motion across the front of the body. Be sure to keep the forearms horizontal.

2. If marching in quick time, at the command: 1. DOUBLE TIME, 2. MARCH, given as either foot strikes the ground, take one more step in quick time and then step off in double time.

3. To resume the quick time from double time, the commands are: 1. QUICK TIME, 2. MARCH. At the command MARCH, given as either foot strikes the ground, advance and plant the other foot in double time; resume the quick time, dropping the hands by the sides. .

Halt

The commands are: 1. SQUAD (PLATOON, COMPANY), 2. HALT.

1. When marching in quick time, at the command HALT, given as

either foot strikes the ground, execute the halt in two counts; advance and plant the other foot, then bring up the rear foot.

2. When marching in double time, at the command HALT, given as either foot strikes the gound, advance and plant the other foot as in double time, then halt in two counts as in quick time.

3. When executing right step or left step, at the command HALT, given as the heels are together, plant the foot next in cadence and come to the halt when the heels are next brought together.

Mark Time

The commands are: 1. MARK TIME, 2. MARCH.

1. Being in march, at the command MARCH, given as either foot strikes the ground, advance and plant the other foot; then bring up the rear foot, placing it so that both heels are on line, and continue the cadence by alternately raising and planting each foot. When raised, the ball of the foot is about 2 inches above the ground.

2. Being at a halt, at the command MARCH, raise and plant first the left foot, then the right as described above.

3. Mark time may be executed in either quick-time cadence or double-time cadence. While marking time, any errors in alignment should be corrected.

4. The halt is executed from mark time, as from quick time or double time. Forward march, halt, and mark time may be executed one from the other in quick time or double time.

Half Step

The commands are: 1. HALF STEP, 2. MARCH.

1. Being in march, at the command MARCH, take steps of 15 inches in quick time instead of the normal 30 inches. The half step is executed in quick time only.

2. To resume the full step from half step, the commands are: 1. FORWARD, 2. MARCH.

Right Step

The commands are: 1. RIGHT STEP, 2. MARCH.

At the command MARCH, carry the right foot 12 inches to the right; then place the left foot beside the right, left knee straight. Continue in the cadence of quick time. The right step is executed in quick time from a halt for short distances only.

Left Step

The commands are: 1. LEFT STEP, 2. MARCH.

At the command MARCH, carry the left foot 12 inches to the left; then place the right foot beside the left, right knee straight. Continue in the cadence of quick time. The left step is executed in quick time from a halt for short distances only.

Back Step

The commands are: 1. BACKWARD, 2. MARCH.

At the command MARCH, take steps of 15 inches straight to the rear. The back step is executed in quick time for short distances only.

To Face to the Right (or Left) in Marching

The commands are 1. BY THE RIGHT (or LEFT) FLANK, 2. MARCH.

1. To face to the right (left) in marching and advance from a halt, at the command MARCH, turn to the right (left) on the ball of the right (left) foot; at the same time, step off with the left (right) foot in the new direction with a half or full step in quick time or double time as the case may be.

2. To face to the right (left) in marching and advance, being in march, at the command MARCH, given as the right (left) foot strikes the ground, advance and plant the left (right) foot; then face to the right (left) in marching and step off with the right (left) foot in the new direction with a half or full step in quick or double time as the case may be.

To Face to the Rear in Marching

The commands are: 1. TO THE REAR, 2. MARCH.

1. Being in march at quick time, at the command MARCH, given as the right foot strikes the ground, advance and plant the left foot; then turn to the right all the way about on the balls of both feet and immediately step off with the left foot.

2. Being in march at double time, at the command MARCH, given as the right foot strikes the ground, advance two steps in the original direction; turn to the right all the way about while taking four steps in place, keeping the cadence, and step off.

To Change Step

The commands are 1. CHANGE STEP, 2. MARCH.

1. Being in march in quick time, at the command MARCH, given as the right foot strikes the ground, advance and plant the left foot; then plant the toe of the right foot near the heel of the left and step off with the left foot.

2. The same movement may be executed on the right foot by giving the command of execution as the left foot strikes the ground and planting the right foot; then plant the toe of the left foot near the heel of the right and step off with the right foot.

To March at Ease

The commands are: 1. AT EASE, 2. MARCH.

At the command MARCH, men adopt an easy natural stride, without any requirement to keep step or a regular cadence; however, they are still required to maintain silence.

To March at Route Step

The commands are: 1. ROUTE STEP, 2. MARCH.

At the command MARCH, men adopt an easy natural stride, without any requirement to keep step or a regular cadence, or to maintain silence.

MANUAL OF ARMS

The manual of arms described here is performed with the M16 rifle. For instruction purposes, it may be taught by the numbers. When marching at quick time, the only movements that may be executed are Right Shoulder Arms and Port Arms. The cadence of all motions is quick time. Recruits learning the manual of arms should concentrate their attention on the details of the motion; the cadence will be acquired as they become accustomed to handling their pieces. The instructor may require them to count aloud in cadence with the motions. See figures 5–2, 5–3, and 5–4 for illustrations.

GENERAL

FALL IN is executed with the rifle at Order Arms. When troops are formed, rifles are immediately inspected. (See commands for Inspection Arms, following.) Prior to executing any movements with the rifle, the magazine is removed and the sling is positioned on the left side

Figure 5–2. Order arms—front and side view.

of the rifle, drawn tight with the keeper lying flat and on top of the pistol grip just below the selector lever. Before starting any movement from the halted position, except for movements requiring the position of Trail Arms, rifles will be at Right Shoulder Arms, Port Arms, or Sling Arms. While at a position other than Sling Arms, the rifle will be brought to Port Arms for marching at Double Time.

Position of Order Arms

This is the basic rifle position. The rifle butt rests on deck, with the toe of the rifle in line with the toe of the right shoe. The left side of the stock is along the outer edge of the right shoe. The magazine well is to the front and the barrel is in a vertical position. The rifle is held with the fingers extended and joined, the junction of the front sight assembly and the barrel rests in the "V" formed by thumb and fingers of the right hand. The right thumb will be on the trouser seam with entire right arm behind the rifle; this may cause a slight bend in the

Figure 5–3. Trail arms—front and side view.

arm. The body is at the position of Attention, as it is executed without arms.

Trail Arms from Order Arms

The commands are: 1. TRAIL, 2. ARMS.

This command is given at the position of Order Arms only. At the command of execution, raise the rifle vertically three inches off the deck. Do not change the grasp of the right hand, keep the right thumb on the trouser seam and the right arm behind the rifle, keep the left hand in position.

Order Arms from Trail Arms

The commands are: 1. ORDER, 2. ARMS.

At the command, lower the butt of the rifle to the deck and assume the position of Order Arms.

The rifle is kept at Trail Arms during any movement of Back Step,

Figure 5–4. Port arms from order arms.

Extending, or Closing ranks; the position of Order Arms is assumed automatically on halting.

Port Arms from Order Arms

The commands are: 1. PORT, 2. ARMS.

At the command of execution, slide the right hand to the barrel with fingers joined and wrapped around it, raise and carry the rifle diagonally across in front of and slightly to the left of your face. The right wrist and forearm are straight, elbow held down without strain. Rifle barrel is up, bisecting the angle formed by neck and shoulder, with magazine well to the left, butt in front of right hip. At the same time smartly grasp the handguard, fingers joined and wrapped around it, little finger above the slip ring, thumb inboard, centered on the chest. Left wrist and forearm are straight, wtih elbow held against the body.

TWO. Release grasp of right hand on the barrel and regrasp the small of the stock. Fingers are joined, wrapped around the small of the stock, parallel to the deck with the elbow pinned to the side, upper arm in line with the back. The rifle should be about four inches from the belt.

Order Arms from Port Arms

The commands are: 1. ORDER, 2. ARMS.

At the command of execution, release the grasp of the right hand from the stock and smartly regrasp the barrel. Fingers are joined, wrapped around the barrel, palm to the rear, little finger just above the bayonet stud. The right wrist and forearm are straight, and the elbow is held down without strain.

TWO. Release the grasp of the left hand from the handguard. With the right hand, lower the rifle to the deck, magazine in front, muzzle in a vertical position. At the same time guide the weapon into the right side with left hand until thumb is on the trouser seam, left fingers extended and joined, thumb along the forefinger. The first joint of the forefinger should touch the metal below the flash suppressor. The left wrist and forearm are straight, elbow against the body.

Figure 5–5. Order arms from port arms.

THREE. Smartly return the left hand to the left side in the position of Attention, and gently lower the rifle to the deck with the right hand, with the toe of the rifle in line with the toe of the right shoe. The magazine is to the front and in a vertical position. The position is the same as described for Order Arms, above.

Present Arms from Order Arms

This is used as a salute to persons and colors during parades and ceremonies, and by sentries. The command is by the numbers: 1. PRESENT, 2. ARMS. On the first count, raise and carry the rifle to a vertical position centered on the body, magazine well to the front. The fingers of the right hand are joined and wrapped around the barrel, thumb on the left side. At the same time, smartly grasp the rifle at the handguard with the left hand, fingers joined and wrapped around the handguard, thumb just above the slip ring, which should be four inches from the body. The left wrist and forearm are straight, parallel to the deck, with elbow held in against the side and upper arm in line with the back.

TWO. Release the grasp of the right hand from the barrel and regrasp the small of the stock, with fingers extended and joined, and the charging handle resting in the "V" of thumb and forefinger. Wrist and forearm are straight, forming a straight line from fingertips to elbow, which is held against the body.

Order Arms from Present Arms

The commands are: 1. ORDER, 2. ARMS. On the command of execution, release the grasp of the right hand from the small of the stock and smartly regrasp the barrel; fingers should be joined and wrapped around the barrel with palm facing left. Right wrist and forearm are straight, the elbow held down without strain.

TWO. Release the grasp of the left hand from the handguard and lower the weapon to the right side until the rifle butt is about three inches from the deck, muzzle in front and in a vertical position, magazine well to the front. At the same time, guide the weapon into the right-hand side with the left hand until the thumb is on the trouser seam. The fingers of the hand are extended and joined, thumb along the forefinger, palm to the rear, and first joint of the forefinger touching the metal just below the flash suppressor. The left wrist and forearm are straight, with elbow held in against the body. The entire right arm is behind the rifle.

Figure 5–6. Present arms from order arms.

THREE. Smartly, in the most direct manner, return the left hand to the left side in the position of Attention. At the same time, lower the rifle to the deck with the right hand so the toe of the rifle is in line with the toe of the right shoe; the magazine should be well to the front, the muzzle in a vertical position. With the butt of the rifle on deck, the right hand takes the position described earlier for Order Arms.

Right Shoulder Arms from Order Arms

The commands are: 1. RIGHT SHOULDER, 2. ARMS.

At the command of execution, slide the right hand to the barrel; fingers joined and wrapped around it, and in continuous motion raise and carry the rifle diagonally across the front of the body until the right hand is in front of and slightly left of the face. The right wrist and forearm are straight and slightly to the left of the face. The rifle barrel is up, bisecting the angle formed by the neck and left shoulder, magazine well to the left, butt of the rifle in front of the right hip. At the

Figure 5–7. Order arms from present arms.

same time, smartly grasp the handguard with the left hand, fingers joined and wrapped around the handguard. The little finger goes just above the slip ring, with the thumb on the inboard side and centered above the chest. The left wrist and forearm are straight and the elbow is against the body.

TWO. Release the grasp on the barrel, regrasp the butt of the rifle, with thumb and forefinger joined on the comb of the stock, remaining fingers joined and wrapped around the butt. The right arm is almost extended; the elbow is against the right side of the body.

THREE. Relax the left-hand grip on the handguard, and with the right hand carry the rifle to the right side. At the same time, rotate the rifle so the magazine is well to the rear, and place it on the right shoulder with the pistol grip in the right arm pit. Guide the rifle into the right shoulder with the left hand by sliding it down the rifle until the first joint of the left index finger touches metal at the base of the charging handle. The left fingers should be extended and joined with the thumb along the forefinger, palm to the rear. The left wrist and

Figure 5–8. Right shoulder arms from order arms.

forearm are straight, the elbow held down without strain. The right hand grasp remains unchanged. The right wrist and forearm are straight, parallel to the deck, with the elbow held into the side and upper arm in line with the back.

FOUR. Return the left hand, in the most direct manner, to the left side at the position of Attention.

Port Arms from Right Shoulder Arms

The commands are: 1. PORT, 2. ARMS.

From the position of Halt, at the command of execution, press the rifle butt down quickly with the right hand so the rifle comes off the right shoulder. At the same time, rotate the rifle with the right hand a quarter of a turn so the magazine is well to the left and let the rifle fall diagonally across the front of the body. Bring the left hand up, grasp the handguard, with left fingers joined and wrapped around it; the little finger is just above the slip ring, thumb on the inboard side and centered on the chest. The left arm and wrist are straight, elbow

Figure 5–9. Port arms from right shoulder arms.

held against the body. Rifle barrel is up, bisecting the angle formed by the neck and left shoulder; rifle butt is in front of the right hip. The right hand grasp is unchanged; the right arm is nearly extended, but held against the body.

TWO. Release the grasp of the right hand, regrasp the small of the stock with fingers joined, thumb on the inboard side of the rifle. Right wrist and forearm are straight, parallel to the deck, elbow held in and upper arm in line with the back. The rifle should be about four inches from the belt.

When the command PORT, ARMS is given while troops are marching at Right Shoulder Arms, it will be given as the left foot strikes the deck. On the next step the first count of the movement is carried out as if done at a halt. With each following step, another count is executed until the movement is complete. The movement is executed in cadence. Troops continue marching in this position until another command is given.

Order Arms from Right Shoulder Arms

The commands are: 1. ORDER, 2. ARMS.

On the command of execution, press the rifle butt down quickly with the right hand so the rifle comes off the right shoulder. At the same time, rotate the rifle a quarter of a turn with the right hand so the magazine well is to the left and let the rifle fall diagonally across the front of the body. Bring the left hand up and grasp the handguard; the fingers of the left hand are joined and wrapped around the guard with the little finger just above the slip ring. The left wrist and forearm are held straight and in against the body, as is the elbow. The rifle barrel faces up, bisecting the angle formed by the neck and left shoulder. The grasp of the right hand remains unchanged. The right arm is extended, with elbow against the body.

TWO. Release the grasp of the right hand, regrasp the rifle with the palm to the rear, fingers joined and wrapped around the barrel, thumb inboard. The wrist and forearm are straight, held down without strain.

THREE. Release the grasp of the left hand from the handguard and lower the rifle with the right hand on the right hand side of the body until the butt is three inches from the deck with the magazine to the front and the rifle in a vertical position. At the same time guide the rifle into the right side with the left hand until the right thumb is on the trouser seam. Left fingers are joined, thumb along the forefinger. The first joint of that finger touches the metal just below the flash

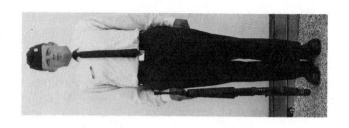

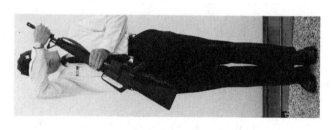

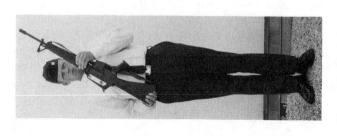

Figure 5–10. Order arms from right shoulder arms.

suppressor. The left palm faces the rear; the left wrist and forearm are straight, with the elbow held in against the body. The entire right arm is behind the rifle.

FOUR. Return the left hand to the left side in a direct manner and assume the position of Attention. Then lower the rifle to the deck, gently, so the toe of the rifle is in line with the toe of the right shoe, magazine well to the front and the rifle in a vertical position. When the butt is on deck, slide the right hand down the barrel so that the front sight assembly and barrel will rest in the "V" formed by the thumb and fingers of the right hand. The fingers of the right hand are joined and extended diagonally across the rifle, with the right thumb on the trouser seam; the entire right arm is behind the rifle.

Right Shoulder Arms from Port Arms

The commands are: 1. RIGHT SHOULDER, 2. ARMS.

At the command of execution release the right hand grasp on the stock and smartly regrasp the butt of the rifle, with thumb and forefinger joined and wrapped around the comb of the stock and the remaining three fingers joined and wrapped around the butt. The heel of the butt will be visible between the forefinger and middle finger. The right arm is nearly extended; the right elbow is held against the body.

TWO. Relax the grasp of the left hand on the handguard, and with the right hand carry the rifle to the right side. At the same time, rotate the rifle a quarter turn so the magazine is well to the rear and place the pistol grip in the right arm pit; guide the rifle into the right shoulder with the left hand by sliding it down the rifle until the first joint of the index finger touches the base of the charging handle. The left fingers should be joined with the thumb along the forefinger; palm to the rear. The left wrist and forearm are straight, the elbow held down without strain. The right hand grasp remains unchanged; the right wrist and forearm are straight and parallel to the deck, elbow to the side, upper arm in line with the back.

THREE. Return the left hand to the side in the most direct way and come to the position of Attention.

Note: This command can be executed while marching at Quick Time, in the same manner as Port Arms from Right Shoulder Arms.

Figure 5–11. Right shoulder arms from port arms.

Order Arms from Left Shoulder Arms

The commands are: 1. ORDER, 2. ARMS.

On the command of execution, bring the right hand across the body in the most direct manner and grasp the small of the stock. The fingers are joined and wrapped around the small of the stock, thumb inboard; right wrist and forearm are straight, with elbow held down without strain.

TWO. Release the grasp of the left hand on the butt of the rifle, and with the right hand bring the rifle from the shoulder to a position diagonally across the front of the body, rotating it a quarter-turn so the magazine is well toward the left. At the same time, smartly regrasp the handguard with the left hand; the fingers should be joined and wrapped around the handguard, with the little finger just above the slip ring and the thumb inboard and centered on the chest. The left wrist and forearm are straight, elbow held in against the body; right wrist and forearm straight, parallel to the deck, elbow held in and in

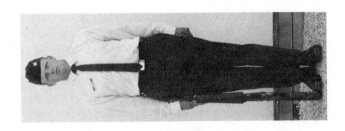

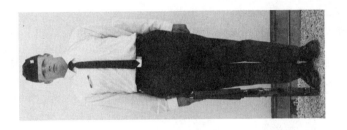

Figure 5–12. Order arms from left shoulder arms.

line with the back. The rifle barrel is up, bisecting the angle formed by the neck and left shoulder, with the butt in front of the right hip.

THREE. Release the right hand grasp on the stock and smartly regrasp the barrel, with fingers joined, wrapped around the barrel, palm to the rear and little finger just above the bayonet stud. The right wrist and forearm are straight, with elbow held down without strain.

FOUR. Release the grasp of the left hand from the handguard, and with your right hand lower the rifle to the right side until the butt is three inches from the deck. The magazine should face the front, with the rifle in a vertical position. At the same time, guide the rifle into the right side with the left hand until the right thumb is on the trouser seam. The left fingers are extended and joined, thumb along the forefinger, with the first joint of the forefinger touching the metal of the flash suppressor. The left palm faces the rear; the left wrist and forearm are straight, with the elbow against the body. The right arm is behind the rifle.

FIVE. Return the left hand to the left side and assume the position of Attention. At the same time, lower the rifle to the deck so the toe of the rifle is in line with the toe of the right shoe with the magazine to the front and the rifle in a vertical position. As the rifle touches the deck, slide the right hand to the front sight assembly; fingers are joined and extend diagonally across the front of the barrel. The right arm is behind the rifle.

Left Shoulder Arms from Right Shoulder Arms

The movement can be made while at Right Shoulder Arms, Marching at Quick Time, or at a Halt. The commands are: 1. LEFT SHOULDER, 2. ARMS. On the command of execution, press the rifle butt down quickly with the right hand so the rifle comes off the right shoulder; rotate the rifle a quarter-turn with the right hand so the magazine well is to the left, and let the rifle fall diagonally across the front of the body. At the same time bring the left hand up and smartly grasp the handguard with left fingers joined and wrapped around it, little finger just above the slip ring, thumb inboard and centered on the chest. The left wrist and forearm are straight; elbow in against the body. The right-hand grasp is unchanged; the right arm is nearly extended, the right elbow held in against the body. The rifle barrel is up and bisecting the angle formed by the neck and left shoulder, with the butt behind the right hip and the rifle about four inches in front of the body.

TWO. Release the grasp of the right hand from the butt and smartly

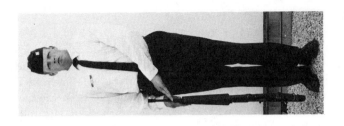

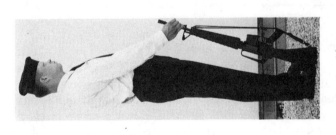

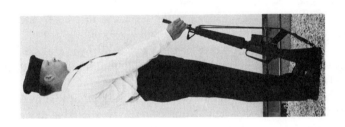

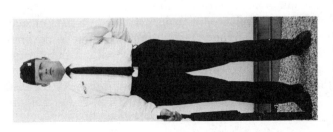

Figure 5–13. Left shoulder arms from right shoulder arms.

regrasp the small of the stock, with fingers joined and wrapped around it, thumb inboard. The right wrist and forearm are straight and parallel to the deck, elbow held into the side, upper arm in line with the back.

THREE. Release the grasp of the left hand from the handguard, and with the right hand carry the rifle to the left side, rotating it a quarter-turn so the magazine is well to the rear; place the pistol grip in the left arm pit. The right wrist and forearm are straight; elbow held down without strain. At the same time, regrasp the butt with the left hand; thumb and forefinger are joined on the comb of the stock with remaining three fingers joined and wrapped around the butt. The heel of the butt will be visible between the forefinger and middle finger.

FOUR. Release the grasp of the right hand from the small of the stock and return it across to the right side in a direct manner for the position of Attention.

Note: This command can be executed while marching at Quick Time, in the same manner as Port Arms from Right Shoulder Arms.

Movements of Rest

Rest movements are used to give troops a change from the position of Attention and still maintain an orderly formation. Parade Rest, At Ease, and At Rest consist of a single count, that of execution. Fall Out has no count at all.

Parade Rest

When the preparatory command PARADE is given, shift the weight from the left leg to the right without any body movement. When the command of execution, REST, is given, move the left foot smartly 12 inches to the left of the right foot—measured from inside the heels. Heels should be on the same line; legs straight but not stiff, with body weight equally on both legs.

The left hand is placed in the small of the back, just below the belt, with fingers extended and joined, thumb along the forefinger, palm to the rear and elbow in line with the body.

The butt of the rifle is kept on deck, in line with the feet, and against the right foot. When the left foot is first moved, relax the grasp of the right hand and move it to a point just below the flash suppressor. The fingers are joined and curled with the forefinger touching the thumb. At the same time, straighten the right arm directly to the front so the rifle muzzle points upward.

Figure 5–14. Parade rest, front and side views.

While at Parade Rest, maintain silence. The only command given to troops in this position is Attention. When that command is given, bring the left foot smartly back against the right foot, lower the left arm back to the side, move the rifle to the position of Order Arms and regrasp the rifle for that position.

At Ease

In this position the right foot remains stationary and the rifle butt remains on deck. The rifle is held as in Parade Rest, but the grip and body stance may be more relaxed. Equipment may be adjusted, but silence must be maintained. The only command given while in this position is Attention, the movement for which is described above.

Rest

This is exactly the same as At Ease, except that troops may talk in conversational tones. The only command given to troops in this position is Attention. On the preparatory command, come to Parade Rest. On the command of execution, come to Attention and Order Arms.

Fall Out

When this order is given, troops may leave the present position and go to a designated area or remain in the general vicinity. The only command that can be given after Fall Out is Fall In, when troops assume the position of Order Arms.

Rifle Salutes

Troops in formation, or individuals who find themselves in a saluting situation, may execute the rifle salute. Salutes are made from Order Arms, Trail Arms, Right Shoulder Arms, or Left Shoulder Arms.

At Order Arms

The commands are: 1. RIFLE, 2. SALUTE.

Carry the left hand across the body in the most direct manner until the first joint of the forefinger touches the metal just below the flash suppressor, left fingers extended and joined, thumb along the forefinger, palm down. The wrist and forearm are straight, with elbow held in against the body.

READY, TWO. Smartly return the left hand to the left side and assume the position of Order Arms.

At Trail Arms

On the command of execution, carry the left hand across the body in the most direct manner until the first joint of the forefinger touches the metal at the base of the flash suppressor. Left fingers are extended and joined, palm down, wrist and forearm straight, elbow held in.

READY, TWO. Smartly bring the left hand back to the side and assume the position of Order Arms.

At Right Shoulder Arms

Smartly carry the left hand across the body until the first joint of the left forefinger touches the metal at the charging handle. The left fingers are extended and joined, palm down, arm parallel to the deck.

READY TWO. Return the left hand to the left side and assume the position of Order Arms.

Figure 5–15. Rifle salute: order arms, trail arms, right shoulder arms.

At Left Shoulder Arms

On the command of execution, smartly carry the right hand across the body until the first joint of the forefinger is touching the base of the charging handle. Fingers of the right hand are extended and joined, with thumb along the forefinger, palm down. The entire arm is parallel to the deck.

TWO. Return the hand smartly to the side and assume the position of Order Arms.

Inspection Arms (Without Magazine)

The commands are: 1. INSPECTION, 2. ARMS.

On the command of execution, slide the right hand to the barrel, fingers wrapped around the barrel. Raise and carry the rifle diagonally across the front of the body until the right hand is in front of and slightly to the left of the face. The right wrist and forearm are straight and held down without strain. The rifle barrel is up and bisecting the angle formed by the neck and the left shoulder, magazine well to the left, butt in front of the right hip. Smartly grasp the handguard with the left hand, little finger just above the slip ring, thumb centered on the chest. The left wrist and forearm are straight, the elbow is in against the body.

TWO. Release the grasp of the right hand on the barrel, regrasp the small of the stock with the thumb wrapped around the inboard portion. The right wrist and forearm are straight and parallel to the deck; elbow against the side, upper arm in line with the back. The rifle should be about four inches from the body.

THREE. Release the grasp of the left hand from the handguard and regrasp the rifle at the pistol grip. The thumb of the left hand is over the lower portion of the bolt catch.

FOUR. Release the grasp of the right hand from the stock and use the thumb and forefinger to unlock the charging handle; at the same time pull it sharply to the rear, apply pressure on the bolt catch, and lock the bolt to the rear.

FIVE. With the thumb and forefinger of the right hand, push the charging handle until it is locked in the forward position. Regrasp the small of the stock with the right hand.

SIX. Elevate the rifle up and to the left with both hands until the rear sight is in line with the left shoulder. At the same time, rotate it a quarter-turn clockwise so the chamber is visible, and turn the head and eyes toward the ejector port to inspect the chamber.

SEVEN. After seeing the chamber clear, or clearing it, turn head and eyes back to the front and lower the rifle to the position of Port Arms. As it is lowered, release the grasp on the pistol grip and regrasp the handguard as in Port Arms.

Port Arms from Inspection Arms (Without Magazine)

The commands are: 1. PORT, 2. ARMS.

At the preliminary command of PORT, release the grasp of the left hand and regrasp the rifle at the magazine well and trigger guard, with fingers extended and joined, thumb inboard, thumb and forefinger forming a "V" at the magazine well and trigger guard. At the same time, press the bolt catch and allow the bolt to slide forward. With the fingertips of the left hand, push forward and close the ejection cover, then slide the left hand toward the pistol grip and place the thumb on the trigger.

At the command, ARMS, push down on the trigger with the left thumb and uncock the hammer. Then release the grasp of the left

Figure 5–16. Inspection arms (without magazine).

Figure 5–17. Port arms from inspection arms (without magazine).

hand and regrasp the rifle at the handguard, with fingers extended and joined, little finger just above the slip ring, thumb inboard. The left wrist and forearm are straight, elbow held in against the body.

FIRING RIFLE IN CEREMONIES

For ceremonial firing, the front rank only of units larger than a squad executes the loading and firing. A squad is always formed in line preliminary to such firing. Rifles are loaded while locked, and are kept loaded and locked without command until the command UNLOAD, or 1. INSPECTION, 2. ARMS.

To Fire by Volley

Being in firing formation with rifles loaded, the commands are: 1. READY, 2. AIM, 3. SQUAD, 4. FIRE. (For ceremonial purposes, blank ammunition is used and only the front rank executes the commands.)

At the word READY, take the loading position, if not already in that position. At the command AIM, raise the rifle with both hands, butt placed and held firmly against the shoulder, left hand well under the rifle and grasping it at or in front of the balance, rifle resting in the palm of the left hand, right elbow at the height of the shoulder, right cheek held firmly against the stock as far forward as it can be placed without straining. The rifle is raised 45 degrees from the horizontal. The left eye is closed, right eye looking over the rear sight.

To continue the firing, the commands are: 1. AIM, 2. SQUAD, 3. FIRE. Each command is executed as previously explained.

To Cease Firing

The command is: CEASE FIRING.

At the command CEASE FIRING, firing stops; rifles not already at the loading position are brought to that position.

CLOSE ORDER DRILL

A group of men in uniform and bearing arms must be under direct control of a senior officer in order for them to move in an orderly fashion. Close order drill will accomplish this. Such drill also serves to teach discipline by instilling habits of automatic and precise response to orders, developing better morale through team spirit, and making it possible for a Coast Guard unit to make a favorable appearance in a parade or other public ceremony.

The basic unit in a military formation is the squad, a group of 8 to 12 men organized as a team. When the squad leader is absent, he is replaced by the second in command. In his absence the command is taken by the next senior member of the squad.

The squad is usually kept intact. Its normal formation is a single rank or file. This permits variation in the number of men in the squad. The original formation is always in line.

The squad marches in line only for minor changes of position.

The squad leader, when in ranks, is posted as the right man of the squad in line or as the leading man in column.

To Form the Squad

The command is: FALL IN.

At the command the squad forms in line. Each man, except the one on the extreme left, extends his left arm to the side at shoulder height, palm down, fingers extended and joined. Each man, except the one on the extreme right, turns his head and eyes to the right and places himself in line so that his right shoulder touches the tips of the fingers of the man on his right. As soon as proper intervals have been obtained, each man drops his arms to his side and turns his head smartly to the front.

To Form at Close Interval

The commands are: 1. AT CLOSE INTERVAL, 2. FALL IN.

At the command, the men fall in as above, except that close intervals are obtained by placing the left hand on the hip, fingers extended downward and joined, thumb along the forefingers, heel of the hand resting along the hip bone, elbow extended to the side.

If the squad is under arms, pieces are inspected.

The squad executes the positions, movements and manual of arms with all men executing the movements together.

To Dismiss the Squad

The commands are: 1. INSPECTION, 2. ARMS, 3. PORT, 4. ARMS, 5. DISMISSED.

If the squad is not under arms, the single command DISMISSED is used (the squad, of course, being at attention or having been brought to attention).

To Count Off

The commands are: 1. COUNT, 2. OFF.

At the command OFF, each man, except the one on the right flank, turns his head and eyes to the right. The right flank man calls out, "One." Each man in succession calls out, "Two," "Three," etc., turning his head and eyes to the front as he gives his number.

To Aline the Squad

If in line, the commands are: 1. DRESS RIGHT (or LEFT), or 1. AT CLOSE INTERVAL, DRESS RIGHT (LEFT), 2. DRESS, 3. READY, 4. FRONT.

At the command DRESS, each man, except the one on the left, extends his left arm (or if at close intervals, places his left hand upon his hip), and all dress to the right. The squad leader places himself on the right flank, one pace from and on the line of the squad. From this position he checks alinement, ordering individuals forward or backward as necessary. Having checked alinement, he faces to the right in marching, and moves three spaces forward, halts, faces to the left and commands: 1. READY, 2. FRONT. At the command FRONT, arms are dropped quietly and smartly to the side, and heads turned to the front.

If in column, the command is: COVER.

At the command COVER, men cover from front to rear with 40-inch intervals between them.

To Obtain Close Interval

The commands are: 1. CLOSE, 2. MARCH.

At the command MARCH, all men, except the right flank man, face to the right in marching and form at close interval.

To Extend to Normal Interval

The commands are: 1. EXTEND, 2. MARCH.

At the command MARCH, all men, except the right flank man, face to the left in marching and form at normal interval.

To March to the Flank

The commands are: 1. RIGHT (or LEFT), 2. FACE, 3. FORWARD, 4. MARCH.

These movements are executed with all men stepping off together.

To March to the Oblique

The commands are: 1. RIGHT (or LEFT) OBLIQUE, 2. MARCH. (The word "oblique" is pronounced to rhyme with "strike.")

At the command MARCH, given as the right foot strikes the ground, each man advances, plants the left foot, faces half right, and steps off in a direction of 45 degrees to the right. He keeps his relative place, shoulders parallel to those of the guide, and regulates his steps so that the ranks stay parallel to the original front.

The command HALT is given on the left foot when halting from the right oblique march, and on the right foot when halting from left oblique march.

At the command HALT (from left oblique march), given as the left foot strikes the ground, each man advances, planting the right foot, turns to the front on the ball of the right foot, and brings the left foot to the side of the right. The opposite is done from right oblique march so that in either case the men end facing front.

To stop temporarily the execution of the movement for the correction of errors, the commands are: 1. IN PLACE, 2. HALT.

All halt in place without facing to the front and stand fast. To resume the movement the commands are: 1. RESUME, 2. MARCH.

If at half step or mark time while obliquing, the full step is resumed by the command: 1. RESUME, 2. MARCH.

To resume original direction, the commands are: 1. FORWARD, 2. MARCH.

At the command MARCH, each man faces half left in marching and moves straight to the front. If at half step or marking time while in oblique march, the full step is resumed by the command: 1. OBLIQUE, 2. MARCH.

To March Toward the Flank

The commands are: 1. BY THE RIGHT (LEFT) FLANK, 2. MARCH.

At the command MARCH, each man simultaneously executes the movements as described above.

In Column, to Change Direction

The commands are: 1. COLUMN RIGHT (or LEFT), (HALF RIGHT), (HALF LEFT), 2. MARCH.

At the command MARCH, the leading man executes the movement immediately; the others in succession as they reach the pivot point.

In Line, to Take Double-arm Interval and Assemble

The commands are: 1. TAKE INTERVAL TO THE LEFT (or RIGHT), 2. MARCH.

At the command MARCH, the right flank man stands fast, extends his left arm at shoulder height, palm down, fingers extended and joined, until the man on his left obtains the proper interval, then drops his arm. Other men face to the left in marching and step out until they have an interval of two arms' length from the man on their right, then halt and face to the front. Each man, except the one on the left who raises his right arm only, extends both arms laterally at shoulder height. Each man, except the right flank man, then turns his head and eyes to the right and places himself in line, so that the finger tips of his right hand touch those of the left hand of the man on his right. As soon as each man alines himself at two arms' length, he drops his right arm to the side and turns his head and eyes to the front. He drops his left arm when the man on his left has obtained the proper interval.

To assemble, the commands are: 1. ASSEMBLE TO THE RIGHT (or LEFT), 2. MARCH.

At the command MARCH, the right flank man stands fast; all other men face to the right in marching and form at normal interval.

To Stack Arms

The squad being in line at normal or close interval, the commands are: 1. STACK, 2. ARMS. Numbers 3, 7, and 11 make the stacks except when there is no one on their left. For squads of more than 14 men, additional stackmen are designated.

The stack is made as follows: At the command ARMS, the man on the left of the stackman grasps his rifle with the right hand at the balance, carrying it to the horizontal position, barrel up, and passes his rifle to the stackman. The stackman grasps it with his left hand between the upper-sling swivel and stacking swivel and places the butt between his feet, barrel to the front, muzzle inclined slightly to the front, the thumb and forefinger raising the stacking swivel. The stackman then throws the butt of his own rifle (the center rifle) two feet in advance of that of his left file and 6 inches to the right of his own right toe; at the same time he allows his right hand to slip to the stacking swivel and engages his rifle with that of his left file.

The man on the right of the stackman raises his rifle with his right hand, regrasps it with his right hand at the small of the stock, steps to the left front, keeping his right foot in place. He carries his rifle well forward, barrel up. His left hand guides the lower hook of the stacking swivel of his own rifle to engage the free hook of that of his left file. He then turns the barrel outward to the angle formed by the other two rifles and lowers the butt to the ground so that it will form a uniform stack with the other two rifles. He then assumes the position of attention. Other rifles of the squad are passed toward the nearest stack and laid on the stack by the stackman.

To Take Arms

The squad being in line behind the stacks, the commands are: 1. TAKE, 2. ARMS.

At the command ARMS, the procedure of stacking arms is reversed. The loose rifles are first passed back. In breaking the stack, the stackman grasps his rifle and that of the man on his left, so that the rifles will not fall when the man on the right raises and disengages his rifle. Each man, as he receives his rifle, resumes the position of order arms.

Column of Twos

When marching small groups, not at drill, the group may be marched in column of twos by forming it in two ranks and giving the commands: 1. RIGHT (or LEFT), 2. FACE.

To Form Column of Twos from Single File and Reform

The squad being in column, at halt, to form a column of twos the commands are: 1. FORM COLUMN OF TWOS, 2. MARCH.

At the command MARCH, the leading man stands fast; the second man in the squad moves by the oblique until he is to the left of and abreast of the squad leader with normal interval, and halts. The third man moves forward until behind the squad leader at normal interval, and halts. The fourth man moves by the oblique until he is to the left of and abreast of the third man at normal interval, and halts; and so on.

To Form Single File from Column of Twos

Being in column of twos, in marching, to reform single file the squad is first halted. The commands are: 1. FORM SINGLE FILE FROM THE RIGHT, 2. MARCH.

At the command MARCH, the leading man of the right column moves forward. The leading man of the left column steps off to the right oblique, and then executes left oblique so as to follow the right file at normal interval. The remaining twos follow successively in the same way.

All military drill is based on the squad. Two or more squads make up a platoon, which is the basic drill unit. Two or more platoons make up a company. Two or more companies make up a battalion, although it is customary to assign four companies to a battalion where possible. When a formation is large enough to form a battalion, orders may be given by bugle or by signal. A regiment consists of two or more battalions; at a minimum it could be made up of 16 squads, although usually it would be far larger. Complete instructions for handling platoons and larger formations are contained in the *Landing Party Manual*.

CHAPTER 6

Uniforms and Awards

The uniform marks a man or woman as being a professional, a member of a military service nearly two hundred years old and, more than that, a person who is devoting years of time to the service of the country. It is designed primarily to identify on sight men and women belonging to the Coast Guard, and to show at a glance their rank, or rating. Over the years there have been many uniform changes.

The biggest change of all came in 1974 when all male personnel, officer and enlisted alike, began wearing the Coast Guard blue uniform. This marked the first time that all enlisted persons, other than CPOs, wore the same type uniform as officers (figure 6–1). While women's uniforms remained initially very similar to those worn by women in the Navy, these were later revised so that they, too, are distinctively Coast Guard blue.

The uniform makes the first big change in a person's appearance upon joining the Coast Guard. A man may still wear sideburns and a woman may still wear eye shadow, but in the Coast Guard uniform they become representatives of the United States government and, overseas, unofficial ambassadors from America. Not only must they wear proper uniforms in a correct manner, they must also set a good example in conduct and deportment at all times.

The matter of ranks, rates, and insignia will appear confusing at first, but after one learns the system, it becomes fairly simple. First, learn

Figure 6–1. A woman member of the Coast Guard Honor Guard in full dress blue.

the marks of rank of all officers and the rating badge chevrons that show the rate of enlisted men. Later you will learn the specialty marks of all enlisted men and the various special identification marks worn by officers.

IDENTIFICATION

The first thing to look for in identifying a person in uniform is the headgear, which is different for flag officers, male commissioned or warrant officers, women, CPOs, and enlisted men. Next, the sleeve markings or shoulder boards for an officer show rank. The rating badges for enlisted people show their rate and rating. The various breast insignia, distinguishing marks, and ribbons tell the details as to special qualifications, awards, and service of officer and enlisted personnel.

Along with learning ranks and ratings in the Coast Guard, you must learn the uniform markings for the Army, Air Force, Marine Corps, and Navy (figures 6–2 and 6–3).

Headgear

All men—officers, warrant officers, and enlisted—wear caps with bills on them. Women, officer and enlisted, wear the same kind of hats with the sides turned up. All hands at sea, and when specified ashore, wear baseball-type working caps with a bill in front. Garrison caps are optional.

Cap devices for commissioned officers, men and women, consist of a shield, eagle, and anchor. Devices for commissioned warrant officers are the same. Chief petty officers wear one anchor mounted vertically, with a shield on it. The device for senior chief petty officers has one star above the anchor; for master chief petty officers, two stars; for the master chief petty officer of the Coast Guard, three stars. The cap device worn by enlisted men is a gold medallion centered over two crossed silver anchors with a silver shield in the center (figure 6–4).

Collar Insignia

There are metal pin-on emblems. Those for line officers consist of the device of rank on both sides. The commissioned officer wears his specialty device on his sleeves or on his shoulder marks, and on his left collar. Collar insignia for CPOs are miniatures of their cap insignia. Petty officers other than CPOs wear a metal collar device consisting of gold chevrons indicating grade, mounted under a silver shield. Non-rated personnel do not wear collar insignia.

Warrant Officer Insignia

These emblems indicate the various specialties. In most cases the insignia is derived from the specialty mark worn by enlisted men rated in the same specialty.

COMMISSIONED OFFICERS

Commissioned officers of the Coast Guard hold commissions granted by the President and signed by the Secretary of Transportation (in wartime they are signed by the Secretary of the Navy). Commissioned officers are assigned to duties commensurate with their rank and experience. The larger Coast Guard units have several commissioned officers assigned. Their duties are command and administrative. Officer ranks, from senior to junior, are:

Fleet Admiral
Admiral
Vice Admiral
Rear Admiral
Commodore
Captain
Commander
Lieutenant Commander
Lieutenant
Lieutenant, junior grade
Ensign

WARRANT AND COMMISSIONED WARRANT OFFICERS

Warrant officers have earned special status by their ability and experience. They are technical specialists in a prescribed occupational area. In addition, they have administrative and supervisory duties. The uniform of warrant officers is the same as that of commissioned officers, except for the insignia.

The warrant categories in the Coast Guard are:

Boatswain
Material Maintenance
Naval Engineering
Finance and Supply
Public Information
Communications

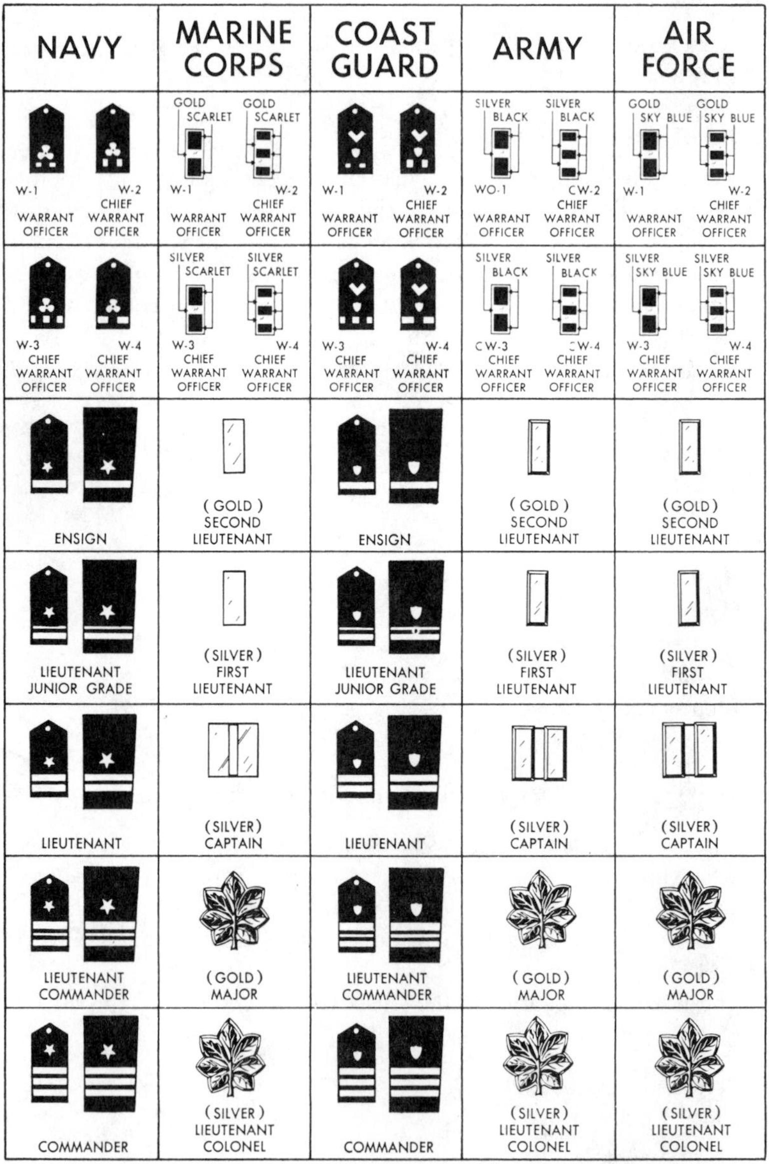

NAVY	MARINE CORPS	COAST GUARD	ARMY	AIR FORCE
W-1 WARRANT OFFICER / W-2 CHIEF WARRANT OFFICER	GOLD SCARLET W-1 WARRANT OFFICER / GOLD SCARLET W-2 CHIEF WARRANT OFFICER	W-1 WARRANT OFFICER / W-2 CHIEF WARRANT OFFICER	SILVER BLACK WO-1 WARRANT OFFICER / SILVER BLACK CW-2 CHIEF WARRANT OFFICER	GOLD SKY BLUE W-1 WARRANT OFFICER / GOLD SKY BLUE W-2 CHIEF WARRANT OFFICER
W-3 CHIEF WARRANT OFFICER / W-4 CHIEF WARRANT OFFICER	SILVER SCARLET W-3 CHIEF WARRANT OFFICER / SILVER SCARLET W-4 CHIEF WARRANT OFFICER	W-3 CHIEF WARRANT OFFICER / W-4 CHIEF WARRANT OFFICER	SILVER BLACK CW-3 CHIEF WARRANT OFFICER / SILVER BLACK CW-4 CHIEF WARRANT OFFICER	SILVER SKY BLUE W-3 CHIEF WARRANT OFFICER / SILVER SKY BLUE W-4 CHIEF WARRANT OFFICER
ENSIGN	(GOLD) SECOND LIEUTENANT	ENSIGN	(GOLD) SECOND LIEUTENANT	(GOLD) SECOND LIEUTENANT
LIEUTENANT JUNIOR GRADE	(SILVER) FIRST LIEUTENANT	LIEUTENANT JUNIOR GRADE	(SILVER) FIRST LIEUTENANT	(SILVER) FIRST LIEUTENANT
LIEUTENANT	(SILVER) CAPTAIN	LIEUTENANT	(SILVER) CAPTAIN	(SILVER) CAPTAIN
LIEUTENANT COMMANDER	(GOLD) MAJOR	LIEUTENANT COMMANDER	(GOLD) MAJOR	(GOLD) MAJOR
COMMANDER	(SILVER) LIEUTENANT COLONEL	COMMANDER	(SILVER) LIEUTENANT COLONEL	(SILVER) LIEUTENANT COLONEL

Figure 6–2. Collar insignia of rank for all armed services, with shoulder marks and sleeve marks for Coast Guard and Navy.

NAVY	MARINE CORPS	COAST GUARD	ARMY	AIR FORCE
CAPTAIN	COLONEL	CAPTAIN	COLONEL	COLONEL
COMMODORE	BRIGADIER GENERAL	COMMODORE	BRIGADIER GENERAL	BRIGADIER GENERAL
REAR ADMIRAL	MAJOR GENERAL	REAR ADMIRAL	MAJOR GENERAL	MAJOR GENERAL
VICE ADMIRAL	LIEUTENANT GENERAL	VICE ADMIRAL	LIEUTENANT GENERAL	LIEUTENANT GENERAL
ADMIRAL	GENERAL	ADMIRAL	GENERAL	GENERAL
FLEET ADMIRAL	NONE	NONE	GENERAL OF THE ARMY	GENERAL OF THE AIR FORCE
NONE	NONE	NONE	AS PRESCRIBED BY INCUMBENT GENERAL OF THE ARMIES	NONE

NAVY	MARINES	ARMY	AIR FORCE	
MASTER CHIEF P.O.	SGT. MAJOR / MASTER GUNNERY SGT.	STAFF SGT MAJOR / COMMAND SGT MAJOR / SPEC. 9	CHIEF MASTER SGT. / CHIEF MASTER SGT OF THE AF	E-9
SENIOR CHIEF P.O.	1ST SGT. / MASTER SGT.	1ST SGT. / MASTER SGT. / SPEC. 8	SENIOR MASTER SGT	E-8
CHIEF P.O.	GUNNERY SGT.	SGT. 1ST CLASS / SPEC. 7	MASTER SGT	E-7
P.O. 1ST CLASS	STAFF SGT.	STAFF SGT. / SPEC. 6	TECHNICAL SGT.	E-6
P.O. 2ND CLASS	SGT.	SGT. / SPEC. 5	STAFF SGT.	E-5
P.O. 3RD CLASS	CORPORAL	CORPORAL / SPEC. 4	SGT.	E-4
SEAMAN	LANCE CORPORAL	PRIVATE 1ST CLASS	AIRMAN 1ST CLASS	E-3
SEAMAN APPRENTICE	PRIVATE 1ST CLASS	PRIVATE	AIRMAN	E-2
SEAMAN RECRUIT	PRIVATE	PRIVATE	BASIC AIRMAN	E-1

Figure 6–3. Enlisted ratings and pay grades, all military services. Coast Guard badges are the same as those worn in the Navy. Chevrons are red on blues with white eagle, blue on whites with blue eagle, blue on khaki with blue eagle. Specialty marks are same color as eagle. Badges worn on dungaree shirts have dark blue chevrons but no specialty mark.

Chief Petty Officer

Senior Chief Petty Officer

Master Chief Petty Officer

Officer or Commissioned Warrant Officer

Figure 6–4. Cap devices for Coast Guard officers and enlisted people.

Weapons
Aviation Engineering
Medical Administration
Personnel Administration
Electronics
Bandmaster

ENLISTED PERSONNEL

The rate, rating, rating-group, special qualifications, length of service, and good conduct records of enlisted men and women are indicated by sleeve and breast insignia. These include group rate marks, striker's marks, rating badges, service stripes, specialty marks, and various insignia denoting special qualifications or designations.

Group Rate Marks

The first distinguishing mark a recruit sews on a uniform indicates his pay grade and, by color, the apprenticeship for which selected. The mark consists of diagonal stripes on square rectangular backgrounds of blue.

Seamen, Seamen Apprentices, Seamen Recruits—white stripes.
Firemen, Firemen Apprentices, Firemen Recruits—red stripes.
Airmen, Airmen Apprentices, and Airmen Recruits—green stripes.

Rating Badges

Rating badges, worn on the left arm, consist of an eagle perched with wings expanded, tips pointing upward, head to eagle's right; chevrons indicating the wearer's rate, and a specialty mark indicating his rating (figure 6–5). Badges are embroidered on a Coast Guard blue background. Rating badges for women are the same size as badges for men, and the space between chevrons is the same—one-fourth inch. For CPOs the eagle and specialty marks are silver, and the chevrons are gold. For all other petty officers the eagle and specialty marks are white and the chevrons are red. Senior chief petty officers wear a star above the rating badge; master chief petty officers wear two stars above the badge (figure 6–6).

Service Stripes

Service stripes (or "hash marks") indicate length of service—one for each full four years of active or reserve service in any of the armed forces, or any combination thereof. Scarlet stripes are worn by nonrated personnel and petty officers, gold stripes are worn by CPOs.

Striker's Marks

Striker's marks are worn by enlisted men and women of the second and third pay grades who are qualified, and have been so designated. The specialty mark of the rating for which qualified is centered immediately above the rectangular background of the group-rate marks.

BREAST INSIGNIA

Metal or embroidered insignia of either gold or silver is worn on the left breast to indicate a special qualification by designation, by both officers and enlisted personnel. The only exceptions are that Command at Sea, Command Ashore, and Officer in Charge insignia are worn on the right breast while so serving. Approved insignia are as follows:

Coast Guard Aviator
Command at Sea
Command Ashore
Cutterman
Officer in Charge
Coxswain
Aircrewman
Only one insignia may be worn at a time except that when ribbons

Aviation Electrician's Mate

Hospital Corpsman

Aviation Electronics Technician

Machinery Technician

Aviation Machinist's Mate

Marine Science Technician

Aviation Structural Mechanic

Musician

Aviation Survivalman

Photo — Journalist

Boatswain's Mate

Port Securityman

Damage Controlman

Quartermaster

Data Processing Technician

Radarman

Dental Technician

Radioman

Electrician's Mate

Sonar Technician

Electronics Technician

Storekeeper

Fire Control Technician

Subsistence Specialist

Fire Fighter

Telephone Technician

Gunner's Mate

Yeoman

Figure 6–5. Coast Guard rating badge specialty marks.

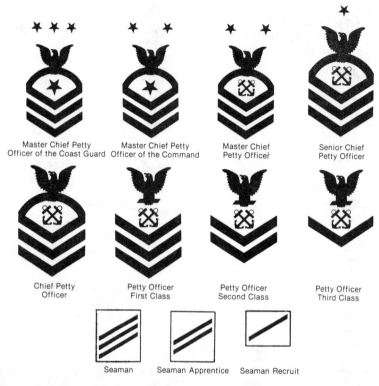

Figure 6–6. Coast Guard rating badges. Specialty marks, worn under the eagle, are shown in figure 6–5.

or medals are worn, two insignia may be worn in addition to the Command at Sea, Command Ashore, or Officer in Charge insignia. When worn alone the insignia is centered above the pocket. When an identification badge is worn, the insignia is worn above it. When two insignia are worn with ribbons or medals, one is centered above and the other below the ribbons or medals; the insignia of the specialty in which currently serving shall be uppermost. Command at Sea, Command Ashore, Officer in Charge, and Coxswain insignia may be worn by officers and men as appropriate even though they are not currently assigned to such duties, but the insignia will be worn on the left breast.

UNIFORM OF THE DAY

This is the uniform prescribed for all personnel within a command or geographical area. Usually the plan of the day for every ship or station lists the uniform for officers and enlisted personnel; a working uniform will be prescribed for "turn-to" hours, and a uniform of the day will be prescribed for after working hours. The uniform for liberty, shore leave, or special occasions or ceremonies will also be prescribed in the plan of the day.

Miscellaneous Uniform Items

Aiguillettes

Worn by officers serving as aide to a flag officer or to the Secretary of Transportation, Vice President, President, and certain other officials. A presidential aide wears his aiguillette on the right shoulder; all others wear it on the left. An aide to a flag officer has as many loops in his aiguillette as there are stars in the flag officer's flag, with four for admiral.

Brassards

These are bands of cloth, marked with symbols or letters to indicate duty of a temporary type. Examples are: OOD, Officer of the Deck; JOOD, Junior Officer of the Deck; MAA, Master at Arms; SP, Shore Patrol, Armed Forces Police; and the Geneva cross, red on white, for ambulance and first-aid parties.

Civilian Clothing

Officers and enlisted personnel are permitted to have civilian clothing in their possession aboard ship and at shore activities, and may wear such clothing while leaving or returning to ships or stations, while on leave of absence or liberty, or in off-duty status ashore. Personnel assigned to marine inspection and marine investigation duties may be required to wear civilian clothing. Men and women may wear current styles and fashions in civilian clothing, provided their appearance is appropriate to the occasion and will not bring discredit upon the service.

Funerals

Officers and enlisted personnel serving as pallbearers at a military funeral, or when attending such a funeral in a military capacity, will wear a three-inch-wide black band around the arm halfway between elbow and shoulder—officers on the left sleeve, enlisted personnel on the right. White gloves may be worn, provided they are furnished to enlisted personnel at no cost.

Name Tags

All personnel wear standard name tags of white letters one-fourth inch high on blue bakelite or similar material, for easy identification. Name tags are worn on the right breast, but not when medals are prescribed. Name tags are provided at no cost to enlisted personnel.

Personal Items

Items worn with uniforms are not to be exposed, except for tie clasps, cuff links, and shirt studs that may be worn as prescribed. Pencils, pens, watch chains, pins, combs, smoking material, or jewelry (except for rings) are not to be worn or carried exposed on a uniform. Wrist watches and identification bracelets are permitted.

Wearing of Uniforms

Along with the military pride, tradition, and dignity involved in the proper wearing of the uniform, some common sense is involved. The hat or cap is part of the uniform, but if a particular duty or operation interferes, it may be removed. Persons riding in motor vehicles with insufficient headroom may remove their headgear; those riding two- or three-wheeled motor vehicles will remove uniform headgear and wear safety helmets, and may wear protective clothing over their uniform. A cap is no longer required to be worn at sea, except on specific watches and specific occasions. It is always worn squarely on the head, bottom edge horizontal.

Shoes must be kept in good repair; those worn on watch, liberty, and for inspections shall be well-shined.

Care of Uniforms

The best way to make uniforms last and keep them looking sharp is to give them proper care and maintenance. Keep them cleaned, and on hangers when possible. No matter how well a new uniform fits, it will soon lose its shape—especially the coat—if the pockets bulge with odds and ends. Trousers should never be tossed over a chair or locker top, but hung to keep the press in. Damp clothing should be carefully hung and smoothed out to avoid wrinkles as it dries.

Most items of uniform wear—woolen, serge, gabardine, or double knit—are best handled by a competent dry cleaning or laundry service. When such service is not available, it is possible to care for your clothing yourself. These hints will help.

Blues

Shiny spots on serge can be removed by first sponging with a 1:20 solution of ammonia, then covering with a damp cloth, pressing with a hot iron, and rubbing gently with "00" sandpaper or emery cloth, but it's best to let an experienced tailor do this. A light singe mark can be removed by rubbing vigorously with the flat side of a silver coin. Some singe marks can be removed by sponging with a 3 percent solution of hydrogen peroxide and drying in direct sunlight. Never use this treatment on wool or dyed fabrics. Cuts, burns, or moth holes can be rewoven by a skillful tailor, who takes threads from another part of the garment; this is an expensive job, but cheaper than buying a new uniform.

Gold Lace, Cap Devices, and Buttons

Gold lace, or braid, will tarnish if left in contact with, or hung near, any substance containing sulphur, such as rubber or ordinary manila and kraft wrapping paper, and is best cleaned by an experienced tailor. However, most uniform shops sell a commercial cleaner that will remove light tarnish. Embroidered cap devices and other insignia may be kept bright by light brushing with a small brush and ammonia diluted in water. This should be done at the first signs of tarnish; after heavy discoloration, the device cannot be restored to its original condition. (In this respect, a few individuals will assume that mouldy sleeve marks or hash marks and crusty green buttons look "salty." Nothing could be further from the truth. All the salty admirals and CPOs wear bright, clean gold.)

Metal cap devices can be kept bright by using soap and water or a soft polishing cloth on the gold and polishing the silver with any silver polish. Buttons will turn green when the gold plating wears off and the copper base becomes covered with copper carbonate due to exposure to moist air. This green stain can be removed by rubbing with acetic acid (found in vinegar and Worcestershire sauce) and washing in fresh water.

Medals

The surfaces of decorations are protected with an oxidized satin finish and a lacquer coating. They will not tarnish, and need no polishing; polishing may remove the finish. Medals may be cleaned with soap and water; the ribbons may be drycleaned, or replaced.

Moths

The best way to discourage moths is to brush clothing frequently and expose it to sunshine and fresh air when possible. If clothing is to be stored for any time, pack items in air-tight plastic bags with camphor balls, naphthalene, paradichlorobenzene, or cedar wood, or spray them with an appropriate insecticide.

Mildew

New mildew can be washed out with cold water. Old stains in white cotton can be removed with a household laundry bleach.

Stains

It is possible to stain a uniform with anything from alcohol to zinc chromate, but if you know what made the stain, an expert cleaner can remove it. In the way of "first aid" to a uniform before it goes to the cleaner, try soap and water—cool water for wool and warm water for cotton. Some stains can be handled as follows.

Oil or Grease. Put clean cloth or absorbent paper under the garment, apply commercial cleaning fluid (or lighter fuel) to the stain, and tamp it, driving the oil or grease through to the cloth or paper. If the stain is heavy, shift the cloth to a clean place and use more cleaning fluid. To avoid a ring around the stain, wet a clean cloth with cleaning fluid and sponge lightly, working outward from the center of the area.

Paint. Fresh paint should be handled as if it were oil or grease. Once it is dry and hard, the uniform should be sent to a cleaner. If this is not possible, apply turpentine and let it stand for an hour, then use a spoon or some other blunt object to break up the paint and flush it out as done for oil and grease. (Never rub when spotting fabric; this will leave a chafed area, with subsequent damage to color and weave. Always use a tamping action with a brush.)

Paraffin or Wax. Put blotting paper over the spot and apply a hot iron. Continue, using clean blotting paper, until the spot is soaked up.

Rust, Ink, or Fruit. Soak the stain in a solution of oxalic acid, or moisten with water and apply powdered oxalic acid or sodium or potassium acid oxalate and rub with a piece of white cotton or linen. When the stain dissolves, wash out with warm water. Remove the oxalic acid solution thoroughly or it will damage the material. Be careful handling oxalic acid, as it is poisonous, but not toxic to breathe.

Iodine. On white uniforms, use a solution of photographic "hypo" or sodium thiosulfate and rinse thoroughly with warm water. A solution of laundry starch or ammonia will also remove iodine.

Stowage of Uniforms

Space is limited aboard ship. You will have to learn how to stow most of your possessions in a small locker so that they take up the least possible space and yet remain neat. Most ships will have standard locker stowage plans posted. There may be special stowage for raincoats and peacoats. In such spaces, take care with your own clothing and be careful with that belonging to others.

Grooming

Regulations concerning dress and general appearance are not nearly as strict as they once were, but men and women are still expected to present a neat appearance at all times.

Ownership Markings

Articles of clothing owned by enlisted men, E-6 and below, shall be legibly marked with the owner's name and service number. Use black marking fluid for white clothes and chambray and enlisted working blue shirts and white marking fluid for blue clothes and dungaree trousers. Use indelible ink when labels are provided. Elsewhere use a half-inch stencil or stamp, if available, otherwise use a stencil not larger than one inch.

Where the word *right* or *left* appears, it means "right" or "left" when wearing the garment. On towels, it means the owner's right or left when standing behind the article laid out for inspection. The individual's name and SSN on all articles, when properly rolled or laid out for inspection, will appear upright to the inspecting officer and upside down to the man standing behind them.

Enlisted personnel shall not transfer or exchange clothing without the authority of the Master-at-Arms. When such transfers or exchanges are authorized, or when clothing belonging to deserters is sold, the name of the former owner shall be obliterated with a stamp marked "DC," and the purchaser's name shall be placed above, below, or next to it. The Master-at-Arms shall keep a record of such changes.

Location of Markings

Bag (Duffel). Along the carrying strap on outer side, and on opposite side from the carrying strap, around the bag about one foot from the top.

Belts. Inside.

Caps.

Blue, Working. Initials only on sweatband.

Combination. Initials only on sweatband.

Garrison. Initials only on sweatband.

Cap Cover. Initials only on inside of band.

Coats.

Blue. On designated nameplate.

Peacoat. On the lining, right side of slit of tail 3 inches from, and parallel to, bottom.

Drawers. On the outside of the right half of the waistband, or immediately underneath the waistband on drawers with elastic waistbands.

Gloves. Initials only on inside, near the top.

Jacket, Blue Working. On the inside of hem at the right of the center line of the back.

Necktie, Black Four-in-Hand. Center back, inside.

Raincoat. Inside on lining, 3 inches below collar seam.

Shirts.

Blue Chambray. On the shirt tail, and last name only on left front, 1 inch above pocket.

Enlisted Working Blue. On the inside hem at the right of the center line at the back and last name only on the left front 1 inch above the pocket.

Light Blue (Long Sleeve). Center back inside on lower part of collar, or on designated nameplate.

Light Blue (Short Sleeve Tropical). Vertically, beginning 1 inch from the bottom on the inner side of the right front fold on which the buttons are sewed.

Shoes. Initials only inside, near top.

Socks. Initials only on the foot.

Towel. Right corner on hem, parallel to end.

Trousers.

Blue (Undress). On label provided or on waistband inside in front at the right of center line.

Blue (Service). On designated nameplate.

Dungaree. On the waistband inside in front at the right of center line; last name only, above the right hip pocket.

Enlisted Working Blue. On the waistband inside in front at the right of center line, last name only above right pocket.

Trunks, Swim. Inside on hem on right center of back.

Undershirt. On the outside of the front, 1 inch from the bottom of the shirt and at right of the center.

Optional articles of clothing shall be marked similarly to comparable items of required clothing.

DECORATIONS AND AWARDS

A *decoration* is a medal awarded to an individual by name for exceptional courage, bravery, skill, or performance of duty; examples are the Coast Guard Medal, Coast Guard Commendation Medal, Bronze Star Medal, Coast Guard Achievement Medal, or Purple Heart. A *unit award* is made to a ship or other unit for a particular action and is worn only by people who took part in that action; examples are Presidential Unit Citation (PUC) or Coast Guard Unit Commendation. *Service awards* are made to those who took part in designated wars, campaigns, or expeditions, or fulfilled specified requirements in a creditable manner; and inside "theater ribbons" such as the Vietnam Service Medal, and awards such as the Good Conduct Medal.

Military decorations and unit awards may be awarded at any time, as fitting and appropriate.

The first American medals were conferred during the Revolutionary War, when military and naval commanders were awarded special gold medals in commemoration of their victories. The first of these special gold medals was presented to General George Washington, in appreciation of his having driven the British from Boston in 1776. The first American decoration for individual meritorious service was instituted by George Washington. It was a badge of purple cloth material in the figure of a heart edged with narrow lace. The first medal for distinguished services—the Medal of Honor—was authorized during the Civil War. In 1874 Congress authorized the awarding of Life-saving Medals. The Commandant has been delegated the authority to award them to civilians and members of the military.

Decorations, medals, and ribbons represent the thanks of the nation for services rendered in its honor. They commemorate entire wars, single campaigns, individual actions, and group and personal heroism.

To have a true meaning, they must be worn correctly; a person wearing a ribbon to which he is not entitled is subject to disciplinary action.

Special honors and awards may be won in peacetime as well as in wartime. While your opportunities to earn service and campaign medals depend to a certain extent on the chances of assignment, your opportunities to earn proficiency awards depend upon how well you apply yourself to the job of being a good Coast Guardsman. The Good Conduct Medal is awarded for above-average service in conduct and proficiency in rating. The Expert Rifleman and Expert Pistol Shot Medals are earned by being a better-than-average marksman. (See appendix A for ribbons of decorations and awards.)

In general, the decorations and service medals that are awarded to Navy personnel may also be awarded to Coast Guardsmen under the same or like conditions. In a few cases the design of the medal is distinctive for the Coast Guard, but the regulations under which it is awarded are similar.

Ribbons for decorations and awards are worn on the left breast. One, two, or three ribbons are centered above the pocket; if not in multiples of three, the top row of one or two is centered over the row below it. Ribbons are worn in order of precedence from the wearer's right to left, and from top down.

In general, Coast Guard personnel are eligible to receive any military decoration or service medal providing the regulations of the service concerned are met and the Commandant approves. The regulations under which other service medals are awarded are similar to Coast Guard regulations. Personal decorations, Letters of Commendation, and the Good Conduct Medal qualify enlisted personnel for additional point credit toward advancement in rating. A maximum of ten points may be credited for awards.

Unit Awards

Coast Guard Unit Commendation may be awarded by the Commandant to any unit that has distinguished itself by extremely meritorious service not involving combat but in support of Coast Guard operations, rendering the unit outstanding compared to other units performing similar service.

Coast Guard Meritorious Unit Commendation is awarded by the Commandant; the Commander, Pacific Area; or Commander, Atlantic Area; it is awarded to any unit that has distinguished itself by either

Individual Decorations, Medals and Awards (In order of precedence)

Name of Award	Awarded to Personnel who	Awarded for
*Medal of Honor	in action with the enemy distinguishes himself conspicuously by gallantry and intrepidity at the risk of his life above and beyond the call of duty and without detriment to the mission	Combat only
Navy Cross	in any capacity with the Naval Service distinguishes himself by extraordinary heroism in military operations against an armed enemy.	Combat action only
Coast Guard Distinguished Service Medal	distinguishes himself by exceptionally meritorious service to the government in a duty of great responsibility.	Noncombat
Silver Star Medal	in any capacity with the Navy distinguishes himself conspicuously by gallantry and intrepidity in action, but not sufficiently for the above medals.	Combat only
*Legion of Merit	distinguishes himself by exceptionally meritorious conduct in the performance of outstanding services.	Combat or noncombat
*Distinguished Flying Cross	distinguishes himself by heroism or extraordinary achievement while participating in an aerial flight.	Combat or noncombat
Coast Guard Medal	while serving in any capacity with the Coast Guard distinguishes himself by heroism not involving actual conflict with an enemy.	Noncombat only
Navy and Marine Corps Medal	while serving in any capacity with the Navy or Marine Corps, including Reserves, distinguishes himself by heroism not involving actual conflict with an enemy.	Noncombat only
*Bronze Star Medal	distinguishes himself by heroism or meritorious achievement or services, in connection with military or naval operations against an enemy. It must not involve aerial flight.	Combat only.
Meritorious Service Medal	distinguishes himself by outstanding meritorious achievement in the performance of duty.	Noncombat only
*Air Medal	distinguishes himself by meritorious achievement while participating in an aerial flight	Combat or noncombat
Coast Guard Commendation Medal	distinguishes himself by meritorious service resulting in unusual and outstanding achievement.	Noncombat only
Navy Commendation Medal	in serving with the Navy or Marine Corps distinguishes himself by meritorious or heroic achievement or service.	Combat or noncombat
Coast Guard Achievement Medal	distinguishes himself by professional achievements that exceed normal expectancy.	Noncombat only

Individual Decorations, Medals and Awards (In order of precedence)—Continued

Name of Award	Awarded to Personnel who	Awarded for
Navy Achievement Medal	distinguishes himself by professional achievements that exceed normal expectancy.	Combat or noncombat
Letter of Commendation	while serving in any capacity with the Coast Guard performs meritorious service resulting in unusual and outstanding achievement rendered while the Coast Guard is serving under the Department of Transportation.	Noncombat only
*Purple Heart	are wounded while serving in action against an enemy of the United States. Wound must be such as to require the attention of a medical officer.	Combat only
Gold Lifesaving Medal	rescues or endeavors to rescue any other person from drowning, shipwreck, or other peril of the water, if such rescue or attempted rescue is made at the risk of one's own life and evidences extreme and heroic daring.	Peacetime or wartime
Silver Lifesaving Medal	rescues or endeavors to rescue any other person from drowning, shipwreck, or other peril of the water. If such rescue or attempted rescue is not sufficiently distinguished to deserve the gold, but evidences the exercising of such signal exertion as to merit recognition, the medal shall be of silver.	Peacetime or wartime
Department of Transportation Gold Medal	are recognized for exceptionally outstanding leadership or service that is distinguished by achievements of marked national or international significance.	Peacetime or wartime
Department of Transportation Silver Medal	distinguishes himself by exceptionally meritorious service to the department or federal government, or for exceptional achievement which substantially contributed to accomplishment of the Department's mission or major programs.	Peacetime or wartime
Department of Transportation Bronze Medal	distinguishes himself by superior achievement which has demonstrated unusual initiative or skill and which has notably contributed to accomplishing the department's or administration's mission.	Peacetime or wartime
Coast Gaurd Good Conduct Medal	has completed four years of continuous enlisted service in the regular or reserve Coast Goard with conduct and proficiency in rating marks that meet requirements and with no disciplinary action.	Peacetime or wartime

Individual Decorations, Medals and Awards (In order of precedence)—Continued

Name of Award	Awarded to Personnel who	Awarded for
Navy Good Conduct Medal	has completed four years of continuous enlisted service in the Regular Navy, Navy Reserve, or as an inductee, if conduct and proficiency in rating marks meet the requirements and the person has no court-martial conviction and not more than one other offense.	Peacetime or wartime

*Under certain specific regulations awarded to Coast Guard personnel while serving under Department of Transportation jurisdiction. Normally these awards are issued only for wartime service, a period when the Coast Guard is operating as a part of the Navy.

valorous or meritorious achievement or service in support of Coast Guard operations not involving combat, which renders the unit outstanding but not sufficient to justify award of the Coast Guard Unit Commendation.

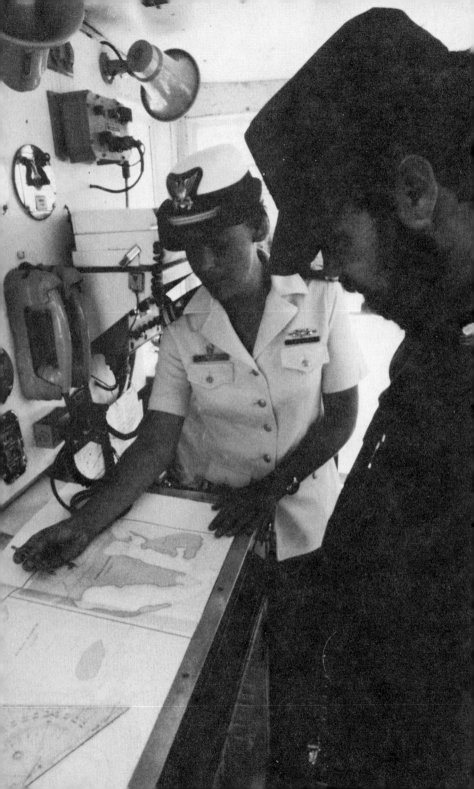

CHAPTER 7

Watches and Routines

For the proper performance of duty, every unit in the Coast Guard—whether a 3-man light-station crew or the entire crew of a high-endurance cutter—must be organized. The organization for similar units throughout the service is similar; to make this organization work, routines and duties in similar units have been standardized. Even time has been standardized.

In the Coast Guard, as in all military services, routines are based on a 24-hour day. Time is counted in hours—1 to 24—and minutes in each hour—01 to 59. The day begins at midnight, when the time is 0000, and ends with 2359. One minute later the time is 0000, or midnight, and the next day starts. Aboard ship, the day is also half-hour periods, marked by the ship's bell, and by watches, which regulate the time on and off duty.

Ship's Bell

Before timepieces were common, time aboard ship was marked by a so-called hourglass, which ran out in 30 minutes. Then the glass would be turned over, to start measuring another 30 minutes, and the bell would be struck so all hands knew a half hour had passed. At the end of each half hour, the bell would be struck one more time; thus it was struck once at the end of the first half hour and eight times at the end of the fourth hour. This practice still continues despite clocks and

Figure 7–1. The basic business of a professional afloat is carrying out the watch routine.

watches. After eight bells are struck, the sequence starts all over again. An odd number of bells marks a half hour, and an even number marks an hour. For the relation between time, bells, and watches, see table below.

mid-watch		morning watch		forenoon watch		afternoon watch		evening watch		night watch	
time	bells	time	bells	time	bells	time	bells	time	bells	time	bells
0030	1	0430	1	0830	1	1230	1	1630	1	2030	1
0100	2	0500	2	0900	2	1300	2	1700	2	2100	2
0130	3	0530	3	0930	3	1330	3	1730	3	2130	3
0200	4	0600	4	1000	4	1400	4	1800	4	2200	4
0230	5	0630	5	1030	5	1430	5	1830	5	2230	5
0300	6	0700	6	1100	6	1500	6	1900	6	2300	6
0330	7	0730	7	1130	7	1530	7	1930	7	2330	7
0400	8	0800	8	1200	8	1600	8	2000	8	2400	8

Watches

A ship in commission always has men on watch. Even when she is tied up in port and receiving steam and electricity from the pier or another ship, it is necessary to have men on watch for communications, security, and safety. Men assigned to watches are called watchstanders. Traditionally, the 24-hour day is divided into seven watches, as follows:

    0000-0400—Mid-watch
    0400-0800—Morning watch
    0800-1200—Forenoon watch
    1200-1600—Afternoon watch
    1600-1800—First dog watch
    1800-2000—Second dog watch
    2000-2400—First watch

The two "dog watches," from 1600 to 1800 and 1800 to 2000, serve to alternate the daily watch routine so that men who have the mid-watch one night will not have it again on the following night.

Watch may refer to the location of the man on watch, as the *forecastle watch, bridge watch,* or to the section of the ship's crew on duty: "second section has the watch."

STANDARD ROUTINE

Ashore or afloat, there are many ways of accomplishing the same purpose. While the commanding officer of a unit is held strictly accountable for producing results, he is allowed considerable latitude in the way he runs his unit. Even so, there is a standard routine both ashore and afloat; changes in this routine are made to meet the local situation.

Time	Daily routine in port
0350	Relieve the watch.
0500	Call the galley force.
0530	Call the relief for the two-hour watches.
0545	Call the officer-of-the-deck, master-at-arms (MAA), mess cooks, and other early risers.

At five minutes before sunrise—Stand by lights.
At sunrise—Turn off anchor, gangway, and other lights about deck.

0550	Relieve the watch.
0600	Reveille. Up all hands.
	Light the smoking lamp.
	Serve out coffee.
	Liberty expires for messmen.
	Discontinue hourly security patrols of ship.
0630	Turn to. Scrub down weather decks. Wipe down deck houses with fresh water. Sweep down compartments. MAA report "crew turned out" to the OOD.
0700	Knock off work.
	Clear the mess deck so the mess cooks can set up for breakfast.
0715	Breakfast.
	Call late sleepers.
	Publish uniform of the day.
0745	Liberty expires.
0750	Relieve the watch.
0755	Quarters for muster.
	Report approach of eight o'clock to the captain.
	Request permission to strike eight bells.
	First call to colors.
0800	Colors.
	"Turn to."
	Breakfast for the watch and late sleepers.
0830	Clear the mess deck for cleaning.
0900	Sick call. OOD is relieved.
1045	Division officers inspect compartments.

1100	Inspection of mess cooks and stewardsmen.
	Liberty expires for watchstanders.
	Report mast.
	Request mast.
1115	Clear the mess deck.
	Knock off the relief watch from work.
1130	Knock off all hands from work.
	Dinner for the watch.
1145	Officer of the deck samples crew's dinner.
1150	Relieve the watch.
1155	Report chronometers wound to the captain; request permission to strike eight bells.
1200	Dinner for all hands.
1230	Clear the mess deck.
1255	Officers' call. All hands fall in for quarters.
1300	Quarters for inspection and drills.
1350	Secure from drills.
1400	Turn to.
	Liberty for watchstanders.
1530	Knock off the relief watch from work.
1550	Relieve the watch.
1600	Clean sweepdown fore and aft. Knock off work.
1630	Liberty for all hands.
1645	Clear the mess deck. Set up for supper.
1700	Supper for all hands.
1730	Supper for the watch.
1800	Clear the mess deck until cleaned up.
One hour before sunset	Electrician test anchor, gangway, deck lights, and searchlights.
Five minutes before sunset	First call to colors, stand by ensign and jack, stand by anchor and deck lights.
Sunset	Colors. Turn on lights.
1900	Movie call.
1945	Muster the night watch.
	Muster eight o'clock reports.
1950	Relieve the watch. Set the anchor watch.
1955	Report the ship secure to the commanding officer.
	Request permission to strike eight bells.
2000	Strike eight bells.
2130	Call the relief.

2150	Relieve the watch.
2200	Start hourly security patrols.
2200	Lights out, silence below deck.
2330	Call the relief.
2350	Relieve the watch.

Daily routine at sea

0150	Relieve the wheel and lookout.
0330	Call the relief watch.
0350	Relieve the watch. Relieve the wheel and lookout. Lifeboat's crew of the watch to muster.
0500	Call the galley force.
0545	Call the MAA, mess cooks, and other early risers.
Five minutes before sunrise—Stand by the running lights and colors.	
Sunrise	Turn off running lights. Hoist colors.
0550	Relieve the wheel and lookout.
0600	Reveille, up all hands. Light the smoking lamp. Serve out coffee. Announce weather. Boatswain's Mate of the Watch secure hourly rounds.
0630	Turn to. Scrub down weather decks. Wipe down deck houses with fresh water. Sweep down compartments. MAA report "crew turned out" to OOD.
0700	Knock off morning work. Clear the mess deck, set up for breakfast.
0715	Breakfast for all hands. Publish uniform of the day.
0750	Relieve the watch. Relieve the wheel and lookout. Lifeboat's crew of the watch to muster.
0755	Report the approach of eight o'clock to the captain. Request permission to strike eight bells.
0800	All hands turn to. Breakfast for the watch.
0830	Clear the mess deck until cleaned. Sick call.
0950	Relieve the wheel and lookout.
1000	Up all sleepers. (varies)
1045	Division officers inspect compartments.

1100	Inspection of mess cooks and stewards.
	Report mast, request mast.
1115	Clear the mess deck.
	Knock off the relief watch from work.
1130	Dinner for the watch.
	Knock off all hands from work. Clean sweepdown fore and aft.
1145	Officer of the deck samples crew's dinner.
1150	Relieve the watch. Relieve the wheel and lookout.
	Lifeboat's crew of the watch to muster.
1155	Report chronometers wound to the captain. Request permission to strike eight bells.
1200	Dinner for all hands.
	Test the general alarm. Test the siren and whistle.
1255	Officers' call. All hands fall in for quarters.
1300	Quarters for inspection and drills.
1330	Secure relief wheel and lookout from drills.
1350	Relieve the wheel and lookout.
	Secure from drills.
1400	Turn to.
1530	Knock off the relief watch from work.
1550	Relieve the watch. Relieve the wheel and lookout.
	Lifeboat's crew of the watch to muster.
1600	Knock off work. Clean sweepdown fore and aft.
1645	Clear the mess deck. Set up for supper.
1700	Supper for all hands.
1730	Supper for the watch.
1750	Relieve the wheel and lookout.
1800	Clear the mess deck until cleaned.
	One hour before sunset—Electrician test the running lights and searchlight.
	Five minutes before sunset—Stand by the colors and running lights.
	Sunset—Colors. Turn on running lights.—Note: Colors may not be made at sea.
	Thirty minutes after sunset—Division officers check to see that proper material condition is set and that watertight integrity is assured.
1900	Movies.

1945	Eight o'clock reports. Department petty officers report the department areas secure for the night to their department officers, who in turn report the department secure to the executive officer.
1950	Relieve the watch. Relieve the wheel and lookout. Lifeboat's crew of the watch to muster.
1955	Executive officer reports the vessel secure for the night to the captain. Report approach of eight o'clock. Obtain permission to strike eight bells.
2100	Lights out, and silence in the berthing compartments. Boatswain's Mate of the Watch start hourly rounds of the ship.
2150	Relieve the wheel and lookout.
2200	Lights out and silence below decks.
2330	Call the relief watch.
2350	Relieve the watch. Relieve the wheel and lookout. Lifeboat's crew of the watch to muster.

Plan of the Day

The executive officer prepares and issues daily a plan of the day, which includes such things as:

The schedule of the normal routine, and any variations or additions.
The orders of the day, detailing the drills, training schedule, duty section, liberty section, working parties, time and location of movies, etc.
Notices of matters that should be brought to the attention of officers and men.
Reprints of regulations and orders that are to be brought to the attention of officers and men.

Copies of the plan of the day are distributed to the OOD, all offices, officers, and division bulletin boards of the ship. Everyone is responsible for knowing what is in the plan of the day.

The plan of the day is carried out by the OOD and the division officers unless modified by the authority of the captain or the executive officer. In case of necessity the OOD may make immediate changes and report his actions later to the executive officer.

Passing the Word

In the case of certain emergency situations, special signals are employed, such as the General Alarm for battle, the siren for collision, and a rapid ringing of the ship's bell for fire. The main reliance for passing the word is placed on the loudspeaker system when one is installed. This system consists of a transmitter on the bridge and others at selected spots. Speakers are located at useful and convenient places throughout the ship. Most ships also have a 21-MC or "Captain's Command" circuit, which consists of several transmitter-receiver units similar to an office intercommunication system. When this system is used, there is always an instrument on the bridge, one in the cabin, and one in the wardroom. There are usually at least three other command circuit transmitter-receiver stations on the ship.

The Boatswain's Pipe

Even though there are loudspeakers and intercommunication systems on modern ships, the boatswain's (pronounced "bosun's") pipe is sometimes used for calling and passing the word. The various calls and their meanings are as follows:

Name of Call	*Purpose*	*When Occurring*
Word to be passed	Piped to command silence before passing an order of information.	As appropriate
All hands	Piped to call all hands' attention.	As appropriate
Boat	Piped to call away a boat; also to call a division or divisions to quarters.	As appropriate
Call mates	Piped by the boatswain to assemble his mates; also to rouse quick notice or attention from a working group.	As appropriate
Mess gear	Piped for mess gear.	At meals
Piping the side	Accompanies appropriate side honors. Signal that official personages are coming aboard.	As appropriate

Tattoo and Taps

Tattoo is the signal for all hands to turn in and keep silence about the decks. Taps is sounded five minutes after tattoo except when circumstances warrant a little longer time.

Special Sea Detail

In getting under way or entering port, a ship has a *special sea detail*. This is composed of experienced men for the different stations that have to be manned. The special sea detail is set about a half-hour before getting under way and remains there until the ship clears the harbor; or it may be set sometime before entering port and remain so until the ship is properly docked or anchored. Special sea detail duty takes precedence over anything else for each man assigned to it.

Sea Watch

Once the ship has cleared the harbor, the special sea detail is relieved and the *sea watch* is stationed; that is, the cruising watches begin and the regular sections of the watch take over their prescribed duties. In the Coast Guard, the five *general degrees of readiness* are:

Condition I. Complete readiness for immediate action.

Condition I-E. Temporary relaxation from the first degree of readiness for purposes of feeding and resting the crew at their battle stations.

Condition III. Part of the armament ready for immediate action, the remainder at prolonged notice.

Condition IV. Condition IV is for peacetime cruising with no armament manned.

Condition V. This condition is defined as ship in port during peacetime with, of course, no armament manned.

In the Navy on large ships *Condition II* is also used. *Condition II* is used by vessels assigned to gunfire support duty in situations such as extended periods of shore bombardment, where only limited action need be provided for.

Smoking Aboard Ship

The commanding officer designates the parts of the ship where smoking is allowed.

The crew may be permitted to smoke at times other than those specified in the normal routine, especially on holidays or Saturday and Sunday afternoons, and for a limited period during night watches.

Smoking in any part of the ship during divine services is forbidden.

Smoking in the ship's boats not on detached service is forbidden.

Smoking is forbidden when ammunition is being received or discharged, or when fuel is being taken aboard.

Lights

All lights, except those in the cabins, offices, officers' quarters, and those designated as standing lights, are extinguished at tattoo.

The lights on the lower decks are reduced in number before tattoo unless they are required for the comfort of the crew. All lights in the holds, storerooms, and orlops (lowest decks) and all open lights in the ship, except those in officers' quarters, are extinguished before 1930 or at the time of the evening inspection by the executive officer.

During the night a sufficient number of lights located throughout the open part of the ship are kept lighted to enable the officers and crew to turn out, to get to the upper decks, or to attend to any duty arising from a sudden emergency. These are known as "standing lights."

Such lights and fires as the captain may deem dangerous are extinguished when the magazines are opened or when handling or passing powder, explosives, or other dangerous combustibles.

In time of war or when necessary to conceal a ship from an enemy, only such lights are used as are deemed advisable by the senior officer present.

Eight O'clock Reports

Each evening the heads of the departments assure themselves as to the condition of security and readiness of their departments. At 2000 the department heads or their representatives muster and report their findings to the executive officer. He in turn passes these reports as to the condition of the ship to the commanding officer. Thus at the end of each day the captain, the executive officer, and all department heads are aware of the exact state of the entire ship.

Visitors

There are two types of visitation: routine visiting and general visiting. Routine visiting means the everyday, informal visits of friends. General visiting occurs on days such as Armed Forces Day, when the ship is open to the public.

Routine Visiting. Members of the crew may have civilian visitors aboard ship on Saturdays, Sundays, and holidays between the hours of 1300 and 1630. For other times, permission must be obtained from the executive officer. Normally, officers and chief petty officers may have visitors on weekdays after working hours. Civilian visitors are not allowed to bring cameras on board. The OOD or his representative will retain custody of all cameras until the visitors leave. A member of the crew who has guests must meet them at the gangway or shipyard gate and escort them at all times while they are on board or within the shipyard. Guests are permitted only in the spaces authorized by the commanding officer. In the event of sickness or accident to any visitor, a report must be made immediately to the medical officer and to the OOD.

General Visiting. Each ship lays out a plan for handling visitors—the general public as well as United States and foreign dignitaries—who may be expected on days of open ship. Prior to visiting hours the word is passed, "Rig ship for general visiting. All hands shift into uniform of the day." While visitors are on board, all officers and men must remain alert that no visitor be permitted in an unauthorized part of the ship, that no visitor endanger himself or herself, and that all guests be treated with special courtesy.

Pets

Pets may be brought on board only with the permission of the commanding officer.

Officers' Quarters and Bridge

Men are allowed on the quarterdeck only when on duty. This is also true of officers' country (wardroom) and the bridges, wheelhouse, and charthouse.

Watch Section

Each man is assigned to a *section* of the watch. These sections are numbered; small ships usually have three sections, large ships may have four sections. Thus, when the word is passed that the first section (or the second or the third) has the watch, each man in that section immediately reports to his watch station. At sea, watches may be either two or four hours in length. Lookout and helmsman watches are usually limited to two hours maximum; under certain conditions they may be shorter. In port, certain watches are also stood on a two-hour basis.

On some ships, especially for watches while in port, the divisions may be divided into a *starboard watch* and a *port watch*. Each of these watches is divided in turn into two sections: the odd-numbered sections, 1 and 3, are in the starboard watch; the even-numbered sections, 2 and 4, are in the port watch.

Men in a three-section watch are spoken of as having a one-in-three watch; those in a four-section watch have a one-in-four watch, and so on. Thus, a man standing a one-in-three is on watch for four hours, off for eight hours, and then back on watch for four more. In all he stands eight hours' watch out of 24 hours.

Relieving the Watch

Watches must be relieved on time. This does not mean at the exact minute the watch changes, but several minutes before—anywhere from 5 to 15 minutes, depending on the type of watch—in order that the relief can receive information and instructions from the man on watch. Some ships muster the oncoming watch to make sure that each man is ready ahead of time.

When reporting directly to the person relieved, a man says, "I am ready to relieve you." The man on watch then passes on any pertinent instructions or information relating to the proper standing of the watch. When the relief is sure that he understands conditions and any instructions given him, he says, "I relieve you." Thereafter he is completely responsible for the watch.

Remember that you must report to the responsible officer (of the deck or engineering watch, for example) that you have been relieved.

Anchor and Security Watches

Men are assigned to the anchor watch to perform emergency work that might arise during the night, and members of this watch are permitted to sleep at their stations until an emergency arises. Members of this watch stand two-hour turns patrolling the deck to see that all is secure.

There is also a security watch that patrols the interior of the ship. This also is usually a two-hour watch in port. Watchstanders are drawn from the duty section.

Persons regularly assigned to four-hour watches are known as "watchstanders." In port they stand watch on and watch off for twenty-four hours, then are off-duty for the next twenty-four hours. Because they get only one day's liberty out of two, instead of two out of three as do the rest of the crew, they are permitted to depart on liberty sooner and return to the ship later than other members of the crew. Men on watch from 0000 to 0400—the mid-watch—have a difficult time getting enough sleep. For this reason they are permitted to sleep in after "all hands" are called. They are the "late sleepers" referred to in the daily routines.

Watch Officers

A watch officer is placed in charge of a watch or a portion of a watch. The commanding officer assigns as a watch officer any commissioned or warrant officer whom he considers qualified. The CO may, when conditions require, assign a petty officer to such duty. The station of the officer or petty officer in charge of the watch is where he can best perform his duties and supervise and control the performance of those on watch under him.

Prisoners at Large (PAL)

For certain reasons, men may be denied liberty or leave. Such men may not leave the ship without specific authority of the executive officer. This group includes those who are:

confined to the limits of the ship by sentence of court-martial
awaiting trial by, or approval of, court-martial
awaiting mast for serious cases (designated PAL by the commanding officer)
restricted to the ship by punishment assigned at mast
on report and awaiting mast for other than serious offenses but not yet made PAL by order of the commanding officer
on the medical restricted list

Restricted Men

These are men under restraint according to the Uniform Code of Military Justice (UCMJ). They are either under *restriction* or under *arrest*.

Restriction is a restraint of the same nature as arrest, imposed under similar circumstances and by the same authorities, but it does not involve the suspension of military duties.

Arrest is the moral restraint of a man, by an order, verbal or written, to certain specified limits pending disposition of charges against him. It is not imposed as punishment, and it relieves him of all his military duties other than normal cleaning and policing.

Liberty

Normally, liberty commences at 1600 or 1630 daily and expires on board at 0745 the following day. Liberty is normally granted to half or two-thirds of the crew, depending on circumstances.

Men on continuous running watches, such as radiomen, may be

granted liberty commencing at 1400 if the head of the department requests it for them.

Special liberty will be granted only for good reasons. A request for such liberty must be made on a form provided, signed by the division officer and the head of the department, and delivered to the executive officer's office prior to 1000. The request, marked "approved" or "disapproved," will be returned to the man.

Liberty may be exchanged in special cases if a man obtains a volunteer relief from the men in his own division who do rate liberty. Such a relief must be of similar rating or with similar qualifications. The man desiring liberty submits a written request to his division officer. If the division officer approves, the request is delivered to the executive officer for final action.

Liberty may be granted more frequently in those commands that have enough men to allow it and still maintain security. Remember, "liberty is a privilege, not a right."

Meritorious Liberty. Extra liberty may be granted to men who, by reason of special effort, have been instrumental in obtaining especially creditable results in gunnery, engineering, communications, or athletics; or it may be granted for especially meritorious conduct.

Quarters for Muster and Inspection

Division Parades

Each division is assigned a parade—a space on deck where men assemble for quarters or inspection. The fair-weather parades are on the uncovered decks; the foul-weather parades are on the covered decks and in the living spaces as designated.

Where possible the departments form with all divisions facing outboard. Those divisions that are aligned athwartships face forward if in the forward part of the ship and aft if in the after part.

Mustering the Division

At the command FALL IN, each section forms in line. Section leaders muster the sections while the division is being formed. When the division is formed, the division leading petty officer then commands: REPORT.

The section leaders in succession from front to rear, without moving from their assigned positions, report, "All present," or "——— absentees."

The division petty officer then commands: 1. DRESS RIGHT, 2. DRESS. After dressing the division he commands: 3. READY, 4. FRONT. The division leading petty officer then resumes his position in front of the division, faces the division officer, salutes, and reports, "Sir, all present or accounted for," or "Sir, ———— men absent," and without command, faces about and moves by the most direct route to his post on the right flank of the front rank of the division.

The division officer then proceeds with the inspection of his division. After his inspection he leaves the division in charge of the junior division officer and falls in with other division officers to report to the executive officer.

Division Inspections

The divisions may be inspected by the division junior officer while the division officer is reporting to his head of department; by the division officer before or after he reports to his head of department; by the head of department; by the commanding officer; or by an inspecting flag officer.

Ranks are opened for inspection unless the division parade space is too limited. The division officer places himself on the right flank of the front rank. Upon the approach of the inspecting officer he presents his division, with the command, 1. HAND, 2. SALUTE; at which the division executes the right-hand salute. He then reports, "Sir, the division is ready for inspection," and when the inspecting officer has returned the salute the division officer commands: 3. TWO.

The inspecting officer, accompanied by the division officer, division junior officer, or division leading petty officer, as the case may be, proceeds to inspect the division rank-by-rank in succession, passing from the right to the left along the front of each rank and from the left to the right along the rear of each rank.

When the front of a rank has been inspected, the command: 1. UNCOVER, 2. TWO is given to that rank in order that the rear of that rank may be inspected with the men uncovered. The inspection completed, ranks are closed and division takes the position of parade rest when commanded.

Forming for Inspection. The command is: FORM FOR INSPECTION. The division junior officer or the leading petty officer, placing himself in front of the division, commands: 1. OPEN RANKS, 2. MARCH. At the command MARCH, the front rank takes three steps forward, halts, and executes dress right; the second rank takes two steps forward, halts, and executes dress right; the third rank takes one step forward, halts, and executes dress right; and the fourth rank, if any, stands pat and executes dress right. The officer in charge alines each rank in succession, moves three paces beyond the right flank of the front rank, halts, faces to the left, and commands: 3. READY, 4. FRONT.

To close ranks the commands are: 1. CLOSE RANKS, 2. MARCH. At the command MARCH, the front rank stands fast; the second rank takes one step forward and halts; the third rank takes two steps forward and halts; and the fourth rank, if any, takes three steps forward and halts. Each man covers his file leader.

To form for inspection, where the restricted space of the parade does not permit normal opening of ranks, the command is: FORM FOR INSPECTION, CLOSE DISTANCE. The division stands fast and, upon the approach of the inspecting officer, is presented to him in the standard manner.

When the front of the first rank has been inspected from right to left by the inspecting officer, the division officer commands: 1. FIRST RANK ONE PACE FORWARD, 2. MARCH. The rear of the first rank is then inspected from left to right, followed by the inspection of the front of the second rank from right to left. The same procedure is followed for the second, third, and fourth ranks.

General Muster (All hands aft)

The general muster or dress parade (sometimes ordered as "All hands aft") is a massed formation of the ship's company at a designated place.

Dress parade is formed as follows: Heads of departments form to the rear of the captain, in order of seniority from right to left, at parade rest. Each division officer marches his division to its designated place in the massed formation and takes his post on the right or left flank of his division, whichever will bring him nearest to the captain. He then commands: 1. PARADE, 2. REST.

When all the divisions are massed, the executive officer commands the boatswain's mate, "Pipe attention." Then the executive officer commands the ship's company: 1. HAND, 2. SALUTE. He faces about, salutes, and reports to the captain, "Sir, all hands are mustered." The captain returns the salute, and the executive officer faces about and commands: 3. TWO.

The executive officer then commands: 1. PARADE, 2. REST, and proceeds with the publishing of orders or with the ceremony, as the case may be.

The ceremony completed, the executive officer orders the "Attention," faces about, salutes, and reports completion to the captain.

The captain returns the salute and commands: "Pipe down, sir," or "Carry on, sir."

The executive officer faces about and commands "Sound the assembly." Division officers then march the divisions to the division parades and await the sounding of retreat.

Enlisted Watchstanders

The two most interesting aspects of Coast Guard life are what you do and what the unit does. There are literally hundreds of different jobs in a large command, each one important to the mission. Because organization and routine are standardized as much as possible, the jobs—what you do—are pretty much standardized, and the mission performance—what the command does—is also standardized to a certain degree. A compartment cleaner's job on a high-endurance cutter is the same as it is on a buoy tender.

A day's work aboard ship, or ashore, involves both professional and military duties. "Turn to on ship's work" means that you carry out the professional duties of your rating. During general drills, and when on watch, you may perform both general military assignments and professional duties. The daily routine, at sea, in port, or ashore, also requires men on duty at all times as watchstanders.

There follows a listing of most enlisted watchstanders, with a brief description of their duties.

Anchor Watch (In Port)

These men are detailed to assist the OOD during the night for such tasks as veering chain or adjusting lines. The number of men assigned and their specific duties vary from ship to ship and according to the type of ship.

Boatswain's Mate of the Watch (BMOW)

The petty officer in charge of the watch is the most important enlisted assistant to the OOD. His status in these respects is the same regardless of the readiness condition in effect.

At sea the normal peacetime deck watch for which the boatswain's mate of the watch is responsible consists of the *helmsman, lee helmsman, OOD messenger, lookouts, orderly, life-buoy watch*, and *lifeboat crew of the watch*. Besides being the principal enlisted assistant to the

OOD, the boatswain's mate of the watch is the watch petty officer. It is his responsibility that all deck watch stations are manned, and that all men in the previous watch are relieved. He reports to the OOD when the deck watch has been relieved.

Boiler, Main Engine and Auxiliaries Watches

These watches are stood by qualified men in the engineering divisions, under the supervision of the engineering officer of the watch.

Bridge and Signal Watch

When stationed, in addition to their regular duties, bridge and signal watches keep the OOD informed of notable changes in the weather, boats approaching the ship, unusual disturbances or signs of distress in the harbor, and movements of other ships. (See also quartermaster.)

Cold Iron Watch

This watch inspects main machinery spaces that are secured and have no regular watch posted, and reports hourly to the POOW.

Combat Information Center

Watchstanders perform duties under the supervision of the CIC officer, and as required by the OOD.

Damage Control Watch and Security Patrols

These are stood by qualified engineering department men, under the supervision of the engineering officer of the watch.

Duty Master-at-Arms

This man is a member of the MAA force who stands his watch under the direction of the executive officer.

Group Command Watches

Men stationed at one of the many groups or units under a group will be assigned numerous watches, including a turn in the lookout tower. The duties of the tower watch include guarding several radio frequencies—the Coast Guard working frequency for the district, the emergency frequency, and very often the local fishing boat frequency—and relaying messages and alerting the station for calls.

Each station posts instructions to guide the lookout tower watch. When a private boat operator is in trouble, he looks to the tower for help, therefore the watch must keep a sharp lookout over the assigned area. When a request for help comes in, *get all the details* and fill out a complete SAR form (Distress Check-off List).

Helmsman

He steers the ship as directed by the OOD or the conning officer. (For details, see *Standard Commands* and *Ship Control* in this chapter.)

Lookouts

Every ship will have at least one lookout. On larger ships additional lookouts may be stationed, when circumstances demand, in the crow's nest, on the fantail and bow, or elsewhere. Bridge lookouts may report orally to the OOD; others will report via telephones. This is a very important job; it may look to an outsider as if all a lookout has to do is stand around and enjoy the view, but actually it takes considerable skill to stand a good lookout watch, and the safety of the ship may depend on just how well the lookout attends to his duties.

The first duty of the lookout is to sight an object and report it. His second duty is to identify it. The report of an object sighted should not be held up until the object is identified. After reporting, the lookout must be certain that the officer of the deck acknowledges his report.

After Lookout. See life-buoy watch.

Bridge Lookouts. These lookouts, port and starboard, stand watch in the wings of the bridge or on the flying bridge. They report ships, aircraft, land, or any object sighted, and at night they make half-hourly reports on the running lights.

Forecastle Lookout. He may be stationed during periods of low visibility—fog or snow—and while entering harbor.

Fog Lookout. He may also be the forecastle lookout. Other fog lookouts may be stationed on the wings of the bridge, to keep watch astern.

Sky and Surface Lookouts. On larger ships, when enemy operations are expected, additional lookouts will be assigned certain sectors of the sky and surface all around the ship. (For proper procedures on reporting objects, see *Standard Commands and Terminology* in this chapter.)

Night Lookouts

Men regularly assigned to lookout duty will receive special training, but as a preparation they should learn some facts in advance. As is the case with day lookouts, the night lookout should scan his sector slowly and regularly so that no point is skipped. But there are certain differences that must be taken into account. These are based on the fact that a man's eyes work differently at night.

Night Vision. Human eyes are adapted to seeing color and distant objects. This is done by light-sensitive nerves in the center of the eye, called cones. Cats and owls, which see well in the dark, cannot see color, but their eyes are sensitive to motion; this is done by nerves around the cones, called rods. Human eyes have rods too, and the way to see at night is not to look directly at an object, because the cones will merely make "spots in front of your eyes," but to look all around an object and give the rods a chance to pick it up.

A simple experiment will help to explain this. Stay in the darkness for 15 minutes. Hold your finger up at arm's length, and look steadily at it. It will disappear. Look a little to one side and it will appear again. Keep staring a little to one side and it will be gone again. Move your eyes to the other side and it will reappear. Practice is necessary to learn the trick of seeing things at night without looking directly at them.

Don't sweep the sky or horizon, as you can't see well while your eyes are moving rapidly. Scan the sky or sea slowly, because night eyes are slow in reacting and you may not notice an object until you have looked near it several times.

The eyes can pick up a moving light or object more easily than one that is standing still. When an object appears, move your head from side to side. This will give the object the appearance of movement even though it is barely seen.

It takes practice and care to become a good night lookout. The following rules for using the eyes at night should be followed:

Don't try working at night until your eyes are dark-adapted. This takes about 20 minutes in darkness or red light.

Avoid *all* light. If necessary to use a light, use only a dim red light.

When seeking an object on the horizon at night, always look for it out of the corner of the eye. Practice this constantly.

Scan the region you are investigating. Be alert for any objects. Practice scanning as much as possible.

If you must go into a lighted place, either blindfold yourself or wear the red dark-adaptation goggles that are available, which permit you to see without disturbing dark-adaptation.

Avoid looking at instrument panels that are illuminated, even by red light. Never stare at lighted instruments.

Use aids, such as night binoculars, as much as possible.

Keep all your optical equipment clean.

Don't keep looking at something you've already spotted.

Above all, keep in good physical shape. Fatigue and alcohol seriously hurt night vision.

Lower Deck Patrol

From tattoo to reveille, one or more men from the various departments, as detailed by the CMAA, make a roving patrol to safeguard personnel and material, maintain order, and correct any irregularity. They report to the OOD hourly.

Messenger

The man assigned to the OOD, either on the bridge when under way or the quarterdeck in port, is commonly called the OOD messenger. He should know the names and locations of the various parts of the ship, department offices and department heads, names and duties of the various officers and senior enlisted men, and he should also know where to find the men. He must also be familiar with standard naval phraseology to understand and repeat a message without making a confusing mistake.

Phone Talker

There may be one or more talkers, depending on the ship and the operation. They use correct phone procedure, know all the stations on their circuit, transmit orders to the stations as directed, and inform the OOD of all information received.

Quarterdeck Watch Officer

This is one of the most responsible jobs an enlisted man can have.

There should be no confusion as to the official status of these petty officers; they are *officers of the deck*, subject only in the performance of their duty to the orders of the commanding officer, executive officer, and command duty officer. The assignment of petty officers as officers of the deck is made in writing either in the ship's organization book, the senior watch officer's watch list, or in the plan of the day.

Quartermaster of the Watch

He assists the OOD in navigation, supervises the helmsman and lee helmsman, instructs the OOD messenger in calling officers and men for the watch, reports to the OOD all changes in weather, temperature, and barometer readings, and makes appropriate entries in the quartermaster's notebook and the ship's log. The QMOW often acts as the JOOD when there are insufficient officers on board, and he may be responsible for keeping the DR plot.

Radioman of the Watch

He maintains required communications in main radio room, receiving, transmitting, and routing traffic as required.

Sounding and Security Patrol

The sounding and security patrol is a petty officer in the engineering department who maintains a continuous patrol of unmanned spaces below decks. He takes periodic soundings of designated tanks and spaces, checks damage control closures, and is alert for evidence of sabotage, theft, fire, and fire hazards. In addition to making his own hourly report to the POOW or BMOW, he frequently relays the report of the *cold iron watch*. Both of these watches are usually manned during nonworking hours at sea and in port.

Enlisted Details

There are many jobs involving work and responsibilities that are not covered by any particular rating description. Men may be detailed to these jobs by a division officer, department head, or the executive officer.

Beach Guard (In Port)

He is a petty officer detailed to control boat traffic and help maintain order at a fleet landing during liberty hours.

Compartment Cleaners

They are nonrated men, detailed by their division officers to be responsible for the cleanliness and good order of their assigned compartments. They do not stand watches, but take part in all drills.

Division Police Petty Officer

These men are assistants to the ship's master-at-arms, and perform their duties in that part of the ship for which their division is responsible. The DPPO makes taps and reveille in his own division spaces, turns standing lights on at sunset and off at reveille, and directs traffic and clears the compartments during drills.

Fresh Water King

He is an engineering department petty officer in charge of the ship's evaporators.

Guard Mail Petty Officer (In Port)

He is a man detailed to carry official mail between the ship and other ships and commands.

Jack o' the Dust

This man is in charge of the provision issue room.

Leadsman

He is detailed to use a hand lead to determine depth of water. (See chapter 9, "Heaving the Lead," for details on this job.)

Master-at-Arms

He is a petty officer detailed to duty as a member of the ship's police force. The chief master-at-arms reports to the executive officer.

Messman

He is one of a group of nonrated men assigned to duty in crew's mess to prepare and serve food.

Oil and Water King

He is a petty officer assigned to keep records of fuel oil and fresh water, make tank soundings, and assist when taking on fuel or water.

Inspections

Inspections are made on a daily, weekly, monthly, quarterly, semi-annual, annual, and when-scheduled basis, and they are made, not so much to find out what is wrong, as to make certain nothing will go wrong. Anyone who keeps himself, his clothing, his cleaning station, and his assigned equipment in good condition has nothing to fear from an inspection. A well-organized and trained ship's crew can take even an admiral's surprise inspection in stride, but in a ship where things have been let go and no one takes in the slack, the announcement of any kind of an inspection can produce near panic. There is no easy way to prepare for an inspection—the best thing to do is to always be ready for it.

Daily Inspection

At quarters for muster, the division officers check their men for general appearance and cleanliness. The also make frequent inspections of the spaces, equipment, and supplies that belong to their divisions. Heads of departments, either by personal or delegated inspections, must make sure that all aspects of their departments are in proper condition or that steps are being taken to make them so.

The executive officer likewise is required to make frequent inspections; usually he inspects a different part of the ship each day. Division officers and department heads, or their representatives, are required to inspect *all* parts of their respective departments each day as far as may be feasible.

Captain's Inspection

This is usually held on Friday and consists of a formal inspection of all divisions at quarters and a topside inspection of the ship and her material. On some ships the captain will also conduct a thorough below-deck's inspection.

General Mess

At least once daily the OOD or his assistant will inspect the general mess and sample a ration to determine that it is well cooked and properly served.

Messmen

Messmen and food handlers may be inspected daily by the OOD or his assistant, and weekly by the medical officer or his assistant.

Bag, or Locker, Inspection

This will usually be made by the division officer, but may be combined with another inspection. Such inspection is to determine that a man has a complete outfit, properly marked, cleaned and stowed.

Inspections by Higher Authority

In addition the the regular inspections made by the captain and other officers, the ship will receive various inspections by district or area staff. These are operational readiness inspections, administrative inspections, material inspections, supply inspections, and medical inspections. Before a ship commences a regular overhaul, she may be inspected by a Board of Survey. At other times there will be security inspections of stowage and conditions of classified material.

Change of Command

When the commanding officer of a ship is relieved, he will make a thorough inspection of the ship—personnel, material, and administration—in company with the new commanding officer.

Customs and Pratique

When a ship returns to the United States from foreign waters, she is liable to inspection by U.S. customs and health authorities, to determine that no unauthorized or contraband items are on board and that there are no contagious or communicable diseases among the crew. Such inspections may be routine, but the inspectors can turn the ship "upside down" if they have reason to suspect anything is being hidden.

Soundings

When a ship enters or leaves port, or approaches an anchorage or shoal area, *Regulations* require that soundings be taken. Usually this is done by the Fathometer, located on the bridge. However, a hand lead and a man who knows how to heave and read it should always be available (see chapter 9, "Heaving the Lead").

Standard Commands and Terminology

There is a correct and proper name for everything and a standard form of order or command for everything that is done. Disregard for proper terms or orders may lead to mistakes, confusion, and perhaps disaster. This applies to communications (proper forms for "words" to be passed are in chapter 10), line handling (see *Commands to Line Handlers*, in chapter 9, and commands to the helmsman and lookout reports, details on which follow here).

Commands to the Helmsman

All commands to the helmsman that specify a change in course or heading will refer to the compass by which the helmsman is steering, and will give the new course or heading in degrees: "Come left to course two seven zero," or "Steer zero zero five." The helmsman repeats most commands that are given to be sure he understands them. Only the following commands are used:

Right (Left) Rudder. Apply right (left) rudder instantly, an indeterminate amount. (Must be followed instantly by the amount of rudder desired.)

Right (Left) Standard Rudder. Put the rudder over to the right (left) the specified number of degrees necessary for the ship to make her standard tactical diameter.

Right (Left) Full Rudder. Put the rudder over to the right (left) the specified number of degrees necessary for the ship to make her reduced tactical diameter.

Right (Left) Five (Ten, etc.) Degrees Rudder. Turn the wheel to right (left) until the rudder is placed at the number of degrees ordered. (This command is used in making changes of course. The helmsman would then be ordered to steer the new course by such command as, "Steady on course ———," in time to permit the helmsman to meet her on the new course. The complete command would be, for example, "Right five degrees rudder. Steady on course two seven five.")

Right (Left) Handsomely. Turn the rudder a small amount. (The command is given when a very slight change of course is desired.)

Increase Your Rudder to ——— Degrees. Increase the rudder angle. (Given with the rudder already over, when it is desired to make the ship turn more rapidly. The command must be followed by the exact number of degrees of rudder desired.)

Ease Your Rudder to ——— Degrees. Decrease the rudder angle. (Given when the ship, turning with right (left) rudder, is turning toward or is nearing the heading desired. The command can be given, for example, "Ease to fifteen.")

Meet Her. Use rudder as may be necessary to check the ship's swing. (Given when the ship is nearing the desired course.)

Steady, or Steady As You Go. Steer the course on which the ship is heading when the command is received. (Given when, in changing course, the new course is reached or the ship is heading as desired. The helmsman responds, "Steady as you go. Course ———, sir.")

Rudder Amidships. Rudder angle zero. (Given when the ship is turning, and it is desired to make her swing less rapidly.)

Shift Your Rudder. Change from right to left rudder (or vice-versa) an equal amount. (Given, for example, when the ship loses headway and gathers sternway, to keep her turning in the same direction.)

Mind Your Rudder. A warning that the ship is swinging off the course because of bad steering. It is also a command to steer exactly, using less rudder.

Nothing to the Left (Right) of ———. A warning to the helmsman that he is not to steer to the left (right) of the course ordered.

How is Your Rudder. A question to the helmsman. He should reply, "Five (ten, fifteen, etc.) degrees right (left)," or "full (standard) right (left) rudder, sir."

Mark Your Head. A question to the helmsman. He should give the ship's head at the time; for example, "Two seven five, sir."

Keep Her So. A command to the helmsman when he reports the ship's heading and it is desired to steady her on that heading.

Very Well. Given to the helmsman, after a report by him, to let him know that the OOD understands the situation.

Come Right (Left) to ———. Put over the rudder right (left) and steady on new course.

Lookout Reports

The proper way for a lookout to let others know exactly where an object is requires that he give its direction with reference to the bow of the lookout's ship, that is, by means of relative bearings (figure 7–2). To locate surface objects, only the direction and the range or distance from the ship need be given. To locate aircraft, the direction and the elevation, or height above water, are required. The elevation is known as the *position angle.*

In reporting objects, a strict form of wording is used. First the object is named: "ship," "buoy," "discolored water," "floating log," "periscope wake," or "aircraft." If the lookout cannot identify the object, he says "object." Next the direction is given as explained below. Lastly, if the object is a surface craft, the range is given; if an aircraft, the elevation, or position angle, is given.

Thus, a full report on a surface object would go something like this: "*Ship*" (the object); "*zero niner zero*" (the bearing); "*fiyuv hundred*" (the range).

How to report relative bearings and ranges.—First, say the word

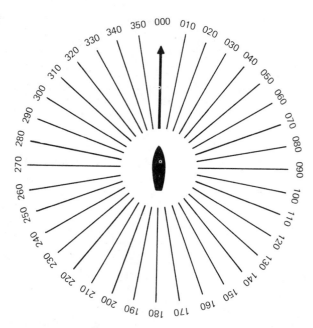

Figure 7–2. Relative bearings, measured clockwise from the ship's head, locate an object in relation to the ship. They have nothing to do with geographical directions.

"bearing"; then give the degrees of the bearing in three digits. Correct wording is "Bearing three five zero" and "Bearing zero one zero." There are no "ohs" in relative bearings; only "zeros" are used. The word "bearing" may be omitted.

Do not add the word "degrees." Since the bearing comes first and is always in three digits, the hearer knows that degrees are intended and it is not necessary to say so.

The range is always given in yards. In making estimates it might be useful to remember that 2,000 yards equals one nautical mile. Where the range is an even hundred or thousand, it is spoken so: "Range eight hundred (800)," "Range twenty thousand (20,000)."

Where the range is below 1,000, and not an even hundred, it is spoken in hundreds and the number of digits. Ciphers are pronounced "zero": "Range nine seven zero (970)."

Where the range is above 1,000 and an even 100, it is spoken in thousands and hundreds: "Range four seven hundred (4,700)"; "Range five zero two hundred (50,200)"; "Range one one zero six hundred (110,600)."

Where the range is above 1,000 and not an even hundred, it is spoken in number of thousands, the balance given as in ranges below a 1,000: "Range three three five zero (3,350)"; "Range three zero two five zero (30,250)."

Distance of Visibility at Sea

Estimating distances at sea takes practice. The table in figure 7–3 will be of assistance. As an example, consider that a 6-foot man standing on a bridge deck 30 feet above sea level will have his eyes a little better than 35.5 feet above sea level, so his horizon is 6.8 miles away. But he can see objects more than 6.8 miles away if they are high enough to be seen above the horizon. A lighthouse 65 feet high has a horizon of 9.2 miles; this means that the man could see the light just at the horizon for a distance of 6.8 + 9.2 miles, or 16 miles.

Position Angle

The position angle is the height in degrees of an aircraft above the horizon (figure 7–4). The horizon is zero degrees (0°) and directly overhead is ninety degrees (90°). For position angles the ordinary way of expressing numbers is used; that is, you say "one," "eight," "twenty," "sixty" and not "zero one," "zero eight," "two zero," "six zero." As with bearing, the word "degrees" is left out, since the hearer automatically understands that with aircraft the numerals stated mean degrees of elevation. Examples of reporting position angles are:

08° "position angle, eight."
10° "Position angle, ten."
30° "Position angle, thirty."

Note that the words "position angle" precede the numerals of the report.

An example of a sighted aircraft report might be:

"Bridge, sky aft, plane, bearing one four five, position angle twenty-five, moving right."

SHIP CONTROL

Two of the most important people in a bridge crew are the helmsman, or steersman, who steers the ship and the annunciator man (usually

Height (feet)	Nautical miles	Height (feet)	Nautical miles
1	1.1	31	6.4
2	1.7	32	6.5
3	2.0	33	6.6
4	2.3	34	6.7
5	2.5	35	6.8
6	2.8	36	6.9
7	2.9	37	6.9
8	3.1	38	7.0
9	3.5	39	7.1
10	3.6	40	7.2
11	3.8	41	7.3
12	4.0	42	7.4
13	4.2	43	7.5
14	4.3	44	7.6
15	4.4	45	7.7
16	4.6	46	7.8
17	4.7	47	7.9
18	4.9	48	7.9
19	5.0	49	8.0
20	5.1	50	8.1
21	5.3	55	8.5
22	5.4	60	8.9
23	5.5	65	9.2
24	5.6	70	9.6
25	5.7	75	9.9
26	5.8	80	10.3
27	6.0	85	10.6
28	6.1	90	10.9
29	6.2	95	11.2
30	6.3	100	11.5

Figure 7–3. Distance of visibility at sea.

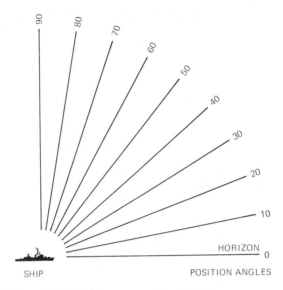

Figure 7–4. Position angles locate an object in the
sky. Measure up, not down.

heading of the ship, and the wheel, steering engine, and rudder to
keep the ship on that course. The helmsman must understand the use
of the compass, wheel, and rudder, and the principles of steering a
ship.

Compass

The magnetic compass consists of a magnetized needle attached to a
circular compass card; both are supported on a pivot set in a cast bronze
bowl that is filled with a mixture of alcohol and water. This liquid
supports the card and magnet, thus reducing the friction and letting
the card turn more easily on the pivot. It also slows the swing of the
card and brings it to rest more quickly. The lubber's line marked on
the bowl agrees with the fore-and-aft line of the ship. The heading
(direction the ship is going) is read from the compass card at the point
nearest the lubber's line.

A magnetic compass can be thrown off the correct heading by the
attraction of any metal near it. Never go on watch as helmsman carrying
a knife, keys, or other metal articles.

Gyrocompass. A gyrocompass is basically a heavy spinning fly-wheel
which, due to the rotation of the earth, will seek a position in which

its axis always points true north and south and is unaffected by variation or deviation.

Gyro repeaters. Set to point the same way as the master gyro, these are located in the wheelhouse, steering stations, and on the bridge wings. If the ship has two master gyros, there will be two repeater stands in the steering station, but only one of these will be used. Be certain that you are steering from the repeater in use, and be especially careful not to confuse them.

The course by gyro, when corrected for any slight mechanical error, is always the true course, but the gyro is subject to mechanical and electrical failure. Report to the OOD at once if it stops swinging as the ship's head changes, or if it starts to jump.

Rudder

All ships or boats are steered by one or more rudders at the stern. When the rudder is moved to one side or the other, the headway of the ship causes water to push against the side of the rudder, creating a force that swings the stern of the ship in the opposite direction. The faster a ship is moving, the greater the pressure against the rudder and the quicker the turning effect. A ship always "answers" her rudder more quickly at high speed than at low speed, and it takes more rudder to turn a slow ship than a fast one. Large rudders are balanced, with part of the rudder forward of the pintle on which it hangs. This is to balance some of the force of the water against the after part, and thus make the rudder easier to turn.

Steering Engine. The rudder of a small boat is moved mechanically by rudder ropes (usually of wire) as the wheel turns. Ships have an engine, steam or electrically powered, that turns the rudder; the engine is controlled by the wheel, either through direct mechanical (wire rope) or hydraulic linkages.

Steering Sense. Many an inexperienced helmsman gets into trouble when bringing a ship to a new heading, trying to make the compass card turn by turning the ship's wheel. *It won't work!* The compass card floats and is not fast to the compass. The compass stand is fast to the ship; the *lubber's line* moves as the ship moves, and always in the direction the wheel is turned. Remember: turn the wheel the way the bow is to swing; if the wheel turns left, the lubber's line moves left, and the ship turns left; everything moves in the same direction, left, or right, from bow to rudder.

Steering a ship is not as simple as driving an automobile, where control is quick and positive. A ship is heavy, slow to start turning, and sometimes reluctant to stop turning. When she reaches the proper heading, you may have to give her a touch of rudder to finally steady her, and you must get the rudder off her before she starts to swing again.

The most common error is using too much rudder. The new steersman turns the wheel a few degrees, but nothing happens; it takes a little time before the ship begins to answer the rudder. After a second or two he turns the wheel a little more. When the lubber's line reaches the course desired, he puts the rudder midships, but the ship keeps on going. Then he puts on opposite rudder, but has to increase it considerably before the swing stops, and starts again immediately in the other direction with increased speed. Remember, the less rudder you use, the better; much less rudder is required to head off a swing than to stop one that has started.

Have the ship steady on her course before you surrender the wheel to your relief. Don't turn it over in the middle of a swing. Give him the course and tell him which compass or repeater you are steering by. Tell your relief about any steering peculiarity you know of; e.g., "Taking a little right rudder," "Taking mostly left," and so on. Relay to him any orders you received that still are standing; as, "Nothing to the left," "Steady as she goes," etc. Before leaving the steering station, report to the officer of the deck the instructions given your relief: "Steering two seven eight, sir," "Steady as she goes, sir," and so forth.

Engine Order Telegraph

Speed orders to the engineroom are handled by an engine order telegraph, which has sectors marked AHEAD: FLANK, FULL, STAND (standard) 2/3, 1/3—STOP—BACK: 1/3, 2/3, FULL. A lever, fitted with an indicator, travels over the circular face of the instrument. When moved to the required speed sector, an answering pointer follows to the same sector as soon as the engineroom has complied with the order.

A ship with one engine has a telegraph with a single handle. Two-engined ships generally have a handle on the port side and another on the starboard side of the telegraph (figure 7–5). Be sure you grasp the handle for the correct engine. If the answering pointer moves to a line between two sectors, so that you are in doubt about the speed set on the engine, repeat your operation on the lever. Report immediately to the OOD if the pointer does not move as ordered.

Orders to the man operating the engine order telegraph are given

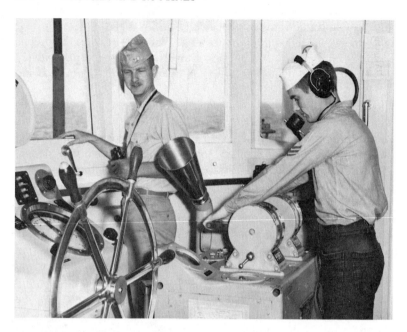

Figure 7–5. This is the engine order telegraph for a twin-engined ship, the cutter *Reliance*.

in this form: First, the engine to be used, *port* or *starboard*; next, the direction, either *ahead* or *astern*; then the speed, *standard, one-third*, etc.

Make sure you have heard an order correctly, and repeat it aloud distinctly before you act, thus: "Starboard engine ahead two-thirds, sir." When the answer appears on the pointer from below, sing out "Starboard engine answers ahead two-thirds, sir."

Ship Control Console

Ship control consoles provided on new ships have controls for the main engines, the bow-thruster (an athwartships propeller up forward used to help steer the ship), and the rudder. Indicators are located on the panel to show engine RPMs, direction, and degrees of thrust (on variable-pitch propellers), and rudder angle and direction of the bow-thruster. Commands relating to propeller pitch are given in so many inches or feet of thrust as "zero pitch," twelve inches ahead, twelve astern or any desired pitch. In ships with control consoles, the conning officer usually handles all the controls.

Emergency Procedures

Emergencies aboard ship happen fast, and they can be dangerous if not met with immediate action. Breakdown (loss of rudder control or engine power) and man overboard are not handled by men assigned to watches for such purpose, but are considered all-hands procedures. Frequent drills train everyone to handle these emergencies.

Breakdown

A breakdown condition requires rapid action by the bridge crew to avoid possible collision. When a breakdown occurs, the FIVE FLAG is displayed, two black balls are hoisted, and a whistle signal of six or more short warning blasts is sounded. At night, two red breakdown lights are turned on. The captain and executive officer are notified immediately.

Man Overboard

When a man goes overboard, the first and most important thing to do is keep track of him. This is a duty of the lifebuoy watch. A life ring or float is dropped on the side nearest the man. The ship hoists the OSCAR flag by day, shows blinking red breakdown lights at night, and sounds at least six short blasts on the whistle. The OOD immediately notifies the captain and executive officer and sees that the lifeboat is ready for lowering. The crew for that boat, if not on station, goes to the boat as soon as the signal sounds.

CHAPTER 8
Ship Construction

Joining the Coast Guard is somewhat like entering any other business or profession—you will have to learn the language that is used there. Most of the words will be familiar, but they will have new meanings. And along with learning a new language, you will have to learn a good deal about ships. A modern cutter is an extremely complicated craft (figure 8–1).

Ship is a general term for any large floating vessel that moves through the water under its own power. A *boat* is essentially the same as a ship, only smaller. There is no absolute distinction between the two. The most common definition is that a boat is any vessel small enough to be hoisted and carried aboard a ship. Another usual difference is that a ship can cross an ocean under its own power, while a boat cannot.

PARTS OF A SHIP

No matter how specialized your professional training may be, you must be thoroughly familiar with basic nautical terminology and ship construction. This is necessary to carry out routine orders and commands and to act quickly during combat or in emergency conditions.

In some respects a ship is like a building. It has outer walls (called the *hull*), floors (called *decks*), inner walls (called *partitions* and *bulkheads*), corridors (called *passageways*), ceilings (called *overheads*), and

Figure 8–1. The mast of a modern cutter carries a complicated array of gear; surface search radar, navigational lights, signal lights, electronic equipment, signal halyards, and the ship's bell.

stairs (called *ladders*). But a ship moves and is never in the same place twice, so you have to learn new terms for directions and getting about. When you go up the stairs from the dock to a ship, you use the *accommodation ladder* to go on board, and what might be an entrance hall or foyer in a building is the *quarterdeck* in a ship.

The forward part of a ship is the *bow*; to go in that direction is to *go forward*; the after part is the *stern*; to go in that direction is to *go aft*. The top, open deck of a ship is the *main deck*; anything below that is *below decks* and anything above it is *superstructure*. The forward part of the main deck is the *forecastle* (pronounced fōc'sul); the after part is the *fantail*. The forecastle and fantail will be on the same deck on a *flush-deck* ship; the fantail will be one deck lower on a *broken-deck* ship. To proceed from the main deck to a lower deck you *go below*; going back up again you *go topside*. As you face forward on a ship the right side is the *starboard* side and the left side is the *port* side. An imaginary line running full length down the middle of the ship is the *centerline*; the direction from the centerline toward either side is *outboard*, and from either side toward the centerline is *inboard*. A line from one side of the ship to the other runs *athwartships*.

If the interior hull of a ship were all one space, a single large hole made below the waterline would quickly cause the ship to flood and sink. To prevent this, the interior of the ship is divided by bulkheads and decks into *watertight compartments*.

In theory, any large ship could be made virtually unsinkable if it were divided into enough small watertight compartments. There is a limit to this, since compartmentation interferes with the arrangement of mechanical equipment and with the operation of the ship. Engineering spaces must be large enough to accommodate bulky machinery and cannot be subdivided.

Hull

The *hull* (figure 8–2) is the main body of the ship below the main outside deck. It consists of an outside covering, or *skin*, and an inside structural framework to which the skin is fastened. In almost all types of modern ships, both the framework and the skin are made of steel. The steel skin is called the *shell plating*. The parts of the hull are usually fastened together by welding, although riveting is still used in some places.

Unarmored hulls are designed and built to withstand only the pressures and strains encountered by a fully loaded ship in the heaviest

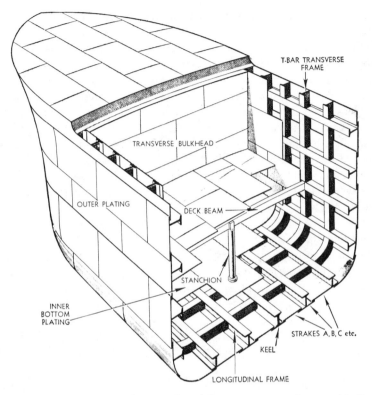

Figure 8–2. This cut-away drawing shows the construction of a typical hull.

seas, with some added structural strength for protection in case the ship runs aground.

Armored hulls have extra layers and thicknesses of steel plating to protect the vital parts of the ship from damage by enemy shells, bombs, and torpedoes.

Keel

The *keel* is the principal structural part of the hull. It runs from the *stem* at the bow to the *sternpost* at the stern. *Frames* are fastened to the keel; they run athwartships and support the shell plating. *Bulkheads, deck beams,* and *stanchions* are joined together and fastened to the frames; they support the decks and resist the pressure of the water on the sides of the hull. The system of interlocking steel bulkheads and decks of a warship furnishes a large part of the whole strength of the hull.

Large ships have an outer and inner bottom, often called *double bottoms*. These are divided into many compartments. In armored hulls the inner bottom may turn up at the turn of the bilge to form an inner side, with similar compartmentation. Many of the compartments aboard ship are used as tanks for fuel oil storage, fresh water, or for trimming ship. Tanks at the extreme bow and stern, used for trimming ship fore and aft, are called *peak tanks*. A heavy watertight bulkhead just abaft the forward peak tank is called the *collision bulkhead*. All compartments and tanks have pump and drain connections for pumping out sea water and for transferring fuel or water from one part of the ship to another.

Hull Reference Terms

Waterline, Freeboard, and Draft. The line to which a hull sinks in the water is the *waterline*. The vertical distance from the waterline to the edge of the lowest outside deck is the *freeboard*. The vertical distance from the waterline to the lowest part of the ship's bottom is the *draft*. The draft may also be thought of as the least depth of water in which the ship will float. The waterline, freeboard, and draft will, of course, vary with the weight of the load carried by the ship; as freeboard increases, draft decreases. (See figure 8–3.)

Draft is measured in feet, and numbered scales are painted on the sides of the hull at bow and stern. The relation between the drafts at the bow and the stern is the *trim*. When the ship is properly balanced fore and aft, she is "in trim." When the ship is "out of trim," because of damage or unequal loading, she is said to be "down by the head"

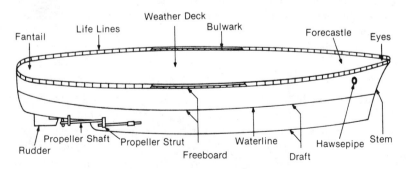

Figure 8–3. Hull of a typical ship, showing principal parts.

or "down by the stern." When the ship is out of balance laterally or athwartships, she has a *list*; she is said to be "listing to starboard" or "listing to port." Both trim and list are adjusted by emptying or filling tanks and compartments in various parts of the hull.

The bow and the stern. The part of the bow structure above the waterline is the *prow*, although this word is not used as generally as the terms *bow* and *stem*. The part of the weather deck nearest the stem is called the *eyes* of the ship. The general area of the weather deck in the forward part of the ship is the *forecastle*, even though the ship may not have a forecastle deck. The edges of the weather deck from bow to stern are usually guarded by removable light wire ropes and stanchions called *life lines*, or by extensions of the shell plating above the deck edge, called *bulwarks*. The main deck area at the stern of the ship is the *fantail*. The part of the stern that literally hangs over the water is the *overhang*. The lower part of the bottom of a ship is called the *bilge*. The curved section where the bottom meets the side is called the *turn of the bilge*.

Propellers. The *propellers*, or *screws*, that drive the ship through the water are attached to *propeller shafts* and are turned by them. Ships with only one propeller are called *single screw*; ships with two propellers are *twin screw*. Ships with more than two propellers, usually four, are called *multiple screw*. In twin- or multiple-screw ships, the exposed length of propeller shafts is so great that they must be supported by braces extending from the hull, called *propeller struts*. Because of the shape of the hull at the stern, the screws may be damaged when the ship is close by a pier. To prevent this, metal frames called *propeller guards* are built out from the hull above the water.

Decks

The *decks* of a ship correspond to the floors of a building. The *main deck* is the highest deck that extends over the entire ship from stem to stern. The *second deck, third deck, fourth deck,* etc., are other complete decks below the main deck, numbered in sequence from topside down (figure 8–4).

A part deck above the main deck is named according to its position on the ship; at the bow it is called a *forecastle deck*; amidships it is called an *upper deck*; at the stern it is called a *poop deck*.

A part deck between two complete decks is called a *half deck*.

A part deck below the lowest complete deck is called a *platform deck*.

The term *weather deck* includes all parts of the main, forecastle,

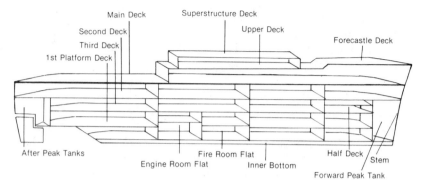

Figure 8–4. Deck arrangement of a typical ship.

upper, and poop decks that are exposed to the weather. The *quarterdeck* is not a structural part of the ship, but is a location on or below the main deck, designated by the commanding officer as the place for masts and ceremonies.

Any deck above the main deck, upper forecastle deck, or poop deck is called a *superstructure deck*.

Compartmentation Numbers for Ships Built before 1949

Compartments aboard ship are numbered from forward aft, starting at each division. Compartments on the starboard side of the ship have odd numbers; those on the port side have even numbers. The number of any compartment locates the exact position in the ship, vertically by decks, and fore and aft by transverse bulkheads.

The first letter of the symbol is always A, B, or C (or D in older ships). A indicates a compartment located forward of the machinery spaces; B refers to amidships or machinery spaces; and C means the compartment is abaft the machinery spaces. In older ships, the machinery spaces are in the B and C areas; D compartments are abaft the machinery spaces. Figure 8–5 shows the divisions of a three-division ship. The lower half of the diagram shows how a new series of compartment numbers begins at the forward end of each division. Note that even numbers are on the port side and odd numbers are on the starboard side.

After the division letter in the symbol comes the deck designation. Main-deck compartments are indicated by numbers such as 102, 109, 117, etc. Second-deck compartments run from 201 through 299, third-deck compartments form a 300 series, etc. A zero preceding the num-

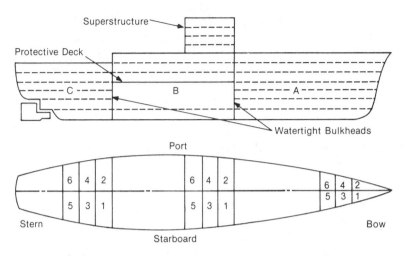

Figure 8–5. Diagram of the principal divisions of a ship (pre-1949).

ber indicates a location above the main deck. The double bottoms always form a 900 series on any ship regardless of the number of decks above.

The use of a compartment is indicated by a letter which follows the symbol number. The letters and their meanings are:

A—Supply and storage
C—Control
E—Machinery
F—Fuel
L—Living quarters
M—Ammunition
T—Trunks and passages
V—Voids
W—Water

All doors, hatches, or manholes leading into a compartment are marked by a label which gives the compartment's use and location.

W.T.D. 4-16-6
C. P. O. Stores
A-412-A

W.T.D. stands for watertight door. The 4 indicates that it is on the fourth deck, the 16 that it is just abaft the sixteenth frame, and the 6 that it is the third opening, from inboard out, on the port side. (Even numbers on the port side, odd on the starboard.) It is a storeroom located in Division A for the use of chief petty officers, and is the sixth compartment on the port side from the bow of the ship.

Compartmentation for Ships Built after March 1949

For ships constructed after March 1949, the compartment numbers consist of a deck number, frame number, relation to centerline of ship, and letter showing use of the compartment. These are separated by dashes. The A, B, C divisional system is not used.

Deck Number

The deck numbers of a ship (with corresponding names) are shown in figure 8–6. Where a compartment extends down to the bottom of the ship, the number assigned to the bottom compartment is used. The deck number becomes the first part of the compartment number.

Frame Number

The frame number at the foremost bulkhead of the enclosing boundary of a compartment is its frame location number. Where these forward boundaries are between frames, the frame number forward is used. Fractional numbers are not used. The frame number becomes the second part of the compartment number.

Relation to the Centerline

Compartments located on the centerline carry the number 0. Compartments completely to starboard are given odd numbers, and those

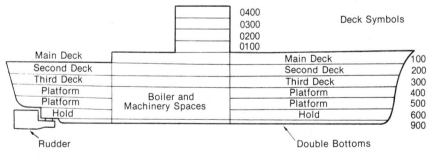

Figure 8–6. The system of naming and numbering decks of a ship.

completely to port are given even numbers. Where two or more compartments have the same deck and frame number and are entirely starboard or entirely port of the centerline, they have consecutively higher odd or even numbers (as the case may be) numbering from the centerline outboard. In this case, the first compartment outboard of the centerline to starboard is 1; the second, 3; etc. Similarly, the first compartment outboard of the centerline to port is 2; the second 4; etc. When the centerline of the ship passes through more than one compartment, the compartment having that portion of the forward bulkhead through which the centerline of the ship passes carries the number 0, and the others carry the numbers 01, 02, 03, etc. These numbers indicate the relation to the centerline, and are the third part of the compartment number.

Compartment Usage

The fourth and last part of the compartment number is the letter that identifies the primary usage of the compartment. On dry- and liquid-cargo ships a double-letter identification is used to designate compartments used for carrying cargo, as follows:

Letter	Type of Compartment	Examples
AA	Stowage spaces.	Storerooms; issue rooms; refrigerated compartments.
AA	Cargo holds.	Cargo holds and cargo refrigerated compartments.
C	Control centers for ship and fire control operations (normally manned).	CIC room; plotting rooms; communication centers, radio, radar, and sonar operating spaces; pilothouse.
E	Engineering control centers (normally manned).	Main propulsion spaces; boiler rooms; evaporator rooms; steering gear rooms; auxiliary machinery spaces; pumprooms; generator rooms; switchboard rooms; windlass rooms.
F	Oil stowage compartments (for use by ship).	Fuel-oil, diesel-oil, lubricating-oil, and fog-oil compartments.
FF	Oil stowage compartments (cargo).	Compartments carrying various types of oil as cargo.
G	Gasoline stowage compartments (for use by ship).	Gasoline tanks, cofferdams, trunks, and pumprooms.
GG	Gasoline stowage compartments (cargo).	Gasoline compartments for carrying gasoline as cargo.
K	Chemicals and dangerous materials (other than oil and gasoline).	Chemicals, semisafe materials, and dangerous materials carried for ship's use or as cargo.

Letter	Type of Compartment	Examples
L	Living spaces.	Berthing and messing spaces; staterooms, washrooms, heads, brigs; sickbays; hospital spaces; and passageways.
M	Ammunition space.	Magazines; handling rooms; turrets; gun mounts; shell rooms; ready service rooms; clipping rooms.
Q	Miscellaneous spaces not covered by other letters.	Shops; offices; laundry; galley; pantries; unmanned engineering, electrical, and electronic spaces.
T	Vertical access trunks.	Escape trunks or tubes.
V	Void compartments.	Cofferdam compartments (other than gasoline); void wing compartments; wiring trunks.
W	Water compartments.	Drainage tanks; fresh water tanks; peak tanks, reserve feed tanks.

The following example illustrates the application of these principles of compartmentation for ships built after March 1949.

M—Ammunition compartment

4—Second compartment outboard of the centerline to port

75—Forward boundary is on or immediately forward of frame 75

3—Third deck

This designation should be expressed as M-4-75-3.

Superstructure

The superstructure of a ship is everything above the weather deck (figure 8–7). There is a great deal of variation in the superstructure layout on different types of Coast Guard ships, but the same elements will be found in all of them in one form or another. A large part of the superstructure in passenger ships consists of living quarters and recreation facilities. The superstructure of a fighting ship is made up of the actual armament and controls necessary for operating the ship.

Bridge

This is the primary control position for the ship when under way, where all orders and commands affecting the ship, her movements, and routine originate. The OOD is always on the bridge when the ship is under way; the captain will be on the bridge during GQ and during most operations.

The ship can also be handled from a secondary control station, called *secondary conn*, the GQ station for the executive officer; thus, if the

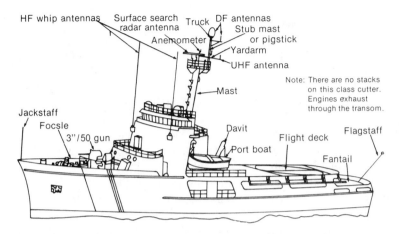

Figure 8–7. Topside arrangement of a typical cutter.

bridge is knocked out or the captain disabled in battle, the executive officer can take over.

Pilothouse

Sometimes called the wheelhouse, the pilothouse contains equipment and instruments used to control the movements of the ship. Usually the bridge extends out on both sides of the pilothouse. Some pilothouse equipment is duplicated on the bridge.

Bridge and Pilothouse Equipment. The ship control console consists of the engine order section and propeller order section that control speed and direction (ahead or astern) of the ship. The engine order section has a dial for each engine, divided into sectors marked flank, full, standard, 2/3 and 1/3 speed ahead, stop, and 1/3, 2/3 and full speed astern. When a hand lever is moved to the speed sector ordered by the OOD, the engine room watch sets the engine throttle for the same speed and notifies the bridge by moving an answering pointer to the same sector. The ship control console is manned by the lee helmsman, who is sometimes 1JV phone talker. The propeller order section enables the OOD to make minor changes in speed by ordering the engine rooms to increase or decrease the rpm of the propellers.

The steering control console contains the controls and indicators required to control the course of the ship. The steering wheel (helm) is operated by the helmsman. On the panel in front of him are various indicators and switches. The ship's course indicator is a gyro compass repeater, which indicates the ship's true course. Another indicator shows the course to be steered. Two more important indicators show the rudder angle (number of degrees left or right or amidships) and the helm angle (number of degrees left or right of amidships).

Tachometer. This is the same type of instrument that is used on a sports model car; it shows shaft RPMs. There is a tach for each propeller.

Lighting Panels. The two primary lighting panels in the pilothouse are the *signal and anchor light supply and control panel* and the *running lights supply control panel.*

Lights installed on combatant ships usually include *aircraft warning lights; blinker lights; breakdown, man overboard* and *underway replenishment lights; steering lights; stern light (blue); wake light;* and *speed lights.* Switches are located on the signal and anchor light supply and control panel.

The location of bridge equipment varies among ship types, and may even be different on ships of the same type. A bridge watchstander has to learn where everything is, so he can find it in the dark.

Charthouse

This is normally just abaft the pilothouse and on the same deck, but it may be on another deck some distance away. It contains charts, a chart desk, and the chronometers. On some ships the dead reckoning tracer (DRT) may be in the charthouse. The charthouse will also contain navigational instruments such as sextants, stadimeters, bearing circles and stopwatches, parallel rulers, protractors, position plotters, and navigational books and tables.

Secondary Conn

This area contains *steering equipment, engine order telegraph, phone circuits,* etc., necessary for ship control in the event the primary control station is unable to perform because of battle damage. The ship's magnetic compass may be located here.

The Signal Bridge

This is an open platform located near the navigational bridge and equipped with yardarm blinker controls, signal searchlights, and flag bags, where signalmen maintain visual communication with other ships.

Message Center

This is the station of the *communication watch officer*, where outgoing traffic is prepared for transmission, and incoming messages are readied for local delivery. All messages, except tactical signals received and sent direct from shipboard control stations, go through the message center.

Cryptocenter

The *cryptocenter* is the exclusive working area of the cryptoboard. Access to the cryptocenter is strictly controlled. There is a single entrance, and an authorized entry list is posted nearby.

Combat Information Center (CIC)

The CIC is the nerve center of the ship. It has a five-fold function: to collect, process, display, evaluate, and disseminate information from sources both inside and outside the ship. A wide range of electronic equipment is installed in CIC: radar, sonar, electronic warfare intercept receivers, IFF (Identification Friend or Foe), radio and visual communications, PPI (Plan Position Indicator) repeaters, display screens, and computers. Radar installations will include both air and surface search and fire control.

Damage Control Central

Damage control central maintains damage control charts, machinery charts, and liquid loading diagrams, and is responsible for seeing that the proper conditions of readiness are set and maintained. The condition of stability and damage throughout the ship are known in damage control central at all times, and reported by direct communication to the bridge. All repair parties report to damage control central.

Masts and Stacks

In some modern ships the masts are included as part of the main superstructure assembly. On older ships and on the smaller types of escort and patrol craft, masts still are a distinct feature of the superstructure. If a ship has two masts, the forward one is the *foremast* and the other is the *mainmast*. On single-masted ships the mast is amidships or forward, is usually part of the main superstructure assembly, and is called the foremast or simply the mast.

Masts vary greatly in size and shape, some being built of several structural steel members and others being a single steel or wooden pole. On all ships, at least one mast, together with a spar running athwartship called a *yard*, is used for flags and other signal devices. These must be rigged in such a way as to be visible from other ships. The lighter type of masts are supported by *standing rigging*, consisting of wire rope *stays* running fore and aft and *shrouds* running athwartships down to the deck or bulwarks.

The small cap at the top of a pole mast or flagstaff is called a *truck*. The top of any mast may be called the *truck*. Above the truck there is frequently a slender vertical extension of the mast, called a *pigstick*. Almost every naval vessel has a pigstick on the mainmast, from which the *commission pennant* or an admiral's *personal flag* is flown. Extending abaft the mainmast is a small spar known as the *gaff*, from which the national ensign is flown when the ship is under way.

The small vertical spars at the bow and stern of a ship are the *jackstaff* and *flagstaff* respectively. When a ship is at anchor or moored, it flies the union jack on the jackstaff and the national ensign on the flagstaff from 0800 to sunset.

Pipes for the expulsion of smoke and gases from the boilers are called *stacks*. There are many different varieties—short, high, vertical, raked, single, double, split trunk, etc. On most vessels, stacks are located on the centerline approximately amidships. Aircraft carriers have stacks located in the "island" on the right side of the flight deck. Many new ships, especially those with diesel or gas turbine propulsion, have twin stacks side by side. Nuclear-powered ships have no stacks. Stacks, their number, and arrangement are important aids in correct identification of ships at a distance.

Macks

In some new ships the mast and stack are combined to form a large tower called a *mack*.

Ladders and Booms

These are not permanent parts of the hull, but are rigged out for use as necessary.

Boat Boom. A spar swung out from the ship's side from which boats can be hauled out or made fast. This permits boats to ride safely alongside when the ship is anchored.

Accommodation Ladder. A "stairway" suspended over the side of the ship, with a platform at the bottom, which serves as a landing for boats and so designed that as it is adjusted up and down the steps remain level. A *boat rope* or *sea painter* is provided to secure boats alongside while they load and unload.

Brow. A form of gangplank used when the ship is moored alongside a pier or "nested" alongside other ships. Its size and construction will depend on the size of the ships and the distance from the ship to the pier.

Chains. A small platform rigged out over the side for use by the leadsman in taking soundings.

Living Quarters

A considerable portion of the interior of a warship must be devoted to living spaces and facilities for the ship's complement of officers and men. Quarters and mess facilities for the officers are generally near the bridge. Quarters for the men may be distributed throughout a large ship. Other facilities include the galleys, washrooms and heads, various storerooms, and sick bay. On a carrier or supply ship the number and variety of facilities are great, while on smaller ships they may be simple. The location, size, and arrangement of living quarters is a secondary consideration in the design of a warship. The location of armament, ammunition handling rooms, magazine, boiler rooms, and other mechanical elements comes before arrangements for the comfort and convenience of the crew, as battle efficiency is always the primary consideration.

Ship's Equipment and Operations

Much of the hull space of most ships is taken up by the engines, engineering equipment, and related piping and electrical systems. Storage and living space may be limited.

Engineering Plant

The engine rooms contain the main engines, which drive the ship; these may be diesel, diesel-electric, steam, or gas turbines. In nuclear-powered ships, the main "engine" room is called the reactor room. Auxiliary engine rooms contain generators that produce electricity, and evaporators and condensers that convert salt water to fresh water. The steering engine room contains the machinery that powers the rudder. Fuel oil tanks carry fuel for the engines.

Electrical System

A large ship has hundreds of electric motors driving everything from fans and tape decks to gun mounts. Every other system in the ship depends on electric motors. The main power supply is produced in the engineering spaces by diesel-driven generators.

Emergency diesel-electric generators in other parts of the ship automatically cut in to the supply power if the main generators are disabled for any reason.

Drainage System

This system includes the piping, valves, and pumps that discharge water from the ship. This includes water in flushing systems, water used in fire fighting, or sea water that enters the hull as the result of damage, collision, or heavy weather. The main eductor is a large pipe in the bottom of the ship to which other drain pipes are connected; the secondary eductor is a smaller pipe running lengthwise of the ship. This system includes connections to all watertight compartments. Boiler rooms have independent drainage systems and sea valves. Motors and valve controls for boiler room centrifugal pumps are located on higher decks so that they can be operated even if the boiler room is submerged. Parts of the system can be used to flood compartments when counterflooding is required for damage control.

Ventilation System

This system includes air supply, exhaust, and air-conditioning equipment. There are many separate systems so that ducts do not have to run through watertight bulkheads.

Fresh-Water System

This system provides water for the crew—for drinking, showers, and cooking—and for the boilers. Fresh-water tanks may be filled in port from shore supplies; at sea, fresh water is made from salt water by condensers and evaporators.

Salt-Water System

This provides water for fire protection, including turret sprinkling, magazine flooding, NBC washdown, and flushing. Flushing water may come directly from the fire main or from separate lines. The fire main is a large pipe running the length of the ship, with risers and branch mains connected to it.

Fuel-Oil System

This includes fuel storage tanks, filling lines, feed lines to the boilers or diesel engines, and lines and connections for pumping oil from one tank to another to control trim or list when the ship is damaged.

Compressed Air System

This includes compressors, storage tanks, and high-pressure lines used for testing and blowing out compartments, and for operating pneumatic tools and other equipment.

Magazines

Ammunition for all guns is stored in magazines, which are placed well below the waterline when possible. Projectiles and powder may be stored in separate compartments. All magazines can be flooded by remote control in case of fire. Ammunition is passed to handling rooms, where hoists take it up to the gun mounts or turrets.

Cargo Holds

Cargo holds are large spaces, with hatches opening on the main deck, from which auxiliaries carry material for other ships.

Storerooms

Storerooms are spaces in which a ship carries her own supplies; these may be clothing, dry or refrigerated provisions, and various types of spare parts and supplies.

Crew Accommodations

There are many compartments throughout the ship, designated as wardroom, officers' cabins, berthing compartments, pantries, messes, heads, washrooms, and sick bay. Other spaces provided for the health and comfort of the crew may include barber and tailor shop, cobbler shop, laundry, galleys, bake shops, butcher shops, library, chapel, ship's store, soda fountain, reception room, and hobby shops, depending on the size of the ship.

Shops and Offices

In addition to offices for the captain and executive officer, a ship has office space, or a separate office, for every department and activity on board. Even a very small ship will have a carpenter's shop and electrical shop; larger ships may have print shops, photographic laboratories, and special repair shops.

Steering

A ship is steered by its *rudder* and by its propeller or propellers acting separately or together with the rudder. The rudder is basically a flat or streamlined metal shape, suspended by a hingelike device from the stern of the ship. Turning the rudder to the right causes the water flowing by the ship to exert pressure against it. This pressure swings the stern to the left, thereby pointing the bow of the ship to the right. The reverse works if the rudder is put over to the left. A rudder has no effect if the ship is not moving. However, if the ship is moving ahead or astern, or if there is a current in the water, the rudder does affect the direction the ship takes. A single screw can affect the ahead or astern motion of the ship by the direction and speed with which it turns. Moreover, the turning motion of the screw tends to push the stern to port or starboard, depending on its rotation direction. In the case of multiple screws, the steering effect is pronounced. For example, a ship with two propellers can turn quickly and in a short space by going ahead on one screw and astern on the other. Many modern ships have twin rudders, each set directly behind a screw in order to receive the full thrust of water; this combination makes a ship highly maneuverable and permits the ship to be turned without moving ahead or astern.

Rudders are turned in the water by the steering engines, and the combination of motors, control instruments, and linkages is called *steering gear*. The steering engines, located in the stern of a ship, are controlled by the *wheel*, located on the bridge. The *helmsman* turns this wheel according to the directions given him by the officer of the deck (OOD), navigator, captain, or pilot—or whoever is conning the course of the ship.

Ground Tackle

Ground tackle is the term for all gear and equipment used in anchoring or mooring with anchors. (*Tackle* is pronounced "tay-kul"—to rhyme with "say-kull.") It includes the anchors, chains, shackles, and stoppers required for these operations. A mooring buoy is a large buoy anchored with one or more large anchors or weights called sinkers. It is equipped with rings or shackles to which the ship may make fast. The use of ground tackle is described in chapter 9—"Seamanship," as are the various *deck fittings* involved in handling lines, chains and cables.

Ordnance

This is an over-all term that takes in all the things that make up a ship's or plane's firepower: guns, gun mounts, turrets, ammunition, guided missiles, rockets, and all the equipment that controls, operates, and supports the weapons. Coast Guard ordnance is usually supplied by the Navy and conforms to plans for possible war or emergency use of cutters as naval vessels.

CHAPTER 9
Seamanship

Seamanship is the oldest of all technical seagoing skills. Long before navigation, gunnery, and steam power were developed, men had learned the basic elements of seamanship. Knotting and splicing, rigging, boathandling, and anchoring and mooring began thousands of years ago. Along with other aspects of going to sea, a modern Coast Guardsman must also learn to be a good seaman (figure 9–1). He must begin with the basic subjects in this chapter.

MARLINSPIKE SEAMANSHIP
This is one of the oldest, and most basic, of all seagoing skills. It includes knot tying and the handling of ropes and lines.

Rope and Line
During the process of manufacturing, the term applied is *rope*, whether fiber or wire. After it has been acquired, but before it has been made up for a specific use, the product is called *line*. When it is placed into use, the *line* takes its name from the purpose it serves. In use, the terms *line, rope, cordage, small stuff, painters,* and so forth are applied according to functions. Some examples are: *mooring lines, manropes, seizing stuff,* and *sea painters*.

Fiber Line or Rope
Line is made of wire strands or fiber. Although metal hawsers have certain advantages in their strength-to-size ratio, fiber lines are much easier to handle, will float unless water soaked, and can be used with

Figure 9–1. Retrieving a ship's boat alongside a cutter at sea requires the best in seamanship.

smaller diameter sheaves. A wire rope must be used with a sheave that is 20 times the diameter of the rope, while fiber line can be used with sheaves 3 times its circumference. For these reasons much more use is made of fiber line than of wire.

Manila. The fiber most used for making line comes from the abaca plant, the principal source of which is the Philippine Islands. It is used with all types of tackles (such as boat falls), and also for towing hawsers, mooring lines, and messengers.

Hemp. Most hemp is grown in the United States. Hemp line is inferior for most uses, although formerly, when tarred, it was extensively used for standing rigging; today, its use is practically confined to *small stuff.*

Nylon. Extensive tests have been made with nylon as a fiber for rope making. Nylon rope is slippery, hard to splice, stretches as much as 30 percent under normal working loads, and is expensive. It is, however, approximately twice as strong as manila of the same size, is more durable, and also rot resistant. These factors make its use desirable under many circumstances—for example, for towing hawsers, sea painters, boat falls, and mooring lines.

Dacron. This synthetic line has characteristics similar to nylon but it will not stretch quite as much. It also is becoming very popular, since it wears well and handles quite well.

Cotton. Cotton line is used for such things as the taffrail log, lead lines, heaving lines, and signal halyards. These lines are usually braided instead of laid.

Polyethylene (etc.). Many synthetic lines of this general type are now in use. They have characteristics similar to nylon, but also will float and can be brightly colored. Two uses are as heaving lines to recover a man overboard and, in deep water, for mooring scientific buoys.

Ropemaking

Ropemaking is essentially a series of twisting operations. The only process that does not involve twisting is the blending and preparation of the fibers into *roping* or *sliver.* Thereafter, rope is put together in three twisting operations. The roping is twisted from left to right to spin the yarn. The yarns are twisted from right to left to form the strand. The strands are then twisted from left to right to lay the rope (figure 9–2). This is the standard procedure and the result is known as "right-laid" rope. When the process is reversed, a "left-laid" rope is

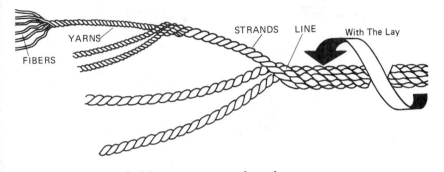

Figure 9–2. Method of forming yarn, strands, and rope.

produced. These ropes may be twisted into a cable. But always the principle of opposite twists is observed.

Opposing twists give a rope stability. They must be kept in the same way in which they were made if the rope is to stay in good condition. "Keep your rope in balance" is the the rule for long rope life. Add twist when it has been taken out; take out twist when extra twist has been added. Double-braided lines are now also in common use.

Size of Fiber Line. The length of fiber line is given in fathoms. The size is specified by the circumference in inches. Thus a 100-fathom coil of 6-inch manila would be a piece of line 600 feet long and 1.91 inches in diameter.

The smaller sizes of cordage are known as *small stuff;* ¾-inch, 1-inch, 1⅛-inch, 1¼-inch, and 1½-inch lines are frequently called 6, 9, 12, 15, and 21 thread stuff. Sizes larger than 21-thread are termed *line,* and those five inches or more in circumference are called *hawsers.* Other terms for small stuff, depending on specific usage, are *ratline stuff, seizing stuff,* and *marline.*

Line Handling

For convenience, the parts of a line are named in accordance with the way it is laying or hanging (figure 9–3). In taking turns around a bitt, take enough so you can hold the line. It is much easier to throw one turn off than to try an extra turn when you find that you cannot hold the line. Always stay out of the bight of a line.

Learning to handle line well is important, since rescue operations, logistics, small boat, and aids to navigation work all involve use of line or rope in some critical part of the operation.

The ends of running rigging not in use, or led out for use, should

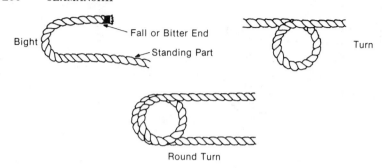

Figure 9–3. Terminology used in working with lines.

always be left *coiled, flemished,* or *faked* down (figure 9–4). This makes them neat and seamanlike, prevents fouling, and prepares them for immediate use. If line must be ready for emergency use, as in the case of the falls of a lifeboat that is ready for lowering, it is coiled down. If the entire length must be run out fairly rapidly, it is faked down. If it is not expected that the line will be needed on short notice, it is flemished down for greater neatness.

Recall that the unit of length for line, wire, rope, or chain aboard ship is the *fathom,* equal to 6 feet. Your two arms spread wide apart will come just about to a fathom, and this fact is made use of aboard ship when measuring line light enough to handle. In measuring a very long line or a heavy line, it is much easier and faster to measure off a stretch on deck and *fake* your line back and forth until the desired length is laid out.

Opening New Coil of Line

The end of a new coil to be drawn out first is supposed to be marked with a tag, but this tag frequently is attached to the wrong end, so don't trust the tag. The inside of every new coil, however, is in the form of a round tunnel, and the inside end of the line is at one end of the tunnel. This inside end *always* comes out first, and from the *bottom* of the tunnel, up through. The coil must set on the deck so that the inside end is at the bottom of the tunnel, next to the deck. You then reach down through the tunnel, draw up the inside end, and the whole coil will run off without a kink. If you open it backwards or from the wrong end, you will have a kink for every turn in the coil.

Once a line has been removed from the manufacturer's coil, it may

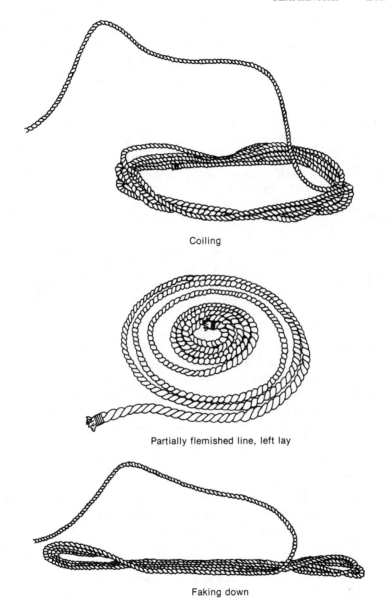

Coiling

Partially flemished line, left lay

Faking down

Figure 9-4. Three essentials in line handling: coiling, flemishing, and faking down.

be made up for storage or for ready use, either by winding on a reel or in one of the following three ways:

Coiling Down. This simply means laying it down in circles, roughly one on top of the other. Remember, right-laid line is *always* coiled down right-handed, or clockwise. When a line has been coiled down, one end is ready to run off. This is the end which went down *last* and which is now on *top.* If you try to walk away with the bottom end, a foul-up will result. If for some reason the bottom end must go out first, you will have to turn your entire coil upside down to free it for running.

Faking Down. This means laying it down in the same manner, except that it is laid out in long, flat bights, one forward of the other, instead of in round coils. With a long line this saves the space a large coil might occupy, and faking down a heavy line is much easier than coiling it down.

Flemishing Down. This means to coil it down first, and then wind it tight from the bottom end so that it forms a close mat. Slack ends of boat painters, boat falls, boat boom guys, or any other short lines about the decks which are not in continuous use should be flemished down for neatness.

Securing Ends. Never leave the end of a line dangling loose without a *whipping* (figure 9–5) to prevent it from unlaying. It will begin to unlay of its own accord. Use tape to whip nylon line ends.

A temporary plain whipping can be put on with anything, even a rope yarn. Lay the end of the whipping along the line and bind it down with a couple of turns. Then lay the other end on the opposite way, bind it with a couple of turns from the bight of the whipping, and pull the end tight.

Care of Line

The lives of the men who use them may depend on whether the lines hold. Lines can be weakened to the breaking point by neglect or mistreatment. Here are a few pointers on keeping them in good condition.

Avoid overloading; it is costly and dangerous. Lighten the load or use a larger line.

When a line is pulled taut between two fixed objects, such as a signal yard and a belaying pin, slack the line off when it rains.

Fiber shrinks when wet, and if the line is not slacked it will surely be overstrained. Sea spray or heavy dew may give the same effect.

1. Bind the end with
   a couple of turns

2. Lay the other end on

3. Bind it with the bight

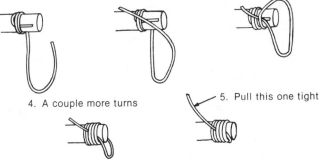

4. A couple more turns

5. Pull this one tight

Plain-whipping a line

1. Right through the
   middle of a strand

2. Wind turns
   toward the end →

3. Through the middle of a
   strand again

Needle comes out
between two strands
in back

4. Follow the groove back
   and pick up a strand

5. Back again and
   pick up another

6. Last one comes through
   the middle of a strand

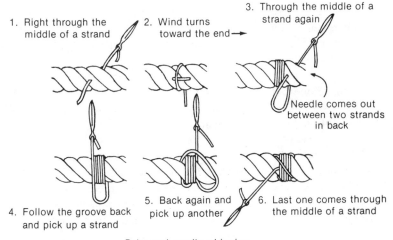

Palm and needle whipping

Note: Use twine doubled. It's shown single here for clearness only

Whipping the end of a hawser

Figure 9–5. Whipping a line is a basic skill for seamen. These diagrams show three procedures.

Always make up line neatly and in the correct direction, else it will kink. This also prevents fouling.

Work kinks and turns out of a line. Avoid removing kinks by putting a strain on the line; the kink will disappear and thereafter the line will look the same, but it will have been seriously weakened.

Always make sure that line is dry before you stow it. Wet line can develop mildew and rot.

Avoid dragging line over sharp objects. Some of the fibers will surely be injured.

Do not allow dirt or sand to work into the strands; it cuts the fibers.

If a section of a line is damaged, cut out the damaged portion, and splice the line together. A line with a good splice in it will hold where one with a damaged section will part. Chemicals can damage a line seriously, as can blocks that are too small.

When line is being used in a position where the wear is not uniform throughout the length of the line, as in tackles, end-for-end it periodically.

Don't use frozen line—ships on arctic runs sometimes come across this problem. Line that freezes after becoming wet is easily broken and cannot be trusted. In this case, thaw it out and dry it thoroughly before using it again.

Handling Nylon Line

Uncoil new nylon by unreeling it as you do wire.

When new nylon hawsers are used and strained, sharp, cracking noises will be heard. This is normal and does not mean the nylon will part unless the line is stretched too much (more than one third of its length).

When wet nylon is strained, it gives off water vapor that looks like steam. This is a normal, not dangerous, effect.

Nylon stoppers (short lengths of line wrapped around a line to stop it from running), not chain or manila stoppers, should be used on nylon lines.

If nylon is badly chafed, cut and splice it, and for heavy work, take an additional backtuck.

Avoid sharp edges and rough surfaces on bitts and chocks when using nylon. Wire or springlay rope should not be used on same bitts or chocks with nylon.

Nylon line will stretch on bitts and chocks, so use several extra turns.

If nylon line is parted by too much strain, it will first have stretched nearly one half its length. When this stretched line parts, the ends whip back with great force and can easily injure any bystander. Stand clear!

In stowing nylon, keep it away from heat, sunlight, and strong chemicals.

Whipping nylon hawsers every 5 or 6 feet will prevent excessive unlaying should the hawser part.

Do not use mooring combinations of nylon and manila. All lines should be one or the other.

Inspecting Line

Line should be inspected carefully before use. A weak place in a line may permit the line to part at an embarrassing moment.

Look for spots. By pressing your fingernail into the line at various places, you can determine a weak spot. This could mean rot.

Look for mildew by separating strands or untwisting and inspecting the yarns.

Look for broken fibers. They show up as small tufts of material.

Splicing

Splicing is a method of permanently joining the ends of two lines or of bending a line back on itself so as to form a permanent loop. If properly done, it does not weaken the line, and a splice between two lines runs over a sheave or other object much easier than a knot does.

There are various forms of splices: the long splice, short splice, and eye splice (see figure 9–6).

Short Splice. For a short splice, both ends of line are unlaid for about a foot and the strands are interlaced, as shown in figure 9–6. Beginning with any one strand, it is tucked from right to left, the lay of the line being opened by a marlinspike, wooden fid, or some other pointed instrument. The other two strands are similarly tucked, from right to left. Threads are then cut away from the ends of each tucked strand until they are two-thirds their original size, and they are then again tucked. After this, the strands are similarly cut away until they are one-third their original size, and a third and last tuck is taken. This produces a neat, tapered splice.

Eye Splice. An eye splice is done by the same method, except that the line is first brought back upon itself enough to give the desired size of eye, and the strands are then tucked into the body of the line.

Long Splice. To make a long splice, unlay both ends to be spliced

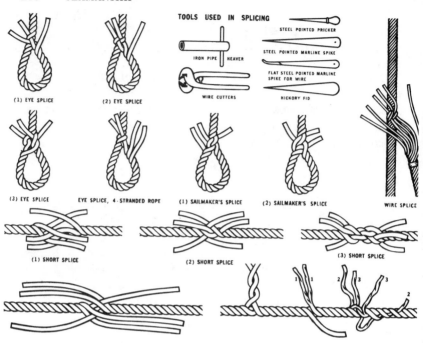

Figure 9–6. Types of splices, and tools required.

15 turns, interlace the strands as for the short splice and seize five strands together. Unlay the loose strand 10 more turns, and lay the opposite strand from the other rope in the groove left by unlaying the first strand. Tie these two strands together with an overhand knot. Cut out the seizing, unlay a strand in the opposite direction and lay in its opposite strand. Tie these two strands together. Unlay one of the two remaining strands one or two turns, and lay in the last strand. Tie these two strands. Next, split the bitter ends of the strands in two and make tucks in the opposite directions with the halves. After all strands have been tucked, the loose ends are trimmed off smooth. By this method a splice is secured that will run over a sheave easily and is hardly noticeable.

In splicing nylon line, use several extra tucks since this fiber is more slippery. It also can be spliced more easily if warmed in a bucket of water.

Seizing

Seizing is the lashing of two parts of line by continuous turns of small stuff. The seizing is then secured by a hitch. When two crossing parts of line are bound, the seizing is called a "throat seizing."

Seizings are used to assist in holding a line loop around a thimble, retaining a loop in the center of a line, holding the short end of a hitch or bend to the main body of the line, or fastening two sister hooks together.

Worming, Parceling, and Serving

Fiber line or wire rope that are to be exposed to the weather or to exceptionally hard usage are protected by worming, parceling, and serving (figure 9–7).

Worming consists of following the lay of the line between the strands with tarred small stuff. This keeps moisture from penetrating to the interior of the line and at the same time fills out the round of line, giving a smooth surface for the parceling and serving.

Parceling consists of wrapping the line spirally with long strips of canvas, following the lay of the line, overlapping like the shingles on a roof, to shed moisture.

Serving consists of wrapping small stuff snugly over the parceling, each turn being hove as taut as possible so that the whole forms a stiff protecting cover for the line. A serving mallet is used for passing the turns; in serving, each turn is hove taut by the leverage of the handle, as illustrated. Remember:

Worm and parcel with the lay,

Turn and serve the other way.

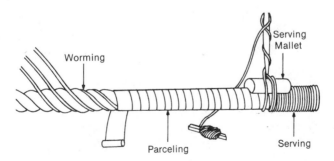

Figure 9–7. Worming, parceling, and serving.

Knots, Bends, and Hitches

Illustrations of the more important knots, bends, and hitches are given in this chapter (figures 9–8 through 9–12). Practice knot tying with these illustrations before you, and you will soon be able to tie them when they are needed.

A *knot* is a pattern of twists, curves, or turns that fastens a line into itself. Here, you have the true pattern of knot, as the square knot, the overhand knot, the figure eight knot, and the bowline. *End rope knots* are formed by working unlaid ends of a line back into itself. None of these knots is illustrated, and all are difficult to tie. The way to learn them is to practice under the supervision of someone who knows. Examples of these are the lanyard knot, the wall knot, the man-rope knot, and the Matthew Walker. The *ornamental knots,* such as the Turk's-head, coxcombing, and MacNamara lace are strictly professional work.

Bends are used for tying the ends of two lines together. Here you have the Carrick bend, the fisherman's knot, the sheet or becket bend, and the reeving line bend.

A *hitch* secures a line to a spar, ring, stanchion, or the standing part of another line. Examples are: the clove hitch, the rolling hitch, the round turn and two half-hitches, the catspaw, and the Blackwall hitch.

Hitches have an additional value in that they can be formed quickly. They afford a fast means of stopping a "running" line, and, by so doing, may prevent an accident. Various methods of securing a line are shown in figure 9–12.

Wire Rope

Wire rope has much in common with fiber line, and its use is important and extensive. Because a knowledge of its properties and uses is not required of all hands, only some general information about wire rope is given here.

Strands of a wire rope are laid up around a core of hemp or wire. Wire with a hemp core is more flexible, but that with a wire core is stronger. Wire is made of various grades of steel; most wire rope is made of plow steel. The length of wire rope is stated in fathoms, and its size is always stated as diameter in inches, while fiber line is always designated by its circumference in inches. Wire cannot be knotted, but it can be spliced.

Wire rope must be properly lubricated to ensure long life and safety.

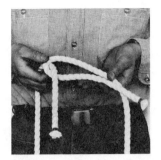

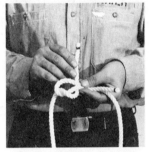

Becket Bend

Also called sheet bend. Good for tying end of small line to end of big line, or to eye splice as in last photo. This bend will jam.

Figure 9–8. Basic knots.

Bowline

The "king of knots" makes a loop that will neither slip nor jam.

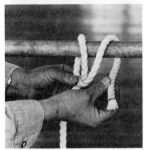

Clove Hitch

A fast way to tie to
a piling or fitting. The
half hitch (last photo) is
added to prevent slipping.

Figure-eight Knot

Used like an overhand knot but easier to untie because it does not jam so hard. Makes a good temporary stopper knot, as in last photograph.

Fisherman's Bend

This is a simple knot to tie, offering great strength and security. Secure the end by a seizing, as shown at right.

Figure 9–9. Basic knots.

Round Turn and Two Half Hitches

Half hitches secure a line quickly to a spar, or ring. The round turn makes the hitch more secure. Both hitches must be left, or right.

Square (or reef) Knot

Common way to tie two lines together. This knot will jam under heavy tension.

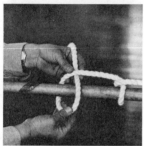

Timber Hitch with Half Hitch

Useful in towing cyclindrical objects. Added half hitches will help keep the object in line when towing.

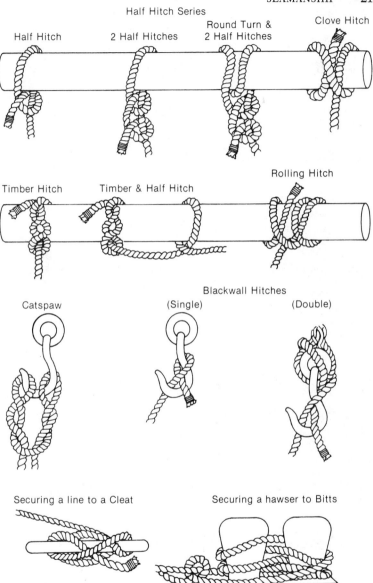

Figure 9–10. Basic knots.

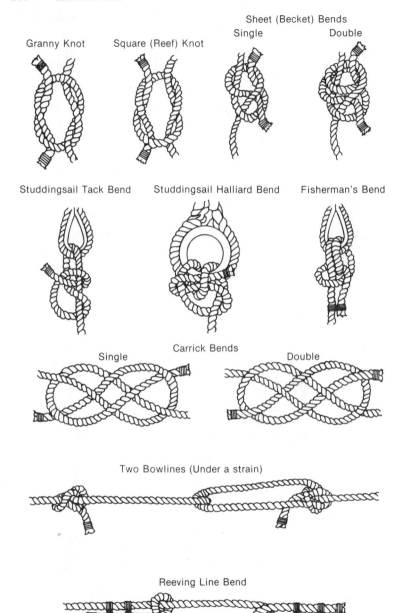

Figure 9–11. Basic knots.

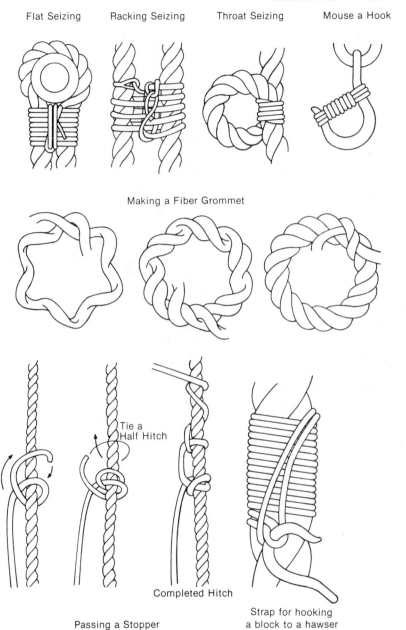

Flat Seizing   Racking Seizing   Throat Seizing   Mouse a Hook

Making a Fiber Grommet

Tie a
Half Hitch

Completed Hitch

Passing a Stopper

Strap for hooking
a block to a hawser

Figure 9–12. Basic knots.

The internal parts of the wires move one against another wherever the rope passes over a sheave or winds on a drum. Each wire rotates around its own axis, and all wires minutely slide by each other. Internal wear can only be minimized by lubrication. The proper lubricant, with the required amount of lubricating qualities, should be used so as to stay with the rope as long as possible without dripping, wiping, peeling, or flaking. The lubricant should be thin enough to penetrate to the core so as to be absorbed by the hemp.

Wire rope is made in much the same way as fiber rope. It is used extensively, especially for heavy lifts, because it is much stronger than natural or synthetic fiber line. A 4-inch manila hawser has a breaking point of 15,000 pounds, while a 1-inch wire, which is approximately the same size, has a breaking point of 46,000 pounds.

Wire rope is made of small steel wires laid together to form strands. Strands are laid together to form the wire rope, which is designated by the number of strands per rope and number of wires per strand, Thus, a 6 × 19 rope has six strands of 19 wires per strand, and a 6 × 37 wire rope has six strands of 37 wires per strand. Wire rope made up of a large number of small wires per strand is more flexible than rope of the same diameter with fewer but larger wires per strand. The more flexible rope is less resistant to external abrasion because its smaller wires break more easily. The rope made of a smaller number of larger wires is more resistant to external abrasion but is less flexible.

Wire rope requires better care than fiber line. A kink will ruin the best wire rope. Kinks are easily seen and are a warning that the wire is weak at that point. Wire should always be stowed on reels; it should be unreeled and never removed in bights. Turns should not be allowed to overlap on a drum or winch. Wire rope should not be run over pulleys in such a way as to make a reverse bend like the letter "S." Sharp bends should always be avoided.

When wire rope is used with sheaves, a good rule-of-thumb is never use a sheave of less than 20 times the diameter of the wire. A wire rope wears faster when run fast over a sheave. Usually it is better to increase the load than to increase the speed.

Wire rope should not be used when the outside wires are worn down to half their original diameter, when there are numerous broken wires, or when there are any other indications that it has been kinked or subjected to excessive strain. *Always wear heavy gloves when handling wire rope.*

BLOCKS AND TACKLES

Blocks

A "block" aboard ship consists of a frame housing one or more sheaves (pulley wheels).

Blocks take their names from the purpose for which they are used, the places they occupy, or from some peculiarity in their shape or construction. They are designated as single, double, or triple blocks according to the number of sheaves they have.

Tackle

An assemblage of ropes (falls) and blocks, for the purpose of multiplying force, is a tackle (figure 9–13).

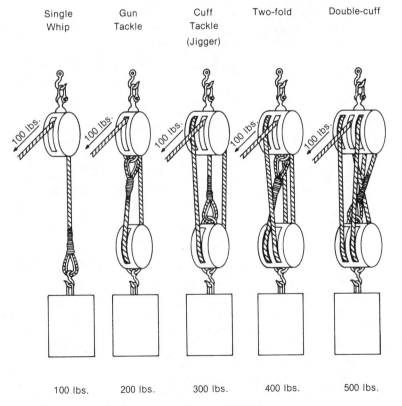

Figure 9–13. Types of tackle. Adding more blocks increases effective force. (Effect of friction disregarded.)

The seaman speaks of "reeving" when he passes lines around the sheaves of the blocks. These lines are called "falls." The "standing part" is that part of the fall made fast to one of the blocks. The hauling part is the end of the falls to which force is applied to handle the weight. To "overhaul" the falls is to separate them. To "round in" is to bring the blocks together. The blocks are said to be "two-blocked" when they are tight together.

Tackles are designated either according to the number of sheaves in the blocks that are used to make the tackle, such as single, two-fold, three-fold purchases; or according to the purpose for which the tackle is used, such as yard-tackles, stay-tackles, and fore-and-aft tackles. Other designations handed down from the past still persist, such as luff-tackles, gun-tackles, and Spanish-burtons. The following types are commonly used aboard ships and you should be familiar with the names and appearances:

Runner. A single movable block attached to the weight and one end of the fall made fast while the other end is used as the hauling part.

Whip and Runner. Obtained by reeving the hauling part of a runner over a fixed block. This would give no advantage in purchase over a runner but might provide a better lead.

Three-fold Purchase. Made with two treble blocks. This is the heaviest purchase commonly used on shipboard.

Ground Tackle

Ground tackle includes all the equipment used in anchoring a ship: anchors, anchor cables (or chains), connecting fittings, anchor windlass, and miscellaneous items, such as shackles of various types, detachable links, mooring swivels, dip ropes, chain stoppers, chain cable jacks, mooring hooks, and anchor bars (figure 9–14).

There are various types of anchors (figure 9-15) and different methods of anchoring. When a ship has one anchor down, she is anchored; when she has two anchors down and swings from a mooring swivel connected to both, she is moored. (A ship secured to a dock with lines or to a buoy with an anchor chain is also moored.) In a Mediterranean moor, a ship usually has the stern moored to a pier, and an anchor out on each bow. A ship's biggest anchor is her *sheet* anchor. An anchor carried aft and used by amphibious ships to pull themselves off the beach (retract) is called a *stern* anchor. A *stream* anchor, now seldom used, is a small anchor dropped off the stern or quarter of a ship to prevent swinging to a current.

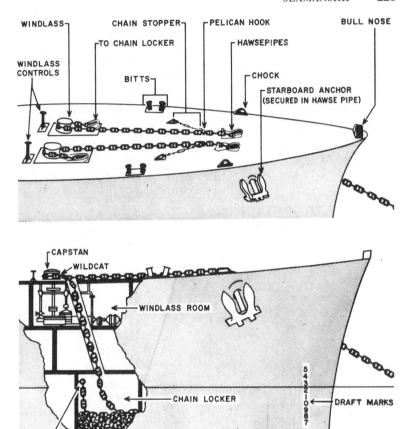

Figure 9–14. Ground tackle installation on typical ship, showing arrangement on forecastle and below decks.

Patent (stockless) Anchors. These are easier to stow and handle than the old-fashioned type. Because they have no stock, they can be raised directly into the hawsepipe. The arms are pivoted on the shank and swing 45 degrees on either side to let the anchor dig into the bottom.

Mushroom Anchors. These anchors are used by submarines and to anchor buoys, torpedo testing barges, and lightships.

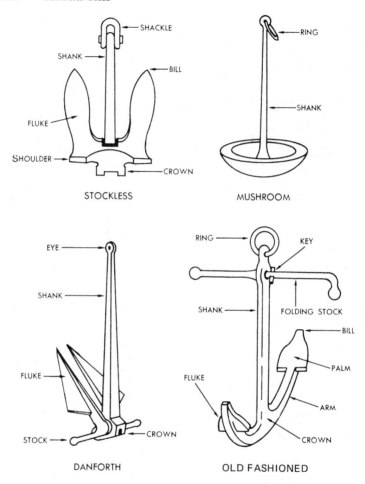

Figure 9–15. Nomenclature for various types of anchors.

Lightweight (LWT) Anchors. These have the stock in the crown. There are two types: the *Northill* anchor, which is used on small boats, and the *Danforth* anchor, which is used on small boats, as a stern anchor for landing craft, and as a bow anchor on some destroyers. The Danforth anchor has the strength and holding power of a patent anchor twice as heavy.

Old-fashioned Anchors. These anchors are exactly that. They are no longer used. You will probably see them only on the lawn of some station.

Anchor Chains. These are made of steel, and the size varies according to the size of the ship and its anchors. Chain comes in 15-fathom lengths (90 feet) called shots. A cutter will have one eight-shot chain and one seven-shot chain. Shots are connected by detachable links; these links, and their adjacent links, are painted red, white or blue, to help the anchor detail know how much chain has run out. Each link of the next-to-last shot is painted yellow; the entire last shot is red. This is to warn that the bitter end of the chain is coming up. When an anchor is hoisted, the chain comes off the anchor windlass and into the chain locker.

Swivel Shots (bending shots). On most ships, standard outboard *swivel shots* (figure 9–16), or *bending shots*, attach the anchor chain to the anchor. They make it possible to stop off the anchor and break the chain between the windlass and the anchor. Outboard swivel shots consist of detachable links, regular chain links, a swivel, an end link, and a bending shackle, and they vary in length up to approximately five fathoms. The taper pins in the detachable links in the outboard swivel shot are secured with a wire locking clip.

Bending Shackles. These shackles are used for attaching the anchor (anchor shackle) to the outboard swivel shot, which in turn is secured to the first plain shot of anchor chain. *Chain swivels* are part of the outboard swivel shot. They help to keep the anchor chain from kinking.

Shot Number	Color of Detachable Link	Number of Adjacent Links Painted White	Turns of Wire on Last White Links
1 (15 fathoms)	Red	1	1
2 (30 fathoms)	White	2	2
3 (45 fathoms)	Blue	3	3
4 (60 fathoms)	Red	4	4
5 (75 fathoms)	White	5	5
6 (90 fathoms)	Blue	6	6

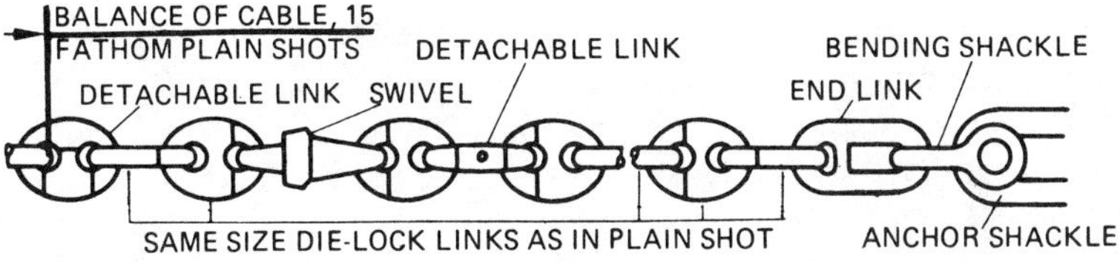

Figure 9–16. Parts of a standard outboard swivel shot assembly.

Riding and Housing Chain Stoppers. These consist of a turnbuckle inserted in a short section of chain, with a slip or pelican hook attached to one end of the chain and a shackle at the other end. The *housing stopper* is the one nearest the hawsepipe; any others are *riding stoppers*. These stoppers are used for holding the anchor taut in the hawsepipe, for riding to an anchor, or for holding an anchor when an anchor is disconnected for any reason. When in use, a stopper is attached to the chain by straddling a link with the tongue and strongback of the pelican hook.

Mooring Shackles. These shackles, made of forged steel, are used for attaching the anchor chain to mooring buoys. Forged steel swivels with two links attached at each end, used in mooring with anchors, are called *mooring swivels* and are inserted in the chain outboard of the hawsepipe, to keep the chain from twisting as the ship swings.

Anchor Windlass. This machine is used to hoist the bow anchor. A ship with a stern anchor has a *stern anchor winch* to hoist it. On combatant ships the anchor windlass is a vertical type, with controls, friction brake handwheel, capstan, and *wildcat* above deck and the electric and hydraulic drive for the wildcat and capstan below deck. On auxiliary type ships, the anchor windlass is a horizontal type, all above deck, with two wildcats, one for each anchor. The wildcat is fitted with ridges called *whelps*, which engage the links of the chain and prevent it from slipping. The wildcat may be disengaged from the shaft so that it turns freely when the anchors are dropped, and it is fitted with a brake to stop the chain at the desired length or *scope*.

Anchor Detail. On most ships, the first lieutenant is in charge on the forecastle, with a boatswain's mate assisting and men detailed to duties by the WQS bill. "Heave around" from the bridge is the order to the anchor windlass to take a strain on the chain and start bringing it in. "Anchor's *aweigh*" from the forecastle means that the anchor is clear of the bottom and the ship is under way, whether or not the propellers are turning.

Scope of Chain. Scope means the amount of chain in use, from the ship to the anchor. In 10 to 15 fathoms, the length of chain used is equal to six times the depth of water. In 15 to 20 fathoms, the length of chain is five times the depth; in 20 to 30 fathoms, the length is four times the depth; and in 30 fathoms or more, the length is three times the depth.

The reason for the lesser scope in deeper water is that if a ship puts heavy strain on her chain in bad weather, more of the length lifts off the bottom and the anchor will break out and drag. With too long a scope, the chain may part before its entire length lifts off the bottom.

Capstans. These are powered devices designed to handle heavy hawsers, mooring, warping, and towing gear. A capstan is fitted with a smooth drum, or gypsy, about which a few turns of the hawser or other line are taken. As long as the line loops loosely around the gypsy, the capstan revolves freely and no pull is taken. The deck end of the line is tended by hand.

When a strain is taken on the line it is pulled taut. The loops tighten around the drum; the harder the pull, the tighter the fit. The drum grips solely by friction. The turning capstan does the actual work; the tending seamen simply reel the line off the gypsy and fake it on the deck or pay it out around the gypsy as needed. Thus the capstan pulls without reeling.

Winches. Hoisting or pulling machines, these do their work primarily by reeling and unreeling a line on relatively large drums. The drums are smooth, but the fag end of the line is secured to the drum, and the line reels up around the drum. Winches are used principally for handling cargo, but most winches are fitted with small gypsies or winch-heads on the end of the shaft supporting the hoisting drum. The winch-heads may be used as capstans for mooring and warping.

MOORING

Mooring a ship to a pier, buoy, or another ship, and unmooring, are the most basic jobs of the deck department. These involve skillful use of mooring lines (called line handling), capstans, and such fittings as cleats, bitts, bollards, and chocks (figure 9–17). Quick, efficient line handling, when coming alongside or getting under way, is one of the marks of a smart ship and well-trained deck force.

Mooring Lines

Mooring lines (figure 9–18) are numbered from forward aft in the order that they are run out from the ship, but their names describe their location, their use, and the direction they tend as they leave the ship.

The *bow line* (1) runs through the bull-nose or chock nearest the eyes of the ship and is led well up the pier to reduce after motion of the ship.

The corresponding line used to reduce stern motion of the ship is the *stern line* (7). A *breast line* (4) leads nearly at right angles to the centerline of the ship; amidships, more than one breast line may be

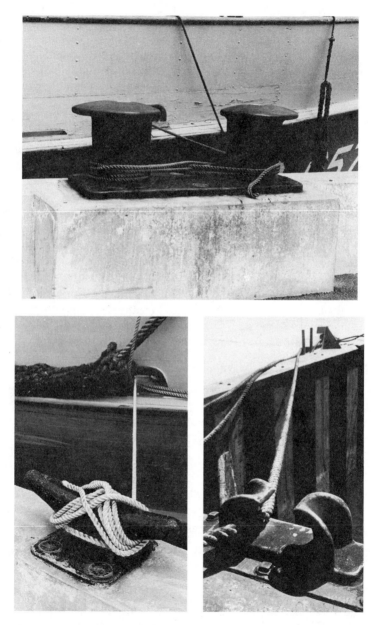

Figure 9–17. Basic line handling: securing a wire to bollards, securing a line to a cleat, running a line through a chock.

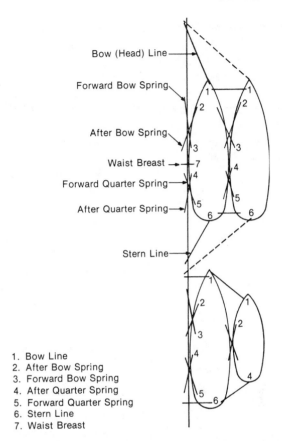

Figure 9–18. Names and number of standard mooring lines.

used, in which case they are named from forward aft: *bow breast, waist breast,* and *quarter breast. Spring lines* lead out from the ship in pairs, at sharp angles, and cross each other; those forward are called *after bow spring* (2) and *forward bow spring* (3); those aft are called *after quarter spring* (5) and *forward quarter spring* (6). Men who work with mooring lines are called *line handlers.*

Deck Fittings

A *cleat* consists of a pair of projecting horns used for belaying a line. *Bitts* are cylindrical shapes of cast iron or steel, arranged in pairs on deck, forward and aft of each chock. A *chock* is a heavy fitting through which mooring lines are led; the lines run from bitts on deck through chocks to bollards on the dock. Chocks are of three types: open, closed, and roller. A *bollard* looks somewhat like half a bitt, but larger; it is on the dock or pier where the bight of a line is placed over it.

Mooring may often involve putting out fenders, handling camels, and placing rat guards. *Fenders* are shock-absorbers of various types placed between ships or between a ship and a pier; they are dropped over the side and tended from on deck. *Camels* are floats used to keep a ship, particularly an aircraft carrier, away from a pier or wharf so that elevators or other overhanging structures will not strike objects on the pier. *Rat guards* are circular metal discs lashed onto mooring lines to keep rats from coming aboard.

In mooring, the messenger (a light line) is first sent over by heaving line, and then is hauled in with the attached mooring line. A *heaving line* is a light line with a weight, called a monkey fist, on one end.

When the ship is secured, the mooring lines are normally *doubled up;* a bight of line is passed to the pier or other ship, giving three parts of line each taking an equal strain, instead of only one part. The size of mooring line used depends on the type of line and type of ship. Cutters generally use six-inch manila or five-inch nylon; smaller ships use five-inch manila or four-inch nylon. Double braided lines are often used.

Commands to Line Handlers

Commands to line handlers are listed here, with the exact meaning following each command.

"Stand by your lines."—Man the lines, ready to cast off or let go.

"Let go," or "Let go all lines."—Slack off smartly to permit those tending lines on the pier or another ship to cast off.

"Send the lines over."—Pass the lines to the pier, place the eye over the appropriate bollard, but take no strain.

"Take ———— to the capstan."—Lead the end of the designated line to the capstan, take the slack out of the line, but *take no strain*.

"Heave around on ————."—Apply tension on line with the capstan.

"Avast heaving."—Stop the capstan.

"Hold what you've got."—Hold the line as it is.

"Hold."—Do not allow any more line to go out. Caution: this risks parting the line.

"Check."—Hold heavy tension on line but render it (let it slip) as necessary to prevent parting the line.

"Surge."—Hold moderate tension on the line, but render it enough to permit movement of the ship (used when moving along the pier to adjust position).

"Double up."—Pass an additional bight on all mooring lines from the ship to the shore so that there are three parts of each mooring line fastened to the pier instead of only one part of each line.

"Single up."—Take in all bights and extra lines so that there remains only a single part of each of the normal mooring lines.

"Take in all lines."—Used when secured with your *own* lines. Have the ends of all lines cast off from the pier and brought on board.

"Cast off all lines."—Used when secured with *another* ship's lines in a nest. Cast off the ends of the lines and allow the other ship to retrieve her lines.

"Shift."—Used when moving a line along a pier. Followed by a designation of which line and where it is to go: "Shift number three from the bollard to the cleat."

If auxiliary deck machinery is to be used to haul in on a line, the command is given, "Take one (number one) to the winch (capstan)." This may be followed by, "Heave around on one (number one)" and then, "Avast heaving on one (number one)."

Rat Guards. After a ship has completed mooring to another ship or a pier, rat guards are put out on all mooring lines. Putting out rat guards is a tiresome job, especially on a cold rainy night, but it is highly essential. Rats carry many contagious diseases, and once they get aboard, it is almost impossible to get rid of them. No one wants to be shipmates with a rat.

TOWING

Many rescue operations become routine towing jobs. Some ships used in ocean towing have an automatic tension towing machine, a powerful electric drive winch mounted in the stern of the ship that automatically heaves in or pays out the towing hawser and maintains the proper tension on it at all times. Most tows are done with hawsers, handled by men.

The length of the towline—hawser and sometimes chain—is adjusted to hang in a deep underwater curve called a *catenary*, which helps to relieve surges on the line caused by movements of the two ships. Proper towing technique, whether with two motor launches or two cruisers, requires that the towline be of such a *scope*, or length, that the two craft are in *step*; both must reach the crest of a wave at the same time, or the towline will be whipped out of the water under terrific strain and may part to do great damage.

Once a towing hawser is properly rigged, it is necessary for the towing vessel to get way on very slowly as the towed vessel commences to move; otherwise, the line may part. Course changes must also be made slowly, as the towed vessel will flounder around at the end of the line and may have difficulty steering a course.

BUOY AND CARGO HANDLING

This sort of work is done mostly by tenders. Aboard such ships, deck seamanship is primarily concerned with handling heavy weights. A knowledge of the principal parts of all cargo gear and the various "rigs" or methods of handling cargo is essential for seamen aboard.

Rigging

This is a general term for all wires, ropes, and chains supporting masts or kingposts, and operating booms and cargo hooks. *Standing rigging* includes all lines that support but do not move, such as *stays* and *shrouds;* *running rigging* includes all movable lines rove (running) through *blocks,* such as *lifts, whips,* and *vangs* (see figure 9–19).

Running Rigging

The booms are moved into position and the cargo is moved into and out of holds by running rigging. *Topping lifts* working on *topping lift blocks* move the boom vertically and hold it at the required height. *Inboard* and *outboard guys,* or *vangs,* move the boom horizontally or hold it in working position over hatch or dock. *Cargo whips* running from *winches* over *heel blocks* near the gooseneck and *head blocks* at the top of the boom raise or lower the *cargo hook.*

Booms

A boom is a long pole built of steel. The lower end is fitted with a *gooseneck,* which supports the boom in a *boom step bracket;* the upper end is raised or lowered and held in position by a *topping lift.* Booms range in capacity from 5 or 10 tons to as much as 30 tons for most tenders. When they are used in pairs, the boom lifting cargo from a hold is called the *hatch boom,* and the boom that positions cargo over the side to lower it to a dock or boat is called the *yard boom.* Booms are used singly, or in combinations, as follows:

Single Swinging Boom. This arrangement is generally used to handle

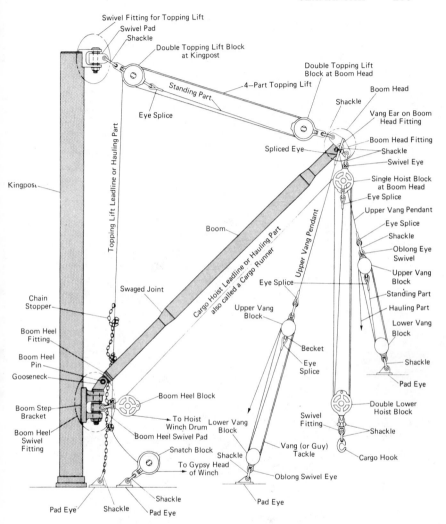

Figure 9–19. Rigging detail for single swinging boom.

buoys. The topping lift is led to a winch that can raise or lower the boom with a full load. The boom is swung over the side by vangs and the hook attached to it. Another winch takes up the *hoist leadline* to raise the load. The boom is swung over the side by the vangs, and the buoy is hooked on. Then the hoist winch raises the buoy clear of the railing, after which the vang on the side opposite swings it in on deck. Cargo, in nets or pallets, can be handled in the same way.

Yard and Stay (or Burtoning). Two booms are used, (figure 9–20) a hatch boom and a cargo boom. The hatch boom is centered over the working hatch; the yard boom is rigged out with its head over the pier or receiving boat. There are two cargo whips, a hatch whip and yard whip, rove through their respective heel and head blocks on the hatch and yard booms and both shackled to the same cargo hook. Each whip has its own winch. With the hatch boom secured above the center of

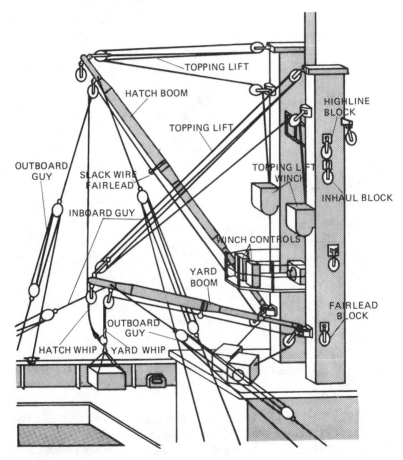

Figure 9–20. Details of yard-and-stay or burtoning rig. Used for medium weight cargo, up to 3,500 pounds.

the open hatch and the yard boom rigged out over the side of the ship, the cargo hook is dropped into the hold for a load. The yard whip hangs slack while the hatch whip hoists the load clear. Then the yard whip heaves round and the hatch whip is payed out, and the load is racked (swung) across the deck and over the side. When the load is under the yard boom, the hatch whip is slacked off, and the yard whip lowers away. In loading cargo, the procedure is reversed.

Inspecting Rigging

A weekly inspection of all booms and their rigging and associated fittings is conducted by the responsible officer of the deck department.

Whenever a boom is to hoist or lower a load equal to its rated capacity as shown on the label plate, the first lieutenant or an officer he designates must make a thorough inspection of the boom, fittings, and rigging before the lift is made.

Underway Replenishment

Cutters operating with the Navy will have to take on fuel and stores by the Navy system, called UNREP for short. In underway replenishment, delivery ships are rigged to transfer general stores, provisions, ammunition, and fuel to receiving ships while both are under way. The basic cargo-handling gear has already been described. UNREP uses various types of cargo transfer rigs, plus several special fuel hose rigs. The following brief descriptions of each rig or system, with diagrams, will give an idea of general UNREP operations. It must be emphasized that all provisioning and fueling operations involve handling heavy weights while ships are moving, and safety precautions must be strictly observed.

Burton Rig. The cargo is moved (figure 9–21) from delivering ship to receiving ship by two *burton whips*, which correspond to the hatch whip and cargo whip. A winch on each ship handles one whip. The delivering ship hoists the load clear, and then the receiving ship takes in her burton whip as the delivering ship slacks hers off. When the load is spotted over the deck of the receiving ship, her whip is slacked and the load is eased to the deck. The entire operation requires skillful teamwork between the two winchmen; they must keep constant tension on both whips at all times, whether they are running in or out, and they must keep the load just clear of the water—if the load is too high, the strain on all rigging is greatly increased. The maximum load is 3,500 pounds.

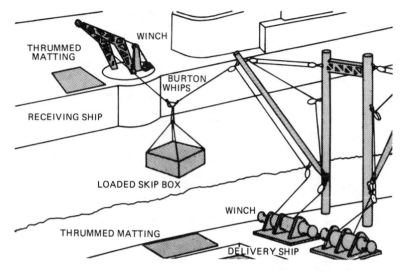

Figure 9–21. Burton rig for underway replenishment; maximum load 3,500 pounds.

Housefall Rig. In this method (figure 9–22), both cargo whips are handled by the delivering ship. The whip that moves cargo to the receiving ship is called the *outboard transfer whip*, (same as yardwhip), and the whip that hauls the cargo hook back to the delivering ship is called the *inboard transfer whip* (same as cargo whip). Both winchmen are on the delivering ship. The maximum load is 2,500 pounds.

Modified Housefall Rig. This method is used when loads must be kept higher above the water than with a housefall rig. A *trolley block* carrying the cargo hook rides back and forth on the outboard transfer whip. Otherwise the rigging is the same as that for housefall rig.

Double Housefall Rig. This is used to speed transfers to ships that cannot handle more than one housefall rig. It is slower than housefalling to two separate receiving stations, but faster than housefalling to one station. In the double housefall method (figure 9–23), the delivering ship uses two adjacent housefall rigs attached to a single point on the receiving ship. In handling cargo with this method, the delivering ship sends over a loaded net with one rig at the same time the other brings back an empty net from the receiving ship; the two nets pass each other in opposite directions each time a load is transferred.

Wire Highline Rig. This method (figure 9–24) involves a trolley mov-

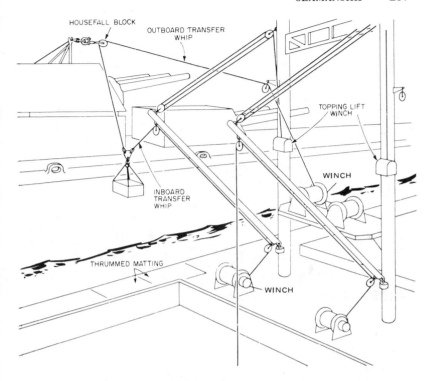

Figure 9–22. Housefall rig; maximum load 2,500 pounds.

ing on a highline that extends from a winch on the delivering ship through a block on a boom head and across to a pad eye on the receiving ship. An *outhaul line* (same as yard whip) is heaved in by hand on the receiving ship to move the load over; a winch-operated *inhaul line* (same as hatch whip) on the delivering ship returns the trolley for another load. The wire highline is the standard procedure in transferring cargo to destroyers and other small ships and at times is the best means of transfer to large ships. In order to use this method, the receiving ship must have a place in her superstructure high enough to attach the line for good working conditions and strong enough to handle the load.

Manila Highline Rig. This is the same as the wire highline rig, except that manila is used instead of wire. Only light cargo can be handled. No boom is needed on the delivery ship; the receiving ship needs only a 12-inch snatch block attached to a pad eye. The highline is kept taut

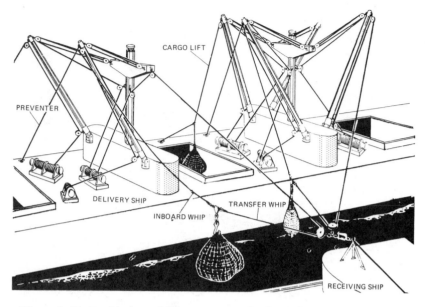

Figure 9–23. Double housefall rig; maximum load 2,500 pounds.

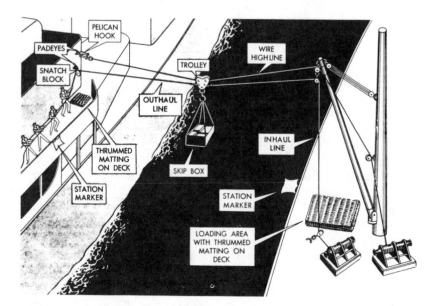

Figure 9–24. Wire highline rig.

during transfer by either 25 men or a capstan; the capstan cannot be used if men are being transferred. The trolley that rides the highline is moved by inhaul and outhaul lines, both handled by men on deck. The rig is easily and quickly set up and is the safest method of transferring men from ship to ship. The maximum load is 600 pounds.

Personnel Transfer. In addition to the manila highline rig, men can be transferred by the burton rig and by helicopter. With the burton rig, used particularly when many men must transfer quickly and time does not allow use of a highline, a skip box is used to send over four or five men at a time. The danger in the burton system is in having the transfer controlled by winchmen on two different ships. The only approved rig for transferring men ship-to-ship is the manila highline (figure 9–25); this is because the line must be tended constantly to prevent parting if the ships roll away from each other, and manila can be tended by hand but wire cannot. The maximum load is 800 pounds.

Fueling at Sea

The two basic systems are *close-in* and *span wire* rigs. The system used depends on the types of ships involved, the kind of fuel being trans-

Figure 9–25. Highline transfer by boatswain's chair.

ferred, and weather and operating conditions. The two rigs differ mainly in the method by which the delivering ship sends the hose over to the receiving ship; for fuel, a 6-inch 230-foot hose is used. Fleet oilers and many major combatant ships have equipment for the span wire method; other ships use the close-in method.

Close-in Method. In this system (figure 9–26), the hose is supported by an inboard saddle whip and an outboard saddle whip attached to the *inboard* and *outboard saddles* and running to booms or other high points on the delivery ship. If an *outer bight* line is used, it runs from the outboard saddle to the receiving ship. The ships steam approximately 60 feet apart.

Span Wire Method. The fuel hose is sent across by a single *span wire* stretched between the two ships. The hose is suspended from a *trolley* which rides along the span wire. This system lets the ships keep 140 to 180 feet apart, which makes ship handling easier and allows use of antiaircraft batteries. The span wire method, because it carries the hose higher above the sea, gives it better protection in rough weather. The hose may be rigged out either by the all-wire rig or the manila rig. The *all-wire span wire* method (figure 9–27) involves a span wire on which a trolley carries the outboard saddle and a retrieving wire

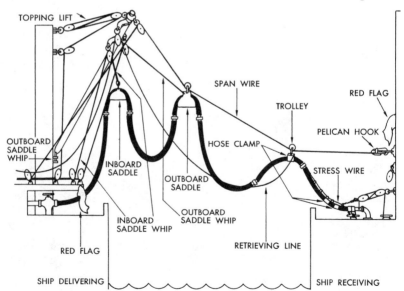

Figure 9–26. Fueling at sea, close-in method.

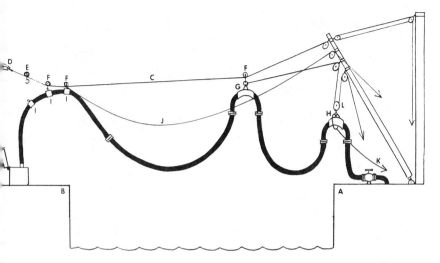

Figure 9–27. Fueling at sea, all-wire span wire method. A, delivering ship; B, receiving ship; C, wire span; D, pelican hook; E, free trolley; G, outboard saddle; H, inboard saddle; I, hose clamps; K, wire pendant; L, wire saddle whip.

line. This method can be used only if there are enough winches at the stations to be rigged. Generally, a minimum of three winches is required. Of the two span wire methods, the all-wire rig is most used.

The Manila Rig. This rig is usually used and is simpler than the all-wire rig, but it requires more men at each station to handle the inboard and outboard saddle whips.

HEAVING THE LEAD

In the old sailing-ship days, a seaman was supposed to be able to "hand, reef, and steer." A few jobs aboard ship are still much the same as they were in the days of sail; one of these is taking soundings, or "heaving the lead." Now ships take soundings electronically, but the lead line is still used, and a seaman should know how to read it.

To make the heave, start by swinging the lead in a fore-and-aft direction outboard of the chains in order to gain momentum. After sufficient momentum has been acquired, the lead is swung in a complete circle over your head. When the force is great enough, let go the lead as it swings forward and at a point about level with the deck.

This makes it fly forward on a line a little above and practically parallel to the deck.

As the ship moves ahead, the spare line is heaved in rapidly. The marker should be read when the lead is on the bottom and the line hauled just taut, up and down.

Ability to heave the lead may be acquired only by practice. It is necessary to practice in both chains, because the right hand is used

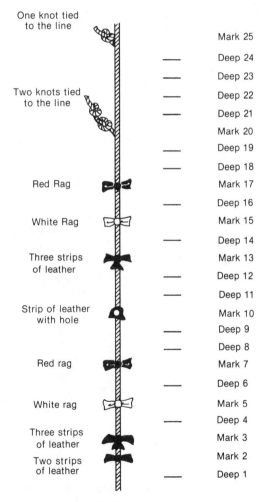

Figure 9–28. Markings of hand lead line.

for heaving from the starboard chain and the left hand for heaving from the port chain.

A good heave has no value unless the depth can be read correctly and quickly. Learn the markings of the line, as shown in figure 9–28.

Also, lead lines are often marked at each half fathom over the range of depth that is most used, and may even have foot marks around the more important depths. Some lead lines are fixed so that the depth may be read at the level of the chain instead of at the water's edge. This makes it simpler to take soundings at night. Learn any special markings of the lead lines that are used on your ship.

When the sounding agrees with one of the markings, it is reported *by the mark*—"By the Mark 7." An even fathom between markings is reported as *by the deep*—"By the Deep 6." If the reading does not give an even fathom, it is reported as "Less a quarter 7" "And a quarter 6" "And a half 6." These reports mean, respectively, that there is ¼ fathom less than 7 fathoms of water, ¼ fathom more than 6, and ½ fathom more than 6. If bottom is not reached, the report "No bottom at 25" is called out.

The lead line may also be used for determining motion of a ship practically dead in the water—the direction of the motion of the ship as shown by the change of direction of the lead line from the up and down. It is also used as a *drift lead* in the same manner to determine if the ship is dragging anchor.

CHAPTER 10
Boathandling

Smart, efficient, and seamanlike boathandling is essential in all operations (figure 10–1). The newer boats in use by the Coast Guard are high-performance craft and require considerable skill and experience to operate properly.

COAST GUARD BOATS

Cutter boats are numbered in accordance with their location on the ship, lower numbers being forward and odd numbers being on the starboard side.

All boats, whether assigned to a cutter or not, have *service numbers* of five digits. The first two digits give the length of the boat and the last three its individual number. Boats with individual numbers of 300 or over are standard to the Coast Guard.

Classes

The Coast Guard uses a wide range of boats, ranging from dinghies and outboard motor boats to amphibious craft. Only a few of them are described and shown in this chapter.

Motor Lifeboats

Motor lifeboats are the standard workhorses of the rescue stations. They are built to withstand the most severe conditions that can be

Figure 10–1. The Coast Guard's new Surf Rescue Boat heading out a coastal inlet on a rough day.

encountered at sea and are capable of effecting a rescue at sea even under the most difficult circumstances. They are self-bailing, self-righting, almost unsinkable, and have an extraordinarily long cruising radius for their size. The standard model motor lifeboat in use today is the 44-foot boat. The modern 44-foot MLB has great speed and power and carries electronics equipment.

Motor Self-bailing Surfboats

These 25-foot boats are also standard equipment on large cutters (figure 10–2). They are not as heavily constructed as the motor lifeboat, but are self-bailing and are rugged indeed. They are designed for all-around assistance work in operations requiring a high degree of maneuverability, such as rescuing persons from the water, in flood operations, and in shallow or obstructed waters.

Motor Buoy Boats

In addition to the five digit number, these boats are identified by the letters "LR." They are beamy, heavily constructed, roundbottom boats built for buoy work in rivers, harbors, and shallow water. Standard buoy boats are 65 feet, 45 feet, and 40 feet in length. Some new boats are jet-propelled.

Figure 10–2. This is an MSB(SV)—motor surfboat, shore version. It is 25 feet 8 inches long.

Motor Launches

Motor launches are found in a variety of shapes and sizes ranging from 16 feet to 40 feet. The classification is usually applied to motor boats assigned to vessels of the Coast Guard as a general utility boat.

Utility Boats

Utility boats are well adapted for such work as patrol, boarding, crash-boat service and rescue missions. Although not capable of withstanding extreme sea conditions, these high-speed craft are quite adequate for operations in moderate seas. They are 30 feet and 41 feet in length.

LCVP (landing craft, vehicle, personnel)

The LCVP was designed to run through the surf to a beach, lower a ramp, unload men or cargo, back off, or retract, through the breakers, and return to the transport or landing ship from which it started. These boats are 36 feet long, with a draft of 12 inches forward and 3½ feet aft, and weigh 8½ tons. They will transport a load of 36 men or 8,100 pounds of cargo at a speed of nearly 10 knots.

Outboard Motorboats

Several types of outboard and out-drive motorboats, mostly under 20 feet in length, are in use for boarding, light rescue and minor aids to navigation work. These may be hauled on trailers to the scene of operations.

Dories, Dinghies and Skiffs

These are small, light, oar-propelled open boats used for miscellaneous duties.

DUKW

The amphibious vehicle commonly known as the "duck" combines the principles of design of a 2½-ton truck with those of the hull of a boat. It can be used on land or water and should be operated in accordance with general principles applicable to vehicles and to water craft, and is especially useful in performing rescue operations off a beach that may be separated from a lifesaving station by a series of inlets cutting through a chain of barrier islands. The DUKW can arrive at the scene much quicker than any boat by utilizing its great land speed in traveling along the beach of each island in the chain. It slows down to its water speed only long enough to cross each inlet.

Surf Rescue Boats

These 30-foot double-ended boats are replacing the 25-foot motor surf-boats and 22-foot motor rescue boats (MRSBs) at rescue stations. The new 30-footer is extremely seaworthy and can handle many of the tasks in surf performed by the 44-foot motor lifeboats.

Barges and Gigs

Boats assigned for the personal use of flag rank officers are called *barges*. Boats used by commanding officers and chiefs of staff not of flag rank are called *gigs*. When an officer embarks in his personal boat, his flag is flown at the bow. Any boat may be assigned this duty.

Boat Equipment and Gear

The equipment supplied with each boat varies with the conditions under which it must operate. Each class of Coast Guard boat comes equipped with certain gear and spare parts that are standard issue.

Figure 10–3. A 32-foot Ports and Waterways Boat, used by Captains of the Port.

Figure 10–4. The 30-foot surf rescue boat (SRB) is a deep-vee, single-screw, diesel-powered, fiberglass reinforced plastic (FRP) boat with self-righting and self-bailing capability. It is designed to accommodate a crew of two and six survivors.

Such equipment ranges from a list of six items (rowlocks, bow painter, oars, etc.) issued with the 10-foot dinghy to a list of more than several hundred articles issued with the larger motor boats. Standard lists for the larger motor boats include engine spare parts, tools, bilge pump, binoculars, navigational equipment, etc. *Boat Outfit Lists* itemize the articles of equipment recommended for each standard service boat. At shore stations, conditions of use may require modification of the list, and this may be accomplished by the commanding officer or officer in charge of the unit. A check should be made at frequent intervals to ensure that all equipment required for the proper operation of the boat is aboard. Lives may depend on this.

The Boat Box

Boats attached to a cutter have, in addition to the gear mentioned above, a boat box. These chests are made to fit under the thwarts and should be kept there at all times, except that when the boats are stowed the chests may be removed and stowed aboard ship in a location where they are readily available for replacing. The equipment carried in these chests includes carpenter's, rigger's, and sailmaker's tools; materials, lantern, matches, signal flags, and flares; fishing gear, sounding lead, and other items that would be necessary or useful in an emergency or in case the boat became separated from its unit for a longer period of time than anticipated. In addition to the boat box, each boat carries a medical kit, water breaker, emergency rations, and lifejackets.

Boat Crews

A good crew is the most important "standard equipment" a boat can have. Necessarily, the crew for a power boat and a pulling boat differ materially, but the fundamental duty of the coxswain is the same in each case. He is in charge of the boat and handles the steering mechanism, whether it be steering oar, tiller, or wheel.

Power boats have, in addition, an engineer whose duty is to handle the engines, and usually two men, one for the bow line (painter) and one for the stern line (stern fast). These men also tend the fenders and serve as lookouts.

Boatkeepers

Aboard a cutter, two men are selected as boatkeepers for each boat each day. Both men turn to and clean their boat during the morning watch so that she is ready by 0800. After 0800, one boatkeeper is on duty at a time. He must be in clean uniform of the day. If the boat is at the boom, the boatkeeper is usually aboard her from morning colors until sunset, except that in bad weather the officer of the deck may order him aboard ship. However, the boatkeeper remains in a position from which he can observe his boat. Boatkeepers do not lounge or read while on duty. They must be constantly on the alert to guard their boat from damage, to keep its gear in place, and to clean it as often as necessary.

Lifeboats

While at sea, cutters always carry two boats, those most suitable for lifeboat duty, rigged out in position for immediate lowering, one boat on each side. (Some very small cutters only use one lifeboat.) Men assigned as lifeboat crew members must be thoroughly familiar with their duties and ready to take their stations on the run when called.

Lowering Lifeboats at Sea

The crew mans the boat and dons lifejackets. Men on deck, who man the falls, frapping lines, sea painter, fenders, etc., take their stations. Boats are carried in davits, standard types of which are shown in figure 10–5. When all is ready, the gripes are tripped and cleared away and

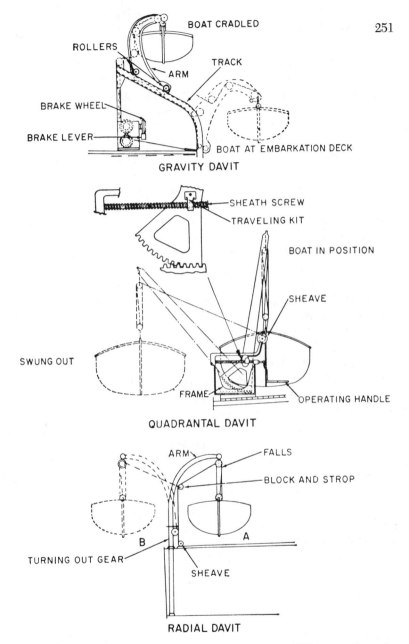

GRAVITY DAVIT

BOAT CRADLED

ROLLERS

ARM

TRACK

BRAKE WHEEL

BRAKE LEVER

BOAT AT EMBARKATION DECK

QUADRANTAL DAVIT

SHEATH SCREW

TRAVELING KIT

BOAT IN POSITION

SHEAVE

SWUNG OUT

FRAME

OPERATING HANDLE

RADIAL DAVIT

ARM

FALLS

BLOCK AND STROP

TURNING OUT GEAR

SHEAVE

B

A

Figure 10–5. Standard types of boat davits. Hoisting and lowering boats by davits requires close teamwork between boat crew and deck force.

fenders lowered. Men in the boat must grasp the knotted lifelines firmly until the boat is waterborne, so that they will not be lost overboard if the boat drops out from under them. Frapping lines are passed around the falls and tended on deck. (Frapping lines prevent the boat from swinging while being lowered.) Members of the boat's crew stand by the releasing hooks of the falls fore and aft to release them at the command of the coxswain. One member of the boat's crew stands by the sea painter ready to release it.

At the command *"Lower away together,"* men manning the falls lower away smartly to a position where the boat is just clear of the tops of the seas. The command *"Let fall"* is then given at the right moment so the boat will be dropped on the crest of a sea. At this command the men on deck let the falls go on the run. When the boat is waterborne, the coxswain orders the *after* falls released first, and then the *forward* falls. At this point the boat is sheered away from the ship's side by use of the sea painter and steering sweep.

Once the boat is clear of the ship's side, the sea painter is released and the boat proceeds on its mission.

Hoisting Lifeboats at Sea

This procedure is practically a repeat of the lowering procedure, *in reverse*. The sea painter is passed from the ship to the boat and secured in the boat. The coxswain then veers the boat under the falls, using the sea painter and rudder. The *forward* fall is hooked first, then the *after* fall. When the falls are hooked and secured, the slack is taken up, and at the command *"Hoist away,"* the deck crew hoists the boat with the utmost speed possible.

Prior to the boat's return to the ship, the deck crew makes full preparations to hoist in without delay; frapping lines are passed, fenders manned, sea painter made ready to pass to the boat, falls led out and all hoisting stations manned.

Notes on handling boats alongside at sea:

Always check the boat plug when the crew first mans the boat.
Always release the *after* falls first when leaving a ship, and hook the *forward* falls first when returning. (A capsize will almost surely result if this rule is not followed.)
Keep your hands off the gunwales. If the boat hits the side of the ship you can lose part or all of your hand.

Heavier power boats also can be lowered and hoisted at sea. Where they are swung from davits, as is the standard practice on large cutters, exactly the same procedure is followed as is used in lowering and hoisting lighter boats. Because of much greater weight, they must be hoisted by the use of a winch. Sometimes motorboats are lowered and hoisted with a winch and boom. When this method is used it is necessary to lead guy lines forward, aft, and sometimes across the ship to prevent the boat from swinging wildly because of the roll of the ship.

Fuel

Most Coast Guard motorboats are powered by diesel engines. However, many gasoline outboard engines are also in use. Gasoline is a highly inflammable, volatile liquid that must be handled with great caution. Diesel fuel, while not as inflammable or volatile as gasoline, is still dangerous, and a boat crew must never develop a false sense of security just because their boat is diesel-propelled. These safety precautions should be followed with both types of fuel.

Power boats should be in the water when fueling.

Engines must be stopped.

No passengers on board while fueling.

No smoking in vicinity of fueling operation.

Have man stand by with CO_2 extinguisher while fueling.

Whenever any fuel is spilled in the bilge or any other place on board, sluice it out at once, pump, and then wipe dry.

Spaces where fuel vapors might accumulate must be ventilated, especially before starting engine.

Compartments and bilges must be cleared of all vapors by use of blower before starting engines and after every fueling.

Except in emergency, no fueling at night.

Always use grounding clips when fueling from hose.

Never fuel boat directly from a drum.

Be careful not to spill fuel and pollute the surrounding water.

Motorboat Handling

The following factors should be considered in handling motorboats:

Normal Effect of the Rudder. When the steering wheel is turned to the right, or the tiller moved to the left, the boat's head is swung to the right if the boat is moving ahead.

Screw Current. With the screw turning ahead, the normal rudder effect is greatly increased due to increased pressure exerted by the water expelled from the screw. When the screw is turning astern, the water expelled from it moves in the reverse direction; hence the result is to lessen the effectiveness of the rudder if the boat is going ahead. However, in the latter case this effect is very slight.

Sidewise Pressure of Screw Blades. As the blades turn, they tend to push the stern in the opposite direction from that in which they are moving. Fortunately, upper and lower blades exert this force in opposite directions. However, there is a difference in water pressure at the top and the bottom of the screw equal roughly to a half-pound for each foot of the diameter of the screw. The lower blades are moving in greater water pressure and therefore exert more sidewise thrust. For this reason, when standard service boats are going ahead, the stern tends to swing to starboard. The reverse effect is noted when going astern. The effect of the sidewise pressure of the blades is hardly noticeable when going ahead. Going astern, there is a strong tendency for the stern to swing to port. For this reason single-screw boats should always make portside landings if possible.

Effect of Wind. The wind has a decided effect on a boat, especially at slow speed. If the bow is high out of the water, it will be difficult to turn into the wind, as the sail area of the bow will have a "wind rudder" effect opposite to that of the rudder. This situation can be helped by increasing the bow weight—a process called "trimming." Despite trim, if the wind is strong and the boat is going astern, her stern will come up into the wind in spite of anything you can do.

Effect of Current. If stopped, the boat will float with the current like a cork. When running, the course made good is a resultant of this motion and the motion imparted to the boat by the effects of screw, rudder, and wind.

Safety Precautions for Power Boats

Have the crew at stations when under way.
Keep crew and passengers off the gunwale.
No "skylarking" in the boat.
Use lifejackets, or have them handy.
Considering sea conditions, avoid overloading.
Approach docks slowly.
Don't take navigational chances.
Observe the Rules of the Road.

Engine Signals

If the coxswain of a boat does not have direct control of the engine, he may have to signal the engineer as follows:

1 bell —Ahead slow.
2 bells—Engine idling, clutch out.
3 bells—Back slow.
4 bells—Full speed in direction propeller is turning when signal is given.

In addition to working with boats, a seaman must be familiar with all the other topside gear aboard ship, such as booms and cranes, capstans and winches, ground tackle, rigging, and cargo-handling gear. A single ship will not have all such equipment, but all ships will have some of it. Check chapter 8 for details.

Small Boat Operations in a Surf

Not all Coast Guardsmen will find themselves in a small boat in a broken sea or in surf. But those Coast Guard people assigned to coastal SAR units will experience that situation many times during their tour of duty.

The Coast Guard specializes in the kind of operation that sends a small boat out to sea in bad weather and then brings it back, usually in worse weather conditions. Coast Guard boats are designed with these operations in mind, but situations can and do develop where the weather exceeds the design of the boat. The safety of the crew and the boat then rests on the surfmanship of the boat coxswain, assisted by his crew.

The greatest danger when running before a broken sea is that of broaching to. In this situation your utmost attention must be directed to proper boat handling.

What causes a boat to broach to when her motion is in the same direction as that of the sea? She opposes no resistance to it, but is carried before it. Thus, the effect of a surf or wave, when overtaking her, is to throw the stern up and depress the bow. If she does not have sufficient inertia (proportional to her weight) to allow the sea to pass under her she is in an unsafe mode.

If a boat being overtaken by a heavy surf or sea is in the unsafe mode described, her stern is raised high in the air and the wave carries her before it on the front, or unsafe side. The bow, being deeply immersed in the hollow of the sea, where the water is fairly stationary, offers resistance while the crest of the sea having motion which causes it to break, forces the stern onward. If the buoyancy is lost forward, while the sea presses on the stern, the boat will be thrown end-over-end (pitchpoled). Or, if the buoyancy forward is such as the 44' motor lifeboat, which inhibits the bow from being submerged, the resistance forward acting on one bow, may slightly turn the boat's head, and the force of the surf would then be transferred to the opposite quarter. This can cause the boat to be thrown broadside (broach to), and possibly capsize.

Much information is available on surf conditions and procedures to follow on open beaches. This is not the case for inlets and bars, although there are some publications that address the subject in part. Below are some primary rules for running before a broken sea or surf. However, no set of rules will provide you with the knowledge and skill required to run before a broken sea or surf. Only through study and understanding of available material, training and practice—coupled with local knowledge—can a coxswain achieve the necessary skill.

Primary Rules

1. Know your boat. Can it match the speed of the sea? If not, can it be maneuvered to let the overtaking sea pass under it. "When in doubt, stay out!"

2. Once the decision is made to enter, stand off and observe the wave trains. Wait until a big one has broken or spent its force and then run through behind it.

3. Position your boat on the back side of a wave (adjust your speed accordingly), staying clear of any breakers fore and aft.

4. Do not overtake the wave. If you do, you will get caught on the dangerous front side.

5. Keep your boat's stern square to the following sea.

6. If a sea begins to overtake you, slow down and let it pass under you and break ahead of you. "Stay out of the curl!"

Towing Operations

Coast Guard boats often end up towing another disabled vessel to safety. Towing is an evolution requiring teamwork for efficient and safe execution. In order to perform towing in a seamanlike and safe manner, personnel *must* be knowledgeable in the fundamentals of towing. Towing preparations vary widely because there are no two tows exactly alike; preparations required include determining the approach, inspecting the tow, the towing bridles, and the towline and applying chafing gear. With knowledge of the fundamentals of towing and experience you will be able to employ the best method of towing and avoid exceeding the stress limitations of your towline, your boat, and that of the boat being towed while performing the towing evolution safely in a professional manner.

Forces Exerted on Towlines (see figure 10–6)

A. Forces encountered in towing are placed into two (2) classifications:
  1. Static
  2. Dynamic
B. These forces act upon:
  1. Towing boat
  2. Towed boat
  3. Deck fittings
  4. Towline and bridles
C. *Static force* is encountered *before and as* the towed vessel begins to move and is minimized by beginning the tow slowly and gradually building up to towing speed.
D. *Dynamic force* is encountered from the time the boats are under way and is continuous until towing speed is reached and during the tow. Dynamic force is caused by any combination or all of the following:

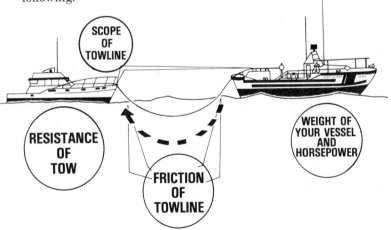

Figure 10–6. Forces exerted on a towline.

1. Frictional resistance, the resistance of the boat's hull to the water immediately next to the hull as the boat moves along the water.
2. Shockloads caused by intermittent force due to waves and/or sea state as the towed boat rides over the seas. Shockloading varies with the frequency of the height of the seas, the speed of the boat, and the *length of the towline.*

The towline is the transmission line connecting all the forces to both boats.

Towline

A. The towline is the most important piece of gear used in the towing rig. A towline leads aft to the tow—not in a straight line, but with a dip in the line termed a catenary. This catenary serves two very important purposes, which are as follows:
   1. It acts as a reserve length of line that prevents the towline from coming up short and taut during periods of surging between your boat and the tow.
   2. Because of the additional weight of line that makes up the catenary, a towline possesses a certain amount of spring and acts as a shock absorber that tends to absorb the energy (shockloads) as a result of the surging on the towline.

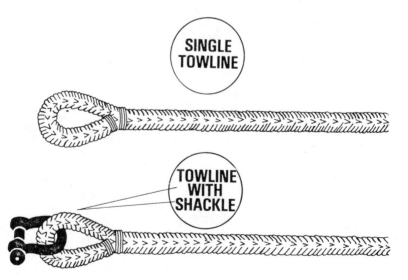

Figure 10–7. Makeup of towlines.

B. In towing it is important to keep both boats in step; adjust the scope of towline so that your boat and tow ride over the seas at the same time (crest to crest) and with at least two wave lengths apart. If one boat is in the trough of a wave while the other is on the crest, the towline will become slack and then become taut with a sudden jerk (jumping the line). Forces exerted on the towline can exceed the tensile strength (breaking strength) of the line. To reduce the strain on the towline it may be necessary to accomplish one or all of the following:

1. Reduce your towing speed;

2. Provide more scope in the towline to provide more spring (catenary);

3. Alter course, quartering the seas.

Passing a Towline

There are four basic approaches that can be used for passing a towline:

1. Crossing the T;

2. The 45° approach;

3. The parallel approach; and

4. The back-down approach.

Any approach used improperly can ruin your day, but number 4 (the back-down) is almost sure to get you into trouble—it should be

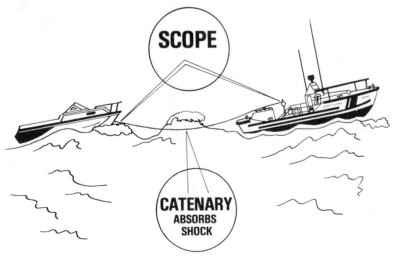

Figure 10–8. Action of the catenary.

reserved for tow trucks, not boats. The tow truck can nicely take a fore-and-aft position in front of a disabled car, back down and stop. The operator can get out, walk aft, pay out the towing rig, hook up and then get back in his truck and drive off. You can't do all that in a boat—besides, you have the screws of the boat ready and waiting to chew up the line if you back down into it.

In addition to that the coxswain just can't see what is happening back aft in most boats. Therefore, the back-down approach is a "No! No!"

One of the first three approaches should be selected depending on the circumstances. Each of these:

A. Keeps you moving forward during maneuver—not backing down;

B. Allows the coxswain and crew to keep an eye on the line;

C. Permits the coxswain to maneuver the towing boat into a fore-and-aft alignment *after* the line has been passed, secured to the towed vessel, and tension has brought the towline clear of the water or to a proper catenary as required.

Towing Check List

1. Assemble and check-out required equipment.

2. Establish communications with the disabled vessel—determine its material condition and the physical condition of persons on board.

3. Consider existing and forecast weather, currents, tidal effects, and sea state for the present position and destination of the tow.

4. Maintain a navigational plot.

5. Determine the relative advantages of placing Coast Guardsmen on board the disabled vessel and/or removing the persons on board. Direct persons on disabled vessel to don PFDs.

6. Determine the best approach to the disabled vessel, brief crew and persons on the disabled vessel on hook-up and breakaway procedures.

7. If no communications exist, provide a portable radio where possible. Otherwise establish visual or sound signals with persons on board the disabled vessel.

8. Ensure that the helm of the disabled vessel is manned.

9. When getting under way: Ensure that there is a proper catenary in towline, keep vessels in step, increase speed slowly.

10. Set towing watch, observe action of tow, select heading or course that minimizes strain on gear and towed vessel.

11. If at night: Illuminate tow, display proper towing lights.

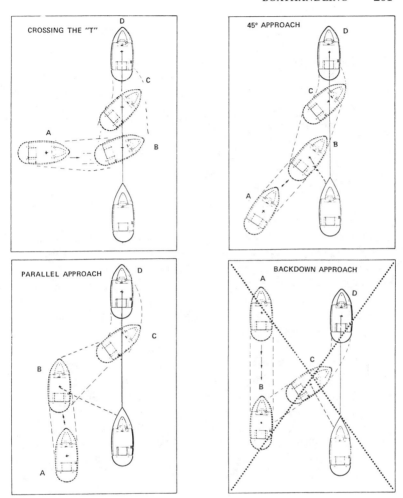

Figure 10–9. Four methods of approaching tow. (A) Approaching. (B) Passing hawser and hooking up the tow (maintaining hawser angle from 090° R to 120° R). (C) Commence towing slowly until the hawser is clear of the water (maintaining hawser angle from 110° R to 135° R). (D) Adjusting course, hawser, and speed as necessary (maintaining hawser angle from 170° R to 190° R.

12. Considerations for transiting bars or inlets: Determine conditions—when in doubt, stay out, request back-up/escort boat, consider removal of persons on board the towed boat; advise home unit of conditions and plan of action; consider use of drogue; adjust towline

as necessary to keep in step while transiting; adjust speed as conditions warrant.

13. When in protected area: Shorten tow as necessary for safe navigation or take tow alongside.

14. When docking towed vessel: Slow down to just enough speed to maintain steerageway and be aware of set and drift; advise disabled vessel of docking plan and/or release of towline.

Towing with the 44' Motor Lifeboat

Recent reports have revealed that a few 44' MLB crews are faking the towing hawser on top of the "turtle" prior to making up a tow. This procedure has several serious drawbacks, one of which is that it greatly increases the chances of fouling the towing hawser in the screws. Another factor to consider is that since working the hawser from the turtle requires a man to be between the towing bit and the towed vessel, the line handler could easily be knocked overboard. The proper method of handling the towline is from the well deck, working the line off the beam and not over the stern. Working off the beam from the well deck greatly reduces the risk of losing a crewman overboard, and also reduces the opportunity to foul the screws.

The 41-foot Utility Boat (UTB)

While the Coast Guard operates many kinds of boats, the 41' UTB is probably the most widely used boat at operational shore units. Many of the characteristics of the 41' UTB apply as well to other boats the Coast Guard operates. Each crew member on every Coast Guard boat should be familiar with the boat in which he or she serves. The guidelines for handling a 41' UTB are important information, not only for 41' UTB coxswains, but for every Coast Guardsman who ever serves in a boat crew.

The 41' UTB is a V-bottom boat with a modified planing hull, constructed of aluminum and fiberglass. It is powered by twin diesel engines. When all systems are working properly, the 41' UTB can easily be operated by one person in the coxswain seat. Twin screws render the boat easily maneuverable; the experienced coxswain can steer, turn, and dock this boat with minimal recourse to rudder controls. Like all boats, however, it is a product of compromises and contradictory effects. Utility boats are designed for speed in relatively smooth water. They are designed with wide transoms for working space and planing lift. Such features, necessary for normal missions, can easily

Figure 10–10. A 44-foot motor life boat. These rugged boats are a mainstay at coastal rescue stations.

be disadvantages in some situations. Use the positive features, but be aware of possible negative reactions and control them or turn them to your advantage.

Speed. The maximum speed of the 41′ UTB is 25-27 knots, depending on engine tuning and operating conditions. However, you should never exceed 90 percent of your boat's capability during normal operations; extra power is the boat's main defense in most threatening situations. If you are at full throttle, you have already squandered half your resources if an emergency should then arise.

Stopping. In an extreme situation, the boat can be stopped very quickly by moving the throttles directly from ahead to full astern. Tests in 45 feet of water showed the boat able to stop from full ahead, within a space of seventy feet, elapsed time approximately 3 to 4 seconds. *Warning: Never use this procedure except in a dire emergency. Each time, some engine and gear damage is likely, and personal injury is possible.*

Weathervaning. The 41′ UTB has a tendency to back into the wind, due to its high superstructure in the fore part. If you sit dead in the

Figure 10–11. A 41-foot utility boat on patrol during the President's Cup Regatta on the Potomac River in Washington, D.C.

water, any breeze will cause the boat to pivot on its propellers until the bow points in the direction the wind is blowing.

Following Seas or Surf. Very careful handling is required when running in a following sea. The 41′ tends to slip down the back of seas and heel strongly; when stern seas exceed 8 feet, the rudder is rather sluggish. If at all possible, avoid running directly before a swell; quarter the seas. The boat's small well deck makes swamping much less likely than in earlier boats where the well deck included the engine spaces, but the possibility is not eliminated.

In waves with a wide, regular pattern, ride the back of the swell. Never let the boat ride on the front of a wave. The UTB's wide, flat stern is more buoyant than the bow and the boat may begin to surf; pushed along on the front of the wave, the boat's tendency will be to dig in at the bow (and pitchpole) or come broadside to the wave (and broach).

Warning: Avoid breaking waves and surf. The 41′ UTB will take a 75° list, far more than other UTBs. However, once past this point, it will capsize. Any close, steep swells will test all your skills. The combination of a sluggish rudder in heavy stern seas, the sail effect of your superstructure, and irregular wave action can easily cause your stern

Figure 10–12. A 30-foot utility boat under way. Utility boats serve in a variety of situations, including search and rescue and law enforcement.

to fall off at a critical moment, resulting in broaching. This boat is not self-righting.

In following seas, a planing boat such as the 41-footer should, where possible, travel as fast as the seas, to prevent seas breaking over the stern. Avoid jumping over crests, for your vision ahead is lost as the bow drops into the trough. If you have to jump a crest, open the throttle as you reach the crest of the wave, to dig in and raise the bow. Close the throttle as you pass the trough, to allow the next swell to lift you and pass more quickly.

Head Seas. Slow down and approach head seas at a slight angle; be prepared to straighten out quickly, to prevent a large wave from pushing you broadside. Adjust your speed as necessary to keep the propellers in the water. This minimizes strain on the hull and allows you to maintain control of the boat; time your progress so that the bow rises to meet the swells. At maximum sea conditions, eight feet and over, the coxswain must maneuver constantly.

Use only enough power to break through the crest; then cut back power to let the boat fall on the back side of the swell. Increase speed as the next wave approaches, to repeat the cycle.

Avoid at all costs, "flying through" the crest; if you are airborne on the back of a wave, severe stresses are placed on the hull and crew as you land; serious injuries are likely. Neither you nor the boat can survive repeated flights of this kind.

Beam Seas. If your course is broadside to heavy swells, tack across at a slight angle, zigzag fashion. Make each tack as long as possible, adjusting for the safest, most comfortable angle. In turning back, allow the boat to lose headway, then wheel hard over and apply power. The less time your stern faces the waves, the better.

Ice Operations. Warning: Avoid ice except in emergencies.

The UTB was not designed as an icebreaker, and the resulting hull stress will shorten the life of the boat, even if the hull is not penetrated.

If you *must* enter an ice field, proceed very cautiously and never exceed 700 RPM. The boat will break ice up to 1½" without much difficulty.

Caution: Operating in ice requires a crewman in the engine space; slush clogs sea strainers every 3-5 minutes, and they must be continuously shifted and cleaned.

The boat is slowed markedly by 2" ice, and will be stopped dead in the water by field ice over 3" thick. It should be noted that the only way to tell the difference between 1" ice and 4" ice is by "feel" or by looking at broken ice at the stern of the boat. Since 4" ice can easily cause severe hull damage, feel your way carefully if you must enter ice.

CHAPTER 11

Communications

Communication is defined as an exchange of information. That includes radiomen sending and receiving dispatches and signalmen making flaghoists, but it also includes people talking to people. Messages, signals, conversations, and written reports are all communications. The bow lookout using a sound-powered telephone to report to the bridge is communicating, just as the OOD using the TBS to advise another ship of a course change is communicating. The lookout is using *internal* communications, and the OOD is using *external* communications; all communications can be classified as one or the other.

INTERNAL COMMUNICATIONS

Internal communications are those that take place within a ship or a shore-based unit. They can include everything from "passing the word" over the MC circuits, to using "squawk boxes," the sound-powered telephone system (figure 11–1), regular dial phones, bell and buzzer systems, boat gongs, or messengers. Internal communications also mean printed or written material such as the plan of the day, visual display systems such as the rudder angle indicator and engine order telegraph on the bridge, the plot in CIC, and even the "On Board-Ashore" display board for officers at the quarterdeck. Everyone must keep tuned in to the internal communications system at all times.

Figure 11–1. Communications—flag hoist, blinker light, and radio antenna—the heart of the cutter's operations.

Passing the Word

Before PA systems were developed, information or orders for the crew were passed by a boatswain's mate, who first sounded the appropriate call and then repeated "the word," fore and aft throughout the ship. Now, on the 1MC system the word is broadcast all over the ship at once. An announcement is usually preceded with "Now hear this," or "Now hear there," unless a boatswain's call is used. When a boatswain's call (or pipe) is used, "All hands" is piped before any word concerning drills and emergencies, and "Attention" before routine words. Common shipboard events are listed here, with the appropriate words following each one:

Air Bedding. "All divisions, air bedding."

Arrivals and Departures. (Title of officer, preceded by proper number of boat gongs.)

Boats. "Away, the motor whaleboat (gig, barge), away."

Church Call. "Divine services are now being held in (location). Maintain quiet about the decks during divine services."

Eight O'clock Reports. "On deck all eight o'clock reports."

Extra Duty Men. "Lay up to the quarterdeck for muster, all extra duty men (or other special group)."

Fire. "Fire! Fire! (state location, including deck, frame, and side)."

Flight Quarters. "Flight quarters. Flight quarters. Man all flight quarters stations to launch (recover) aircraft (helicopters)."

General Quarters. "General quarters! General quarters! All hands man battle stations."

Hoist Boats. "First division stand by to hoist in (out) number ——— — motor launch (gig)."

Idlers. "Up all idlers." (At sea.)

Inspection (personnel). "All hands to quarters for captain's personnel inspection."

Inspection (material). "Stand by all lower deck and topside spaces for inspection."

Knock Off Work (before noon meal). "Knock off all ship's work." (First pipe "All hands.")

Knock Off Work (before evening meal). "Knock off all ship's work. Shift into the uniform of the day." (First pipe "All hands.")

Late Bunks. "Up all late bunks."

Liberty. "Liberty to commence for the (first) and (third) sections at 1600; to expire on board at (hour, date, month)."

Mail. "Mail call."

Meals. "All hands, pipe to breakfast (noon meal or dinner; evening meal or supper)." (First pipe "Mess call.")

Mess Gear (call). "Mess gear (call). Clear the (all) mess decks." (First pipe "Mess call.")

Mistake or Error. "Belay that last word."

Muster on Stations. "All divisions muster on stations."

Pay. "The crew is now being paid in the mess hall."

Preparations for Getting Under Way. "Make all preparations for getting under way."

Quarters for Muster. "All hands to quarters for muster."

Quarters for Muster (inclement weather). "All hands to quarters for muster. Foul weather parade." (First pipe "All hands.")

Rain Squall. "Haul over all hatch hoods and gun covers."

Readiness for Getting Underway Reports. "All departments, make readiness for getting underway reports to the officer of the deck on the bridge."

Relieving the Watch. "Relieve the watch. On deck the ——— section. Lifeboat crew on deck to muster. Relieve the wheel and lookouts." (First pipe "Attention.")

Rescue and Assistance. "Away rescue and assistance party, ——— section."

Reveille. "Reveille. Reveille, all hands heave out and trice (lash) up." Or "Reveille. Up all hands, trice up all bunks." (First pipe "All hands.")

Shifting the Watch. "The officer of the deck is shifting his watch to the bridge (quarterdeck)."

Side Boys. "Lay up on the quarterdeck, the side boys."

Smoking. "The smoking lamp is lighted (out)." (Unless the word applies to the whole ship, the location should be specified.)

Special Sea Detail. "Go to (man) your stations, all the special sea detail." Or "Station the special sea detail."

Sweepers. "Sweepers, start (man) your brooms. Make a clean sweep down fore and aft." (First pipe "Sweepers.")

Taps. "Taps. Lights out. All hands turn in to your bunks and keep silence about the decks. Smoking lamp is out in all living spaces." (First pipe "Pipe down.")

Turn to. "Turn to (Scrub down all weather decks) (Scrub all canvas) (Sweep down compartments) (Dump trash)."

Under way. See *Preparations* and *Readiness.*

Sound-Powered Telephones

These phones are used on all ships. They do not require outside electrical power; the user's voice acts on a carbon-filled cell and diaphragm to generate enough current to power the circuit. All handset phones look much like ordinary desk telephones and are used for routine ship's business; headset phones are somewhat more complicated and are used for drills and exercises. The handset phone has a button on the bar between receiver and mouthpiece that must be depressed to talk or listen. On the headset phone this button is in the top of the mouthpiece.

The headset phone consists of a headband that holds receivers over the ears, a breastplate supported by a cloth neckstrap, and a yoke that holds the transmitter in front of the mouth. The phone has a lead, which may be up to 50 feet long, ending in a jack that plugs into a jackbox connected to the circuit.

To use the phone, hold the entire unit in the left hand, then unhook the right side of the neckstrap from the breastplate, run it around your neck, and hook it back to the breastplate. Put the headband over your head, adjust the earphones, push the jack into the jackbox, and turn the collar up tight to make a good connection. Adjust the mouthpiece so it is about one inch from your lips. Be careful in all adjustments not to break any cords running into the function block. Remember that with the phones on you can go no farther than the length of the cord. Keep the cord slack so it lies flat on deck and will not trip anyone; don't get yourself twisted around a piece of equipment.

Testing

Always test the phone immediately; press the mouthpiece button and transmit (for example: "Bridge, fantail, testing"). If the phone does not work, immediately notify the person in charge of your station; use a spare phone if one is available. Never turn an earphone away from your head; it will pick up and transmit all noise in the area and drown out the circuit. If the mouthpiece is damaged, you can talk through one earphone and listen through the other; if both earphones become damaged, you can talk and listen through the mouthpiece.

Securing

Remove the jack from the jackbox by holding it in one hand and backing off the collar with the other. When the collar is free, pull the jack out.

Don't pull on the lead cord or drop or bang the jack or you will have a bad connection the next time you use the phone. Replace the jackbox cover finger-tight, otherwise dust, dirt, and salt-air corrosion will soon short circuit the jackbox.

To make up the phone, remove the headband and drape it over the yoke, then coil the lead cord beginning from the headset, making 10-inch clockwise loops in one hand. Next, remove the headpiece from the yoke and hold it with the lead cord; hold the mouthpiece in the same hand. Unhook the neckstrap from the breastplate, fold the yoke flat (being careful not to bend the mouthpiece cord) and wrap the strap around the coiled cord and the headband, leaving a short end that hooks to the breastplate again.

The phone should now be in a compact package, ready to hand up or stow in the storage box provided at the station. Be careful not to crowd or jam any cords.

Caution—Remember that the jack must always be unplugged when the phone is not in use, otherwise the phone will transmit any noises through the circuit. Don't lay the phone on deck for the same reason; besides, someone could step on it.

Telephone Circuits

Sound-powered phones are hooked up in circuits, according to their use. Most ships will have these circuits:

JA	Captain's battle control
JC	Ordnance control
JF	Flag officer
1JG	Aircraft control
JL	Battle lookouts
2JC	Dual-purpose battery control
1JS	Sonar control
1JV	Maneuvering, docking, catapult control
JW	Ship control, navigation
JX	Radio and signals
JZ	Damage control

Every outlet on a circuit will have a number. Some circuits may have auxiliary circuits; these have the same letter designation, prefixed by an X. All circuits feed into main switchboards where more than one can be tied together, or certain stations on a circuit can be cut out.

Telephone Technique

The way you talk in ordinary conversation is not the way to use a telephone. The person on the other end of the line cannot see you, he may not know you, and he may be unfamiliar with the things you say. Telephone talkers must speak clearly, be specific, and act businesslike; they are not on the circuit for social chitchat. Follow these suggestions:

Use a strong, calm voice. Speak slowly, pronounce words carefully.
Don't mumble, run things together, or talk with gum or a cigarette in your mouth.
Use standard terms and phraseology. Avoid slang or "in" words.
When transmitting numbers and letters, use approved communication procedure. The expression "Item 5C" may sound like "Item 9D," but "Fi-yuv Charlie" will not be mistaken for "Niner Delta."

Circuit Discipline

Circuits are like a "party line"—everyone can talk, and listen, at the same time. To prevent such a confusing state of affairs, strict circuit discipline must be maintained.

Send only official messages.
Keep the button on the *off* position except when actually talking.
Do not leave your station or engage in other work or pastimes without permission.
Use only standard phraseology.
Never show anger, impatience, or excitement.

Each phone talker is a key link in the ship's interior communications chain. Unauthorized talking means that the chain is weakened. Don't do it; don't permit it.

Circuit Testing

To find out if stations on the circuit are manned and ready, the control station talker says:
"All stations, control, testing."
Each talker then acknowledges in the assigned order (or sequence). Here's how it would go on a gun circuit:

Gun one—"One, aye, aye."
Gun two—"Two, aye, aye."

Gun three—"Three, aye, aye."

Normally each station answers up in order, but does not wait more than a few seconds if the station ahead of it fails to acknowledge. If you are on gun three, and gun two fails to answer up, acknowledge for your gun. Gun two then can come in at the end.

The test is not complete until each station has answered and any equipment faults have been checked.

Message Form

Most messages have three parts: the name of the station being called, the name of the station calling, and the information to be sent. This order must always be followed. Call the station the message is for, identify your own station, then transmit the message. Remember this order: *who to, who from, what about.* If you are on the anchor detail and want to call the bridge, the message is "Bridge (who to), forecastle (who from), anchor secured (what about)."

Messages are acknowledged when understood by identifying the station and adding "Aye, aye." This lets the sender know the message has been received by the station he sent it to, and that it is understood. If you don't understand, ask for a repeat. If the sender wants to make certain an important message has been received correctly, he may ask you to repeat it back to him.

Sending a Message

First name the station being called. Next name the station doing the calling. Then the message:

"Bridge, forecastle; anchor ready for letting go."

Receiving a Message

First, identify your own station; then acknowledge for the message. If your station is the forecastle, and the bridge has just ordered the anchor "let go," acknowledge with "Forecastle, aye, aye."

Sometimes there are three or four steps involved, for example:

"Forecastle, bridge; how many lines are to the pier?" If you don't know, you say, "Forecastle, aye, aye; wait."

After getting the desired information, call the bridge:

"Bridge, Forecastle; five lines to the pier."

The bridge will acknowledge:

"Bridge, aye, aye."

Requesting Repeats

If an incoming message is not clear, the receiving station says "Repeat." When the message is repeated and understood, the receiving station acknowledges by repeating the name of the second station and adding "Aye, aye."

Spelling Words

Difficult or little-known words are spelled out, using the phonetic alphabet: "Stand by to receive officer from NASA. I spell NOVEMBER ALFA SIERRA ALFA—NASA.

Securing the Phones

Never secure until you have permission from the control station:
Forecastle—"Bridge, forecastle; permission to secure?"
Bridge—"Bridge, aye, aye; wait."
The bridge talker learns that the forecastle may secure; he says:
"Forecastle, Bridge; you may secure."
"Forecastle, aye, aye; securing."
Remember to make the phones up properly and stow them before leaving your station.

Squawk Boxes

Intercommunication voice (MC) units, or "squawk boxes," are installed in most important stations of most ships. They are normally used only by officers, and should be limited to emergency use if paralleled by sound-powered telephones. No matter who uses the MC system, circuit discipline and standard phone talker's procedure must be observed. A complete list of MC circuits follows.

Circuit Announcing System

	One-way system
1MC	Battle and general
2MC	Engineers
4MC	Damage control
6MC	Boat control
11MC	Turret
16MC	Turret
17MC	Antiaircraft
18MC	Bridge

Two-way system
Two-way system

19MC Readyroom
21MC Captain's command
22MC Radio room
23MC Distribution control
24MC Flag officer's command
25MC Wardroom
26MC Machinery control
27MC Sonar control
29MC Sonar information
31MC Escape trunk

EXTERNAL COMMUNICATIONS

External communications are all those between a ship and another ship, aircraft, or command whether it is afloat or on shore. They may be visual—flaghoist, semaphore, signal searchlight or blinker; sound—whistles, bells, foghorns; or even a gun (for distress signal); physical delivery—guard mail, officer-messenger mail, and U.S. mail; and electrical and electronic—CW and voice radio, TTP, FAX, RATT, telegraph and telephone when possible to hook into shore circuits, and even walkie-talkie radios.

With ships operating 24 hours a day around the world, there must be rapid, accurate communications, not only for tactical and strategic control in war time, but also for administrative and logistic purposes at all times. No ship is ever out of touch with its base of operations or its tactical, type, or administrative commander.

Visual Signals

Visual signals began centuries ago, when flags and pennants were given special meanings. Columbus hoisted a lantern in the rigging to let his ships know land had been sighted. Even with dozens of radios on a ship, visual signals are still used extensively, especially in fleet operations, for two reasons—speed and security. Radio messages may be intercepted by anyone with a receiver, perhaps hundreds of miles away. Visual signals are limited to line-of-sight transmissions—the receiver and sender have to be where they can see each other—and do not require complicated equipment.

The three main systems of visual signals are: flashing light, semaphore, and flaghoist.

Flashing Light Signaling

This system uses short and long flashes of light to spell out dot-and-dash messages. The transmitting signalman sends one word at a time, with a slight pause between each letter. The receiving signalman flashes a dash after each word, meaning it was received and he is ready for another.

Directional Method. In this method the sender aims his light directly at the receiver. Only people near the receiver can see the light. The signalman controls the length of the flash by a shutter on the face of the light. Other types of directional gear are the blinker tube (or blinker gun) and the multipurpose lamp—both battery operated with trigger switches to control the light flashes.

Non-Directional Method. Another term for this type of signaling is "All-around." Most of it is done by yardarm blinkers, lights mounted high on a mast and controlled by a signal key on the signal bridge. This method is best for sending a message to several ships at once.

Nancy. While other signal systems use "white" light, Nancy uses invisible infra-red light, which can be seen only by those who have a special Nancy receiver, which gathers the infra-red rays and converts them to visible light. Nancy has a range of from 10,000 to 15,000 yards, and can be used only at night. It is a very secure method of communication.

Semaphore

This requires the least equipment of all—two small hand-held flags, but a man can send semaphore using only his arms. A good signalman can send or receive about 25 five-letter groups a minute. Only 30 positions need to be learned (figure 11–2).

Flaghoist

This is the most rapid system of visual signaling, but like semaphore it can be used only in the daytime. Usually it is used for tactical orders; the meanings of each signal must be looked up in a signal book. There is a signal flag for each letter of the alphabet, one for each numeral from 0 through 9, and others with special uses. A complete set of signal flags will have 68 flags and pennants (see appendix B), with them, thousands of different signals can be sent. Most ships carry only two

Figure 11–2. The semaphore alphabet is easily learned and can be used by anyone.

O

P

Q

R

S.

T

U

V

W

X

Y

Z

ERROR

FRONT

NUMERALS

ATTENTION

or three complete sets of flags, and substitutes are used when particular flags are already flying: the *first substitute* repeats the first flag or pennant in the same hoist, the *second substitute* repeats the second flag or penant, and so on.

The following five flags, and their meanings, should be known to every man, whether he stands bridge watches or not:

BRAVO—ship is handling explosives or fuel oil
OSCAR—man overboard
PAPA—all hands return to ship
QUEBEC—all boats return to ship
FIVE FLAG—breakdown.

Absence Indicators

When the commanding officer, or any flag officer, is absent from his command, an "absentee pennant" is flown as follows:

First Substitute (starboard yardarm) The admiral or unit commander, whose personal flag or pennant is flying, is absent.

Second Substitute (port yardarm) The chief of staff is absent.

Third Substitute (port yardarm) The commanding officer is absent. (If he is to be gone more than 72 hours, then the pennant shows the absence of the executive officer.)

Fourth Substitute (starboard yardarm) The civil or military official whose flag is flying is absent.

Other Visual Signaling Systems

Other visual systems involve special methods for special occasions. Here are some of them:

Speed Indicators. These are flags and pennants, or red or white lights in combinations of flashes, used to show a ship's speed.

Pyrotechnics. These are colored smoke and flare signals usually used for distress or emergency purposes.

Panels. Large strips of colored cloth laid out in different designs on the ground or the deck of a ship to signal aircraft.

Procedure Signs

Procedure signs (prosigns) are a form of communication shorthand. They provide, in brief form, certain orders, requests, instructions, and other types of information used often in communications. Shown below are some of the more common ones—prosigns that may be sent by radiotelegraph, radioteletype, semaphore, or flashing light.

Prosign	Meaning
AA	Unknown Station
AR	End of transmission
AS	Wait
B	More to follow
BT	Long break
DE	From
EEEEEE	Error
F	Do not answer
HM HM HM	Emergency silence sign
IMI AB (word)	Repeat all before (word)
IMI AA (word)	Repeat all after (word)
IMI WA (word)	Repeat word after (word)
IX	Execute to follow
K	Invitation to transmit
NR	Number
R	Received (*also* Routine)
T	Transmit to

The International Morse Code

All radiotelegraph and flashing light signaling use the International Morse Code, a system in which letters and numbers are formed by combinations of dots and dashes, or "dits" and "dahs." A skilled radioman or signalman sends code in evenly timed dots and dashes, in which a dot is one unit long, a dash is three units long; there is a one unit interval between dots and dashes in a letter, three units between letters, and seven units between words.

Letter	Code
A	· —
B	— · · ·
C	— · — ·
D	— · ·
E	·
F	· · — ·
G	— — ·

Letter	Code
H	· · · ·
I	· ·
J	· — — —
K	— · —
L	· — · ·
M	— —
N	— ·
O	— — —
P	· — — ·
Q	— — · —
R	· — ·
S	· · ·
T	—
U	· · —
V	· · · —
W	· — —
X	— · · —
Y	— · — —
Z	— — · ·

Number	Code
1	· — — — —
2	· · — — —
3	· · · — —
4	· · · · —
5	· · · · ·
6	— · · · ·
7	— — · · ·
8	— — — · ·
9	— — — — ·
0	— — — — —

Electronic communications include radio, wire, or telegraph. Wire communications go directly from sender to receiver and cannot be intercepted except by physically cutting into the circuit. Radio uses electromagnetic waves broadcast through the atmosphere in all directions; it includes radiotelegraph (CW), radiotelephone (RT), radio teletype (RATT), and facsimile (FAX).

Radiotelegraph (CW)

Radiotelegraph uses International Morse Code. If the transmission is in plain language, anyone can intercept and read. Important messages may be encrypted and sent in code or cipher systems known only to the sender and receiver. A coded message may be copied by anyone, but without the code system it cannot be read.

Radiotelegraph messages are called *traffic*, and are sent out in two ways. In the *broadcast method*, one station transmits traffic for many ships, and every ship copies all traffic. Ships do not acknowledge the traffic, so an enemy can not determine how many ships are listening or where they are.

In the *receipt method*, each station acknowledges its traffic; this way there is no doubt that it has been received. The disadvantage of the receipt system is that an enemy can locate the sending and receiving stations by radio-direction finding.

Radiotelephone (RT)

The *radiotelephone*, or voice radio, is one of the most useful military communication systems. Because of its directness, convenience, and ease of operation, voice radio is used almost exclusively between ships and aircraft for short-range tactical communications (up to 25 miles). RT transmissions are on high frequencies with line-of-sight characteristics, which provides some security. Most transmissions are in plain language, so strict circuit discipline is necessary.

Radioteletype (RATT)

Radioteletype is basically an electrically operated typewriter which, either by radio or telegraph line, can operate another similar typewriter elsewhere. RATT is used extensively on ships at sea as well as at shore stations. A typewriter keyboard produces printed letters simultaneously at both sending and receiving machines, no matter how many receiving machines may be on the circuit. RATT tapes can be prepared and stored for future transmission.

Facsimile (FAX)

Facsimile is a method for transmitting pictorial and graphic information electronically by wire or radio, reproducing it in its original form at the receiving station. The image to be sent is scanned by a photoelectric cell, and electrical variations, corresponding to light and dark areas being scanned, are transmitted to the receiver that reproduces the picture. The process is similar to television, but is slower and cannot produce a moving picture. FAX signals may be transmitted by wire or radio. The most useful application of FAX is transmission of complete weather charts.

Because voice radio is used so widely—not only in ships and aircraft but in motor vehicles and even by recruits directing vehicle traffic at the training center—everyone must understand the basics of circuit discipline (discussed earlier) and transmitting techniques. Because voice radio can be heard by anyone with the proper equipment, the following are strictly prohibited:

violation of radio silence;
unofficial conversation or prowords;
transmitting without permission;
unauthorized plain language;
profane, indecent, or obscene language.

Transmitting Techniques

Listen before transmitting. Don't break in on another message.

Speak clearly, distinctly, and slowly, but transmit phrase by phrase, not word by word.

Use standard pronunciation, use standard terminology, and always use prescribed procedures.

Procedure Words

Procedure words (prowords) are words and phrases used to speed up radio traffic. They perform the same functions and are used in the same manner as prosigns. Many prosigns and prowords have the same meaning.

Prowords	Meanings
Correction	An error has been made.
I say again	I am repeating transmission or portions indicated.
I spell	I shall spell the next word phonetically.
Message follows	A message that requires recording will follow.
Out	End of transmission, no receipt required.
Over	Go ahead; or this is end of transmission, reply is necessary.
Roger	I have received your last transmission.

Prowords	Meanings
Say again	Repeat.
Wilco	I have received your message, understand it, and will comply.

Pronouncing Numbers

Always pronounce numbers as follows:

Number	Pronunciation
0	Zero
1	Wun
2	Too
3	Thu-ree
4	Fo-wer
5	Fi-yuv
6	Six
7	Seven
8	Ate
9	Nin-er
44	Fo-wer fo-wer
90	Nin-er zero
136	Wun thuh-ree six
500	Fi-yuv hun-dred
1478	Wun fo-wer seven ate
7000	Seven thow-zand
16000	Wun six thow-zand
16400	Wun six fo-wer hun-dred
812681	Ate wun too six ate wun

Decimal is pronounced "day-see-mal."

Ranges, *distances*, and *speeds* given in miles are transmitted as cardinal (whole) numbers, such as "range two thousand," "speed twenty," and so on.

Altitude is given in feet (except for weapons orders, which are always in yards) and transmitted in cardinal numbers.

Pronouncing Letters

In all communications, a phonetic alphabet is used to avoid confusion between letters that sound alike, such as C, D, or T. Each letter is designated by a word, as follows:

Letter	Name	Spoken
A	ALFA	*AL*-FA
B	BRAVO	*BRIAH-VOH*
C	CHARLIE	*CHAR*-LEE
D	DELTA	*DEL*-TAH
E	ECHO	*ECK*-OH
F	FOXTROT	*FOKS*-TROT
G	GOLF	GOLF
H	HOTEL	HOH-*TEL*
I	INDIA	*IN*-DEE-AH
J	JULIETT	*JEW*-LEE-*ETT*
K	KILO	*KEY*-LOH
L	LIMA	*LEE*-MAH
M	MIKE	MIKE
N	NOVEMBER	NO-*VEM*-BER
O	OSCAR	*OSS*-CAH
P	PAPA	PAH-*PAH*
Q	QUEBEC	KAY-*BECK*
R	ROMEO	*ROW*-ME-OH
S	SIERRA	SEE-*AIR*-RAH
T	TANGO	*TANG*-GO
U	UNIFORM	*YOU*-NEE-FORM
V	VICTOR	*VIK*-TAH
W	WHISKEY	*WISS*-KEY
X	XRAY	*ECKS*-RAY
Y	YANKEE	*YANG*-KEY
Z	ZULU	*ZOO*-LOO

Standard Phraseology

Because of the specialized and technical nature of most operations, it is necessary that in all communications everyone "talk the same language." There is one correct, proper way to say things, and it must be used to avoid confusion, which in many high-speed operations can easily lead to danger and disaster.

Cryptography

Since all communications may be intercepted by an enemy, messages that contain vital information must be "disguised" so that they cannot be read. This is done by putting messages in codes or ciphers.

Cryptography is the science of enciphering and deciphering messages; *cryptanalysis* is the breaking of enemy ciphers or codes. All ciphers are designed to allow a large volume of traffic to be handled, and at the same time to defeat enemy cryptanalysts.

Codes are word-for-word substitutions of letter or number groups, with prearranged meanings for entire phrases (such as are found in signal books). They are used where speed is preferred to security and are changed frequently, since they are subject to compromise.

Ciphers offer letter-for-letter substitutions, greater flexibility and security than codes, and are easier to use in rapid communications. Most ciphers are changed periodically. Simple tactical codes and ciphers are changed frequently; those considered more secure may be used for months or years.

Sound Signals

Sound signal devices include the ship's bell, whistle, siren, gong, and sometimes underwater sound devices (sonar). The bell is sounded when the ship is at anchor in fog, mist, snow, or heavy rain. The gong is sounded under certain conditions when the ship is in international waters. The whistle or siren is sounded in fog and whenever required by *Rules of the Road* either as a signal of intent or as a danger signal. See chapter 14, "Rules of the Road," for more details on whistle signals. Whistles, sirens, and bells are used by ships for transmitting emergency warning signals (such as air raid alerts) and, in wartime, for communications between ships in convoy.

On most small vessels, the voice tube is the primary means of interior communication. The voice tube requires only lung power; its effectiveness decreases according to its length and the number of bends in it. On large ships, voice tube communication is for short distances only, as between an open conning station and the pilothouse.

MAIL

A vast amount of administrative detail concerning personnel, supplies, logistics, and operations is handled by *official mail*, which is carried through the U.S. postal system. Official mail between ships or stations in the same port is carried by guard mail. Guard mail petty officers are designated in writing. They carry registered-mail log books, and must take care to see that all mail they handle is logged and receipted. Classified mail is carried by officer couriers. Personal mail is handled much as it is in a civilian community. Always have your correspondents use the correct zip code.

Censorship

In time of war, all letters written by personnel on ships and at overseas bases must be examined by official censors.

When censorship is in effect, censors must delete such information as:

location, identity, and actual or prospective movements of ships or aircraft;

information on the forces, weapons, military installations, or plans of the United States or her allies;

information regarding the employment of any naval or military unit of the United States or her allies;

effects of enemy operations, including casualties to personnel or material of the United States or her allies;

criticism of equipment or morale of the United States or allied forces.

ZONE TIME

The solar day contains 24 hours, the time it takes the earth to turn once on its axis. The world is divided into 24 different time zones (see figure 11–3), so at any moment of the day there are 24 different times around the world. The United States has four time zones—Eastern, Central, Mountain, and Pacific. When the time is 0800 in Boston it is 0500 in San Francisco, 0600 in Denver, and 0700 in Chicago.

The standard time zones begin at Greenwich, England, the point from which all longitudes east and west are measured. All navigation and most communication is based on Greenwich Mean Time (GMT), the time at the 0, or Prime, Meridian at Greenwich. Time zones are numbered from 1 to 12, east and west of Greenwich; those west are + and those east are −. (The line between east and west is the 180th meridian, halfway around the world from Greenwich.)

If your ship is in Boston, which is Zone +5, and you need to know GMT at 0800 Eastern Standard Time, you add 8 and 5 and find that it is 1300 GMT. In Hawaii, which is five zones further west, the local time is naturally 5 hours earlier than in Boston, or 0300. To check on this, note that Hawaii is in zone +10, and 0300 plus 10 equals 1300, the GMT.

The 180th meridian is also called the *International Date Line*. When it is Saturday east of the line, it is Sunday west of the line. As a ship steaming around the world crosses each time zone, it has its clocks *advanced* one hour if it is steaming *east,* and *set back* one hour if

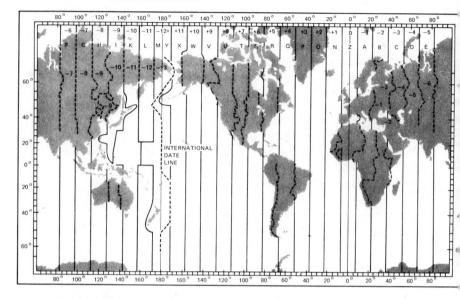

Figure 11–3. Standard time zones, showing latitudes east and west from Greenwich (the prime meridian), time zone numbers (+ and −), and GMT or Zulu time designations used in radio communications.

steaming *west*. To compensate for this gain or loss of 24 hours, the date is changed when crossing the date line. A ship steaming west and setting the clocks back an hour for each time zone it crossed will advance the calendar one day when it crosses the International Date Line; a ship going east will set the calendar back and have the same day twice.

This change does not have to be made the instant the ship crosses the date line; it may be delayed for a reasonable period. It would not be desirable to lose a Sunday, nor to have Sunday twice in a row. Usually, a ship will advance the clocks (shorten the day) during the mid-watch, and retard the clocks (lengthen the day) during the second dog-watch.

In the accompanying diagram of world time zones, note that the zones are also lettered. When a date-time group ends in ZULU, the time used is GMT. If your ship is operating out of Hawaii, which is in time zone WHISKEY (+ 10), you add 10 to the local zone time to find GMT.

The navigators determine GMT, which is used in celestial navigation, by a chronometer, described in chapter 13. The 24-hour system of bells and watches used at sea is described in chapter 7.

CHAPTER 12

Weapons

Coast Guard units are armed with various types of weapons, according to their missions. Law enforcement and military readiness both require the use of weapons, and individuals may be armed, depending on their duty assignments. This chapter offers an introduction to weapons in general use by the Coast Guard.

TERMINOLOGY

Ordnance. An overall term including everything that makes up a ship's firepower.

Gun. Basically a tube closed at one end from which a projectile is propelled by the burning of gun powder.

Rocket. A weapon containing an explosive section and a propulsion section. A rocket is unable to change its direction of movement after it has been fired.

Missile. A vehicle containing an explosive section, propulsion section, and a guidance section. A missile is able to change its direction of movement, after it is fired (launched), to hit the target.

Torpedo. Self-propelled underwater missile used against surface and underwater targets.

Mine. An underwater explosive weapon put into position by surface ships, submarines, or aircraft. A mine explodes only when a target comes near or into contact with it.

Figure 12–1. Gunners on the USCGC *Sherman* (WHEC–270) clean their lone 5"/38-caliber gun.

Depth Charge. Antisubmarine weapons fired or dropped by a surface vessel or aircraft, and set to either explode at a certain depth or in proximity to a submarine—no longer used by surface ships.

Bomb. Any weapon other than torpedoes, mines, rockets, or missiles, dropped from an aircraft.

GUNS

The caliber of a gun is its inside diameter, measured from the tops of the lands. Caliber is expressed in inches and the length of the gun barrel in calibers, as 5-inch 54 caliber (5″/54 cal), a gun 270 inches long with a bore of 5 inches. Guns are grouped as major (8 inches and larger), intermediate (less than 8 inches and larger than 4 inches), and minor (less than 4 inches in diameter), except small arms. The various types of guns are described hereafter.

Bag Guns. These are guns in which the projectile is loaded first, then the powder in silk bags is inserted. The USS *New Jersey* (BB 62), one of the last bag gun ships in service, carries nine 16″/50 cal. guns.

Case Guns. All modern naval guns are of the case type; the propelling charge of powder is contained in a metal cartridge or case. Ammunition for case guns is either fixed or semifixed. Fixed ammunition has a propellant powder case and projectile attached as one unit. Small arms and minor caliber guns use fixed ammunition. Semifixed ammunition is in two parts, powder case and projectile. All 5-inch guns (figure 12–1) and larger use semifixed ammunition.

Automatic Guns. These use the recoil of the gun to eject the fired case and reload the gun; 5-inch 54 caliber and 3-inch 50 caliber guns are of the automatic type.

Semiautomatic Guns. These guns eject the fixed case and leave the breech open in a proper position for hand loading, as in the 5-inch 38 caliber gun.

Dual-Purpose Guns (DP). These are designed for use against both surface and air targets. The 5-inch 54 caliber and 5-inch 38 caliber guns are classified dual-purpose guns.

Saluting Gun. The saluting gun fires gun salutes, normally black powder blanks.

Line-throwing Guns. These guns are used to shoot a light line across a space that is too great to throw a heaving line.

Battery. A group of guns of the same size, normally controlled from the same point. The main battery of a ship consists of the largest size gun aboard. The secondary battery consists of dual-purpose guns or guns of the next size aboard. An antiaircraft (AA) battery consists of small-caliber guns, and is usually called the machine-gun battery.

Parts of a Gun

The function and size of a gun mount will govern its major parts, but all guns have the following components: stand; carriage; slide; housing; barrel; breech assembly.

The *stand* is that part firmly attached to ships' superstructures and contains the roller bearings upon which the mount rotates.

The *carriage* is normally of two parts, the base and gun carriage. The base is a platform that supports the gun carriage and rotates on the stand. The gun carriage supports the gun assembly in the pivot points, called trunnion bearings.

The *slide* does not move, but it contains the bearing surfaces that support and guide the moving (recoiling) barrel and housing. The slide also contains the trunnion (pivot point), which enables the gun to elevate.

The *housing* moves within the slide during firing. The housing contains the breech assembly and barrel (which is locked to the housing by a bayonet joint and a locking key).

The *barrel* is a rifled tube closed at one end to contain the pressure of the rapidly burning powder. The rear end of the barrel is attached to the breech housing, which contains the breechlock—sometimes called a plug. Forward of the breech end is an enlarged chamber that holds the propelling charge. The forward end of the chamber is tapered down to guide the projectile into the rifling where it is seated prior to firing. The bore of the barrel is rifled with a right-hand twist of a uniform diameter end to end. Rifling in a barrel (figure 12–2) causes a projectile to spin. This spinning motion keeps the projectile from tumbling once it leaves the barrel, and ensures greater accuracy. The slide cylinder area is a bearing surface on the slide during recoil and counter-recoil. The chase area is the tapered part of the barrel. Some guns have an enlarged area at the muzzle called the bell, which prevents any tendency of the barrel to split.

The *breech assembly* is the plug or block that closes off the chamber end of the barrel. The breech assembly contains the firing mechanism, which ignites the powder primer in the propellant cage, and the extractors, which remove the fired case from the gun chamber.

Guns now in use are:

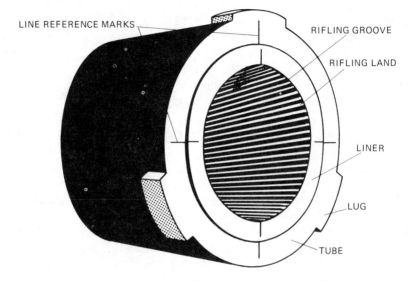

Figure 12–2. View through barrel of a rifled gun, showing lands, grooves, and right-hand twist.

Size	Range	Type	Projectile Weight
5"/38 cal	17,300 yds	CASE-Semi Fixed	55 lbs
3"/50 cal	14,000 yds	CASE-Fixed	13 lbs

Ammunition

Ammunition is either fixed or semifixed (figure 12–3), and consists of the propellant charge (powder), the primer which sets off the propellant charge, and the projectile.

All naval guns use smokeless powder shaped into cylindrical grains. This shape, with holes through the powder grain, ensures complete and predictable burning of the powder to develop propelling pressures.

Projectiles

A projectile consists of five distinct parts (figure 12–4). The *ogive* (Pronounced o-jive) is the streamlined forward part. The *bourrelet* is the forward bearing surface of the body, which steadies the projectile in the gun barrel. The *body* is the main part of the projectile, and it carries the explosive charge. The *rotating band,* normally of brass, seals the projectile in the bore of the gun so that the full force of the

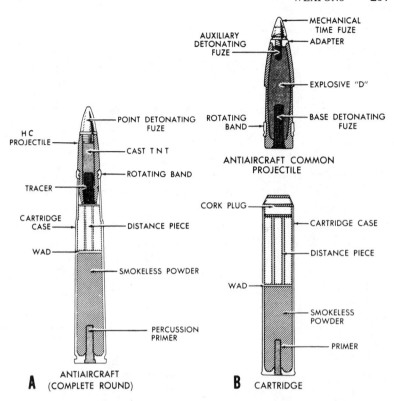

Figure 12–3. Details of case ammunition, showing (A) cross section of 40-mm fixed ammunition and (B) semifixed ammunition, 5-inch cartridge, and projectile.

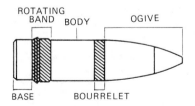

Figure 12–4. External details of gun projectile.

propellant gases are exerted on the projectile, and it also engages the rifling so as to impart the spin to the projectile. The *base* houses the base fuse tracer, or solid base plate. Projectiles include these general types:

Thin-walled projectiles designed to cause damage by blast effect and fragmentation. The two sub-divisions of this projectile type are High Capacity (HC) for use against troops or surface targets, and Antiaircraft (AA) for use against aircraft.

Thick-walled projectiles such as Armor Piercing (AP), which are designed to penetrate armor plating or thick concrete before exploding.

Common (COM) projectiles whose wall thickness is midway between thin-walled projectiles and AP projectiles.

Special-purpose projectiles, which are not intended to inflict damage by explosion or fragmentation.

Illumination, called starshells, which drop a flare attached to a parachute.

Smoke projectiles, which provide a smoke screen using white phosphorus.

Window projectiles, which scatter metal foil strips to confuse radar.

Target projectiles, which do not contain explosives and are used for target practice firings. Target ammunition is also said to be inert loaded.

Projectiles may be fitted with any one of the following type fuzes or any combination of them:

Point detonating fuze (PDF), which explodes on impact.

Mechanical time fuze (MTF), which contains a clock mechanism to explode the projectile at a preset time.

Proximity fuze (VT) contains a miniature radio transmitter that explodes the projectile when it senses a nearby target.

Auxiliary detonating fuze (ADD) acts as a booster fuze in conjunction with a nose fuze.

Base detonating fuze (BDF) is set to explode a fraction of a second after impact to obtain penetration of the projectile before it explodes.

All fuzes in naval guns begin to function or arm themseves after the projectile leaves the gun barrel and has traveled a safe distance.

Ammunition Handling

Ammunition is perfectly safe to handle, as long as it is handled carefully and cautiously. Ammunition safety precautions are posted in handling areas, and strict compliance with them is necessary for safety. These rules are based upon past experiences and unfortunate disasters that resulted in loss of life, ships, and port facilities.

Small Arms

Any weapon with a bore diameter of .60 inch or less is called a small arm. The military classifies any hand-held or carried weapon as a small arm. The largest such weapon used by the Coast Guard is the .50-inch machine gun, and the smallest is the .22-inch training weapon. The bore size of small arms is designated by caliber (cal) or gauge (ga) in the case of shotguns. All small arms approved for military use prior to 1958 have the caliber of the bore measured in hundredths of an inch— a .50 cal machine gun has a bore of one-half (.50 inch) in diameter. Since 1958, the bore diameter is expressed in millimeters—the caliber 7.62 mm M14 rifle has a .30-inch bore diameter. Small arms have one of the following firing systems:

A semiautomatic weapon unlocks the bolt, extracts the fixed case from the chamber, ejects the fired case from the mechanism, cocks the hammer, and reloads automatically. The trigger must be released and pulled again to fire the weapon.

Automatic weapons follow the same chain of events as semiautomatic weapons, except that as long as the trigger is held in the fire position the weapon will continue to fire.

Double action weapons, such as revolvers, operate off the trigger pull. When the trigger is pulled back, the cylinder rotates to align a chamber with the barrel, the hammer is cocked and then released to fire the weapon. To fire again, the trigger must be released and pulled again.

The *.45 caliber M1911A1 automatic pistol* (figure 12–5), in use for over 60 years, is one of the most dependable small arms ever made. It is a recoil-operated, air-cooled, magazine-fed, semiautomatic hand weapon, and the only gun in use with left-hand rifling. It contains five safety devices; two automatic safeties (disconnector and grip safety), two manual safeties (safety lock, thumb safety), and the half-cock notch.

Proper care of the pistol is a requirement of the user, and the

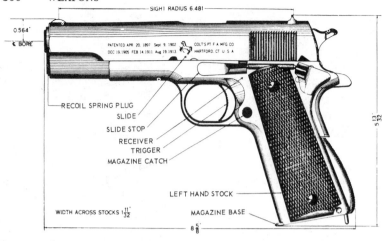

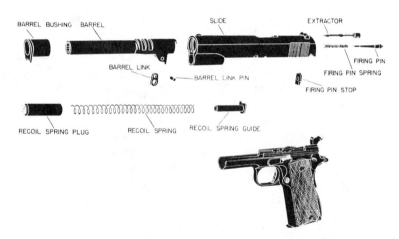

Figure 12–5. Details of .45-caliber automatic pistol, and pistol in field-stripped condition.

following steps outline the procedure for field-stripping the weapon for maintenance:

Clear the weapon of all ammunition.

Push in magazine catch to remove magazine.

Cock the hammer and push the safety lock up to the safe position.

Push the recoil spring plug in and turn the barrel bushing about a quarter turn clockwise while holding the recoil spring plug inward.

Slowly release the pressure on the recoil spring plug, removing it from the gun. Return the safety lock to the fire position.

Pull slide rearward until the projection on the slide stop is directly below the half-moon recess on the slide. Push the slide stop out from right to left using finger pressure.

Holding pistol upside down, draw the receiver to the rear, removing it from the slide. Lay the receiver on a padded surface—don't let it fall on deck.

Remove the recoil spring and guide out the rear of the slide. Remove barrel bushing by turning counterclockwise as far as it will go, then pull out with your fingers.

Tilt slide, upside down, downward and pull barrel out of the muzzle end of the slide.

The *M16 Rifle* (figure 12–6) is a gas-operated, magazine fed, air-cooled, lightweight shoulder weapon, capable of either semiautomatic or automatic fire through the use of a selector lever on the left side of the receiver. When the last round is fired from the magazine, the bolt is held open by the bolt catch. The weapon is equipped with a manual safety and a three-position fire selector lever on the left side of receiver

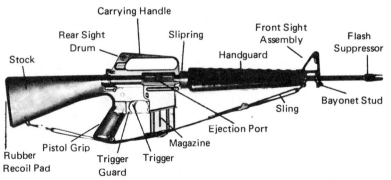

Figure 12–6. M16 rifle, right side view.

Small Arms

Model	Caliber	Capacity	Weight	Barrel Length	Type of action	Max Range	Effective Range
Pistol M1911A1	.45 cal	7 rounds magazine	2½ lbs	5 inches	semiautomatic	1,600 yds	55 yds
Revolver 38 CAL	.38 Special	6 rounds	1½ lbs	4 inches	single/double action	1,600 yds	50 yds
M16 Rifle	5.56 mm	20 rounds magazine	7½ lbs	20 inches	semiautomatic/ automatic	2,900 yds	500 yds
Shotgun	12 gauge	5 rounds	7½ lbs	20 inches various	pump	748 yds	40–50 yds
Machine Gun M2	.50 cal	50 or 300 round belt	84 lbs	45 inches	semiautomatic/ automatic	7,400 yds	2,250 yds
Machine Gun M60D	7.62 mm	100 rounds belt	22 lbs	24 inches	automatic	3,500 yds	1,200 yds
Line-throwing Gun	.45 cal Blank	single Shot	N/A	N/A	N/A	100 yds	100 yds

(safe, semiautomatic, and full automatic). It is classified as safe *only* when the magazine is out, the chamber is empty, the bolt carrier is to the rear, and the selector is on safe.

The *Machine Gun M2 Caliber 50* is an air-cooled, belt-fed, recoil-operated, 84-pound weapon fired from stand or tripod.

The *M60 Machine Gun* is an air-cooled, belt-fed, gas-operated weapon firing the 7.62 mm (NATO) cartridge. The M60 machine gun may have either a bipod or tripod mount.

Marksmanship. The two keys to accurate shooting are correct sight alignment and trigger control. To make them work, the weapon must be held firmly. Above all, know your weapons and follow all the rules of safety when handling them.

Safety Precautions

A weapon is just as safe as the man behind it, regardless of how well built it is or how many safety features it has. Unless the man who handles it regards it as a deadly weapon, it is a source of danger to him and everyone near him. Accidents don't just happen; they are usually caused by carelessness. Observe the following firearm safety precautions at all times and insist that those around you do likewise:

Consider every firearm to be loaded until you examine it and find it to be unloaded. Never trust your memory in this respect.

Never point a weapon at anyone unless you intend to shoot, nor in a direction where accidental discharge may do harm.

Never fire a weapon until it has been inspected to see that the bore or chamber is clear. Firing a weapon with any obstruction in the bore may burst the barrel, resulting in serious injury to you or your shipmates.

On the firing line, if a weapon is loaded, keep it locked until you are ready to shoot, and do not turn around on the line with a loaded weapon in your hands.

Never put your trigger finger within the trigger guard until you intend to fire and the weapon is pointed toward the target.

On leaving the firing line, open the chamber and keep it open.

Never leave a loaded firearm or one with cartridges in the magazine where it can be picked up by somebody else.

Never carry a loaded pistol in the holster with the hammer cocked and safety lock on, except in an emergency or unless directed by proper authority.

Figure 12–7. Coast Guardsmen learn to repair and clean M–16 rifles.

When pistols are issued to men on watch, the following applies:

The pistol is carried in the holster unloaded but with a full magazine.
On relieving the watch, the relief will avoid standing in front of the
man armed with the pistol, but will stand to one side.
The previous watchstander will come to raised pistol, remove magazine, lock slide open, and inspect chamber. If the chamber is
empty, he then turns the pistol over to the relief.
The relief assumes the raised pistol position, lowers the slide gently
after seeing that the chamber is empty, and releases the firing
pin.
The relief then checks the number of rounds in the clip, re-inserts
it in the pistol, and returns the pistol to the holster.
The pistol must not be removed from the holster during a watch
except for the inspection as required above and for actual use.
Men entrusted with pistols may not use them when off watch for
any purpose, except when specifically ordered to do so and when
adequately supervised.

TORPEDOES

The torpedo is a self-propelled, explosive-carrying underwater weapon that carries its own automatic guidance system.

A torpedo consists of *tail, afterbody, midsection,* and *head.* The tail section includes the *screws, fins,* and *control* surfaces. The propulsion system is contained in the afterbody. The *midsection* houses *batteries, compressed air,* or *liquid fuel.* The head contains the *explosive charge, fuze,* and any *acoustic* or *magnetic sensing devices.*

Guidance systems are either preset, wire-guided, or homing. Preset torpedoes follow a set course and depth after they are launched. Wire-guidance torpedoes have a thin wire connecting the torpedo and the firing ship through which signals can be transmitted to the torpedo to intercept the target. Homing torpedoes are either active or passive types. Active types depend on the sensing signals generated and returned to the torpedo through a sonar device contained within the torpedo. Passive types listen for the noise generated by the target and home in on it.

The only Coast Guard cutters armed with torpedoes are the WHEC 378-foot-class cutters.

MINES

Most information on mines is classified, so only a very general discussion can be given here. Mines are of several types, and can be described according to the method of actuation (firing), method of planting, and position in the water.

Method of Actuation. A contact mine fires when a ship strikes it. Usually it has lead horns containing glass tubes filled with an electrolyte. When the horn is struck, the glass breaks and the electrolyte generates enough current to fire the mine. *Influence* mines may be actuated by underwater sound generated by a passing ship, a ship's magnetic field, or by sensitivity to the reduction of water pressure caused by the passing of a ship.

Method of Planting. Mines may be planted by surface craft, submarines, or aircraft. Surface ships planting mines are subject to enemy interception. Submarines can plant mines in secret, but cannot return to plant more mines until those planted have been destroyed or have become inactive. Aircraft can plant mines in shallow waters where submarines and surface craft can not operate.

Position in the Water. Moored mines are anchored in place and float near the surface of the water, where a ship can strike them. They are usually contact types. Bottom mines lie on the bottom, so they can only be used in shallow water; they are usually influence types, set off by sound, magnetism, or pressure.

TYPES OF ARMAMENT ABOARD COAST GUARD CUTTERS

5"/38 cal single mounts: WHEC 378' class; 327' class; 311' class. *Note:* The 378' class is scheduled to have its 5"/38 mount and accompanying MK 56 Gun Fire Control System (GFCS) replaced by a 76-mm single mount and a MK 92 Fire Control System (FCS). The 327' and 311' class WHECs presently do not have a GFCS.

76-mm single mounts: WMEC 270' class (includes the MK 92 FCS).

3"/50 cal single mounts: WMEC 210' class; 205' class; and the *STORIS*.

40 mm MK 19 machine gun/grenade launchers: WHECs; WMECs; WAGBs; and WLBs.

20 mm MK 16 machine guns: WHEC 378' class; some WLB 180' class (*SASSAFRAS, IRONWOOD, SEDGE, SWEETBRIAR, BITTERSWEET*).

MK 32 triple torpedo tubes: WHEC 378' class.

Unarmed: All Coast Guard Cutters operating on the Great Lakes; all WYTMs; all WYTLs.

USE OF FORCE

Coast Guardsmen, both during military operations and peacetime law enforcement, must often resort to the use of weapons. Training in "use of force" policies is a vital part of weapons training, particularly in the area of law enforcement. It is not appropriate to deal with those policies in this manual inasmuch as they are subject to legal interpretations and continuing reevaluation. Before a Coast Guardsman is given a weapon for use, he or she will be trained in all aspects of the use of that weapon, including *how* and *when* to use it.

CHAPTER 13

Navigation

There are three kinds of navigation: marine navigation, air navigation, and space navigation. Only marine navigation, which includes four methods of determining position—*piloting, dead reckoning, electronic navigation*, and *celestial navigation*—will be discussed here. Even though you are not a navigator, you should understand the basic elements of navigation (figure 13–1).

All navigational methods depend on exact measurements of distance, speed, direction, and time. Marine navigation sometimes requires the measurements of the depth of water, called *soundings*. The final result, in any method, is position or location, usually called "fix."

The location anywhere on earth is determined by latitude—the distance north or south of the equator—and longitude—the distance east or west of the prime meridian, which runs from the North Pole to the South Pole through Greenwich, England. Latitude is measured in degrees north or south of the equator, with 0 degrees at the equator and 90 degrees at each pole. Longitude is measured in degrees from Greenwich, 180 degrees east and 180 degrees west. The place where 180 degrees east and 180 degrees west meet, halfway around the world from Greenwich, is called the International Date Line. The location of a ship at sea is established on a chart.

Charts. Charts, which show ocean areas and shore lines, and maps, which show landmasses, are marked off in parallels of latitude—degrees

Figure 13–1. The ship's navigator must be an expert at using the sextant, even with all the electronic navigational equipment on board.

north or south—and meridians of longitude—degrees east or west. Each degree (°) is divided into 60 minutes (') or nautical miles. A nautical mile measured along the equator or a meridian is 6076.11549 feet, or roughly 2,000 yards. Any position at sea or place ashore is stated in degrees and minutes north or south and east or west; Cleveland, Ohio, is 41° 30'N. and 81° 45'W., the island of Funafuti in the South Pacific is 8° 30'S. and 178° 30'E.

Distance. Distance at sea is measured in nautical miles. A nautical mile is one minute, or one sixtieth of a degree. Speed is measured in *knots*, a seaman's term meaning nautical miles per hour. A ship makes 27 knots, but never 27 knots per hour. In electronic navigation, distance measured by radar is called *range*.

Direction. This is determined by a compass, either magnetic or gyro, which will be described later. The four cardinal directions are north, east, south, and west. All directions are measured from north on a system of 360 degrees, in which east is 090 degrees, south is 180 degrees, west is 270 degrees, and north is either 360 or 000 degrees.

Time. There are two kinds of time predominantly used at sea: local apparent time as determined by the passage of the sun across the sky, and Greenwich mean time (GMT), which is mean time (time based on the sun) at the prime meridian in Greenwich, England, from which all meridians of longitude east and west are measured. All standard time is also measured from that meridian (see *Zone Time*, chapter 11). GMT is used for observations in celestial navigation and is shown by chronometers (highly accurate clocks).

The world is divided into 24 standard time zones, each covering 15 degrees of longitude, or 900 miles at the equator. Each standard time zone bears a number, as well as a plus (+) or minus (−) sign and a letter. The number refers to the difference in time between that zone and the Greenwich zone. The sign tells whether the time is earlier (+) or later (−) than the Greenwich zone time; the sign shows how to find Greenwich time from the standard time in any zone. If a ship is in zone + 4, and the clock showed the time to be 1300 aboard the ship, it would be 1300 + 4 or 1700 in the Greenwich zone. In radio traffic, when the time of origin of a dispatch is expressed in GMT, it is indicated by ZULU after the date-time group.

In recent years a new basis of timekeeping has been developed, required by the exacting needs of modern science, electronics, and navigation. Called *Universal Coordinated Time (UTC)*, it is based on the frequency of vibrations of a radioactive element, usually cesium.

Because UTC is based upon an unchanging atomic time standard, while GMT can be affected by small variations in the motion of the earth, there can be at times as much as a .9-second difference between the two. However, the two systems are kept in close agreement by the periodic insertion of a "leap second" by international time authorities, so that the actual difference rarely approaches this maximum and can be disregarded for most normal navigational purposes. Most *radio time signals* broadcast by various maritime nations by which navigators check their chronometers use UTC.

Soundings. Soundings are made with an electronic device, usually an echo sounder. A ship is said to be "on soundings" when she is in water shallow enough that a lead line can be used to determine depth. Deep-sea soundings show when a ship crosses a submarine canyon, sea mount, or other bottom feature, and when a chart shows bottom contours, soundings may be used to establish the ship's position by an actual fix.

METHODS OF DETERMINING POSITION

Piloting

This is the oldest method of navigation, used before men ventured out of sight of land and across the seas. It is a method of directing the movements of a ship by referring to landmarks, navigational aids such as lighthouses or lightships, or soundings. Piloting is generally used when entering or leaving port and in navigating along the coast (figure 13–2) and may be used at sea when the bottom contour makes the establishment of a fix possible.

Navigational aids used in piloting include the *compass*, to determine the ship's heading; the *bearing circle*, to determine direction of objects on land, buoys, ships, etc.; *charts*, which depict the outlines of the shore, as well as the positions of land and seamarks, and the standard depths of water at many locations; *buoys; navigational lights;* the *echo sounder*, which determines the depth of water under the ship's keel by measuring the time it takes a sound signal to reach the bottom and return to the ship; and the *lead line,* which determines the depth of the water by actual measurement. The *Coast Pilot* and *Sailing Directions* are books containing detailed information on coastal waters, harbor facilities, etc., for use in conjunction with the chart of the area. *Tide Tables* predict the times and heights of the tide, and *Current*

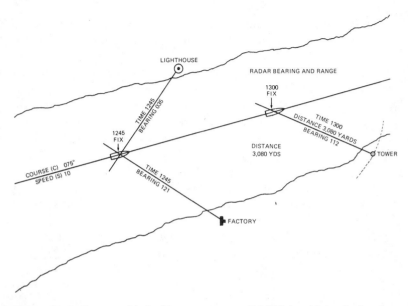

Figure 13–2. Fixes established by gyrocompass (1245 fix) and by radar bearing and range (1300 fix).

Tables predict the times, direction of flow, and velocity of tidal currents in harbors, bays, and inlets.

Bearing, Range, and Fixes. In clear weather piloting, the ship's position is usually determined by taking simultaneous gyrocompass bearings on two objects of fixed position. As a backup, radar may be used to obtain ranges and bearings to landmarks and some seamarks.

Figure 13–2 shows how the ship's position can be fixed by simultaneous visual bearings of two known objects, and also by a radar bearing and range on a single object, which are *plotted* or drawn on the chart. The lighthouse bears 035° from the ship, so the navigator draws a *line of position (LOP)* in the reverse direction, or 215° (180° + 35°) from the lighthouse in the direction of the ship. The factory bears 121°; a line of position 301° is similarly drawn *from* the factory. Each line is labeled with the bearing, 035° and 121°, below the line as shown.

The intersection of these two lines represents the actual position of the ship on the chart. A position that has been accurately established is called a *fix*, and is so labeled, together with the time that it was established. The symbol used to represent a fix is a small circle, placed over the intersection of the LOPs.

A line drawn from the fix in the direction in which the ship is steaming is called a *course line*. The direction, or *course*, is labeled above the line; speed in knots is labeled below the line.

The manner of obtaining a fix by radar bearing and *range* or distance is also shown in figure 13–2. Radar gives a bearing of 112° on a prominent tower and a range of 3,080 yards. The navigator again plots a line from the tower, uses dividers to measure 3,080 yards on the chart scale, then puts one leg of the dividers on the tower location on the chart, and marks the bearing line with the other end. This establishes the fix by bearing and range.

Good piloting permits almost continuous position fixing to a high order of accuracy but demands great care and judgment.

Dead Reckoning (DR)

This is a method in which the position of a ship is calculated by plotting the course steamed and distance covered by the ship from the last well-determined position. DR gets its name from "deduced reckoning," used in the old days when navigators "deduced" a new position mathematically, rather than determining it graphically, as is the modern practice. Today, the navigator determines the DR position on a chart by plotting courses and distances run from the last known position.

When celestial navigation or piloting is used, dead reckoning provides a check and helps uncover errors. If other means of navigation fail, the navigator must rely solely upon dead reckoning.

Figure 13–3 shows the DR *plot* on the chart. The 1200 fix is plotted and labeled. A course line is drawn from the fix on the ship's course of 073°. Course is labeled above the line and the speed of 15 knots below the line. At 15 knots, in one hour the ship will cover one-quarter degree, or 15 minutes on the chart. To determine the 1300 position, the navigator uses dividers to measure 15 minutes of *latitude* on the vertical latitude scale printed on either side of the chart. (One degree of latitude equals 60 nautical miles; one minute of latitude equals one mile.) This distance is marked off from the fix along the course line, and the resulting spot is labeled "1300 DR," as shown.

The captain orders the OOD to put the ship on a new course, 117° at 1330. Using his dividers, the navigator marks a spot seven and one-half miles from the 1300 DR position along the direction in which the ship is steaming, labels it "1300 DR," and draws in a new course line in the direction 117°.

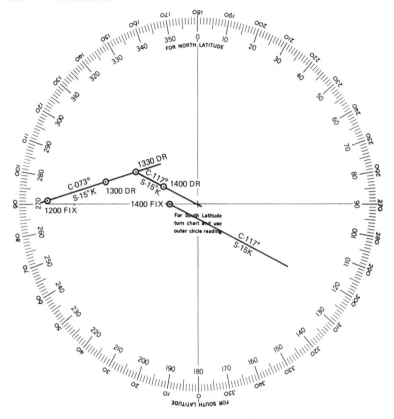

Figure 13–3. Dead reckoning plot, showing 1200 fix, 1300, 1330, and 1400 DR position. At 1400 a new fix is taken and ship's position on the chart is changed accordingly.

When properly maintained, the DR plot permits the ship's approximate position to be quickly determined.

Electronic Navigation

This division of navigation will be further developed during the coming years. As far as basic techniques are concerned, it is analogous in many respects to piloting, differing primarily in the methods by which the data are collected. *Radar,* SINS, *Omega,* and *Loran* are examples of electronic navigation equipment.

Increasing use is also being made of satellite-based electronic navigation systems for mid-ocean navigation. There are currently two systems in widespread use: the Transit or NAVSAT system consisting of some seven operational satellites in polar orbits that yield periodic fixes as the satellites pass overhead, and the GPS system, which by 1987 will consist of 18 satellites in synchronous orbits capable of furnishing continuous fix information worldwide.

Celestial Navigation

This is the determination of position by the observation of celestial bodies (sun, moon, planets, and stars) and is still the most widely used offshore navigation method, though electronic and satellite-based navigation are fast becoming predominant. Observations, made with a sextant, involve measuring the altitude above the horizon of navigational stars or other bodies and are called sights. When the navigator and quartermaster take a sight, they usually say they are "shooting a star."

Many of the navigational aids used in piloting are used in celestial navigation, but additional equipment, such as chronometers and sextants, is required. A DR plot is always maintained. On some ships this is done automatically by a Dead Reckoning Tracer (DRT).

NAVIGATIONAL INSTRUMENTS AND EQUIPMENT

Sextant. The sextant is a precision instrument that can measure angles in degrees, minutes, and seconds. Through a system of mirrors, the image of a star is brought down to the horizon; then very exact scales allow the navigator to read the angle between the actual star and the horizon. This angle is called the *altitude* and is the basis of all celestial navigation.

In establishing a position by star sight, several observations are taken. Each one is *reduced* or worked out by means of the Nautical Almanac and the reduction tables and results in a single *line of position*, a line passing through the ship's position. The ship's location is represented by the point at which the various lines of position intersect on the chart. This is the ship's location at the time of observation and is marked "2000 posit," "0530 posit," etc.

Stadimeter. The stadimeter measures the distance of an object of known height, such as a masthead light, between heights of 50 to 200 feet at distances of 200 to 10,000 yards. Like a sextant, the stadimeter operates on the principle of measuring an angle. The height of an object is set on a scale, and then the reflecting image is brought into coincidence with the actual direct image and the distance is read off another scale.

Azimuth Circle and Bearing Circle. An azimuth circle is a metal ring that fits over a compass bowl and measures bearings of objects on the surface of the earth and *azimuths* (or bearings) of celestial bodies.

Plotting Equipment. Position plotting on a chart is usually done with a universal drafting machine, also called a parallel motion protractor (PMP), which is clamped to a chart table and allows both distance and bearing to be plotted at once. Sometimes a simple plastic protractor and straight edge is used.

Chronometer. This is a highly accurate clock, mounted in a brass case, which is supported in gimbals in a wooden case, so as to eliminate much of the ship's motion. The chronometers are kept in a cabinet in the chart room, usually on the centerline of the ship, where they are protected against shock and temperature changes. Chronometers are set to show GMT; they are wound every day at exactly the same time, and this fact is always reported to the captain with the noon reports. Once a chronometer is started, it is never allowed to stop, and it is not reset while aboard ship. A record is kept of whether it is running fast or slow, but a good chronometer will never deviate more than a hundredth of a second from its average daily rate. Chronometers are checked against radio time signals, which are broadcast all over the world. To do this, a quartermaster uses a comparing watch, or hack watch, and he calls the process "getting a time tick." The exact GMT time, as determined by radio, is *never* used to change the chronometer, but only to show whether it is running fast or slow.

The necessity for exact time, as indicated by the chronometer, is because all celestial navigation is based on tables using Greenwich mean time. The time of a celestial observation, anywhere in the world, must be converted to GMT before the navigator proceeds to work out his position.

COMPASSES, COURSES, AND BEARINGS

Compass

A *compass* is a device for determining directions on the surface of the earth. There are two main types of compasses: *magnetic* (figure 13–4) and *gyroscopic*. In each there is a *compass card* from which the directions can be read.

Figure 13–4. A modern compass; this one is installed aboard the cutter *Active*. The card is marked in 360 degrees, with North at 0°, South at 180°.

Magnetic Compass

These compasses have the following general characteristics. The magnetized compass needles align themselves with the earth's magnetic field and are fastened to either a disk or a cylinder marked with the cardinal points of the compass: north, east, south, and west. North, on a magnetic compass, points to the magnetic North Pole, which is several hundred miles from the geographic North Pole.

The card and needles are supported on a pivot. No matter how the ship, aircraft, or boat swings, the card is free to rotate until it has realigned itself to magnetic north.

The moving parts are contained in a bowl or housing provided with a window through which the compass card may be seen. Ship's compasses usually have a flat glass top for all-around visibility and for taking bearings.

The *lubber's line*, a mark in the window of the compass, or on the compass bowl, indicates the fore-and-aft line of the ship or boat. The compass direction under the lubber's line tells the ship's heading.

A *deviation card* is attached to the binnacle (the stand in which the compass is housed) or near it. The card gives the deviation for various headings in this form:

Ship's Heading (Magnetic)	Dev	Ship's Heading (Magnetic)	Dev	Ship's Heading (Magnetic)	Dev
000°(360°)	14°W	120°	15°E	240°	4°E
015°	10°W	135°	16°E	255°	1°W
030°	5°W	150°	12°E	270°	7°W
045°	1°W	165°	12°E	285°	12°W
060°	2°E	180°	13°E	300°	15°W
075°	5°E	195°	14°E	315°	19°W
090°	7°E	210°	12°E	330°	19°W
105°	9°E	225°	9°E	345°	17°W

Compass Error. The magnetic North Pole and the true, or geographic, North Pole are not at the same location, so the magnetic compass does not point directly north in most places. Usually there is a difference of several degrees, known as *compass error*, which is made up of variation and deviation. The *variation* of a compass is caused by changes in the magnetic field of the earth from place to place; hence the needle follows the magnetic field and "varies" from the real north. The *deviation* of a compass is caused by the presence of metal objects around the compass, such as the iron and steel of the ship and her equipment. Even a knife in the pocket of the helmsman can cause the compass to deviate. Never bring a metal object near a compass.

Variation. This is the difference between geographic north and magnetic north (figure 13–5). Variation for any given locality, together with the amount of yearly increase or decrease, is shown on the *compass rose* of the chart for that particular locality. Variation remains the same for any heading of the ship at a given locality.

Deviation. This error is caused by the magnetic effect of any metal near the compass. It is different for different headings of the ship.

Every so often, the navigator and quartermaster go through an operation called "swinging ship." The ship steams in a complete circle from 0° to 360°, and the amount of her compass deviation is noted at every 15°. The results are compiled in a Deviation Table that is kept

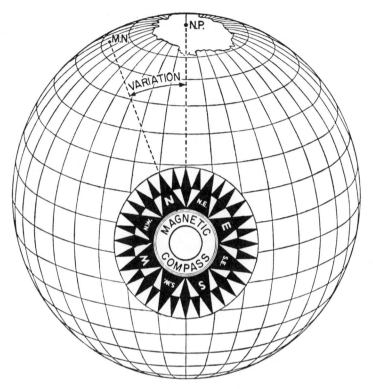

Figure 13–5. Diagram showing how variation affects the compass. The magnetic needle points to the magnetic pole (MN) instead of the geographic north pole (NP).

near the compass. There is a similar table near the magnetic compass in every aircraft. Compass error for any compass is the final effect of the variation of the locality and the deviation of the ship's heading. In some cases these must be added; in other cases one is subtracted from the other, as explained above.

True Course. This is the heading of the ship or boat in degrees measured clockwise from true north.

Magnetic Course. This course is the heading of the ship in degrees measured clockwise from magnetic north.

Compass Course. The reading of a particular magnetic compass, that is, the course the compass actually indicates, is called the compass course.

Correcting for Compass Error

Variation and deviation combined gives what is known as magnetic *compass error*. The course on which the ship is to head is the *true course*, worked out from the chart, on which only true courses and bearings are given. Given the true course, it is necessary to find the *compass course* that you must steer to make good the true course. Do this by applying variation and deviation to the true course. This is done by a simple rule, remembered as a nonsense statement: *Can Dead Men Vote Twice?*

In order to change from true to compass course, or vice versa, set up the columns as follows:

Can	Compass
Dead	Deviation
Men	Magnetic
Vote	Variation
Twice	True

Going *up*, or changing from true to compass, is called *uncorrecting*. Coming down, or changing from compass to true, is called *correcting*. Just remember this rule:

When *correcting, add* easterly and *subtract* westerly error.
When *uncorrecting, subtract* easterly and *add* westerly error.

All compass errors are either easterly or westerly. (There are no northerly or southerly errors.) To correct a compass course of 270° to the true course, first correct for deviation, and then correct for variation. An example is given below. The deviation table described earlier shows that the deviation for 270° is 7° west. Assume that the chart shows the variation to be 12° east. Make a table as follows:

Compass	270°	Compass	270°
Deviation	7°W	Deviation	7°W
Magnetic		Magnetic	263°
Variation	12°E	Variation	12°E
True		True	275°
Total error		Total error	5°E

To find *true course*, the 7°W deviation is subtracted from the compass course of 270°, (column two), which gives a magnetic course of 263°. The variation, 12°E, is then added to the magnetic course, giving the true course of 275°. The total compass error is 5°E, which is the difference between the 7°W and the 12°E.

But how do you decide whether to add or subtract the deviation or variation? Remember: when *correcting*—going from compass course to true course—*add easterly errors and subtract westerly errors*.

Note that *true* differs from *magnetic* by the amount of *variation*, and that *magnetic* differs from *compass* by the amount of *deviation*.

Uncorrecting

The process of finding the *compass course* from the *true course* is called *uncorrecting*. Suppose that the given true course is 180° and variation is 10°W.

Apply variation	Compass	
	Deviation	
	Magnetic	190°
	Variation	10°W
	True	180°
	Total error	
to true course	Compass	176°
	Deviation	14°E
	Magnetic	190°
	Variation	10°W
	True	180°
	Total error	4°E

This is *uncorrecting*, so reverse the rule and *add* westerly variation, giving a *magnetic course* of 190°.

Refer to the deviation table previously discussed. Take the deviation nearest the heading you are on. In this case the nearest deviation is 14°E, or that shown for 195°. Remember: when *uncorrecting*—going from *true to compass*—add westerly errors and *subtract* easterly errors.

Gyrocompass (Gyro)

This instrument is essentially a heavy fly wheel driven at high speed by an electric motor and mounted on gimbals so that it is free to move in all directions. It is usually located in a well-protected place below deck. *Repeaters*—compass cards electrically connected to the gyrocompass and placed on the bridge and in other parts of the ship—show the same readings as the master gyrocompass.

Gyro Error. The gyrocompass is not affected by either variation or deviation. The motion of the earth will cause the rotor to move so that its axis lies in a north-south direction. For mechanical reasons and because of the vibrations of the ship, the best gyrocompass will vary from time to time from true north. This *gyro error* is rarely more than a few degrees, and normally it is constant over a long period of time and on any heading of the ship.

Correcting for Gyro Error. Gyro error is determined by taking an azimuth, or bearing, on a celestial body where the exact bearing can be determined. This error is applied every time the compass is used, and the rule for the magnetic compass is followed: when *correcting, add* easterly errors and *subtract* westerly errors.

Bearings

Bearings are lines drawn, pointed, or sighted from one object to another. For accurate navigation, a system of true and relative bearings has been worked out so that all directions at sea are given in bearings that are measured in degrees.

True bearings are based on a circle of degrees with true north as 000° (or 360°), east as 090°, south as 180°, and west as 270°.

Relative bearings are based on a circle drawn around the ship itself, with the bow as 000°, the starboard beam as 090°, the stern as 180°, and the port beam as 270° (figure 13–6). Thus, if a ship is on a course true north (000°), another ship sighted dead ahead would bear 000° *true* and 000° *relative*. But if the ship were on a course true east and sighted a ship dead ahead, it would bear 090° *true* but would still be dead ahead or 000° *relative*.

Relative Bearings

Relative bearings are used wherever there is no compass. Lookouts cannot have accurate compasses at hand, nor can they be expected to know the course of the ship and the true directions that lie about it. They need a way to point out where objects lie, and this method must be fast, accurate, and unmistakable. By using the Navy system of relative bearings measured in degrees from the bow of the ship, a man can soon learn to report objects in such a way that anyone can locate them immediately.

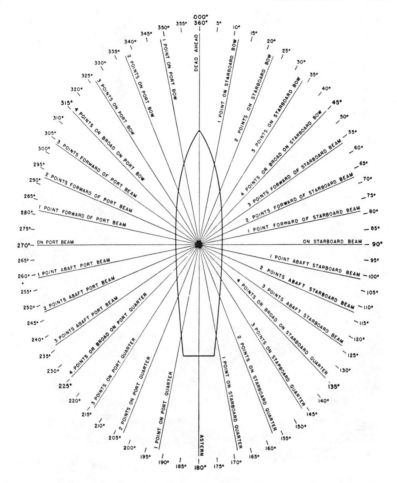

Figure 13–6. Relative bearings from a ship. The old system of giving bearings by the 32 "points" of the compass is indicated, but no longer used.

True Bearings

True bearings can be obtained directly from a gyro repeater, from a magnetic compass situated so as to make bearings on outside objects possible and with the appropriate corrections applied, or by calculation from a *relative* bearing.

Pelorus. This is a flat, nonmagnetic metal ring mounted on a vertical stand about five feet high (figure 13–7). The inner edge of the ring is

Figure 13–7. A pelorus.

graduated in degrees from 0° at the ship's head clockwise through 360°. This ring encloses a gyro repeater. Upon the ring is mounted a pair of sighting vanes. These vanes are sighted through on an object much like the sights on a rifle.

Gyro Bearings. Since the gyrocompass, and therefore the gyro repeater in the pelorus, are already closely lined up with the true geographic directions, taking a true bearing over the gyro card is the easiest and most common method. Merely line the vane sights of the bearing circle on the object, steady the compass bowl in its gimbals (rings that compensate for the roll of the ship) until the leveler bubble shows that the vanes are level, and then read off the bearing in degrees on the compass card.

TIDES

Tides are very important in many shiphandling operations. In some harbors, deep-draft ships may be able to enter only at high tide. Large ships are usually launched, or dry-docked, at high tide. Ships going alongside piers in channels subject to strong tidal currents will usually wait for slack water, when the tide is neither ebbing nor flooding. Every Coast Guardsman who is concerned with the handling of a vessel, from the largest cutter to a motor whaleboat, must understand what causes *tides* and the meaning of the names given to different tidal conditions.

The term *tide* describes the regular rise and fall of the water level along a seacoast or in an ocean port. Gravitational attraction of the moon is the primary cause of tides (figure 13–8); it exerts a very considerable pull on the sea, piling the water up on that part of the earth nearest the moon. There is an almost equal *bulge* of water on the opposite side of the earth, because the centrifugal force of the earth piles the water up where the pull of the moon is weakest.

As the moon orbits the earth every 24 hours and 50 minutes, there are two low and two high tides at any place during that period. The low and high tides each are about 12 hours and 25 minutes apart. The

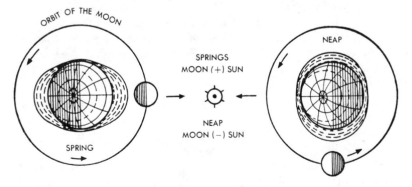

Figure 13–8. Relation of positions of the sun and moon to height of tides.

sun also affects the tide, but it is so much farther away than the moon that its pull is not nearly so great. A tide rising or moving from low to high water is said to be *flooding;* when the tide is falling, after high tide, it is said to be *ebbing*.

The difference in water depth between a high and the next low tide is considerable in many harbors; areas that are safe for a power boat at high tide may be completely dry at low water.

CURRENTS

In most harbors and inlets, the tides are the chief causes of currents; however, if the port is situated on a large river, its flow may have a marked effect on the tidal currents. The flow of such a river will prolong the duration of the ebb current as compared to that of the flood, and the velocity of the ebb current will be considerably greater than that of the flood.

Where the currents are chiefly caused by the rise and fall of the tide, their direction and speed are largely governed by the shape of the shore lines and the contour of the bottom. Where there is a long *reach,* or straight section of the waterway, the current will tend to flow most rapidly in the center and considerably slower in the shoal water near either shore. If a boat goes with the current, the coxswain will generally want to stay near the center of the waterway; if the boat goes against the current, he will stay as near shore as the prevailing water depth will allow.

In many wide inlets, near the time of *slack water,* when the current is at the end of the ebb or flood, the current may actually reverse itself in part of the inlet; while the ebb is still moving out in the main channel, a gentle flood current may start near one shore. This condition, where it exists, can be very helpful to a small boat operator.

Where there is a bend in the channel, the current will flow strongest on the outside of the bend. This effect is very marked, particularly with a strong current.

In some areas, a strong current can create areas of very rough water, called *tide rips*. These are usually shown on charts, and should be avoided.

Every vessel, regardless of her size, must make some allowance for the set and drift of the current, or this will affect the course to steer.

One more thing to bear in mind about currents is that only on the seacoast does the time of the turn of the current agree with the turn of the tide; that is, only on the seacoast does the current *flood* until the time of high water and *ebb* until the time of low water. At many ports owing to the effect of the shape of the land on the water flow, there may be a very considerable difference between the time of high or low water and the time that the current starts to ebb or flood.

A strong wind, blowing for a considerable period of time, will increase the speed of the current if they are both moving in the same direction. A wind will also prolong somewhat the duration of that current. Similarly, a strong wind may blow so much water out of a harbor that the water level will be considerably lower than its predicted depth for that time.

NAVIGATIONAL PUBLICATIONS

The principles of all methods of navigation can be learned, but much detailed information necessary in working navigational problems must be obtained from complicated charts and tables. One of these is the *Nautical Almanac,* which enables the navigator to determine the exact location in the sky of the planets, sun, moon, and major stars for any second of GMT. *Tide Tables* show the predicted times and height of high and low tides. This publication also shows the exact time of sunrise and sunset. A ship will carry a large number of charts, and an important duty of the quartermaster is to keep them corrected and up to date.

Wind and Currents

For the greatest part, the movement of a raft will be governed by prevailing winds and currents. These, of course, cannot be altered but they sometimes can be intelligently utilized if the survivor knows the direction in which he desires to go.

Wind and current do not necessarily move in the same direction in a given area. One may be favorable, the other unfavorable.

The lower the raft rides in the water and the lower its occupants remain, the greater will be the effect of current. This effect can be increased by the use of a sea anchor or drag if the current is setting toward land or toward an area in which your patrols are operating.

On the other hand, if the wind should be favorable, the raft should be lightened as much as practicable. Survivors should sit erect to offer wind resistance. Any sort of makeshift sail would be of help.

To use wind or current advantageously, two things are required:

Knowledge of the direction you wish to go.
Knowledge of the direction of wind and current.

Certain types of life rafts are equipped with charts printed on water-resistant paper. They show the direction of prevailing winds and currents at different periods of the year and also land and water areas. To use them it is necessary to have a general idea of your position at the time you ditch. In the case of aircraft, it is the responsibility of the officers to give out this information in the event of a forced landing. But in case they might be unlucky in the landing it is a good idea to carry a rough—necessarily very rough—plan of overwater flights in your mind, whatever your duty in a plane crew may be.

The wind and current map may not have reached your outfit on the date you need it most; or the plane captain may have it stuck in his bunk instead of the raft you find yourself in. Therefore, form the habit of studying maps and charts of the area in which you are operating. Get a general picture in your mind of the locations of lands and islands in the vicinity.

The Sun

The sun rises in the east and sets in the west. If you are north of latitude 23°27′ N. the sun will invariably pass to the south of you on its daily trip across the sky.

Latitude 23°27′ N. is an imaginary line passing approximately through the Marcus Islands, Formosa, the tip of Lower California, along the northern shore of Cuba, and through the northern part of the Arabian Sea (figure 13–9).

The sun follows the upper path at about the 21st of June each year before starting slowly south.

If you are south of latitude 23°27′ S. the sun will *always* pass to the north of you on its daily trip from east to west. Lat. 23°27′ S. passes roughly through Noumea, Rio de Janeiro, and the southern part of Madagascar.

About March 21 and September 21 of each year the sun travels across the sky directly along the equator. If you should be a few miles north of New Guinea, or in the center of the Macassar Strait, or around the northern Galapagos Islands on those dates the sun would pass directly overhead.

Planets

Planets such as Mars, Jupiter, and Venus resemble stars—except that they do not twinkle. Planets are known as wanderers, since they move about among the stars, and are not much help to the survivor in

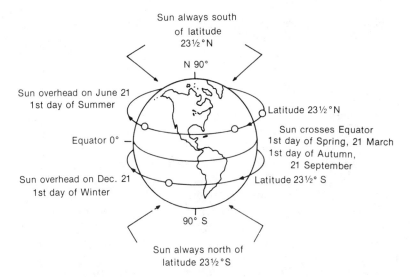

Figure 13–9. Diagram showing the sun's apparent path around the earth.

determining direction. If possible, learn something about the planets and how and where they usually appear, so that when a planet appears in some constellation you will not think that you have mistaken the order of the stars and therefore of the constellation.

Stars

Like the sun, the stars also move across the sky from east to west. Their position relative to one another remains fixed. This is a convenience in locating them, once you learn the relationship of stars and groups of stars to one another. Upon locating one or more stars or constellations in the sky you can use them as markers telling you where to look for others.

You won't find the same stars in the same part of the heavens every night. This is because the sun moves westward around the earth at a slightly greater speed than do the stars.

Consequently, stars that may be just appearing over the horizon at midnight in one month may be high in the heavens at midnight another month. Or they may not appear at all. The latter happens when they travel across the sky within a few hours of the sun, which, of course, would be during daylight—for the stars travel across the sky in daylight just as they do at night.

Groups of stars are known as constellations. Some of the most prominent and easily identifiable constellations and single stars are described in the following pages. Train yourself to recognize them.

Orion

The constellation of Orion (figure 13–10) always rises true east, sets true west, and follows a path directly over the equator. Notice how the three stars forming the belt are almost parallel to the equator. The two brightest stars of the constellation, Betelgeuse and Rigel, lie approximately the same distance north and south of the line respectively. Orion can be seen from any position on earth.

On a clear night around Christmas, Orion is visible for almost the entire night, rising around 1800 and setting about 0600. Each month thereafter, it is visible for a shorter period of time, appearing at dusk in a progressively higher position until March when it first appears near its zenith (highest position in relation to you). From then until June it can be first seen in a lower position to the west of you. In June, Orion is not visible at all as it makes its passage during daylight hours.

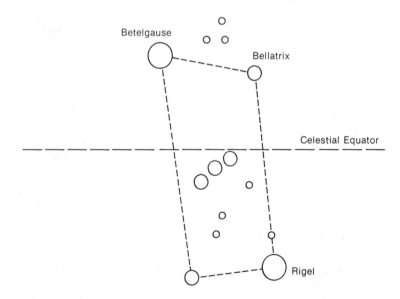

Figure 13–10. The constellation of Orion is the biggest and brightest in the Northern Hemisphere; it includes several navigational stars.

Then in July it once more makes its appearance in the east around 0400 and each month thereafter appears about two hours earlier.

The Dipper

The Dipper is a distinctive constellation containing seven stars. If you are in northern latitudes it will be the most important constellation in the heavens for you to identify.

Polaris (the North Star)

As the Dipper is the most important constellation in northern latitudes, Polaris is the most important star. Since it is almost directly over the North Pole, for practical purposes it can be considered to be due north of you wherever you may be.

Polaris is not very bright and is sometimes hard to locate if the sky is hazy. Without the Dipper it would be very hard to find. But the two "pointers" of the Dipper, whatever its position, "point" to Polaris.

As shown in figure 13–11, the Dipper moves slowly around Polaris— occupying in turn the position shown.

Hold the page above you—and face north to view it. That should give you an idea of the way the Dipper and Polaris will appear.

Now that you know how to locate Polaris—if you are north of the equator (if you are south of the equator you won't be able to see it)— remember this rule. *The number of degrees Polaris is above your horizon will always be nearly equal to your latitude* (figure 13–12).

This means that if Polaris is 30° above the horizon, you are in latitude 30° N.; if it is 50° above the horizon, you are in 50° N. It would be directly overhead at the North Pole.

To estimate the angular distance of Polaris above the horizon you must first estimate the point in the heavens that is exactly overhead. From the horizon to that point is 90°. Halfway from the horizon to the zenith (the point overhead) would be 45°, one-sixth (or one-third of halfway) would be 15°, and so on.

One degree of latitude is 60 miles, so if you are 10 degrees off in estimating the altitude of Polaris you will be 600 miles off in your estimate of latitude. If you ever have to use this, measure the star's altitude as exactly as you can—and then don't place too much confidence in the accuracy of your estimate.

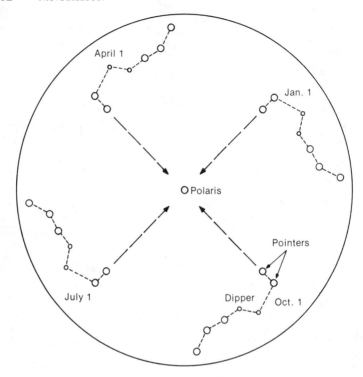

Figure 13–11. Rotation of the Dipper around the north celestial pole, showing how the pointer stars locate Polaris.

Southern Cross

In the Southern Hemisphere Polaris is not visible. There the Southern Cross is the most distinctive constellation. As you go south the Southern Cross appears shortly before Polaris drops from sight astern. An imaginary line through the long axis of the Southern Cross points toward the South Pole (figure 13–13). The Southern Cross should not be confused with a larger cross near-by, known as the False Cross. The latter, though the stars are more widely spaced, is less bright. It has a star in the center, making five stars in all, while the Southern Cross has only four. Two of these are among the brightest stars in the heavens.

There is no star at the South Pole to correspond to Polaris at the North Pole. In fact the point where such a star would be, if one existed, lies in a region devoid of stars. This point is so dark in comparison with the rest of the sky that it is known as the Coal Sack.

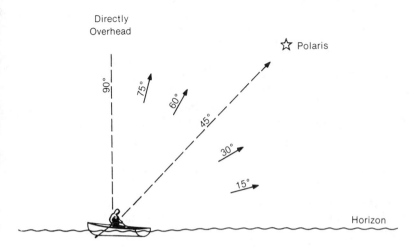

Figure 13–12. Estimating latitude by observation of Polaris. When the star is 45 degrees above the horizon, the observer is at latitude 45 North.

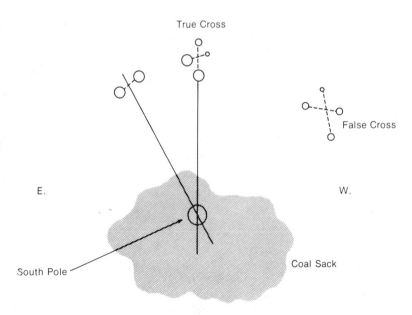

Figure 13–13. Locating south celestial pole by stars in the Southern Cross.

First, extend an imaginary line along the long axis of the Cross to the south. Join the two bright stars to the east of the Cross with an imaginary line. Bisect this line with one at right angles. Where this east line intersects the one through the Cross is (approximately) the point above the South Pole.

This point can be used to estimate latitude in the same manner as is Polaris in northern latitudes—by its height above the horizon.

Orientation

It is possible to determine north, south, east, and west by day or night. If you can determine any of the cardinal directions, you can easily determine the others.

Well out to sea the prevailing winds from about 8°-10° N. to about 40° N. (look this up on a map or globe and see where it is) are from the northeast—blowing toward the southwest. They are called the northeast trades and will carry you in a southwesterly direction.

North of 40° N. and south of 40° S. the winds are usually from the west and will tend to carry you eastward.

These are only general rules. There are many local and some seasonal exceptions. Learn as much as you can by observations and questions about the winds and sea currents in the areas in which you operate.

Learn to pick out the stars that have been mentioned and many more. Learn where to look for them in the heavens. This is how the first navigators found their way, and without navigational instruments it is still the best method.

CHAPTER 14

Rules of the Road

Just as an automobile driver must know traffic signals and the laws governing speed, parking, and passing on curves, so people who handle ships and boats must know the signals, lights, laws, buoyage systems, and other matters governing traffic on the high seas and their connecting waters and in crowded harbors. The rules are not just for big ships—they apply to boats and ships of all sizes (figure 14–1).

SEAGOING TRAFFIC RULES

The nautical traffic laws are embodied in a set of rules, termed collectively the Rules of the Road. On the high seas and in the navigable inland waters of countries without special local rules of their own, ships are governed by a set of laws established by agreement among maritime nations, known as the *International Rules* (Convention on the International Regulations for Preventing Collisions at Sea, 1972—COLREGS). Along the coasts and in adjacent rivers and harbors of the United States, its territories, and possessions, however, ships are subject to local regulations known as *Inland Rules* (Inland Navigational Rules Act of 1980).

Content of the Rules

The Rules of the Road are hard to think of in terms of automobile operation, because cars and trucks are mostly limited to roadways.

Figure 14–1. The crew of the cutter *Papaw* tends an ice-damaged buoy. Buoys and other aids mark the nation's waterways. The rules of the road govern the vessels moving on those waterways. Both are critical to safe navigation.

Roadways can have lanes marked with paint, have signs for directions and warnings, be controlled by signal lights, and be illuminated by street lights. Except in harbors with marked channels for deep-draft vessels, navigating a ship or boat on open water is a lot like driving a car around a large, mostly empty parking lot. The nautical Rules of the Road, to be useful, must provide for both day and night situations, and when vessels can see each other and when, because of poor visibility, they cannot. The rules should let one vessel know something about the other, what it is doing, where it's going, its size, whether or not it can maneuver, and on congested waters, its intentions. Information like this may not be important to a driver on a roadway, but in a large, nearly empty parking lot—if you think about it—that information might be very useful.

The Rules of the Road apply to a vessel when it is "under way," meaning it is not at anchor, made fast to the shore, or aground, and they also apply when it is at anchor or aground. They do not apply when it is moored to the shore.

There are rules that are mostly common sense such as keeping a lookout, being cautious, going at a safe speed, using the equipment you have to minimize risk, avoiding dangerous situations before they happen, considering the need for other vessels to move in narrow waterways because of their draft and not blocking them or embarrassing them, keeping to the right in narrow channels, and obeying special navigation rules and regulations. There are other rules that govern power-driven vessels and sailing vessels and other vessels that have limited maneuverability when they are in sight of one another. Certain rules describe which vessels have the right-of-way. The vessel with the right-of-way is called the "stand-on vessel," and the one that has to keep out of the way of the other is called the "give-way vessel." Then, there are also rules for vessels in restricted visibility, rules for lights and shapes, rules for sounds and light signals, and rules for distress signals.

The Basic Rule of Safety

The basic rule of safety for ships and boats is practically the same as that for automobiles: safety first, keep to the right, and proceed cautiously when in doubt. And while doing this, report immediately to the officer in charge of the ship or boat all lights, sounds, and signals of any sort.

Application and Scope of the Rules

For many years, the International Rules of the Road and the Inland Rules were quite different. This caused a lot of confusion. On December 24, 1981, a new set of Inland Rules came generally into effect, which are very similar to the International Rules of the Road. While there are a few areas in U.S. waters where some parts of the old rules still apply, most navigators of oceangoing vessels will not be faced with the confusion of the past. Some important differences still do exist, however, such as the use of maneuvering signals, which mean "intent" on inland waters, but which mean an actual maneuver is taking place on international waters. And there are some towing light differences as well as minimal vessel length requirements.

New mariners will find that the new rules and their similar terms are easy to absorb, but more seasoned sailors, used to the old differences, will have to be careful not to get mixed-up. There are a group of general definitions in the rules, (Rule 3) such as what the word "vessel" means. There are also some more precise definitions in the different parts of the rules as well as whole sections of "definitions" on lights (Rule 21) and sounds (Rule 32). It is important that persons who navigate vessels have a full and complete understanding of the Rules of the Road. But every seaman should realize the purposes of the rules, and being aware of their importance, take an intelligent and active interest in his or her duties as a lookout, crew member, or passenger in a boat. The professional mariner *must* realize that all lights and sounds at sea have a meaning, and that no light or sound signal must ever be overlooked. This chapter gives an idea of the importance of the rules and some details as to their application to small boats. A section on buoys is included. While not actually part of the Rules of the Road, the buoyage system (the traffic lights and signals of harbors and channels) also governs water traffic.

Navigation Lights

At the same time as the new mariner learns the meaning of the words "port" and "starboard," the colors red and green pop up. Red for port and green for starboard are two of the four colors used in navigation lights. Sometimes navigation lights are called "running lights." The other two colors are white and yellow. The white navigation lights on a vessel are used along with the red and green navigation lights to let an observer know in which direction a vessel is going when only its lights can be seen. The yellow light is used in special circumstances such as in towing situations.

As we know, the red port and green starboard lights are used to mark the sides of the vessel, while the white lights are usually located on the vessel's centerline. The navigation lights are not used by the navigator to see with, as are the headlights of a car, but rather to allow navigators and lookouts on other vessels to see his vessel. The red and green are called "side lights." A white light at or near the stern is called a "stern light" and one, and sometimes two, white lights are placed on the vessel's superstructure, or on masts, and called "masthead lights."

These navigation lights are allowed to show only in certain sectors around the vessel. Using the 360-degree system, each of the two side lights are positioned to show from right ahead to 22.5 degrees abaft the beam on each respective side for a total of (90° + 22.5°) 112.5 degrees on the horizon on each side. The stern light is installed to show from right aft to 67.5 degrees on each side of the vessel for a total of (67.5° + 67.5°) 135 degrees over the arc of the horizon. The masthead light(s) are positioned to show from right ahead to 22.5 degrees abaft the beam on both sides or (22.5° + 90.0° + 90.0° + 22.5°) 225 degrees over the arc of the horizon. The masthead light(s) combined with the stern light show at least one white light all around the vessel, (masthead 225° + stern 135° = 360°). When two masthead lights are required, such as on vessels 50 or more meters in length, or when they are optimally installed on vessels less than 50 meters, the aftermost masthead light is higher than the forward one.

The side lights let the observer know which side of another vessel he is seeing and in that way the observer knows in which general direction the other vessel is heading. If the observer doesn't see the side lights, then he knows that he is looking at the stern of the other vessel. When both side lights are visible, the other vessel is headed right at the observer. The use of two masthead lights on larger vessels lets the observer see changes of heading on the part of the other vessel. If the two white lights get closer together, the ship is changing its heading toward the observer. If the white lights separate, it is heading away.

A single white light seen on another vessel that is under way is usually the vessel's stern light. That means that the observer is astern of the other vessel. But when a side light is visible, that means that the observer is nearly abeam the other vessel or forward of it. The masthead lights and side lights on another vessel should be visible at the same time while the other vessel's stern light should never be visible to an observer at the same time as one of its side lights.

There are a lot of other kinds of lights shown by vessels at night. Some are used for towing, some for anchoring, and some show a special purpose or situation of the vessel displaying the lights.

Sound Signals

There are two reasons for using sound signals. One is to let a vessel, which is aware of the presence of another, announce the direction of his maneuver or intended maneuver. On the Inland Waterways of the U.S., and under overtaking situations in international narrow channels and fairways, agreement with the other vessel's intentions is also signaled by sound. Warning signals are also used when needed in connection with maneuvering signals. The other reason for sound signals is so one vessel can let other vessels know of its presence when visibility is restricted. The sound signals are made by blasts of the ship's whistle. A short blast is about 1 second in duration, a prolonged blast is 4 to 6 seconds in duration.

Maneuvering and Warning Signals

On the high seas under the International Rules of the Road one short blast means "I'm altering my course to starboard" and two short blasts means, "I'm altering my course to port." On U.S. Inland Waters the one-short-blast signal means that the vessel *intends* to leave the other on its port side; two short blasts means an intent to leave the other vessel on the starboard side. The direction of the maneuver is the same for both U.S. Inland and International Waters, but on U.S. Inland Waters, the vessel being signaled must repeat the signal when in agreement or sound the danger signal of five or more short and rapid blasts.

Three short blasts, both inland and international, means a vessel is operating astern propulsion. The danger signal for both rules is the same; five or more short and rapid blasts.

On international waters in narrow channels or fairways, overtaking signals that include intent signals and agreement signals are exchanged. Intent to overtake on the starboard side is signaled by two prolonged blasts followed by one short blast; on the port side, the signal is two prolonged and two short. The agreement signal is one prolonged, one short, one prolonged and one short (or "Charlie" in Morse Code).

On U.S. Inland Waters, one prolonged blast is sounded when other vessels may not be observed, such as at a bend of a channel, or behind other obstructions, and when leaving docks.

Lights may be used in conjunction with whistle signals to visually show the sound signal. The light is flashed for the same duration as the whistle is sounded. The lights used are all around (360°) lights; International Rules specify the color white of five miles minimum visibility and Inland Rules specify white or yellow of two miles visibility.

On U.S. waters when agreement is reached by bridge-to-bridge radiotelephone (Channel 13 VHF, 156.65 MHz), a vessel in a meeting, crossing, or overtaking situation is not obliged to sound whistle signals but may do so. If agreement is not reached, whistle signals shall be exchanged.

Sound Signals in Restricted Visibility

Whether day or night, in or near an area of restricted visibility, sound signals, often called "fog signals," shall be sounded. A power-driven vessel making way through the water shall sound, at intervals of not more than two minutes, one prolonged blast. If the vessel is under way but stopped, it shall sound, not more than two minutes apart, two prolonged blasts with a two second interval between the blasts. These signals are required on both International and U.S. Inland Waters.

There are additional special signals for vessels at anchor, vessels not under command, fishing vessels, pilot vessels, sailing vessels, towing and towed vessels, and vessels aground. There are also some exceptions for vessels less than 12 meters. Basically, the "fog signals" for both U.S. Inland and International Waters are the same.

Rights of Way

A vessel having the right of way, is the "stand-on" vessel. Instead of doing whatever it wishes, the stand-on vessel has a number of obligations. Likewise, the other vessel—the "give-way" vessel—has its own obligations.

Deciding which vessel is stand-on and which is give-way depends upon a number of factors. Manner of propulsion, or lack of it, is one factor; whichever vessel is to the port of the other is another; and sailing vessels approaching one another are governed by the position of the wind. Moreover, Narrow Channel situations, Vessel Traffic Regulation situations, and overtaking situations create their own requirements. But both U.S. Inland and International Rules are alike with few exceptions on the matter of determining stand-on and give-way vessels.

The rules involving two sailing vessels are somewhat complicated and may require a detailed explanation. Except where a power-driven vessel is confined to a narrow channel, or is being controlled by a traffic service, or is being overtaken, a sailing vessel is the stand-on vessel in a power-driven–sailing vessel encounter. The power-driven vessel is, thus, the give-way vessel. The give-way vessel must keep out of the way of the stand-on vessel and so far as possible take early and substantial action to keep well clear.

In any overtaking situation, the overtaking vessel must keep out of the way of the overtaken vessel; therefore the overtaken vessel is the stand-on vessel, the overtaking is the give-way vessel. Overtaking means when one vessel is coming up on another vessel so that at night the vessel coming up would only see the other's sternlight. That would mean it was coming from a direction more than 22.5 degrees abaft the overtaken vessel's beam.

In a head-on situation where two power-driven vessels are meeting on reciprocal or nearly reciprocal courses, each must alter its course to starboard so that each shall pass on the port side of the other. There is no give-way nor stand-on vessel in this situation.

Whenever two power-driven vessels are crossing so as to involve risk of collision, the vessel that has the other to starboard becomes the give-way vessel and, hence, shall keep out of the way. If the circumstances of the case allow, the give-way vessel must avoid crossing ahead of the other vessel. On the Great Lakes, U.S. Western Rivers, or other specified waters, a vessel crossing a river shall keep out of the way of a power-driven vessel ascending (going upstream) or descending (going downstream) the river.

Stand-on vessels must keep their course and speed. Otherwise, the give-way vessel's maneuver to keep clear could result in a collision. A stand-on vessel can take action to avoid a collision by its maneuver alone as soon as it becomes apparent that the give-way vessel is not taking appropriate avoiding action. If it is necessary for the stand-on vessel to take this action, it shall not alter course to port for a vessel on its port side. The stand-on vessel shall take such action to avoid a collision when it is so close that action by the give-way vessel alone would not avoid a collision.

Except in vessel traffic service controlled situations, narrow channel situations and overtaking situations, a power-driven vessel shall keep out of the way of a vessel not under command, a vessel restricted in its ability to maneuver, a vessel engaged in fishing, and a sailing vessel. Sailing vessels under way shall keep out of the way of a vessel not under command, a vessel restricted in its ability to maneuver, and a vessel engaged in fishing. A vessel engaged in fishing when under way shall so far as possible keep out of the way of a vessel not under command and a vessel restricted in its ability to maneuver. Seaplanes on the water shall generally keep out of the way of all vessels and avoid impeding their navigation. When a risk of collision exists between a seaplane and a vessel, the seaplane shall comply with the Rules of the Road.

Rule of Good Seamanship

Nothing in these Rules shall exonerate any vessel, or the owner, master, or crew thereof, from the consequences of any neglect to comply with these Rules or of the neglect of any precaution which may be required by the ordinary practice of seamen, or by the special circumstances of the case.

General Prudential Rule

In construing and complying with these Rules due regard shall be had to all dangers of navigation and collision and to any special circumstances, including the limitations of the vessels involved, which may make a departure from these Rules necessary to avoid immediate danger.

Submarine Distress Signals

A yellow smoke bomb fired into the air indicates a submarine is coming to periscope depth from below periscope depth. A red smoke bomb fired into the air indicates the submarine is in trouble and will surface immediately if able to do so. In any case it requires assistance. Any colored smoke bomb fired into the air at short intervals indicates that a submarine is in trouble and requires assistance.

Special Aircraft Signals

The following signals are used by aircraft in emergency conditions involving a forced landing; if a Very's pistol is not available, red tracer bullets may be used to attract attention:

Figure 14–2. Failure to understand and observe all the rules of the road can result in disaster.

White Very's Signal meaning "Can proceed shortly. Wait if practicable."

Green Very's Signal meaning "Need help or parts. Long delay."

Red Very's Signal meaning "Need medical assistance; land, if possible." Or: "Pick us up; plane abandoned."

It is against the law for anyone to use emergency signals, or any other signal that may be confused with them, except for the purpose of indicating that a vessel or an aircraft is in distress.

AIDS TO NAVIGATION IN U.S. WATERS

Buoys Presently Used in U.S. Waters

Buoys are plastic or metal floats of various types. They direct the course of sea traffic in the same way that road markers direct automobiles on highways (Appendix D). There are seven types of buoys.

Nun Buoy. A conical-shaped buoy, used principally to mark the right-hand side of a channel, that is, the right-hand side when facing inland. When speaking of right hand or left hand with regard to buoys, it is understood that the ship or boat in question is approaching land from seaward.

Can Buoy. A cylindrical buoy, used principally to mark the left-hand side of the same channel. The nun and can buoys are the only buoys whose shape has a special significance. When a ship is going

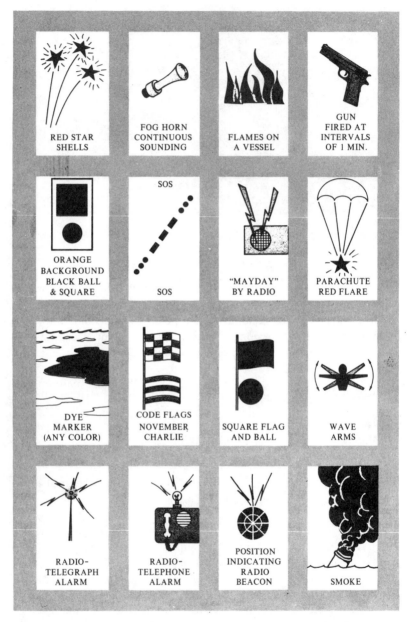

Figure 14–3. Distress signals—1972 Colregs. (See International Rules, Annex IV.)

toward land, the nun buoys should be to starboard, the can buoy to port.

Bell Buoy. A float with a flat top surmounted by a framework in which a bell is fixed. The motion of the sea causes the bell to ring.

Gong Buoy. Similar to a bell buoy, but has four gongs, each of a different tone.

Whistle Buoy. Usually a conical-shaped buoy bearing a whistle that generally is sounded by the motion of the sea.

Lighted Buoy. A buoy that contains batteries. It is surmounted by a framework supporting a light of some sort. Shapes of lighted buoys are not uniform.

Combination Buoy. A buoy in which a light and a sound signal are combined, such as a lighted bell buoy, lighted gong buoy, or lighted whistle buoy. Shapes of combination buoys follow no set pattern.

Purposes of Buoys

Buoys of many shapes and colors are used to mark sides of channels, junctions of one channel with another, obstructions, anchorages (including quarantine anchorages), areas where fish nets and traps are permitted, and areas where dredging operations are being conducted.

All types of buoys are used for all the purposes listed, except that nun buoys are not found on the left-hand side of a channel and can buoys are not found on the right-hand side of a channel as viewed from seaward.

At night or in fog the nun and can buoys are difficult to locate; therefore, other types of buoys may replace them at important points.

Colored Buoys

Buoys are painted in various colors and combinations of colors, according to location and purpose as follows:

Red: Right-hand side of a channel (as seen from seaward).

Black: Left-hand side of the same channel.*

Red and black horizontal bands: Obstructions in the channel, or

---

*On 15 April 1982 the U.S. Coast Guard signed an agreement with the various member nations of the International Association of Lighthouse Authorities (IALA), whereby during the period 1982–1989 most black buoys in U.S. waters will become green buoys. Certain other changes involving other types of buoys and buoy shapes, and the use of top marks on some of them, are also to be phased in under the agreement.

junction where two channels meet. If the top band is red, the better channel is to the left of the buoy, which usually is a nun buoy. If the top band is black, the better channel is to the right of the buoy, which usually is a can buoy. Such marking always means that there is a channel on either side of the buoy. A junction where a secondary channel leads off from the main channel at a right angle usually is not marked by a junction buoy.

Black and white vertical stripes: Middle of the channel. Buoy may be passed on either side.

White: Anchorages.

Yellow: Quarantine anchorages.

White with green tops: Areas in which dredging is being carried on.

Black and white horizontal stripes: Special local meaning. For example, in the Norfolk area, a fish-net location.

Numbered Buoys

In addition to being colored, some buoys are numbered, lettered, or marked with combinations of numbers and letters. Red buoys bear even numbers, black buoys odd numbers, with numbers running from seaward toward the shore. If there are more buoys on one side of the channel than on the other, some numbers are omitted so as to keep these buoys numbered in approximate sequence.

Numbers are not given to banded or striped buoys, but letters are assigned to some of them for identification purposes. An example of such a buoy is the East Rockaway Inlet Bell Buoy, which carries black and white vertical stripes and the letters ER. Some buoys bear a number combination, such as Governors Island West End Shoal Bell Buoy, which is black and carries the combination 1GI.

"Red, Right, Returning"

"Red, right, returning" is a widely used phrase that helps in remembering the significance of the color on channel markers. The *red* buoys should be on the *right* when a ship is *returning* from the sea.

Lighted Buoys

Lighted buoys are used in important locations, particularly where they must be located and identified at night. If the lights are off longer than they are on—that is, if the period of darkness is longer than the period of light—they are called *flashing lights*. If the lights are on more than they are off, they are called *occulting lights*.

Any regularly flashing or occulting lighted buoy on which the light goes on every 2 or 3 seconds marks the side of a channel. If it goes on and off regularly but at a much faster rate, it marks a point on the side of a channel where special caution is required, such as a turn. Colors used for such buoy lights are red or white on the right side of the channel, and green or white on the left side of the channel (Appendix D). Note that white may be used for either side, but a red light is used only for the right side, and a green light only for the left side.

Lights that flash rapidly a number of times, pause, and then repeat the flashes are called *interrupted quick-flashing lights*. They are used on lighted obstruction and lighted junction buoys. A white light means there is no preferred channel. If the light is red, the preferred channel will be followed by keeping the buoy to starboard; if green, keep the buoy to port (as viewed from seaward).

Finally, there is a timing that produces groups of short-long flashes, each group appearing at regular intervals. Such a light is called a *short-long flashing light*. It is always white and always represents a black and white vertically striped lighted midchannel buoy.

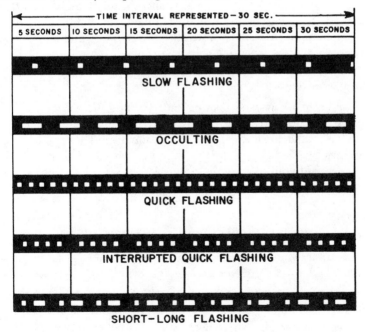

Figure 14–4. Characteristics of lights on lighted buoys.

Fixed Aids

Fixed aids called daymarks are often positioned along U.S. inland waterways in place of buoys. Sometimes these aids are located on pilings over water, sometimes they are located on shore. Fixed aids are occasionally placed in line with other fixed aids to form a "range" to mark the center of a channel. Aids, buoys and fixed, use the same system of numbers, lights, and colors.

Temporary Markers

Temporary channel markers usually consist of floats carrying lights, pennants, or lights and pennants. Red pennants mark the right side of the channel and black pennants mark the left side. Red and black vertically striped pennants mark obstructions and channel junctions, and black and white vertically striped pennants mark the midchannel (also called the fairway). If lighted, the right side of the channel will be marked by red lights, the left by white lights, obstructions by blue-over-red combination lights, and fairways by green lights.

Boat crews must keep on the alert and not rely too much on these sea markers. Buoys have a way of shifting about; lights burn out, or the blinking mechanism fails; whistles, bells, and gongs fail to sound loudly when the sea is calm.

Storm Warnings

In United States waters, information regarding the weather and the approach of storms is furnished by the Weather Bureau by means of bulletins, radio broadcasts, and in certain seaport towns, by storm warnings signaled by a system of flags, pennants, or lights (Appendix E). The night equivalent of these signals consists of lights in a vertical line.

Small Craft

When conditions dangerous to the operation of small craft are forecast for the area (winds up to 33 knots), a red pennant will be displayed by day, and a red light over a white light will be displayed at night.

Gale

Two red pennants or a white light over a red light indicate that winds ranging from 34 to 48 knots are forecast.

Whole Gale

A square red flag with a black center or two red lights indicate that winds from 48 to 63 knots are forecast.

Hurricane

Two red flags with black centers or three lights (red, white, red), indicate that winds of 64 knots and above are forecast.

CHAPTER 15

General Drills

General drills aboard ship are designed to prepare the crew to handle emergencies. At shore stations, drills are based on shipboard practices. By using a standard system of drills throughout the Coast Guard, it is possible for a man to move from one ship or unit to another and still know generally what to do in an emergency.

On board ship, a general drill means all hands—everyone. You must know exactly where your station is, and what your job is, for each drill or emergency (figure 15–1). This important information is clearly stated on the Watch, Quarter, and Station Bill for each division and is usually posted in the division's living compartment. Your job may be important, or perhaps you may only be required to stand at quarters waiting to be assigned as a relief. No matter what it is, no one is excused from any drill unless permission has been granted by the executive officer through the department head.

General drills develop teamwork so that every man in every department, every division, and every section knows and does exactly what must be done in every emergency. Every job has been assigned for a purpose. By drilling together, the ship's crew develops unity of action and teamwork. For this reason, all hands must participate wholeheartedly in all emergency drills.

STANDARD ORGANIZATION MANUAL

A bill is written to cover a certain emergency or job. It describes the duties involved and stations to be manned, and lists the rates required to perform the duties and man the stations. The Organization Manual

Figure 15–1. *Gallatin's* OD discusses simulated battle problems facing the ship with bridge personnel during general quarters.

for each ship describes *administrative bills, operational bills,* and *emergency bills.*

Administrative Bills

These bills set forth procedures for the everyday administration of the ship's company, where a specific assignment for each member of the crew is required; they include the bills listed below.

Personnel Assignment

The executive officer is responsible for carrying out this bill. He assigns officers to departments, to collateral duties, and to deck and CIC watches, and assigns enlisted men to the various offices. Division officers assign men to battle stations, duty sections, and regular watches. Under this bill nonrated men are assigned to messman duties for three months; designated men are assigned to the master-at-arms force for six months.

Berthing and Locker

This bill assigns all bunks, lockers, and rooms for enlisted men and officers. Division officers assign bunks and lockers for men within their divisions.

Cleaning and Maintenance

Cleaning stations and duties are assigned by division officers, except that side cleaners are assigned by the first lieutenant to care for the ship's exterior.

Operational Bills

These bills detail procedures and specific assignments of men for evolutions of a periodic nature.

Special Sea Detail

The first lieutenant, under the executive officer, is responsible for maintaining this bill, which covers both getting under way and entering port.

Replenishment at Sea (UNREP)

The first lieutenant prepares this bill. Each department has definite responsibilities. In normal peacetime operations, Coast Guard cutters do not perform UNREP operations.

Flight Operations

This sets up the procedure for launching and recovering helicopters in vessels carrying them.

Search

This provides for extended surface searches, or working with aircraft to locate wrecks or survivors. Such searches may continue for days.

Steering Casualty

This sets up emergency procedures for steering the ship if the usual system fails.

Rescue and Assistance

The engineer officer maintains this bill, under the supervision of the executive officer. It sets up procedures for the rescue and assistance detail in case of a plane crash close aboard, distress of another ship or distress ashore, and rescue of a large number of survivors.

Landing Party

This provides a nominal force equipped and organized to perform field functions ashore, to police an area during an emergency, and to take part in parades or ceremonies. It is maintained by the weapons officer.

Visit and Search, Prize Crew, and Boarding and Capture

Such operations were much more liable to take place in the old days of square riggers and muzzle loaders, but they can still happen, and it's the responsibility of the operations officer to keep the bill up to date. Visit and search involves sending a party of armed officers and men aboard a ship to determine her nationality, type of cargo, and nature of employment. A prize crew is organized to take over a seized and captured merchant ship and take her to port. A boarding and capture party is organized to perform the same duties as a prize crew, and it is also able to control prisoners. Law enforcement duties frequently involve boarding; the vessel to be searched might be a jumbo tanker suspected of carrying drugs, or merely a 16-foot "puddle jumper" being checked for required safety equipment.

Towing

Cutters frequently have to tow other vessels in rescue operations. The method of rigging for tow varies in each class and type of ship. The fixed towing method is usually used, involving hawsers and careful handling of engines to make proper speed.

All-Hands Drills

These are the emergency drills: General Quarters, Man Overboard, NBC Defense, and Emergency Destruction. When the alarm for one of these sounds, go to your station on the double—FORWARD and UP the STARBOARD side, AFT and DOWN the PORT side. Maintain silence; only men in charge will speak.

Alarms

GQ

Continuous sounding of the general alarm, or (on smaller ships) siren; horn, or bell, plus the word "General Quarters! General Quarters! All hands man your battle stations," over the 1MC system.

Fire

Word passed twice over general announcing system, giving compartment location, followed by rapid ringing of the ship's bell, followed by one stroke if forward, two if amidships, three if aft.

Man Overboard

Word passed twice "Man overboard, port (starboard) side," followed by six or more short blasts of the whistle.

Collision

Words "Collision, port (starboard) side, forward (aft, amidships), all hands man your battle stations," followed by general alarm. Some ships have a special howler for collision alarm.

Rescue and Assistance

Word passed over the general announcing system, as appropriate: "Plane crash, starboard side," "Away, the Rescue and Assistance Detail, rescue survivors."

Emergency Bills

These bills detail procedures and specific assignment of men to perform an evolution on short notice, when there is danger of loss of life or of the ship itself.

General Emergency
Man Overboard
Nuclear, Biological, and Chemical Defense
Emergency Destruction

General Emergency

This bill organizes the crew to handle the effects of a major emergency, such as collision, grounding, explosion, earthquake, storm, or battle damage. It also provides for an orderly process of abandoning ship if this becomes necessary, and for salvage of the ship if feasible. It is set up to assign men to necessary duties, whether a full crew or partial crew is on board.

The general emergency bill will not give detailed duties for every emergency, because it is impossible to plan for all emergencies. The one thing every man must remember is that he must carry out all orders from persons in authority with speed and precision. As it is possible that any emergency may result in casualties, every man must learn the general duties and responsibilities of those senior to him, because he may have to take them over.

Man Overboard

The first necessity when a man goes overboard is prompt action. Anyone who sees a man go overboard should immediately give the alarm "Man overboard, port (or starboard) side," drop a life ring or life jacket if possible, and try to keep the man in sight. If a smoke float and dye marker are available, they should also be dropped. Make sure the officer of the deck is informed immediately.

Every underway watch is organized to handle this emergency. The OOD will maneuver the ship to reach a recovery position, at the same time having the word passed twice, sounding six or more short blasts on the whistle, hoisting OSCAR by day or showing two pulsating red lights at night. These signals apply to naval task force operations and are practiced by all cutters. The lifeboat crew will stand by to lower away when directed. A helicopter may be launched, if available, as the helicopter can quickly spot a man in the water and can pick him up even if he is unable to help himself. A muster of the crew must be held in order to find out who is missing.

There is always the possibility that the man overboard may be *you*. If this should happen, keep your head. Don't panic or despair. Hold your breath when you hit the water and the buoyancy of your lungs will bring you to the surface. Don't swim frantically away from the ship—the screws won't suck you under, because they are too deep in the water. Just keep afloat and try to stay right where you went in. The ship will maneuver so as to come right back down her track to you.

Even if no one saw you go over, keep afloat. When a man is missed, ships and aircraft commence hunting for him. Men have been found and picked up after several hours in the water. In at least one case, a man was picked up after an entire day.

If a man goes overboard in port, the alarm is sounded as usual, and the OOD uses the best available method of rescue. Boats in the water will assist in any emergency without orders.

Emergency Destruction

This is action, ordered by the commanding officer, to burn or otherwise destroy registered publications and cryptographic material to avoid its falling into enemy hands. Personnel assigned duties under this bill will be given specific and detailed instructions. In shallow water (less than 100 fathoms) papers must be burned; in deep water (more than 100 fathoms) they may be permitted to go down with the ship.

Abandon Ship

This is one emergency in which many senior officers and petty officers may be lost as battle casualties, and full responsibility may fall on the shoulders of very junior men.

Abandon ship stations and duties are noted on the Watch, Quarter, and Station Bill. Additional details are listed in the Organizational Manual. Careful planning takes care of who goes in which boat or raft, what emergency equipment is to be supplied, and who supplies it. Know your abandon ship station and duties. Know *all* escape routes from berthing spaces or working spaces below decks to topside, how to inflate a life jacket, lower a boat or let go a life raft, how to handle survival gear, and how to do it all in the dark if necessary.

Only the commanding officer can order the ship abandoned, and he will do so only after all efforts to save the ship prove futile. When the abandon ship alarm sounds, *act fast*. It's your last chance. Survival at sea depends on knowledge, equipment, training, and self-control; it is your only aim after you do abandon ship, but you have to prepare and train for it before the emergency comes. Disaster can strike suddenly at sea; a ship can go down within three minutes after a collision or explosion. On the other hand, men with very little equipment but plenty of self-control have survived for more than 40 days in an open boat.

Remember that it is a seaman's duty to "maintain hope, perseverance, and obedience." If men cooperate in keeping high morale, they will be happier and more comfortable, and most important, they will survive. When you have to abandon ship, that's the name of the game—survive!

THE BATTLE BILL AND WATCH, QUARTER, AND STATION BILL

Two documents devoted to organizing and assigning men on a ship that are common to all ships, but not included in the *Organization Manual*, are the *Battle Bill*, or the Ship Manning Document, and the *Watch, Quarter, and Station Bill*.

The Battle Bill

This bill assigns men with certain qualifications to specific jobs on a ship while at general quarters (figure 15–2); also applies in all conditions of readiness. This complements the organization of watches for conditions of lesser readiness when all hands are not at a battle station.

In the battle bill, each station and duty is assigned to an enlisted man by a billet number—a combination of numbers and letters indicating a man's division, section within the division, and his seniority within the section. Each man reporting aboard ship, when he is assigned to a division, will be given a billet slip by his division officer, on which his billet number and duties for the various bills are listed. It is his responsibility to know his stations and duties for each bill.

The Watch, Quarter, and Station Bill

This bill displays in one place the duties of each man in each emergency and watch condition. It also shows his duties in the administrative and the operational bills.

The readiness conditions are:

Condition I. General quarters: All hands at battle stations.

Figure 15–2. A *Gallatin* crew member mans one of the 20-mm guns during general quarters at REFTRA.

Condition II. Modified general quarters: Used only in large ships, permits some relaxation among personnel.

Condition III. Wartime cruising: Usually only a third of the crew on watch and only certain stations manned or partially manned.

Condition IV. Peacetime cruising: Only necessary personnel on watch, remainder available for work and training.

Condition V. Peacetime watch in port: Enough personnel on board to get ship under way if necessary or to handle fires and similar emergencies.

Condition VI. Peacetime in port: No armament manned.

Variations in these conditions include:

Condition 1A. Amphibious battle stations. All hands on station to conduct amphibious operations and limited defense of the ship.

Condition 1AA. All hands at battle stations to counter an air or surface threat.

Condition 1AS. All hands at battle stations to counter a submarine threat.

Condition 1E. Temporary relaxation from general quarters for brief periods of rest and the distribution of food at battle stations.

Condition 1M. All hands are at battle stations to take mine countermeasures.

General Quarters

The ship is in Condition of Readiness 1, with all hands at battle stations and all equipment ready for instant action; GQ is sounded whenever battle is imminent or when the highest state of readiness to meet an emergency is desired. For example, the OOD should immediately sound the general quarters alarm when a lookout sings out that a periscope has been sighted; when CIC reports that an unidentified plane has been picked up by radar; or for precaution at dawn and dusk, when there is an increased chance of enemy attack.

When men reach their stations they throw off gun covers, break out ammunition or prepare for action the equipment to which they are assigned. GQ must be set in seconds, not minutes. When each station is manned and ready, the man in charge notifies his control station. When all stations in the control group are ready, the bridge is notified.

When the danger has passed or the drill is over, "Secure" is announced over the general announcing system and sound-powered telephone circuits, and may also be sounded by bugle. No man leaves his station until "Secure" is sounded or until he has permission from his control station. All gear on hand must be stowed or secured as necessary.

Fire

Alarm for a real fire may be given at any time. For drill purposes, a fire may be assumed to be in a specified place—for example, in an ammunition space.

The man who discovers an actual fire must give the alarm. The most important thing is to notify at least one other person who can go for help. Too often a fire has gotten out of control because a man tried to put it out by himself without calling for help.

Use any means at hand to spread an alarm. Use the telephone, messenger, or word of mouth to notify the OOD in port, or the OOD or damage control central when under way.

Once the alarm has sounded, men nearby should act promptly to check or extinguish the fire, using the means nearest at hand. All other men respond to the alarm in accordance with the Watch, Quarter, and Station Bill. If you and several other men have begun to fight the fire, do not leave the scene until the fire or repair party arrives.

Fire During Condition I

When the ship is in Condition I, the damage control organization is ready to fight several fires at once, and little assistance will be required from other stations. Damage control central will direct a repair party to fight the fire and will keep the captain and the OOD informed as to progress.

Fire During Condition II, III, IV, or V (under way or in port)

When the ship is in any of these conditions of readiness with all hands aboard, Condition I is set immediately so that the highly trained damage control organization may be used most effectively to fight the fire.

In port when Condition IV or V is set, the duty section shall furnish the fire party. This fire organization is made up of some of the key people from the regular damage control parties.

Special steps to be taken when the fire alarm is sounded:

Main engine control must maintain fire-main pressure. All electrical circuits in the vicinity of the fire are shut off.

Supply department sends a storekeeper to the scene of the fire, with keys to the supply storerooms in the area.

Medical department sends a corpsman with first-aid kit to the scene of the fire.

Air crews stand by their helicopters if any are on board.

Weapons department stands by all magazine spaces and inspects bulkheads for rise in temperature. The magazine sprinkling-system valves are constantly manned.

Summary

Drills are held to train you to cope with real emergencies: bills tell you where to go and what to do in a drill or emergency.

NBC DEFENSE

NBC warfare refers to the use of nuclear, biological, or chemical weapons, which are termed mass weapons because they can affect great numbers of people. NBC defense is planned for in the NBC bill, which provides an organization and procedures to follow in case an enemy attacks with any of these weapons or in the event of an accident involving any NBC weapon in use by friendly forces.

The effects of an NBC attack may extend over large areas of land or water. Some effects—air blast, thermal radiation, and ionizing radiation of nuclear weapons—end almost instantly. Other effects—base surge and fallout of nuclear weapons—can contaminate an area for a long time and spread to other areas if carried by wind or water currents. The hazards of biological and chemical agents can also move with the winds. All NBC contamination remaining in an area can affect personnel in the area where it occurs, or those entering the area later.

Nuclear Warfare

Nuclear warfare, the use of a weapon armed with a nuclear warhead, may produce these effects:

Shock wave, a blast, as in any explosion, followed by rapid movement of air or water away from the explosion, the force of which can wreck ships, smash buildings, and kill or severely injure people at a considerable distance.

Shock wave protection is similar to general damage control precautions against any explosion: keep loose gear secured, be prepared for the effects of heavy shock and blasts, maintain WT integrity, and make repairs as fast as possible.

Thermal Radiation, heat so intense that everything touched by the fireball melts, and buildings at a great distance burst into flames.

Radiation (both Initial and Residual), which cannot be seen or felt, but is more dangerous than the shock or heat. The radiation is composed of invisible Alpha and Beta particles of energy, neutrons, and Gamma rays. Alpha particles can be stopped by a sheet of paper; Beta particles can be stopped by a thin sheet of aluminum; the other particles travel at the speed of light and therefore are more difficult to stop.

Initial Radiation from the detonation of a nuclear weapon consists mostly of neutrons and Gamma rays, both injurious to human tissue. It lasts only one-tenth of a second. Heavy shielding is required as a protection, depending on distance from the burst and the "yield," or size of the bomb.

Residual Radiation, the radioactive "fallout" from a nuclear explosion, can contaminate large areas. (Fallout from bomb tests in China can be detected in the United States.) This contamination can only be detected and measured by special instruments; if it is hazardous, the area must be decontaminated (washed clean) before unprotected personnel can enter.

Ships may be exposed to three types of bursts: air burst, in which the fireball does not touch the earth; surface burst, in which the fireball touches the surface; and subsurface, in which the explosion is underground or underwater. An air burst produces blast, heat, intense light, and initial radiation, but no fallout requiring decontamination of ship or personnel. In an air burst 85 percent of the damage is due to shock, 10 percent due to thermal radiation, and 5 percent due to initial or residual radiation. A surface burst will produce shock, heat, intense light, and initial and residual radiation. The fallout, especially over water, will spread radioactive contamination over a much wider area than the base surge of an underwater (or subsurface) explosion. A subsurface blast normally produces no heat or light and very little initial radiation. The danger in this type of explosion is in the intense underwater shock and heavy residual radiation from the highly contaminated base surge of earth or water created when the column formed by the explosion falls back to the surface.

NBC Attack at Sea

The alarm for an NBC attack is the 1,000-cycle chemical alarm. When it sounds, *take shelter* at once. The actions of men on duty, of course, must be determined by circumstances and their orders. The air blast can knock people around like ping pong balls, so *hang on* to something solid to reduce chance of injury. The same warning goes for men below decks, as the shock wave transmitted to the hull by water can smash them against bulkheads and overheads. Never lie flat on the deck, but rest on the balls of your feet and flex your knees. Thermal radiation from an air or surface burst will produce skin burns and eye damage only among those directly exposed. Men can reduce the chance of burns by dropping out of direct line of sight of the fireball and covering exposed skin surface.

Attack without alarm is always possible, and the only warning will be a very bright flash or the sky lighting up. When you see the flash, close your eyes, cover your face with your hands, drop to the deck if you can, or crouch and bend down, and after two to five seconds, or after you feel a sudden wave of heat, grasp something solid and *hang on*. Otherwise, the air blast could blow you over the side. You may suffer from flash blindness, but will be able to see perfectly well in 30 minutes.

NBC Attack Ashore

If there is warning, *take shelter*. Get into a depression in the ground, a dugout, the lowest floor of a building, or the crawl space under a house. In a house, the safest place is in a basement, near walls; the next best place is on the lowest floor in an interior room, a hall, or away from windows and near a supporting column. If you have time, draw the blinds or shades to reduce heat and blast and get under some piece of furniture.

Tunnels, storm drains, and subways provide shelter and will usually withstand blast and fire, but perhaps not severe underground shock.

Surface explosions produce much radioactive dust or mist. As protection against this, use a gas mask or breathe through a folded handkerchief or other cloth.

Radiation Measurement

The effect of nuclear radiation on any living thing depends on the intensity of radiation and the time exposed to it, and can be determined by multiplying one by the other. The result, called *dosage*, is measured in RADs or Roentgens, and is used to determine the treatment required after exposure to radiation. It is important that no one is exposed to a greater radiation dose than the body can absorb without permanent damage. For practical purposes, a 5 RAD dose can be considered negligible; a 200 RAD dose in one day or a 400 RAD dose received in a month is generally considered the upper permissible limit. Some individuals have greater resistance to radiation injury than others. Men previously exposed may require less radiation to become ill. Radiation injury normally does not become apparent for some time. This delay is called the "latent period." The amount of radiation received affects the degree of injury and the length of latent period—the larger the radiation dose, the quicker symptoms are noticeable. The latent period is important, because a person exposed to a large amount of radiation may still be able to perform his duties for hours and even days. Killing doses of radiation may reduce the period to less than an hour.

Radiation sickness is *not* a communicable disease; you get it only by exposure to radiation. Sometimes, for psychological or other reasons, an individual may develop symptoms that are similar to radiation sickness, such as nausea and vomiting, but that are actually not due to radiation exposure.

Maximum Permissible Exposure

There is a limit on RADs established by competent authority. Ships will use appropriate maneuvers and countermeasures (washdown, shelter, rotation of personnel between topside and deep shelter stations, etc.) to limit radiation exposure as much as possible.

Detection Equipment

This is designed to be worn by individuals in certain cases, or to be used by monitors. Individuals will use a *pocket dosimeter,* which looks like a fountain pen and records radiation by deflection of a needle on a roentgen scale; a *film badge,* made of lead or cadmium, in which the film records radiation but must be removed and developed to determine the amount; or a *glass dosimeter,* which replaces the film badge. The film badge will be seen most often, as it is primarily for use in nuclear reactor rooms or around any radiation generating equipment. The glass dosimeter is a plastic disc worn on a dog tag chain. The important fact about the dosimeter is that it measures *total dose* received.

Monitoring Equipment

This is usually handled by trained teams, and is used to locate and monitor "hot spots." The purpose in monitoring is to measure the *instantaneous* intensity of radiation; once this is known, it is possible to control the amount of time any man spends in any area so as to keep his total dose below the maximum permissible exposure. Monitoring equipment, generally known as *radiac sets,* has no popular names, but carries "short titles" such as AN/PDR-45 or AN/PDR-56. The various types are designed to measure high-range Gamma radiation, lower-range Gamma and Beta radiation, Alpha radiation, and neutron radiation. A monitoring team consists of a man in charge, called the monitor, who measures intensity of radiation, a recorder who records intensity of readings and time and location, a marker who marks intensity and time of contamination and places warning signs, and a talker or messenger who relays readings to damage control central.

Shipboard Decontamination

This consists of three phases. The first two—tactical decontamination—take place immediately, at sea, and reduce contamination so the ship can carry out its mission without subjecting the crew to more than maximum permissible exposure. Phase one—primary gross decontamination—consists of a salt-water washdown of the entire topside. This will remove 98 percent of contamination if the surface was wet prior to contamination and washdown commences while it is still wet; if the surface has dried, only 50 percent of contamination will be removed. Washdown should commence before the base surge or fallout reaches the ship and should be completed within 15 minutes after contamination occurs. Hose squads wear protective clothing and gas masks. Salt-water washdown commences even if the sea is contaminated, in which case it will continue until the ship reaches a clear area.

The second phase—conducted by individual ship departments—involves reducing contamination of equipment vital to the ship's mission, by use of steam lance and detergents, scrubbing paint work, scraping with abrasives, or removing with flame.

The final phase of decontamination is normally conducted by advanced bases, repair ships, tenders, and shipyards, using flame burning, acid dips and sandblasting.

Personnel Decontamination

Preliminary decontamination is done immediately; exposed personnel wash down under firehoses or topside showers. Detailed decontamination is done in stations divided into three sections where all possible precautions are taken to prevent contamination spreading from one section to the other. In the undressing area all contaminated clothing is removed; in a washing area each man scrubs thoroughly with soap and water; in the clean dressing area they are provided with uncontaminated clothing. Radiation detection devices at each section ensure that contamination is not spread throughout the center. Decontamination priority is as follows: repair party and damage control teams, uninjured men, injured men. Injured men are usually handled last because of the extra time required for medical personnel to assist them.

Biological Warfare (BW)

This is the military use of living organisms or their toxic products to diminish the ability of an enemy to wage war through destruction or contamination of food sources, such as crops and domestic animals, and through infliction of disability or death on the population by spreading an epidemic. A BW attack is most probably conducted by producing a biological agent that can be spread by an aerosol released into air currents or water supplies; this can be done by aircraft, bombs, long-range missiles, or even by people trained to infiltrate enemy territory, as the quantity of material needed could be very small.

It is nearly impossible to see, smell, or taste any BW agent, and because of their various incubation periods, there may be no immediate effects on people, animals, or crops to indicate that an attack has been made. The only way to detect and identify a BW agent is for trained experts to examine specimens of air, food, water, or human and animal blood and excretions. Most BW agents are not fatal; they will cause illness if taken into the body, but the victims will recover. Depending on their type, BW agents may be absorbed through the skin, taken in with food or water, or inhaled. The best defense against them is to keep yourself and your living areas clean, and report any sickness immediately. Action under known attack is much the same as for NW; wear protective clothing and a gas mask, or breathe through a folded cloth. Decontamination and washup procedures are the same as for NW.

Most BW agents will die or lose their effectiveness after a few days of exposure to ordinary weather conditions, but there are some which may remain dormant for a long period. All clothing should be boiled in soapy water or exposed to the sun for a few days before wearing. Food in sealed containers should be safe, but food or water that has been exposed should be avoided until tested. Play it safe; don't assume danger is past after a BW decontamination team has done its work.

Chemical Warfare (CW)

This is the military use of any chemical that can produce powerful casualty or harassing effects, and includes screening smokes and incendiaries. With proper protection, such as clothing and gas masks, a person has an excellent chance of surviving any chemical attack. Chemical smoke screens are used to hide enemy targets or troop movements, but they might also disguise other types of CW agents. Incendiaries— chemical compounds that burn with terrific heat—may be dropped by aircraft, fired in shells, or used with flame throwers, and include napalm, jellied gasoline, and thermite and magnesium bombs. The most dangerous aspect of chemical warfare is the use of casualty or harassing agents against troops or civilian populations.

Casualty Agents

These agents can kill or seriously injure large numbers of people. They include:

Nerve agents, which upset the nervous sysem, produce headache, sweating, muscular reaction, and difficulty in breathing. One whiff of a nerve gas can kill. A mask is not adequate protection, as nerve agents can enter through exposed skin anywhere on the body.

Blister agents are liquids that produce clouds of vapor; as liquids they burn the skin wherever they touch; as vapors they will burn eyes and most skin and injure lungs if inhaled.

Choking agents, or lung irritants, will inflame and irritate the respiratory system if inhaled, and may cause death from the collection of fluid in the lungs.

Blood agents are liquids that cause a chemical change in high concentrations in the blood, making it useless to carry oxygen, and producing a sort of internal suffocation. Smaller amounts will result in headache, giddiness, and nausea, but recovery is usually complete.

Harassing Agents

These are not as dangerous as casualty agents, but produce effects that harass an enemy by reducing his efficiency. Principal types are:

Tear gases, which affect the eyes, causing considerable flow of tears, and irritate the skin. Their action is usually temporary and slight. Ordinarily, tear gas casualties do not require medical attention. A newer agent, CS, has a very rapid action and also produces a choking sensation.

Vomiting agents produce violent coughing and sneezing followed rapidly by severe headaches, chest pains, nausea, and vomiting. On leaving the contaminated area, severe discomfort ceases in about half an hour; in three hours recovery is complete.

Detection of CW Agents

This is easier than with BW agents. The most important to detect are the nerve gases, which can kill very quickly. Several chemical agent detector kits are in use, but some of them identify only certain gases, and some do not give warning soon enough for personnel to don protective clothing.

As a final resort, learn to note clues that might indicate CW agents: presence of oily liquids after an explosion; drying and browning vegetation; a spray from aircraft; a vaporous cloud that remains close to the ground or water. Any unusual enemy operation that does not involve conventional projectiles and explosives should be treated as possible CW or BW attacks.

Defense against CW attack is much the same as for NW or BW attacks. The main difference will lie in the speed with which nerve and blood agents act. At the first sign of a nerve gas, *hold your breath* until your mask is on and properly adjusted. Any liquid on your skin should be blotted with cloths from a Protective Ointment Kit, or some other cloth. Do not rub; that will only increase skin absorption. Flush exposed skin with water for about half a minute and then apply the ointment from the kit, but *not near or in the eyes*. If drops of nerve agents get into your eyes flush with water immediately, even if you have to remove your mask. While unmasked do not breathe contaminated atmosphere. Symptoms of nerve poisoning are local sweating and muscular twitching of contaminated skin area, or the contraction of the pupils of the eyes; if these are observed, use atropine syrette in the Protective Ointment Kit, but *not* until you are *sure* that the symptoms are nerve agents.

Protective Mask

This important part of NBC defense is designed to protect your face, eyes, nose, throat, and lungs by filtering the air, removing particles of dust and smoke that may be radioactive or contaminated with BW or CW agents, and purifying the air of many poisonous gases. It will not protect against ammonia, carbon monoxide, carbon dioxide (CO_2), cooking gas, sulphur dioxide, and certain other industrial gases or fire-produced fumes. It will not produce oxygen, and is useless where there is not enough oxygen to breathe, even after the mask has purified what air there is. In such places the oxygen breathing apparatus (OBA), or air-line hose mask, must be used.

Because of the great importance of the protective mask, it should receive careful attention. Perspiration should be dried out completely, as moisture will cause rotting, corrosion, deterioration of the canisters, and mildew. Only authorized equipment, such as the Protective Ointment Kit, should be stowed in the carrier. The mask should be inspected periodically, tested in a gas chamber, and stored in a cool, dry place away from solvents, such as cleaning fluid, and their vapors.

Protective Clothing

This clothing, provided for monitoring and decontamination teams, must have the best possible care. Check for tears, holes, broken or missing buttons, broken or jammed zippers, and other such defects that might leave you unprotected during an attack.

Special protective clothing made of rubberized cloth is air tight and provides the most complete protection against BW and CW agents. Liquid CW agents will penetrate it after a few hours, so wearers should go through decontamination as soon as possible. Permeable clothing has been chemically treated to neutralize blister agents, but provides little protection against nerve gas and only limited protection against any other contamination. Regular stock issue wet weather clothing, and ordinary work clothing, will keep some contamination away from the skin, and is easily decontaminated by washing. All contaminated clothing should be removed as soon as possible.

Successful NBC defense involves early warning of attack, effective monitoring of contamination, and thorough decontamination procedures. All ships are equipped with instruments and gear to accomplish this. Proper training and preparation will greatly reduce the after effects of an NBC attack, and enable a ship to continue with her assigned duties.

CHAPTER 16

Damage Control and Fire Fighting

Damage control includes all efforts to prevent damage to a ship, as well as all action taken to reduce the harmful effects of damage after it happens. The primary purpose of damage control is to keep a ship in condition to perform its assigned mission; a secondary purpose is to return the ship to port after damage so it can be repaired. The need for damage control is not limited to combat operations; any routine operation (figure 16–1) can result in an accident calling for prompt damage control.

DAMAGE CONTROL

The three main objectives of the damage control organization of a ship are:

To take all necessary action before damage occurs. This means making the ship watertight and gas-tight in those parts that were so designed, removing all fire hazards, and maintaining as well as distributing necessary emergency equipment.

To reduce damage by controlling flooding, fighting fires, and providing first-aid treatment to injured personnel.

To provide emergency repairs or restore services after damage occurs. This means manning essential equipment, supplying emergency power, and repairing important parts of the ship that were damaged.

Figure 16–1. A fire drill afloat must exercise all parts of the fire-fighting system; pumps, waterlines, hoses, and crew.

The ship's ability to perform any assigned duty depends upon the actions of its damage control organization. It is important that you realize your responsibility in damage control procedures. Damage control must be considered an offensive as well as a defensive weapon.

Damage control is concerned not only with battle damage but also damage from fire, collision, grounding, or explosion. It may be necessary in port as well as at sea.

Learn all you can about your ship—the whole ship, not just the part to which you are assigned. In an emergency you may have to work anywhere on the ship, depending on the location and the extent of the damage.

The important damage control systems are: drainage and flooding, fire main and sprinkling, ventilation, fuel and fresh water, compressed air, and communications. An effective man in any repair system is one who can find his way to any compartment in the dark and close any valves, doors, or hatches by touch alone. Much of this you will learn from drills and practical experience.

Damage Control Parties

When a ship is placed in commission, damage control parties are set up in the ship's organization. The number of such parties depends upon the size and type of ship and the number of men available for assignment. A Coast Guard Cutter will probably have two parties.

Each damage control party contains a number of different ratings in order to provide skilled men for any type of work. For example, an engineer repair party may also include machinist's mates, electrician's mates, boilermen, and others.

The engineer officer, as the *damage control officer,* is responsible for damage control. The *damage control assistant,* who is under the engineer officer, is responsible for establishing and maintaining an effective damage control organization. Specifically, the damage control assistant is responsible for the following:

The prevention and control of damage, including control of stability, list, and trim. He shall supervise placing the ship in the material condition of readiness (to be explained later) ordered by the commanding officer.

The training of the ship's personnel in damage control, including firefighting, emergency repairs, and nonmedical defensive measures against gas and similar weapons.

The operation, care, and maintenance of auxiliary machinery, piping, and drainage systems not assigned to other departments.

Duties of Repair Parties

All repair parties must be able to:

Control and extinguish all types of fires.
Correctly and promptly evaluate the extent of damage in their area and make accurate "on scene" reports.
Repair electrical and sound-powered telephone circuits.
Detect, identify, and measure dosage and intensity of radiation, and decontaminate after NBC attack.
Give first aid and transport injured to battle dressing stations without seriously disrupting other functions.

In addition to the general functions required of all repair parties, certain repair parties are additionally responsible for maintaining the ship's:

Stability and buoyancy
Offensive power and maneuverability
Propulsion
Ordnance and magazine protection.

Available personnel are assigned to repair stations. A main propulsion repair party will consist largely of machinist's mates, boilermen, enginemen, and firemen. Repair parties assigned to areas in which magazines are located will have gunner's mates as part of their personnel. Storekeepers are assigned to repair parties that have storerooms located in their areas.

The number and ratings of men assigned to a repair party or station, as specified in the Battle Bill, are determined by: the locale of the station, the portion of the ship assigned to that party, and the total number of men available for all stations.

Each repair station has an officer in charge, who may in some cases be a chief petty officer. The second officer in charge of a repair party is in most cases a chief petty officer who is qualified in damage control and is therefore capable of taking over the supervision of the repair party.

Damage Control Equipment

This is stowed in repair lockers and includes patches for ruptured water lines, steam lines, broken seams, and for the ship's hull; plugs, made of soft wood in sizes from one-half inch to 12 inches for stopping the flow of liquids in a damaged hull or in broken lines; wedges for shoring, made of soft woods in various sizes; radiological defense equipment; an electrical repair kit for isolating damaged circuits and restoring power; and such tools for forcible entry as axes, crowbars, wrecking bars, claw tools, hacksaws, bolt-cutters, and acetylene cutting torches. Such equipment is reserved for damage control use only.

Battle Dressing Stations

Most ships have at least two battle dressing stations equipped to handle battle personnel casualties. These stations are manned by personnel of the medical department and are so located that stretcher cases may be brought directly to the station by the repair party stretcher bearers. Besides the battle-dressing station, emergency supplies of medical equipment are placed in first aid boxes at various stations throughout the ship.

Decontamination Stations

A minimum of two decontamination stations are provided in widely separated parts of the ship, preferably in the vicinity of battle dressing. These stations provide a place where, after NBC attack, personnel go through decontamination. Stations are manned by medical department and repair party personnel who make certain that proper decontamination procedures have been followed.

Damage Control Communications

Effective communications are of vital importance to the damage control organization. Without adequate means or proper procedures of communications between the different units of the damage control organization, the whole organization would break down and fail in its primary mission.

The normal means of damage control communication aboard large ships are:

Battle telephone circuits (sound-powered)
Inter-station two-way systems (4MC intercoms)
Ship's service telephones

Ship's loud-speaker system (1MC general announcing)
Voice tubes (where installed)
Messengers.

Watertight (WT) Integrity

One of the most important aspects of any operation at sea is to keep the ship watertight. It may sustain any degree of damage, but if the proper degree of watertight integrity is maintained, the ship will stay afloat.

Entering Closed Compartments After Damage

Watertight doors, hatches, manholes, and scuttles should be opened only after making sure that the compartment is dry or so little flooded that no further flooding will be produced by opening the closure. They should never be opened until permission is obtained from the damage control officer. Extreme caution is always necessary in opening compartments below the waterline in the vicinity of any damage.

Closing and Opening Watertight Doors

Doors, hatches, and manholes giving access to all compartments must be securely dogged. Double-bottom manhole covers should be bolted at all times except when they must be open for inspection, cleaning, or painting. They must never be left open overnight or when men are not actually engaged in work.

You must obtain permission from the OOD or Damage Control Central before opening any secured watertight fitting, and you must report back to him when you have secured the space.

Watertight doors and hatches will retain their efficiency longer and require less maintenance if they are properly closed and opened. To close a door, first set up a dog opposite the hinges, with just enough pressure to keep the door shut. Then set up the other dogs evenly to obtain uniform bearing all around. To open a door, start with the dogs nearest the hinges. This procedure will keep the door from springing and make it easier to operate the remaining dogs.

General drill orders call for closing all watertight doors, hatches, and ventilator openings designed to be closed during maneuvers, in fog, or as a matter of routine at night.

The strongest doors are those classified as *watertight doors (WT)* (figure 16–2). Many of these are used in watertight bulkheads of the compartments of the second deck. They are designed to resist as much

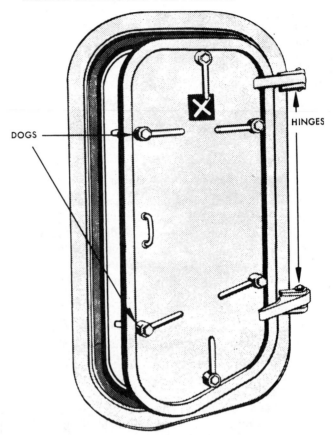

Figure 16–2. Watertight door with individually operated dogs.
Dogs are shown in closed position, but would have to be opened
before door could be closed.

pressure as the bulkheads through which they give access and usually
have 10 dogs. Some doors have dogs that must be individually closed
and opened; others, known as *quick-acting watertight doors* (figure
16–3), have handwheels that operate all the dogs at once.

Non-watertight doors (NWT) are used in non-watertight bulkheads.
Usually they have fewer dogs than WT doors and are made with dogs
that require individual operation.

Airtight doors are also fume-tight and gas-tight. When such doors

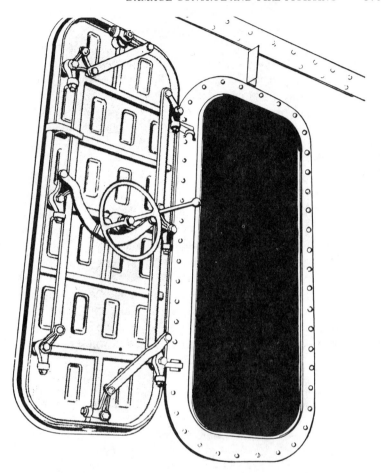

Figure 16–3. On a quick-acting WT door, a control wheel operates all dogs at once.

are used in air locks, they usually have lever-type quick-acting closures, but most others have individually operated dogs.

Passing scuttles may be placed in some doors through which ammunition must be passed. These are small, tube-like openings, watertight and flashproof.

Spray-tight doors are used topside in vessels with low freeboard, to prevent spray and seawater from entering.

Panel doors are ordinary shore-type doors that are made of metal and used to provide privacy closures for staterooms, wardrooms, etc.

Hatchways are access openings in decks; hatches are the coverings for the hatchways (figure 16–4). Raised lips called coamings encircling the hatchways keep water and dirt from entering the compartment when the hatch is not secured. Hatches operate with quick-acting devices or may be secured with individually operated drop bolts or individual dogs. Quick-acting escape scuttles are often provided for rapid access through a hatch (figure 16–5).

Manholes are small openings to the water and fuel tanks and voids. They are usually secured by bolting steel plates (provided with gaskets) over them. Occasionally, however, manholes are provided with hinged covers and dogs or drop bolts. Manholes may also be placed in bulkheads, but they are not so common as those in decks.

Gaskets are rubber strips mounted in the covering part of doors or hatches to close against a fixed position *knife edge* (figure 16–6). Gaskets of this type are either pressed into a groove or secured with retaining strips held in place by screws or bolts.

Watertight closures also must have clean, bright (unpainted), and smooth knife-edges for gaskets to press against. A well-fitted WT door

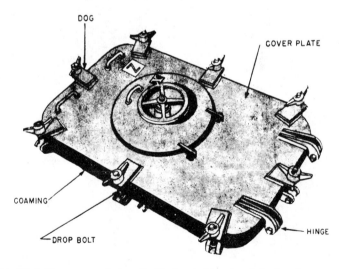

Figure 16–4. Escape scuttle installed in hatch. Note hatch is closed by drop bolts instead of dogs.

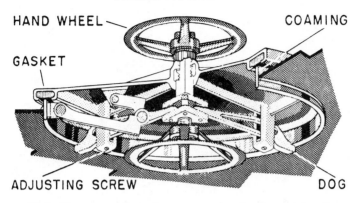

HAND WHEEL

COAMING

GASKET

ADJUSTING SCREW

DOG

Figure 16–5. Cut-away section of escape scuttle, showing quick-acting wheels above and below.

with new gaskets will still leak if knife-edges are not properly maintained.

Investigating and Reporting Damage

In order to make a complete, thorough investigation of any damage, you must know your ship and be familiar with the basic principles of investigating and reporting damage:

Be Cautious

Each investigating team should consist of two or more men who must take care not to lose control of watertight fittings and who must use safety equipment (oxygen breathing apparatus, explosimeter, flame safety lamp) in case toxic or combustible gases are present.

Be Thorough and Determined

Find out what type of damage exists, its location and extent, and how it can be best repaired or controlled.

Report the Damage

A report should be made to DCC, promptly, accurately, and by either telephone or messenger.

Damage Repair

Repairs made to a vessel damaged while the vessel is in action, or otherwise in operation, are termed *damage repairs*. These are emer-

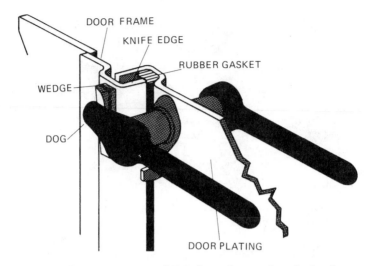

Figure 16–6. Cut-away section of WT door, showing how knife edge sets up against rubber gasket for tight seal.

gency, usually temporary, repairs necessary to allow the vessel to continue its mission and permit its return to port for permanent repairs. Such repairs are made with whatever material is at hand. The important thing is keeping the ship afloat and maintaining as much of its operational capability as possible.

Holes in the Hull

Small holes in the underwater hull result from near-miss bombs or violent explosions in other parts of the ship. Temporary repairs can be made by driving wooden plugs or wedges into small holes. Plugs wrapped in cloth also make good seals. Care should be taken before driving wedges into cracks; the cracks might enlarge.

Large holes through which water is pouring are difficult to control. The only control possible may be to close off near-by watertight boundaries and isolate the damage from the water.

Hull holes above the waterline may be more dangerous than they look. When the ship rolls, these holes may admit water into spaces above the center of gravity, thus seriously affecting the stability of the ship. Holes like this are not difficult to patch; either inside or outside patches may be used. Inside patches might be pillows and mattresses backed up with boards or mess-table tops. Inside patches are preferred since outside patches are hard to tend and may be knocked about by the action of the sea.

Patches and Shorings

There are many types of patches and shorings that have been developed to combat leaks and holes in the hull. Crew members must learn how to make these repairs. A member of a damage control repair party must learn what the ship has available in the way of damage control equipment. It is then up to him to do his best with what he has in an emergency. If he is calm, alert, and works fast with the tools at hand, he can do much to help keep the ship afloat.

Material Conditions of Readiness

All ships are classified as three-condition ships: Condition XRAY is set and maintained at all times, as a division responsibility; Condition YOKE is set, when damage is probable, as a division responsibility; Condition ZEBRA is set before going to sea or entering port during wartime, or for general quarters or collision, and is a repair party responsibility.

If it is necessary to break the material condition in effect, permission must be obtained from the OOD or DCC. In DCC a log is maintained at all times to show where the existing condition has been broken, the number, type, and classification of fittings involved, the name, rate, and division of the man requesting permission to open or close the fitting, and the date the fitting was opened or closed.

It is the responsibility of all hands to maintain the material condition in effect to prevent fires from getting out of control and spreading from one space to another, to keep flooding from getting out of control, and to prevent NBC agents from being admitted into the internal parts of the ship. *Remember:* When general quarters is sounded, setting condition ZEBRA is an all hands responsibility. Circle X and Y fittings may be opened without special permission when proceeding to battle stations or during action if it is necessary to do so to fight the ship. Fittings must be kept closed when not in use. Red circle Z fittings may be opened during prolonged periods of General Quarters to permit the distribution of food, the use of sanitary facilities, the ventilation of various parts, and similar necessary functions. However, these fittings are guarded for immediate closure. Circle W fittings, normally opened, are closed only to prevent NBC contamination or smoke from entering a vent system.

It is obvious that the ship's watertight integrity has much to do with damage control. When she is going into battle, or at any time when damage may be sustained, such as in fog or ice, or at night, she must be as "tight" as possible. So proper preparation of the ship is the most important part of damage control procedure.

Damage Control Markings

All doors, hatches, scuttles, valves, and fittings are classified and marked as follows:

XRAY. Used only in well-protected harbors. All XRAY fittings closed at all times, except when actually in use, such as for issuing stores, repairs, or cleaning.

YOKE. Used in unprotected ports and for wartime cruising. All YOKE and XRAY fittings closed.

ZEBRA. Used for maximum battle protection. All XRAY, YOKE and ZEBRA fittings closed.

Classification of fittings

XRAY. Closed at all times except when actually in use.

YOKE. Fittings for which alternate ZEBRA accesses exist, and which are closed during condition YOKE, thus providing a higher degree of readiness and reducing number of fittings to be closed under condition ZEBRA.

ZEBRA. Normally open for operation of the ship, habitability, and access to battle stations. Closed during battle or emergencies.

WILLIAM. Normally open during all conditions of readiness. Examples are sea suction valves and ventilation fittings in systems servicing heat-generating spaces.

Black circle XRAY or YOKE. May be opened without special authority while proceeding to or from battle stations. Other fittings so marked permit ammunition transfer and operation of vital systems. All such fittings opened only when actually in use.

Red circle ZEBRA. May be opened on authority of the commanding officer to set modified condition ZEBRA to distribute food, open limited sanitary facilities, or ventilate battle stations and other vital areas such as magazines. When open, must be guarded for immediate closure if necessary.

Black "D" ZEBRA. Closed for darkening ship.

Circle W. Normally open during action, but may be closed, or stopped, as defense against NBC attack. Includes nonvital sea suction valves which, if secured, would not impair mobility or fire protection of the ship.

FIRE FIGHTING

The danger of fire is always present. Fire can start in the aviation fuel stowage area of a cutter, or it can start in an office wastebasket. If not handled promptly and properly, one can be as dangerous as the other. There are three basic elements in fire fighting:

Prevention. Eliminate the possibility of fire before it starts.

Equipment. Ships and stations are supplied with the items needed to fight fire. Know where they are.

Technique. The best equipment is useless if not handled properly. Know how to use it.

No one wins against a fire. It may be fought efficiently and well, the damage may be minimized, and the fighters may receive commendations for their work. The fact remains that in any fire some property is lost, men may be injured and lives may be lost, and valuable time is lost for all concerned (figure 16–7).

Fire Prevention

The best way to combat fires is to prevent them. Fire prevention must become a daily habit. Keep equipment squared away; keep working areas shipshape. When things are properly stowed and handled, they don't start fires. Remember:

Keep containers of volatile liquids tightly closed.

Prevent the accumulation of oil and grease in the bilges or in the exhaust from galley hoods.

Keep quarters and workshops free of waste material.

Properly stow bedding, unseasonable clothing, flammable liquids, paints, acids, gases, and chemicals.

Be careful in the use of open lights and electrical equipment where an explosive vapor might exist.

Factors Causing Fires

The three elements necessary for fire are fuel, heat, and oxygen. They form a dangerous triangle. Eliminate any one side of the triangle, and you put out the fire. The *fuel* side of the triangle may be eliminated

Figure 16–7. There was plenty of water to fight this fire on an oil-well platform in the Gulf of Mexico, but even so it burned for over four months.

by shutting off valves in gasoline or oil lines or jettisoning (throwing overboard) combustible materials. The *heat* side of the triangle may be removed by using water, water sprays, or fog, and ventilating heat to the outside. The *oxygen* side of the triangle may be removed by forcing a noninflammable gas into the area and so diluting the atmosphere that fire cannot continue. Chemical foam may also be used; it forms a blanket over the fire, prevents oxygen from reaching it, and will also prevent heat from reaching some materials.

Kinds of Fires

All fires can be classed under four general types. It is important to know what type of fire you are fighting, in order to know how best to fight it.

Class A Fires. Fires in ordinary combustible materials (such as bedding, clothing, wood, canvas, rope, and paper). Here the cooling effect of water is needed to kill the fire. Class A fires leave hot embers or ashes. Material of this type must be cooled throughout to make certain the fire does not start up again.

Class B Fires. Fires in flammable liquids (such as gasoline, oil, grease, paint, and turpentine). These materials burn at the surface where the vapors are given off. The burning liquid should be smothered or blanketed with foam, CO_2, steam, certain dry chemicals, or fog.

Class C Fires. Fires in electrical equipment. Here the use of a "nonconducting" extinguishing agent is of first importance. In most electrical fires it will be necessary to cut the circuits before any progress can be made. Carbon dioxide is a nonconductor and will not damage electrical equipment. Water fog would be the second choice, because it would probably do less damage than foam.

Class D Fires. Burning metals. Light metals used in ship construction and aircraft will ignite at high temperatures. These fires produce their own oxygen and burn at such high temperatures that conventional cooling methods result in explosive reactions. Twin agent systems (foam/light water and dry chemical) are somewhat effective on large fires. When under way on the high seas, disposal of the burning metal object over the side is recommended.

Fire Prevention Rules

General

Be fire prevention conscious.

Keep fire-fighting equipment handy and in good working order.

Keep all gear properly stowed, and areas and spaces clean and shipshape.

Don't take fire- or spark-producing items (matches, lighters, metal objects) into places where flammables are located, and vice versa.

If you have one or two of the fire factors—heat, air, fuel—present, be careful that the others aren't brought into the area.

Class A Fires

Don't throw lighted cigarettes or matches into trash cans.

Don't smoke in bunks.

When welding or burning, keep Class A materials protected against the flame and hot droppings. Inspect opposite bulkheads and maintain a fire watch.

Be careful of spontaneous combustion—where and how you stow rags and, particularly, oily, or paint-smeared cloth and paper.

Remember that Class A materials give off flammable gases when heated.

Class B Fires

Expect all low places, bilges, tanks, bottoms, to have accumulations of gasoline or oil vapors. These vapors are extremely flammable or explosive.

Remember the danger of flashback where gasoline is concerned.

Use only non-sparking tools in areas where Class B substances have been or are stowed.

Don't carry matches, lighters, or keys, or wear metal buttons or nylon clothing, when you are in the vicinity of gasoline or oil vapors.

Don't turn on lamps, flashlights, or electrical equipment that have not been certified sparkproof in any area where gasoline or oil fumes can accumulate.

Class C Fires

Do not paint or splash paint, oil, grease, or solvents of any sort on electrical equipment or wires.

Report all frayed or worn wires.

Report all sparking contacts, switches, and motors.

Report any electrical equipment that becomes hot, smokes, or makes unusual noises.

In case of fire, cut off all unnecessary electric lights and equipment. In the immediate area of the fire, turn off all electrical circuits.

Don't try to use unauthorized equipment. For example, don't plug in hot plates, shavers, extension lights, or radios except in the spaces and at the times authorized.

FIRE-FIGHTING EQUIPMENT

There are many kinds of fire-fighting systems and equipment. Some of it is permanently installed and some is portable. These systems and devices must be maintained at maximum efficiency. All fire-fighting equipment is distributed in readily accessible locations. It is inspected frequently to ensure its reliability and readiness for instant operation.

Fire-main System

The fire-main system is made up of piping, pumps, fireplugs, valves, and controls. The system is designed to supply plenty of water for fire

fighting, sprinkling the magazines, washing the decks, or other purposes for which salt water is normally used.

The *piping* in a fire-main system is either a single line or a loop
system. *Risers* are pipes leading from the fire main, which is usually
located below the main deck, to *fireplugs* on the upper deck levels
and to others located throughout the ship. The fire-main system is so
designed that any damaged section of piping can be isolated (figure
16–8). That is why there are so many cross connections and shut-off
valves at various locations throughout the piping system.

Standard fireplugs usually have outlets either 2½ inches or 1½
inches in diameter. Some 2½-inch plugs are equipped with wye-gates,
which provide two hose outlets, each 1½ inches in size. In other cases
a reducing fitting is used so that a single 1½-inch hose line can be
attached to a 2½-inch outlet.

Fire Hose

There are two fittings or couplings on each length of hose—a female
fitting at one end for coupling to the fireplug, and a male fitting at the
other for connecting another length of hose or a nozzle.

Connected to the fireplugs, and faked down in adjacent racks, are
two 50-foot lengths of either 1½-inch or 2½-inch hose with nozzle
attached. The 1½-inch hose is used at all fireplugs on smaller ships,
and at all below-deck fireplugs on larger ships.

Before connecting a hose, check to be sure the coupling gaskets are
in place. Two men working together can quickly make up a fire hose.
To do the job alone, lay the hose out flat on the deck and hold it down
with your foot just behind the male fitting. This will cause the fitting
to point upward, so that you can screw on the nozzle, or female end
of the coupling.

In connecting threaded parts, first take a half turn to the left to set
the threads. Be careful not to cross the threads. Then turn to the right
until the joint is tight.

Fire hose is usually faked down on a bulkhead rack near a fireplug.
Nozzles, applicators, and spanner wrenches (for tightening fittings) are
racked on the bulkhead near the hose. When two lines are faked down
separately on the bulkhead, one is connected to the fireplug; the other
is left unconnected. Always fake the lines with their free ends hanging
down so that they will be ready for instant use. The end of the line
should be equipped with an all-purpose nozzle.

To roll a hose for stowing, lay it out straight, then double the male

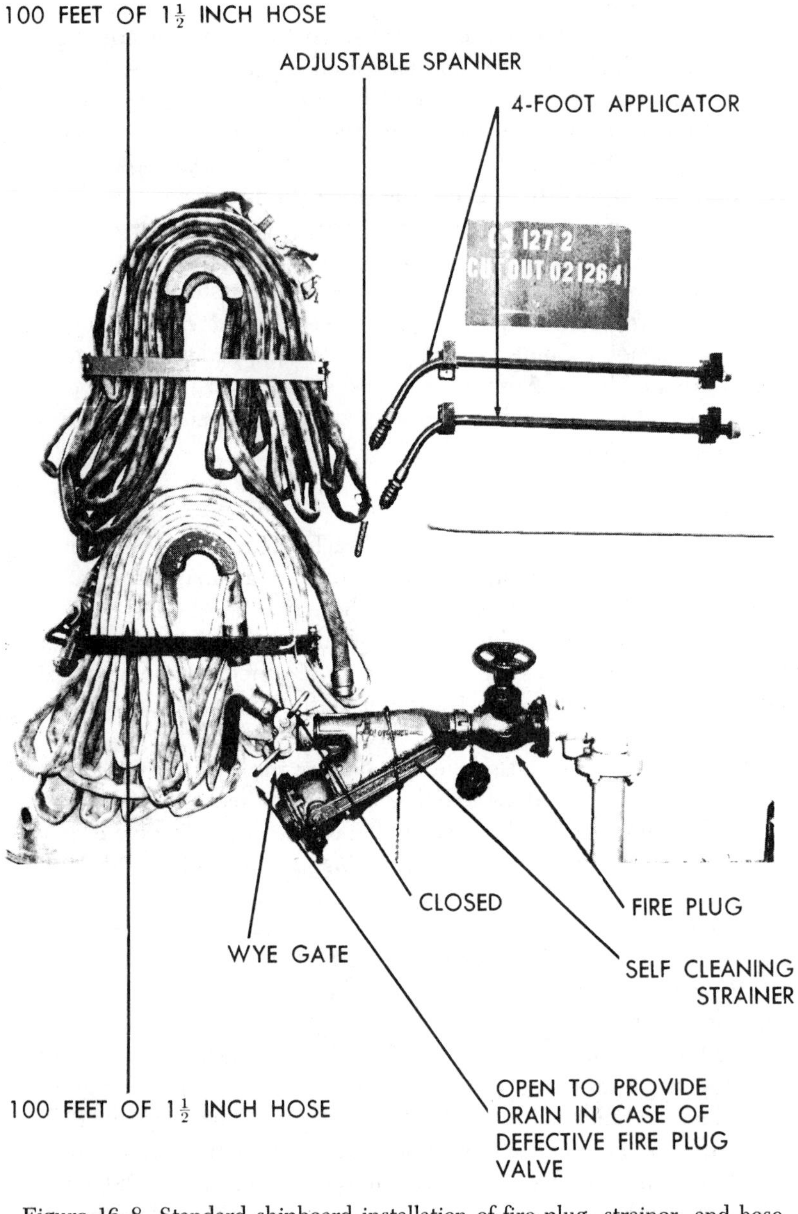

100 FEET OF 1½ INCH HOSE

ADJUSTABLE SPANNER

4-FOOT APPLICATOR

CLOSED

FIRE PLUG

WYE GATE

SELF CLEANING STRAINER

100 FEET OF 1½ INCH HOSE

OPEN TO PROVIDE DRAIN IN CASE OF DEFECTIVE FIRE PLUG VALVE

Figure 16–8. Standard shipboard installation of fire plug, strainer, and hose sections. Lower valve on wye gate is open to provide drain in case of defective fire plug valve.

end back on top until it reaches within 4 feet of the female end. Start rolling the hose at the fold, with the male end inside. When the roll is finished, secure it in place with light line or a strap. Thus the female end will be on the outside ready for connecting to a male end. The male end is always stowed inside the roll where its threads will be protected.

All-purpose Fire Nozzles

The Navy all-purpose nozzle (figure 16–9) can produce either fog or a solid stream of water. It can be adjusted or shut off quickly and easily by means of a lever.

Fog comes out through an opening in the lower part of the nozzle. When a straight stream is used, the water shoots out of the upper part, above the fog outlet.

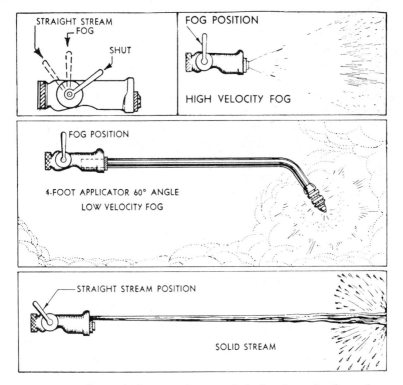

Figure 16–9. All-purpose hose nozzle in use for high-velocity fog, low-velocity fog, and straight stream.

The all-purpose nozzle is usually set to produce a high-velocity fog. For this use, a removable high-velocity nozzle tip is installed in the fog outlet.

For a low-velocity fog, the high-velocity nozzle tip is removed and replaced with an applicator that is equipped with a fog head. The three uses of the all-purpose nozzle are shown in figure 16–9. With the applicator in place, it is still possible to get a solid stream of water by pulling the nozzle control handle all the way back. Some variflow nozzles are now in use.

Know the fire-main system in your ship: know the location of the fire main proper and the riser piping that carries water to the upper decks; the location of the plugs where fire hoses can be attached; and the location of the pumps, valves, and controls.

Foam Equipment

Foam is a frothy mixture of water and chemicals used to fight Class B fires. The foam provides a "blanket" that floats on top of burning oil or gasoline and smothers the fire; it sticks better to a flaming area than water, which runs off quickly, or CO_2, which blows away. However, because of the mess left by the foam after the fire has been put out, it is not used unless absolutely necessary on Class C (electrical equipment) or Class A (wood, cloth, etc.) fires. A little foam will do the work of a lot more water, but the mess it leaves makes it a last resort— except for large Class B fires, when it usually is a *must*.

Foam is produced by:

Foam proportioner (portable or installed).
Water motor proportioner (portable).
Straight-type pickup tube proportioner (portable, with a pickup tube attached directly to mechanical-foam nozzle).
S-type proportioner (for use with gasoline-engine-driven handy billy pump) (figure 16–10).

The straight-type pickup tube proportioner and the S-type proportioner use the Navy pickup unit (NPU). All three use the *mechanical foam nozzle* (MFN). This nozzle has a 21-inch length of flexible metal or asbestos composition hose attached. It is 2 inches in diameter, has a solid metal nozzle outlet, and a suction chamber and air port in the butt end. The foam is a mixture of water, liquid-foam solution, and air. Figure 16–10 shows the arrangement by which the pickup is joined

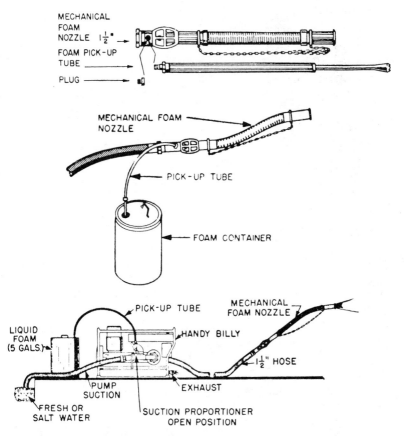

Figure 16–10. Foam fire-fighting equipment. (A) Mechanical foam nozzle; (B) Straight-type proportioner; (C) S-type suction proportioner used with handy-billy.

to the mechanical foam nozzle in the straight-type pickup tube proportioner.

The pickup is also used by proper attachment to a handy billy pump. In this system the foam liquid is drawn into the suction chamber of the handy billy and forced into the water stream.

Carbon Dioxide (CO_2) Extinguishers

Carbon dioxide extinguishers are used mainly in putting out electrical fires (figure 16–11). However, they are effective when used on burning

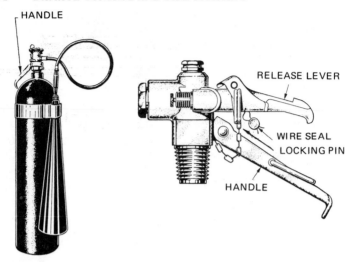

Figure 16–11. Portable CO_2 extinguisher, with detail of handle, release lever, and locking pin.

fuel oil, alcohol, and paint. They smother a fire with a layer of carbon dioxide (CO_2), which will not burn, is heavier than air, and puts out a fire by cutting off its air supply. It is quick to use, does not leave the after effects of water or foam, but can be blown away by any wind or air blast. It is not poisonous, but will not support life, and can smother men in confined places. It gives no warning of its presence because it can't be seen, smelled, or tasted.

Operation of CO_2 Extinguisher

The portable extinguisher holds 15 pounds of CO_2. It has a disk-type release valve. To operate, carry it by the handle, pull out the locking pin, and turn the valve wheel. Some extinguishers have a squeeze-grip type release valve. With this type, release the CO_2 by squeezing the release lever. This type is standard in the Navy and is replacing the former cutter type.

When CO_2 is released, its volume rapidly increases 450 times. This rapid expansion causes the temperature to drop to 110° below zero. Most of the liquid CO_2 turns to gas, but some of it forms "snow," which will produce painful blisters if it touches your skin.

Large cylinders of carbon dioxide installed on ships are connected to a manifold and are used with a hose and reel or a fixed piping system. Operation may be by local control, nozzle control, or remote control.

When using CO_2, keep the compartment closed and shut off the ventilation. Except in an emergency, don't open a compartment flooded with CO_2 for at least 15 minutes; this will allow time for burning materials to cool down below ignition temperatures and prevent starting another fire when air is let into the compartment.

A compartment filled with CO_2 may be entered if you wear an approved oxygen-breathing apparatus or hose (air line) mask. Otherwise don't enter it until a safety lamp, placed in the compartment, burns without flickering. Don't use a canister-type gas mask in place of an oxygen-breathing apparatus, as it merely filters the air but does not add the oxygen you need.

Dry Chemical Extinguishers

This type of extinguisher is supplied in 18 and 22 pound sizes. It is effective against Class B and Class C fires. The chemical—usually sodium bicarbonate—is discharged by the pressure of carbon dioxide, nitrogen, or dry air, and acts on a fire by smothering it.

P-250 Pump

This portable pump is self-priming, driven by a gasoline engine, and delivers up to 250 gallons of water per minute. It is used for fire fighting or pumping water out of flooded compartments. It is supplied with a special trigate which, when attached to its regular 2½-inch outlet, can supply three 1½-inch fire hoses. The pump is equipped with 3-inch suction hoses and is self-priming for suction less than 20 feet. Greater suction distance requires manual priming.

Eductor

The efficiency of a P-250 pump can be increased by using the eductor. Water pumped through a venturi-tube in the eductor produces a low-pressure area around the tube. This low pressure causes additional water to enter the eductor. Then both the water pumped through and the water sucked up are either discharged through a 4″ discharge hose or forced back into the pump through a 4″ hard-rubber suction hose. In the latter case, the eductor takes the place of a suction valve and strainer and serves to increase the suction life of the pump.

Electric Submersible Pumps

These pumps are used for dewatering, to increase the suction lift of the P-60 pump, and may be semi-permanently installed as a part of the ship's secondary drain system. They have a capacity of 200 GPM at 15 feet, which is reduced to 50 GPM at 100 feet. The water-cooled motor operates on 440 volts in AC ships and 220 volts in DC ships.

Always observe all electrical safety precautions with these pumps, check the direction of rotation when energizing, make certain the switch on the portable controller is off when connecting a power source, and never pump oil, gasoline, or hot or contaminated water. Use a basket strainer, and always flush the pump with fresh water after use.

There are also a variety of other small portable pumps in use. Become familiar with the types at your unit.

Sprinkler Systems

Sprinkler systems are installed in magazines, spaces where flammable materials are stowed and, in some ships, in airplane hangar spaces. Water for this system is piped from the fire main. The system is not automatic; all valves must be operated by hand. In most cases, however, they can be operated at a distance by reach rods or by some mechanism driven by electricity, by compressed air, or hydraulically.

Fixed Fog-spray Installations

Fixed fog-spray installations are used aboard certain types of naval vessels—such as carriers, transports, and cargo ships—where there is great danger of gasoline fires. The installation is made up of overhead fixed piping equipped with fog heads. To operate, this nonautomatic system is connected by 2½-inch hose to a convenient fire plug.

Transverse fog curtains, composed of nonautomatic fog heads installed at specific boundary bulkheads, are provided on certain decks of such vessels as transports and cargo ships, to prevent the rapid spread of fire.

Steam Smothering

Oil and gasoline fires in confined spaces can be extinguished with steam. The steam smothers the fire in much the same manner as fog does. However, steam generally is used only when other methods such as foam or fog are not available or as a last resort. The use of steam carries the danger of injury to personnel or damage to equipment, plus the danger of a reflash when oxygen is admitted after a fire is out. Steam systems are gradually being phased out.

Fire Fighting Chart

Extinguishing agents are listed in the order of their preferred use.

	Class Fire	Extent	Extinguishing Agent
Woodwork, bedding clothes, combustible stores	A	Small	Low-velocity fog Solid water stream Portable CO_2 or dry chemical extinguishers Foam
		Large	High-velocity fog Solid water stream Foam CO_2 (fixed system)
Explosives	A		Water immersion Magazine sprinkling Solid water stream
Combustible metals (magnesium, etc.)	D		Special powder agents with light water foam High-velocity fog Water immersion
Gasoline, JP–4 type jet fuel	B	Small	Portable CO_2 or dry chemical extinguishers Foam Low-velocity fog (prevent spread) Installed fog spray (prevent spread)
		Large	Foam High-capacity foam system CO_2 (fixed system) Fog spray (prevent spread) Sprinkler curtains (prevent spread)
Fuel oil, diesel oil, JP–5 type jet fuel & kerosene	B	Small	Portable CO_2 or dry chemical extinguishers Low-velocity fog Foam

	Class Fire	Extent	Extinguishing Agent
		Large	Foam
			High-capacity foam system
			CO_2 fixed system
			Steam smothering (boiler casings)
Paints, spirits, flammable stores		Small	Portable CO_2 or dry chemical extinguishers
			Low-velocity fog
			Foam
		Large	CO_2 (fixed system)
			High-velocity fog
			Foam
			Installed sprinkler system
Electrical & electronic equipment	C	Small	(shut off power)
			Portable CO_2 or dry chemical extinguishers
			High-velocity fog
		Large	(shut off power)
			Portable CO_2 or dry chemical extinguishers
			High-velocity fog
			Foam

Protective Clothing and Breathing Equipment

Any clothing that covers your skin—even a skivvie shirt—will protect it from flash burns and from other flames of short duration. Whenever there is any possibility of a fire or explosion, keep your body covered as much as possible.

Wear anti-flash goggles to protect your eyes. Have them ready to slip on when the alert sounds.

If your clothes catch on fire, don't run. This fans the flames. Lie down and roll up tightly in a blanket, coat, or anything at hand that will smother the flames. If nothing is available, roll over slowly, beating out the flames with your hands.

If another person's clothes are on fire, throw him down and cover him (except his head) with a blanket or coat.

Proximity Fire-Fighting Suit

This combination glass fiber and asbestos suit—with its aluminized surface—replaces the asbestos suit. It is lightweight and resists penetration of liquids. Its hood provides a protective cover for the oxygen breathing apparatus normally worn with it. The suit will allow men to enter overheated compartments and to make crash fire rescues.

Navy Oxygen Breathing Apparatus (OBA)

You may use several types of breathing equipment:

Type A Navy oxygen breathing apparatus. Parts are supplied to permit conversion to Type A-1.
Type A-1 oxygen breathing apparatus.
Type A-2 Navy oxygen breathing apparatus.
Type B Navy oxygen breathing apparatus.
Air-line mask or hose mask.
Navy service gas mask.
Type A-3 Navy oxygen breathing apparatus.
Navy oxygen rescue breathing apparatus (oxygen cylinder type).

Except for the air-line mask, all these devices use a canister that contains chemicals, although the function of the chemicals is different in the gas mask from the OBAs. The gas mask canister does not generate oxygen but aids as a filter against most poisonous gases and provides only a limited protection against smoke. It does not protect against carbon monoxide (CO), which is extremely poisonous and odorless, and which is almost always present where there is any fire or smoke, nor does it protect against carbon dioxide (CO_2).

Types A-1, A-2, and A-3 are in general shipboard use. The A-1 and A-3 are pretty much alike in operation and maintenance. The A-2 has a main valve so designed as to permit changing the canisters in a toxic or smoke-filled atmosphere; this feature has been eliminated in the Type A-3. Coast Guard units are usually equipped with Type A–3 OBAs.

The Type B OBA is designed to protect men who are engaged in hard work. It is of lighter construction and its canister has only about half the life of the other types. It protects the face and eyes, and supplies oxygen for breathing in smoke-filled, gas-filled, or fume-filled spaces— or in spaces where any sort of bad air is suspected. The OBA provides you with a closed breathing circuit. Your breath is circulated through a canister filled with chemicals. The chemicals react with the carbon dioxide and the moisture in your breath to produce oxygen.

Then you breathe this fresh oxygen into your lungs. The process, once started, is continuous until the oxygen-producing capacity of the chemicals is used up—from 20 to 40 minutes—depending on how hard the wearer is breathing. Since the canisters are powerful oxygen producers, they should be kept away from all flammables, such as oil, grease, gasoline, paint thinner, etc. Even when the cans are exhausted, they still contain enough oxygen to start or fan a fire.

Starting, wearing, and changing canisters in the various types of OBA require special instructions and practice. Don't try to use an OBA until you have been properly instructed.

To start Navy oxygen-breathing apparatus be sure that the canister is properly inserted *with seals removed*. Each type of canister has instructions for its use stenciled on it. Read them carefully.

> Adjust the facepiece and test it by inhaling while pinching both breathing tubes. If the facepiece collapses, it is airtight. If there is any leak at all, adjust the facepiece further.
>
> Grasp both breathing tubes with one hand and squeeze tightly; depress the starter valve and inhale deeply. Release the starter valve and tubes and then exhale into the apparatus.
>
> Repeat this procedure until the breathing bags are fully inflated. This will usually take three or four breaths.
>
> Lift one side of the facepiece with one hand and deflate the breathing bags with the other hand.
>
> Repeat the above—further adjustment of the facepiece may be omitted if there are no leaks—until the canister becomes warm at the *top and bottom.* This is absolutely necessary before you risk your life in smoke- or gas-filled spaces. Oxygen is not produced until the chemical reaction starts; and the chemical reaction makes the canister warm. In cold weather this procedure may take much longer, but you may hurry the process by exercising (jumping, squatting, simulating running) with the breathing bags full.
>
> Immediately after inflating the bag, turn the pointer on the timer dial to number 45. The pointer will return to zero as the apparatus is used, and at zero a warning bell will ring. When the bell rings, or if breathing becomes difficult, leave the area and charge the canister.
>
> To remove a spent canister, spread your legs apart, bend slightly

forward, turn the handwheel counterclockwise to the extreme DOWN position, depress the canister stop, and, with a quick forward motion, swing the bail (bottom frame) outward. The canister will then drop out.

Changing canisters in a gas- or smoke-filled area. This can be done only with the Type A-2 and B apparatus. When wearing the Type A, A-1, or A-3, you must go to a safe area to change the canister.

In using oxygen breathing apparatus observe these precautions:

Keep out of the danger area until you are sure the apparatus is working correctly. Start the timer each time you start a new canister.

If the bag takes extra time to fill and yet deflates rapidly, do not use the apparatus unless you first find and stop the leaks.

Excessive fogginess of the facepiece lenses and increased resistance to exhalations indicate that the bag is over-inflated, or that the canister is exhausted. If the canister is exhausted, get a new one, or go into fresh air.

Don't touch a canister with bare hands—they get *hot*.

Don't throw a used canister into the bilges or onto a deck where oil, grease, or gasoline may be present. Don't throw a canister overboard if there is an oil slick on the water, or if the ship is not under way.

Never let any liquid, especially oil or grease, enter the opening of a used canister. Never hold your face or hands over a canister opening; they can burn or explode after use. Handle open canisters with care; the chemicals they contain are caustic and can burn.

The procedure with a quick-starting canister is the same, except that breathing bags are inflated by the chlorate candles in the canister bottom. It is not necessary to inflate the bags by breathing into them. In weather below 50°F, canisters should be stowed in a warm area to ensure quick starting.

Hose (Airline) Mask

This provides breathing and eye protection in spaces contaminated by any type of gas or vapor, and in a space where there is a lack of oxygen. All that is needed is an air-line hose, which will give a continuous supply of pure air to the face-piece at a pressure slightly above the surrounding pressure. The hose mask is useful when conditions make it difficult to use the bulkier oxygen breathing apparatus.

The most common source of air supply is the low-pressure ship's service line. The full pressure of the low-pressure line can be admitted to the control valve, and the wearer can regulate the flow to suit his needs. You cannot get too much air into the mask. All excess air escapes around the face mask. Never use an oxygen bottle with this equipment. A small amount of oil, grease, or oily water in the apparatus might combine with the oxygen to cause an explosion.

Before entering a space filled with toxic gases or smoke, check the hose mask to be sure it is working properly. Take a deep breath to determine whether the airflow is sufficient.

Life Line

This is a 50-foot length of woven steel-wire cable with snap hooks at each end. There is a *back loop* on the oxygen breathing apparatus harness to which the life line may be secured.

The life line should be attached to the *upper part* of the body, preferably to the back of a shoulder harness. A cardinal rule is: *Never attach a life line to the waist.* If the line were pulled, it might interfere with the stricken man's breathing, or might injure him internally. Only as a last resort should the life line be used to drag a man out of a space. Instead, another man should be sent in to bring him out.

The life line is also used as a means of communication between tender and wearer. Signals used follow the basic diving signals:

	Pulls on life line	*Meaning*
Tender to Wearer	1	Are you OK?
	2	Advance
	3	Back out
	4	Come out now
Wearer to Tender	1	I am OK
	2	I am going on in
	3	Keep slack out of my line
	4	Send help

FIRE FIGHTING TECHNIQUE

Ships are in constant danger of sudden fire, which can spread quickly and place the ship and its crew in the gravest danger. Fire on board ship must be handled promptly and effectively wherever it may occur. Every moment of delay increases the danger that the fire will spread.

Fighting fire on board ship is complicated. It involves the teamwork and efficiency of all shipboard personnel. All hands must learn their fire fighting duties thoroughly. Then when the fire strikes, they will be prepared to fight it promptly and efficiently.

A fire party consists of two groups. The attacking group includes a nozzle man, several hose men, a plug man, and two auxiliaries—one to man the CO_2 system and the other with forcible entry tools. The "backup" fire party gives protection to the attacking group as it approaches the fire. This second group includes a hose man to operate an applicator, an electrician's mate to isolate circuits, and a hospital man to render first aid. A fire party follows these steps in fighting a fire:

Locates and reports the fire.
Isolates the area and fights the fire.
Overhauls the area.
Sets a reflash watch.

Locating the Fire

Many fires break out in unattended spaces such as storage areas, and gain considerable headway before they are discovered. The first sign of fire may be smoke seen pouring from a ventilating system outlet, or seeping around a door or hatchcover. Smoke may have traveled a considerable distance from the fire, so locating the fire is usually the first job.

Members of the fire party examine all bulkheads, decks, and vents for abnormal heat. A compartment may be clear, but a hot bulkhead would indicate a fire in the next compartment. Follow up any odor or trace of smoke. Even though the main fire is located, there may be fires in other compartments, and they must all be fought at the same time. When the fire has been definitely located and its extent determined, a complete report of the situation is made to the captain.

Isolating the Fire

While the fire party fights the fire, it also sets up fire boundaries to isolate the fire. If a single compartment is involved, it is isolated from above and below, as well as from all four sides. If a number of compartments are involved, the fire party treats them as a unit, and protects all adjacent spaces, to keep the fire from spreading. Sprinklers in such spaces are turned on as necessary.

Materials on the deck above are removed or thoroughly cooled to prevent the spread of fire. Usually, about an inch of water on the deck is enough to absorb the heat from the burning compartment below. Spaces below the fire must not be neglected or paint on the overhead may blister and ignite. Fog should be used to cool the overhead and prevent ignition of materials in such spaces.

All ventilation systems in the fire area are secured to prevent heat and unburned vapors being carried to other compartments, and to help starve the fire by cutting off its air supply.

If there is any doubt that the fire can be kept within the established boundary, a secondary or emergency boundary is set up. Additional hose lines and standby sprinkling systems are made ready for use at the secondary boundary.

Fighting the Fire

While the fire is being isolated, it should also be fought. The first step is to de-energize electric circuits in the compartments to protect personnel against shock. Always check fire-hose water pressure at the nozzle before entering any space. As a standby emergency provision, at least one member of the fire party should be dressed in a fire-protection suit. Heat and unburned gases build up pressure that should be vented by undogging the door before it is opened completely for entry.

Overhauling the Area

After all fire is extinguished, the area must be overhauled to prevent a reflash of the fire. To do this, members of the fire party break up all smoldering or charred material and saturate it thoroughly. Whenever possible, materials are immersed in buckets of water.

Foam should be washed into the drains. All compartments involved are checked for explosive vapors or liquids that may remain. Dewatering operations are then begun. At this time, a full report is made to the captain on fire and smoke damage, and flooding.

Reflash Watch

Fires that seem to be out may start again from a smoldering fragment of material or through vapor ignition. The final step in fighting a fire aboard ship is to set up a reflash watch for each compartment involved, and to maintain it as long as the possibility of reflash exists.

Special Problems

In some spaces of the ship, fire fighting is more hazardous than in others, and special equipment is needed. Magazine fires are extremely dangerous. In these spaces, sprinkling systems are installed, which are either automatically or manually operated to cool the ammunition and bulkheads until the fire can be extinguished by fire fighters.

Dangerous oil fires may occur in machinery spaces. Therefore, a steam smothering system is installed in addition to standard firefighting equipment. Smothering is used first to smother the fire. If the fire spreads, water-fog and foam must be used to extinguish it.

Bedding and other combustibles in living and berthing spaces are potential sources of fire. Some of these spaces contain fixed fog systems that are manually connected to fire plugs with hose lines. The fog will beat down the surface flames until fire hoses can be turned on the fire.

Caution

Some plastics and curtains or carpets used in living areas, can burn easily and produce toxic gases. Fire parties must be aware of such dangers. The man in charge must know what is burning and how best to handle it, in order to protect his men.

CHAPTER 17

Survival

Normally, the Coast Guard helps others who get into trouble, and you will be trained to handle such emergencies. But there may come a time when your own ship, boat, or aircraft is in trouble, and the problem of doing something about it may be pretty much up to you (figure 17–1). This chapter gives basic information on survival if you should be shipwrecked. Special instructions will be given to members of rescue boats or aircraft crews. No matter where you are, you must familiarize yourself with such other instructions as are available. Perform drills diligently, learn the use of available survival equipment, keep your life jacket and other lifesaving gear in good condition, and regularly review instructions so that you can manage in an emergency. Refer to the Coast Guard Rescue and Survival Systems Manual, Commandant Instruction M10470.10 series for detailed information.

PERSONAL FLOTATION DEVICE (PFD)

Personal flotation devices (PFDs) come in a number of forms. Shipboard military personnel are usually provided with specially designed PFDs that are inherently buoyant, meaning they are filled with a substance such as fibrous glass or kapok that provides flotation. Other military PFDs include less cumbersome, inflatable, and formed plastic types. Commercial-type PFDs are also used by Coast Guardsmen in certain situations. These are referred to as Type I, II, III or IV PFDs and are assigned a Coast Guard Approval Number. Details on each can be found in Title 46 of the Code of Federal Regulations beginning in part 159. Type I commercial PFDs provide similar flotation to mil-

Figure 17–1. Personal flotation devices are donned during most emergency situations.

itary PFDs that are inherently buoyant. PFDs are often termed "life preservers," "life jackets," or "life vests." The official definitions for these terms are somewhat tricky, so if you become involved with this terminology in a legal sense or in a written report, be sure to use the correct term. Generally speaking, the term "life preserver" is correct for those PFDs provided on board Coast Guard vessels. The typical Coast Guard life preserver is the Navy Vest Type with collar. It is an inherently buoyant PFD. This PFD is designed to provide superior flotation characteristics and reliability. It will support the head of an unconscious person except when worn with the full wet suit.

Navy Vest-Type PFD with Collar

The vest-type PFD uses fibrous glass or kapok pads to provide buoyancy, and has tapes to pull tight for a close fit. Leg straps prevent it from riding up in the water. A webbing body strap helps toward a snugger fit and provides a hold for lifting you out of the water. You can also use the strap to attach yourself to life craft or to other individuals.

Put the vest preserver on over your other clothes. Tie the upper tape at the waist fairly tight; it helps keep the preserver from sliding

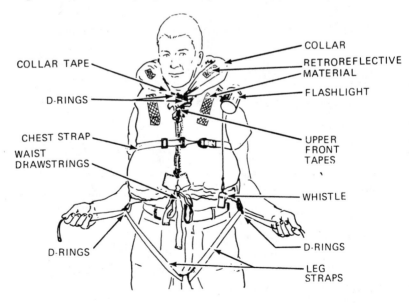

Figure 17–2. U.S. Navy vest-type PFD, with collar.

up in the water. Then adjust the chest strap and fasten the snap hook into the ring. Tie the collar tapes to keep the collar under your chin, threading the tapes through the D-rings to hold the collar in the proper position.

The leg straps may be adjusted in the water, but if a man is injured or unconscious, they should be adjusted before he is put overboard. Pull the straps between the legs from behind. Pull the leg straps as tight as possible without producing discomfort. While aboard ship and not in danger of going overboard, you need not use the leg straps.

Care Aboard Ship

When the outer covering or envelope of the vest preserver becomes soiled, the pads should be removed, the envelope— *not the pads*— cleaned, and the pads reinserted. Don't scrub kapok-filled life preservers lest you impair the fire-resistant qualities of the cloth. You can wipe them off, but that is all. Fibrous-glass life preservers do not have fire-retardant cloth, and their envelopes may be laundered. The pads should never be removed except for laundering the outer covering. Don't tamper with any jacket, or handle it roughly. Keep all jackets away from heat, moisture, oil, and dirt—or you may have a jacket that won't support you when you want it to.

Navy Vest-Type PFD Without Collar, Work Type (Inherently Buoyant)

This is a lightweight PFD that is formed-plastic filled and provides 17½ pounds of buoyancy. The unit, illustrated in figure 17–3, is composed of three cotton drill-covered sections that are assembled through

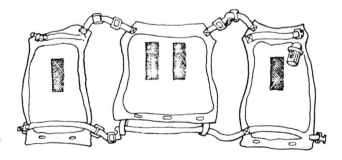

Figure 17–3. U.S. Navy vest-type PFD, without collar; work type (inherently buoyant)

a series of straps to form the completed PFD. Each section has a formed or molded pad two inches thick, notched for flexibility, allowing the PFD to more closely conform to the shape of the body. Because this vest type PFD is light in weight, the wearer is able to work in comparative comfort.

The work-type PFD is buoyant enough to keep the wearer afloat; it has no self-righting capability and will not keep an unconscious wearer's head out of the water while awaiting rescue.

Coast Guard-Approved Type III PFD, (Inherently Buoyant)

The main advantages of type III PFDs are wearability, ease of donning, simple construction, and neat appearance. The disadvantages are poor flotation characteristics (no righting movement), and minimum buoyancy (approximately 15 pounds). Therefore, type IIIs should only be worn where greater freedom of movement is required, and the mission and environment are less hostile.

Coast Guard-approved type III PFDs are authorized for use by Coast Guard personnel to meet the requirements of paragraph 4-1-27B of

Figure 17–4. Coast Guard-Approved Type III PFD.

COMDTINST M5000.3 and as a substitute for the work-type preserver.

Type III PFDs are not normally universally sized. Two or three different sizes will be required to fit adults properly.

Navy Inflatable Yoke-Type PFD

This is a lightweight preserver that can be blown up either by a CO_2 cylinder or by mouth. It is fastened around your waist by a web belt. When blown up, it holds itself closely around your neck. An extra piece of webbing provides a handhold for assisting you out of the water. A length of line with a wood T-toggle enables you to attach yourself to a boat, or to float lines, or to other survivors. When not needed, the inflatable preserver is carried in a pouch, normally worn at your back.

When you need the preserver, pull the pouch around to the front, remove the preserver, slip it over your head and inflate it. To inflate the preserver, grasp the lanyard attached to the inflater and jerk downward as far as possible. This will release the carbon dioxide gas into the air chamber. If the preserver has two inflaters, pull both lanyards. For more buoyancy, push in the mouthpiece or the oral inflation valve and blow up the preserver yourself. To deflate the preserver, open the oral valve.

Inflatable preservers should not be tied tightly together or otherwise compressed when stowed; they should be stowed in dark, cool, dry places. They should be kept away from oil, paint, and greasy substances. Sharp edges increase wear and tear, so keep the preservers clear of them. Don't stow the preservers near steam lines or radiators. Inflatable preservers should never be cleaned with commercial dry-cleaning solvents; they should be washed with mild soap solutions and dried thoroughly.

ABANDONING SHIP

Preparations

There are two important things to do if time permits; find out the distance and direction to the nearest land, and see that your equipment is in good condition. What clothing and gear to take with you will depend on whether you are in a hot or cold climate and whether you will take to a boat or raft, or depend upon your life jacket to keep you afloat.

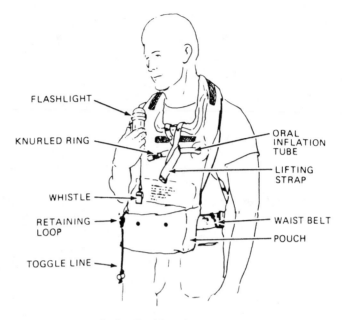

Figure 17–5. Navy standard inflatable yoke-type PFD.

Clothing

This is especially important in cold weather, but even in hot weather you need protection from the sun. In cold weather, you need:

Long woolen underwear, woolen socks, to keep body warm.
Windproof jacket to protect shoulders and arms.
Helmet or cap to keep head warm and water out of ears.
Gloves to warm hands and to prevent burning them on lines.
Anti-exposure suit, if available.

Equipment

The more you have, the better. Take this as a minimum:

Flashlight, knife, and whistle;
Line, at least six feet long, tied under arms with snap-on free end
   to make fast to line on raft, boat, or rescue ship;
Sunglasses;
Wallet, money belt.

Actions Before Leaving Ship

This depends on the amount of time you have. Remember to:

Keep calm.

Test life jacket valves and inflating tubes; don't leave the ship with a leaking jacket.

If it's available, drink hot tea or coffee to reduce effects of cold.

Abandon Ship Procedure

The following procedure is a guide to be followed whenever practical.

Leaving the Ship

For survival it is best that you abandon ship fully clothed. If possible, get away from the ship in a lifeboat or life raft. If it is impossible to leave the ship on a life raft, lower yourself into the water using a firmly anchored hose or line. When you have a choice, leave the ship from the windward side and from whichever end of the ship is lower in the water. If it is necessary to jump into the water, hold the legs together and the body erect. Injured personnel should always have leg straps adjusted before they are lowered into the water. Inherently buoyant type PFDs must be securely fastened and kept close to the body by folding the arms across the chest and gripping the jacket with the fingers. This procedure will prevent buoyant PFDs from riding up and striking your chin or neck when you hit the water. If you are wearing an inflatable PFD, it must not be inflated until you are in the water. The same procedure is followed for jumping with an uninflated PFD as with the inherently buoyant PFD. The PFD should be inflated as soon as you are in the water and clear of flames.

In the Water. When in the water, you should swim away from the ship as rapidly as possible and climb into a lifeboat if one is available. If depth charges or underwater explosions are occurring in the vicinity, you should swim or float on your back, keeping your head and chest as far out of the water as possible, because underwater explosions are particularly threatening to body cavities such as lungs, abdomen, sinuses, and eardrums.

Ship Surrounded by Flames. When the ship is entirely surrounded by burning oil, and abandonment is essential, you should jump feet first through the flames and swim to windward under the surface of the water for as long as possible. When the air in your lungs is exhausted, you should spring above the water in a vertical position, push the flames away with a circular motion of your hands, quickly take a deep breath, and with back to the wind, submerge feet first in a vertical position and swim under the surface again. This procedure should be repeated until you are well clear of flames. Any buoyant articles of clothing and shoes should be discarded. Only the inflatable PFD should be worn, insofar as possible during this abandon ship procedure, and the preserver should be inflated only after the person is clear of the flames. Inherently buoyant PFDs will not permit the wearer to swim beneath the surface. They should, therefore, be discarded before leaving the ship, should it be surrounded by flames.

Survival in Cold Water

When forced to abandon ship in cold waters put on as much clothing as possible (including hat and gloves), or anti-exposure suit, if available, and be sure your life jacket is properly adjusted. Once in the lifeboat or raft, huddle up close to your shipmates to conserve body heat. If there is water in the lifeboat, immersion-foot can be prevented by untying shoe laces, elevating legs, and exercising ankles and toes at regular intervals. However, if you develop frostbite or immersion-foot, do *not* rub the affected parts.

If you must enter the water, make sure you are heavily dressed and wearing a life jacket. Enter the water as slowly as possible in order to reduce the shock of initial entry. Once in the water remember that any movement will only increase the rate of body-heat loss and reduce your chance for survival. Swim only to a nearby boat, raft, or piece of debris that you may be able to use to escape from the water. If you must remain in the water, cross your legs and bring your knees up towards your chest while at the same time holding your arms around your chest (heat-escape-lessening posture). This posture will help reduce body-heat loss. Do not use the "drown proofing" method of floating, as this increases loss of body heat.

If you should find yourself in the water, especially cold water in a survival situation, follow these tips:

Keep as much of your body out of the water as possible. If you can, climb onto an overturned hull or piece of debris. Do so immediately.

Wear a personal flotation device. This will eliminate the need for physical activity to stay afloat, thereby saving body heat.

If you have time, put on extra clothing and be sure to cover your head.

Protect yourself against the wind by staying to leeward.

If forced to remain in the water, keep your head above water and as dry as possible. Swimming will produce a faster cooling rate; therefore, once flotation is assured and essential survival actions have been taken, stop swimming and assume the heat-escape-lessening posture. Hold your upper arms against your sides with the wrists placed over the chest. Your legs should be drawn up as close as possible to the chest, with ankles crossed, much like a fetal position. If there are other people in the water with you, assume a huddle position. All survivors face inward, with sides and chests close together and arms around each other. Either of these two actions will increase survival time up to 50 percent.

Hypothermia is a killer. Its danger is not restricted to freezing the body to death. Prolonged exposure to cold renders the body incapable of coordinated movement and the mind incapable of rational thought. Long before victims are unconscious, they may be unable to take the steps necessary to save their own life.

Survival in Hot Climate

Wear a shirt, trousers, and shoes. They may be a hindrance in the water, but if you are adrift for any time, they are necessary to protect against the effects of sun, wind, and salt water. Take the same equipment as for cold weather, and take the same actions before leaving the ship.

Avoid panic—keep calm. If you panic, others may, and you are going to be in trouble. Nonswimmers are most likely to lose their heads after

Wear PFD to maintain position

Keep head and neck out of water

Conserve heat by huddling

Figure 17–6. Heat-preserving postures. (Commandant's Bulletin 12–82)

abandoning ship, so encourage them, help them, and keep talking to them. Keep your wits about you, keep control of the situation, and you will come through.

ADRIFT IN A BOAT OR RAFT

Ingenuity and foresight are required to make the most of all available equipment. In a powerboat, use the fuel for making the most distance, not speed. The best mileage will be made at the slowest speed that can be held with the clutch fully engaged. If the boat has sails, use them and save the fuel for an emergency. If there are no sails, try to jury-rig a mast and sail with oars, boat hooks, pieces of wreckage, clothing and tarpaulins.

The most serious situation is to be adrift in a life raft with no means for rigging a sail. In that case, try to make your rations and water last as long as possible. The longer you hold out, the better your chances of rescue or a safe landing. Men have endured for more than a month in a raft, with practically no rations.

Rescue units will start looking for you at your last-known position. Don't leave that area unless you can make it to shore or to a well-traveled shipping lane.

Organizing for Survival

The first thing to do is to secure all gear to the raft or boat. Anything not lashed down is liable to go overboard and be lost.

Rig a tarp or sail for protection from the sun, and get under it. The water will reflect enough sun to burn your skin, so don't get any more sunburn than necessary. Remember that the same tarp or sail will provide drinking water when there is rain.

Inventory the provisions on board, and store them where they will be safe, even against high seas. Plan for rationing food and water. No one should eat or drink during the first 24 hours. However, in cold climates, eating every two hours will help a man to stay warm.

Don't get excited and don't rush. Do things deliberately to conserve energy and to avoid perspiring.

Save your clothes. Although it is warm during the day, you may need something to wear at night.

Arrange watches and cooperate in standing them. Stow your signaling gear—mirror, marking dye, flares, and smoke signal—where they can be reached in a hurry.

First Aid

In general, the first-aid procedures afloat are the same as on shore. There are some special considerations, however, which apply to survivors at sea.

Fuel oil from a sinking ship will float on the water and accumulate on the skin of survivors. If swallowed it may cause vomiting. In the eyes it will cause redness and smarting. Ordinarily these symptoms will disappear in a day or two. Wipe oil carefully from the eyelids with a clean cloth or bandage.

Survivors may not evacuate their bowels for many days at a time. This condition is to be expected, and no first aid or medication is necessary to correct it.

Petrolatum (vaseline) may be used to ease chapped skin and cracked lips. But it is better to prevent sunburn by wearing or rigging whatever protection is available against the sun. Even a dark tan is not a sure protection against sunburn. Reflected light from the ocean may burn the eyeballs as well as the skin. Guard against the sun when it is directly or almost directly overhead.

Boils often appear on the skin of men who have been in lifeboats or rafts for several days. Unless skilled medical assistance is at hand, no treatment should be attempted. Simply cover them with protective bandages and do not try to open them. Resist exhaustion and conserve strength by sleeping and resting as much as possible.

Coast Guard-Approved and Navy MK-5 Rafts

Presently Coast Guard cutters are equipped with Navy MK-5 life rafts. Coast Guard-approved rafts have been procured and are being distributed to some cutters. In the future, only Coast Guard-approved life rafts (figure 17–7) will be procured. The standard features of Coast Guard-approved rafts are listed below.

Constructed of neoprene-coated nylon;
CO_2 overpressurized inflation system with relief valves that provide for cold inflation;
Two independent buoyancy tubes;
Self-erecting canopy;
Boarding ladder/towing bridle;

1. Canopy Arch
2. Pump
3. Rain Catcher with Tie-Down Line
4. Exterior Canopy
5. Inner Canopy
6. Outside Light (Recognition)
7. Canopy Closure
8. Boarding Ramp
9. Boarding Handles
10. Hull Tube
11. Gunwale Tube
12. Life Line
13. Paddle Bag
14. Righting Line
15. Equipment Container
16. Hull CO_2 Bottle
17. Gunwale CO_2 Bottle
18. Sea Anchor

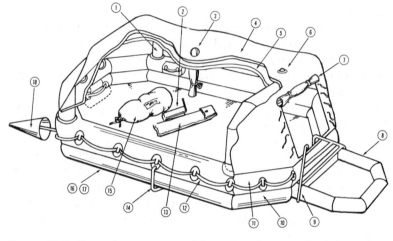

Figure 17–7. General arrangement of Coast Guard approved raft (typical).

Survival equipment (drinking water, signal flares, etc.);
Inflatable floor;
Exterior and interior lights;
Stabilizing pockets (water);
Rainwater catchment assembly;
Rescue line (throwable);
External/internal life line;
Sea anchor.

The crew survival rafts can be released and inflated either manually or automatically by use of the hydrostatic release.*

Note: Some installations may not be equipped with hydrostatic releases.

The operating painter line is attached to the stowage rack. As the raft container is released and drifts away, the painter line is pulled from the container. The inflation cable is attached near the raft end of the painter line. The painter line pulls the cable from the inflation valve, resulting in the release of the CO_2 from its cylinder, which inflates the raft. The painter line keeps the raft near the vessel unless sufficient pull is applied to break the 500-pound weak link, such as when the vessel sinks.

On the Navy MK-5 life raft stowed in the flexible (valise) cases, neither the sea painter nor the manual CO_2 release shall be secured to the ship in any manner.

The life rafts can be deployed manually by releasing the raft from the stowage rack and pulling the operating painter line from the raft container. The container should preferably be placed in the water prior to inflation to allow ample room for expansion of the raft. If practical, personnel should board the raft directly from their vessel to avoid unnecessary boarding problems and exposure to the water, especially in cold oceans. Immediately upon boarding the raft complete these steps:

1. Get clear of sinking vessel in case of explosion or surface fire.

2. Search for any possible survivors.

3. Salvage any floating equipment that may be useful; stow and secure all items.

4. Ensure sea anchor is properly deployed.

5. Check raft for proper inflation, leaks, and points of possible chafing. Bail out any water that may have entered the raft. Be careful not to snag the raft with shoes or sharp objects.

6. In cold oceans, inflate floor immediately, put on exposure suit, if available. Rig entrance cover. If with others, huddle together for warmth.

7. Check the physical condition of all aboard. Give first aid if necessary. Take seasickness pills if available. Wash oil or gasoline from clothing and body.

8. If there is more than one raft, keep close together to expedite rescue operations. If possible, rafts should be tied together about 50 feet apart bow to stern from towing bridle to towing bridle.

9. Make a calm estimate of situation and plan course of action carefully.

10. Ration water and food; assign duties to the survivors.

11. Keep a log. Record time of entry into water, names, and physical condition of survivors, ration schedule, winds, weather, direction of swells, times of sunrise and sunset, and other navigation data. Inventory all equipment.

Rescue and Assistance

Although shipboard rafts are intended for crew survival, these rafts may be used, at the discretion of the commanding officer, for other purposes such as rescue and assistance. If the raft is used as a rescue platform for recovering survivors, the canopy fabric may be cut away.

Caution. When cutting away the canopy fabric, exercise care to avoid cutting or puncturing the buoyancy tube and canopy supports.

Training

Inflation of a crew-survival raft due for its annual inspection would provide an opportunity for crew familiarization and training as well as useful information regarding raft reliability.

Caution. A clean, clear area large enough to allow unrestricted inflation is necessary. Care must be taken to prevent damage to the raft. Avoid sharp objects and abrasion from dragging the raft on rough surfaces.

Adequate protection should also be provided for shipment if the raft is shipped out of its container.

Inspection and Test Requirements

Coast Guard life rafts and hydrostatic releases shall be inspected annually by an approved raft servicing facility. Refer to COMDTINST M16714.3 for a listing of approved servicing facilities.

Four-Man Rescue and Survival Raft

The four-man rescue and survival raft (RR-4) was modified to provide SAR boats with a multipurpose raft. The rescue and survival raft is a basic Coast Guard-approved raft modified to incorporate a stowable canopy and a heavy, water ballast system for stability. The four-man rescue and survival raft incorporates most of the features required for Coast Guard-approved rafts (figure 17–8). However, there are the following exceptions:

The canopy is stowable. This raft is packed with the canopy stowed. The exterior and interior lights, as well as the rainwater catchment assembly, have been removed from the canopy.

A heavy, water ballast system has been added for increased stability in heavy weather. Because of this system, the raft will not be as affected by wind as conventional rafts would be.

The inflation of the raft can be accomplished either manually or automatically by action of the operating painter line, as mentioned previously.

Deployment

To deploy the four-man rescue and survival raft, complete these steps:
1. Remove the raft container from its stowage rack.
2. Place raft into the water on the down-wind side of the boat.

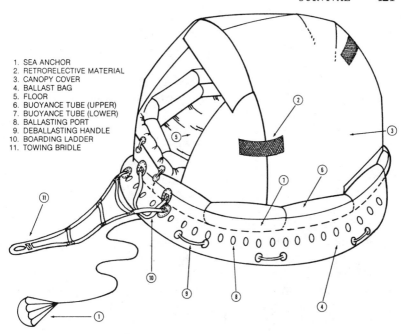

1. SEA ANCHOR
2. RETRORELECTIVE MATERIAL
3. CANOPY COVER
4. BALLAST BAG
5. FLOOR
6. BUOYANCE TUBE (UPPER)
7. BUOYANCE TUBE (LOWER)
8. BALLASTING PORT
9. DEBALLASTING HANDLE
10. BOARDING LADDER
11. TOWING BRIDLE

Figure 17–8. Life raft, four-man (RR–4), SAR boat, rescue and survival (typical).

3. Pull the operating painter line (50 feet) from the raft container. This action should inflate the raft.

4. If practical, pull the raft along side the boat and board the raft directly from the boat.

5. If time permits, take extra equipment and supplies aboard the raft. Signals, portable radios, immersion suits, and water and food should be used to supplement the raft's equipment, as this raft is equipped with a limited service survival kit.

6. Deploy sea anchor.

7. Untie the canopy and pull it over the support tubes. Then, retie it in the closed position. In most cases, try to remain in the general area of the boat. If the boat does not sink immediately, it is best to leave the operating painter line attached to the raft stowage rack. If the boat should sink rapidly, the painter line could be cut. Otherwise, it will break at the weak link.

8. Refer to the section on the MK-5 raft for action that should be taken immediately upon boarding the raft.

Rescue and Assistance

This raft can be capsized by large, breaking waves. Although it is heavily ballasted and very stable in most sea states, alternate rescue methods (e.g., a helicopter) should be considered if large breakers are present. Due to its heavy ballast system, the raft will not be as affected by wind as conventional rafts would be.

The use of this raft should be considered for evacuation of persons stranded in areas where the rescue boat cannot be safely operated.

1. Complete steps 1 through 3 of the previous section on "Deployment."

2. Attach two lines of sufficient length to the raft's towing bridle. Pass one line to the persons in distress for use in pulling the raft to them. The second line will be retained by the boat crew and payed out as the raft is pulled by the distressed persons. Once boarding has been completed, pull the raft to the boat with the second line.

3. Deballast the raft by slowly lifting one side of the raft. Handles are located on the ballast bags for assisting in dumping (figure 17–8) of water from raft's ballast bags. Prior to shipment for inspection and repacking, the raft and ballast bag system should be completely dried.

Inspection and Test Requirements

The following inspections and tests shall be completed as required.

Weekly. Visually inspect the exterior of the raft container, stowage rack, and operating painter line at least once a week by completing these steps:

1. Inspect the exterior of the raft container for damage to the case and seal.

2. Inspect the stowage rack for general condition.

3. Inspect the operating painter line for proper attachment, cuts, and fraying.

Annual. Return the raft, container, and hydrostatic releases to an approved servicing facility for inspection once a year. Refer to COMDTINST M16741.3 for a listing of approved raft servicing facilities.

Survival Kit and Items

Boatcrew Signal Kit

This kit is designed to be worn around the waist and will not interfere with the wearing of the PFD or wet suit. The boat's pyrotechnics and signals are not accessible to the crewman in the event the boat capsizes, sinks, or a crewman is lost overboard. For these reasons a personal signal kit for boatcrews was developed.

The kits consist of two MK-13 day/night distress signals, one MK-79 flare kit, one strobe light SDU-5/E, one emergency signaling mirror, and a pouch with adjustable belt. Survival items must be attached to the pouch grommets with 3-foot lengths of type I nylon cord to prevent loss. The strobe light (SDU-5/E) carried in this kit must be removed from the nylon pocket.

The coxswain makes sure that the boatcrew signal kit is worn at all times when operating the boat during hazardous operations, heavy weather, and darkness, unless signals are carried in the PFD or wet-suit pockets.

Signal Whistle

The signaling whistle emits an audible signal to rescue ships or personnel. It is made of plastic with a lanyard attached for easy access and to prevent loss. This whistle is used to attract the attention of rescue ships or personnel in foggy weather or at night. Whistle range is 1,000 yards.

Survival Knife

The survival knife is a multipurpose survival tool stowed in its sheath when not in use. It is a hunting knife with a 5-inch steel blade. One side of the blade is honed while the other side is serrated. The grip

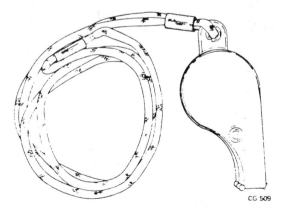

CG 509

Figure 17–9. Signaling whistle.

is made of leather washers ⅛-inch thick, layered in a row up to the guard. At the end of the grip there is a still butt. The sheath is constructed of leather with a pocket to carry the sharpening stone. There is a metal tip on the sheath to protect from injury.

The survival knife is the most valuable general-purpose survival tool. It can be used for cutting wood and material, opening cans, and it is a hunting knife as well as a weapon. At all times the survival knife should be kept clean, sharpened, and returned to the sheath when not in use.

Signal Kit; MK-79 MOD-0

The MK-79 MOD-0, containing a pencil-type launcher and cartridge flare, is used to signal rescue parties and aircraft. This illumination signal kit consists of seven MK-80 screw-cartridge flares and one MK-31 pencil-type launcher. Each cartridge flare has a duration of 4½ seconds minimum. Included with the flares and launcher is a bandolier,

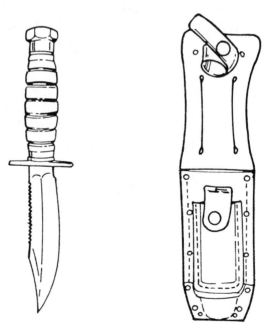

Figure 17–10. Survival knife and sheath.

which stores the flares until use, protective caps for the flares, and an instruction sheet.

The MK-79 MOD-0 illumination signal kit is designed to be used by personnel as a distress signaling device. It is small and light in weight so that it can be carried in pockets of flight suits or on life rafts. The projector aims and fires the signals. Each signal contains a red pyrotechnic star. On activation, this star is propelled upward to a height of from 250 to 650 feet. The star burns for a minimum of 4½ seconds. Candlepower of the MK-80 star is 12,000.

This kit is actuated by release of the firing pin, which strikes the percussion primer in the base of the signal. The primer ignites a black-powder expelling charge that ignites the first-fire composition of the star and propels the star to the desired altitude.

To operate the MK-79 MOD-0 illumination signal kit, proceed as follows:

1. Remove the bandolier and projector from plastic envelope.

2. Cock the firing pin of the projector by moving the trigger screw to the bottom of the vertical slot and slipping it to the right so that it catches at the top of the angular (safety) slot.

3. Bend protective plastic tab away from signal in bandolier to allow

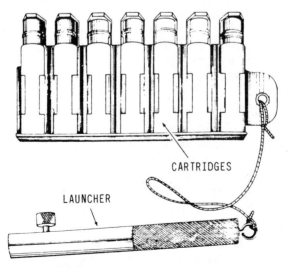

Figure 17–11. MK-79 MOD-0 illumination signal.

attachment of projector. *Warning*. The plastic tabs over the signals in the bandolier protect the percussion primers from being struck accidentally. They should be kept intact until just before loading signal into projector.

4. Mate projector with signal and rotate projector clockwise until signal is seated.

5. Hold projector over head with arm fully extended. The projector should be pointed at a slight angle away from the body.

6. While firmly gripping the projector, fire the signal by slipping the trigger screw to the left out of the safety slot and into the firing slot. This action must be one continuous movement so that the thumb does not interfere with the forward motion of the trigger screw when it is brought into the firing slot.

7. If a signal fails to fire, two more attempts should be made to fire it; then unload the cartridge only after waiting at least 30 seconds to eliminate the possibility of a hangfire.

8. Unscrew spent signal case or signal that failed to fire. Discard by throwing overboard.

9. To fire another signal, repeat steps 1 through 8.

The MK-79 MOD-0 must be stored in a dry, well-ventilated location and shielded from direct sunlight. Observe the following safety precautions when handling MK-79 MOD-0 illumination kits:

1. Signals in this kit are ignited by percussion primers that must be protected from accidental striking. Protruding tabs of the bandolier that extend over signal bases prevent accidental striking of the primers. They must be torn off or bent back except when loading a signal into the projector.

2. The projector must not be loaded until immediately before firing. If a signal is loaded into the projector and is not fired immediately, it must be returned to the bandolier.

3. Signals must be inspected periodically to ensure that they are not dented or otherwise damaged. *Warning*. Dented or damaged signals must not be used. Dents or other imperfections might result in violent action of the signal when fired.

4. Signals must be kept away from fires and other heat sources.

5. The projector trigger screw must be checked frequently to ensure that it is tight. A loose trigger can release the firing pin prematurely and cause injury or can fall out and become lost during emergency loading, making the projector useless.

6. The trigger screw must be in the safety slot while the signal is being loaded.

7. In firing the projector, care must be taken to raise the arm well above the head with the projector held in the vertical position. A loaded projector must *never* be pointed toward the user or other personnel.

Smoke and Illumination Signal; Marine MK-13 MOD-0

The MK-13 MOD-0 is used for day or night signaling with smoke or flare. This marine smoke and illumination signal consists of a metal cylinder approximately 5 inches long and slightly more than 1.5 inches in diameter, each end of which is fitted with a protective plastic cap. The cap on the flame (night) end is molded so that there are three prominent protrusions or beads across its face. These beads positively identify this end, by the sense of touch, for nighttime use. The face of the cap at the smoke end is smooth. A label adhered to the outer surface around the whole body of the signal further identifies the smoke (day) and flame (night) end and provides precise instructions for use. Beneath each plastic end cap is a pull ring to which is tied a nylon cord or lanyard. A large washer on the cord at the flame end provides additional identification in darkness. The pull ring at each end is attached to a pull strip seal, which in turn is attached to a friction wire that extends inward through a pull wire igniter cup containing ignition composition.

A small percentage of MK-13 MOD-0 signals were manufactured without the three beads on the flange end cap for night identification. However, the flange end can be identified by touch in night use by the flange around the tubular portion of the end cap.

The MK-13 MOD-0 illumination signal is intended for either day or night signaling by personnel on land or sea. Because of its weight (6.4 ounces) and size, the MK-13 MOD-0 may be carried in life vest, flight

Figure 17–12. MK-13 MOD-0 marine smoke and illumination signal.

suit, or life raft. The MK-13 MOD-0 emits orange smoke for day use and a red flare for night use. Burning time is approximately 20 seconds.

A sharp, quick pull on the pull ring of the MK-13 MOD-0 causes a friction wire, which is attached to the pull strip seal, to move through the ignition cup and ignite the flare mixture (night) or the smoke mixture (day), depending on which type of display is desired. After choosing the type of display desired—smoke for day or flare for night—operate the signal as follows:

1. Tear paper or plastic cap from end to be ignited.

2. Flip pull ring over signal rim.

3. Push pull ring downward to break seal. *Warning:* Do not break seal until just prior to ignition. Premature breaking of the seal could result in non-ignition due to water reaching the igniter.

4. If seal does not break, continue to push ring downward until it bends against case.

5. Flip bent ring back to original position and use as lever to break seal. *Caution:* Do not twist pull ring in an effort to break seal. Twisting may tear ring loose at solder joint and leave signal useless.

6. After seal is broken, ignite signal with quick pull on ring. Ensure that firing end is not pointed toward face or body.

7. Hold signal firmly at arm's length at an angle 45 degrees from the horizontal to prevent burns from hot drippings. *Warning:* After ignition, the outer case may overheat and burn the hand. Dropping the signal will not lessen its effectiveness.

8. If smoke signal changes to flames at sea, douse signal in water for a moment; if on land, place burning signal against the ground momentarily. Smoke will resume after immersion or smothering.

9. After using one end, douse signal in water to cool; if on land, place signal on ground to cool. Save for use of other end.

The MK-13 MOD-0 signal must be stored and handled in accordance with procedures found in CG 272, Coast Guard Ordnance Manual, and NAVORD OP 2213, Pyrotechnic Screening and Dye Marking Manual. Under no circumstances shall both ends of the MK-13 MOD-0 signal be ignited at the same time.

Emergency Signaling Mirror

The emergency signaling mirror is used to attract rescue ships or aircraft. It measures 2 inches by 3 inches and replaces the 3-inch by

5-inch mirror. There is a hole in the corner of the mirror through which a lanyard passes so that the mirror may be looped around the neck.

The emergency signaling mirror is intended to reflect sunlight at passing ships, aircraft, or rescue parties. Instructions for using the mirror are printed on its back.

Signal Distress Lights

SDU-5/E

The SDU-5/E is a battery-operated strobe light used to signal rescue parties. The light is a lightweight, compact, battery-operated portable unit with all circuitry encapsulated within the case. The case is fabricated of high impact-resistant thermoplastic material with provisions in the bottom end for receiving the 4RM1B mercury cell battery. The battery entry and the case are completely watertight when the battery is installed in place. The case is also provided with a push-ON, push-OFF type switch to permit one-handed operation. A flexible switch boot further ensures watertight integrity. A 3-foot nylon cord serves to attach the light to the equipment case by either of two attachment loops on the light case.

The table below lists the leading particulars of the light.

Item	Characteristic
Dimensions	4½ in. by 2 in. by 1 in.
Weight	8 oz. with battery installed
Light Output	100,000 peak lumens per flash
Flash Rate	50 ± 10 flashes per minute
Visibility	5 miles minimum

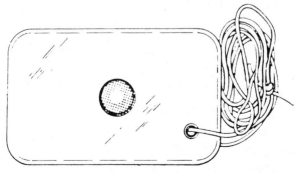

Figure 17–13. Emergency signal mirror.

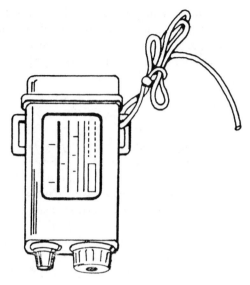

Figure 17–14. Distress marker light (SDU–5/E strobe light).

Item	Characteristic
Duration	9 hours continuous; 18 hours intermittent (w/o battery change)
Battery Type	4RM1B (NSN 6135–00–073–8939)
Battery Volts	5.0 volts dc

The SDU-5/E is intended for equipping aircrewmembers and shipboard personnel with a high-intensity, visual distress signal in the event of abandonment of aircraft or man overboard. Operate the signal as follows:

1. Turn ON. Push switch in until click is heard, then release. Light should begin flashing within a few seconds.

2. Turn OFF. Push switch in until click is heard, then release. Light should stop flashing.

761-A Matrix

The 761-A matrix light emits a steady light that is beamed by a special lens at the horizon, 45 degrees and straight up. It can also be used as a flashlight. There is no established shelf life for the 761-A matrix light.

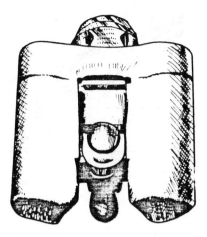

Figure 17–15. Matrix light, 761–A.

To inspect the 761-A matrix light, complete these steps:
1. Replace batteries annually.
2. Inspect battery contacts for corrosion.
3. Inspect lens and case for cracks.
4. Replace damaged parts as required.
5. Activate light to ensure proper function.

Personnel Marker Lights

The personnel marker light (PML) is a chemical light developed for use on personal flotation devices. It is used to attract the attention of SAR aircraft, ships, or ground parties; once activated it provides light for approximately 8 hours. The PML is equipped with a pin-type clip and should be attached in the same location on the PFD as the one-cell flashlight. *Note:* The PML is the only chemical light authorized for use and is to replace the one-cell flashlight on an attrition basis.

To activate the PML, slide the protective sleeve from the PML breaking the sealing band. Firmly squeeze the lever against the light tube until the ampule inside the light breaks.

The inspection should be performed quarterly and should consist of examining the sealing band for security and checking the expiration date stamped on the sealing band (2½ years from the date of mfg.). The safety pin-type clip should be examined for deformity and to ensure that the clip is in the closed position.

Note: The protective sleeve must be kept in place to protect against

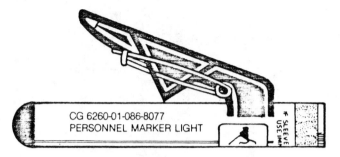

Figure 17–16. Personnel marker light (PML).

accidental breaking of the glass ampule and to protect against deterioration of the chemical by ultraviolet light.

Equipment in Rafts and Boats

The following items should be in all rafts or lifeboats:

Air pump
Canned water
Dye marker
First aid kit
Flashlight (waterproof)
Food packet
Knife
Paddles
Sea anchor
Signal gear
Signaling mirror
Sponge
Water desalting kit
Whistle

Note: The ship will provide items such as additional rations, battle lanterns, blankets, charts and navigation equipment, and small arms and ammunition.

Other Survival Kit Items

Many of the items listed in the section entitled "Survival Kit and Items" will be included in the survival equipment provided on boats and rafts.

Concentrated Food. The Navy emergency rations for life craft meet minimum nutrition requirements for men shipwrecked with limited supplies of water. Each can contains a total of 15 sugar-type tablets, 8 malted milk tablets, 2 multivitamin tablets, and 2 packs of chewing gum. The daily ration would normally be one of these cans per man.

Dye Marker. The dye marker consists of a can of *fluorescein* (a material that glows in very little light) packed in a waterproof container. On the water it forms a yellow-green patch that usually is visible for 2 hours for a relatively long distance. At night it can be seen only in bright moonlight, and rough water quickly disperses it.

First-aid Kit. The Army-Navy camouflaged kit for life rafts contains an assortment of bandages and some tubes of petrolatum (for burns). The bandages consist of compresses to cover open wounds, long strips of gauze to hold the compresses in place, and triangular all-purpose gauze bandages, which may be used to hold other bandages in place, or as slings, head bandages, and so on.

Fishing Kit. The fishing kit contains gloves, a knife that will float, sinkers, pork rind for bait, an assortment of hooks and fishing rigs, a dip net, a bib with pockets to hold the equipment, and directions printed on waterproof paper. The kit is enclosed in a can with a key opener.

Flashlight. One of the most commonly used night signals as well as a most useful piece of equipment is the flashlight. A waterproof model is standard; but any flashlight should be kept out of the water to ensure the best service and longest life. The equipment containers are provided with spare batteries; nevertheless, flashlights should be used only when necessary.

Food and Water in the Environment

Fish caught in the open sea are healthful and nourishing, cooked or raw, and will supplement and even replace canned rations as long as sufficient drinking water is available.

When fish are caught near shore, avoid the poisonous kinds. One of these, the parrot fish, has large teeth like a parrot's beak. Poisonous porcupine and puffer fish swell up like a balloon if they are scratched on the belly. Poisonous fish can be used as bait but must not be eaten.

Drying Fish

Well-dried fish will stay unspoiled for several days. To dry large fish, clean them, cut them in thin narrow strips, and hang them in the sun.

Small fish, a foot long or less, should also be cleaned before drying, the backbone removed, and slits cut across the inside about a quarter of an inch apart. They should then be hung in the sun. Fish not cleaned will spoil in a half day. Do not eat dried fish unless you have plenty of drinking water.

Fishing Tips

Never tie line to finger, hands, feet or boat. A big fish can cut or break your line or carry off your tackle. Don't pay out all your line, but leave slack in the boat. Have someone hold the end of the slack line.

Don't lean over the side of the boat when a fish is hooked. A boat can be capsized in this fashion.

Try to catch small fish rather than big ones.

Keep the bait moving to make it look alive.

Keep a part of any bird or fish you catch and use it for bait.

Clean hooks and lines of fish and fish slime. Dry them in the sun.

Don't get your lines tangled or let hooked fish tangle them. Two men can fish at the same time, but they must be careful.

In a rubber boat, be careful that your knife and fishing hook never get a chance to prick, stick, or make a hole in your boat.

Make a fair division of your catch.

Keep fishing. You never know when fish may bite.

Fish will be attracted by a light at night. Often a bright moon or flashlight shining on a cloth will draw fish.

Solar (Sun) Stills

Solar stills are sometimes provided. They can distill about two pints of water each day (figure 17–17). Usually a still is provided for each man the boat is designed to accommodate. The stills operate most efficiently in direct sunlight; they will function to a certain degree during cloudy or overcast days, but they cannot distill water at night, on dark days, in polar waters, or during inclement weather. The solar still is one of the most reliable sources of water while at sea. The water is pure, but may appear somewhat milky because of talc sprinkled on the inside of the plastic cover to keep it from sticking to itself.

The procedure for operating the still is as follows:

Wet the cloth drain on the bottom thoroughly. The cloth acts as a safety valve: when wet, the openings in the fabric are closed and no air escapes while the still is being inflated; upon overinflation, however, the excess air forces its way through the drain and keeps the still at

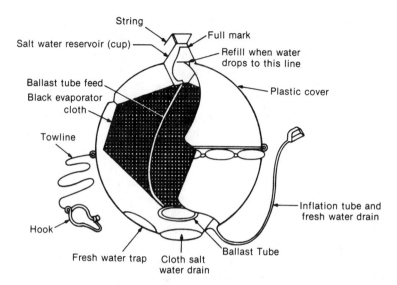

String

Salt water reservoir (cup)

Full mark

Refill when water drops to this line

Ballast tube feed

Black evaporator cloth

Plastic cover

Towline

Inflation tube and fresh water drain

Hook

Fresh water trap   Cloth salt water drain   Ballast Tube

Figure 17–17. A solar still will provide enough water to keep a man alive.

normal inflation pressure. Inflate the bag, either orally or with the hand pump, using the inflation tube. Place the still in the water. While holding it upright, fill the reservoir until the water level remains at the full mark (part of the water you first put in will flow down to the ballast tube). The still is now ready for operation. Refill the reservoir periodically and keep the still firmly inflated. Remove fresh water through the drain at least three times daily.

The sun's rays heat the water causing some of it to evaporate. The moisture condenses on the cooler walls of the plastic cover and runs down to the fresh-water trap. The still has a silvery appearance caused by condensation of the water; if the bag loses this appearance in spots, pull on the string in the reservoir to clear the water feed of foreign matter.

Eating on Land

Most tropical fruits are good to eat. It is safe for humans to eat the same things that monkeys eat. Unknown roots, fine shoots, and other herbs must be experimented with cautiously. Eat any unfamiliar plants in very small quantities until their effect is ascertained. In general, a man should eat only what he is sure of, as long as it exists in sufficient amounts to sustain him.

Turtles and their eggs may be eaten cooked or raw. All animals are safe to eat. Snakes, even poisonous ones, are edible, but their heads should be removed. Grubs and grasshoppers can be eaten if the wings and legs are picked off before cooking. Caterpillars should not be eaten.

All birds are good to eat, cooked or raw. Their blood and liver are edible. The feathers, meat, guts, and even the toes make good lures or bait for fish. Birds can sometimes be caught in nets; the larger ones will often take a bait of fish on a hook dragged on top of the water. Some birds will go after a baited hook tossed into the air.

Water Discipline

If possible, take a drink of water before abandoning ship. After abandoning ship, conserve body water; try to keep cool and avoid sweating. Take it easy.

Unless you become very thirsty, drink no water for the first 24 hours on the raft. Thereafter, drink a pint (16 ounces) of water a day if your supply is limited. Drink a pint and a half (24 ounces) a day, or more if necessary, if you have an abundant supply of rain water and the 1-pint allowance does not satisfy you. It is better to keep up the rate of 16 ounces a day (4 ounces—half a glass—4 times a day) until only 10 ounces are left, rather than to use smaller amounts for a longer time. When only 10 ounces are left, use it only to moisten the mouth. (Sea water and urine should never be drunk. Sea water will cause vomiting, diarrhea, and delirium.)

When the supply of water is limited, bird and fish flesh should be consumed sparingly. The moisture in fish flesh is more than offset by the increase in urine resulting from the body's assimilation of the fish protein. Use fish for food, not water.

On land, water can be obtained from a hole dug at low tide just below the high-water mark. The water in the hole may be salty and discolored, but it can be drunk in small quantities. Large amounts will cause sickness.

To summarize: Conserve water by keeping the body from perspiring. In the beginning, do not make the daily water rations too small. Do not eat much food when water is scarce. Avoid swallowing any salt water.

Mental Attitude

The most important factor in survival after shipwreck in any except the coldest waters is the human factor of mental and emotional stability.

How well men adjust to the psychological stress of being cast adrift may mean the difference between eventual rescue and loss. Superior equipment will be useless when men are emotionally and mentally disorganized.

Emotional Reactions

There are certain symptoms to expect of shipwrecked men. Combat them in yourself, and when you observe them in others, cooperate immediately with whatever efforts are made by your leaders to alleviate them. Some of these symptoms are:

A man may stand still and weep or scream for help, or fight for a place in a lifeboat or on a raft, or become sick at his stomach. Keep obeying orders and sizing up the situation; as long as you are busy there is less chance that you will get into such states.

A man may become pale, tense, and agitated, and may stutter. Again, the thing to do is to keep yourself and others busy with proper preparation.

After some time on the raft, a man may become delirious or exhibit behavior dangerous to himself and others. He may suddenly attack other men in the party. He may dive off the raft "to go below for a cup of coffee." He is liable to drink sea water or eat the few rations left on the raft. This type of person must be closely watched all the time. Cheerful conversation may keep him interested. When necessary, restrain him until his symptoms subside.

Most survivors will not reach the states just described, but many will exhibit to some extent a strained emotional attitude. Once away from the sinking ship, they may show relief, elation, and even excitement. This stage is succeeded by other feelings: sorrow for lost shipmates, speculations as to chances of being picked up, and uneasiness over growing physical discomfort.

Before long the attitudes worsen into irritability, preoccupation, moroseness, and withdrawal from the rest of the group. Ideas of food and drink dominate thinking and dreaming.

The answer for everyone lies in a rule first formulated 150 years ago: *The seaman has the duty as well as the good counsel to maintain hope, perseverance, and obedience.*

Morale

A man noting in himself any of the symptoms described above must "snap out of it." Morose or hopeless thoughts once started grow rapidly worse and harder to overcome. If these danger signs are noted in others, immediate efforts should be made to cheer up the group; fortunately, the effort to help others always helps oneself. The moods of depression, hopelessness, and helplessness are not permanent or unchangeable. They can be offset by good morale. When each man makes an effort towards good morale, the group will be happier, better conducted, more comfortable, and the chance of rescue is much greater.

CHAPTER 18

Swimming and Lifesaving

Anyone who goes to sea, whether in a high-endurance Coast Guard cutter or merely across a harbor in a 14-foot puddle-jumper, should know how to swim. Old-timers used to wear a tattoo of a pig and rooster, which was supposed to save them from drowning, but many of them drowned anyway. Many emergencies—shipwreck, flood relief, and other types of rescue work—require the use of expert swimmers (figure 18–1). Just being able to swim is often not enough—you have to be a good swimmer.

Good swimming must not be confused with a lot of speed and splash. The purposes of emergency swimming and of swimming for health and recreation are different from those of competitive swimming, although one can help the other. Keep these points in mind:

You must train so as to be able to pass the required tests.
It is not enough merely to know how to swim; you must build up strength and endurance to help in an emergency.
Exercises such as floating, breathing, sculling, and kicking contribute to all-around body-building, lengthen the profitable practice period by keeping many muscles in action, and in time of emergency will keep a man going much longer in the water.
A "one-stroke" man might look good in a race, but in case of shipwreck he could be at a great disadvantage. A man going over the side may have to swim fast, slow, or under water, may have to

Figure 18–1. A team of Coast Guard swimmers executes a practice rescue drill.

put on or take off clothing, hold up his head and look around, carry or search for objects, or float patiently for hours. There is no end to what he might have to do.

Control of Position and Buoyancy

Jellyfish or Tuck Float

Double up, hugging legs, with face submerged. Float like a ball with only part of your back above the water. This is a good exercise for beginners; it acquaints them with body buoyancy, and develops ability to hold breath. From this position the beginner can learn to open his eyes under water and familiarize himself with floating. From this position, too, a person can slowly but firmly massage cramps in legs or toes. At times it may serve as a rest for muscles tired from the stretch-out of swimming.

Back Float

Lie on your back with your head thrown back, chin and nose above water, arms and legs relaxed. (Some people can float well this way, others keep sinking as they exhale.) Try to keep your lungs full of air. Do not become panicky if your face does sink. Gently work your hands so as to raise your chin enough for a quick breath, and then let yourself sink. Your face will soon rise above the surface. Gulp a breath while drifting, rest and relax while sinking. This is the preparatory position for learning the backstroke, and an excellent way of resting and floating during long periods in the water.

Dead Man's Float and Glide

Lean forward, face down in the water, and relax completely. Play "dead man" all over. This float leads to the crawl, or speed stroke, and to the breast stroke, or froglike stroke. It teaches relaxation in the water, how to swim under water with eyes open, and how to get the most out of a glide.

Breathing

In general, breathing for swimming is the same as for any other sport. Try to keep it regular, don't hold breath too long, don't pant. Breathe through your mouth when your face is out of water; exhale by blowing out through your mouth and nose to keep them clear of water. Try to take air in fast, blow it out slowly.

Treading

Being able to tread water is a vital skill and should be practiced until you can do it for minutes at a time, not just a few seconds. It is required for every situation in which you need to raise your head to look around, or call for help, or use your hands.

There are several methods of treading. Practice all of them, and by changing from one to the other you will be able to stay afloat longer. The most commonly used methods are mentioned here.

Modified Frog Kick for Treading. Stand upright in the water. Draw legs up together with the knees spread out to the sides. Then separate and extend legs. Finally press the legs together until the feet are about 10 to 20 inches apart. The movement of drawing, spreading, and pressing is then repeated. Pushing the legs out and pressing them together gives the upward thrust to the body. This kick can be practiced hanging on to the edge of the pool; its advantage is that the slow movement is not so tiring as some of the other treading kicks and it is adjustable; you can tread low in the water or thrust up high by this same kick.

Scissors Kick for Treading. This is similar to walking and is easy to learn. It is best practiced at first on land. Lie on your side with feet together and legs extended, then draw them slowly up in a semi-tucked-up position. Now separate the legs, one moving forward, the other backward, then squeeze them together. The movement should be slow, steady, and continuous. Practice for a while, holding on to the edge of the pool or firm object. The scissors kick is easy to learn and is a natural movement, effective but not tiring. It also leads to the side-stroke, which is important in distance swimming and lifesaving.

Sculling

Sculling with the hands enables a man to control his body in the water in a number of positions, with or without the help of his feet. Sculling and treading combined will save more energy than using the feet or hands alone. Sculling also has the advantage of teaching a sense of balance in the water. It develops the muscles of the hands and arms needed for pushing against the water, and it teaches a man how to get a "grip" on the water.

Vertical Sculling. One method of sculling while holding oneself upright in the water is to weave the hands vigorously back and forth in front of and to the sides of the body in a figure-eight movement. This forces the water downward and keeps the body up.

Another method is to drop the hands down near the hips in the water; then turn them to about a 45-degree angle away from the body, thumbs downward. With the palms of the hands, push the water away from the body until the hands are about two feet out from the sides of the body. Immediately rotate the hands so that the thumbs are up, then turn to the starting position, pulling water toward the sides of the body. When the hands reach the sides they are again rotated until the thumbs are down, and the movements are repeated. The emphasis is on the push-away part of the stroke.

A third method is to place the hands palms down on the water, press down on the water several feet in depth, and recover again.

All these methods, or combinations of them, will be useful at different times.

Flutter-back Sculling. This is one of the best sustaining strokes to stay afloat for a long time or to move slowly and easily in some direction. Lie on your back and kick slowly up and down, with legs and feet in a knock-kneed and pigeon-toed position, and make a slow sculling movement at the hips with your hands.

Swimming Strokes

In general, there is no need for speed swimming. There may, however, be occasions where speed is needed, such as in swimming away from a sinking ship, catching up with a boat or raft, or swimming against a rapid current.

In the crawl, or speed strokes, it is necessary to lift the arms out of the water, and water-soaked clothing would make this very difficult and tiring. At the same time, a life jacket and other gear would hamper the freedom required for the crawl strokes. The strokes satisfactory for emergencies are those with underwater arm recoveries, as discussed in the sections that follow.

Dog Paddle or Human Stroke

The dog paddle is a valuable sustaining stroke for men fully clothed or wearing life jackets. It is particularly useful in crowded or narrow places because most of the movements are under the body, and the position of the head enables a man to look about him.

In the dog paddle the legs execute a slow up-and-down kick; the knees are bent and the feet are extended in a pigeon-toed manner. The arms are also moved alternately. Each arm is pushed ahead in the water until extended, then brought downward and backward, held straight the whole time, and strong grip is taken on the water. At the end of the pull the arm is bent, drawn up, and shoved forward again. Avoid the tendency to hold breath and to stroke too fast.

Sidestroke

The sidestroke is a good relief stroke after one has become tired from the other strokes. A slight modification enables a swimmer to tow or carry objects, and it can be used for a lifesaving carry. The side overarm stroke is excellent for use in rough water. Since it is practically noiseless it is less likely to attract attention.

The sidestroke or scissors kick has already been described. Either the scissors kick or the inverted scissors kick may be used. In the standard scissors kick, the top leg goes forward while the bottom leg goes backward; in the inverted scissors kick, the bottom leg goes forward while the top goes back.

The whole sidestroke is performed as follows: Lie on one side, whichever side feels natural, with legs extended and side of face in the water.

The trailing or top arm is extended along the side of the body, with the hand resting on the thigh. The opposite or under arm is extended beyond the head. On the count of one, the legs are drawn up together toward the waist while the under arm begins to pull toward the chest; the trailing or top arm recovers from the thigh up to the chest under water. On the count of two, the legs separate in a wide spread, the trailing arm begins to push the water, and the under arm begins to recover. On the count of three, the legs (now straight and separated) begin to squeeze or thrust together while the arms finish pushing and recovering. This movement returns you to the starting position. This is the point where a coast or glide should be taken, the body relaxing and resting momentarily.

The inverted scissors kick is best done lying partially on your back. The inverted scissors kick seems easier to most swimmers; in any case choose what feels best.

The sidestroke is easily converted into the *overarm sidestroke* by simply recovering the top or trailing arm over the surface of the water instead of under the surface. This is speedier, though more tiring than the regular sidestroke, and is well adapted to rough water swimming.

To use the sidestroke for lifesaving carries or for towing equipment or materials, it is necessary only to pull the under arm with a wide, sweeping motion in a shallower horizontal plane than in the deep, vertical plane. The inverted scissors kick has the advantage here of making it easier to avoid kicking the person or object being towed.

Backstroke

There are several types of backstrokes which may and should be learned, but only the *elementary backstroke* is described here. It is a good relief stroke, and it allows a man to rest other muscles while making considerable progress over a long distance if necessary. Beginners and mediocre swimmers find it easy to master. It is a stroke of power and endurance. The underwater recovery makes it possible for the swimmer to use the arms easily even though fully clad. In addition the face is out of the water so there is less of a breathing problem. Where there is danger of underwater explosions, the backstroke should alway be used, as it is the best protection against internal injuries from the shock waves of underwater concussions.

Either the scissors kick or the frog kick may be used. The frog kick is probably best. It is similar to that already described for the purposes of treading. It is divided into three movements. While lying on the back, legs together and extended, the legs are drawn up toward the waist, with the soles of the feet in contact with each other. This keeps the legs in the same plane and the knees are turned out. Next, the legs are separated and spread quite widely apart; at the end of the movement they are in an extended position. Then the legs are squeezed vigorously until they come together in the original extended position. At this point the glide or coast is taken.

The arm stroke is started with the arms extended along the thighs. The arms recover by allowing the thumbs to travel up along the side of the body from the thighs to the armpits. Next they extend sideward and outward from the shoulders, and then sweep vigorously from the shoulders to the thighs, where they are held momentarily during the glide. The hands are kept beneath the water throughout the stroke.

Breaststroke

The breaststroke is energy-conserving, yet it provides power and reasonable speed. It has many uses. With simple modifications it is probably the best stroke for swimming under water; through oil or debris-covered water; in extremely rough water; with clothes on; with head high out of water; pushing a tired swimmer.

The breaststroke is similar to the elementary backstroke in the kick, total recovery underwater, and the moving of legs in unison and arms in unison.

The frog kick is used with the breaststroke. The swimmer lies on his stomach, with his face down in the water except when he raises his head for breathing or for some other reason. The swimmer should realize that every time he lifts any part of his body out of the water he expends extra effort. Normally, then, he should raise himself—or do anything else requiring a lift out of the water—for the shortest time possible.

The kick is executed in three movements. First, draw legs up toward waist, with soles of feet together and knees separated and turned out. The second movement consists of the extension of the legs outward, with the lower portion of the leg from the knee down rotating outward. The legs then push the water and spread apart as far as feels comfortable. At the end of the spreading movement the legs are in an extended position. The final movement is the thrust or squeeze of the legs, in which they give the water a vigorous whip resulting in forward progress of the body. At the end of this thrust, the legs are extended and almost together—touching or not touching as comfortable. They then relax and rest while the body glides on the momentum given. This final position is the same as the starting position.

The arms start from the position of being extended in front of the head. The arms pull backward and somewhat downward in the water until they are back as far as the shoulders. Next, they are brought together, palm to palm, under the lower part of the chest. For the final recovery the arms are slid forward smoothly through the water until they reach out in front of the head. At this point the arms relax and advantage is taken of the glide. Try to glide as far as possible when doing the breaststroke.

It is possible to swim the breaststroke with the head held out of water the whole time, or to stay underwater for as many strokes as one has breath to hold for. However, the best form consists in breathing rhythmically throughout the stroke. As the arms start their pull from the ahead position to the shoulders, the head is passed up enough to inhale once through the mouth. During the rest of the cycle the head is dropped slowly into the water. The exhalation begins gradually and is so timed that all the breath is out just before the head is raised for the next inhalation.

Special Instructions

Cramps

Cramps are rarely as dangerous as people believe. Take a deep breath and float quietly for a while. If cramp is in an arm or leg muscle, massage it slowly and firmly (figure 18–2).

Removal of Clothes

If it is necessary to remove clothes in the water, the heaviest articles should be removed first. To remove trousers, assume a back float position, unzip them, and slide them down, then flutter-kick out of them.

Remember that shoes are a real protection against sharks and sunburn, and that clothing in general is a protection against exposure. Remove only clothing that interferes with keeping afloat.

Using Clothing to Keep Afloat

The jumper or shirt may be inflated by tying the cuffs and collar, blowing air in the opening, and then holding the garment under water. Trousers make better floats than jumpers. After the trousers are removed, they should be floated on the surface with the fly turned up. A single knot should be tied in each leg, then one side of the waist of the trousers should be grasped with each hand, and the garment should be worked around on the surface until the legs are at the back of the head and neck. When this position is reached, the trousers should be flipped over the head, and the waist brought down smartly on the surface, trapping a good pocket of air in each leg. The waist should then be gathered under the water and held in one hand.

Figure 18–2. A muscle cramp in the foot can be worked out by massage.

Mattress covers, sea bags, laundry bags, pillow cases, and sacks may also be used for support by capping the openings on the surface.

Swimming in Dangerous Waters

There are several emergency techniques that should be studied and practiced (figures 18–3, 18–4, and 18–5). The illustrations and captions will help one learn these techniques.

Underwater Swimming

Ability to swim underwater is very important in avoiding surface hazards such as floating debris, oil, or flaming oil or gasoline. It has lifesaving value, for it enables a swimmer to rescue a shipmate who has gone under. There are occasions, too, when it is necessary to recover articles lost overboard in shallow water.

Almost any swimming stroke can be used underwater. The breaststroke and the sidestroke lend themselves particularly well to underwater swimming. The main thing is to learn breath control. Practice holding your breath and keeping your eyes open as much as possible.

Swimming in Burning Oil

It is not possible to swim through burning oil, flames, or debris, but it is possible to swim under them. If it is necessary to jump into oil or flames, the jump should be made to windward of the vessel, feet first. To make the jump, a deep breath should be taken, the nose held and the mouth covered with one hand, and the eyes covered with the other. The feet should be held close together. A kapok jacket or inflated life belt should never be worn when it is necessary to swim under water. Clothing should be worn as a protection against flames or debris, but the shoes should be removed, as they will slow underwater progress.

The swimmer should stay under water as long as he can. When it is necessary to take a breath, he should come to the surface with his arms above his head. When his hands break the surface, he should begin beating away the burning oil with a circular thrashing motion. When the upper part of his body breaks the surface, he should turn, with his back to the wind, continuing to beat away the burning oil, take a deep breath, and submerge, using a feet-foremost dive. He should then swim underwater as before, to windward, until he is out of the burning oil or until it is necessary for him to come up for air as before.

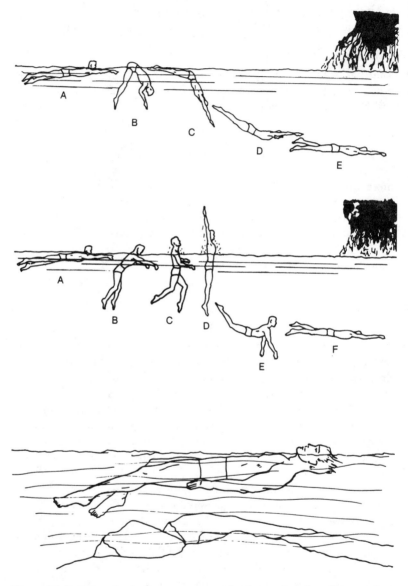

Figure 18–3. Swimming in dangerous water; (top) procedure for making surface dive; (center) alternate procedure for submerging; (bottom) in shallow rapids, swim feet first on your back, "fin" the hands at hip level to protect against rocks.

Figure 18–4. Use side stroke or breast stroke in surf to preserve strength. Ride small waves; surface-dive to end the ride before the wave breaks.

Figure 18–5. In shark-infested waters, swim as quietly as possible. Always wear shoes. Try to hold onto some floating object, especially in cold water. Keep moving to maintain circulation. In a current, either swim parallel to the shore or diagonally to it in order to get out of it. In seaweed or underwater plants, move calmly; don't thrash about.

Swimming in Shark Infested Waters

A lot of research has been done on shark attacks in recent years. Back during World War II, people in the water were told to splash wildly to drive away sharks, but more recently it has been discovered that sharks seem attracted to frantic movements. Sharks are extremely dangerous, unpredictable predators and have extraordinary sensory receptors. Species of sharks vary in their feeding habits, with the result that some are considered more dangerous to man than others. Sharks seem to sense fright exhibited by creatures in the water. They also seem to be attracted to bright colors, but most of all, sharks are attracted by blood. Some recent experiments indicate that sharks exhibit a characteristic "S" twist before striking, and immediately before biting they roll their eyes upward losing sight of their prey. These experiments indicate that during the last phase of the attack, the sharks are guided by sensors located in their snouts. For some reason, in these experiments, the presence of metal objects caused the shark to divert that last phase of his attack toward the metal object and away from the original object of the attack.

While there is no good advice on how a swimmer might avoid shark attacks, except by avoidance, the information that is currently available indicates that the following actions may reduce the risk of shark attack.

Avoid, at all costs, the entry of any blood into the water.

Wear shoes and other protective clothing, particularly clothing of dark drab shades; save the bright colors to show above the surface of the water to attract rescuers.

Try to remain calm, remembering that all species of sharks are not the same, nor do all sharks have the same level of aggressiveness.

Swim slowly and as quietly as possible to minimize attracting the attention of sharks.

In the presence of non-attacking sharks, do not strike at them, because that may provoke an attack that might not otherwise occur.

If the water is clear enough to see sharks swimming beneath the surface, watch for a tell-tale "S"-like twisting by a shark, which may indicate that an attack is imminent.

If a shark is about to attack, its jaws may possibly be diverted at the last moment by thrusting an object toward the shark's mouth, such as a piece of driftwood or a large metal object.

Do not confuse sharks with dolphins and porpoises, both of which are mammals, known in fact and legend to be friendly and helpful to sailors in the sea.

Research is continuing on shark attacks with the possibility that a major discovery may be made to positively reduce the risk of such attacks.

Swimming in Surf

Along the coastlines and on reefs, ocean waves steepen and break, turning into what are called "breakers." Surf consists of more than one of these breakers. Recreational surfers develop their skills with surfboards so that they may catch and ride surf waves for their enjoyment. Others have learned to "body surf" and similarly enjoy the fun of surf play. Operationally, the Coast Guardsman is most likely to encounter surf while manning Coast Guard boats, usually during rescue attempts. In the old days, Coast Guardsmen were trained to launch boats from open beaches and row out through the surf to make rescues, then to return back through it to the beach. The expression, "You have to go out but you don't have to come back," comes from the old Life Saving Service and was directed toward those surfmen and their missions. Today, Coast Guard boats frequently cross bars in leaving and entering coastal inlets and harbors, and often encounter broken waves at sea, on bars, and in inlet channels; seldom, however, do Coast Guard boats proceed deliberately inshore into the surf, except during special emergency operations.

The kind of condition that a Coast Guardsman is likely to experience in the surf, operationally, would result from the foundering of a Coast Guard boat, or his or her being swept overboard from a boat near a beach. The surf conditions in such circumstances are probably going to be very rough. Theoretically, the Coast Guardsman would be wearing a PFD. Recreationally, Coast Guard people may encounter any kind of surf condition, but good sense should prevail and dangerous surf should be avoided. Breakers generated by offshore waves usually proceed in a direction to the beach generally perpendicular to the shoreline, becoming more so as the dry beach is approached. In storms, waves usually are angled toward the beach according to wind direction. There are three basic classes of surf: spilling breakers, plunging breakers, and surging breakers.

The spilling breaker breaks gradually over a considerable distance. The ocean bottom is usually flat and gradually rises to the beach. All waves become breakers when the depth of water is about 1.3 times the height of the waves above the level of still water. Spilling breakers are somewhat similar to waves that break at sea, where the waves crest and then the tops spill forward. Some air is entrapped in the wave crests, and the broken waves become "white water" or "white caps." Spilling breakers usually lack the violence and crest force of the other two classes of breakers. A swimmer wearing a PFD encountering a spilling breaker is likely to be pushed by the wave upward and ahead of it for a short distance before the wave passes. The swimmer, under such circumstances, should continue swimming toward shore, riding small "spillers," while keeping track of all waves approaching from the rear. When a large "spiller" approaches, the swimmer wearing a PFD should prepare to rise over the wave by facing shoreward, taking a deep breath and bending forward in a squatting position until the wave passes over. Without a PFD, the swimmer should surface dive perpendicular to the direction of the wave's motion to minimize the time of his or her submergence, and to avoid spinal damage that might result from diving in the direction of wave movement. When submerging under waves, swimmers should open their eyes to aid them in rising up through the water's surface, and to locate the next wave. A strong onshore wind tends to flatten the crests of waves that might otherwise be plunging breakers, giving them some of the characteristics of spillers. As breakers of any classification move across bars into deeper waters, they will often recrest as spillers. When the swimmer approaches the beach, it may become possible to stand with feet touching bottom, but it would be more practicable to treat "white water" breakers approaching shore as spillers, regardless of their wave class. The swimmer should let the wave's energy do the work of pushing the swimmer toward the beach.

Plunging breakers tend to have peaked crests that curl over and break with a single crash. In such surf, a "tunnel" is created on the face of the wave where the curl falls forward in front and in advance of the wave's face. A large amount of air is usually entrapped in the tunnel, and this air will often explode out the back face of the wave. Such plunging waves are typical on moderately steep beaches. Strong offshore winds also tend to make some spilling breakers crest higher, giving them the appearance of plunging breakers. While a moderately steep beach is a general requirement for plungers, the presence of plunging breakers does not mean that dry land is always close at hand. Waves steepen as the bottom becomes shallow, because the ocean bottom slows down the wave's forward progress. This is not noticeable until the depth of water becomes equal to about one-half the distance between the waves. Then the waves begin to steepen, with their front faces becoming steeper than their back faces, and the crest becomes narrower and narrower; when the wave crest height is about ¾ as high as the depth of the water, it breaks. This phenomenon can occur anywhere where the bottom shoals. Cresting of plungers is sudden and dramatic, often producing great and spectacular surf. Although the steepness of the bottom approaching the beach is the important factor in determining the class of wave encountered, an offshore sand bar can cause the required steepness for plunging surf many hundreds of yards away from the beach itself. In handling plungers, the swimmer must be careful to conserve energy; at the same time, high plungers must be dealt with before the swimmer is caught up in them. Low plungers, three to four feet in height, will usually occur in relatively shallow water. In such conditions the swimmer wearing a PFD should treat low-plunging breakers as if they were spilling breakers. The swimmer without a PFD should do likewise, but would do well to surface dive under the wave to a greater depth than would be done for spilling surf. It may be possible to stand on the bottom immediately before the wave breaks; if so, the dive can be directed toward the base of the front face of the wave to further decrease the time of submergence, but at the same time, taking care not to move offshore. When encountering high plungers, a PFD wearer is likely to experience severe turbulence, with the result that the swimmer will be slammed and tumbled as he is floated upward toward the crest, tossed forward down the curl, then rotated and exploded through the back face of the wave, only to continue rolling forward in the white water until the wave passes. Since plungers usually come in "sets," or series of 5 to 7 waves, additional following waves in the sea will pummel and push the swimmer shoreward. The PFD-equipped swimmer's best chance of avoiding injury is to ensure that the PFD is properly secured, to protect his back, neck, and limbs by assuming a rolled-forward position, to take deep breaths whenever possible, and to keep the eyes open underwater to aid in reorienting to the surface. The PFD will provide flotation, but the swimmer must also protect his or her body and maximize the opportunities for breathing while retaining the protection position.

A non-PFD-equipped swimmer must avoid being caught on the surface by a large plunging breaker. That means that such a swimmer must dive under approaching crested waves, then surface soon enough after the passage of each wave to allow time to get air before diving, in turn, under the next waves in the set. Dives should be as deep as possible to prevent being trapped in the surface water as it plunges forward from the back face of the wave over the curl. There is a temptation for a PFD-equipped swimmer to remove the PFD to permit diving under plunging waves. Unless conditions are ideal, and the swimmer is an expert surfer, such an action could be fatal!

There is a good aspect to plunging breakers; they usually break in a line at about the same distance from the shore. This means that if a swimmer can time his or her crossing the breaker line to coincide with the last wave of a set, he or she may successfully be pushed far enough toward the beach with that last wave; hopefully, plungers of successive sets will break sufficiently to seaward to reduce the danger to the swimmer. Broken plungers become "combers," or masses of turbulent white water with a front face only a fraction of the height of the wave when it crested. Since combers decrease in height and strength as they move toward shore, they should be treated like spilling breakers by swimmers.

Surging breakers peak up, but surge onto the shore without spilling or plunging. For a moment they frequently have a deep, low tunnel at still-water level at the point of surge where they hit the beach. They generate foam and froth even though they do not actually break. Surging breakers occur where the bottom rises very steeply toward the land. This kind of steepness is typical along rocky coasts and on other shorelines where headlands rise directly above the beach. High tides on both flat and moderately steep beaches can also create surging breakers of heights of about three or four feet. These occur just at the point where the beach drops into the sea. The swimmer who encounters a surging breaker should be prepared to land on a firm surface when tossed forward by the breaker at the place of surge. Heavy surging breakers are extremely dangerous to swimmers because of the mass of sea water contained above the tunnel, and the usual absence of anything but a few inches of water, then solid beach or rock, beneath the tunnel. A swimmer must be prepared to protect his or her body from both the weight of the water crushing down, and the hard surface beneath. The swimmer should roll or bend forward in a squatting position, but be prepared to use his or her hands and forearms to protect the head, while allowing the legs to absorb the shock of landing on a hard surface. With medium-height surging breakers, the swimmer should try to ride squatting, feet down, up onto the beach on the back face of the wave, while avoiding the wave's forward face and tunnel. Properly executed, the surging breaker can provide all the energy necessary to propel the swimmer up and onto the beach, quickly and safely. Once ashore, the swimmer must move quickly up onto the safety of the beach to avoid the back rush of water that will feed successive surgers.

Many combinations of breakers can be encountered in a storm surf; they can be of all three classes described. Waves can be flattened by strong onshore winds, yet retain all the force of much higher seas. The swimmer in such a surf must always watch for approaching seas and rise with them or dive as necessary to conserve air and strength. Strong inshore feeder currents will set parallel to and along the shoreline usually in the direction of the wind and surf. These currents are formed from the waves that have been pushed onto the beach, which must find paths or outlets to return to the level of the sea. Generally these outlets are marked by the reduced heights of waves, retarded wave speeds, confused current swirls, and foam. Around rocky headlands and jetties, these outbound currents move offshore from the windward sides of land or rock formations. On flat beaches, they may form anywhere along the beach cutting outward across inner sand bars and out to sea hundreds of yards. Where feeder currents turn toward sea, they are called "rip currents," known in some areas as "sea-pusses." They flow seaward at angles of anywhere from 45° to 80° from the direction of the inshore feeder currents. Rip currents sometimes migrate along the beach, or they may remain fairly stable, depending upon the beach. Old-time Coast Guard and Life-Saving Service surfmen used these rip currents to their advantage when launching boats from the beach. They timed their passage across the surf line to coincide with the slack periods, or "slatches," between sets of breakers. Surf fishermen cast their lines into the cuts (or holes) formed by rip currents, because they're known to be good places for game fish.

These rip currents are not good places for swimmers! Many recreational swimmers have lost their lives after being caught by them in even light summer surf. If the swimmer seaward of the breaker line can determine the direction of wind, or the angle that the surf is approaching the beach, he or she may be able to select the place where a rip current is least likely to be encountered. That place will be just downwind of the place in the surf line where the waves seem lower and break farther to sea. This will also be downwind of the offshore terminus of the rip current, which is usually marked by an abundance of foam and swirling currents. Should a swimmer be caught in a rip current, the best strategy is to swim gently at right angles to the direction of the current, but *never* against the rip current. Because most all rip currents are angled away from the beach, and seldom perpendicular to it, gently swimming at right angles to the current, down the beach and in the general direction that the wind and surf is moving, will enable the swimmer to make slow progress toward the shore and still retain strength, even though the swimmer may be carried somewhat out to sea for a short while in the rip current. Once clear of the current, the swimmer should head directly toward the shoreline.

Further information on breakers and surf can be obtained from *Knights Modern Seamanship* and the *American Practical Navigator, Bowditch.* Swimming in surf can be a frightening experience at night and in storm seas. While the sea must always be respected, it is panic that must be feared. Coast Guardsmen, because of their unique profession, should take every opportunity to learn to swim comfortably in surf, to experience its rhythm and to study its movements. Under adverse emergency conditions, those things learned and experienced about the surf may make survival possible.

Lifesaving

Successful lifesaving in the water depends on the rescuer's presence of mind, his knowledge of the methods that may have to be used, and his strength and skill in carrying out these methods. A drowning person usually panics. His one idea is to keep his head above water. The whole technique of lifesaving is centered around that fact. A drowning person will try to grab some part of the rescuer's body or clothing as he approaches; the rescuer should then sink, taking the drowning man with him. Under water, he will usually let go. Under no circumstances should a rescuer strike a drowning person; his system has already had sufficient shock to cause severe physical reactions, and a severe blow may cause heart failure.

Lifesaving Approaches

There are several ways to approach a drowning person. Practice all of these.

Front Approach. The rescuer should swim slowly toward the victim and, if he is not too far gone, attempt to calm and reassure him by talking to him. The victim should be told exactly what the rescuer is going to do and must be instructed to follow orders. Then the rescuer should reach with his right hand for the victim's left wrist, turn the victim's body slowly, and use one of the carries described below.

Rear Approach. If the victim is too excited to pay attention to directions, the rescuer should swim behind him, grasp his chin with the right hand, apply pressure to his back with his left hand, and use one of the various carries.

Underwater Approach. The underwater approach is by far the safest because the drowning person does not have a chance to get a grip on his rescuer. The rescuer should swim within ten feet of the victim and surface-dive to a depth at which the victim's legs can be easily reached. If the victim is facing the rescuer, he should be turned in the opposite direction by pressure on his upper legs. The rescuer should slide his right hand up the drowning person's back and grasp him by the chin, applying pressure to his back with the left hand. He should be brought to the surface as quickly as possible and one of the various carries used.

Lifesaving Breaks. If the victim does succeed in getting a grip on his rescuer there are several methods of breaking the grip (figure 18–6). The first step is to sink with the victim. The rescuer should take his time and keep calm. When he goes into the actual movement of breaking the grasp, he should do so suddenly and with all his strength so that it works the first time.

Wrist Lock. If the victim has grasped the left wrist, the rescuer should seize the victim's right wrist with his free right hand. Then the rescuer should move close to him, doubling up the right leg, placing the right foot on the victim's left shoulder. He should then apply pressure suddenly with his foot, twisting himself away from the drowning man and breaking the grip. The victim's body should then be turned by the right wrist to the left, brought to the surface, and one of the

Figure 18–6. A rescuer must know how to break the hold of a drowning victim—either wrist lock (left), front stranglehold (center); or back stranglehold (right).

carries should be used. If the victim has grasped the right wrist rather than the left, the procedure should be reversed.

Front Stranglehold. If the victim's chin is over the left shoulder of his rescuer, the rescuer should seize the victim's left elbow with the right hand. He should then slide his left hand between the victim's face and his own, along the drowning man's left cheek. Pressure should be applied suddenly to the victim's head with the left hand, simultaneously shoving up with the right hand and twisting to the right from his grasp. The rescuer should continue to hold the victim's left elbow with his right hand, turning the victim's body to the rescuer's right and passing the victim's elbow from the right hand to the left. The drowning man should then be brought to the surface and one of the carries should be used. If the victim's chin is over the rescuer's right shoulder instead of the left, the hands should be reversed and the procedure followed otherwise as described.

Back Stranglehold. If the victim grabs the rescuer by throwing his arms around him from the rear and holding his right wrist or arm with his left hand, the rescuer should grasp the victim's right elbow. He should then suddenly twist the victim's right wrist down, at the same time exerting pressure on his right elbow and turning his own head to the left. The rescuer should then push up, bringing the victim's arm around from behind his back. Next, he should release the right hand from the victim's elbow and place it over the victim's right shoulder and under his chin, bringing him to the surface. If the victim has seized the rescuer from behind with the opposite grip, the procedure should be reversed.

Breaking Two Drowning People Apart. In this case, decide quickly which of the two victims is to be rescued first. This victim should be approached from the rear. Both of the rescuer's hands should be placed over the victim's shoulders and gripped together under his chin. The right or left leg, depending upon which is more convenient, should be used to apply pressure on the chest of the other victim over the shoulder of the first to be rescued. The rescuer should shove suddenly and pull the victim he has grasped upward to the surface.

Lifesaving Carries

All of these methods should be practiced.

Hair Carry. This is the easiest of the carries because it allows the most freedom of movement on the part of the rescuer. The rescuer should turn on his left side, slide his right hand up the back of the victim's head to the top and grasp the hair tightly, using the left arm and legs for swimming sidestroke. The rescuer may swim on either side, changing hands when necessary in order to rest.

Head Carry. The rescuer should swim on his back, holding the victim's head above the water with both hands meeting under his chin (figure 18–7).

Cross-chest Carry. The rescuer should turn on his left side, place his arm over the victim's right shoulder, across the chest and under the left arm. The victim's body should be supported on the rescuer's right hip, and the rescuer should swim sidestroke, using his free left arm and both legs. This carry may be done from either side, but should not be used unless the victim is in bad condition, nor should it be used for long distances, because it is most tiring (figure 18–7).

Tired Swimmer's Carry. If the victim has enough control of himself to obey orders, he should be ordered to turn on his back, face his rescuer, spread his legs, and place both of his hands on the rescuer's shoulders with his arms stiff. The rescuer then assumes the position for the breaststroke and swims, pushing the victim ahead of him. The breaststroke is useful because it leaves the arms and legs unhampered for swimming and is only slightly more tiring than ordinary swimming (figure 18–7).

Carries from the Water. The most common carry is the *fireman's carry.* On reaching shallow water, the rescuer stands the victim up temporarily, places his right arm between the victim's legs, and throws the helpless man's body over his right shoulder. In this position the victim's right wrist is grasped in the right hand of the rescuer, whose left arm is free.

A convenient carry for short distances is the *saddle back.* After bringing the victim into waist-deep water, the rescuer moves the victim's body around behind him, with the head to the right. He then throws his arms around the body of the helpless man, hoists him across his back, leans forward, and carries him ashore.

Snorkel and SCUBA Diving

Both of these techniques are being used more and more, in military operations and as a form of recreation. Each offers many dangers to an untrained swimmer, and no one should attempt to snorkel or dive

A

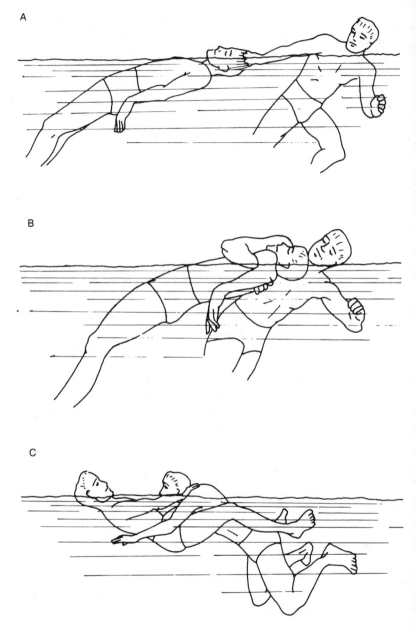

B

C

Figure 18–7. Approved methods of carrying a person in the water are: (A) head carry; (B) chest carry; (C) tired swimmer's carry.

with SCUBA gear without adequate training. Certification courses are available and will greatly benefit any swimmer. Any diving done for the Coast Guard under orders must be performed only by trained swimmers.

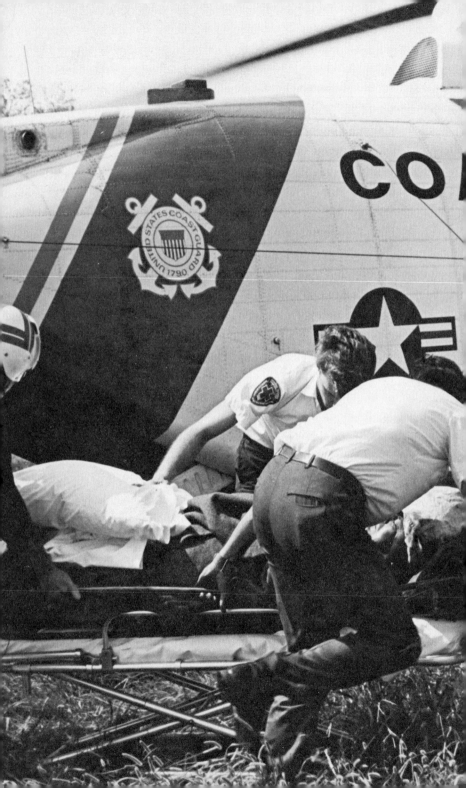

CHAPTER 19

First Aid

First aid is emergency treatment for injured or wounded people. It consists only of immediate, temporary assistance (figure 19–1) to save life, prevent further injury, and preserve the victim's vitality and resistance to infection. The three things to do first in giving first aid are: stop severe bleeding, begin artificial respiration, and prevent or reduce shock.

TAKE IMMEDIATE ACTION

Know what to do, and do it. Serious bleeding must be stopped; if a man is bleeding from the mouth (or vomiting), roll him on his belly with his head turned to one side, lower than his feet. If he is in shock, place him on his back, head lower than feet. Clear his mouth or throat, start artificial respiration if needed, then treat for shock.

Don't move patient unless absolutely necessary to save him from fire, gas, drowning, or gunfire. A fractured bone may cut an artery or nerve; a broken neck or back may result in spinal cord injury and paralysis, or death. Make an injured person comfortable; cover him to keep him warm. If a man must be moved, know how to do it (see "Transportation of the Injured").

Control the Situation

Ask for medical assistance. Use telephone, radio, messenger, or send someone in a car. Have someone keep bystanders clear. Loosen clothing about the patient's neck, chest, and abdomen.

Examine the patient to determine the extent of his injuries. Look

Figure 19–1. Coast Guardsmen and Red Cross workers on a rescue mission after hurricane Camille hit Mississippi in 1969.

for bleeding, wounds, fractures, or burns. Notice the color of his face. Determine whether he is conscious by asking him questions. Bleeding from the nose and ears is often a symptom of a *fractured skull*. Bloody froth coming from the mouth often indicates *damaged lungs*. Check the pulse rate and strength. Check dogtags for blood type; see if the man carries anything (bracelet, tag, or card) about drugs or medicines he must or cannot take.

Frequently, loss of blood is not as serious as it may look, but lack of breathing is very dangerous to a patient. Breathing must be restored first. For that reason, artificial respiration is covered first in this chapter. After this section, all other first-aid treatments follow in alphabetical order.

RESUSCITATION OR ARTIFICIAL RESPIRATION

When breathing stops for any reason, a condition results that is known as asphyxia. Asphyxia may be present also in victims of shock or collapse, of extreme exposure to heat or cold, and chemical poisoning. A few seconds' delay in starting artificial respiration may result in death.

With a highly toxic chemical, a person applying mouth-to-mouth resuscitation could be poisoned by the downed person. The use of adjunctive equipment or the placement of a cloth barrier over the victim's mouth will minimize contamination.

Symptoms

The symptoms which indicate the necessity for artificial respiration are: Cyanosis (blueness of the skin and membrane), suspension of breathing, or shallow breathing in some cases of poisoning.

Treatment

The first step is to remove the cause, or to remove the patient from the cause. Then administer artificial respiration. Later treat as for shock. In most cases artificial respiration should be administered while the patient is being removed to more suitable surroundings. The treatment for shock can often be started while artificial respiration is being administered.

The patient's mouth should be cleared of any obstruction, such as chewing gum, tobacco, false teeth, or mucous, so that there is no interference with the inhaling and exhaling of air from the lungs.

Artificial respiration should be started immediately and continued until normal breathing is established, until the patient is pronounced dead by a doctor, or until you are unable to continue.

Not infrequently the patient, after a temporary recovery of respiration, stops breathing again. The patient must be watched, and if natural breathing stops, artificial respiration should be resumed at once. Perform artificial respiration gently and at the proper rate. Roughness may injure the patient.

General Principles

Time is of prime importance. Seconds count. Do not take time to move the victim to a more satisfacotry place; begin at once. Do not delay resuscitation to loosen clothes, warm the victim, or give stimulants. These are secondary to the main purpose of getting air into the victim's lungs.

As soon as the victim is breathing by himself, or when additional help is available, see that the clothing is loosened (or removed if wet), and that the patient is kept warm, but do not interrupt the rhythmic artificial respiration to accomplish these measures.

Do not wait for a mechanical resuscitator; but when one is available, use it as an inhalator. The important advantages of good mechanical resuscitators are that they are not fatiguing, and can furnish 100 percent oxygen. Because a resuscitator need only be applied to the patient's face, it can be used when physical manipulation of the body is impossible or would be harmful, as during surgical procedures, in patients with extensive burns, broken vertebrae, ribs and arms, for victims trapped under debris of excavations, or under overturned vehicles, and during transportation of the victim. Furthermore, some resuscitators signal when the airway is obstructed and provide an aspirator. These may only be used by qualified personnel.

Remember, it is all-important that artificial respiration, when needed, be started quickly. A check should be made to ascertain that the tongue or foreign objects are not obstructing the passages. A smooth rhythm in performing artificial respiration is desirable, but split-second timing is not essential. Shock should receive adequate attention, and the subject should remain recumbent after resuscitation until seen by a physician or until recovery seems assured.

Cardiopulmonary Resuscitation

This is an emergency first aid procedure that combines *artificial respiration* with *artificial circulation*. It is known as the *heart-lung* method, and is the one method usually authorized for Coast Guard use. Remember:

> The best technique for *artificial respiration* is mouth-to-mouth breathing.
>
> The best technique for *artificial circulation* is external cardiac massage.

Artificial respiration should be started at once in any case where breathing has ceased. This may be due to any one of many causes including:

Drowning
Suffocation
Electrocution
Poisonous gases
Heart attack

Mouth-to-Mouth Breathing

This is *always* started first, and then the necessity for external cardiac massage is determined (see figure 19–2).

Place victim on his back. (A)
Kneel beside his head. (F)
Place one hand under his neck. (G)
Place other hand on his forehead so that your thumb and forefinger can close his nose. (H)
Lift gently with hand under neck while pushing down with hand on forehead. This will extend the neck and open the air passages in the vast majority of cases. (I)
Take a deep breath (about twice the normal), open you mouth widely, place your mouth over the victim's mouth and blow, giving four quick breaths. (J)
Watch for victim's chest to rise. As soon as this happens remove your mouth from victim's and let natural recoil expire from victim; check then for a pulse and breathing.
Repeat 12–14 times a minute for adults, 18–20 for children and infants.
If chest does not rise, one or more of the following conditions exist and must be corrected:

Airleak. Make sure that there is an airtight seal between your mouth and the victim's.

Airway obstruction (more likely). Insert finger into victim's mouth and remove any foreign bodies (false teeth, etc.), vomit, and/or blood clots. If chest still fails to rise, remove hand from neck, insert thumb into mouth and grab lower jawbone (mandible) between thumb and fingers and lift jawbone upward holding it in this position while you continue to perform mouth-to-mouth breathing.

In children and infants, a lesser amount of air is necessary. In infants the amount of air that can be held in your cheeks may be sufficient. However, if your mouth is removed quickly as soon as the chest begins to rise, no damage will be done.

Mouth-to-nose breathing may be carried out using much the same technique except, of course, the victim's mouth is held closed while your mouth is placed over the victim's nose.

If you would hesitate to place your mouth over the victim's, satisfactory mouth-to-mouth breathing may be carried out through a handkerchief. Airways and tubes should be used only by those personnel trained in their use by physicians. Not only are they dangerous when used by untrained personnel, but usually are not available when such an emergency arises.

Only *after* mouth-to-mouth breathing has been started and only *after* it has been determined that the heart has stopped, should external cardiac massage be started and combined with mouth-to-mouth breathing to give cardiopulmonary resuscitation.

It is most important to realize that external cardiac massage is unnecessary and actually dangerous unless the heart has stopped beating. Many cases will be encountered in which the person has stopped breathing but whose heart is still beating, and these cases require only mouth-to-mouth breathing.

Cardiopulmonary resuscitation (figure 19–2) must be started without delay. You have only 4–5 minutes in which to initiate this rescue technique. After that time irreparable damage has occurred in the victim's vital organs. Therefore, *do not* leave the victim to summon aid. If another person is present, send him for help, but start resuscitation immediately. Don't waste time moving the victim except when

(A) Victim on back on firm surface.

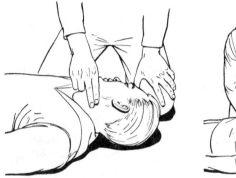

(B) Carotid pulse.

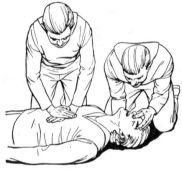

(C) Position of hands.

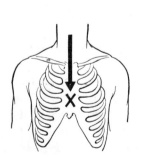

(D) Sketch of sternum.

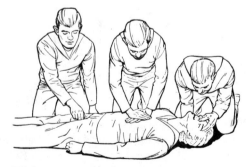

(E) Resuscitation by three rescuers.

Figure 19–2. Artificial respiration involves both mouth-to-mouth breathing and external cardiac massage.

Mouth-to-Mouth
Breathing

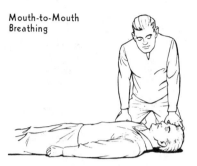

(F) Rescuer in position.

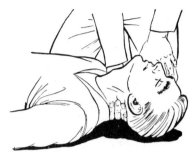

(G) Hand under neck.

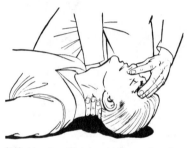

(H) Hand on forehead. Nose closed.

(I) Neck extended.

(J) Actual inflation.

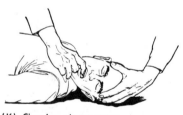

(K) Cleaning air passages.

(L) Elevation of jaw.

(M) Mouth to nose breathing.

External Cardiac Massage

After mouth-to-mouth breathing has been instituted with 4 quick breaths, and only then, check to see if external cardiac massage should be started. It is needed only if the heart has stopped.

In many cases mouth-to-mouth breathing will cause resumption of the heartbeat.

Check for a pulse. The best place to check is the carotid artery in the neck, (B) close to the surface on either side of the Adam's apple. Practice feeling your own.

Check the pupils. If the pupil is widely dilated and doesn't contract when light hits it, then the blood flow to the brain is insufficient. Start external cardiac massage.

Locate notch at top of breastbone. (D)

Locate lower end of breastbone. (D)

Place heel of one hand over the lower one-third of breastbone, point "X" in (D), and other hand on top of first. (E)

Compress breastbone against backbone by exerting downward pressure on hands with the weight of your upper body.

Pressure is then released quickly. The cycle is repeated 60–80 times per minute in adults, 80–100 in children.

Breastbone should move 1½ to 2 inches in adults. Children's chests are not as strong, and external cardiac massage in infants can be done with 2 fingers while in older children up to age 10 one hand usually suffices.

Fingers should be kept *away* from the ribs to avoid fractures.

Check pulse frequently to see if heart has restarted.

If three rescuers are available after someone has been sent for help, one administers mouth-to-mouth breathing, one administers external cardiac massage, and one monitors the pulse, preferably in the groin (to check adequacy of massage).

Rhythm may be adjusted by giving 5 strokes on the breastbone followed by one lung inflation: stroke, stroke, stroke, stroke, stroke, breath, etc. Timing may be estimated by repeating "one thousand and one" for each stroke; this will closely approximate one second.

If two rescuers are present, one administers mouth-to-mouth breathing and one administers external cardiac massage.

If only one rescuer is present, he must of necessity administer both mouth-to-mouth breathing and external cardiac massage. This can be managed by interrupting external cardiac massage every 15 beats to give 2 lung inflations.

The stomach may become distended with air. This is especially true if airway is not clear. It is not dangerous and can be remedied by applying pressure over the stomach with the palm of one hand. This expels the air but may also lead to regurgitation of the stomach contents, so you must be ready to turn the head to one side and clean out mouth with fingers or cloth. (K)

Cardiopulmonary resuscitation, once started, must be continued until spontaneous breathing and heartbeat occur or until victim is turned over to a physician. In many cases this will mean that the procedure must be continued while victim is being transported to medical facilities.

In cases of submersion (apparent drowning) do not attempt to drain fluid from lungs. If possible have head lower than body, but even this is not essential.

Summary

Cardiopulmonary resuscitation should be started at once in any case where breathing and the heart have stopped. If only breathing has stopped, use mouth-to-mouth breathing. Don't waste time seeking help or equipment. Begin at once.

Resuscitation should be performed where the victim is found. Don't waste valuable time moving him, finding special equipment, seeking additional help, getting him out of the water, etc. It is necessary to move him only if gases or fumes are present. Follow these simple instructions:

Put victim on firm surface, face up.
Start mouth-to-mouth breathing.
Check for heartbeat, pulses, dilation of pupils.
If heart has stopped begin external cardiac massage.
Continue cardiopulmonary resuscitation until a physician takes over, until victim's breathing and hearbeat have started again, or until you are unable to continue.

Alternative Methods

Sometimes the mouth-to-mouth method cannot be used; for example, when there are injuries to the face with bleeding around the mouth or when gas masks must be worn in contaminated areas. Rather than stopping efforts to help a patient breathe, try one of the following manual methods. They are not alway effective because of failure to maintain a free and unobstructed airway. In all manual methods, the first consideration must be proper positioning of the head to avoid airway obstruction. The steps for this method are shown in figure 19–3.

Chest-Pressure, Armlift Method

Place the victim in a face-up position, and put something under his shoulders to raise them and to allow the head to drop backward (step A).

Kneel at his head. Grasp his arms at the wrists. Cross them, then press them over the lower chest (step B). This should cause the air to flow out.

Immediately release the pressure and pull the arms outward and upward over his head and backward as far as possible (step C). This should cause the air to rush in.

Repeat this cycle about 20 times a minute, checking the mouth frequently for obstruction. A victim in a face-up position may aspirate vomit or blood into his lungs, so you must keep his head extended and turned to one side. If possible, the head should be a little lower than the trunk. If there is a second rescuer on hand, have him continuously check the victim's head so that the jaw is jutting out and the mouth is kept as clean as possible.

Back-Pressure, Armlift Method

Follow these steps for the back-pressure, armlift method (figure 19–4):

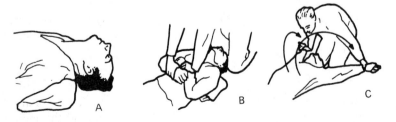

Figure 19–3. Chest pressure, armlift method of artificial respiration.

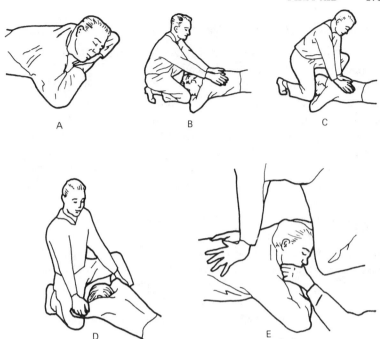

Figure 19–4. Back-pressure, armlift method of artificial respiration.

Place the victim face down. Bend his elbows and place his hands one upon the other under his chin. Turn his head slightly and extend it as far as possible, making sure that the chin juts out (step A).

Kneel at the head of the victim. Place your hands on the flat of his back so that the palms lie just below an imaginary line running between the armpits (step B).

Rock forward until the arms are approximately vertical, and allow the weight of the upper part of your body to exert steady, even pressure downward on your hands (step C).

Immediately draw his arms upward and toward you, applying enough lift to feel resistance and tension at his shoulders (step D). Then lower his arms to the ground. Repeat this cycle about 20 times a minute. If a second rescuer is available, have him hold the victim's head so that the jaw juts out (step E). Check the mouth for any stomach contents, and keep it as clean as possible.

Special Treatment for Water Cases

It is vital to keep a possible drowning victim from becoming chilled; his body temperature is already dangerously low.

Time your pressure application to coincide with the victim's first attempt to breath for himself. If he vomits turn him on his side, wipe out his mouth, then reposition him. Normally, recovery should be rapid—except in cases where the victim has also suffered from electric shock, drug poisoning, or carbon monoxide poisoning, when the nerves and muscles that control the breathing system may be paralyzed or deeply depressed, or carbon monoxide may displace oxygen in the blood stream.

Artificial respiration must continue for long periods in such cases. When the victim is revived, he should be kept as quiet as possible until he is breathing regularly. He should be kept covered and otherwise treated for shock until suitable transportation is available. Since respiratory and other disturbances may develop, a doctor's care is necessary during the recovery period. Mouth-to-mouth resuscitation can be given to a person in the water. Divers must learn to do this.

Cold-Water Drowning

Sudden face contact with cold water (below 70° F) sometimes touches off a primitive response called the "mammalian diving reflex." This complex series of body responses shuts off blood circulation to most parts of the body except the heart, lungs, and brain. Thus, what little oxygen remains in the blood gets transported to the brain where it is needed the most. Even though there may be very little oxygen in the blood, it can be enough since the cooled brain requires much less oxygen than normal.

While we know little about the human diving reflex, scientists know that diving mammals like whales, porpoises, and seals depend on a similar mechanism to survive long periods underwater.

By itself the diving response won't protect everyone of course.

Survival depends on:

How long the person is under water
How cold the water is
The age of the victim
How well the rescuers do their jobs

GENERAL FIRST AID TREATMENT

Animal Bites

Wash the wound under running water, then wash with soap and water. Apply antiseptic. Treat for bleeding and shock as necessary. The danger in an animal bite is rabies; if the bite is by a pet, it must be kept under observation to determine if rabies treatment is required. Bites by wild animals or unknown domestic animals should be checked by a doctor to determine if rabies treatment is necessary.

Asphyxiation

This is loss of consciousness due to lack of oxygen. Drowning, electric shock, and gas poisoning are the most common causes, but suffocation, strangulation, and choking will produce the same results. Breathing stops, but the heart may continue to pump blood for some time. Even if a heartbeat cannot be felt, artificial respiration must be administered.

Bandages

Bandages may consist of gauze, a gauze square, an adhesive compress, a bandage compress, or a plain strip of cloth. The compress, which directly covers the wound, must be sterile. Bandages need not be sterile, as they do not contact the wound. They should not be made of anything adhesive that will stick to the skin. The bandage may be applied in turns: circular, spiral, figure eight, or recurrent. Triangular bandages may be tied on the head or face, shoulder or hip, chest or back, foot or hand. Cravat bandages are employed for wounds of the head, neck, eye, temple, cheek, ear, elbow, knee, arm, forearm, or palm of hand. Roller bandages are wrapped on hand and wrist, forearm or leg. The *First Aid Textbook* prepared by the American Red Cross is invaluable for application of bandages and any first aid problem.

Bleeding

An average human body contains five quarts of blood. One pint can be lost without harmful effect. A loss of two pints will usually produce shock. If half the blood is lost, death almost always results. Bleeding must be stopped quickly.

In arterial bleeding, bright red blood spurts out; this bleeding is very serious. In venous bleeding dark red blood flows steadily; this also can be very serious. Capillary bleeding—usually not serious—comes from a prick or small abrasion.

Practically all bleeding can be stopped if pressure is applied *directly to the wound*. If direct pressure does not stop the bleeding, pressure should be applied at the right *pressure point*. Where severe bleeding cannot be controlled by either of these methods, pressure by means of a *tourniquet* should be applied.

Direct Pressure

Use a sterile dressing or the cleanest cloth available—a freshly laundered handkerchief, a towel, or an article of clothing. Fold it to form a pad, place it directly over the wound, and fasten it in position with a bandage (figure 19–5).

If the bleeding does not stop, try applying direct pressure by hand steadily, for five or six minutes, over the pad of cloth.

In cases of severe bleeding, don't worry about infection—stop the blood. If nothing else is available, jam a shirt into the wound. Remember, *direct pressure* is the first method to use to control bleeding.

Pressure Points

Bleeding from a cut artery or vein may often be controlled by applying pressure to the right pressure point (figure 19–6).

A pressure point is a place where a main artery lies near the skin surface and over a bone. Pressure there compresses the artery against the bone and shuts off the flow of blood to the wound.

Face, below the eyes. Pressure point is the lower jawbone (A), at a notch you can feel with your finger.

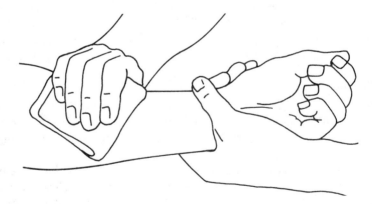

Figure 19–5. Control of bleeding by direct pressure on the wound.

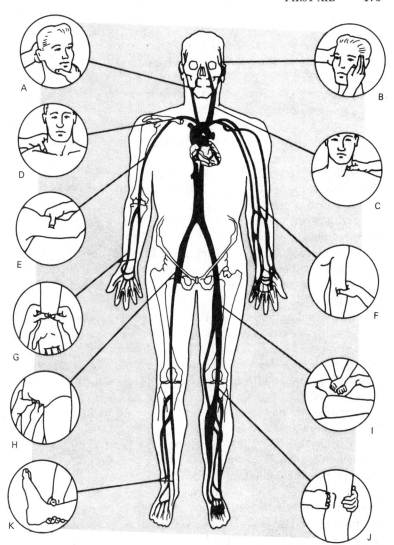

Figure 19–6. Control of bleeding by application of pressure at points where artery lies near the skin and over a bone.

Temple or scalp. Pressure point is just in front of the ear. Your finger can feel the pulse in the artery there. (B)

Neck. Apply pressure below the wound, just in front of the neck muscle (C). Press inward and slightly backward. Apply pressure here only if absolutely necessary, since there is danger of pressing on the windpipe and choking the victim.

Shoulder or upper part of the arm. The pressure point is back of the collarbone (D). Press forward against the collarbone or down against the first rib.

Middle of the upper arm and elbow. Pressure point is on the inner side of the arm, about halfway between shoulder and elbow (E).

Lower arm. Pressure point is at the elbow (F).

Hand. Pressure point is at the wrist (G). If the arm can be held up, bleeding will stop sooner.

Upper part of thigh. Pressure point is middle of the groin (H). Sometimes it is better to apply pressure on the upper thigh (I); it takes heavy pressure here; use a closed fist and press the fist down with the other hand.

Between foot and knee. Use firm pressure at the side of the knee, or else push one fist against the back of the knee and hold one hand in front of the knee (J). As a last resort, fold a bandage behind the knee and bend the leg back against it.

Foot. Pressure point is at the ankle (K). Elevating the leg will help control bleeding.

Remember to apply pressure at the point nearest the wound and between the wound and the heart.

It is very tiring to apply finger pressure, and it can seldom be maintained for more than 15 minutes. As soon as possible, use a compress held securely over the wound by a bandage.

If the bleeding is still severe, you may have to apply a tourniquet. Remember—they may result in gangrene when left on too long.

A tourniquet (figure 19–7) consists of a pad (pressure object), a band, and a device for tightening the band so that the blood vessels will be compressed. The type found in many first aid kits consists of a web band approximately two inches wide by five feet long, with a buckle for fastening. Wrap it once about the limb, then run the free end through the slit in the felt pad and through the buckle. Draw the band tight enough to stop the flow of blood. In an emergency, any round, smooth pressure object may be used—a compress, roller bandage, stone, rifle shell—and any long, flat material may be used as the band.

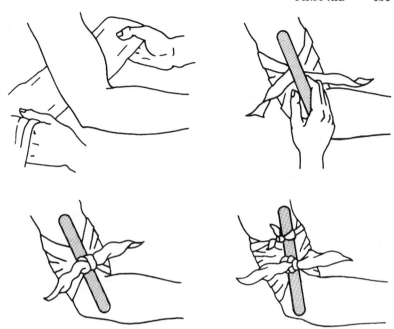

Figure 19–7. Applying a tourniquet: tie bandage with overhand knot, tie square knot over stick, twist to tighten the tourniquet.

At the pressure point, place a thick compress or folded cloth from four to six inches square. Do not use rope, wire, string, or very narrow pieces of cloth; they will cut into the flesh. A short stick may be used to twist the band and tighten the tourniquet. A tourniquet is *never* used unless bleeding cannot be controlled in any other way. By the time the tourniquet is put on, the victim has already lost a considerable amount of blood. The additional loss resulting from loosening the tourniquet may easily cause death. Once a tourniquet has been applied, it should be released only by medical personnel. If a tourniquet is used, mark the patient's forehead with a T and the time, using felt tip pen, lipstick, or iodine so there is no doubt about how long it has been in place. Improper use may produce gangrene. Do not use one if there is any other choice.

Internal Bleeding

If the patient is bleeding internally, he may be thirsty, restless, fearful, and in shock.

Nothing should be given by mouth, even if the victim is thirsty, for if anesthesia has to be given the patient might vomit and aspirate material into his lungs.

Bleeding in the stomach is indicated by the location of the wound and bloody vomiting. The treatment to be administered for internal bleeding is the same as for shock, except that stimulants must not be given. Immediate medical care should be sought, since internal bleeding may be rapidly fatal, or may cause death by slower bleeding over a period of time.

Blisters

The skin covering a blister is better protection than any bandage. If the blister is where it might be broken, open it with a sharp knife or needle that has been heated in flame. Press out fluid with a bit of sterile gauze and apply a sterile bandage.

Burns and Scalds

Burns and *scalds* are caused by exposure to intense heat (fire, bomb flash, sunlight, hot metal solids, hot gases, or hot liquids). Contact with electric current may also cause severe burns.

Burns are usually classified according to the depth of injury to the tissues. A burn that reddens the skin is called a *first-degree burn*. A burn that raises a blister is a *second-degree burn*. When the skin is destroyed and the tissues are actually charred or cooked, the injury is described as a *third-degree burn*. In some third-degree burns the destruction extends down to muscles and bones.

The size of the burned area may be far more important than the depth of the burn. *Third-degree burns*, for many hours after the injury, frequently appear as blanched areas surrounded by reddened or blistered skin. A *first-degree burn* that covers a very large area of the body is almost always more serious than a small third-degree burn.

Rule of Nines

The Rule of Nines is used to establish the extent and percentage of burn for determining the amount of fluid the body would need during the first 24 hours after injury. The front and back of the trunk and the lower legs are each rated as 18 percent for a total of 72 percent. The arms and head are individually rated at 9 percent and the genital area at 1 percent for a total of 28 percent. A first-degree burn over 72 percent of the body is more serious than a third-degree burn on the arm.

Treatment of Burns and Scalds

The main dangers from burns are shock and infection. First aid treatment must be directed toward relieving pain, combating shock, and preventing infection.

Minor Burns

Dress the burns immediately. Do not apply ointments or other medicines to the burned area. Cover the burn with a sterile bandage to prevent infection. The pain will be greatly lessened if the bandage is airtight and fairly firm.

Cold-water treatment has proved both comforting and effective. Use compresses wrung out of ice water, or submerge the burned part in water containing sufficient ice to chill (but not freeze); continue until no pain is felt when the burned part is withdrawn from the water. An ounce or so of germicidal detergent in the chilled water will help control infection.

Serious Burns

Extreme pain increases the severity of the shock. Relieve pain with morphine if available. Treat for shock immediately, before making any attempt to treat the burns.

Relieving pain is highly important in treating for shock. Keep the patient's head slightly lower than his feet, and see that he is warm enough. Do not remove clothing immediately. Cover him with a blanket if he appears to be cold. Do not overheat him. Remember that exposure to cold will increase shock.

A seriously burned person has an overwhelming need for fluids. If a person is conscious, able to swallow, and has no internal injuries, give him water or sweet tea, fruit juices, or sugar water.

Burns of the Eye

See "Eye Injuries."

Chemical Burns

Chemicals in various contact with the skin or other body membranes may cause *chemical burns,* by direct chemical destruction of the body tissue. This kind of injury can be caused by acids, nitric acid, sulphuric acid, hydrochloric acid, etc., and *caustic alkalies*, such as potassium hydroxide (lye), sodium hydroxide (caustic soda, soda lye), and calcium oxide (quicklime). Phenol (carbolic acid) also causes chemical burns. Strong concentrations of various bleaches and disinfectants cause chemical injuries to the skin. Chlorine, ammonia, and other industrial gases (whether in liquid or vapor form) may cause serious chemical burns of the skin or of the eyes. *White phosphorus* causes a burn that is a combination of a true heat burn and a chemical injury.

These are some guidelines for treating chemical burns.

Wash off the chemical *immediately* with large amounts of clean, fresh, cool water. If it is not possible to put the victim under running water, immerse the affected areas in water, or pour great quantities of water over the burns.

Neutralize any chemical that remains on the skin. For *acid* burns, apply a solution of sodium bicarbonate (baking soda) or some other mild alkali; for *alkali* burns, apply vinegar, lemon juice, or some other mild acid; and for *phenol* (carbolic acid) burns, apply alcohol. *Do not attempt to neutralize any chemical unless you are sure that you know what the chemical is and what substance will effectively neutralize it!* Flooding with great amounts of cool water will suffice when doubt exists.

Wash the affected areas again with fresh water, and dry gently with sterile gauze. Do not break the skin or open any blisters.

Do what you can to relieve pain and treat for shock. See also "Eye Injuries."

Information on chemicals can be obtained through the Chemical Hazards Response Information System (CHRIS), Commandant Instruction M16465.12 series.

Electrocution

A person knocked unconscious by electrical current needs artificial respiration at once. If he is still in contact with any object that might carry current, *cut the contact*. Pull the switch if you know where it is, but don't waste time looking for it. Pull or push him away from contact with a dry rope, piece of clothing, pole, oar, or board. Rubber gloves are good if you have them, but they will not protect against very high voltage. Most work gloves will be damp and sweaty; don't use them. Don't touch the victim until he is clear of contact. Commence artificial respiration, and keep it up. Send for medical assistance.

Exposure to Extreme Cold

This can result in *loss of body heat, frostbite,* and *immersion foot.*

In the treatment of all injuries from exposure to extreme cold, it is essential to get the victim into a warm place as soon as possible. It is almost impossible to give effective first aid treatment while the victim is still exposed to the cold.

Remember that there may be other injuries that must be treated *before* he can be moved into a warmer place.

General Loss of Body Heat (Hypothermia)

This abnormally low body temperature usually results from total immersion in cold water and loss of consciousness. The person will appear pale and unconscious and may be taken for dead. Breathing is slow and shallow and the pulse faint or unobtainable. Body tissues feel semirigid, and the arms and legs may be stiff.

First aid treatment consists mainly of bringing the body temperature to normal: The patient should be wrapped in warm blankets in a warm room. Be alert for further complications such as respiratory or cardiac arrest.

Frostbite

Exposure to dry cold causes *frostbite,* especially in the cheeks, nose, chin, ears, forehead, wrists, hands, and feet. The skin turns white or gray, then bright pink.

Frostbite may also be caused by contact with certain chemicals that have a rapid freezing action—such as liquid oxygen, carbon dioxide, Freon, and other industrial gases. Injuries caused by these substances are often referred to as chemical "burns," but the body tissue is actually frozen rather than burned.

When the frostbitten area is warmed up, it immediately becomes red and swollen, and large blisters develop. Severe frostbite causes *gangrene,* in which soft body tissues—and sometimes even bone—are permanently destroyed. If deep tissue has been destroyed, the injured part may have to be amputated.

The first aid treatment for frostbite is *rapid* thawing of the frozen tissues.

Get the victim into the warmest available place as soon as possible and get him undressed. If his feet or legs are frostbitten, *do not allow him to walk.* Do not handle the frostbitten area unnecessarily, and do not exert any pressure against it. Do not thaw a frozen extremity until you can transport the patient to a place where the following steps can be taken.

Immerse the injured part in water kept at a temperature of 107° to 109° F. If you have no thermometer, make sure that the water is just comfortably warm. Warming should not continue after thawing is complete. Keep the water in motion by using a paddle or similar device.

Dry the victim carefully. Place him in bed and keep him covered. Don't let anything touch the frostbitten parts. Keep sterile gauze or cloth pads between toes and fingers, and keep frostbitten parts elevated. Obtain medical assistance as soon as possible.

Caution: Never rub or massage frostbite with ice or snow. Do not apply cold water. Do not expose a frostbitten area to cold air.

Immersion Foot (or Trench Foot)

This results from prolonged exposure to a combination of moisture and cold. Men on life rafts or in unprotected lifeboats are most likely to get immersion foot from exposure to near-freezing sea waters, but cases have occurred as a result of longer immersion in warmer water. This condition sometimes affects other parts of the body, such as knees, hands, buttocks, etc.

A person who remains for a long time in a cold, wet place, standing or crouching in one position, is also very likely to develop this condition.

Immersion foot causes a feeling of heaviness or numbness. All sensitivity may be lost. The affected areas become swollen. The skin is first red, then waxy white, then a yellowish color, and finally a mottled blue or black. The injured parts remain cold, swollen, discolored, and numb; or they thaw, with the swelling increasing and the skin becoming hot, dry, red, and blistered. In severe cases there may be gangrene.

This first aid treatment should be given while medical aid is being summoned.

Get the victim off his feet as soon as possible; keep him as warm as possible.

Expose the injured part to warm, dry air.

If the skin is not broken or loose, the injured part may be left exposed;

however, if it is necessary to move the victim, cover the injured part with loosely-wrapped, fluff bandages of sterile gauze.

Do not apply salves or ointments. Be careful not to rupture blisters. If severe pain is present, give the victim no more than one-fourth grain of morphine.

Eye Injuries

For wounds of the eye, apply thick, dry, sterile bandages. If the eyeball is injured, do not allow any pressure of the bandage against the eyeball. If soft tissue around the eye is injured, apply a pressure bandage. Keep the patient lying down while he is being transported and until he receives medical aid.

To remove an object in the eye, have the patient look upward, and remove the object with the corner of a clean handkerchief or with a cotton swab moistened in clean water. Either gently pull the lower lid down with your finger, or turn the upper lid back over a match stick or cotton swab applicator by grasping the lashes of the upper lid between the fingers and everting it. If these methods fail, use a sterile syringe or medicine dropper to irrigate the eye gently with sterile water at body temperature, holding the lids apart with the fingers. If the object still cannot be removed, cover the eye by bandaging and obtain medical help. Never attempt to remove a foreign body from the eyeball.

Heat Burns

Drop clean mineral oil or olive oil into the eye, and cover it with a thick gauze compress. Do not allow the patient to rub the eye. Get medical help.

Chemical Burns

Flush the eye immediately with large quantities of fresh, clean water. Hold the victim's head over a drinking fountain so that the water flows from the *inside* corner of his eye toward the *outside* corner, or have the victim lie down with his head turned slightly to one side; then pour water into the *inside* corner of his eye and let it flow gently across the eyeball to the *outside* corner. If he is unable to open his eyes, hold the eyelids apart so that the water can flow across the eyeball. Do not use anything except water.

Another way to wash chemical substances from the eye is to have the victim open and close his eyes several times while his face is immersed in a pan of fresh water.

Cover the eye with a small, thick compress; fasten the compress in place with a bandage or an eyeshield, and get medical care as soon as possible. Refer to CHRIS.

Choking

Follow the directions shown on the American Red Cross poster, reproduced here as figure 19–8.

Fainting

This is a reaction of the nervous system that slows down the flow of blood to the brain. A worried or tired person suffering a mental setback may faint. To prevent fainting a person should lie flat for ten minutes with the head lower than the rest of the body. If a person who appears to have fainted does not recover consciousness almost immediately, he has not simply fainted. Unconsciousness may also be caused by asphyxia, deep shock, poisoning, head injury, heat stroke, heart attack, apoplexy, or epilepsy. Get medical help at once.

Fish Hooks

If the barb is buried in the flesh, clean the area, paint with antiseptic and then push the hook entirely through so the barb comes out on the other side. Then cut off the barb; the rest of the hook can be backed out. Watch out for infection. Check your medical record to see if you need a tetanus shot.

Fish Stings

Many sea creatures (Portuguese man-of-war, jellyfish, stingray, scorpion fish, toadfish) are poisonous. The symptoms range from burning, stinging, reddening of the skin, hives, pus sores, abdominal cramps, numbness, dizziness, pain in the groin and armpits, nausea, muscular pain, difficulty of breathing, and constriction of the chest, to prostration and shock.

For Portuguese men-of-war stings, remove the tentacles immediately and wash the skin with alcohol. Then apply calamine lotion or ammonia water. The treatment for jellyfish is about the same. Apply ammonia water, vinegar, or a soothing lotion. If available, an excellent

FIRST AID FOR
CHOKING

If victim can cough, speak, breathe ➡ *Do not interfere*

If victim cannot cough speak breathe

Have someone call for help. Telephone : _____
(Number)

⬇

TAKE ACTION: FOR CONSCIOUS VICTIM

4 QUICK BACK BLOWS   4 MANUAL THRUSTS

Repeat steps until effective or until victim becomes unconscious.

TAKE ACTION: FOR UNCONSCIOUS VICTIM

TRY TO VENTILATE   4 BACK BLOWS   4 MANUAL THRUSTS   FINGER PROBE

Repeat steps until effective.

Continue artificial ventilation or CPR, as indicated.

Everyone should learn how to perform the above first aid steps for choking
and how to give mouth-to-mouth and cardiopulmonary resuscitation. Call
your local Red Cross chapter for information on these and other first aid
techniques.

Caution: Abdominal thrusts may cause injury. Do not practice on people.

Figure 19–8. First aid for choking. (Courtesy American Red Cross)

remedy is meat tenderizer, which contains papain from papaya. Make
a paste with it and apply to the sting area. Treat for shock.

A stingray wound should be washed immediately with cold salt water.
Much of the toxin will wash out, and the cold water causes blood vessels
to constrict, slowing circulation, and acts as a mild pain-killing agent.

The wound should then be immersed in hot water for 30 miutes to an hour, with temperature as high as the victim can stand without injury. (Hot compresses can be applied for wounds in areas that cannot be immersed.) A sterile dressing should then be applied.

Fractures

A *closed fracture* is one in which a bone is broken, but there is no break in the skin. An *open fracture* is one in which the broken bone protrudes through the skin. All fractures require careful handling; send for medical aid as soon as possible. Don't move a fracture victim until the fracture has been splinted, unless necessary to save life or prevent further injury. Do not attempt to set a broken bone.

Treat for shock if the victim shows signs of shock. But don't give morphine if there is a head injury. Stop the bleeding in a compound fracture—use direct pressure or the pressure point system.

Apply splints over clothing if the patient is to be moved a short distance or if a doctor will see him soon. Otherwise, apply well-padded splints after the clothing has been cut away. Be careful when you handle any fracture to avoid additional shock or injury. Splints vary according to the area and nature of the fracture. Follow these rules.

Forearm

Two well-padded splints, top and bottom, from elbow to wrist. Bandage in place. Hold the forearm across the chest with a sling.

Upper Arm

For a fracture near the shoulder, put a towel or pad in the armpit, bandage the arm to the body, and support the forearm in a sling. For a fracture of the middle upper arm, use one splint on the outside of the arm, shoulder to elbow. Fasten the arm to the body and support the forearm in a sling. For a fracture near the elbow, don't move the arm at all—splint it the way you find it.

Thigh

Use two splints—the outside one from armpit to foot, the inside one from crotch to foot. Fasten the splints around the ankle, over the knee, below the hip, around the pelvis, and below the armpit. Tie both legs together. Don't move the patient until this has been done.

Lower Leg

Use three splints, one on each side, one underneath. They must be well padded, especially under the knee and at the ankle bones. Or use a pillow under the leg with edges brought around in front and pinned, and add two side splints.

Kneecap

Carefully straighten the leg, place a four-inch-wide padded board under it, reaching from buttock to heel. Fasten it in place just below the knee, just above the knee, at the ankle, and at the thigh. *Do not cover the knee.*

Collarbone

On the injured side, place the forearm across the chest, palm turned in, thumb up, with hand four inches above elbow, and support the arm in this position with a sling. Fasten the arm to the body with several turns of bandage around the body and down over the hand to keep the arm close against the body.

Rib

There is danger of a broken rib puncturing a lung; if it has, the patient will cough up frothy bright red blood. If there is no pain, no action is required. To relieve pain, put a wide bandage around the upper part of the chest and tie in a loose knot on the uninjured side. Place two more bandages a little lower down, and tie loosely. Put a compress or pad under each knot on the uninjured side. Then tighten each bandage, one at a time, starting at the top, after the patient has exhaled.

Nose

Stop the nosebleed. Have the patient sit with head tipped forward and breathing through his mouth. If bleeding does not stop in a few minutes, cauterize the nose with cotton dipped in lemon juice or vinegar. Do not let the patient swallow blood. It will cause vomiting. A cold compress or ice bag over the nose will ease pain and reduce swelling.

Jaw

If the injury interferes with breathing, pull the lower jaw and tongue forward and keep them forward. Apply a four-tailed bandage under the jaw, with two ends tied on top of the front of the head and the other two on top at the back, so the bandage pulls the jaw forward. It must support and immobilize the jaw but not press on the throat.

Skull

It is not necessary to determine whether or not the skull is fractured when a person has a head injury. The primary aim is to prevent brain damage. Do not let the patient move. Try not to move him more than necessary. Do not let him get cold, do not give him anything to drink, and do not give him morphine. Stop any bleeding and get immediate medical assistance.

Spine

Pain, shock, and partial paralysis result from damage to the spine. Severe pain in the back or neck after injury should be treated as a fractured spine. Treat for shock. Keep the patient flat, and do not move his head.

If the patient cannot move his legs, feet, or toes, the fracture is probably in his back; if he cannot move his fingers, it is probably in his neck. If the patient must be transported, carry him face up on a backboard, rigid stretcher, door, or wide frame. Never try to lift such a patient with less than four men; pick him up by his clothing and slide him onto the stretcher.

Pelvis

Treat a patient with a pelvis injury for shock, but do not move him unless absolutely necessary. If a patient must be moved, handle him the same as for a victim of a fractured spine. Bandage legs together at ankles and knees; place a pillow at each hip and fasten them in place. Fasten the patient securely to the stretcher.

Heatstroke (Sunstroke)

Heatstroke and heat exhaustion are caused by excessive exposure to desert or jungle heat, direct rays of the sun, or heat of machinery spaces, foundaries, bakeries, etc. Under similar circumstances, one person may develop heatstroke and another heat exhaustion. There are important differences between the two afflictions.

Each represents a *different* bodily reaction to excessive heat, and for this reason the symptoms and treatment are also different.

Heatstroke results from a failure of the heat-regulating mechanism of the body. The body becomes overheated, the temperature rises to between 105 and 110 degress Fahrenheit, but there is no sweating or cooling of the body. The victim's skin is hot, dry, and red; he may have preliminary symptoms such as headache, nausea, dizziness, or weakness; but very often the first signs are sudden collapse and loss of consciousness. Breathing is likely to be deep and rapid. The pulse is strong and fast. Convulsions may occur. Heatstroke may cause death or permanent disability; at best, recovery is likely to be slow, and complicated by relapses.

The longer the victim remains overheated, the more likely he is to die. Follow these first aid measures to lower body temperature:

Move the victim to a cool place, remove his clothing, and place him on his back with head and shoulders slightly raised.

Sponge or spray his body with cold water, and fan him so the water will evaporate rapidly.

When he regains consciousness, give him cool (not cold) water to drink. Don't give stimulants or hot drinks.

Get him to a medical facility as soon as possible. Keep him cool while he is being transported.

Heat Exhaustion and Heat Cramps

In *heat exhaustion,* there is no failure of the heat-regulating mechanism, but there is a serious disturbance of the blood flow, similar to the circulatory disturbance of shock. Through prolonged sweating, the body loses large quantities of salt and water.

Heat exhaustion may begin with a headache, dizziness, nausea, weakness, and profuse sweating. The victim may collapse and lose consciousness, but can usually be aroused rather easily. His temperature is usually normal or even below normal; sometimes it may go down as low as 97 degrees Fahrenheit. The pupils of the eyes are usually dilated; the pulse is weak and rapid; and the skin is pale, cool, and sweaty. Sometimes there may be severe cramps in the abdomen, legs, and arms.

Follow these first aid measures:

Move the victim to a cool place, but not where he will be exposed to strong drafts or become chilled.

Loosen his clothing and make him as comfortable as possible. Keep him quiet. Keep the victim lying down, with feet and legs somewhat elevated. Be sure that he is kept comfortably warm. You may have to cover him with blankets, even if the air around him is quite warm. The pain of severe cramps may be relieved by the application of heat to the affected muscles or by firm pressure of the hand against the muscles. If the cramps are exceedingly painful, it may be necessary to give morphine. If the victim is conscious and able to swallow, give him plenty of warm water to drink with one-fourth to one-half teaspoonful of salt in each glass. This is probably the most important part of the treatment; replacement of the salt and water that has been lost by sweating often brings rapid recovery.

Give hot coffee or hot tea when the patient is able to take it. If recovery is not prompt, get medical attention as soon as possible.

Insect Bites

Wash insect bites with soap and water and apply a paste of baking soda and water. Itching can be relieved by using hot-water compresses. Ice, ammonia, or papain (meat tenderizer) applied to bee stings will prevent pain and swelling. Some persons experience severe allergic reactions to bee and other insect stings. The person stung should be carefully observed and given immediate medical attention if allergic reactions are either observed or are part of that person's medical history. Ticks can be dislodged by applying a lighted cigarette; be careful not to crush the insect or leave its jaws embedded in flesh. Certain types of ticks carry Rocky Mountain or Spotted Fever, which can be fatal. Inflamed bites require medical assistance.

Morphine

Morphine relieves severe pain and helps prevent shock. It should not be given if there is a head injury, chest injury, any injuries or burns that impair breathing, if there is evidence of severe or deepening shock, or if there is massive bleeding. Morphine should never be given to an unconscious man. Morphine should not be given if a doctor can be in attendance within four hours. If morphine is given, it must not be repeated within four hours.

Ordinarily, there is no need for anyone giving first aid to administer morphine. If it must be used, follow these steps.

Inject morphine on the outer surface of the upper arm or into the thigh if the arms are injured. In very cold climates, morphine is sometimes injected into the back of the neck to avoid undressing the victim. If a tourniquet has been applied, the morphine must be injected above the tourniquet.

Sterilize the skin with an antiseptic, alcohol, soap and water, or plain tap water. Pick the tube of the syrette up at its shoulder with the fingertips. Remove the shield, grasp the wire loop and push the wire into the tube to break the seal. Pull out the wire and discard.

Push the needle through the skin for its full length, and slowly squeeze out the contents of the syrette.

Withdraw the syrette; remove and discard the needle.

Pin the empty syrette tube to the man's shirt collar to show that morphine has been given. Also, with a skin pencil, colored antiseptic, ballpoint pen, etc., write the letter M and the time of the injection on his forehead.

Poisoning

First aid treatment for poisoning depends partly upon whether the poison enters the body by ingestion—taking the poison into the stomach by way of the mouth or by inhalation—breathing poisonous gases, by skin contact, and by injection. (Poisoning by injection is covered under "Snakebite" and "Spiders and Scorpions.")

Symptoms

Intense pain frequently follows poisoning; nausea and vomiting may occur. The victim can become delirious, or he may collapse and become unconscious; he is almost always likely to have trouble breathing. Some poisons characteristically cause paralysis; others cause convulsions. Shock is always present in cases of acute poisoning.

Emergency treatment is usually required, bcause poisons act very rapidly. Treatment by a physician should be obtained as soon as possible.

Ingested Poisons

Many substances are poisonous, if swallowed. Refer to CHRIS. *Corrosives* (substances that rapidly destroy or decompose the body tissue they contact) may be *acids* (hydrochloric, nitric, sulfuric); *phenols* (carbolic acid), creosol (Lysol, creosote); or *alkalies* (lye, lime, ammonia). Iodine is also a corrosive.

Corrosives cause burning pain in the mouth, severe burning pain in the esophagus and stomach, retching, and vomiting. The inside of the mouth is eaten away. Swallowing and breathing are difficult, the abdomen is tender and distended with gas, and body temperature is high.

Irritants (substances that do not directly destroy the body tissues, but cause inflammation in the area of contact) are potassium nitrate, zinc chloride, zinc sulfate, arsenic, iodine, and phosphorus. Irritants cause faintness, nausea, vomiting, and diarrhea, and pain with cramps in the abdomen.

Depressants (substances that depress the nervous system) include atropine, morphine and its derivatives, bromides, barbiturates, alcohol, and most local anesthetics.

They usually have an initial stimulating effect, soon followed by drowsiness and stupor; slow breathing, snoring; cold, moist skin with the face and fingers a bluish color; relaxed muscles; and dilated or contracted pupils.

Excitants (substances that stimulate the nervous system) are strychnine, camphor, and the fluorides. They cause delirium (mental disturbance, physical restlessness, and incoherence); a feeling of suffocation and inability to breathe; hot dry skin; rapid, weak pulse; convulsions or jerking muscles; and dilated or contracted pupils.

Some relatively common substances are effective emetics, demulcents, or antidotes that can be used to treat poisoning.

Emetics cause vomiting. Some effective emetics are: powdered mustard—1 to 3 teaspoonfuls in a glass of warm water; salt—2 teaspoonfuls in a glass of warm water; warm water with soapsuds (not detergents); and large quantities of warm water.

Emetics are not very effective in depressant poisoning because depressants inhibit vomiting. In such cases, vomiting may be brought on by tickling the throat.

Demulcents are substances that will soothe the stomach and delay absorption of poison. Periodically, after the victim has vomited, he should be given raw egg whites, milk, or a thin paste of cooked starch or flour.

A universal antidote, especially effective against irritants, excitants, and depressants, consists of two parts of activated charcoal, and one part each of magnesium oxide and tannic acid.

The dose is one-half ounce in a half glass of water, given by mouth. It should be followed by an emetic, *except when the poison is a corrosive*. You can substitute burned toast or charred wood for activated charcoal, milk of magnesia for magnesium oxide, and strong tea for tannic acid.

Antidotes for acids are milk of magnesia, magnesium oxide, lime water, or soap given in large amounts of water. This should be followed by a demulcent. *Do not give emetics.*

Antidotes for alkalies are diluted vinegar, lemon juice, or grapefruit juice. This should be followed by a demulcent. *Do not give emetics.* In the treatment of poisoning by mouth, identify the poison if possible. Give an emetic (except for corrosives), then give an antidote. Repeat both procedures every ten minutes. Give a demulcent after the patient has vomited. *Get medical assistance immediately.*

Inhaled poisons can come from refrigeration machinery, fire-fighting equipment, paints and solvents, photographic materials, and many other types of shipboard equipment that contain volatile and sometimes poisonous chemicals. Fuel oil and gasoline vapors constitute special hazards.

Other poisonous gases are found in voids, double bottoms, empty fuel tanks, and similar places.

Carbon monoxide, the most frequent cause of gas poisoning, is colorless, odorless, and tasteless, and so gives no warning of its presence. Carbon monoxide is present in all exhaust gases of internal-combustion engines.

First aid treatment for carbon monoxide, and *for all gases,* follows:

Get the victim out of the toxic atmosphere into a well-ventilated space. Remove his contaminated clothing.

Watch his breathing. Give artificial respiration if necessary.

Give oxygen, or an oxygen-carbon dioxide mixture, if it is available and if you know how to use it.

Keep the victim lying down. Keep him quiet. Treat him for shock. *Call a medical officer as soon as possible.*

Gasoline, benzene, naphtha and other petroleum products are poisonous if they are ingested, inhaled, or if they come into prolonged contact with the skin. Inhaling gasoline fumes causes a kind of intoxication similar to that produced by alcohol. Standard first-aid treatment should be used, but it may be difficult to keep the patient quiet. He may become extremely violent and self-destructive, or he may cause injury to others unless he is very carefully guarded. *Caution:* Do not give morphine.

Carbon tetrachloride and other chlorinated hydrocarbons such as methylene chloride, chloroform, dichloromethane, and tetrachloroethane are used for dry cleaning, for degreasing metal articles, for cleaning electrical and electronic equipment in various manufacturing processes, and in some fire extinguishers. It is extremely dangerous as a fire-extinguishing agent because it decomposes in the presence of heat and forms phosgene gas.

A person exposed to these vapors may not realize his condition until he becomes dangerously ill with nausea, mental confusion, and in some instances a kind of drunken behavior similar to that caused by alcohol.

Persons who are required to work with chlorinated solvents *must not drink alcoholic beverages*. The use of alcohol greatly increases susceptibility to this type of poisoning.

There is no known antidote for poisoning by carbon tetrachloride and the other chlorinated hydrocarbons. Standard first aid instructions should be followed.

Freon, a colorless, odorless gas used as a refrigerant, is toxic in high concentrations. First aid is the same as for other gases. Because even a very small amount of freon can freeze the delicate tissue of the eye, medical attention must be obtained as soon as possible in order to avoid permanent damage. In the meantime, put drops of clean olive oil, mineral oil, or other nonirritating oil in the eyes, and make sure that the victim does not rub his eyes.

Hydrogen sulphide smells like rotten eggs. Its presence cannot always be detected because the gas paralyzes the sense of smell. It is flammable as well as poisonous.

The general signs of hydrogen sulphide poisoning are eye, nose, and throat irritation, and an abundant flow of tears. Breathing is at first deep, noisy, and gasping; later it is feeble and irregular. Death is caused by paralysis of the brain. First aid treatment is standard.

Ammonia, an industrial gas used in many ways, is pungent, biting, and extremely irritating. Personnel cannot remain in a concentration of one-tenth of 1 percent ammonia. The irritation causes coughing and a spasm of the air passages. Death may occur from asphyxiation.

Give standard first aid treatment. In addition, hold vinegar or a weak solution of acetic acid close enough to the victim's face so that he can inhale the fumes, but discontinue this if it does not give relief.

Poisoning by skin contact is not usually a first aid problem. Such poisoning frequently is fatal, but it builds up over a long period of time. There is no real cure. Know the substances that can poison by contact and be careful in handling them. They include gasoline, benzene, naphtha, lead compounds, mercury, arsenic, carbon tetrachloride, and TNT.

Shock

When the nervous system is subjected to excessive shock, the nerves lose control of the blood vessels, allowing them to relax and reduce the supply of blood to the brain. Unconsciousness or "fuzzy headedness" may result. The heart quickens its beat, but the pulse is weak. All injury is attended by shock, which may be slight, lasting only a few seconds, or serious enough to be fatal. Shock may begin immediately, or it may be delayed as much as several hours.

How to Recognize Shock

The pulse is weak and rapid; breathing may be shallow, rapid, and irregular; the skin feels cold to the touch, and may be covered with sweat. The pupils of the eyes are usually dilated. A shock victim may complain of thirst. He may feel weak, faint or dizzy, and nauseated. He may be very restless and feel frightened and anxious. As shock deepens, these signs gradually disappear and he becomes less and less responsive, even to pain. A man in shock may insist he feels fine, and then pass out.

Treatment

These are the most important considerations in the treatment of shock. Keep the patient flat on his back, with feet higher than his body. Keep the patient warm by use of blankets. Do not use artificial heat. Do all you can to relieve pain, but do not try to give any drugs.

A person in shock is often thirsty. Moisten his mouth and lips with cool water, but don't give him anything to drink unless medical personnel will not be available for an excessively long period of time.

Never give alcohol to a person in shock or who may go into shock. Alcohol increases the blood supply to surface vessels and so diminishes the blood supply to the brain and other vital organs.

Snakebite

Poisonous snakes in the United States include "pit vipers"—rattlesnakes, copperheads, water moccasins—and coral snakes.

The Armed Forces Medical Supply provides an antivenom kit that neutralizes the venom of snakes of North and South America, including the rattlesnake, cottonmouth, copperhead, fer-de-lance, and the bushmaster. Throughout the world, other antivenoms have been developed that neutralize the venoms of snakes peculiar to certain areas.

Antivenoms should be given only by medical personnel. But if professional help is not available, the antivenom should be given to save a life. Be certain you have identified the snake and have the right antivenom.

Identifying the snake, in some cases, is not easy. Check these points:

Fangs mean the snake is poisonous (figure 19–9).

Rattles identify rattlesnakes, but not always; sometimes a rattler looses his rattle.

Snakes with a sensory organ—a "pit"—between nostrils and eyes are "pit-vipers," and are poisonous.

Snakes striped fore-and-aft are not poisonous—except for one very rare native of the Far East.

Pit-viper bites may produce the following symptoms:

Tissue swelling at the bite gradually spreading to surrounding areas. (Swelling occurs between three to five minutes following the bite, but may continue for as long as an hour and be so severe as to burst the skin.)

Severe pain.

Escape of blood from the capillaries. (Accumulation of blood in the tissues may cause severe pain.)

Severe headache and thirst.

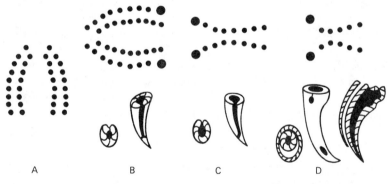

Figure 19–9. Identification of snake bites: (A) nonpoisonous—no fangs (U.S. garter snake, European ringed snake, black snake); (B) poisonous—posterior fangs (boomslang of Africa); (C) poisonous—anterior fangs (kraits, mambas, water cobras, cobras, coral snake, sea snakes); (D) poisonous—anterior fangs widely separated from teeth (various vipers, puff adder, rattlesnake, copperhead, water moccasin, fer-de-lance).

Bleeding from internal organs into the intestines, and blood in urine or stools.

Bites of coral snakes, cobras, or kraits may produce some of the following symptoms:

Irregular heartbeat, generalized weakness and exhaustion, shock.

Severe headache, dizziness, mental disturbances such as incoherent speech, stupor, mental confusion, and possibly unconsciousness. (Extreme pain is not characteristic.)

Muscular incoordination, such as inability to reach for and pick up an object or to move from place to place; sometimes muscle spasms and twitching.

Difficult or labored breathing and even respiratory paralysis.

Numbness and tingling of the skin, particularly of the lips and soles of the feet, and excessive sweating.

Chills and fever.

Nausea, vomiting, and diarrhea.

Treatment

A snakebite victim should be advised to lie down and keep calm. Remind him that very few people are even disabled by snakebite.

Keep him at rest (dry, warm, and quiet), and immoblize the affected part below the level of the heart.

For a bite on the arm or leg, place a tourniquet two to four inches closer to the heart than the bite. The tourniquet should be tight enough to stop the flow of blood in the veins but not in the arteries. *Exception:* in Africa, India, Burma, Thailand, or Australia, the tourniquet should be tight enough to restrict arterial flow and should be placed on the upper arm or upper leg where single bones make restriction possible. The tourniquet should be released for 30 seconds every 20 minutes to allow fresh blood to enter the extremity.

If more than an hour will elapse before antivenom can be injected, use incision and suction. With a sharp, sterile instrument (sterilized with a match if no other means is available) make two cuts, each not more than ½ inch long and ¼inch deep. The cuts should be made over the fang marks, lengthwise along the arm or leg, and must not injure tendons, muscles, blood vessels, or nerves. Suction may be performed by suction cup, if available, or by mouth and continued for at least 30 minutes. The sooner suction is started the better. If an hour has passed since the bite was inflicted, incision and suction should not be used.

Antivenom should be given as soon as possible. This is best done by a physician because of difficulties that may arise from reactions to the serum. It should be administered as first aid only if medical assistance is not available and it is necessary to save the life of the victim.

Treat the victim for shock. It may be necessary to give artificial respiration. Men have been kept alive for two hours after they became unconscious and have been saved by delayed injection of antivenom.

What not to do: Morphine should not be given for pain when the venom is the type that affects the nervous system. Don't give alcohol, or use ice pack or ice water.

If you are alone and have been bitten by a snake, keep your emotions under control. If you can kill the snake and look for fangs, do so. If not, apply a tourniquet two to four inches above the site of the bite, incise the wound, and suck to remove the poison. Remain as quiet as possible and keep the wound lower than your heart.

If pain is great, if there is swelling, numbness, tingling, or continued oozing of blood at the bite site, you can be fairly sure that the snake is poisonous. If it is evident that no help is coming, then walk slowly with a minimum of exertion.

Spiders and Scorpions

Tarantulas and black widows are probably the most common of the poisonous spiders. The black widow spider bite causes pain almost at once, and the pain spreads quickly from the region of the bite to the muscles of the back, shoulders, chest, abdomen, and limbs. The pain is usually accompanied by severe spasms of the abdominal muscles.

A bite from any other poisonous spider may be felt as a sharp sting, but it is not usually accompanied by severe pain. About half an hour after the bite, the victim begins to feel painful muscle cramps near the bite, which soon spread to other muscles of the body. Shock usually develops at about the same time, though it may be delayed for as much as an hour or two. The victim becomes restless and anxious. He may be very thirsty. Nausea and vomiting may occur.

Scorpions have a stinger and venom sac located in their tail. Their sting causes immediate, intense pain. The area near the sting will become numb and paralyzed.

First aid measures for spider bites and scorpion stings are limited. Clean the wound and surrounding area with alcohol to rid them of bacteria. Treat the victim for shock; keep him lying down, quiet and warm. Severe muscle cramps and pain may somtimes be relieved by warm-water baths. Do not apply suction and do not incise (cut the wound in an attempt to remove the poison. It does no good.

Splinters

If a splinter is under the skin where it can be seen, it can be removed by pulling it out the same way it went in. Clean the broken skin, paint with an antiseptic, and cover with a sterile dressing.

Transportation of the Injured

Take these precautions before transporting an injured person:

Give necessary first aid. Locate all injuries to the best of your ability. Treat serious bleeding, breathing trouble, shock, fractures, sprains, and dislocations. Relieve the victim's pain, and make him as comfortable as possible.

Use a regular stretcher. If you must use an improvised stretcher, be sure that it is strong enough to hold the victim. Have enough men to carry the stretcher; don't drop the victim.

Fasten the patient in the stretcher so that he cannot slip, slide, or fall off. Tie his feet together unless injuries make this impracticable (figure 19–10).

Use blankets, garments, or other material to pad the stretcher and to protect the victim from exposure.

An injured person should usually lie on his back while being moved, but one having difficulty in breathing because of a chest wound may be more comfortable if his head and shoulders are slightly raised. Fracture cases should be moved very carefully, so that the injury will not be made worse. A man with a severe injury to the back of the head should be kept on his side. A patient should always be carried feet first, unless there is some special reason for carrying him head first.

The *three-man lift* and the *fireman's lift* are recommended ways to lift an injured person, and the *tied-hands crawl* is used to transport a patient under special circumstances.

Figure 19–10. Stokes stretcher being lifted into a rescue helicopter.

Three-Man Lift 1 (Figure 19–11)

Number one man takes head and shoulders of victim; number two, back and buttocks; number three, legs and feet. Number one says, "Ready, lift," all lift together and keep man's body straight. If the man has a chest wound, he is placed on his stomach; if a stomach wound, on his back with knees bent.

Fireman's Lift (Figure 19–12)

Turn the patient face down. Kneel above his head, facing his shoulders (A). Pass both your hands under his armpits and lift him to his knees, then slide your hands down lower and clasp them around his back (B). Raise him to a standing position, stick your right leg between his legs (C), take his right wrist in your left hand and swing his arm around the back of your neck, holding him close to you. Put your right arm between his thighs (D), stoop quickly, pull his trunk across your shoulders, and straighten up (E).

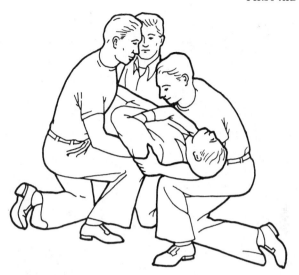

Figure 19–11. Transporting an injured man; three-man lift.

To lower the patient, kneel on your left knee. Grasp his left knee with your right hand. Slide him around in front of you and down your right thigh into a sitting position. Shift your hands to his head and place him gently on his back.

Tied-Hands Crawl (Figure 19–13)

Use this method when you must remain close to the deck, or when you must have both hands free for climbing a ladder.

Lay the patient on his back. Lie on your back alongside him and to his left. Grasp his right arm above the elbow with your right hand. With your left hand, grasp the same arm below the elbow. Entwine your legs with his and roll over upon your chest, pulling him over onto your back. Now pull his free hand (the left one) under your armpit. Tie his wrists together with a handkerchief or any other available material, then crawl forward.

Stokes Stretcher

This is a wire basket supported by iron or aluminum rods. It is adaptable to a variety of uses, and will hold a person securely in place even if it is tipped or turned. The Stokes stretcher is generally used aboard ship,

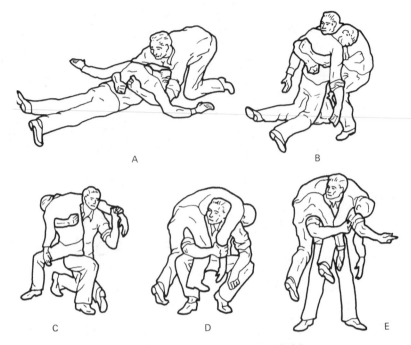

Figure 19–12. Transporting an injured man; fireman's lift.

Figure 19–13. Transporting an injured man; tied-hands crawl.

and especially for transferring injured persons to and from boats. It can be used to rescue men from the water and for direct ship-to-ship transfer of injured persons.

The stretcher should be padded with two blankets placed lengthwise, so that one will be under each of the victim's legs, and a third folded in half and placed in the upper part of the stretcher to protect the patient's head and shoulders. He should be lowered gently into the stretcher and made as comfortable as possible. His feet must be fastened to the end of the stretcher so that he will not slide up and down, and he must be fastened into the stretcher by straps over his chest, hips, and knees. The straps should go *over* the blanket or other covering.

CHAPTER 20
Safety

Safety must be practiced 24 hours a day. Danger exists in every operation ashore and afloat. Going to sea involves working with powerful machinery, high-speed equipment, intensely high-temperature-pressure steam, volatile and exotic fuels and propellants, heavy lifts (figure 20–1), expolsives, high electrical voltages, and the unpredictable, elemental forces of wind and wave. It is the responsibility of everyone to observe all safety precautions.

Every piece of machinery and equipment must be operated in a safe manner. Special safety precautions have been provided for all equipment. Other specific safety regulations are contained in various manuals, the *Ship's Organization Manual* for each type of ship, and station orders. Learn those that pertain to your job, ship, or station.

Accidents are caused by inattention to the job, lack of good preparation, and failure to comply with known and specified safety rules. Overanxiousness causes many accidents. So do weakness and fatigue—in machinery, materials, and in human beings. Remember, accidents don't happen—they are caused.

Calculated Risks

Much of the work you do in the Coast Guard will be purely routine in nature, but at times, in order for your ship or unit to reach its objective, there will be risk involved.

If the objective is important enough, and if the chance of success is a reasonable one, the risk must be taken. This is called a calculated risk. Coast Guardsmen often must take calculated risks. But there is a big difference between a calculated risk and an unnecessary risk. If

Figure 20–1. Working aloft—one hand for the ship, one for yourself.

you go out in a storm in a small boat to effect a rescue, you must take the calculated risk of the boat capsizing. If, however, you fail to wear a life jacket on such a mission, you are taking a wholly unnecessary risk of drowning. The man who opens a hatch cover, fails to secure the stanchion with a toggle pin, and then walks away, is not taking a calculated risk; he is setting a trap for a shipmate.

FUNDAMENTALS OF SAFETY

The following common-sense guides are the fundamentals of safety: constant planning for safe conditions; education to create safety awareness and recognition of observed hazards; training in safe practices and methods of operation; supervision to enforce proper procedures; and inspections leading to the removal of hazards and unsafe methods.

Neglect of minor safety details and failure to follow proper procedures in small matters can build up into major disasters. Good housekeeping practices can promote safety. Safety shoes, hard hats, life vests and goggles, if used at the required times, will help prevent many injuries and deaths.

Observance of the following general safety instructions will help both you and your shipmates.

Aircraft Handling

Most of the common-sense precautions required around motor vehicles apply to working with aircraft, but jet engines and helicopter rotors present special safety hazards, as do flight-deck operations.

Propellers and helicopter rotors may be nearly invisible. A helicopter's rotor tips cover a wide area and may dip close to the deck when it lands. Keep clear of all props and rotors.

Engine noise of the plane you are watching will drown out the noise of the one you are not watching. Don't move without looking in all directions; don't direct all of your attention to one aircraft.

Jet blast can burn a man, knock him to the ground, or blow him over the side.

Jet suction is equally dangerous. Keep clear of the intake scoops; men have been sucked into them and badly injured.

Jet engines and their exhausts may take a half hour to cool down after shutoff. Don't touch them without asbestos gloves.

Aviation gasoline and all jet fuels are dangerous. See precautions under "Volatile Fuels."

Aircraft Passengers (see "Smoking")

Life vests must be worn during all landplane flights made beyond gliding distance of land.

A safety belt and shoulder harness should be secured before takeoff and during flight, except when their removal is authorized by the pilot or when necessary activities require that they be removed temporarily.

Parachutes or an attachable-type parachute harness must be worn by all personnel in all single-engine airplanes. They may be omitted in multi-engine transport types operating in air carrier status and able to maintain level flight with 50 percent of the engines inoperative.

Passengers and flight personnel must obey all orders of the pilot or officer in charge of the flight.

Passengers are forbidden to carry photoflash bulbs or any explosive materials.

Ammunition (see "Underway Replenishment")

All persons required to handle ammunition must be instructed in safety regulations, methods of handling, storage, and uses of all ammunition and explosive ordnance with which they may work.

No one will be permitted to inspect, prepare, or adjust live ammunition and explosives until he thoroughly understands the duties, precautions, and hazards involved.

Before beginning any operation involving ammunition, men must be familiar with the characteristics of the materials involved, the equipment to be used, safety regulations, and the hazards of fire or explosion.

All persons supervising the inspection, care, preparation, handling, use, or disposal of ammunition or explosives shall see that all regulations and instructions are observed, remain vigilant throughout the operation, and instruct and warn subordinates of the need for care and constant vigilance.

Smoking is not permitted in magazines or in the immediate vicinity of handling or loading operations. Matches, lighters, and spark- or flame-producing devices are not permitted in spaces in which ammunition or explosives are present.

Crews working with explosives or ammunition shall be limited to the minimum number required to perform the operation. Unauthorized personnel shall not be permitted in magazines or in the vicinity of handling or loading operations, except for inspections. Only inert ammunition should be used for drills.

Supervisors should require the maintenance of good housekeeping in explosives spaces and should allow only explosives, containers, and authorized handling equipment in such spaces.

Authorized Operators (see "Hot Work" and "Special Equipment")

Boats, General Operation

In motor launches, only the coxswain and the boat officer or senior line officer may ride on the coxswain's flat. No more than two persons may be on the deck at one time.

Boat crews must keep their stations, especially in bad weather; during such times vigilance is most needed.

Boats must always be properly loaded for the sea state. In heavy weather, boats are loaded down slightly by the stern, and passengers and crew wear life jackets. Passengers must remain seated when a boat is under way and keep arms inboard of gunwales.

The coxswain, or boat officer when assigned, shall be responsible to the commanding officer for the enforcement of these regulations.

No boat shall be loaded beyond the capacities established by the commanding officer and published in the boat bill without specific permission of the command duty officer, and then only in an emergency.

No person shall smoke in a boat under any circumstances.

No person other than those specifically designated by the engineer officer shall operate or attempt to operate a boat engine; test, remove, or charge a boat's battery; tamper in any way with the boat's electrical system; or fuel a ship's boat.

No person shall be assigned as a member of a boat crew unless he is a qualified swimmer; has demonstrated a practical knowledge of boat seamanship, Rules of the Road, and boat safety regulations; and has been duly qualified for his particular assignment by the first lieutenant.

All persons in boats being hoisted in or out or hung in the davits shall wear vest-type, inherently buoyant life preservers properly secured and safety helmets with the chin straps unbuckled.

No person shall board a boat from a boat boom unless someone is standing by on deck or in a boat at the same boom.

All members of a boat's crew shall wear rubber-soled canvas shoes in the boat.

Fueling instructions must be posted in all boats, and passengers must be kept clear of the boat while it is being refueled.

Maximum operating speeds must be posted permanently in all boats.

Standard equipment listed in the allowance list must be in boats at all times.

Prescribed lights must be displayed by all boats under way between sunset and daylight or in reduced visibility.

Life buoys must be carried in each boat, secured in such a manner that they can be easily broken out for use.

All boats must carry enough life preservers to accommodate each person aboard. The life preservers must be readily available when rough seas, reduced visibility, or other hazards threaten.

All boats leaving a ship shall carry local charts with courses to and from their destination, boat compasses, and fog signaling equipment.

No boat will be dispatched or permitted to proceed unless released by the OOD, who must determine that crew and passengers are wearing life preservers, when advisable, and that weather and sea conditions are suitable for small-boat operations.

Recall and lifeboat signals and standing orders must be posted in boats where they may be easily read by the coxswains.

Boats, Hoisting and Lowering

The slings used for lifting a boat with a crane are given a 100 percent overload test when made up and are marked with a copper band certifying that the test was conducted. Slings for one type of boat should not be improvised for use on another type.

Slings must be inspected before each lift and should never be used if they look worn. Fittings must be inspected before each lift to see that cotter pins are in place and nuts tightened and secured on the shackle bolts used with the main hoisting slings.

When hoisting or lowering a boat, all unnecessary people must be kept clear of the area. Only qualified operators will handle any lifting equipment. Only those men who are absolutely necessary shall be in the boat, and they must use the life lines. Lifting hooks and hoisting fittings must be secure.

Cargo Handling (see also "Underway Replenishment")

Open hatches in use should be cleared of any adjacent loose equipment that might fall into them, and traffic about the hatch must be restricted to the off side from where cargo is being worked. The working area must be roped off from traffic.

Hatch beams or other structures in the way of hatches where cargo is being worked must be secured by bolts or removed. Men moving hatch beams must wear a safety line, which must be tended at all times.

Experienced personnel must supervise the topping and lowering of booms. Before making any repairs or replacing any of the gear, booms should always be lowered on deck. When life lines are removed, emergency lines should be rigged and everyone cautioned to keep clear.

Closed Compartments

Danger of explosion, poisoning, and suffocation exist in any closed compartment or poorly ventilated space, such as tanks, cofferdams, voids, and bilges. No person shall enter such compartment or space until applicable safety reglations have been complied with, all danger has been eliminated or reduced to the lowest practicable minimum, and the following precautions have been observed.

The seal around the manhole or other opening should be broken before all holddown bolts or other fastenings are completely removed, to reduce any pressure built up inside, and to make it possible to quickly secure the cover again if gas or water is present.

No person should enter any such space without permission from the responsible division officer.

No naked light or spark-producing electrical apparatus should be carried into a closed space.

Safety lamps used in closed compartments must be in good operating condition. If the lamp fades or flares up, the space is dangerous and should not be entered.

No person should work in such a compartment without a life line attached and a responsible man stationed outside the compartment to tend the line and maintain communications.

Compressed Gases

Compressed gas cylinders used aboard ship are identified by color.

Yellow: flammable materials—acetylene, hydrogen, and petroleum.

Brown: poisonous materials—chlorine, carbon monoxide, sulphur dioxide.

Green: oxidizing material, particularly pure oxygen.

Blue: anesthetics and materials with similarly harmful fumes.

Gray: physically dangerous materials; gas under high pressure or gas that asphyxiates if breathed in confined areas, such as CO_2, nitrogen, and helium.

Red: fire protection materials, especially carbon dioxide.

Black, with green striping: compressed air, helium-oxygen, and oxygen–carbon dioxide mixtures.

All flammable gases become highly explosive when mixed in certain proportions with air. Even an inert gas like CO_2 can cause an explosion if the cylinder becomes too hot or cracks because of rough handling. The following rules should be obeyed without exception:

Gas cylinders and air cylinders must be kept away from high-temperature areas. Oil should never be allowed to come in contact with oxygen cylinder valves, since a violent explosion could result.

Gas cylinders must not be handled roughly, dropped, clanked against each other, or handled or transported without the cylinder valve caps in place.

Flames or sparks should not be permitted in any closed spaces where acetylene or oxygen tanks are stored. Ammonia and poisonous gases must be handled with caution. There is always the possibility that the gas is leaking from a loose valve or seeping through a defective connection.

In case of fire or other disaster, gas cylinders should quickly be moved from the danger area and, if necessary, thrown overboard.

Dangerous Materials (see "Semisafe and Dangerous Materials")

Electrical and Electronic Equipment

This includes generators, electrically powered machinery and mechanisms, power cables, controllers, transformers and associated equipment, radars, radios, power amplifiers, antennas, electronic warfare equipment, computers, and associated controls. The most important safety precaution with all such equipment is *never work alone.*

No person shall operate, repair, or adjust an electrical or electronic equipment unless he has been assigned that duty, except in definite emergencies, and then only when no qualified operator is present. (Electric light and bulkhead electric fan switches are exempted.)

No person shall operate, repair, or adjust electrical and electronic equipment unless he has demonstrated a practical knowledge of its operation and repair and of all applicable safety regulations, and then only when duly qualified by the cognizant head of department.

No person shall paint over, destroy, or mutilate any markings, name plates, cable tags, or other identification on any electrical or electronic equipment.

No person shall hang anything on, or secure a line to, any power cable, antenna, wave guide, or other electrical or electronic equipment.

Only authorized portable electric equipment that has been tested by the electric shop shall be used.

Electric equipment shall be de-energized and checked with a voltage tester or voltmeter to ensure it is de-energized before servicing or repairing it, if possible. Circuit breakers and switches of de-energized circuits shall be locked or placed on the "off" position while work is in progress, and a suitable warning tag shall be attached thereto.

When work on live circuits or equipment is required, the person performing the work must be insulated from the ground and must follow all practical safety measures. If possible, rubber gloves shall be worn. Another man shall stand by to cut the circuit and render first aid.

Personal electrical or electronic equipment used aboard ship must be approved by the engineer officer and the executive officer.

Never intentionally take a shock of any voltage. Even 115 volts can kill.

Bare lamps or fixtures with exposed lamps shall not be installed in machinery spaces. Only enclosed fixtures shall be installed in such spaces to minimize the hazard of fire caused by flammable fuels making contact with exposed lamps.

No person shall go aloft near energized antennas unless it is determined in advance that no danger exists. If any danger exists from rotating antennas, induced voltages in rigging and superstructure, or from high-power radiation causing direct biological injury, the equipment shall be secured and a suitable warning tag shall be attached to the main supply switches. These precautions shall also be observed if any other antenna is in the vicinity, as on an adjacent ship (see "Radiation Hazards" and "Tagout Procedures").

Electrical and electronic safety precautions must be conspicuously posted in appropriate spaces, personnel must be instructed and drilled in their observance, and all electrical and electronics personnel must be qualified in first aid treatment for electrical shock. Emergency resuscitation procedures must be posted in all spaces containing electronic equipment.

Rubber matting must be installed in front of and behind propulsion control cubicles, power and lighting switchboards, IC switchboards, test switchboards, fire control switchboards, ship announcing system amplifiers, and control panels; areas in and around radio, radar, sonar, and countermeasures equipment spaces that may be entered while servicing or tuning energized equipment; and around work benches in electrical and electronic shops where equipment is tested or repaired. A "shorting stick" should be available in every working space for electronic equipment.

Electrically Powered Tools

Electric shock and physical injury from flying particles accompany the use of portable electrically powered or pneumatic tools. The rough use that electrically powered tools receive and the metal construction of the ship increase the possibility of shorts and grounds and present a constant hazard to users.

No person shall be issued or use a portable power tool unless specifically authorized by his division officer, and then only after he has demonstrated knowledge of the tool's operation and applicable safety regulations.

No portable electric tool shall be issued unless it has been carefully inspected and checked for proper insulation resistance.

No person shall use a portable electric or pneumatic tool for any purpose other than those specifically authorized by his department head.

No person shall use a portable electric tool unless it is equipped with a three-conductor portable cable and a three-prong grounded plug. The equipment must be checked by an electrician for proper connections and conductivity.

Sparking portable electric tools must not be used in any place where flammable vapors, gases, liquids, or exposed explosives are present. These tools should be stored in a clean, dry place with the cord loosely coiled.

Cords to electrical tools must not come in contact with sharp objects, oil or grease, hot surfaces or chemicals. Cords must not be allowed to kink and must not be left where they might be run over, be pinched by a hatch cover or closing door, or cause a tripping hazard. Damaged cords should be replaced, not patched.

All persons using electrically powered or pneumatic wire brushes, chippers, sanders, or grinders shall wear goggles or eye shields.

Fire and Explosion Prevention

Stow and protect all essential combustibles so as to reduce the probability that they will cause or contribute to destructive fires.

Avoid accumulation of oil or other flammable materials in bilges and in inaccessible areas. Any such accumulations must be flushed out or removed at the first opportunity.

Stow paint, paint brushes, rags, paint thinners, and solvents only in authorized locations.

Do not use compressed air to force oil, gasoline, or other combustible liquids out of containers.

Make regular daily inspections for fire hazards.

Fire Watch (see "Hot Work")

Forklifts

Only authorized personnel should operate forklifts.

Check the condition of the equipment prior to operation.

Keep feet and hands inside the running line of the forklift.

Drive with dry hands; ensure hands are not greasy or oily.

Slow down on wet or slippery decks and corners.

No person other than the forklift operator should ride the forklift, unless an additional permanent seat is provided.

Do not stand under loads being hoisted or lowered by forklifts.

Transport all cargo "upgrade" whether going upgrade or downgrade (i.e., back down the grade with the load facing "upgrade"). Transport all loads with the lifting rails tipped back. Lower and rest forks on the deck when not in operation. Keep forks four to six inches above deck, empty or loaded, when moving. Do not exceed the load capacity.

Never bump or push stacks of cargo to straighten them. Forks must be all the way under the load. Inspect load before lifting; an unstable load should be repiled or banded. Once the load is lifted and moving, it is too late.

Come to a full stop before reversing direction of travel.

Set the parking brake when parking the forklift, park it in a fore-and-aft position near the center of the ship, and secure it with adequate chains or cables. Use only special personnel pallets for lifting personnel.

Fuel Oil

While oil is being received on board, no naked light, lighted cigarettes, or electrical apparatus that is liable to spark should be permitted within

50 feet of an oil hose, tank, or compartment containing the tank or the vent from a tank. Matches or cigarette lighters shall not be carried by anyone involved in the operations.

No naked light, lighted cigarettes, or electrical fuzes, switches (unless enclosed type), steel tools, or other apparatus that is liable to cause sparks should be permitted at any time in a compartment that contains a fuel-oil tank, fuel-oil pumps, or fuel-oil piping. Smoking may be permitted in the engine rooms and on the fireroom floor in front of the furnaces of a boiler that is in operation. Electric lamps used in such compartments must have gas-tight globes. The term "naked light" includes oil lanterns, open lanterns, lighted candles, and matches. Flashlights must not be used inside a fuel compartment.

No person shall be allowed to enter a fuel-oil tank until the tank has been freed of vapor, until he has obtained permission from the safety officer or CO, required precautions have been taken, and he is wearing a life line attended by a person outside of the tank.

Fuel oil must not be heated to a temperature higher than 120° F.

Compartments and tanks used for storage of fuel oil should not be painted on the inside.

Whenever a fuel-oil tank is to be entered, or any work is to be done in it, or any lights other than portable explosion-proof electric lights are used, and when work is to be done in the vicinity of an open tank or of pipes, all such tanks and pipes must be cleared of vapor after the fuel oil has been removed.

Gasoline (see "Volatile Fuel")

Hand Tools (see also "Electrically Powered Tools," "Pneumatic Tools")

Chisels

Cold chisels should be held between the thumb and other four fingers; on horizontal cuts, the palm should be up. Do not use a burred chisel, or one with a mushroomed head, or one that is not properly tempered or sharpened. Wear goggles, and allow no one near enough to be hit by flying chips.

Wood chisels should be free of cracks. Don't use one with a mushroomed head. Cup the chisel handle in the palm of your hand and exert pressure *away* from your body. Make all cuts in the direction *away* from your body. Be sure that no other person is close enough to be injured if the chisel should slip.

Hammers

Select the right hammer for the job. The head should be wedged securely and squarely on the handle and neither the head nor the handle should be chipped, cracked, or broken.

Keep the hammer clean and free of oil or grease; otherwise, it might slip from your hands or the face of the hammer might glance off the object being struck.

Grasp a hammer handle firmly near the end, and keep your eye on the point to be struck. Strike so that the hammer face hits the object squarely.

Heavy Weather

During heavy weather conditions, do not go onto weather decks except for urgent duties.

Extra life lines, protective nets, and snaking should be in place during heavy weather, particularly for replenishment or recovery of a man overboard.

Helicopters

Only authorized personnel shall be allowed in the helicopter area; all others shall remain clear or below decks. Personnel engaged in flight operations shall wear appropriate safety helmets. Passengers shall be led to and from a helicopter by a member of the handling crew or flight crew. Loose gear in the vicinity shall be stowed or secured to the deck. All personnel shall be instructed concerning the shrapnel effect caused when rotor blades strike a solid object.

Hot Work

Hot work includes welding, flame cutting, the use of open-flame equipment, or any heating of metal to or above a red heat. Hot work must be done only by qualifed men. Hot work near flammable or explosive materials can create a dangerous situation. No person shall undertake a job involving hot work unless and until the marine chemist (or his authorized representative) has inspected the place on the day the job is to be done, indicated that the applicable safety regulations have been complied with, indicated that men can work in the area without danger of poisoning or suffocation, and indicated that the hot work can be undertaken without danger of fire or explosion.

No hot work shall be permitted without the permission of the CO when under way or the duty officer when in port.

Where flammable or explosive materials will be exposed to welding or cutting operations, a fire watch must be posted on both sides of a deck or bulkhead if necessary. Fire watches must remain on their stations for at least 30 minutes after a job is completed to ensure no smoldering fires have been started. Fire extinguishing equipment shall be maintained near all welding and cutting operations.

Welding or burning is not permitted in compartments where explosives are stored.

Personal Flotation Devices

PFDs must be worn at times when there is a possibility that men could slip, fall, be thrown, or be carried into the water, and always under the following conditions:

Working over the side in port and at sea, on stages, on boatswain's chairs, or in boats or punts. "Over the side" means any part of the ship outside the life lines or bulwarks.

On weather decks during heavy weather, even to go from one station to another.

Handling lines or other deck equipment during transfers between ships, fueling under way, and towing.

During buoy, rescue, or towing operations.

In boats being raised or lowered, while entering boats from a boom or Jacob's ladder, in boats under way, and in rough water or low visibility. Ring buoys with a line and a light attached must be available for use when a sea ladder or a Jacob's ladder is being used.

Transfer by highline or helicopter. Don life jackets prior to getting into the transfer seat or sling.

Life Lines and Ladders

No person shall lean on, sit on, stand on, or climb over any life line either in port or when under way. Men working over the side in port may climb over life lines when necessary, but only if they are wearing life preservers.

No life line shall be dismantled or removed without specific permission of the first lieutenant, and then only if temporary life lines are promptly rigged. Life lines must remain rigged from sunset to sunrise *without exception*.

No person shall hang or secure any weight or line to any life line unless authorized by the commanding officer.

Ladders must not be unshipped (removed) without permission from the department head in charge, and all accesses must be carefully and adequately roped off, or suitable railings installed.

Work on ladders must, when possible, be performed during the hours of least traffic.

Lights

When in port at night, weather decks shall be well lighted. All accommodation ladders, gangways, and brows shall also be well lighted.

Lines and Rigging (see also "Synthetic Lines")

Lines or rigging under heavy strain should be eased to prevent overstress or parting. Men must keep clear of heavily stressed line or wire, and under no circumstances stand in the bight of a line or on a taut fall.

When hoisting heavy loads overhead, the person responsible shall warn everyone away from the area directly beneath.

Boat falls, highlines, and mooring lines should be end-for-ended or changed at the first indication of wear or overstress to avoid damage or serious injury.

Lines not in use should be carefully made up and stowed clear of walkways and passages.

Lines must never be made fast to capstans or gypsy heads, but only to fittings provided for that purpose, such as cleats or bitts.

Steadying or frapping lines should be used on boat falls and large lifts to prevent uncontrolled swinging or twisting.

Line-Throwing Gun

A line-throwing gun may be used in replenishment or in rescue operations. Line-throwing gun-crew members must wear red helmets and highly visible red jackets for easy identification.

Gun lines must be properly prepared for running. For the gun line, a loose coil in a bucket is preferable to a spindle, but a faking board is better. Reel-wound shotline is best.

Special instructions will be issued for UNREP operations.

Machinery

This includes all engines, motors, generators, hydraulic systems, or other apparatus supplying power or motive force.

Except in definite emergencies, and then only when a qualified operator is not present, no person shall operate, repair, adjust, or otherwise tamper with any machinery and associated controls, unless assigned by his head of department to perform a specific function on such machinery.

No person shall be assigned to operate, repair, or adjust any machinery unless he has demonstrated a practical knowledge of its operation, repair, and safety regulations, and then only when qualified by the cognizant head of department.

Machinery undergoing repair shall have its power or activation sources tagged-out to prevent accidental application of power.

Materials Handling

Safety shoes or toe guards must be worn when handling heavy stores or equipment (figure 20–2).

Gloves must be worn when carrying, lifting, or moving objects that have sharp edges or projecting points; always remove rings when wearing gloves.

Materials must not be thrown from platforms or trucks to the floor or ground. Use suitable lowering equipment.

When lifting or lowering operations are being performed by several persons, they shall be done only on signal from one man and only after everyone is in the clear.

Don't overload hand trucks. On a ramp or incline keep the load below you—*pull* the *load up,* and *push* it *down*.

To lift objects, stand close to the load, with your feet solidly placed and slightly apart. Bend your knees, grasp the object firmly, and lift by straightening your legs, keeping your back as straight as possible.

Motor Vehicles

At times you may be assigned to drive an official car as part of your duty. Sooner or later almost everyone in uniform acquires "wheels," either a car or motorcycle, for use on liberty. Whatever you drive, and whether on duty or liberty, handle the vehicle with care, because the most dangerous place in the world is out on the public highways.

It is commonly believed that young people make good drivers be-

Figure 20–2. A Coast Guard buoy tender setting a standard radar reflecting, lighted buoy. Note that men handling a buoy wear hard hats, life jackets, and gloves.

cause they have faster reaction time than older people, but the casualty figures for those under 25 prove that good reactions are not nearly as important as good judgment.

There is no prohibition against anyone owning a vehicle, but base and station regulations will make it difficult for an irresponsible or reckless driver to keep his vehicle on government property. Traffic violations off base, of course, can put you in jail.

The usual statistics on safe stopping distance, number of highway deaths, and amount of annual property loss are not quoted here because statistics will not make you a safe driver. The only thing that can make you a safe driver is determination to become one, rather than a statistic. Use seat belts and shoulder harness if the vehicle has them. Take a course in defensive driving if your unit offers it.

Motorcycles

If you are a biker, wear a helmet and observe these rules.

Ride as though you were invisible—some car drivers may not see you.

Keep your distance—50 feet from another vehicle at 20 mph, more than 300 feet at 50 mph.

Keep alert. Be prepared for sudden stops, traffic coming from the left at intersections, and vehicles pulling out from the curb.

Brake properly; rear brake first. Brake gently on slippery surfaces, and brake before entering a turn, not in it.

Watch out for objects in the road, children playing, dogs and other animals, vehicles at the curb opening left-hand doors.

Never carry anything in your hands; use saddlebags or a rack.

When possible, cross railroad tracks and bridge expansion joints at a 90-degree angle; when crossing steel gratings, reduce speed and do not accelerate or brake unless necessary.

Painting

Pigment in paint usually contains lead, which is poisonous if absorbed through the skin or inhaled as dust or particles, as when a spray gun is used. The vehicle in paint is a volatile solvent that can cause irritation of the nose and throat, headache, dizziness, apparent drunkenness, loss of memory, and a staggering gait. If any of these symptoms appear, remove the victim to an area of clean, fresh air, or unconsciousness and death may result.

When painting, parts of the body not covered by clothing should be coated with vaseline.

When spray painting, use respirators and change the filter frequently; use fresh air supplied through a face mask.

Wash hands and clean under fingernails to avoid lead poisoning; use soap, not solvent.

Change soiled clothing as soon as possible.

Keep flames away from open paint.

Spark-producing operations are prohibited in compartments when spray painting.

Protective Clothing

When working on or near moving machinery, do not wear clothing with loose ends or loops that might be caught by shafts, gears, belts, or pulleys.

Leather or other heavy gloves shall be worn when working on steam valves or other hot units.

When working near steam equipment, keep your shirt buttoned and sleeves rolled down to reduce the danger of steam burns.

Protective goggles or helmet and a leather welding jacket must be worn when brazing, welding, or cutting. Goggles shall be worn whenever working with substances dangerous to eyes. Respirators shall be worn when working where fumes or paint dust are present.

Only shoes with rubber heels will be worn aboard ship, except that boat crew members shall wear rubber-soled canvas or boat shoes in ship's or shore unit boats. Safety shoes must be worn in designated foot-hazardous areas. No shoes with taps or other metal devices shall be worn aboard ship.

Pneumatic Tools

These tools are powered by high-pressure compressed air and include chipping hammers, drills, wire brushes, etc. Operate a pneumatic hammer in a careful and safe manner, and never point it at another person. All hammers are equipped with a safety tool holder to keep the tool in place. These devices are frequently inspected; the man who loses one is subject to disciplinary action. Never play around with an air hose or try to "goose" someone with one. Don't let an air hose under pressure get away from you; it can whip about like a loose fire hose and cause serious injury.

All persons using pneumatic hammers, chippers, drills, or brushes shall wear goggles or eye shields (figure 20–3).

Wear gloves when operating an air hammer, and reduce body shock by grasping the hammer as lightly as possible.

Figure 20–3. The first lieutenant can always issue another pair of eye goggles; there are no spare eyes in the sick bay.

Radiation

Radioactive material is present in nuclear reactors and warheads, in the sources used for calibration of radiation monitoring equipment, and in certain electronic tubes.

Radiation sources shall remain installed in the radiation detection equipment or shall be stowed in their shipping containers in a locked storage.

Spare radioactive electronic tubes and fission chambers shall be stored in clearly marked containers and locked stowage.

All hands shall scrupulously obey radiation warning signs and shall remain clear of radiation barriers.

Radiation Hazards (RadHaz)

The power generated by electronic equipment can result in biological injury to men. Where such danger is possible, an *r-f (radio frequency) radiation hazard* exists, and *warnings* must be posted.

Before a man goes aloft to work on masts or stacks, he must obtain permission from the OOD. He will usually have to have a chit stating that radio and radar transmitters have been secured and tagged, "secured, men aloft." The following specific precautions must be observed to avoid hazardous intensity levels.

No visual inspection of any opening, such as a wave guide, that emits r-f energy, is allowed unless the equipment is definitely secured for inspection.

Operating and maintenance men must inspect all r-f hazard signs posted in the operating area to ensure that the equipment is operating in such a manner that nearby personnel are not subjected to hazardous radiation.

All personnel must be aware of and observe r-f warning signs in a specific area.

When the possibility of accidental exposure exists while the antenna is radiating, a man must be stationed topside, within view of the antenna (but well out of the beam), and in communication with the operator.

Radiation hazard warning signs must be permanently posted and also used to temporarily restrict access to certain parts of the ship where equipment is radiating.

Safety Devices

Mechanical, electrical, and electronic safety devices shall be inspected at suitable regular intervals and additionally as unusual circumstances or conditions warrant. When practicable, such inspection shall include operation of the safety device while the equipment or unit is in actual operation. Machinery or equipment shall not be operated unless the safety devices are in proper working condition.

No person shall tamper with or render ineffective any safety device, interlock, ground strap, or similar device intended to protect the operators or the equipment.

Semisafe and Dangerous Materials

Semisafe materials are considered safe so long as contained in unopened, nonleaking containers. In the event of leakage, any spilled material must be cleaned up with reasonable promptness and the leaking containers disposed of. Common semisafe materials are diesel oil, grease, lubricating oil, metal polish, paint, safety matches, and wax.

Dangerous materials are materials involving a considerable fire hazard or having other dangerous characteristics, whether or not in sealed containers. Common dangerous materials are acids, alcohol, anticorrosive paint, bleaching powder (chlorinated lime), calcium hypochlorite, compressed gases, gasoline, kerosene, lacquer, paint thinner, paint stripping compound, paint drier, rust preventive compound, storage battery electrolyte, turpentine, and varnish.

All such materials shall be stowed in the paint and flammable liquids storeroom unless other designated stowage is provided. Naked lights and spark-emitting devices must not be used in compartments containing semisafe or dangerous materials.

Calcium hypochlorite and bleaching powder (chlorinated lime) must be stowed in a clean, cool, dry compartment or storeroom not adjacent to any magazine and safe from exposure to heat or moisture, isolated from flammable materials, and not in the same compartment with acids or other chemicals. Containers shall be inspected periodically to ensure they are tightly sealed and that exteriors of cans are free of rust. All defective containers must be removed from storage and the contents consumed by immediate use or otherwise disposed of. Bleach in plastic containers must be stowed in a covered metal container.

Sleeping Topside

Sleeping topside when the ship is under way shall be carefully supervised to ascertain that no cots are used and that there is no possibility of men rolling over the side.

Small Arms

Small arms are hand-held pistols, rifles, machine guns, line-throwing guns, and flare guns, of less than .50-caliber bore diameter.

No person shall be issued small arms unless he has demonstrated full knowledge of refined operational procedures and safety regulations.

No person shall load any small arm unless he intends and is required to use the weapon in the performance of duty.

Only designated personnel shall clean, disassemble, adjust, or repair small arms.

A small arm shall never be pointed at anyone unless it is intended to shoot him, nor in any direction where accidental discharge may do harm.

Smoking

No person shall smoke in any area or during any evolution described as follows:

> In holds, storerooms, gasoline tank compartments, gasoline pump rooms, voids, or trunks; in any shop or space where flammable liquids are being used or handled; in boats; in bunks or berths; in magazines, handling rooms, ready service rooms, or gun mounts; in gasoline control stations, oil relay tank rooms, and battery and charging rooms; in the film projection room, motion picture stowage, or photographic laboratory; when bleeding oxygen; in any area where vinyl or saran paint is being applied.
>
> In any area of the ship where ammunition is being handled, or when loading or unloading ammunition.
>
> In any part of the ship when receiving or transferring fuel oil, diesel oil, aviation gasoline, or other volatile fuel, except in spaces designated as smoking areas by the commanding officer.
>
> During general quarters, general drills, or emergencies, except as authorized by the commanding officer.
>
> When the word "the smoking lamp is out" is passed.

Smoking in Aircraft

Smoking is forbidden during fueling operations and whenever any gas fumes are detected in the aircraft; during all ground operations, take-offs, and landings; in the fuselage or in hull compartments that contain gasoline tanks, and in the cabin when cargo of a flammable or explosive nature is aboard; whenever oxygen equipment is in use; and during inspection of compartments where gas or other flammable fumes may have collected.

Special Equipment

All personnel handling special equipment such as gravity boat davits, winches, or booms must be thoroughly indoctrinated in the safety precautions for such equipment. Applicable safety precautions must be posted in the immediate vicinity. Only personnel who have been instructed in their duties and who have been specifically authorized by the first lieutenant are permitted to operate cranes, capstans, winches, and windlasses. Except in an emergency, operation of the machinery must be supervised by a responsible officer.

Synthetic Lines

An extra turn is required when securing synthetic fiber line to bitts, cleats, capstans, and other holding devices.

When easing out synthetic fiber lines from bitts, cleats, or other holding devices, extreme care shall be exercised owing to its high elasticity, rapid recovery, and low coefficient of friction.

No one shall stand in the direct line of pull of nylon line when heavy loads are applied.

Towing hawsers are usually nylon, and especially dangerous if they part under strain.

Tagout Procedures (see also "Electrical and Electronic Equipment," and "Working Aloft")

Proper use of tagout procedures for equipment and instruments can greatly improve the safety of personnel and help prevent costly accidents. Once a piece of equipment has been tagged, it cannot be untagged, operated, or used normally except by specified competent authority. General practice is as follows:

Red tag: used on valves or switches whose operation, owing to test condition or derangement, would cause danger to personnel or damage to equipment.

Orange-yellow tag: used for precautionary purposes where temporary special instructions or unusual precautions apply.

Red and orange tags: used to indicate defective, disconnected, or unreliable equipment, or uncalibrated instruments, respectively.

Toxic Materials

The issue and use of all materials that are potential health hazards shall be strictly controlled by the medical officer or other designated person.

Methyl alcohol, commonly used as duplicator fluid, paint thinner, cleaner, and antifreeze, is hazardous if inhaled, absorbed through the skin, or swallowed, and can cause permanent blindness or death. Methyl alcohol and products containing methyl alcohol shall only be released in the amount required and at the time needed to perform a specific job and used only in well-ventilated spaces and in such a manner that contact between alcohol and skin is avoided.

Halogenated hydrocarbons, normally used in solvents, refrigerants, fumigants, insecticides, paint removers, dry cleaning fluids and as propellants for pressurized containers, are hazardous if inhaled, swallowed, or absorbed by the skin. They shall be used only with adequate ventilation, by authorized personnel under close supervision, and in such a way that contact with the eyes and skin is prevented.

Underway Replenishment

Only essential personnel shall be allowed in the vicinity of any transfer station.

Life lines shall not be lowered unless absolutely necessary; if lowered, temporary life lines shall be rigged.

When line-throwing guns or bolos are used, all hands on the receiving ship shall take cover.

Topside personnel handling stores and lines shall wear safety helmets and orange-colored, inherently buoyant, vest-type life preservers. If safety helmets are equipped with a quick-acting, break-away device, the chin strap shall be fastened and worn under the chin. If not so equipped, the chin strap shall be fastened behind the head or worn unbuckled. Between-ship phone talkers must not secure neck-straps around their necks.

Cargo handlers must wear safety shoes. Those handling wire-bound or banded cases must wear work gloves.

Personnel shall keep clear of bights, handle lines from the inboard side, stay at least six feet from any block through which the lines pass, and keep clear of suspended loads and rig attachment points until loads have been landed on deck.

Care shall be taken to prevent the shifting of cargo. Personnel shall not get between any load and the rail.

Deck space in the vicinity of transfer stations shall be covered with a slip-resistant covering.

A lifebuoy watch shall be stationed well aft on the engaged side.

Provisions shall be made for rescuing a man overboard (i.e., if a life-guard ship is not available, a boat shall be kept ready).

Suitable measures must be taken to avoid hazards associated with radio frequencies. This is especially important when handling ammunition, gasoline, and other petroleum products.

Dangerous materials shall be transferred separately from one another and from other cargo, and stowed in designated storerooms as soon as possible.

When transferring personnel by highline, only a hand-tended manila line shall be used. All personnel being transferred shall wear orange-colored inherently buoyant life preservers (except patients in litters equipped with flotation gear). When water temperature is extremely low, immersion suits shall be worn, if possible.

When fuel oil is being received or transferred, no naked lights or electrical or mechanical apparatus shall be permitted within 50 feet of an oil hose in use, an open fuel tank, the vent terminal from a fuel tank, or an area where fuel oil or fuel oil vapors are or may be present. Portable electric lights used during fueling shall have explosion-proof protected globes and shall be thoroughly inspected for proper insulation and tested prior to use. On ships being fueled, portholes on the receiving side shall be closed and secured.

When transferring gasoline, a ground wire shall be connected between the two ships before the hose is brought aboard and shall be disconnected only after the hose is clear. Gasoline hoses shall be blown down by an inert gas upon the completion of any transfer.

Voids and Bilges (see "Closed Compartments")

Volatile Fuels

Aviation gasoline, motor gasoline, JP-4, and JP-5 give off a vapor that may travel along an air current for a considerable distance and then be ignited, the flash traveling back to the source of supply and causing an explosion or fire.

All spaces into which volatile fuel vapors issue shall be constantly and thoroughly ventilated.

No smoking and no naked lights shall be permitted in the vicinity of volatile fuel tanks or filling connections, drums, cans, stowage, piping, or spaces through which such piping passes.

Care shall be used to prevent the striking of sparks in locations where volatile fuel vapors may collect.

When carried in cans for ship's-own use, gasoline shall be stowed in the paint and flammable liquids storeroom or, if no such storeroom is provided, on the weather deck, so that the containers may be readily thrown overboard.

Gasoline shall be issued only under the supervision of a reliable man who shall make sure that all containers are securely closed and that all safety regulations are observed.

The metal nozzle at the end of a fuel hose shall be properly grounded to prevent sparks from static electricity.

Gasoline shall not be used for cleaning purposes under any circumstances.

Upon completion of loading or delivery, piping and hoses shall be carefully drained back into the ship's tanks or into containers which can be closed and sealed.

Welding (see "Hot Work")

Working Aloft

Men wishing to go aloft must obtain permission from the OOD, who must see that the following safety precautions are observed.

Power must be secured on all radio and radar antennas in the vicinity, and power switches tagged, "SECURED! MEN ALOFT."

The engineer officer must be instructed not to lift safety valves and, if men are to work in the vicinity, to secure steam to the whistle.

Men exposed to stack gases must wear protective breathing masks and remain there for only a brief time.

Men must use a short safety line secured around their waists and attached to the ship's structure at the same level.

Tools, buckets, paint pots, and brushes should be secured by a lanyard when used in work on masts, stacks, upper catwalks, weather decks, or sponsons that overhang areas where other men may be present.

Burning and welding, blowtorch operations, or the presence of any open flame are not permitted on or near a boatswain's chair unless the suspension ropes and sling are of steel. In such cases the sling shall be at least 1-inch diameter wire rope.

Every man using a boatswain's chair must be provided with and use a safety belt. This belt should be attached to a hanging life line secured to a fixed object.

Figure 20–4. When working over the side, safety lines tended on deck are a necessity; life preservers are added insurance.

Working Over the Side

Men working over the side must be instructed in all safety precautions before they will be permitted on scaffolding, stages, or in boatswain's chairs (figure 20–4), and the following precautions must be observed.

Men must be supervised by a competent petty officer, and qualified men must be assigned to tend safety lines.

Men working on stages, in boatswain's chairs, or in boats alongside shall wear life preservers and, with the exception of men in boats, shall be equipped with safety lines tended on deck.

Tools, buckets, paint pots, and brushes used by men working over the side shall be secured by lanyards to prevent their loss overboard and injury to personnel below.

Burning and welding, the use of a blowtorch, or the presence of any open flame are not permitted on or near float scaffolds unless suspension ropes are made of steel. No more than two men should work on a scaffold at the same time.

No person shall work over the side of the ship while under way without permission of the CO or without life jackets with safety lines around them, properly tended by someone on deck. Men working outside the life lines at sea or in port must wear life jackets with the straps fastened.

CHAPTER 21

Maintenance

The maintenance of material, aboard ship or at a shore station, is a full-time job; proper maintenance is highly important if the unit is to perform its assigned tasks properly. Maintenance involves more than just cleaning and painting, it also involves *planned* upkeep and repair of all equipment. For safety and efficiency, every item at the unit, from the most simple latch or valve to the most complicated electronic equipment, must be clean and operable (figure 21–1).

Every Coast Guard unit ashore or afloat has a planned system of maintenance that also includes cleanliness and safety.

GENERAL INSTRUCTIONS

Sweeping

The sweepings should never be swept into a scupper, but always into a dustpan, and then should be thrown into the trash or slop chute. The sweepers also clean out all ashtrays and wipe off all ladders in the ship. The ladders should be wiped off with a damp swab.

Swabbing

Spaces are cleaned with swabs and fresh water. Drying can be speeded by dry mopping afterwards and by having maximum ventilation. On topside decks, buckets of fresh water are used, or fresh water or fire-main salt-water hoses may be rigged. Scrubbing is done with long-handled brushes. On wooden decks, which very few ships have today, sand is sprinkled. Squilgees ("squee-gees") can be used to push water

Figure 21–1. Main propulsion machinery can be diesel-electric, steam turbine, direct diesel, or even outboard motors. All must be properly maintained if they are to provide power to Coast Guard operations.

into scuppers. A swab may be used after the squilgee to wipe up remaining water from corners. All swabs should be stowed in racks topside, never belowdecks or in cleaning lockers. Wear rubber boots to protect your shoes; salt water especially will shorten their life.

Brightwork

Brightwork is the term applied to all metal objects, whether steel or brass, that are polished rather than painted or covered with grease. The term can also apply to varnished wood, sometimes found aboard ship. Never use emery cloth, a wire brush, or sandpaper on brightwork. Use brightwork polish sparingly, and with clean rags remove all traces from adjacent paintwork or gaskets. Polish and rags should be properly stowed after use.

Scrubbing Paint Work

In cleaning paint work, sand and canvas will take off the paint as well as the dirt unless great care is taken. Fresh water and very little soap often save much work. Lye should not be used. Rust spots can be removed by canvas and fresh water if care is taken. Greasy dirt is hardest to remove. After washing down decks, all paint work that has become wet must be wiped dry. If this is not done, the drops of salt water will evaporate and leave the paint work speckled with white salt marks, which are not only untidy but also spoil the paint. Sand soap (or similar material) should be used instead of coarse abrasives to clean label plates, aluminum, brass, bright steel (CRS) or porcelain insulators.

Compartment Cleaners

Compartment cleaners are detailed by their division officers and are responsible for the cleanliness and tidiness of the compartments assigned to them. They are also responsible for the proper placing and care of the equipment of the compartments. They are excused from cleaning any other part of the ship, but must attend all quarters and drills.

The section leaders on the upper decks are responsible to the division officers for the equipment in their parts of the ship.

Electrical Equipment

Never attempt to alter or repair any electrical gear. Electrician's mates are trained for this duty, and they alone should touch it. Never paint screw threads, label plates, hinges, or other parts of electrical fittings. Avoid using steel wool near electrical equipment, since particles may cause "shorts."

Fire Hose and Canvas

Never use sand, holystone, or stiff-wire brushes on fire hose or canvas. If oily or greasy, fire hose or canvas can be washed with mild soap, a soft-bristle brush, and fresh water. Hose and canvas must be triced up and dried thoroughly at normal temperature before being stowed.

Ventilators and Air Ducts

Ventilators and air ducts should be inspected periodically and cleaned to prevent the accumulation of rubbish and trash. They should not be used as stowage spaces.

Gaskets, Dogs, Air Ports

Rubber gaskets used for watertight, weather-tight, and airtight purposes should not be painted. The metal-bearing edges that come in contact with the gasket should be kept free from rust, grease, and paint. Emery should not be used. The dogs, dog-bolts, nuts, hinges, and hinge pins or other parts of watertight doors, and the hatches, manholes, and air ports upon which the watertight security of vessels depends must not be removed except for repair or adjustment. The removal of these parts for other purposes, such as cleaning or polishing, is prohibited, as this practice often results in the loss of the parts or their replacement without correct adjustment.

Standing Rigging

Wires that support the masts are called standing rigging. The fore-and-aft supports are stays, and the thwartships supports are shrouds. Formerly all standing rigging was protected from the weather by coating it with tar. Tar has given way to more satisfactory commercial preservatives, but the preservatives are applied in the same fashion as the tar was. A man seated in a boatswain's chair supported by a shackle over the wire being covered is lowered by means of a gantline. As the man is lowered, he applies the preservative to the wire with a rag or a brush. The deck should be wet down or tarpaulins placed under the rigging before starting to apply the preservative.

PAINTING

Paints and varnishes are used to protect and decorate surfaces. The protection of metal surfaces is the chief object of much of the painting done on warships.

Keeping a cutter in first-class condition means a constant battle against rust, and the only effective protection against rust is good paint properly applied (figure 21–2) to metal surfaces that have been carefully prepared for painting.

The *Paint and Color Manual* provides excellent information on surface preparation and the proper application of all coatings authorized for use. Since there are many different materials that you may be maintaining with a variety of special coatings, be sure that you know specifically how to handle your particular job.

Figure 21–2. Paint is used not only for appearance, but for protection of metal surfaces.

Preparing Surfaces

Even the most expensive paint is of little value if it is applied on an insecure foundation. Loose old paint, rust, dirt, dust, moisture, or grease on any surface will prevent new paint from adhering to it.

Before painting steel, it is necessary to remove all scale, grease, rust, and moisture. Rust spreads even when it is covered by paint. In time it will cause the paint to flake off.

Removing Rust and Old Paint from Steel Surfaces

Rust and old paint may be removed in several ways, depending on the thickness of the coating, the thickness of the steel underneath, the materials stored on the other side of the steel plating, and the available equipment for scaling. In normal operations portable power sanders, wire brushes, air-driven jitterbugs, and scrapers and hammers may be used. Electrically heated devices for blistering paint should be used where available. Torches are satisfactory if used by a skilled operator. The flame should be hot enough to blister the paint, but not to burn wood underneath nor to discolor metal. The flame should not play long enough on the surface of the paint to produce smoke. The fumes and powder from oil paints are poisonous if inhaled.

When the ship is equipped with portable power tools such as sanders and wire brush wheels, you may be issued one. Their operation is relatively easy, but in any case instructions on how to use them will be given. It is probable, however, that the average man will most often use hand tools, such as scrapers and chipping hammers.

Chipping is not recommended for removing rust and paint, and surfaces are chipped only when other equipment is not at hand. Care must be taken that the chipping does not result in irregularities—"hills and valleys"—in the surface since they make it difficult to produce a smooth film. It has happened, too, that careless men have chipped through the skin of a ship. There is less danger in doing harm with scrapers, but care still must be taken that all paint and rust are removed without unnecessarily scratching the surface underneath.

Oil and grease are removed by compounds such as paint thinner, which dissolve them sufficiently to be washed and wiped off the steel surface. Instructions will be given in the use of solvents at the time they are issued.

An inexperienced person must never undertake the removal of paint from wooden surfaces, except under the immediate direction of a competent man.

Types of Paint

Anticorrosive paint is used on underwater hull areas to prevent salt water from acting on metal, and for boot topping. It is always used with antifouling paint and *must* go on first. It contains heavy pigments and must be stirred frequently. It dries very rapidly, so it must be applied in short quick strokes.

Antifouling is applied to a ship's bottom to prevent marine growth—barnacles, worms, and plants. It contains copper oxide, which will pit steel plating wherever it touches, as it must always be used *over* anticorrosive paint.

Boot topping is a special paint applied to the hull at the waterline, covering the area between light load and full load drafts.

Pretreatment coating is applied to all bare metal surfaces, if possible, before the primer coat is applied. It dries fast—within 30 minutes—and if not used within eight hours, must be discarded. It is highly flammable; observe all safety precautions.

Primers are base coats applied to wood and metal to make a smooth surface for final coats. Principal primers used are zinc chromate and red lead. Only zinc chromate is used on aluminum and galvanized surfaces. Always apply two coats of a primer, and a third at all outside edges and corners; allow at least eight hours between coats.

Exterior topside paints consist of white or haze gray for vertical surfaces and deck gray for horizontal surfaces; spar is used on certain other areas.

Deck paints are green for officers' quarters and wardrooms, gray for other living and working spaces, and red for machinery spaces and shops.

Interior bulkhead and overhead paint is usually fire retardant. White is commonly used on both bulkheads and overheads; other colors are green for offices, radio rooms, pilothouses and medical spaces; gray for electronic and flag offices; acid-resisting black for compartments in which acids are used; and various pastel shades in crew's living and messing compartments.

Machinery paint is usually gray enamel. Before painting any machinery, read in this chapter "what not to paint."

Canvas preservative comes in several colors: deck gray, haze gray, and white for general use, and international orange for life jackets and life rings. When painting canvas, let one side dry for at least an hour before painting the other side.

Varnishes are either oil varnish or spirit varnish. Oil varnish must dry for at least 24 hours before the next coat is applied; spirit varnish will dry in one hour. Make certain you know which kind you are using.

Aluminum paint is mixed from a paste and a special mixing varnish; it must be prepared just before using and stirred frequently. Any paint left over at the end of the day must be discarded, so never mix more than will be needed.

Application of Paint

Most painting is done by brush (figure 21–3). The following rules should be followed:

> Hold the brush by the handle and not by the stock. If the brush is held by the stock, the hands become covered with paint, which may cause poisoning, especially if small cuts are exposed and lead paints are used.
>
> Hold the brush at right angles to the surface (figure 21–4), with the ends of the bristles alone touching, and lift it clear of the surface when starting the return stroke. If the brush is held obliquely to the surface and not lifted, the painted surface will be uneven, showing laps and spots and a generally dauby appearance.
>
> Do not completely fill the brush with paint. Dip only the ends of

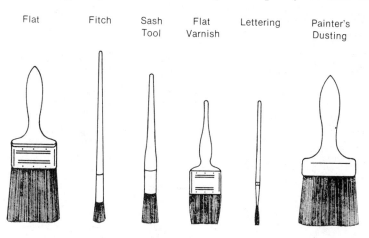

Figure 21–3. There are many kinds of brushes; use the right brush for the job.

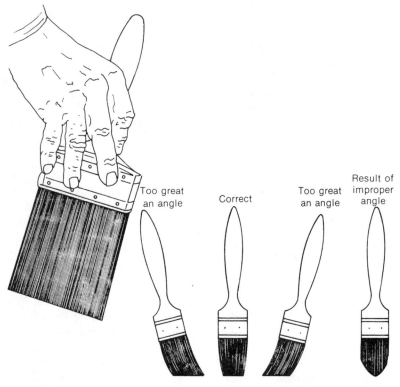

Figure 21–4. Proper technique with a brush saves paint, time, and the brush.

the bristles into the paint. Do not charge the brush with paint until the preceding charge has become sufficiently exhausted.

Apply the paint with long strokes parallel to the grain of the wood. When painting along smooth surfaces, draw the brush along the whole surface if convenient, so that there will be fewer breaks in the lines.

Cross the work by laying off the paint over a small section with parallel strokes and then crossing the first application with parallel strokes at right angles to the first ones. A medium pressure should be applied during the crossing and a light pressure during the final laying-off. All final laying-off should be lengthwise on the work.

In painting an overhead surface, the ceiling panels should, as far as possible, be laid off fore and aft and the beams athwartship. Where panels contain a great many pipes running parallel with the beams it would be difficult to lay off the ceiling panel fore and aft. In such cases better results can be obtained by laying off parallel with the beams.

When painting vertical surfaces, bulkheads, etc., the work should be laid off vertically. In all cases each succeeding coat of paint should be laid off in the same direction.

Keep the paint in the pot well mixed while the work is proceeding.

Remember that paint applied in too heavy a coat will show brush marks and produce an uneven finish. Better results can be obtained by applying two coats of thin or medium body paint than one coat of heavy paint.

Do not apply a succeeding coat of paint before the previous one is sufficiently dry. Paint dries because of its contact with the air, and the drying of the first coat will be retarded if the second coat is applied too soon.

Care of Brushes

Modern brushes should not be soaked in water to tighten the bristles. The bristles are generally set in rubber or similar compositions that do not swell when wet. Soaking in water may cause the metal ferrule to rust and weaken, and when the wooden handle part does swell, the ferrule will split.

Before use, rinse a brush with thinner. After use, if the brush is to be re-used the next day, mark whether it is to be used for white, light colors, or dark colors. Remove excess paint and suspend it with bristles completely immersed in thinner or linseed oil in a closed container. If the brush is not to be used soon, clean it with thinner, wash it with soap and water, and rinse it well with water. Then store it suspended from the handle or laid flat on a rack. Never let any weight of the brush rest on the bristles.

Spray-Gun Painting

A spray gun is a precision tool that mixes air under pressure with paint, breaks it up into spray, and shoots it out in a jet. There are several types, either with a container attached to the gun or connected by a hose. Spray guns for small areas use feedcups of paint; large areas call for pressure tanks of from two to sixty gallons. The two main assemblies of the spray gun are the gun-body assembly and the spray-head assembly. Most guns are now fitted with a removable spray-head assembly. This type allows easier cleaning and permits quick change of the head if it is damaged or if the paint color is changed.

Spray Painting Techniques

Paint is shot out of the nozzle in a thin jet, and compressed air spreads it in a fine spray (figure 21–5). The spray pattern is changed by adjusting the air control screw. If a wide pattern is used, the flow of paint is increased accordingly with the fluid control screw. Follow these rules in spray painting:

Before starting to spray, test the gun on a surface similar to the one you will work on.

Use the minimum pressure for the job, and hold the gun from six to ten inches from the surface.

Hold the gun perpendicular to the surface and at a constant distance at all times on the strokes. Start the stroke before squeezing the trigger, and release it before finishing the stroke.

Spray up to within one or two inches of a corner and stop. Then

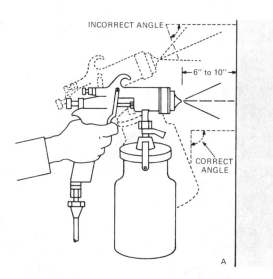

Figure 21–5. (A) Hold the gun perpendicular to the surface. (B) Keep the gun the same distance from the surface during an entire stroke. (C) Spray into a corner, not past it.

turn the gun sideways and spray downwards, spraying both sides at once.

If small pieces protrude from a large area being painted, paint them first, and then do the entire area.

Thoroughly clean the spray gun, paint container, and hoses after each use, as described in the training course for Boatswain Mate 3 and 2.

Common Spraying Defects

The most common defects in sprayed paint result from improper cleaning, improper technique, and poor material.

Orange peel. This is a painted surface that has dried with a pebble texture resembling an orange peel. This may be caused by using improper thinners or a spray that is not fine enough, by holding the gun too far from (or too close to) the surface, by improperly mixing the material, by drafts, or by low humidity.

Runs and sags. *Runs* usually are the result of using material that is too thin; *sags* result from too much material. Both can also be caused by allowing too big a lap in spraying strokes and by poor adjustment of the spray gun or pressure tank. Dirty or partially clogged passages for air or fluid will also cause runs or sags.

Pinholes. These may be caused by the presence of water or excessive thinner in the paint, or by quick-drying paint that has been applied too heavily. In either case, small bubbles form and break in drying, leaving small holes.

Blushing. This resembles a powdering of the paint. What happens is that the cellulose material in the paint separates from its solvent and returns to its original powder form. Water is usually the cause of this—either moisture on the sprayed surface or excessive moisture in the air. When blushing occurs, the defective coating must be removed, because moisture is trapped within the material and will remain there unless the coating is removed.

Peeling. This problem is almost invariably due to carelessness in cleaning the surface. Before any spraying is attempted, the surface must be absolutely clean. Poor adhesion will occur with cheap materials, but never with standard issue paints.

Bleeding. This defect occurs when the color of the previous coat discolors the finish coat. A paint containing a strong aniline dye (synthetic organic dye) will bleed when another color is sprayed over it.

Respirators

Spray painting releases fumes, pigment, and vehicle into the air. You may inhale or otherwise absorb these substances into your body when spraying or when in the vicinity of spray work. Respirators are especially designed to give you maximum protection. The following are the most common types.

Filter respirator. Equipped with filter pads, it can be used in spraying, grinding, or dust-blowing work, when dust and fumes are not too severe.

Cartridge respirator. This is designed for more severe conditions than can be met by a filter respirator. It uses a filter pad and also a large purifying cartridge made of chemically treated charcoal.

Dust respirator. One of the most common types, it contains a replaceable cartridge and is easy to wear owing to its light weight.

Air supply respirator. This respirator provides complete protection when you are working in holds, tank interiors, and other areas where no ventilation is possible. This type is supplied with fresh air, purified by a charcoal cartridge and then fed to the breathing compartment of the respirator through a compressed air line.

Hood respirator. This consists of a flameproof hood, a headgear of fiber with a metal eyepiece, an air filter, and an air hose. The neck cloth at the bottom of the hood ties snugly around the neck to prevent the entrance of fouled air. The opening in front of the hood is the only outlet for the constant flow of air entering from a hose attached to the back of the hood. Foul air cannot enter because the pressure inside is slightly greater than the pressure outside. A maximum range of vision is permitted by the generous opening.

Safety precautions concerning ventilation and approved solvents should be observed.

A Few Don'ts

Don't use shellac as a protective paint on steel surfaces or where it comes in contact with water or damp conditions.

Don't use shellac as an undercoating for outside varnish work.

Don't do any puttying until the first or priming coat has been applied and is dry.

Don't use boiled linseed oil for priming.

Don't forget that no paint will give good results when applied over a wet or damp surface, whether such surface is wood, metal, plaster, or cement.

Don't forget that painting or varnishing over a damp or "tacky" surface will cause blistering and "alligatoring" of paint and cracking of varnish.

Don't apply varnish over a glossed surface. Haircloth or sandpaper will quickly remove the gloss and also improve the general appearance of subsequent coats.

Don't expect to produce a successful job of rubbing with water or oil and pumice stone, or of polishing with rottenstone, before the varnish is thoroughly dry.

Don't forget that each coat of varnish must be thoroughly dry before you apply another. If this fact is neglected, cracking will surely result.

Don't expect to be able to preserve steel surfaces unless frequent and careful examinations are made, surfaces thoroughly cleaned before painting, and repainting carefully done.

Don't forget that the volatile thinners used in paint are flammable. Keep all flames away from open containers of paint.

What Not to Paint

Aboard ship it's also important to know what *not* to paint. In general, *nothing should be painted that can be kept bright* (fig. 21–6). This doesn't mean that all such surfaces must become brightwork. But it does mean that except for camouflaging, the following should never be covered with a coating of paint:

Galvanized iron or metals with a special noncorroding finish.

Metal lagging on turbines, reciprocating engines, piping, pumps, tanks, coolers, heaters, evaporators, and boilers.

Machined metal surfaces of reciprocating engines or pumps, such as columns, moving parts, flanges, bolts, bolt heads, studs, and nuts, blower fans, sliding contacts, and pivotal points.

Turbine casing points, nuts, and bolts.

Sliding feet of turbines and boilers.

Exposed composition parts of any machinery.

Valve bonnets, glands, nuts, or any machined parts of valves.

Heads and outside surfaces of condensers (when of composition), bell pulls, sheaves of all types, and annunciator chains.

Cylinder heads of reciprocating engines and pumps, except those parts that are exposed to water in bilges.

Figure 21–6. Knowing what *not* to paint is as important as knowing how to paint.

Name plates.

Radio antennas. The wires of antennas should be brushed and cleaned thoroughly. Petrolatum should then be applied and the excess wiped off. Every six months all the grease should be wiped off and fresh petrolatum applied. This will prevent corrosion and the consequent dropping of copper sulphate, which ruins awnings.

Floor plates, gratings, and handrails.

Gaskets.

Rubber packing.

Jointing of watertight work.

Electric insulators and insulation of all kinds (special insulating paint coatings may be specified).

Zincs wherever fitted.

Strainers.

Panels, coils, cabinets, and in general all parts of radio and underwater sound transmitters, receivers, testing equipment, frequency meters, etc. The original enamel, lacquer, or crackle finish on radio and sound equipment should be retained unless damage makes refinishing essential.

ACCOUNTABILITY FOR EQUIPMENT

Some men will assume that because they can draw government property with a chit, no one is really paying for it, and it can be wasted, lost, or even stolen with no regard for consequences. They may get away with it for a while, but in the end the records must balance, and the never-ending inspections and inventories will show who is responsible.

The Coast Guard maintains accurate records of all equipment and supplies. It is possible to predict on the average the amount of various materials each unit should use. This means that when a unit or a ship begins to use more paint, tools, food, or anything else in the way of equipment or supplies than is reasonable for its operations, an investigation is soon in order. If inquiries prove that the equipment or supplies were lost, wasted, or stolen, the next step is to find out who is being inefficient, careless, or criminal.

For the performance of routine duties a person will be issued the necessary tools and supplies to accomplish the job. In the beginning this may be no more than a paint brush and bucket; later, it may mean signing a custody card for valuable equipment. In all cases you are required to treat the article with care and to return it when possible in good condition to the issuing authority.

Types of Equipment

In general there are two ways of classifying all government property: as items of *equipage* and items of *consumable supplies*.

Items of equipage (and other gear requiring special handling even if not strictly termed equipage) are relatively permanent, such as binoculars, typewriters, rifles, gas masks, and special clothing. These things are not consumed by use but may be returned unchanged to the supplying officer. In case of loss, breakage, or wearing out, final disposition and accounting must be made in accordance with existing regulations.

Consumable supplies such as paint, paint brushes, soap powder, wiping rags, and stationery are not expected to last, and they are not normally returned to the supplying officer. However, their *rate of use* is closely watched, investigated, and accounted for.

No one can be careless of public property without getting into trouble. The usual result of inefficiency in using equipment and supplies is delay in promotion or loss of promotion where a rate is already held. The usual result of carelessness or of pilferage is captain's mast or a court-martial, depending on the seriousness of the offense. As both a Coast Guardsman and citizen, don't waste your own money.

TA GRAYS HARBOR

41314

CHAPTER 22

Security

Security, as used in most training manuals and publications, refers to the safeguarding of classified information. The security of the United States in general, and of military operations in particular, depends greatly upon the success attained in the safeguarding of classified information. But security takes in more than classified information, which generally refers to printed information—classified or registered publications, manuals, and charts—but may include such forms of communication as radio, visual signals, and mail, as well as knowledge of ships' movements. Security, in the full sense of the word, also has to do with the safeguarding of materials and techniques and the physical safety of ships and stations. The latter subject will be discussed later in this chapter under the headings of external and internal security.

As the first discussion of security involves classified information, it is important that everyone understands what classified information is, its importance, how to safeguard it, how to obtain clearance to work with or have access to it, and the penalties for security violations.

Security Classifications

Classified information is generally classed as top secret, secret, or confidential. Other special classifications are used in some naval and government activities; for example, the Coast Guard uses the classi-

Figure 22–1. A major portion of the Coast Guard's national purpose is law enforcement. That can mean the enforcement of drug laws, safety laws, pollution laws, fisheries laws, and port security laws, such as shown in this photo when demonstrators attempted to interfere with a Navy submarine. Security is a serious matter!

fication "for offical use only" (FOUO) in its law-enforcement functions. These will become known to you only if you are assigned to very special kinds of work. Standard definitions for the various security classifications follow.

Top Secret

Of such importance to the defense of the United States that unauthorized disclosure would result in exceptionally grave damage to the United States or her allies. The damage might range from a break in diplomatic relations to an armed attack on the United States or her allies, even to an all-out war. A less serious result might be the compromising of military or defense plans, intelligence operations, or scientific or technical information vital to national defense. *Compromised* means that classified knowledge or information becomes available to persons not authorized to have access to it.

Secret

Unauthorized disclosure would endanger national security or cause serious injury to the interests or prestige of the United States. The result of such disclosure might be to jeopardize international relations, endanger the effectiveness of a program of vital importance to national defense, compromise important military or defense plans or technical developments, or reveal important intelligence operations.

Confidential

Unauthorized disclosure would be prejudicial to the national interests or prestige of the United States.

For Official Use Only

Information that does not concern the safety of the nation is still sometimes of such a nature that it cannot be divulged. The results of investigations, examination questions, bids on contracts, and proposed plans to buy or lease real estate is "privileged information," and the government and the Coast Guard have the right and duty to keep it from becoming public. Such information is marked *For official use only,* and must not be made available to anyone whose duties do not officially require him to know it.

Disciplinary Actions for Security Violations

Anyone who is responsible for the loss or unauthorized disclosure of classified matter, and anyone who violates security regulations, will be subject to disciplinary action, which may include trial by court martial.

Security Clearance

Before you are allowed to receive classified information you must have a *security clearance*, a statement or document indicating that you have been "cleared" to receive classified information, and also indicating the classification to which you are cleared—top secret, secret, or confidential.

Standards for Clearance

These are listed in the *Security Manual*. You must be trustworthy, of excellent character, and able to show discretion and good judgment. A man loyal to his country may not be eligible for clearance because he cannot meet requirements for a position of trust and confidence. Bad conduct, such as excessive drinking, gambling, promiscuity, and poor credit can lead to withholding of security clearance. This could result in failure to be promoted. A clearance may be denied or terminated at any time due to emotional disturbance, homosexuality, general ineptitude, drug abuse, general disciplinary cases, AWOL, or larceny.

Clearance Procedures

Security clearance is granted or denied by the commanding officer of each activity, according to a person's ability to meet the standards for the level of clearance his work requires. A confidential clearance may be granted upon the completion of a review of personnel, health, and legal records at the command level. Clearances for top secret and secret always require an investigation. This investigation will be either a National Agency Check (NAC) or a Background Investigation (BI), which will ask questions about your military and civilian history. *These questions must be answered completely and correctly.*

Clearance Requirements

The following requirements must be met before military personnel can be cleared to handle classified information.

Top Secret

Final clearance. A Background Investigation plus review of personnel, medical and other records immediately available to the command issuing the clearance to determine if any derogatory information exists concerning the individual. Exceptions to these requirements must be requested from the Commandant.

Interim clearance. A National Agency Check plus review of personnel, medical and other records available to the command.

Secret

Final Clearance. A National Agency Check plus review of personnel, medical and other records immediately available to the command issuing the clearance to determine if any derogatory information exists concerning the individual.

Interim clearance. Must have continuous honorable active duty as a member of the Armed Forces for a minimum of two consecutive years immediately preceding the date of the current clearance (re-enlistment within a one-year period is considered continuous active duty), plus a Headquarters Record Check and review of personnel, medical and other records available to the command.

Note: An Interim Secret Clearance shall not be issued to military personnel having less than two years active duty unless authorized by the Commandant.

Confidential

Final clearance. A formal investigation is not required provided a Local Records Check (personnel, medical or other records immediately available to the command issuing the clearance) contains no derogatory information concerning the individual that would indicate that permitting access to classified information may not be clearly consistent with the interests of national security.

Interim clearance. Not authorized except in the case of immigrant aliens.

Security investigations remain valid and may serve as the basis for issuance of future clearances unless:

Derogatory information becomes available, indicating a need for
    further investigation; or
The individual is assigned to a particularly sensitive billet requiring
    a greater clearance criterion than indicated by the foregoing; or
Continuous active service in the Armed Forces or civilian employ-
    ment in the government service is broken by a period longer than
    one year.

You will be cleared only for the level of information your work requires. This clearance may be revoked by the commanding officer who issued it at any time. Upon transfer you must sign a "Security Termination Statement," which outlines your responsibility for the protection of information obtained during your duty at the issuing ship or station. When you are transferred, your new command will determine your eligibility for access to classified material.

The technical nature of naval operations requires many jobs in which a person must have knowledge of classified information and equipment. In some cases the very existence of such equipment must be kept secret. Accordingly, classified information is made available only to those who are cleared to have access to it, and *who need to know* it to perform their duties.

Clearance for a certain level does not entitle you to see and work with all information or equipment classified at the level. Though you may have a secret clearance, you are not automatically eligible to have access to secret information in other locations or departments not related to your billet.

When you are entrusted with classified material, it will be plainly labeled with its classification. There will never be any excuse for carelessness with classified material.

Sometimes you will be exposed to classified information that you do not "need to know." You may also occasionally hear conversations not intended for your ears. It is best not to pry into the details of this information. There is too much risk that the classified information will become public, and this may result in a security compromise. It is important that a balanced and common-sense outlook be maintained in any situation regarding security.

Compromise of Classified Information

Each person to whom classified matter is entrusted or made known is responsible for protecting it against loss or compromise—letting material be so displayed or revealed that any unauthorized person might become aware of it, or allowing release of classified matter to unauthorized persons. Any loss or compromise of security may become a case for disciplinary action, as stated earlier. Don't talk about classified information to unauthorized persons, which includes family, friends, and shipmates, as well as strangers. It can be revealed unintentionally in many ways. Avoid all of the following.

Bragging

This can snowball into a dangerous situation. A person brags of how much he knows, in order to impress friends or family. They in turn brag of how much he knows, and the next step is for him to reveal classified information.

Talking Too Freely

It is natural to talk with shipmates, but classified subjects should be avoided. The fact that you may be entrusted to certain classified information gives you no right to divulge it to anyone else.

Enthusiasm

Interest in your own job is natural and desirable, but is must not lead to revealing classified information to unauthorized persons. In an argument, enthusiasm may cause a man to blurt out classified facts and figures to prove his point. Such a situation may develop from a discussion of some news item. Never add to a news story that appears to be incomplete, no matter how much more you may know. By so doing, you may make public exactly what has been kept secret.

Intelligence Collection Methods

Unfriendly foreign nations are always interested in classified information on new developments, weapons, techniques and materials, as well as on ship and aircraft movements and their operating capabilities. The people who collect such information will not look or act like spies in TV thrillers, and that is why they are successful in their work. A person who has access to classified material should never talk to any stranger about any classified subjects. A foreign intelligence agent collects many odd little bits of information, some of which might not even make sense to him, but when they are all put together in his own country, they may tell experts much more than we want them to know. Don't make their work easier for them.

Safeguarding Classified Information

If you accidentally come across some classified matter—a letter, booklet, or a device—which has been left unguarded, misplaced, or not properly secured, do not read or examine it or try to decide what to do with it. Notify the nearest officer or petty officer in charge, and then stand by to keep unauthorized personnel away until a responsible person arrives to take charge.

Security Areas

In some ships, depending on the type of equipment installed, there will be various types of security areas, as follows.

Exclusion Area

This is an area where access to the area constitutes access to classified information because the equipment cannot be covered.

Limited Area

This is an area that contains classified information that a visitor could gain access to, such as uncovered gauges, etc.

Controlled Area

This is an area adjacent to or surrounding an exclusion or limited area.

All these areas will be clearly marked by signs reading "Security Area—Keep Out."

A ship with a proper topside (quarterdeck or gangway) watch that requires everyone coming on board to identify himself is in itself a controlled area. A man on watch in such an area must not be reluctant to ask for identification; no responsible person will object to being stopped politely but firmly until he can be identified.

Censorship

In time of war or under certain peacetime emergency conditions, censorship of personal mail may be imposed. The main intent of censorship is to avoid security violations that might occur through carelessness or lack of judgment in writing letters. Under such emergency conditions, all letters written aboard a ship, or in a forward area, must be passed by a censor. When censorship is imposed, instructions will be issued detailing subjects not to be discussed in letters. These will include ships' movements, mention of combat actions, details of weapons, and other subjects.

The use of cameras may also be subject to censorship. Cameras may be barred completely, or all pictures taken aboard ship may require clearance for release.

External Security

Every man aboard ship, whether he is on watch or not, must always be security-minded and on the alert for any sign of danger to the ship. A ship in port should be relatively safe, but nevertheless it can be threatened by many things—hurricanes, tidal waves, flooding, fire, explosion, sabotage from within the ship, saboteurs, sneak attack, civil disorder, or riots.

Threats to security may originate outside the ship. Strangers who approach the ship should be regarded with suspicion, even though they appear to be ordinary visitors, salesmen, agents, newsboys, or delivery men. All individuals coming on board must be identified by the officer of the deck or his representative, and packages, parcels, brief cases, tool boxes, etc., should be inspected. Men standing gangway or quarterdeck watches assist the OOD in identifying approaching boats, screening visitors, and checking packages.

Sentries and Guards

These men, posted for security purposes, are guided by written instructions and must know how to challenge boats in order to identify occupants before they come alongside. All sentries may be armed when the situation demands. An armed guard should be reasonably proficient in the use of his weapon; one who does not know his weapon is useless at his post and a danger to his ship and shipmates.

Sneak Attack and Sabotage

Particularly at night, ships moored or at anchor are vulnerable to sneak attack or sabotage. The ship could be approached by swimmers, small boats, a midget submarine, or a submarine. Boarders may pose as bumboat crews; saboteurs may mingle with the returning liberty party, pose as visitors, or sneak aboard when ships are moored to a pier. Where such dangers of attack exist, the operations officer will organize special watches and issue instructions to them.

The Signal Bridge

In port the bridge and signal watches perform the following functions with regard to security:

Report to the OOD any boats approaching the ship, or operating in the vicinity of the ship in a suspicious or aimless manner.

Report to the OOD any unusual disturbances or signs of distress in the harbor, aboard other ships, or ashore.

Internal Security

The safety of a ship may also be threatened from within. Sabotage is possible particularly in times of great international tension. Abrasives in oil, nails driven into multiple conductor cables, or foreign objects placed in turbines or reduction gears can cause great damage. Fire or flooding, accidental or otherwise, is always a danger. All ships maintain watches to help maintain internal security.

Emission Control (EMCON)

This is necessary in wartime because modern science enables an enemy to detect almost any electronic emission. When EMCON is set, personal radios aboard ship cannot be used if they have signal-emitting characteristics.

Darken Ship

This order demands rigid observance by everyone going topside. The glow of a cigarette can be seen for miles on a dark night, or the loom of light from an improperly shielded hatchway will let a submarine make a successful periscope attack.

Quiet Ship

Observance of this order is most important. Banging or hammering can give away the position of an otherwise perfectly silent submarine.

Trash, Garbage, and Oil Slicks

Orders covering trash disposal and pumping bilges must be carefully observed. A ship littering the ocean with floating debris can be tracked down by an alert enemy. It is also violating both U.S. and international law.

Keys

The commanding officer is custodian of all keys to the magazines, but he may designate others to have duplicate keys. Heads of departments are responsible for keys to locked spaces under their cognizance. Keys to other spaces are kept in the custody of designated officers or petty officers. Each department head maintains a key locker containing all the keys to spaces in his department. Keys to these key lockers are available to the OOD at all times for use in emergency.

Every man must provide a lock for his own personal locker and should carry his locker key at all times. Any other keys with which he may be entrusted should never be carried off the ship.

Shipyard Security

When a ship is in a shipyard, all workmen coming on board must be identified. Compartments containing classified matter must be secured, either by locking or by sentries. Fire watches are normally assigned each welder and burner who comes on board. Also, special precaution must be taken after each shift to inspect spaces for all fire hazards.

Prisoners of War

If a man is captured by the enemy, he will be questioned at great length. Enemy interrogators are clever and persistent and will use every trick they can to obtain classified information. Article 1223 of *U.S. Navy Regulations* states that any member of the naval service who is captured shall not disclose any information other than his name, rate, number, and date of birth. Since the Coast Guard operates with the Navy in time of war or national emergency, this regulation would also apply to the Coast Guard.

GENERAL SECURITY MEASURES

Security refers to all measures taken to protect a ship or station against damage by storm or fire, and to guard against theft, sabotage, and other subversive activities. Security involves sentry duty, fire watches, guard duty, and barracks watches. *Sentry duty* is a formal, military duty, governed by specific orders. *Guard duty* may be the same as sentry duty, or, at times, a guard may be permitted to relax military bearing so long as he is on the job and ready for action. A *fire watch* may cover an assigned area on foot, or with a vehicle, or simply an assignment to a certain place for a certain period. A *barracks watch* may sometimes stand a sentry watch, or sometimes merely be available to answer a phone, check people in and out, turn lights off and on, and preserve order and cleanliness.

Sentry Duty

The requirements for standing sentry duty are the same as for all watches: keep alert, attend to duty, report all violations, preserve order, and remain on watch until properly relieved. The rules or orders for sentries form the basic rules for all security watches.

Detail to a sentry watch involves two sets of orders, which follow.

Special Orders

These cover duty as a sentry, with regard to the specific watch in question, and will be passed on and explained to you by the petty officer of the watch or corporal of the guard.

General Orders

These never change. You will always be responsible for carrying out general orders, whether or not anyone explains them to you or reminds you of them. The eleven general orders, with an explanation of each, follow. You must memorize them and be able to recite them whenever called on to do so.

1. To take charge of this post and all government property in view.

2. To walk my post in a military manner, keeping always on the alert, and observing everything that takes place within sight or hearing.

3. To report all violations of orders I am instructed to enforce.

4. To repeat all calls from posts more distant from the guard house than my own.

5. To quit my post only when properly relieved.

6. To receive, obey, and pass on to the sentry who relieves me all orders from the commanding officer, field officer of the day, officer of the day, and officers and petty officers of the guard.

7. To talk to no one except in line of duty.

8. To give the alarm in case of fire or disorder.

9. To call the corporal of the guard in any case not covered by instructions.

10. To salute all officers and all colors and standards not cased.

11. To be especially watchful at night, and during the time for challenging, to challenge all persons on or near my post, and to allow no one to pass without proper authority.

Orders 1, 2, and 3 mean that all persons in the service, whatever their rank, are required to respect you in the performance of your duties as a sentinel and a member of the guard.

You report immediately, by telephone or other means, every unusual or suspicious occurrence.

You apprehend and turn over to proper authority all suspicious persons involved in a disorder occurring on or near your post, and all parties who try to enter your post at any time without authority. You report violations of orders when you are inspected or relieved. If it is urgent and necessary, apprehand the offender and call the corporal of the guard.

Order 4 means that you "pass the word" by calling "corporal of the guard, number ———," giving the number of your post, when you need the corporal for any purpose other than relief, fire, or disorder.

Order 5 means that if you become sick or for any reason must leave your post, you call "corporal of the guard, number ———, relief." You must not leave your post for meals or any other reason unless properly relieved. If your relief is late, telephone or call the corporal, but do not leave your post.

Order 6 names the officers whose orders you must obey. However, any officer can investigate apparent violations of regulations when he observes them.

You give up possession of your rifle only on receiving a direct order to do so from the person who can lawfully give you orders while on your post. No other person can require a sentinel to hand over his rifle or even require it to be inspected.

When challenging, or holding conversation with any person, you take the position of Port Arms if you are armed with a rifle, and take the position of Raise Pistol if you are armed with a pistol.

Order 8 means that if fire is discovered, you must immediately call, "Fire, Number ———," then turn in the alarm, or make certain that it has been turned in, and, if possible, extinguish the fire.

Order 10 covers saluting. (There are more details on saluting in chapter 5.) A sentry salutes as follows:

If walking post, he halts, and if armed with a rifle, he salutes by presenting arms; if otherwise armed he renders the hand salute.

If doing patrol duty, he does not halt, unless spoken to, but renders the rifle salute (at Shoulder Arms); if otherwise armed, he renders the hand salute.

If in a sentry box, he stands at Attention in the doorway upon the approach of the person or party entitled to the salute, and if armed with the rifle, he salutes by presenting arms; if otherwise armed, he renders the hand salute.

During the hours when a sentry is required to challenge, he salutes an officer as soon as he is recognized.

The sentry salutes an officer as he comes on the post. If the officer stops to hold conversation, the sentry assumes the position of Port Arms if armed with a rifle, or the position of Attention throughout the conversation, and salutes again when the officer leaves.

In talking to an officer, the sentry does not interrupt to salute another officer unless the officer being addressed salutes, then the sentry follows his example.

When the flag is raised at morning colors or lowered at evening colors, the sentry stands at attention at the first note of the National Anthem or "To the Colors" and renders the prescribed salute. A man engaged in some duty that would hamper him need not salute. One should face the flag while saluting; but if duty requires, it is permissible to face in another direction.

When a person approaches a post during challenging hours, the sentry should advance rapidly toward him, and at 30 paces, challenge sharply: "Halt! Who is there?" Unless circumstances prevent it, the sentry should continue to advance while challenging. He then takes the best position to pass or apprehend the person, and requires him to advance, remain halted, or face toward the light, in order to determine whether he should be passed or turned over to the guard.

If a person is in a vehicle, the same procedure is followed. If necessary, the sentry may require him to get out of the vehicle.

A sentry permits only one out of a group of people to approach to be recognized. If he is not satisfied with the identification, he detains a person and calls the corporal of the guard.

When two or more individuals approach from different directions at the same time, a sentry challenges each in turn and requires him to halt and remain halted until told to proceed.

A sentry must never allow himself to be surprised or permit two persons to advance at the same time.

A sentry should always say, "Advance one to be recognized." If the party has replied properly, he says "Advance, friend (or officer of the day, etc.)" As soon as recognition is sure, he salutes and permits the person to pass.

Guard duties aboard ship will differ somewhat from those ashore. Some of the variations follow.

Guard duty, if required, is performed by details from the ship's divisions and is known as the *security watch*. The OOD performs the functions of the officer of the day.

The guard of the day is mustered only at morning and evening colors and in the daylight hours in between when honors may have to be rendered.

Sentries do not challenge.

The guard does not raise and lower the colors.

CHAPTER 23

Ships and Aircraft

At the beginning of the calendar year 1983, the Coast Guard had approximately 245 vessels of various types, sizes, and shapes in service. Some of them are described and pictured in the following pages. The types of ships in service, their designations, and the numbers of each type are tabulated here. A summary of all Coast Guard ships, listing their chief characteristics, follows this section.

High Endurance Cutter	(WHEC)	17
Icebreaker	(WAGB)	6
Medium Endurance Cutter	(WMEC)	26
Patrol Craft, Large	(WPB)	76
Harbor Tug, Medium	(WYTM)	9
Harbor Tug, Small	(WYTL)	15
Oceanographic Cutter	(WAGO)	1
Icebreaking Tug	(WTGB)	6
Buoy Tender, Seagoing	(WLB)	27
Buoy Tender, Coastal	(WLM)	15
Buoy Tender, Inland	(WLI)	6
Construction Tender, Inland	(WLIC)	18
Buoy Tender, River	(WLR)	18
Lightship	(WLV)	2
Training Cutter	(WIX)	1
Reserve Training Cutter	(WTR)	1
Surface Effect Ship	(WSES)	1

Figure 23–1. *Polar Star* (WAGB–10), the biggest ship in the Coast Guard fleet. One of the world's most powerful icebreakers, she can ram ice 21 feet thick.

COAST GUARD SHIPS

Desirable Characteristics

The characteristics of ships are built into them. In designing a ship, many factors must be considered to result in a ship that can do the job for which it is intended. However, each ship must be a compromise in which desirable features are obtained only at the sacrifice of some other desirable feature.

Seaworthiness. This characteristic must be possessed by every ship in the Coast Guard. It means the ability to put to sea and stay there regardless of the weather conditions, without danger of structural failure or of capsizing. This characteristic is affected by a ship's size, the type of materials used in the construction, the weight distribution, and the shape of the hull.

Cruising Radius. Some Coast Guard duties require that ships remain at sea for long periods, and travel long distances. The fuel consumed per mile, for any ship, varies with the speed. The most economical speed is that at which the ship travels the greatest distance for the expenditure of a given amount of fuel. Unless specified otherwise, whenever the cruising radius of a Coast Guard ship is given, it is understood that it is for the most economical speed. Cruising radius is affected by the hull structure, the cleanliness of the hull, the efficiency of the engines, the fuel capacity, and, of course, the speed.

Speed. The ability to sustain high speed is most valuable to a ship that is en route on a rescue mission or which is chasing a suspected smuggling vessel. Speed is influenced by the shape and condition of the underwater body, and the weight of the ship in relation to the power.

Maneuverability. When a Coast Guard cutter is trying to take people off a disabled ship, it has to get in close. The action of the sea tends to throw the ships together or apart. It takes quick action on the bridge of the cutter and a maneuverable ship to get the job done and to avoid disaster. Maneuverability means the ability to start and stop quickly and to turn rapidly.

Habitability. Ships are operated by men; there must be space and facilities for them to live as comfortably as possible under the conditions of the duty assigned. Food and water must be provided. The ship must not roll, pitch, or pound to a point where sleep becomes impossible. The ship must be steady enough in a rough sea to ensure that men will not be injured.

A ship cannot have all desirable characteristics. A stiff, highly stable ship is jerky and rolls too deeply and rapidly for comfort. A fast ship needs too much space for machinery to allow livability and uses fuel too rapidly to have a large cruising radius. A large beam-to-length ratio for maneuverability reduces speed and cruising radius.

The 270- and 210-foot medium endurance and 378-foot high endurance cutters embody the best of these characteristics. Older ships are being refitted to provide better living conditions for their crews.

Types of Coast Guard Ships

High Endurance Cutter (WHEC)

The 378-foot *Hamilton*-class cutters are next to the largest craft in the Coast Guard. They are powered by diesel engines and gas turbines, and have controllable-pitch propellers. The 327-foot class of WHECs are geared turbine ships named for former secretaries of the treasury. The lead ship of the class, the *Alexander Hamilton,* was lost in an antisubmarine action during World War II.

Medium Endurance Cutter (WMEC)

The Coast Guard is buying a new class of cutters that will be considered medium endurance cutters. These new ships are 270 feet in length and will be designed to carry helicopters. They will be used during peacetime mainly in law enforcement and search-and-rescue missions. The new WMEC 270-foot class cutter will also have wartime capability to conduct coastal surveillance, antisubmarine warfare, and wartime search-and-rescue tasks.

Another class of medium endurance cutters is the 210-foot class. These vessels first went into service in the mid-1960s. The first four are powered with both diesel and gas turbines but later versions have only diesels. These vessels are designed for law enforcement and search-and-rescue duties. They can and do operate with helicopters.

Oceangoing tugs of the 213-foot and 205-foot classes, as well as the specially constructed Arctic duty vessel, *STORIS*, are also considered to be medium endurance cutters. The Coast Guard's oceangoing tugs were augmented by three additional Navy vessels of similar type in 1980. The fleet tugs *UTE* and *LIPAN*, and the fleet salvage tug *ES-CAPE*, were loaned to the Coast Guard to engage in law enforcement activities. These vessels have a special capability in search and rescue

Figure 23–2. *(top to bottom)* U.S. Coast Guard cutters *Dauntless* (WMEC–624), *Storis* (WMEC–38), *Taney* (WHEC–37), and *Sherman* (WHEC–720).

Figure 23–3. *(top to bottom)* U.S. Coast Guard cutters *Westwind* (WAGB–281), *Bear* (WMEC–901), *Mackinaw* (WAGB–83), and *Glacier* (WAGB–4).

because their original design included special provisions for towing and heavy weather endurance.

Icebreakers (WAGB)

The biggest ships in the Coast Guard fleet are the two icebreakers of the *Polar Star* class—the *Polar Star*, which went into service late in 1975, and the *Polar Sea*, which followed in 1976. They are 399 feet long, displace about 12,000 tons at full load, and have a combination diesel and gas turbine power plant rated at 60,000 horsepower that drives the ships at 17 knots.

Other icebreakers are the *Mackinaw*, 290 feet long, and the *Wind*-class ships, 269 feet long, and the *Glacier*, 309½ feet long, all with powerful diesel-electric drive. All icebreakers have reinforced hulls, special ice-breaking bows, and fast ballast-shifting systems to increase their effectiveness at this work. The *Mackinaw* works in the Great Lakes to keep shipping lanes open as long as possible. The *Wind*-class ships are seagoing and have done important work in the polar regions.

Icebreaking Tug (WTGB)

This relatively new class of cutter is designed for domestic icebreaking missions on the Great Lakes and other commercially used waterways that are affected by ice. They are 140 feet long and driven by a single screw, diesel-electric main propulsion system.

Patrol Boat (WPB)

The Coast Guard has a continuing need for a fast, sturdy, highly maneuverable boat that is capable of withstanding any seas. Such a boat is very valuable as a rescue craft and for general law enforcement duties. Steel-hulled 95-foot and 82-foot patrol boats are used for this purpose. They are powerful, capable vessels, carrying various armament. WPBs are named for capes and points of geographic interest.

Buoy Tenders (WLB) (WLM) (WLI) (WLR)

One of the most important types of Coast Guard ship is the buoy tender. These hard-working vessels have the difficult task of servicing the more than 44,000 aids to navigation that the Coast Guard maintains to provide safe navigation in the inland, coastal, and territorial waters of the United States. They range in length from 65 feet to 180 feet, and in displacement from 45 tons to 1,025 tons, and have various types of propulsion. Some are designed for ocean work and are equipped for

Figure 23–4. *(top to bottom)* U.S. Coast Guard harbor tug *Shackle* (WYTL–65609); patrol craft *Point Herron* (WPB–82318) and *Cape Cross* (WPB–95321); harbor tug *Yankton* (WYTM–72).

Figure 23–5. *(top to bottom)* U.S. Coast Guard cutter *Cherokee* (WMEC–165); buoy tenders *Red Birch* (WLM–687) and *Primrose* (WLIC–316); the training barque *Eagle* (WIX–327).

icebreaking, while others are shallow-draft river boat types for duty in such waters as the Mississippi and Ohio rivers. They are named for trees, flowers, and shrubs. In addition to tending aids to navigation, these vessels also do a great deal of district patrol and rescue work.

Construction Tenders, Inland (WLIC)

The Coast Guard's system of aids to navigation on inland coastal waters requires the construction and maintenance of many different kinds of structures. A special class of cutters called "Construction Tenders, Inland" are employed in this service. These vessels usually operate with a construction barge, or they are equipped with pile drivers to assist in positioning fixed aids to navigation as well as maintaining aids on inland coastal waters.

Harbor Tugs (WYT)

Harbor tugs range in length from 65 feet to 110 feet. They are equipped for fighting fires, they carry out rescue operations and perform customs and anchorage duties.

Lightships (WLV)

Only two of these remain in service, one stationed off Nantucket I., Mass., and one in Boston as relief ship. They anchor at a charted position and thus mark the location of a reef or shoal or an important navigational point. To be readily visible, they are painted bright red with white superstructure. At night a characteristic light is shown so that the vessel is really a floating lighthouse. Radiobeacon transmitters and sound fog signals make the lightships a useful, in fact vital, aid to navigation, regardless of visibility or weather conditions. All but the two lightships mentioned above have been replaced with offshore platforms or large navigation buoys (LNB), from which signals can be made.

Special Vessel (WIX)

The *Eagle*, formerly the *Horst Wessel*, is a training vessel built in Germany in 1936. She is assigned to the Coast Guard Academy in New London, Connecticut, where she is used each summer for the training of cadets. The *Eagle* is 295 feet in length, displaces 1,600 tons, and has a steel hull and a 700-horsepower diesel engine. Maximum speed under power is 10 knots. Under sail she has topped 18 knots. She is ideal for practical training of cadets in seamanship and shipboard activities. Being used primarily under sail, she serves to give future officers the experience so necessary to make them well-trained seamen for all types of vessels and duties. (See table on page 584)

COAST GUARD AVIATION

To aid in accomplishing its varied duties more effectively, the Coast Guard operates a number of various types of aircraft, including both fixed wing and rotary wing (helicopters). The requirement for a particular task may be for long range, large cargo capacity, high speed, low speed, long endurance, ability to land on the water, ability to operate in and out of small fields or normally inaccessible places, ability to become airborne in a hurry, or some combination of these or other specific capabilities. No one aircraft has the characteristics to perform all of these functions.

Aircraft Markings

All Coast Guard aircraft have an overall glossy white finish. The wing tips, tail, and nose of all fixed-wing aircraft are painted fluorescent red-orange. Helicopters are now painted in a combination of red and white. All aircraft are marked USCG and U.S. COAST GUARD in large letters.

Aircraft Designations

The Coast Guard uses the standard DOD system of designating aircraft. A typical example follows:

HC 130B

H	C	130	B
(Modified Mission Symbol)	(Basic Mission Symbol)	(Model Number)	(Modification)

Search-and-Rescue Equipment

Within the limits of its capacity, each Coast Guard aircraft carries as much search-and-rescue gear as may be needed to accomplish the mission. In addition to the life rafts provided for the protection of the crew, special rafts are carried, ready for dropping to any survivors who may be sighted. These rafts will inflate during their descent and they can be entered as soon as they drop to the surface. Packets attached to them contain a small amount of emergency equipment. Other equipment is delivered by additional droppable kits containing radios, flares and smoke signals, emergency rations, and medicine. Pumps can be air-dropped for salvage purposes.

Kinds of Coast Guard Aircraft

The Coast Guard operates both fixed wing and rotary wing (helicopters) aircraft. The service is also considering the future use of lighter-than-air (blimps) aircraft for surveillance activity. Coast Guard aircraft vary with the needs of the service. Some Coast Guard aircraft and their designs were borrowed from other armed services, others were designed solely for Coast Guard use. The Coast Guard pioneered the use of the helicopter in World War II.

HC-130 Hercules

This is an all-weather, medium speed, long-range, long-endurance, four-engine, turbo-propeller driven land plane. In the Coast Guard, the primary mission of this aircraft is search and rescue. A secondary mission for which the aircraft is well suited is the transport of emergency equipment, personnel, and cargo from or to unprepared as well as prepared runways. It is also used in carrying out the International Ice Patrol. The Coast Guard operates the HC-130B, E, and H modifications of the Hercules.

HU-25A Guardian

This all-weather, high-speed, medium-range twin-jet aircraft entered Coast Guard service in 1982. Its primary purpose is air surveillance (electronic) in support of law enforcement, search and rescue, and enviromental protection missions. This aircraft is the Coast Guard's first pure jet fixed-wing aircraft.

HC-131

This aircraft, obtained from the U.S. Air Force, served in the early 1980s, replacing the HU-16 Albatross in advance of the purchase of HU-25As. It has a twin reciprocating engine and is a medium-range, cargo aircraft used for law enforcement surveillance and search and rescue.

HH3F Helicopter

This twin-turbine rotary-wing aircraft has sufficient range to permit extended offshore searches. It can hover and lift survivors or land on water during search-and-rescue operations. Its weight, however, gen-

Coast Guard Ships

Class	Number	No. in Class	Full Load Displ.	Length Overall	Max. Draft	Ext. Beam	Propulsion (code)*	Screws/ SHP	Max. Speed (Kts.)
Hamilton	WHEC–715	12	3,050	378'	21'	42'	DOG	2/36,000	29.0
Bibb	WHEC–31	5	2,656	327'	15'	41'	TR	2/6,200	19.8
Unimak	WHEC–379	1	2,800	311'	14'	41'	DR	2/6,080	19.0
Polar Star	WAGB–10	2	12,000	399'	28'	83'6"	DOG	3/78,000	17.0
Glacier	WAGB–4	1	8,449	310'	29'	74'	DE	2/21,000	17.6
Mackinaw	WAGB–83	1	5,252	290'	19'	74'	DE	3/10,000	18.7
Bear	WMEC	13	1,730	270'	14'	38'	DR	2/3,500	19.5
Westwind	WAGB–281	2	6,515	269'	29'	64'	DE	2/10,000	16.0
Storis	WMEC–38	1	1,925	230'	15'	43'	DE	1/1,800	14.0
Yocona	WMEC–168	1	1,745	213'	15'	41'	DER	2/3,000	15.5
Resolute	WMEC–620	11	1,007	211'	10'	34'	DR	2/5,000	18.0
Diligence	WMEC–616	4	970	211'	10'	34'	DAG	1/3,000	18.0
Cherokee	WMEC–165	3	1,731	205'	17'	39'	DER	2/5,000	16.2
Katmai Bay	WTGB–101	6	662	140'	12'	37'	DE	2/2,500	14.7
Dorado	WSES–1	1	121	110'	8'	39'	DR	2/2,880	33.0
"Cape" (C)	WPB–95321	6	105	95'	6'	20'	DR	2/2,324	21.0
"Cape" (B)	WPB–95312	8	105	95'	6'	20'	DR	2/2,324	20.0
"Cape" (A)	WPB–95300	8	105	95'	6'	20'	DR	2/2,324	20.0
"Point" (D)	WPB–82371	9	69	83'	6'	18'	DR	2/1,600	22.6
"Point" (C)	WPB–82318	40	66	83'	6'	18'	DR	2/1,600	23.7

"Point" (A)	WPB–82302	4	67	83'	6'	18'	DR	2/1,600	23.5
Arundel	WYTM–90	3	370	110'	11'	27'	DE	1/1,100	11.2
Apalachee	WYTM–71	6	370	110'	11'	27'	DE	1/1,100	11.2
Bitt (D)	WYTL–65613	3	72	65'	6'	19'	DR	1/400	9.8
Hawser (C)	WYTL–65610	3	72	65'	6'	19'	DR	1/400	9.8
Bridle (B)	WYTL–65607	3	72	65'	6'	19'	DR	1/400	9.8
Capstan (A)	WYTL–65601	6	72	65'	6'	19'	DR	1/400	10.5
Evergreen	WAGO–295	1	1,025	180'	13'	37'	DE	1/1,000	12.9
Basswood (C)	WLB–388	18	1,025	180'	13'	37'	DE	1/1,200	13.0
Ironwood (B)	WLB–297	6	1,025	180'	13'	37'	DE	1/1,200	13.0
Laurel (A)	WLB–291	3	1,025	180'	13'	37'	DE	1/1,000	12.8
Fir	WLM–212	3	989	175'	12'	34'	DR	2/1,350	12.0
Red Wood	WLM–685	5	512	157'	6'	33'	DR	2/1,800	12.8
White Sumac	WLM–540	7	600	133'	9'	31'	DD; except WLM–547, DR	2/600	9.8
Buckthorn	WLI–642	1	200	100'	4'	24'	DR	2/600	11.9
Cosmos	WLI–293	4	178	100'	5'	24'	DR	2/600	10.5
Bayberry	WLI–65400	2	68	65'	4'	17'	DR	2/400	11.3
Blackberry	WLI–65303	2	68	65'	4'	17'	DR	1/220	9.0
Pamlico	WLIC–800	4	413	160'10"	4'	30'	DR	2/1,000	11.5
Clamp	WLIC–75306	5	145	76'	4'	22'	DR	2/600	9.4
Sledge	WLIC–75303	3	145	75'	4'	22'	DR	2/600	9.1

Coast Guard Ships—Continued

Class	Number	No. in Class	Full Load Displ.	Length Overall	Max. Draft	Ext. Beam	Propulsion (code)*	Screws/ SHP	Max. Speed (Kts.)
Anvil	WLIC–75301	2	145	75'	4'	22'	DR	2/600	8.6
Sumac	WLR–311	1	478	115'	8'	30'	DR	2/2,250	10.6
Dogwood	WLR–259	1	310	114'	5'	26'	DR	2/800	11.0
Lantana	WLR–80310	1	235	80'	6'	30'	DR	3/945	10.0
Gasconade	WLR–75401	9	141	75'	4'	22'	DR	2/600	8.7
Ouachita	WLR–65501	6	139	66'	5'	21'	DR	2/630	11.5
Lightship I	WLV–612	2	607	128'	11'	30'	DR	1/550	11.1
Eagle	WIX–327	1	1,784	295'	17'	40'	Sail/DR	1/700	10.5
Reliance	WTR–615	1	970	211'	10'	34'	DAG	2/5,000	18.0

*Propulsion Code

DD   Diesel Direct
DE   Diesel-Electric
DER   Diesel-Electric Reduction
DR   Diesel Reduction Gear
TE   Turbo-Electric
TR   Turbine Reduction
REC   Reciprocating
RU   Reciprocating Uniflow
DAG   Combined Diesel & Gas Turbine
DOG   Combined Diesel or Gas Turbine

Figure 23–6. *(top to bottom)* HC–130H Hercules, HH65A helicopter, HH3F helicopter, HH52A helicopter, HU25A Guardian.

erally prevents it from operating from the flight decks of WHEC 378 and WMEC 210 class cutters.

HH-52A Helicopter

This medium-range, single-turbine helicopter is used primarily for search-and-rescue missions. It can operate at sea from the flight decks of WHEC 378-, WAGB- and WMEC 210-class cutters.

HH-65A Dolphin Helicopter

This twin-turbine helicopter is used for short-range recovery operations as well as for law enforcement surveillance missions. The HH-65A entered Coast Guard operations in 1982. It can operate at sea from all cutters equipped for flight operations.

Air Stations

The bases from which Coast Guard aircraft operate are known as air stations. The operational mission of an air station is to operate and provide maintenance for Coast Guard aircraft and shipborne air units. Air stations have their own facilities such as hangars, shops, and barracks. At present, air stations are located at or near these places:

Large
Cape Cod, Mass.
Brooklyn, N.Y.
Elizabeth City, N.C.
Miami, Fla.
Clearwater, Fla.
Corpus Christi, Tex.
Traverse City, Mich.
San Diego, Calif.
Barber's Point, Hawaii
Kodiak, Alaska
New Orleans, La.
Sacramento, Calif.

Small
Borinquén, Puerto Rico
Detroit, Mich.
Los Angeles, Calif.
Cape May, N.J.
Chicago, Ill.

Savannah, Ga.
Houston, Tex.
Astoria, Oreg.
North Bend, Oreg.
Port Angeles, Wash.
Sitka, Alaska
San Francisco, Calif.
Arcata, Calif.

CHAPTER 24

Customs and Ceremony

The customs and ceremonies observed in the Coast Guard have developed over long years. Some are common to all military services, and some are naval in nature, because the Coast Guard is at first essentially a seagoing service. Coast Guardsmen should learn and observe all the customs and ceremonies of the service and take pride in carrying them out in proper fashion. Like wearing the uniform, they are a mark of the select group of citizens who have taken a special oath to support and defend their country.

In one sense, service etiquette is simply the Coast Guard way of observing the rules of good manners, which prevail in some form everywhere. To reduce these rules to their essence, well-mannered persons always show respect and politeness toward each other, and it is always the duty of the junior to take the initiative. But the senior is equally obligated to respond.

Personnel of the Coast Guard have a special reason for observing the rules of courtesy. Their uniform makes them representatives of the United States and their service, wherever they are.

Customs and ceremonies of the armed forces show courtesies of several kinds. Some of the most important are:

Respect toward the emblems of our nation and toward its officials.
Courteous behavior aboard a ship of the Coast Guard or Navy.
Mutual respect and courtesy between enlisted personnel and officers.

Figure 24–1. The cutter, regardless of size, follows the age-old customs and ceremonies of the naval service.

Respect and courtesy toward the flags, ships, officials, and other personnel of friendly nations.

Honors and ceremonies are prescribed in *Coast Guard Regulations*.

National Ensign and Anthem

The *national ensign*—the Stars and Stripes—is the flag of the United States. The *national anthem* is the song called "The Star Spangled Banner." These symbols represent the nation, and are always treated with great respect. Similarly, the anthems and flags of other countries whose governments are formally recognized by the U.S. are treated with respect. You render the same salutes for other national flags and anthems as are described here for our own.

Colors

Every Coast Guard shore command and every ship *not under way* performs the ceremony of *colors* twice a day—at 0800 and at sunset. This ceremony consists of paying honor to the national ensign as it is hoisted at 0800 and lowered at sunset.

At 5 minutes before 0800, and before sunset, *first call* is sounded on the bugle (if the ship or station has a bugler), or a recording of first call is played. If not, then the boatswain's mate pipes and passes the word, "First call to colors." PREP is hoisted close-up.

At 0800, Attention is sounded on the bugle. Commands without buglers or records will pass the word "Attention to colors" over their loudspeakers, or the quartermaster will blow a blast with a whistle. PREP is executed.

The national ensign is hoisted smartly to the top of the flagstaff. While it is being hoisted, the band, if there is a band, plays the national anthem. If there is no band, but a bugler, then the bugler plays "To the colors." Everyone within sight or hearing renders honors as follows:

If in ranks, you will be called to attention or to present arms.

If you are in uniform but not in ranks, you stop whatever you are doing, face the colors and salute until "Carry on" is sounded.

If you are in a vehicle and traffic safety permits, you stop and sit at attention, but do not salute. If conditions permit, the senior man in the vehicle gets out and salutes. The driver remains seated.

If you are a passenger in a boat, you remain at attention, seated or standing. The boat officer or coxswain salutes for the boat.

If you are in civilian or athletic gear at colors, you stop and face the colors at attention. If you have a hat, you hold it in your right hand, over your heart. If you have no hat, you salute by holding your right hand over your heart. A woman in civilian clothes, with or without a hat, stands at attention and places her right hand over her heart.

At sunset a similar ceremony takes place. Each day a quartermaster calculates the time of sunset, and at five minutes before that time, "First call" is sounded. At sunset, "Attention" is sounded and the band, if there is one, plays the national anthem. The flag is lowered slowly, so that it reaches the bottom on the last note of the music. If there is no band, but a bugler, then the bugler plays "Retreat."

Your behavior during evening colors is the same as that for morning colors. You face the ensign at attention and hold your salute until "Carry on" is sounded.

Commissioned vessels not under way also hoist and lower the jack at morning and evening colors. This is a square flag with white stars on a blue background, the same as the small square in the national ensign. It is hoisted on the jackstaff, a small flagpole at the bow of a ship.

Ships that are under way do not hold morning or evening colors. They hoist the national ensign at the gaff as they get under way, but the jack is not flown.

Shifting Colors. On unmooring, the instant the last mooring line leaves the pier or the anchor is aweigh, the BMOW will blow a long whistle blast over the 1MC and pass the word "Shift colors." The jack and ensign, if flying, will be hauled down smartly. At the same instance the "steaming" ensign will be hoisted on the gaff and the ship's call sign and other signals flags will be hoisted or broken. On mooring, the instant the anchor is let go or the first mooring line is made fast on the pier, the BMOW passes the same word as for unmooring, the ship's call sign and the "steaming" ensign are hauled down smartly, and the jack and ensign are hoisted.

Half-Masting the Ensign

The ensign is half-masted as a tribute to the dead. Whenever the ensign is to be half-masted, it first is closed up and then is lowered to the half-mast position. The same procedure is used when lowering the ensign; it first must be closed up and then lowered.

On Memorial Day, the ensign is half-masted from 0800 until completion of the 21-gun salute at 1200, or until 1220 if no salute is fired.

During burial at sea, the ensign is at half-mast from the beginning of the funeral service until the body is committed to the deep.

The SOPA may prescribe a longer period for displaying the ensign at half-mast, depending on circumstances, and after the death of a nationally known figure, all ships and stations may be directed to half-mast the ensign for a stated period.

Dipping the Ensign

Merchant ships "salute" naval ships by dipping their ensign. They seldom fly an ensign at sea so this will normally occur in or near a port.

A merchant ship of any nation formally recognized by the United States salutes a ship of the U.S. Navy or Coast Guard by lowering its national colors to half-mast. The Navy ship, at its closest point of approach, will lower the ensign to half-mast for a few seconds, then close it up, after which the merchant ship raises its own flag. If the salute is made when the ensign is not displayed, the Navy ship will hoist her colors, dip for the salute, close them up again, and then haul them down after a suitable interval. Naval vessels dip the ensign only to answer a salute; they never salute first.

Coast Guard Ensign

Secretary of the Treasury Oliver Wolcott described the ensign and pennant in a letter to his collectors in 1799 as "consisting of sixteen perpendicular stripes, alternate red and white, the Union of the Ensign to be the Arms of the U.S. in dark blue on a white field." The stripes stood for the states that comprised the nation at that time. The original 13 states were commemorated by an arch of 13 blue stars in a white field. The only major change in the ensign was made in 1927 when the Coast Guard seal of shield and anchors was centered on the middle of the seventh red stripe. The Coast Guard ensign is required to be displayed by a Coast Guard vessel whenever that vessel takes active measures in connection with law enforcement. Usually, Coast Guard vessels display the Coast Guard ensign continuously. At shore units, the Coast Guard ensign may be displayed on the yardarm, or just below the national ensign when on the same hoist, from 0800 to sunset.

Commission Pennant

The commission pennant is a long, narrow pennant flown from the time a ship goes into commission until she goes out of commission (except as noted below); it is hoisted at the after truck or, in a mastless ship, at the highest and most conspicuous point of hoist. A commission pennant is also flown from the bow of the boat in which the commanding officer makes an offical visit. The commission pennant is not flown when a ship flies a personal flag or command pennant.

The commission pennant is not a personal flag, but sometimes it is regarded as the personal symbol of the commanding officer. Along with the ensign and the union jack, it is half-masted upon the death of the commanding officer of the ship. When a ship is decommissioned, the commanding officer keeps the commission pennant.

Personal Flags

The ship carrying an officer of flag rank who commands a fleet or a unit of a fleet flies his personal flag from the main truck at all times unless he is absent for more than 72 hours. This is a blue flag, carrying five white stars for a fleet admiral, four for admiral, three for vice admiral, and two for rear admiral. A commodore (one white star) flies a *blue* pennant.

An officer below flag rank, when in command of a force, flotilla, squadron, carrier division, or aircraft wing, flies a broad command pennant, white with blue stripes top and bottom.

An official in command of any other division, such as a mine division or destroyer division, flies a burgee command pennant, which is white with red stripes top and bottom.

Absence Indicators

When the commanding officer, or any flag officer, is absent from his command, an "absentee pennant" is flown as follows:

First Substitute (Starboard Yardarm). When the admiral or unit commander, whose personal flag or pennant is flying, is absent.

Second Substitute (Port Yardarm). When the chief of staff is absent.

Third Substitute (Port Yardarm). When the commanding officer is on an official absence of more than 72 hours, then the executive officer, serving as acting commanding officer, is accorded the use of this pennant as if he were the commanding officer.

Fourth Substitute (Starboard Yardarm). When the civil or military official whose flag is flying (such as Secretary of Defense) is absent.

Speed Pennant

This pennant, flown where it can best be seen, indicates that the official or officer whose personal flag or command pennant is flying will leave ship officially in about five minutes. It is hauled down as he departs.

These pennants are not flown when a ship is under way, nor between sunset and sunrise. They show an absence of less than 72 hours.

Church Pennant

The church pennant is the only flag ever flown over the national ensign at the same point of hoist. It is displayed only during church services conducted by a chaplain, both ashore and afloat.

Red Cross Flag

Hospital ships in wartime fly the Red Cross flag instead of the commission pennant. Boats engaged in sanitary service and landing parties from hospital boats fly the Red Cross flag from a staff in the bow.

Other Flags and Pennants

Both in port and at sea, ships fly many single flags or pennants with special meanings. The Senior Officer Present Afloat (SOPA) may prescribe certain flag hoists for local use, such as requests for garbage or trash lighter, or water barge. At anchor, ships awarded the Presidential Unit Citation (PUC), Coast Guard Unit Commendation, Navy Unit Commendation (NUC), or Coast Guard Meretorious Unit Commendation should fly the pennant at the fore truck from sunrise to sunset.

Other Honors to the Flag and Anthem

There are many occasions other than colors when you will render honors to the ensign or national anthem. The usual rule is, face the flag if it is displayed; face the music if the flag is not displayed. Hold your salute until the anthem ends or, if there is no anthem, until the flag has been hoisted or lowered, or has passed your position.

Anthem Played Outdoors, Flag Not Displayed

Men and women not in formation stand at attention, facing the music, and salute, hand salute, or present arms, or hold hat or hand over heart. Formations are brought to a halt and the officer in charge faces the music and renders the salute, the ranks remaining at attention facing the direction they were in at the halt.

Anthem Played Outdoors and Flag in View

The salutes are the same, except that the officer in charge of a formation faces the flag instead of the music and salutes; the ranks remain at attention facing in the direction they were in at the halt.

Flag Ceremony Inside a Building

If the anthem is played during a ceremony inside a building in which the flag is brought forward and presented to the audience, or is then retired, the procedures are:

All personnel face the flag.

Civilian and uncovered military personnel stand, face the flag, and render the right-hand-over-heart salute from the first note of the anthem to the last.

Men with rifles execute present arms.

Men covered or with side arms, in uniform, render the hand salute.

Military formations stand at attention; their officers in charge render the salutes.

If the audience is all or almost all military, the officer in charge will call "Attention." Then he may order all to salute, or he may salute for the audience.

Salutes are held until the flag is placed and its bearer steps aside.

Anthem Played Inside a Building, Flag Not Displayed

All persons stand and face the music. Men and women in uniform, if covered, render the hand salute; if not covered, they simply stand at attention. Men and women in civilian clothes render civilian salutes.

Men in Boats

During the playing of the national anthem, only the boat officer (or coxswain, if there is no boat officer) stands and salutes. Crew and passengers remain standing or seated at attention. If in civilian clothing, they simply remain at attention and do not salute. This is an exception to the general rule.

Passing in Parades

If you are in a formation, simply obey orders. Your officer in charge will render the salute for the formation. If you are not in formation and the flag is hoisted, or lowered, or passes in a parade, obey the following procedures:

If seated, rise, come to attention, face the flag, and salute.
If standing, come to attention, face the flag, and salute.
If walking, halt at attention, face the flag, and salute.
If riding in a vehicle, remain seated at attention.

The rules for saluting the anthem apply only if it is played or broadcast as a part of a public ceremony. If you hear it in private or as you walk past a radio, you need not stop or salute.

Hail to the Chief

The song "Hail to the Chief" is played when the President of the United States is being honored. When "Hail to the Chief" is so played, render the same honor given during the playing of the national anthem.

Boarding and Leaving Ship

Large ships will rig two accommodation ladders (small ships, one) for use in coming aboard (boarding) and leaving the ship. The forward ladder or the starboard one will usually be reserved for officers; the after one or the port one, for enlisted men. During bad weather, all will use the lee (downwind) ladder. At the gangway the officer of the deck (OOD) or his representative—who may be an officer or petty officer—will always be on duty to greet persons leaving or boarding the ship.

The procedure for *boarding your own ship* is: At the gangway, if the national ensign is flying, turn aft and salute the ensign. Then turn to the OOD or his representative, salute and say, "I report my return aboard sir." The OOD will return both salutes and say, "Very well," or "Very good."

The procedure for *leaving your own ship* is: You step to the OOD, salute, and say, "I have permission to leave the ship, sir," if you have such official permission. Or, if you are only going to the pier to handle some work detail and do not need the permission of your division officer and the executive officer, you salute and ask the OOD, "Permission to leave the ship, sir?" or "I request permission to go on the pier to check the after mooring lines, sir."

When the OOD says, "Very well," or "Permission granted," and returns your salute, you drop your salute and step to the gangway. If the ensign is flying, you salute in its direction and then leave.

When you go aboard a ship other than your own, you must obtain permission from that ship's OOD. Stand at the gangway and salute the ensign, if it is flying, then turn to the OOD or his representative, salute, and say, "I request permission to come aboard, sir."

On leaving the ship you have been visiting, turn to the OOD or his representative, and say, "With your permission, sir, I shall leave the ship." After he has said, "Very well," or "Permission granted," and has returned your salute, step to the gangway, and, if the ensign is flying, salute in its direction before leaving.

If you are in a party of men, only the man in charge makes the requests to the OOD to board and leave the ship. However, you salute the ensign, if flying, and the OOD as you file by, both coming and going. If you are making many trips bringing stores aboard, then you salute only the first and last times over the gangway.

Shipboard Customs

Quarterdeck Customs

The quarterdeck is not a specific deck like the forecastle deck or the poop deck. It is an area designated by the commanding officer to serve for official and ceremonial functions. Therefore, the quarterdeck is treated as the "sacred" part of a ship, and you must obey the following rules:

Do not be loud or sloppy in its vicinity.

Never appear on the quarterdeck unless wearing the uniform of the day or as a member of a working party.

Never smoke on the quarterdeck.

Never cross or walk on the quarterdeck except when really necessary.

Do not lounge on or in the vicinity of the quarterdeck.

Sickbay Customs

In the old days, conditions of medicine and sanitation were so bad that sickbay usually meant a place for dying rather than for getting well—particularly after a battle. Accordingly, it became customary to remove one's cap when entering sickbay, out of respect for the dying and the dead. Nowadays, medicine is so highly developed that we less commonly think of death in connection with sickbay. However, the custom of removing one's cap has remained. And, of course, you maintain quiet, and you do not smoke without permission in the sickbay or its immediate vicinity.

Messdecks and Living Areas

The messdeck is where the enlisted men eat; the wardroom is where the officers eat. If you enter any of these areas while a meal is in progress, you uncover. Even if you are on watch and wearing the duty belt, you uncover while a meal is in progress.

Officers' country is the part of a ship where the officers' staterooms and the wardroom are located. CPO country is where the chief petty officers have their living spaces and mess. You enter these areas only on official business. Never use their passageways as thoroughfares or shortcuts. If you enter the wardroom, or any compartment or office of an officer or CPO, you remove your cap. If you are on watch and wearing the duty belt or sidearms, then you remain covered—unless divine services or a meal is in progress in one of the spaces. Always knock before entering any officer's or chief petty officer's room.

Divine Services

When divine services are being held, the ship flies the church pennant above the national ensign and the word is passed, "Divine services are being held (in such and such a space). Maintain quiet about the decks during divine services."

If you enter the area where divine services are being held, uncover. Even if you are wearing duty belt and sidearms, you uncover. There is one exception: for a Jewish ceremony, remain covered.

The Salute

The military custom you will learn first and use most is the hand salute. This is a courtesy that has been observed for centuries by military men of every nationality. It exists by more than force of custom; the occasions and methods of saluting are specified by detailed orders in *Regulations for the U.S. Coast Guard*.

Whom to Salute

All uniformed members of the armed forces recognize and greet each other. However, military organization as well as custom requires that this recognition take the form of the official hand salute or rifle salute to any of the following:

> Commissioned and warrant officers of the Navy, Marine Corps, Air Force, Army, and Coast Guard.
> Officers of foreign armed services whose governments are recognized

by the United States. (In practice this means all foreign officers, unless we are actually at war with the country in question.)

Officers of the National Oceanic and Atmospheric Administration and the Public Health Service when they are serving with the Armed Forces of the United States.

If in doubt, salute. It is better to be over-courteous than to fail to salute when you should have. Always hold your salute until it is returned or acknowledged (figure 24–2).

Saluting Rules

The hand salute is given with the right hand (figures 24–3 and 24–4). If a person has an injury that makes this impossible, the salute may

Figure 24–2. Follow all saluting rules in meetings with senior officers; if uncertain as to the rule, salute.

be made left-handed. Also, if a man is doing something that makes a right-handed salute impractical—using a boatswain's pipe, for instance—it is permissible to salute left-handed (figure 24–5). (The Army and Air Force never salute with the left hand; the Coast Guard, Navy, and Marine Corps do so *when necessary*.)

Accompany your salute with a cheerful, respectful greeting.
"Good morning, sir," "Good afternoon, Commander," "Good evening, Miss White," as appropriate.

Always come to attention. If on the double, slow to a walk when saluting a passing officer. You need not stop walking, but hold yourself erect.

Don't bow your head; don't stare off in the distance; look directly at the officer as you salute.

If both hands are occupied and you are unable to salute, face the officer as though you were saluting and greet him as described above.

Figure 24–3. A Coast Guardsman demonstrates the hand salute.

Don't salute with pipe, cigar, or cigarette in your mouth.

If you are accompanying a commissioned officer, do not salute another officer until the officer with you salutes. Then salute at the same time he does.

Salute an officer even if his hands are engaged and he cannot return the salute. He will acknowledge your salute by saying either, "Good morning," "Good afternoon," or "Good evening."

Prisoners do not salute.

Distances for Saluting

Since the salute is basically a courtesy, it should be used in a manner similar to civilian greetings: an officer should be recognized and saluted at about the same distance and at about the same time as one would recognize and greet a civilian acquaintance—six paces away is a good general rule. Remember—an officer must pass near enough to be identified as rating a salute, and the man giving the salute should start

Figure 24–4. Back view of the same man, same salute. With practice, the salute becomes a natural motion, as shown in figure 24–5.

while far enough away for the officer to have time to see and to return it.

Salutes in Civilian Dress

Since the salute is the military form of greeting and is the same as tipping one's hat, and since Coast Guard personnel do not uncover when out of doors, it follows that you use the military salute when recognizing officers in civilian dress or when greeting civilian friends.

The same holds for meeting women. You do not tip your hat, but acknowledge their greeting with the hand salute. Keep your uniform cap on even when ladies are present.

When you are in civilian dress, you naturally follow the rules of civilian courtesy and tip your hat to other gentlemen (officers or not), and to women. While in the presence of women, you remove your hat unless you walk with them. There is always the problem of what to do when not wearing a hat, as most men in civilian clothes customarily go bare-headed. The answer is simple: if failure to salute would cause embarrassment or misunderstanding, salute anyway, even if not wearing a hat.

If you have occasion to salute the flag while in civilian clothes, remove your hat with your right hand and hold it over your chest, with your hand over your heart.

If you are not wearing a hat, place your right hand over your heart. Women in civilian dress salute in this manner also.

Etiquette for Boats, Vehicles, and Passageways

The basic rule in service etiquette as in civilian etiquette is to make way for a senior quickly, quietly, naturally, and without fuss.

Thus, the rule for entering boats and vehicles is, seniors *in* last and *out* first. The idea is that the captain should not have to wait in a boat for a seaman to amble down the accommodation ladder. When reaching his destination, the senior is allowed to get out first because normally his business is more important and more pressing than that of the men under him.

Remember, juniors *enter* a boat or vehicle *first*; that is, they don't make last-minute dashes to reach the boat, but get in a minute or so before the boat gong, or as soon as the OOD says the boat is ready. Similarly, they are ahead of time and *enter* buses, cars, and other vehicles well in advance of the arrival of a senior. When the boat docks or the vehicle arrives at the destination, the juniors wait until their seniors have disembarked before disembarking themselves.

Generally, seniors take the seats farthest aft. If officers are present, do not sit in the stern seats unless invited to do so. Also, enlisted men maintain silence as long as officers are in the boat. (For reasons of safety, you should never become noisy and boisterous in a boat, regardless of the hour, condition of sea, or who is present.)

If boats with officers on board pass within view, the senior officer and the coxswain of each boat render salutes. Other crew members and passengers remain seated at attention. The coxswain stands and salutes all officers entering or leaving the boat.

Men seated in boats in which there is no officer, petty officer, or acting petty officer in charge, rise and salute all officers passing near. When an officer, PO, or acting PO is in charge of a boat, he alone renders the salute.

Enlisted men seated well forward in a large boat do not rise and salute when officers enter or leave the stern seats. However, men who are passengers in the after section of a boat always rise and salute when a commissioned officer enters or leaves.

A boat takes rank according to rank of the highest grade officer embarked in the boat. A barge with an ensign is junior to a motor whaleboat with a lieutenant on board. When junior boats are passing seniors, the junior boats salute first. The coxswain and senior officer in each boat render the hand salute. Other members of the crew not concealed by canopies stand at attention, facing the senior boat. Passengers sit erect at attention. Boats passing U.S. or foreign men-of-war during "colors" on board must lay to, and their crews face the colors and salute.

For entering and leaving through doors, the rule is to let the senior go *first*. If possible, you hold the door for him. If, however, the junior is a woman, and the senior motions her to go first, she should do so.

On meeting a senior in a passageway, you should step aside and let him pass. If he is a commissioned officer and other enlisted men or officers junior to him are present, you should call "Attention" so that the others can make way for him.

You should not overtake and pass an officer without permission. When necessary to walk past him, overtake him *on his left side*, salute when you are abreast, and ask, "By your leave, sir?" When the officer returns the salute and says, "Very well," or "Permission granted," you drop your salute and continue past him.

When walking with a senior, you always walk *on his left*. That is, you put him on *your* right. This rule also applies when seated in an automobile.

Addressing Officers

Senior officers—commanders, captains, and admirals (who wear gold oak leaves or "scrambled eggs" on their cap visors)—are always addressed and referred to by their titles of rank, "Admiral," "Captain," or "Commander." If several officers of the same rank are seated or working together, it is proper to use both title and name, as "Admiral Taylor," or "Captain Smith," to avoid confusion.

Junior officers—lieutenant commanders, lieutenants, lieutenants (junior grade), and ensigns, are addressed and referred to by their last name, preceded by "Mister," as "Mister Taylor," or "Mister Smith." In speaking to a junior officer whose name is not known, address him as "Sir, . . ." Warrant officers are treated in the same manner as junior officers. Midshipmen and aviation cadets are addressed as "Mister."

By tradition, the commanding officer of any ship or station, no matter what his rank, is addressed and referred to as "Captain." Other captains or commanders in the same command should be addressed by rank and name.

Officers in the Medical and Dental Corps are addressed and referred to by titles or as "Doctor," if they are commanders and above; if of junior officer rank, they are addressed as "Doctor" instead of "Mister." A chaplain may be called "Chaplain," regardless of rank.

An officer below the rank of admiral who is in command of a squadron, task unit, or convoy of ships is customarily addressed and referred to as "Commodore." The rank of commodore, between captain and admiral, was reinstated in the U.S. Navy in 1982. It is now under consideration for reinstatement by the U.S. Coast Guard.

Officers of the Army, Air Force, and Marine Corps of and above the rank of captain are addressed and referred to by their titles, as "General," "Colonel Howes," "Major," and "Captain Farrow"; others are addressed and introduced as "Mister," unless circumstances make it advisable to use their rank to inform other persons present of their status.

Women officers in all ranks may be addressed as "Miss" or "Mrs.," but it is proper to call captains and commanders by their rank. The title, no matter what the rank, may be used alone, while "Miss" or "Mrs." must be used with the last name.

When replying to an order, the only correct reply is "Aye, aye, sir." This means you heard the order, you understand it, and will carry it out to the best of your ability.

"Sir" is a military expression, always used with "Yes" or "No" in addressing officers. In addressing a woman officer, where a male officer would be addressed as "Sir," use her rank, as "Yes, Commander," or "Good morning, Lieutenant." Also use "Sir" in addressing other enlisted men when they are performing a military duty, such as junior officer of the deck or in reporting a muster to a chief petty officer. At such times, you also exchange salutes.

Addressing Enlisted Personnel

A chief petty officer is addressed as "Chief Petty Officer Smith" or more informally as "Chief Smith," or as "Chief" if you do not know his name. But in Recruit Training Command, all chiefs acting as company commanders rate "Mister" and "Sir." Master chief petty officers and senior chief petty officers are customarily addressed and referred to as "Master Chief Smith," or "Senior Chief Smith." Other CPOs are introduced by rate, rating, and last name: "Chief Radioman Price." Introduce other POs by stating the rate and rating first, followed by the last name; "Machinists's Mate First Johnson," or "Petty Officer Johnson."

Introduce "nonrated" men by rate and name; "Seaman Wells," "Fireman Clifton," etc.

When introducing first-, second-, and third-class petty officers to civilians, use the term petty officer: "This is Petty Officer Brown."

Civilians generally address enlisted people as "Mr.," "Miss," or "Mrs."

Seniors may call juniors by their first names, but juniors never address a senior by his first name. If a petty officer tells you to use his (or her) first name, do so only in privacy or on liberty. While on duty in the presence of others, use only last names with the appropriate rank.

In civilian life, it is customary to introduce men to women and youth to age; for instance, a young man to an older one, and a girl to an older woman.

The same general rules are followed in military life, except that in most cases, rank establishes the order of introduction: introduce the junior to the senior, whether male or female, except that all other people, no matter the rank or sex, are introduced to a chaplain. If one

Person Addressed or Introduced	To Military Personnel		To Civilians	
	Introduce as:	Address as:	Introduce as:	Address as:
Officer (CDR or above)	Captain (or appropriate rank) Smith	(same)	Captain Smith	(same)
Officer (LCDR or below)	Mr. (Mrs., Miss) Smith	(same)	LCDR Smith	Mr. (Mrs., Miss) Smith
Medical Corps Officer (CDR or above)	Commander (or Doctor) Smith	(same)	Commander (or Doctor) Smith	(same)
Medical Corps Officer (LCDR or below)	Dr. Smith	(same)	LT Smith of the Naval Medical Corps	Dr. Smith
Chaplain Corps Officer	Chaplain Smith	(same)	Chaplain Smith	(same)
Navy Nurse Corps Officer (CDR or above)	Commander Smith	Miss (or Mrs.) Smith	Commander Smith, of the Navy Nurse Corps	Miss (or Mrs.) Smith
Navy Nurse Corps Officer (LCDR or below)	Miss (or Mrs.) Smith	(same)	LT Smith, of the Navy Nurse Corps	Miss (or Mrs.) Smith
U.S. Public Health Service Officer (M.D. or dentist)	Dr. Smith	(same)	Dr. Smith of the Public Health Service	Dr. Smith
U.S. Public Health Service Officer (Sanitary Engineer)	Mr. Smith	(same)	Mr. Smith, of the Public Health Service	Mr. Smith
Commissioned Warrant Officer	Mr. Smith	(same)	Warrant Officer Smith	Mr. (or Miss Smith)
Midshipman	Mr. Smith	(same)	Midshipman Smith	Mr. Smith
Warrant Officer	Mr. Smith	(same)	Warrant Officer Smith	Mr. (or Miss) Smith
Chief Petty Officer	Chief Yeoman Smith	Chief Smith	Chief Yeoman Smith	Chief (or Miss) Smith
Aviation Cadet	Aviation Cadet Smith	Mr. Smith	Aviation Cadet Smith	Mr. Smith
Petty Officer	Petty Officer Smith	(same)	Petty Officer Smith	(same)
Seaman	Seaman Smith	(same)	Seaman Smith	(same)

of the persons is a civilian, follow the civilian rules. In making any introductions, name the honored or higher ranking person first, then the name of the person being introduced or presented: "Admiral Jones, this is Ensign Smith," or "Mrs. Jones, this is Master Chief Williams."

The accompanying table summarizes the forms for addressing and introducing naval personnel.

There may be times when unofficial letters are exchanged between officers and enlisted men; a coxswain might write to a former skipper to congratulate him on promotion. The salutation would be "My dear Commander Meader," and the complimentary closing should always be "Very respectfully." An officer would not address an enlisted man in writing as "Dear Smith," but as "Dear Chief Petty Officer Smith."

All officers should be addressed by their title of rank, except that officers in the Medical, Dental, Nurse, and Medical Service Corps with doctoral degrees may be addressed as Doctor. Modifiers may be dropped: address a lieutenant commander as "Commander", a lieutenant (junior grade) as "Lieutenant." When a captain or lieutenant is not in uniform, he would be introduced as "of the Coast Guard" or "of the Navy," in order to avoid confusion with Army or Air Force ranks.

HONORS

Gun Salutes

In olden days it took as much as 20 minutes to load and fire a gun, so a ship that fired her guns first did so as a friendly gesture, making herself powerless for the duration of the salute.

The gun salutes prescribed by Regulations are fired only by such ships and stations as are designated. A national salute of 21 guns is fired on Independence Day and Memorial Day, and to honor the President of the United States and heads of foreign states. Salutes for naval officers are: fleet admiral, 17 guns; admiral, 17 guns; vice admiral, 15 guns; rear admiral, 13 guns. Salutes are fired at intervals of five seconds, and always in odd numbers.

Manning the Rail

This custom evolved from that of "manning the yards," which is hundreds of years old. In sailing ships men stood evenly spaced on all the yards and gave three cheers to honor a distinguished person. Now men are stationed along the rails and superstructure of a ship when honors are rendered to the President, the head of a foreign state, or a member of a reigning royal family. Men so stationed do not salute.

Dressing and Full-Dressing Ship

Commissioned ships are *full-dressed* on Washington's birthday and Independence Day and *dressed* on other national holidays.

When dressing ship, the national ensign is flown from the flagstaff and, usually, from each masthead. When a ship is full-dressed, in addition to the ensigns a "rainbow" of signal flags is displayed from bow to stern over the mastheads, or as nearly so as the construction of the ship permits. Ships not under way are dressed from 0800 to sunset; ships under way do not dress until they come to anchor during that period.

Side Boys

Side boys are a part of the quarterdeck ceremonies when an important person or officer comes on board or leaves a ship (figure 24–5). Large ships will have side boys detailed to the quarterdeck from 0800 to sunset. The custom of having side boys originated centuries ago in the

Figure 24–5. Sideboys salute as officer comes aboard ship. Note that the boatswain is saluting left-handed.

Royal Navy when officers were hoisted aboard in a sort of basket, and since senior officers usually weighed more than juniors, more boys were needed on the line. When the side is piped by the boatswain's mate of the watch, from two to eight side boys, depending on the rank of the officer, will form a passageway at the gangway. They salute on the first note of the pipe and finish together on the last note.

Side boys must be particularly smart in appearance and grooming, with polished shoes and immaculate uniforms.

Boat Hails

During hours when side boys are stationed, the officer of the deck challenges an approaching boat by raising his hand with fist closed. The coxswain replies by holding up his fingers to show how many side boys are needed to honor the senior officer in his boat, or gives a wave-off if no side boys are required.

At night, the gangway watch hails an approaching boat with "Boat ahoy." The coxswain replies, according to the following table, to indicate the rank of the senior person aboard his boat.

Coxswain's Reply	Officer or Official
"United States"	President or Vice President
"Defense"	Secretary of Defense, Deputy or Assistant Secretary of Defense
"Navy"	Secretary, Under Secretary, or Assistant Secretary of the Navy
"Naval Operations"	Chief or Vice Chief of Naval Operations
"Fleet" or abbreviation of administrative title	Fleet or Force Commander
"General Officer"	General Officer
"Staff"	Chief of Staff
"__Flot__"*	Flotilla Commander
"__Ron__"*	Squadron Commander
"__Div__"*	Division Commander
"Brigade Commander"	Marine Officer Commanding a Brigade
"(Name of Ship)"	Commanding Officer of a Ship
"Regimental Commander"	Marine Officer Commanding a Regiment

*The type and number abbreviation is used, i.e., DesFlot–2, DesRon–6, DesDiv–22

Coxswain's Reply	Officer or Official
"Aye, Aye"	Other Commissioned Officer
"No, No"	Warrant Officers
"Hello"	Enlisted Men
"Passing"	Boat Not Intending to Go Alongside

Passing Honors

When ships pass each other, all hands who are topside or who are visible from outboard and are free to do so, should face the ship being passed, stand at attention, and salute on signal, whether in ranks or not.

Coast Guard and Navy ships use the following whistle signals when exchanging passing honors:

Attention—2 blasts
Ship is passing to starboard—1 blast
Ship is passing to port—2 blasts
Salute—1 blast
End salute—2 blasts
Carry on—3 blasts.

Distinguished Persons

Salutes may also be given to distinguished visitors. If so, "Attention" is sounded, and all men on deck face outboard at attention. If you can see the visitor, salute at the signal to do so.

If a gun salute is rendered, men on the quarterdeck (or in the ceremonial party, if ashore) render the hand salute. Others simply stand at attention.

When any of the above-mentioned honors are rendered, men inside the ship or on covered decks, if not in sight, are not required to obey the call, but they must remain silent until "Carry on" is sounded.

Ceremonies

Change of Command

On any ship or station, when a new commanding officer takes over, all hands will fall in at quarters in dress uniform. The skipper will read his detachment orders and then the new captain will read his orders to take over the command. Both officers will then inspect the crew and the ship.

Ship Launching Ceremony

When a new ship is launched, she does not actually belong to the Coast Guard yet; but there will be flags, a band, a sponsor who christens the ship, and a reception for distinguished visitors.

Commissioning Ceremony

This is the day a new ship actually joins the Coast Guard. The entire crew will be present in dress uniform. The ceremony will be simple for a small ship. The ensign, jack, and commission pennant will be hoisted for the first time; the commanding officer will read his orders and assume command, the executive officer will "Set the watch," the boatswain's mates will pass the word "On deck, the first section," and the OOD will commence the official log. Families and friends are invited to a commissioning ceremony, and there will be receptions for guests in the various messes.

Decommissioning Ceremony

When a ship is taken out of service, either to go into "mothballs" or to be transferred to a foreign navy, the ceremony is smaller and simpler. The commanding officer will read the decommissioning orders to officers and crew at quarters, and the ensign, jack, and commission pennant will be hauled down. By tradition, the captain keeps the commission pennant. In some ships, names of officers and men are put in a hat from which the skipper draws the names of two people who will be given the ensign and jack.

Crossing the Line

When a ship crosses the equator, all "pollywogs"—those who have never crossed before—are initiated into the "Ancient Order of the Deep," and become shellbacks. Men will be issued a wallet-sized card with the name of the ship, date, and longitude, and a larger certificate. On large ships, the shellbacks may spend days planning an elaborate "Neptune party" in which King Neptune, Davy Jones, and a group of "royal" police, judges, surgeons, barbers, bears, and other characters initiate the pollywogs. A Neptune party is an all-hands affair during which the shellbacks take over the ship to a certain extent and initiate all pollywogs, whether they are E2s or admirals.

Golden Dragons

When a ship crosses the 180th meridian—the International Date Line—going west, it enters "the realm of the golden dragon," and men will be issued a card to mark the occasion.

Blue-nose Polar Bear

When a ship crosses the Arctic Circle, all hands will be issued a wallet-sized card, similar to the shellback card, stating the circumstances, and naming them "Blue-nose Polar Bears."

Christmas Lights

Ships in port during the Christmas holidays sometimes display strings of lights or other illuminated signs of the holiday season.

New Year's Log

It is traditional that the log for the first mid-watch of the new year—1 January—must be written in verse. In recent years, some such log entries have been published, especially in the weekly *Navy Times*.

Ship's Bell

On some ships the oldest member of the crew strikes the old year out with eight bells, and the youngest member of the crew is given the privilege of striking eight bells for the new year.

Homeward-bound Pennant

No ship carries this flag; it is made up only when needed. It is flown by a ship that has been overseas for nine months or more, when she gets under way to return to the United States. The homeward-bound pennant flies until sunset of the day of arrival in a U.S. port.

The pennant next to the hoist is blue and has one white star for the first nine months overseas, and an additional star for each six months. The rest is divided lengthwise; the upper section is red, the lower is white. The pennant is one foot long for each person on board who has been outside the U.S. for at least nine months, but is never longer than the length of the ship.

After being hauled down, the pennant is cut up. The blue part goes to the commanding officer. The remainder is divided equally among all hands.

Burial at Sea

During combat, or at other times when operations prevent holding a body for services ashore, the dead will be buried at sea. When schedules permit, retired persons may also be buried at sea. The ceremony may be very simple in combat or more elaborate when time permits. The body is covered by a U.S. flag, which is removed as the body is committed to the deep and then presented to the next of kin.

CHAPTER 25

Rates and Ratings

The Career Compensation Act of 1949, as amended, established uniform pay grades for officers and enlisted people in the armed forces. Under this law the pay in a given grade is the same in any of the services. Officer ranks in the Coast Guard are the same as they are in the Navy. Most enlisted ratings are the same as in the Navy, although the Coast Guard does not have all the Navy ratings. Those described here are authorized for normal peacetime operations; in times of war or national emergency other ratings may be necessary.

General

Rating

A rating is a name given to an occupation in the Coast Guard that requires basically related aptitudes, training, experience, knowledge, and skills. A person holding a rating is a petty officer.

Rate

A rate is a pay grade, reflecting a level of aptitude, training, experience, knowledge, skill, and responsibility.

Pay Grades

The order of pay grades is as follows:

Rates	Pay Grade
Seaman Recruit, Fireman Recruit	E–1
Seaman, Fireman, and Airman Apprentice	E–2
Seaman, Fireman, Airman	E–3

Figure 25–1. A petty officer 2nd class salutes an officer at the gangway.

Rates	*Pay Grade*
Petty Officer, third class	E–4
Petty Officer, second class	E–5
Petty Officer, first class	E–6
Chief Petty Officer	E–7
Senior Chief Petty Officer	E–8
Master Chief Petty Officer	E–9
Master Chief Petty Officer of the Coast Guard	E–10

Duties of Nonrated Men (E-1—E-3)

Recruits (SR, FR)

Recruit training.

Apprentices (SA, FA, AA)

Perform simple duties of seamen, firemen, and airmen, but under close supervision.

Seaman (SN)

Training for a rating in deck, ordnance, electronics, precision equipment, administrative and clerical, or miscellaneous groups: Perform general deck and other detail duties; maintain equipment, compartments, lines, rigging, and decks; act as lookouts, members of gun crews, and security and fire sentries.

Fireman (FN)

Training for engineering groups: lighting-off boilers, operating pumps, motors, and turbines; recording readings of gauges; maintaining and cleaning engineering machinery and compartments; standing security and fire room watches.

Airman (AN)

Training for a rating in the aviation group: assist in the maintenance of aircraft and associated aeronautical equipment and in the maintenance of aircraft support equipment; service and clean aircraft; assist in aircraft handling; perform other apprenticeship duties required in the operation of aviation activities.

Duties of Petty Officer Ratings (E-4—E-9)

The following brief descriptions of the duties and responsibilities of ratings in the Coast Guard is based on the rating structure in effect in 1981. The insignia for all ratings are shown in figure 6–3.

Deck Group

Boatswain's Mate (BM). The boatswain's mate serves aboard all types of ships and at most shore stations. In battle, he acts as gun captain, a member of a damage control party, or is stationed on the bridge; he must have a thorough knowledge of seamanship, and understand all deck work connected with boatswain's mate and anchor watches, as well as be familiar with rigging, hawsers, winches, hoists, tackle, lines, and cargo nets. He may take a turn at the wheel, sew canvas, or double as gun captain; he must know signal flags, lights, and navigation instruments. He directs handling and stowage of cargo, maintains and operates hoisting gear, must know how to handle small boats, and directs boat crews in landing or rescue operations.

Quartermaster (QM). Quartermasters (figure 25–1) are assigned to all types of ships and serve in the pilothouse, on the bridge or signal bridge, or in the charthouse. A quartermaster takes care of the ship's navigation publications, charts, and tables; he must know how to use and care for navigational instruments. He trains and supervises helmsmen, checks bearings and soundings, and plots course. He must know whistle, bell, and light signals, Rules of the Road, visual communications, blinker signaling, semaphore, and signal flags. QM school is a ten-week course at the Naval Training Center, Orlando, Florida.

Radarman (RD). Radarmen are stationed on all types of ships and small craft and at some shore stations. The radarman must know the function and operating principles of all radar equipment on board and be able to use such equipment in tracking and searching, in intercepting aircraft and surface vessels, and where indicated, in tracking weather balloons. He interprets and plots all information received, makes routine tests and adjustments, and performs minor repairs. Radar school is a 19-week course at CG Training Center, Governors Island, New York.

Sonar Technician (ST). They serve on ships fitted with sonar equipment, at training stations, and at certain district offices. They interpret sonic and magnetic information received by electronic and magnetic defense equipment; they may use international Morse code in transmitting and receiving messages on sonar equipment; operate sonar countermeasures equipment where installed; perform routine tests and adjustments on equipment, and make minor repairs. Training begins with a 36-week course at Fleet ASW Training Center, San Diego, California.

Ordnance Group

Gunner's Mate (GM). Gunner's mates are assigned to all fighting ships. In battle they may be at guns or in magazines to supervise ammunition handling. The gunner's mate is responsible for operation and maintenance of guns, rocket launchers, and mounts; he maintains and stows ammunition, projectiles, powder bags, fuzes, rockets, bombs, and pyrotechnics. He repairs and maintains recoil mechanisms, bearings, breech mechanisms, firing attachments, loading mechanisms, and hoists. He inspects magazines for proper temperature, and tests powder, and acts as demolition expert in placing and firing explosives. The school for gunner's mates is an 18-week course at Governors Island, New York.

Fire Control Technician (FT). Fire control technicians operate, repair, and perform maintenance on fire control equipment including computers, fire control radars, directors, switchboards, control components of ordnance power drives, and associated units aboard Coast Guard vessels. They conduct operational tests and alignment checks. They must possess general knowledge of ordnance equipment, ammunition, and magazines. Training begins with 27 weeks at the Naval Training Center, Great Lakes, or at the Naval Schools Command, Mare Island, California.

Engineering and Hull Group

Damage Controlman (DC). Damage controlmen are assigned to all but the smallest ships and shore stations, and are specialists in the theory, techniques, skills, and equipment of fire-fighting, chemical warfare, carpentry, painting, and general damage control. They maintain and repair damage-control equipment, perform all types of carpentry work, and repair and maintain woodwork aboard ship, including small boats. School: 15 weeks at Governors Island, New York.

Machinery Technician (MK). Machinery technicians may be assigned to both ships and shore stations. They operate, maintain, and repair internal combustion engines, propulsion boilers, steam turbines and main propulsion power transmission equipment. They also operate, maintain and repair auxiliary, fireroom, refrigeration, air-conditioning, electrical and machine shop equipment. They organize, lead, and participate in damage-control repair parties and perform engineering-related administrative functions. School: 16 weeks at CG Reserve Training Center, Yorktown, Virginia.

Electronics Technician (ET). The electronics technician serves on all types of ships and at shore stations having electronic equipment. He is responsible for maintenance and repair of all shipboard electronic equipment, and other types of communication, detection, and ranging equipment employing electronic circuits. He uses many types of precision test equipment—such as cathode-ray oscilloscopes, frequency meters, and vacuum-tube testers. School: 12 weeks at Governors Island, New York.

Electronics Technician (Communications) ETN. (Rating badge same as ET.) He is responsible for the maintenance and operation of communications equipment, radio aids to navigation, teletype and cryp-

Figure 25–2. An Electronics Technician repairs equipment.

tographic terminal equipment, data transmission systems, and equipment using digital logic circuits. School: 12 weeks at Training Center, Governors Island, and 22 weeks at Naval Schools Command, Mare Island, California.

Telephone Technician (TT). He maintains telephone equipment, including switchboards, electronic repeaters, instruments, teletypewriters, etc. He also maintains telephone lines and cables, including poles and underground lines. This rating serves both ashore and on board ships. Training consists of 12 weeks ET school plus 14 weeks TT school at Governors Island.

Electrician's Mate (EM). The electrician's mate serves on all types of ships and at bases. He installs, maintains, and repairs generators, electric motors, searchlights, yardarm blinkers, and the general lighting and power distribution system employed aboard ship. He locates and repairs defects in wiring; he uses electrician's hand tools and electrical measuring instruments, and performs soldering and brazing operations. In addition to maintenance and repair duties, he may stand an engineroom watch, being at such time responsible for the proper operation of all electrical equipment and control panels. Training for EM consists of 16 weeks at Governors Island.

Aviation Group

Aviation Machinist's Mate (AD). The aviation machinist's mate (figure 25–3) may be assigned to an air station or other air activity; he sometimes serves on a cutter and may fly as a member of an air crew. He is familiar with the theory of flight and the various technical aspects of engine repair and operational maintenance, as well as with work in aircraft shops and hangars. He works with hand and machine tools, assists in the handling of planes on the ground or deck, performs periodic checks, engine repairs, and trouble-shooting. School: 21 weeks at Coast Guard Aircraft Repair and Supply Center, Elizabeth City, North Carolina.

Aviation Survivalman (ASM). Aviation survivalmen inspect, maintain, and repair parachutes, survival equipment, and flight protective clothing. They pack and rig parachutes and pack and equip life rafts, as well as operate and handle small arms, aviation munitions, and pyrotechnics. They service and maintain oxygen-breathing equipment, droppable pumps and all search-and-rescue equipment carried by Coast Guard aircraft. School: Naval Air Technical Training Center, Lakehurst, New Jersey, for 16 weeks.

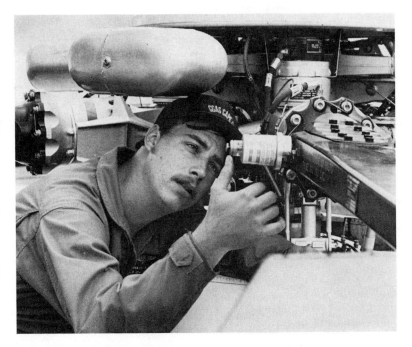

Figure 25–3. An Aviation Electronics Technician who serves as a radioman on a helicopter crew inspects parts on the rotor system.

Aviation Electronics Technician (AT). Aviation electronics technicians are stationed wherever Coast Guard aircraft are based; during flight operations, they check and repair airborne electronic equipment. They maintain, adjust, test, install, and repair all airborne electronic equipment. School: 28 weeks at Coast Guard Aircraft Repair and Supply Center, Elizabeth City, North Carolina.

Aviation Electrician's Mate (AE). Aviation electrician's mates inspect, maintain, adjust, repair, and replace all aircraft electrical power generating, converting, investing, indicating, and actuating systems and components. They maintain, test, adjust, and replace aircraft flight and engine instruments, propellers and propeller accessories. School: 23 weeks at Naval Air Technical Training Center, Memphis, Tenn.

Aviation Structural Mechanic (AM). Aviation structural mechanics (figure 25–4) may be assigned to cutters or to Coast Guard air activities ashore. They maintain and repair aircraft surfaces, structures, and hydraulic systems; they construct, repair, and align structural parts,

Figure 25–4. An Aviation Electronics Technician preflights the avionics package in the nose of the HH-sF helicopter.

such as wings, elevators, ailerons, tabs, rudders, and fuselage structures. They fabricate sheet metal and install, maintain, and repair tubing systems and flexible hose. They perform oxyacetylene and arc-welding operations, repair and maintain rubber equipment, such as tires and tubes, and repair fabric-covered surfaces. They make all periodic checks and inspections on aircraft. School: as above.

Administrative and Scientific Group

Marine Science Technician (MST). Marine science technicians observe, collect, analyze and disseminate meteorological and oceanographic data. They make visual and instrumental weather and oceanographic observations and conduct routine chemical analysis. This analysis and interpretation of weather and sea conditions furnishes advice used in search-and-rescue operations and helps direct merchant, pleasure, and military vessels safely. School: 16 weeks at Coast Guard Reserve Training Center, Yorktown, Virginia.

Yeoman (YN). A yeoman must be familiar with official letter and report forms, routing and correspondence, and with the Coast Guard filing system. He performs typing and clerical duties, prepares reports, maintains office records and files, and operates office machines. He is an expert on Coast Guard regulations, manuals, circular letters, and directives, is in charge of personnel records, and furnishes information on ratings, insurance, transportation, and promotions. Yeoman school is a 12-week course at Coast Guard Training Center, Petaluma, California.

Storekeeper (SK). All shore activities require storekeepers, as do all ships except the smallest types. A storekeeper procures, stows, preserves, packages, and issues clothing, spare parts, provisions, technical items, and all other supplies needed. He keeps inventories, prepares requisitions, and checks incoming supplies and stocks for quantity; he may perform some disbursing duties. He operates a typewriter and other office machines. In the higher pay grades he processes all matters pertaining to Coast Guard pay rolls and the disbursing of funds for various payments. He prepares and types financial accounts and reports, has knowledge of the basic principles of Coast Guard accounting system, and is familiar with allowances for subsistence, uniforms, reenlistment pay, family allowances, longevity, etc. School: 12-week course at Coast Guard Training Center, Petaluma, California.

Radioman (RM). Radiomen serve aboard all ships and at all radio stations ashore, operating radios, radio direction finders, teletypewriters, and facsimile equipment; transmitting and receiving messages in international Morse code. The radioman makes adjustments and performs upkeep in equipment, and obtains bearings with radio direction finders. He stands watches on teletypewriters, voice radio, and telegraph circuits, and copies broadcasts and keeps required logs. He lubricates, cleans, and detects mechanical difficulties in radios and typewriters and rigs emergency antennas. School: 20 weeks at Coast Guard Training Center, Petaluma, California.

Photo-Journalist (PA). Photo-journalists are assigned to certain shore stations. They are trained in photography and write news stories and press releases. They also edit copy and art, write captions, and prepare page layouts, as well as operate and maintain various types of motion-picture and still cameras and television equipment. No school; on-the-job training and correspondence courses.

Subsistence Specialist (SS). Subsistence specialists serve at shore stations and aboard ship in both the general mess and officers' mess.

They ordinarily serve as cooks and bakers, but at large shore stations and in large ships they may also serve as butchers. They prepare menus, keep cost accounts, assist in ordering provisions, and check deliveries for quantity and quality. They are responsible for proper storage of all food products and for the care of galleys, bake shops, refrigerator spaces, and provision issue rooms. School: 18 weeks at Coast Guard Training Center, Petaluma, California.

Hospital Corpsman (HM). Hospital corpsmen serve in sick bays, dental offices, or dispensaries of any ship or shore station (figure 25–5) and may be assigned to a Public Health Service Hospital for duty as liaison officer. The corpsman performs medical, dental, and clerical duties, gives first aid, and performs ward and operating room duties. He may be a technician in such fields as X-ray, pharmacy, or epidemiology. He may serve independently on small ships, performing all but major surgical duties. He serves as assistant to the medical officer in preventing and treating warfare injuries and in giving physical examinations. School: 16 weeks at Coast Guard Academy, New London.

Dental Technician (DT). He performs dental, clinical, and administrative duties; he assists dental officers and maintains and repairs equipment. He is qualified in dental X-ray techniques, clinical laboratory procedures, and other dental specialities. School: 12 weeks at Coast Guard Training Center, Cape May, New Jersey.

Port Securityman (PS). (Open only to members of the Coast Guard Reserve.) The port securityman supervises and controls the safe handling, transportation, and storage of explosives and other dangerous cargo. He is expert in fire prevention and fire fighting, knows regulations and uses equipment necessary for security of vessels, harbors, and waterfront facilities. School: 12 weeks at Coast Guard Reserve Training Center, Yorktown, Virginia.

Master Chief Petty Officer of the Coast Guard (MCPOCG)

The senior enlisted member of the Coast Guard is assigned to the office of the Commandant for a four-year tour of duty and serves as senior enlisted representative of the Coast Guard. He acts as the senior enlisted adviser to the Commandant in all matters pertaining to enlisted people, and serves as an adviser to many boards dealing with enlisted personnel. He sometimes serves as the Coast Guard representative at special events, celebrations, and ceremonies.

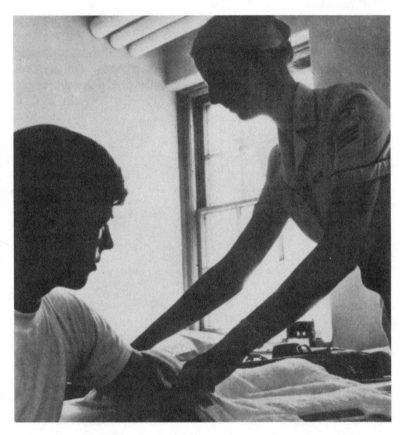

Figure 25–5. The duties of a hospital corpsman range from simple first aid treatment to highly specialized jobs such as X-ray technician.

Precedence

No one rating takes precedence over another rating. All ratings are equally important. Among enlisted people present and regularly assigned to the same activity, or among those present in any gathering, the one with the longest period of continuous service in the highest pay grade shall take the highest precedence and be considered senior, regardless of rating.

CHAPTER 26

Career Information

Enlistment in the Coast Guard offers you a choice of many careers. The one you finally select will depend in part on your own aptitudes and the needs of the service. This chapter will help you determine what occupation you are best suited for and point out how you can start on a Coast Guard career. Remember that the amount of responsibility and self-discipline you display in your work will have a great effect on your duty assignments.

Recruit Training

Your cruise in the Coast Guard begins when you report to a Recruit Training Center. Here, in a few short weeks, you must learn to make the difficult change from school and home life to a strict military routine. You may be upset and confused at first, but so will almost everyone else with you. Your instructors have all been through the mill before and are there to help you get organized and learn to do things the Coast Guard way.

One of the biggest problems the average recruit has, on entering any military service, is learning how to live with a large group of people. Recruit training is designed to assist you in solving this problem, but it cannot do it all alone. You must assist yourself by being tolerant of other people's peculiarities. You probably have some of your own.

While you are in recruit training you will learn many things. Some of them are taught in formal classes, others you gradually absorb in your daily work. Recruit training is designed to provide the basic

Figure 26–1. The crew chief on a Coast Guard helicopter always stands outside the aircraft with a fire extinguisher and watches the engine closely when it is started.

knowledge necessary to help you learn the various skills required in the Coast Guard: boatmanship, visual signaling, infantry drill, personal hygiene, traditions, care of the uniform, marlinspike seamanship, and many others. You will also learn the main essential of good citizenship—living with others.

Basic Tests

All recruits are given the Navy Enlisted Qualification Tests, sometimes called the Navy Basic Battery. These tests are used to measure your basic aptitudes—in other words, to find out what things come naturally to you. Test scores are arranged to show how you compare with all others who have taken the test. There are no "passing" or "failing" scores—the tests are designed to guide you into what you can do best rather than measure how much you have learned. On each test 50 is an average score, with 77 about the highest and 22 the lowest.

Recruits entering the Coast Guard all take these basic tests:

General Classification Test (GCT). This measures ability to think and to reason *in terms of words*.

Arithmetic Test (ARI). This does the same, *in terms of numbers*.

Mechanical Test (MECH). This shows potential ability for work of a mechanical nature. It gives an idea of familiarity with mechanical and electrical tools.

Clerical Test (CLER). This measures the ability to observe quickly and accurately.

Other tests used are: Electronics Technician Selection Test (ETST); Radio Code Test; Sonar Pitch-Memory Test; and Advanced Technician Test (ATT). These are used to screen candidates for advanced technical training, and include four categories—reading comprehension, mathematics, physics, and electricity.

Test scores are used in determining assignments to petty officer schools. Do your best the first time, because classification tests are usually not given a second time. These tests are important, but they are not the only factor; your own determination and ability will determine your success in the Coast Guard.

First Duty Assignments

On completion of training, recruits are granted ten days' leave before reporting for duty. This usually allows time to visit your family and friends for a few days. They may base their entire impression of the

Coast Guard on what you do and how you show off the training you have received.

First duty assignments may be either sea duty or shore duty. Sea duty may mean a 378-foot cutter, an icebreaker, buoy tender, patrol boat, or any of many other vessels. Shore duty may be with a station, light station, base or group. Wherever you go, you will find new and exciting experiences.

Petty Officer Training

Petty officer training consists of basic or Class A petty officer schools, advanced or Class B petty officer schools, and specialized or Class C petty officer schools.

The basic petty officer schools give men in pay grades E-3 and E-2 the theoretical knowledge and practical work necessary for advancement to petty officer third class in a specific rating. Assignment to Class A schools is often made upon completion of recruit training. However, personnel may obtain assignment to a specific basic petty officer school when serving on board a ship or station.

At present the Coast Guard conducts these Class A schools:

Training Center, Governors Island, New York

Damage Controlman (DC)
Electrician's Mate (EM)
Electronics Technician (ET)
Gunner's Mate (GM)
Radarman (RD)
Telephone Technician (TT)

Aircraft Repair and Supply Center, Elizabeth City, North Carolina

Aviation Electronics Technician (AT)
Aviation Machinist's Mate (AD)

Training Center, Petaluma, California

Radioman (RM)
Storekeeper (SK)
Subsistence Specialist (SS)
Yeoman (YN)

Reserve Training Center, Yorktown, Virginia

Machinery Technician (MK)
Marine Science Technician (MST)

Academy, New London, Connecticut

Hospital Corpsman (HM)

Training Center, Cape May, New Jersey

Dental Technician (DT)

Navy Schools

The Coast Guard uses Navy schools for training the following ratings:
Aviation Electrician's Mate (AE)
Aviation Structural Mechanic (AM)
Aviation Survivalman (ASM)
Electronics Technician Communication (ETN)
Fire Control Technician (FT)
Quartermaster (QM)
Sonar Technician (ST)
The length of school courses varies from about eleven weeks to as
long as nine months.

Advanced PO Schools

The advanced or Class B petty officer schools are available for second-
class petty officers and above and are designed to provide both theoretical and practical knowledge required of a rate higher than petty
officer third class. Coast Guard and other service Class B schools are
utilized (figure 26–2).

Specialized or Class C petty officer schools provide training in special
skills that are in addition to the qualifications for a specific rate. Both
service and civilian schools are utilized. Eligibility is determined by
the needs of the specific unit.

Selection for Training

In order to attend advanced schools, a man must have made certain
scores in his classification tests, must have a good conduct record, and
must be recommended by his commanding officer. No mechanical
aptitude is necessary to be a yeoman, but the trainee for this rating
should have clerical aptitude. For certain other schools, high scores

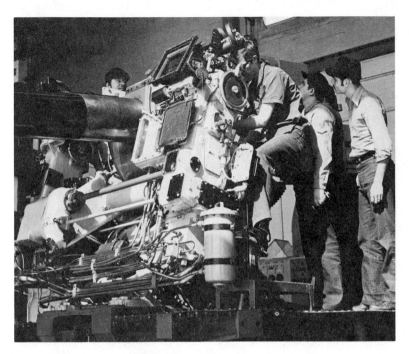

Figure 26–2. Men are checked out on the complicated mechanism of a 5-inch gun mount.

in the mechanical and arithmetic tests are needed (figure 26–3). A high GCT score helps a person's chances for any school. Your commanding officer's recommendation will be based on observation of your work by himself, the executive officer, and your division and petty officers. They will judge you by your work and your attitude.

Class A schools offer theoretical and practical training in the rating you have chosen, and leadership training for your future role as a petty officer. These schools combine classroom lectures with shop or laboratory work where you will use the tools of your future trade.

Graduates of Class A schools may be promoted to petty officer third class, provided there is a vacancy in their rating and they have the required one year of service, counted from day of enlistment. Those not advanced on graduation will be given a school-assigned designator. This allows them to work in their new rating and be promoted when they have the required time in service, provided there is a vacancy and their conduct is satisfactory.

Figure 26–3. Engine overhaul and maintenance is one job that requires high mechanical aptitude.

The advanced courses for petty officers are not required for later advancement, but they certainly help. If you want to advance, you must study.

Some of the knowledge you need can only be gained by experience. The rest comes by study of various publications, including this manual. Remember that knowledge alone will not give you promotion. You must have a record of satisfactory performance in your present duty, your conduct record must be satisfactory, and you must be reliable. The officers and petty officers of your unit must be able to depend on you.

Ratings Qualifications

After reaching pay grade E-3, you should decide what rating you prefer to enter. Most ratings are covered by Class A schools, but for others you make your own preparations.

In addition to the actual knowledge requirements for advancement in rate, you must serve a certain minimum time in the lower rate, be recommended for advancement, and have completed the practical factors for the rating. The *Enlisted Ratings Qualifications Manual*, gives details on practical factors.

Correspondence Courses

The Coast Guard Institute furnishes correspondence courses covering the requirements for advancement in practically all ratings. These courses enable you to study for a rating at your own unit. Completion of one of them is usually required for advancement. Class A school graduates do not have to complete correspondence courses for advancement to pay grade E-4.

On-the-Job Training

On-the-job training goes hand-in-hand with correspondence courses. What you learn in your courses in theory, you can practice in your daily work. In many of the ratings, experience is an absolute necessity. For instance, a boatswain's mate must have experience as a leading seaman. Here, while serving an apprenticeship, you actually learn while doing, under an experienced petty officer. Whether you train on the job or in a formal school, both theoretical knowledge and practical experience are necessary.

Leadership

You need more than knowledge and experience to hold a rating in the Coast Guard. The device on the petty officer badge means more than that he is a specialist—the eagle shows that he is a petty officer, a leader. A petty officer is both a *specialist* in his rating and a *military leader*. Military duties and responsibilities as a petty officer take precedence over skill in rating. Leadership is a quality that few people are born with. The acquisition of leadership requires study and practice. Some of the study can come from a book or formal course. Much of it must come from observation of good leaders. In your daily life you will come in contact with many leaders. Watch them, note the qualities that make them good leaders, and copy them.

A good leader must have a good conduct record. Conduct itself is an integral part of leadership. You cannot expect a higher standard of conduct from your subordinates than you yourself display.

Advancement in Rating

Most petty officer promotions are the result of successfully passing examinations in service-wide competition. A few people are advanced to third-class petty officer after finishing a basic petty officer school. Promotion examinations are usually held twice a year; only persons recommended by their commanding officers may take the examinations.

Eligibility

To be able to take the promotion examination, you must have a certain minimum time in service, or time in present pay grade. You must complete the required correspondence course, fulfill the practical factors qualifications for your rating, and be recommended by your commanding officer.

Multiples

Your examination mark will be assigned by the Coast Guard Institute, where your examination will be graded. You will be given additional credits for performance marks, time in service, time in grade, and awards. The total score is called "final multiple." People are promoted in "final multiple" order—highest man first. If there are not enough vacancies to allow the promotion of everyone who passed the examination, those who didn't make their rate will have to take another examination. This gives them a chance to make a better score next time.

Promotion to Warrant and Commissioned Grades

Every petty officer rating has a normal path of advancement to warrant officer rank. Selections for warrant officer are made from among first class and chief petty officers on the eligibility list who apply for this advancement. An applicant must have the required service, must make satisfactory scores on warrant qualification and specialty examinations, and must be recommended by his commanding officer. A selection board of commissioned officers then chooses those considered best qualified to fill the existing vacancies in the various warrant categories. Selected candidates are promoted to W-2.

To qualify for promotion to chief warrant officer, W-3, a warrant officer must have completed the required length of service in grade satisfactorily. He must then be approved by a selection board. Similar procedures are followed for promotion to W-4.

Advancement does not end here. Many warrant and chief warrant officers have been promoted to higher commissioned grades.

Officer Candidate School

In periods of expansion or national emergency, selected enlisted men (figure 26–4) are ordered to the Officer Candidate School (OCS) at the U.S. Coast Guard Reserve Training Center, Yorktown, Virginia. This training leads to appointments for temporary service as ensigns, providing certain requirements are met. Many such temporary officers eventually receive permanent commissions, after meeting service requirements and after having been selected for promotion to lieutenant. Also, at certain times enlisted men with the necessary educational qualifications are given the opportunity to become commissioned officers in the Reserve. The *Personnel Manual* lists the eligibility requirements for this program.

Coast Guard Academy

Cadets are selected annually by competitive examinations. To qualify for the examinations, a candidate must be between the ages of 18 and

Figure 26–4. Trainees reporting to the Officer Candidate School at Yorktown, Virginia, include both civilians and enlisted men.

22, be of good character, be a U.S. citizen, and be a high school graduate with school credits in the required subjects. These examinations are open to enlisted people in all the armed forces.

Recreation

The Coast Guard plans a comprehensive program of recreation for the crews of all ships and shore stations. In addition, Headquarters or district offices provide for motion pictures, libraries, sports equipment, etc. Not all of such material, of course, goes to every ship or station. Each ship or station, however, does develop a recreation program aimed at keeping the crew contented, amused, and healthy. Such activities cover a wide variety of projects, depending on the location of the station and other factors.

Morale and Recreation Officer

On large ships and stations, an officer is specifically assigned additional duty as morale and recreation officer. An officer may also serve as morale and recreation officer on smaller ships and stations.

The morale and recreation officer has many resources upon which to draw in order to provide recreation. See him about anything of this nature that you or your shipmates consider desirable.

Sports

All forms of athletics are encouraged. In this connection the Navy permits the entry of Coast Guard personnel in the Navy Sports Program. In addition, every ship and station does what it can to provide athletic facilities on a competitive and noncompetitive basis so that every sailor, regardless of his physical prowess, can engage in healthful, body-building athletic activities.

Entertainment

Various forms of entertainment, including motion pictures, are provided for Coast Guard personnel. Nearly all ships and stations have stereo equipment and color TV. Some of the smaller ships and stations may not provide a regular hobby shop, but you will usually have the opportunity to keep up a hobby in which you may be interested. The recreation officer may be able to assist you in this regard.

Libraries

Almost every Coast Guard unit has a library. The size of the library will depend on the personnel strength of the unit. Most libraries stock fiction, nonfiction, a variety of technical books, and many popular magazines. They will help you in off-duty studies, and in studying for a rating.

Information and Education Program

It is possible to study almost any subject in your off-duty time through the Coast Guard's educational program. The principal sources of off-duty education are the U.S. Coast Guard Institute (USCGI), and various educational and commercial institutions.

The Coast Guard Institute

This organization provides correspondence courses and conducts service-wide examinations for enlisted advancements and warrant officer selection. Most of the courses are directly related to the knowledge and skills that Coast Guardsmen in the various ratings and pay grades must possess. As a general rule, a Coast Guardsman must complete an Institute correspondence course before he can compete for advancement to a higher pay grade.

The unit's educational services officer has a copy of the Institute's *Correspondence Course Manual,* which contains the rules and procedures of the program and a list of the courses available. He will take care of the details for your enrollment, keep track of your progress, and give instruction and guidance if you have any problems while you are completing the course. You are eligible for enrollment in any course offered by the Institute. Enrollment is usually limited to one course at a time.

In addition to enlisted rating courses, the Coast Guard Institute offers a number of special courses, among which are oceanography, meteorology, boating safety, and search and rescue. All courses are furnished without cost, and you may keep most of the materials for future reference. Satisfactory course completion is recorded in your service record.

Coast Guard Tuition Assistance Program

This program covers courses taken during off-duty hours at accredited colleges, universities, junior colleges, high schools, and commercial schools, but not correspondence courses. (See Veterans Administration Tuition Assistance concerning these.) In order to qualify for assistance, the desired course must be one that would broaden your technical and academic background and increase your usefulness to the service. Generally, any course that will increase your chances for promotion—shorthand for a yeoman, bookkeeping for a storekeeper—will meet this requirement. However, funds must be available and your attendance at the course must not interfere with your assigned duties. Duty comes first.

Coast Guard Mutual Assistance

This organization provides financial assistance to active duty and retired personnel in times of need or emergency, in the form of interest-free loans, or grants. It is not a loan agency where money may be borrowed as a convenience or for the purchase of automobiles or TV sets. Rather, it is established to assist in cases of real hardship beyond the control of an individual. If you find yourself in such a situation, Coast Guard Mutual Assistance is one of the first activities to go to for help.

Coast Guard Mutual Assistance can help with loans for down payments on homes. Within certain limits, such as the amount of your monthly bills and the cost of the home you desire to purchase, the loan may cover all or a portion of the required down payment.

The American Red Cross

This organization provides several services to Coast Guard units and individual personnel. Among these are verification of requests for emergency leave or leave extensions based on emergencies, assistance with the unit blood program, and individual counsel, guidance, and financial assistance in the form of a loan or grant. Any financial assistance given will depend on whether the emergency is real and how serious it is.

Non-Appropriated Fund Activities

Many of the larger units have a base or ship's exchange, laundry, tailor shop, barber shop, snack bar, enlisted men's club, etc. These functions are called non-appropriated fund activities (NAFA), because they are supported by their own profits rather than by government funds. Part of the profits are used by the commanding officer for recreational equipment for the crew, for holding crew's parties, etc. Part of the profits are distributed to smaller units not having NAF activities in order that they may also benefit. You are entitled to use the exchanges or stores at any Army, Navy, Marine, Air Force, or Coast Guard base.

Legal Assistance

The district legal officer is designated as the legal assistance officer. He will interview, advise, and assist members of the Coast Guard and their dependents who have legal problems and, in certain cases, refer them to competent attorneys. All matters are treated confidentially and will not be disclosed without your permission. The legal assistance officer can draw up wills, powers of attorney, deeds, affidavits, contracts, and many other documents. He also deals with cases of transfer of property, questions of marriage and divorce, adoption of children, taxation, personal injury, and any other legal problems.

Post Office

Most large shore units and the major ships have post offices that usually sell stamps and money orders. Money orders are a good way to pay bills or send money home. Never send cash through the mail.

Benefits

Veterans Administration Tuition Assistance

After serving 181 days on active duty you become eligible for VA tuition assistance. Under this program you may take off-duty courses that are not directly related to your rating. Correspondence courses may also be taken. Any course must be state approved and may be offered by a college, vocational, business, or high school, or correspondence school. The amount of financial assistance received is determined by the VA regulations in effect at the time. Courses paid for by the VA while you are in the service will reduce your benefits after you are discharged or retired. Your education officer can provide detailed information on this program.

Social Security

All service personnel participate in the Social Security program. A small portion of your pay is deducted each month for this purpose. The amount of deduction is matched by the Coast Guard. These funds will earn Social Security benefits for you and your dependents.

Insurance Programs

Dependency and Indemnity Compensation (DIC) is a form of insurance payable to the survivors of personnel who die in the line of duty while on active duty. As a member of the Coast Guard you automatically receive this coverage, free of charge.

Servicemen's Group Life Insurance (SGLI). This is a government-sponsored term insurance program. Upon joining the Coast Guard you are automatically insured. A small amount of your pay is deducted each month to pay for this insurance. You may reduce your coverage or cancel it; however, this is seldom done since the cost is so low. This insurance is good only while you are on active duty, or for certain categories of reservists. The Survivors' Benefit Plan (SBP) applies to retired personnel. Under this program a service member agrees to a reduced retirement pay upon retirement, and in return his widow continues to receive a portion of his retired pay after he dies.

Mortgage Insurance for Servicemen. Some time during your career you may decide to purchase a residence. If you obtain a conventional mortgage loan, you will have to make a down payment of as much as 20 or 30 percent of the purchase price. As a member of the Coast Guard you are eligible to apply for an FHA in-service loan, or a VA in-service loan, which allows you to purchase a home with a greatly reduced down payment. Detailed information on mortgages and rates of interest may be obtained from any major lending institution.

Medical Care. Free medical and dental care is provided all members of the Coast Guard on active duty. This care includes surgery and emergencies, as well as routine immunizations, physical exams, etc. Dependents are eligible for medical care in the facilities of any of the armed services; they pay a small daily charge when they are hospital-ized. Another medical care program is CHAMPUS (Civilian Health and Medical Program of the Uniformed Services). Under this program dependents may receive outpatient treatment, and in some instances inpatient care, from civilian facilities. The government pays most of each CHAMPUS bill, but the individual must pay part of it.

Off-duty Employment. Personnel on active duty are in a 24-hour duty status, and their military duties take precedence at all times. However, you can hold a part-time job, or work for yourself in off-duty hours. Anyone doing such work must remember that even though they are on leave or liberty, they are subject to recall and duty at any time. The Coast Guard Personnel Manual covers the conditions under which civilian work or employment is prohibited.

Soldiers' and Sailors' Civil Relief Act. There are wide differences in some of the laws of the various states, particularly those laws regarding taxes. If you were stationed in one state for part of a year and in another state for the remainder of the year and all the while claimed a third state as your legal residence, you could find yourself in a complicated tax situation. The Soldiers' and Sailors' Civil Relief Act was enacted to help you in such a case, and to protect you if you have signed a lease, as lessee, and are subsequently transferred, provided the lease contains a military clause. For more information on this, see the Coast Guard Personnel Manual.

Pay and Allowances

The pay of all members of the armed services is determined by Congress. Your pay consists of basic pay, basic allowances (one for quarters and one for subsistence or meals), incentive pay or hazardous duty pay, and miscellaneous pay and allowances.

You will be paid twice a month, generally the fifteenth and the thirtieth. The actual amount you receive each pay day is equal to basic pay, plus certain allowances, minus taxes and minus any allotments you may have made. Your basic pay is determined by your rank or rate and your total years of creditable service. Basic pay and basic allowances are computed on a monthly basis.

Basic Allowances for Subsistence and Quarters

As a member of the Coast Guard you are entitled to food and shelter in addition to basic pay. Also, regardless of your pay grade, you are entitled to certain allowances in cash to provide quarters for your wife or legal dependents. If you have no legal dependents, you will usually be provided subsistence and quarters "in kind." This means that you will eat in a government mess and will sleep on board ship or in government barracks or quarters. Your food costs you nothing, so you receive no cash allowance for it. There may be times when it is impracticable to furnish you with either subsistence, quarters, or both in kind. In that case you will receive a cash allowance in lieu of those items not furnished.

Commuted Rations

When a regular mess is available, but you would rather eat in your own home, your commanding officer may authorize payment of a daily allowance for this, in which case you lose the right to eat in the regular mess. The conditions under which "ComRats" may be paid will be explained by your pay officer.

Incentive Pay for Hazardous Duty

For pay purposes the following duties have been designated as hazardous:

> Duty involving frequent and regular participation, as a crew member, in aerial flights.
> Duty involving frequent and regular participation, *not* as a crew member, in aerial flights.

Men assigned to such duties will be entitled to monthly incentive pay, which varies from $50 to $105, depending on rate and time in service. For all other hazardous duties, the additional pay is $55 a month. The directives on hazardous duties and incentive pay change from time to time. Check with your pay office.

Sea and Foreign Duty Pay

The rates for this pay vary with your pay grade. Instructions covering the places where duty entitles you to such pay change from time to time; check with your pay officer.

Clothing Allowance

All recruits get an initial cash clothing allowance, enough for a complete outfit. After six months, you begin receiving a monthly allowance for clothing maintenance. Special clothing, such as arctic clothing, is furnished to you at no cost when you are required to use it.

Proficiency Pay

This was established as an incentive to help fill shortages in certain ratings, or special duty assignments, and is classified either as Shortage Specialty pro pay or Special Duty Assignment pro pay. Each year Coast Guard headquarters determines which ratings, skills (identified by qualification codes), and special duty assignments will be authorized awards of pro pay.

Family Separation Allowance

This is paid to help offset additional expenses you might have when stationed away from your family. The rate of pay varies, and eligibility is involved. See your pay office.

Military Incentive Awards Program

This is a system offering cash awards for suggestions that improve techniques in the service. Awards range from $25 to $5,000 and up, depending on the extent of application and value of the suggestion, which must be for something outside your assigned duties.

Allotments

You may assign or allot a part of your pay regularly to a spouse, parent, bank, or insurance company. You can also use this method to buy Savings Bonds. The money you allot is paid each month, and is deducted from your pay.

Deposits for Safekeeping

The executive officer may hold money for you in his safe, but is not responsible if his safe is robbed. Money so deposited may be drawn out at will (though this privilege must not be abused) and does not earn interest.

U.S. Savings Bonds

A wise way to save money is by buying U.S. Savings Bonds, preferably by a monthly allotment. Bonds provide savings for family emergencies and for return to civilian life. They may be cashed at any time 60 days after purchase.

Travel, Transportation, and Per Diem

When traveling under orders, you are entitled to do so at government expense. You may be authorized to travel by automobile, or by government or commercial transportation. In addition, a per diem (daily) allowance may be paid to cover the cost of food, lodging, and other expenses. With the exception of those personnel in the lowest pay grades, transportation of dependents and household goods at government expense is authorized on a permanent change of station. Orders to a new duty station involve many expenses. The Coast Guard recognizes this and reimburses you through a dislocation allowance, trailer allowance, mileage allowances, dependents' transportation, and shipment of household goods. The rules and regulations covering transportation and travel expenses are complicated and subject to frequent changes. You are only entitled, however, to allowances authorized or directed in the orders, so to determine what these are—check with the transportation officer.

Enlistments

Requirements for enlistment are established by the Commandant, in accordance with broad standards established by Congress. At present an applicant for original enlistment must:

> Be a native-born or naturalized citizen of the United States.
> Be between 17 and 26 years of age.
> Pass the physical examination.
> Be of good character.
> Meet certain mental requirements. (Attain a specified minimum score in qualification test.)
> Present written consent of parent or guardian if under 18 years of age.
> In some cases, have written references from at least three responsible persons plus school or employment records.

Extension of Enlistment

You may extend any enlistment voluntarily for any number of years up to four.

Reenlistment

If you desire to reenlist on the same ship or station, you must do so on the day following discharge. If honorably discharged, you may reenlist any time within three months at a regular recruiting station. Your commanding officer must recommend you for reenlistment.

A reenlistment on the same ship or station on the day following discharge is in the same rating held on date of discharge. All other reenlistments are effected under conditions prescribed by the Commandant, and very often at a lower rating. You should reenlist at the same unit on the day following discharge.

There are other requirements for enlistments by men with prior military service, as well as a limit on the number of dependents they may have.

Reenlistment Leave

All men who reenlist immediately may be granted reenlistment leave in an amount not to exceed 90 days. This includes leave from previous enlistment for which payment has not been made, and up to 30 days "advance leave." If payment has been received for accrued leave in the previous enlistment, 30 days "advance leave" may be taken as reenlistment leave. Reenlistment leave shall be taken as soon as possible after reenlistment or voluntary extension of enlistment. It may be granted only once during the period of enlistment or voluntary extension of enlistment. Reenlistment leave is chargeable against the leave account of the individual concerned in the same way as regular leave.

Cash Settlement for Unused Accrued Leave

On discharge, leave accounts are balanced; unused leave may be carried over into the new enlistment or paid for in cash. The amount paid includes basic pay, subsistence allowance, and quarters allowance for the period of the unused leave. However, the Coast Guard encourages men to take all their leave; the rest and relaxation makes for better work.

Selective Reenlistment Bonus (SRB)

When there are shortages of trained petty officers in certain ratings, a reenlistment bonus may be established to encourage men in those ratings to remain in service. The amount paid on reenlistment depends on the actual petty officer shortage, the amount of training required to serve in the ratings involved, and a man's length of previous service; it may run into thousands of dollars.

Duty Tours

In general, you may expect to get the duty or training you desire, unless the needs of the Coast Guard make it impossible. Sometimes you may have to wait, but eventually your requests will be taken care of. It is important to keep up to date on changes in rules and regulations, so as to take advantage of all opportunities for either duty or schools.

Sea Service

Sea duty for pay, promotion, and rotation is defined by the Commandant. The length of duty tours beyond the continental limits of the

United States varies, according to the location, degree of isolation, and the needs of the service.

Shore Duty

After a certain amount of continuous sea duty, or overseas duty, or combination of both, you become eligible for transfer to shore duty. The interests of the service come first, but every effort is made to give everyone a fair share of shore duty.

Time Not Creditable for Service

You will not be paid, or credited for time served, if you were not performing duty. In counting time served, days in which you were absent from duty due to misconduct will be deducted from the total. The following count as time not served:

Absence over leave, absence without leave, and desertion.

Absence from duty due to injury, disease, or sickness resulting from own intemperate use of drugs or alcoholic liquor, or other misconduct.

Absence due to arrest and serving of sentence imposed either by civil or military authorities. If the arrest results in no conviction, the time spent under arrest is not deducted.

Duty Assignments

All enlisted men list their personal data, training, previous assignments, and duty preferences on the Enlisted Assignment Data Form (CG-4526). Reassignments to duty are based on this form, so be sure to have one filled out and up to date on file.

Petty Officer Assignments. These are handled by the Central Assignment Control (CAC) program, at Headquarters. They are based on the billet requirements for each unit, the needs of the service, the enlisted qualification code of certain billets, and billet vacancies.

Non-rated Assignments. These are controlled either by Headquarters or district personnel officers, in much the same way petty officer assignments are handled.

Autogenous Transfers. On first duty assignments, it is not always possible to match duty stations with personal preference; men are sent where they are needed the most. Later, changes in personnel at various stations make it possible for a man to be sent to a station he prefers, but because there is no advantage to the Coast Guard in such a transfer, it must be made at no expense to the government. The man wanting the transfer must find someone at the other station with the same rating and experience, who will "mutual" with him—swap duty stations with both paying their own expenses. If a "mutual" exchange can not be made, a unilateral change of station may be requested—this is always a transfer to sea duty unless you are in a rating that doesn't have sea billets. Again, a man making a unilateral transfer pays the costs himself.

Humanitarian Assignments. These are special assignments made to help a man handle a hardship of such nature that it cannot be taken care of by emergency leave. Such transfers are usually for four months, but in special cases a permanent change of station will be considered. These assignments are at government expense. Details are contained in the Personnel Manual.

Discharges

There are five types of discharges for enlisted personnel:

Type of Discharge	Character of Separation	Given by
Honorable	Honorable	Administrative action
General	Under honorable conditions	Administrative action
Undesirable	Conditions other than honorable	Administrative action
Bad conduct	Conditions other than honorable	Courts-martial
Dishonorable	Dishonorable	General courts-martial

The formal reasons for discharge of enlisted personnel are:

    Expiration of enlistment
    Convenience of the government
    Dependency or hardship
    Minority
    Disability
    Unsuitability
    Security
    Unfitness
    Misconduct
    Sentence of courts-martial

Honorable Discharge

To obtain an honorable discharge, you must fulfill certain conditions described in detail in the *Personnel Manual.* Your record must show high standing in performing the duties of your rate, in industry, and in conduct.

General Discharge

A general discharge is given for the same reasons as the honorable discharge. If your conduct and performance of duty have been satisfactory, but not high enough to warrant an honorable discharge, you will receive a general discharge.

Undesirable Discharge

An undesirable discharge is given for reasons of unfitness, security, and misconduct.

Bad Conduct Discharge

A bad conduct discharge is given, only by approved sentences of special or general courts-martial, for offenses which, although serious, are not sufficiently grave to warrant dishonorable separation.

Dishonorable Discharge

A dishonorable discharge is given only by approved sentences of general courts-martial. It is one of the consequences of serious offenses.

Importance and Benefits of an Honorable Discharge

The kind of discharge you receive may affect you for the rest of your life. Eligibility for veterans' preference in federal employment, for payments for service-connected disability, for a pension, and for many other benefits and privileges—state and federal—will depend upon the type of discharge you receive. Civilian employers may refuse to hire a person with the "wrong" kind of discharge. Do all you can to earn a discharge under honorable conditions.

Formal Reasons for Discharge

Expiration of Enlistment

Normally, enlisted personnel are promptly discharged on the date of expiration of enlistment. However, they may continue on duty for some time after that date if they extend their enlistment, are undergoing medical treatment, or awaiting trial, or are required to make up lost time. They may also be held past discharge date if the ship is at sea, or in time of war or national emergency.

Disability

This discharge is given to men who are found unable to carry out their duties because of mental or physical disability.

Convenience of the Government

This term covers such reasons as general demobilization or the acceptance of a permanent commission.

Own Convenience

Generally, the Coast Guard will not discharge enlisted personnel merely for their own convenience.

Dependency or Hardship

Discharges given for reasons of dependency or hardship, sometimes called "hardship discharges," are authorized when it is shown that undue and general hardship exists at home; that the hardship is not a temporary one; and that the conditions have arisen or become worse since the person joined the Coast Guard. A dependency discharge is not authorized merely for financial or business reasons or for personal convenience. However, a man's discharge will not be held up because he is needed in his assigned duties, or because he is indebted to the government or to an individual.

Minority

Discharge for minority is of interest only to enlisted personnel who are under 18 years of age. Instructions regarding such discharges may be found in the *Personnel Manual*.

Unsuitability

The Commandant may authorize or direct the discharge of personnel for unsuitability. Among the good and sufficient reasons for such a discharge are inaptitude for service life, psychiatric or neurological handicaps, enuresis, alcoholism, and personality disorders or defects.

Security

A discharge for reasons of security is directed only when it is determined that the enlisted person cannot continue in service without risk to the national interest.

Unfitness

A person will be recommended for an unfitness discharge only after he has demonstrated total unfitness, and after disciplinary action has been taken for any offenses he may have committed. A discharge for unfitness should not replace appropriate disciplinary action. Unfitness includes acts such as drug addiction, sexual perversion, frequent involvement with military or civil authorities, habitual shirking, financial recklessness, and other good and sufficient reasons.

Misconduct

A discharge for misconduct may be directed for desertion, conviction by civil authorities, or fraudulent enlistment.

Sentence of a Court-Martial

In addition to other punishments, a court-martial can award a discharge from the Coast Guard. Not only does this rid the service of unwanted persons, but it puts—by way of punishment—a black mark of serious consequences forever in the person's record.

Service Record

Your service record is a large manila folder that holds the official papers and records concerning you and your Coast Guard career. It is the Coast Guard's official file on you.

Actually you have two records. One is kept in the personnel office of your ship or station and goes with you when you are transferred from one command to another. The other is kept at Headquarters in Washington. At the end of your service the two records are combined and then sent to a records storage center.

Your record is important, during your service career and later in civilian life, so "keep it clean." Even after you have been discharged, or retired, information from your record may be needed for collecting veteran's benefits, for employment, or for school credits.

Contents

The record contains copies of birth certificates, school certificates, and letters of commendations, but it is, primarily, a series of "pages," which are as follows:

Page 1—Enlistment Contract
Page 2—Record of Emergency Data (CG-4113)

This is one of the most important in your record, and should be kept up to date at all times. It shows those persons you want notified in case of emergency; any insurance company to be notified in case of death; persons or banks to receive special allotments in case you are missing, interned in a foreign country, or otherwise unable to return to Coast Guard jurisdiction. You should make out a new CG-4113 on reenlistment, recall to active duty, promotion, change of permanent address, changes in name or address of those who are to receive the death gratuity or a percentage of your pay if you are missing, and on any change in your status such as marriage, additional children, or divorce.

Page 3—Classification, Training, and Rating

This is a summary of your education, advancement, and special qualifications.

Page 4—Court Memorandum, used in event of courts, nonjudicial punishment, other disciplinary actions.

Page 5—Leave Record

Page 6—Performance of Duty Marks

Page 7—Administrative Remarks—entries on medals, absences, injuries, etc.

Page 8—Motor Vehicle Operator's Record

Pages 9-10—Separation from Service

Page 12—Personal Action Sheet

Identification Card

The green *Armed Forces of the United States Identification Card*— "ID card" for short—identifies you as an active member of the armed forces. It shows your name, social security number, rate, fingerprints, photograph, and date of expiration of enlistment. It is not a pass, but you should carry it at all times.

"Non-Petty Officer" is typed on the cards of people in pay grades E-1, E-2, and E-3. Cards for those in higher pay grades are marked PO3, PO2, PO1, POCS or POCM, as appropriate. If you lose your ID card, you will have to sign a statement explaining how it was lost. If you were neglectful, disciplinary action will follow. The card is government property; if you alter, damage, or counterfeit it, or use it in an unauthorized manner, you will be subject to disciplinary action. The same warning applies to lending your card or borrowing another person's card. When you are discharged, your ID card must be turned in. People in an inactive status are issued a red ID card, while those who are retired get a blue one.

ID Tags

Metal "dog tags" are issued to all hands. Make certain yours are correct, and wear them when required—generally, this is when operating under hazardous conditions. The *Personnel Manual* lists all specific instances when dog tags must be worn.

Special Requests

When a man wants a transfer to another ship or station, assignment to school, change of rating, permission to bring some piece of personal property on board, or some other consideration, he submits a special request slip, or "request chit." Such slips are submitted in a "chain of command" fashion so that the officer to take final action will know the decisions of those immediately above you. If your request is reasonable and valid, and your performance of duty has been good, your request will probably be granted.

Requests Through Channels

Anyone may make a request or an appeal to higher authority (senior to your CO). Appeal from censure, request for transfer or school, or forwarding of a suggestion are possible reasons for "going up the line." The general rule is that all requests are usually in letter form (see *CG Correspondence Manual*) and must go through the "chain of command," via the CO, the Group Command, District, and finally to the Commandant. Do not by-pass the chain of command; this is a violation of a basic military principle. You are permitted to make requests; just make them through channels.

Liberty

Authorized absence from duty for periods up to 96 hours is classed as liberty. Most liberties consist of leaving the ship or station around 1630 and returning before 0730 or 0800 the next morning. The normal 48-hour liberty that is granted for weekends may be extended to 72 hours if the period includes a national holiday. A 96-hour liberty must include two consecutive nonwork days and shall not, under any circumstances, extend beyond 96 hours.

Various ships and stations will have different types of liberty schedules. For example: "port and starboard liberty" (1-in-2, or liberty every other evening); "three section liberty" (2 liberty nights for each duty night); and even "six-section liberty" (five liberty nights and 1 duty night).

All liberty is controlled by your commanding officer, and is granted as work loads and operating schedules permit. Remember, it is a privilege, not a right.

Leave

Leave is authorized absence from duty for a period of longer than 96 hours. Leave is earned at the rate of two and one-half days per month of duty, but not for periods of training duty without pay (Reservists), any period of less than 30 consecutive days of training duty (Reservists), while confined as sentence of court-martial, or while in an unauthorized absence status for 24 hours or more.

Earned Leave

This is the amount of leave you have credited "on the books" at any given date. If you have taken more leave than you were entitled to, then you have *minus leave* on the books. Any minus leave over that which you would normally earn during the rest of your enlistment is treated as *excess leave*. Excess leave is leave over and above your earned leave and any *advance leave* granted you. Advance leave is leave granted out of the amount of leave you will earn during the rest of your enlistment.

Here is how advance and excess leave works. Say you have 10 days' earned leave on the books and 4 months to go on your enlistment. Because of an emergency you are granted 20 days' leave. Those 20 days are half earned leave and half advance leave. Suppose those 20 days were extended by your commanding officer for 10 more days. Those last 10 days are excess leave.

On a yearly basis, the 30 days you earn are figured from 1 October of one year to 30 September of the next year. As your leave builds up, it is carried over from one fiscal year to the next, to a maximum of 60 days. If you have 67 days on the books on 30 September, you lose 7 days and start with just 60 days.

If you are discharged with leave still on the books, you will be paid a lump sum equal to your daily pay (plus "daily leave ration") for each day on the books. If you are discharged with minus leave on the books— in other words, owing the Coast Guard for leave time—your pay will be checked by an amount roughly equal to a day's pay for each day's leave you owe.

Your commanding officer has the authority to grant you (on a yearly basis) all your earned leave plus up to 30 days' advance leave. However, you may not have more than 60 days of leave at one time—except for *reenlistment leave* or *emergency leave*, both of which may go up to 90 days. Persons lacking enough earned leave during an emergency can be granted advance and excess leave.

Sick Leave

Also known as "convalescent leave," this is authorized absence while under medical care and treatment. It usually follows a period of hospitalization and is not charged on the books as leave.

Emergency Leave

In the event of a personal emergency—the death of your father, for example, with no brothers or sisters to assist your mother, or the serious illness of your wife, with no one to care for the children—you will normally be granted emergency leave to take care of important personal matters that no one else can handle. Emergency leave is not granted merely because of death or serious illness in your family. You have no *right*, as such, to emergency leave.

How Leave Is Counted

The day you depart on leave, whatever the hour, is counted as a day of duty. If on your day of return you check in by 0900, that day counts as a day of duty (not chargeable against leave). But if you return after 0900 it is counted as another day of leave. Remember—"The day you leave is a day of duty; the day you return is a day of leave."

Compensatory Absence

This is a form of liberty granted to personnel at isolated units where normal liberty cannot be granted. Compensatory absence is granted insofar as possible for rest and rehabilitation, usually on the basis of 7 days absence for 14 days of duty. There are limits on how much can be accrued. At isolated overseas units, credit is earned at the rate of 2½ days per month.

Retirement

Retirement means that a person is released from active duty but continues to draw a certain fixed pay for the rest of his life. The exact amount of this retired pay depends on many factors. Length of service is the greatest governing factor in the case of most retirements. Degree of disability is the controlling factor in the case of disability retirements. In time of war or national emergency, retired personnel may be called to active duty.

There are several classes of retirement, including compulsory retirement at the age of 62, voluntary retirement after 20 or more years' service, involuntary retirement after 20 or more years' service, and retirement for disabilities incident to service. Retired people are entitled to medical treatment in government facilities and are also entitled to use commissary and exchange facilities at any military base.

U.S. Coast Guard Reserve

A person, who upon an original enlistment in the Coast Guard, incurs a statutory obligation as described in Section 4(d) (3) of the Universal Military Training and Service Act must, upon release from active duty, be transferred to the Coast Guard Reserve to complete his obligated service. Such a person incurs a six-year period of obligated service and on his release must be transferred to the Ready Reserve.

CHAPTER 27
Other Mariners

In order to fulfill the traditional national purposes of the Coast Guard, our personnel have always had to deal directly with other mariners. Most of these other mariners have been people trying to make a legitimate living on the water, or people seeking relaxation and enjoyment out of boating. Invariably, there have been others who were out to turn a dishonest buck or whose desires were to get around the marine safety laws. Generally speaking, Coast Guard people have done well in dealing with other mariners. And while the relationship has not always been one of affection and admiration, it has usually been marked with respect for the "Smokies of the Sea."

The purpose of this chapter is to better acquaint new Coast Guard personnel with other mariners and the vessels they operate. While space will not permit a complete run-down on each type of boating and shipping activity, this chapter should provide some good general information to both new Coast Guardsmen and those who have been around a few years.

Vessels might be characterized as fitting into one of three general categories. These categories, as listed, do not pretend to be the "legal" categories, which are the subject of volumes of decisions and memoranda developed by people paid to worry about such things. Rather, these categories have been chosen because they seem to be generally descriptive of the vessels concerned, and for no other reason. They are:

Figure 27–1. A familiar sight at every harbor entrance is the pilot boat. Pilots are expert licensed civilian mariners who control and direct merchant ships on coastal waterways. (Courtesy Charleston Branch Pilot's Association)

1. commercial vessels.
2. private vessels.
3. public vessels.

Commercial vessels are owned and operated to make money. Private vessels are owned and operated for pleasure, research work, and supporting private enterprise, but not to make money as a direct result of their operations. Public vessels are owned and operated by governments for nonprofit purposes; this category includes military vessels.

Before going into descriptions of the vessels that fit into these three categories, it must be stated that all vessels are described in two other ways:

1. by their method of propulsion.
2. by their size.

Method of Propulsion

Method of propulsion is relatively easy to explain. Commercial or private vessels propelled by steam are called "steamships," and the letters "SS" are used before their names. Commercial or private vessels propelled by motors, usually diesel, are called "motor vessels"; "MV" is the prefix before the name of such a vessel. Public vessels are not identified by method of propulsion; for example, "USS" means "United States Ship," which is a U.S. Navy vessel, "USCGC" means "United States Coast Guard Cutter," "HMS" means "Her Majesty's Ship," a vessel of the Royal Navy. There are a few additional designations for propulsion such as Nuclear Ship, (NS) and the types of sailing ships are schooner (Sch.), brig (Bg.), bark (Bk.), ship (Sh.), etc. Barges are usually referred to as "unrigged" on vessel documents, while sailing vessels are referred to by rig. Self-propelled vessels have been referred to in such papers as "oil screw," "steam screw" and "gasoline screw," depending on the type of fuel providing the vessel's motive force. Method of propulsion (i.e., "MV") often becomes confused with the abbreviations used within the Coast Guard. For example, "M/V" is used to mean "Merchant Vessel" not "Motor Vessel."

Size

While the descriptions for method of propulsion are relatively simple, those for size are more complicated. Generally, size is indicated by a ship's length and its tonnage.

Length

While describing the length of a vessel seems to be a straightforward matter, it's not! The given length of a commercial vessel varies, not because it is elastic, but because of the different legal definitions of length. The "register length" is measured between perpendicular structural members of the vessel's hull, hence is often less than "length over all (LOA)," which is the straight-line distance from one end of the outside hull to the other, parallel to the waterline. Length over the deck also is measured on occasion and includes the extra length of the curvature of the deck as a result of sheer. Again, generally speaking, the length over all (LOA) is the dimension most often used in describing a vessel, and is the length that is used in the Rules of the Road. A "motor boat" is a power-driven vessel less than 65 feet in length, as measured along the deck, exclusive of sheer, parallel to the vessel's centerline. A motor-driven vessel 65 feet and over is called a "motor vessel." This measured length could be slightly different from LOA depending upon the difference between the freeboard at the bow and the stern. Vessel designers are careful not to plan vessels that would be controversial and usually are conservative in order to ensure that the vessel's dimensions give the greatest advantage to the vessel owner when it comes to the vessel's complying with various rules and regulations.

Where register length differs from length over all, so does a vessel's registered breadth and depth. These measurements placed on a vessel's certificate of documentation are exactly defined by regulations and have special meaning in the determination of a vessel's gross and net tonnage. There is also such a thing as "tonnage length."

Tonnage

In its application to vessels, tonnage is difficult to describe. The word "ton" today is used to express a weight; 2,000 pounds equals a "short ton" while 2,240 pounds equals a "long ton." The original spelling of the word "ton" was "tun," a variation of the old French word *tunne* meaning "cask." In the late middle ages, England imported its wine from French vineyards, and the wine was shipped in casks. Duties were paid on the quantity of casks (or *tunnes*) imported, with the result that the vineyards put their wine in increasingly larger casks. A vessel's capacity to haul wine as cargo was measured in the number of *tunnes* the vessel could carry. Ultimately, the size of a wine cask was standardized as an expression of volume, and thus the cargo capacity of a vessel became the number of standard-sized tunnes (or tons) that could be stored below decks. Today the register tonnage of vessels is still based upon volume rather than weight. The register ton equals 100 cubic feet. There are two expressions of register tonnage, *Gross Tons* (G.T.) and *Net Tons* (N.T.). Both tonnages are recorded on U.S. vessel certificates of documentation. The exact determination of register tonnage is very detailed and the subject of federal regulations, but simply speaking, gross tonnage is the legal term for the underdeck volume of a vessel, and net tonnage is that same volume reduced by the volume of certain noncargo spaces such as the engineroom. The term *gross tons* is used in a number of U.S. laws and regulations to define the application of various federal standards to certain sized vessels, and to exempt other vessels from these standards. The term *net tonnage* is often used internationally in establishing the charges vessels must pay for pilotage fees, port fees, canal fees, etc. Net tonnage is also used to establish the minimum size (5 net tons) that a U.S. vessel can be documented. The exemption of engine spaces from gross tonnage to obtain net tonnage helps explain why enginerooms on commercial vessels are often so spacious compared with those on Coast Guard cutters. The rules and regulations for determining gross and net register tons are the subject of international agreements and are fairly standard throughout the world. While the use of gross tons and net tons satisfies the many legal requirements associated with a vessel's size, the use of a volume measure of the internal spaces of a vessel to describe that vessel's ability to "lift" cargo is not realistic. Under the register tonnage method of measuring size, 100 cu. ft. of feathers is the same "ton" as is 100 cu. ft. of lead ore. This situation explains why the original measurement of a ton (tunne) was changed from one of volume to one of weight in every application except shipping.

Military vessels are routinely measured in displacement tons. At an established loaded capacity, drawing a given depth of water (draft), the military ship is calculated to displace a certain quantity of sea water. Using standard densities of sea water, this quantity of water can be calculated in terms of weight. In fact, 35 cubic feet of sea water weighs about one long ton. Thus, military vessels with a given draft (loaded with its stores, fuel, and ammunition) can be "weighed" in displacement tons and be considered to be of a certain size. Commercial vessels, along with some private and other public vessels, however, do not always draw the same amount of water. The drafts of these vessels vary depending upon the quantity of cargo. And having tonnages on documents that vary with draft would not suit the needs for a size description that reflected cargo capacity.

Concern over the safety of commercial vessels led to the establishment of international load-line requirements that assign a minimum freeboard for each vessel depending upon its hull type and watertight structure. A load-line mark is positioned on the side of each vessel about midships; the mark is called a Plimsoll Mark. The load line that has been assigned to the individual vessel must not be submerged, or a monetary penalty can be assessed. Of course, there are allowances for fuel consumption, fresh water, and other factors that permit a certain amount of submergence, provided that the exception conditions are met. Responsibility for assignment of load lines rests with different nations who, in turn, usually delegate this responsibility to nonprofit organizations called "classification societies." Next to each Plimsoll Mark are two letters that identify the classification society that assigned the load line. These societies are internationally recognized bodies that have prepared structural and machinery standards for commercial vessels. If a vessel conforms to a society's standards, the vessel owner contacts the society and requests that the society classify his ship. The cost of the classification is paid by the ship owner. Classification society employees who perform the task of comparing the vessel with the society's standards are called "surveyors." When the survey is completed and the vessel is considered to be "in class," various documents are awarded to the vessel by the society, and usually include a load-line certificate. The vessel owner presents these various documents to a marine insurer, including one that certifies that his vessel meets the standards of a classification society. Based on the loss record of the vessel owner, and the fact that the vessel meets established standards, the insurer negotiates an insurance premium for hull and machinery insurance with the vessel owner. Other insurance concerning liability for personnel, called "P and I" (protection and indemnity) and for a vessel's cargo are handled separately. It is important to a large number of interests that a vessel comply with all the applicable standards. The Plimsoll Mark is one evidence of the involvement of those interests.

The load line of a vessel permits it to be loaded to a given amount of weight. But that doesn't mean that the vessel has to be right on the load line in order to operate. Commercial vessels frequently operate "light," or without a full load of cargo. Thus, the amount of water displaced by the ship varies with the amount of cargo it carries. The amount of ship's bottom paint that shows on the "wind and water" area of a vessel's hull, as well as draft marks exposed at the bow and stern, give the observer an idea of a vessel's cargo capacity or "cargo lift." The calculated lift of a ship, from a certain minimal displacement of the ship when it is light, up to its load line, can be expressed in terms of the number of tons of sea water that are displaced when the vessel is loaded down from that given light condition to its Plimsoll Mark. This tonnage is called deadweight tons (DWT). Deadweight tonnage is a good way to measure the cargo capacity of a vessel, particularly when the cargo is liquid or granular. Tank ships, ore carriers, and other bulk cargo carriers are, in fact, categorized by deadweight tonnage. Since the maximum deadweight tonnage depends upon the load line, and the load line upon a minimal freeboard allowance, a vessel owner can opt to increase his freeboard and, thus, decrease his vessel's deadweight tonnage. As a result of the ease with which deadweight tonnage can be reduced, the regulation of vessels on the basis of deadweight tonnage is not very effective. For that reason, the volumetric based gross tons and net tons have withstood the tests of time as being the ways commercial vessels are legally "sized."

Documents and Certificates

Method of propulsion and size for each vessel are recorded on vessel documents. So are other important facts concerning each individual vessel. Before proceeding, we should take a look at some of the documents and certificates vessels and their crew members are issued. The various documents carried on board a vessel seem endless in number. A load-line certificate is one, and a classification society certificate is another; both were mentioned previously. Among a U.S. commercial vessel's documents, the most important is its Certificate of Documentation. While foreign flag vessel requirements vary, each commercial vessel, regardless of flag, has its "ship's papers," which attest to the ownership and home nation of the vessel. Other data that may be found in these papers are the ship's home port, register length, gross and net tonnage, the place and date she was built, and her trade. The types of trade are registry, coastwise, Great Lakes, fishery, and pleasure. On U. S. vessels, one that is engaged in foreign trade is certified as being under "registry" and must enter and clear U.S. Customs at each U.S. port visited, as do foreign vessels at U.S. ports. U.S. vessels engaged in coastwise trade carry certificates of documentation stating that trade. Coastwise trade is restricted to U.S. vessels. Vessels in coastwise, Great Lakes, fishery, and pleasure trade do not have to enter and clear U.S. Customs. Most commercial U.S. vessels, 5 net tons and over, are required to have certificates of documentation in order to engage in trade. Private craft 5 net tons and over are not required to have vessel documents, but many owners obtain them. If not documented as pleasure craft, such vessels must have state numbers. A documented pleasure craft is called a yacht. A yacht can usually enter and clear foreign Customs much more easily than U.S. state-numbered pleasure craft. A yacht may also obtain a "preferred mortgage" from a bank, which means that the lender's lien, once recorded, can not be forfeited merely by taking the vessel across a state line.

The "service" of a vessel means what the vessel does. In the case of documented fishery and pleasure craft, service is the same as trade. A commercial vessel may engage in carrying freight, carrying passengers, towing, fishing, etc. Private vessels may be engaged in research, pleasure, dredging, etc. Service is important because it defines the nature of a vessel's business. It is possible for a vessel to be engaged in more than one service. It can also be engaged in more than one trade. The definition on U.S. vessel documents, however, will state the trade but not the service. Coast Guardsmen should consult with a Coast Guard marine documentation office whenever a question arises concerning a vessel document.

In addition to the ship's papers, other documents of importance to Coast Guardsmen include the vessel's safety certificates, its cargo manifest, its declaration of inspection (on tank vessels), its official log and oil record book, the previously mentioned load-line certificate, and officers' licenses. A vessel's safety certificates will depend upon its flag and the service the vessel is in. If the vessel has radios and electronic gear, it will have a radiotelegraphy certificate of some description. If it is over 1,600 gross tons, it will have Safety of Life at Sea (SOLAS) Convention Safety Construction and Safety Equipment Certificates. Cargo gear certificates may be required, and so may certain other papers dealing with stowage of grain. The Dangerous Cargo Manifest will identify and list the dangerous cargo and where on the ship it is stowed. Besides those documents mentioned, there are more that may be of specific interest to vessels engaged in specific kinds of trade. And some U.S. flag vessels have Coast Guard safety certificates in addition to the SOLAS certificates.

Coast Guard Certificates of Inspection

U.S. vessels are sometimes grouped into one of two additional categories. They are referred to as "inspected" or "uninspected." Inspected vessels for the most part are commercial vessels, although a few private and public vessels carry Coast Guard Certificates of Inspection. Uninspected vessels include some commercial vessels, along with most all private and public vessels. Whether or not a vessel is inspected depends upon a number of things:

1. Does it carry passengers? how many? and what is its gross tonnage?
2. Does it carry freight for hire? and if so, what is the vessel's gross tonnage?
3. Does it carry bulk inflammable or combustible cargoes?
4. Is the vessel propelled in whole or in part by steam?
5. If it is a motor-driven vessel, what is its gross tonnage?
6. If it is a barge that goes on the high seas, what is its gross tonnage?
7. What is the vessel's service?
8. What is the vessel's route?

A table that appears in the federal regulations has been reproduced as table 27–1 and demonstrates the complexity of the various U.S. vessel inspection laws. But while it is complex, it is also practical. The vessel inspections performed by the Coast Guard are done by Coast Guardsmen under authorities delegated by the Commandant of the Coast Guard to regional, decentralized Coast Guard commands known as Officers in Charge, Marine Inspection (OCMI). Trained and experienced Coast Guard inspectors use their practical experience afloat to carry out the U.S. vessel inspection effort. People that operate inspected U.S. vessels bear the burden for the safety of their vessels, but the Coast Guard is concerned with their compliance with federal safety standards from the time the vessels are on the designers drawing tables until the vessels are scrapped or sold to foreign interests.

The term "uninspected vessel" sounds as though that vessel is immune to the scrutiny of the Coast Guard. That is not the case. Virtually all U.S. vessels, inspected or otherwise, must meet minimal safety equipment and operating standards. The degree of federal concern is expressed by inspection laws that bring certain kinds of vessels under more rigid standards. These are vessels that pose a significant risk to their passengers, port populations, other vessels, their own paid crews, or the marine environment. The degree of risk is measured by major accidents that have already happened, accident trends, near misses, and new technologies. Uninspected vessels can also pose risks to their crews and passengers, but to a lesser degree.

When a vessel required by U.S. law to be inspected has been inspected and found satisfactory, it receives from the Coast Guard a Certificate of Inspection that is good for one, two, or three years for a particular service. The "route," meaning the waters on which the vessel may operate, is also specified on the certificate. A vessel with an OCEANS route can operate on any waters, but aside from that route, other waters become more and more restrictively specified. The period of certificate validity depends upon the kind of vessel. When a Certificate of Inspection is issued to a U.S. vessel, that also means that all other required forms, such as SOLAS documents, ship's papers, etc., were in order at the time the certificate was issued. Routine checks of inspected vessels are made at intermediate times during the period of validity of a certificate. If a vessel is found not in compliance with the applicable safety standards, remedial action is taken by the cognizant Coast Guard OCMI. Without a Certificate of Inspection, a U.S. vessel required to be inspected cannot operate legally in trades that require certification. Under the concept of inspection applied to vessels required by law to be inspected, it is the responsibility of the vessel operator or owner to come to the Coast Guard and apply for a certificate. He must comply with all federal standards in order to receive and retain the Certificate of Inspection. The burden of compliance with federal standards rests with the vessel, not with the Coast Guard. If something goes wrong with the ship that affects its safety, the master must report that deficiency to the Coast Guard. It is not the Coast Guard's role to "catch" the vessel in a state of noncompliance, but if that occurs, the Certificate of Inspection may be withdrawn by a Coast Guard OCMI until the deficiencies are corrected. In the meantime, civil penalty action may be taken against the vessel owners, or license suspension and revocation proceedings may be initiated against the responsible persons.

Uninspected vessels boarded by Coast Guard law enforcement officers while the vessels are operating are also subject to remedial actions such as civil penalties. When licensed or documented personnel are required to man an uninspected vessel, suspension and revocation proceedings may be directed against the documents or licenses held by the responsible crew members of the vessel.

Certificates of Inspection also specify the minimum manning requirements of inspected U.S. vessels. They carefully state the mini-

Table 27-1.

Method of propulsion[1]	Size or other limitations[1]	Classes of vessels (including motorboats) examined or inspected under various Coast Guard regulations[1]					
		Vessels inspected and certificated under Subchapter D—Tank Vessels[2]	Vessels inspected and certificated under either Subchapter H—Passenger Vessels[2,3,4,5] or Subchapter T—Small Passenger vessels[2,3,4]	Vessels inspected and certificated under Subchapter I—Cargo and Miscellaneous Vessels[2,3]	Vessels subject to provisions of Subchapter C—Uninspected Vessels[2,3,6,7,8]	Vessels subject to provisions of Subchapter U—Oceanographic Vessels[2,3,6,7,9]	Vessels subject to the provisions of Subchapter O—Certain Dangerous Bulk Cargoes[10]
Column 1	Column 2	Column 3	Column 4	Column 5	Column 6	Column 7	Column 8
Steam........	Vessels not over 65 feet in length.	All vessels carrying combustible or flammable liquid cargo in bulk.	All vessels carrying more than 6 passengers.[7]	All tugboats and towboats.	All vessels except those covered by columns 3, 4, 5, and 7.	None..............	None.

	Vessels over 65 feet in length.	All vessels carrying combustible or flammable liquid cargo in bulk.[5]	1. All vessels carrying more than 12 passengers on an international voyage, except yachts.[7]
			2. All vessels of not over 15 gross tons which carry more than 6 passengers.[7]
			3. All other vessels carrying passengers,[7] except:
			   a. Yachts.
			   b. Documented cargo or tank vessels issued a permit to carry not more than 16 persons in addition to the crew.
			   c. Towing and fishing vessels, in other than ocean and coastwise service, may carry persons on the legitimate business of the vessel, in addition to crew, but not to exceed one for each net ton of the vessel.
				All vessels except those covered by columns 3 and 4.	None..............	All vessels engaged in oceanographic research.	None.

Motor.......	Vessels not over 15 gross tons.	All vessels carrying combustible or flammable liquid cargo in bulk.	All vessels carrying more than 6 passengers.[7]	Those vessels carrying dangerous cargoes when required by 46 CFR Part 98 or 146.	All vessels except those covered by columns 3, 4, 5, and 7.	None.............	None.
	Vessels over 15 gross tons except seagoing motor vessels of 300 gross tons and over.	All vessels carrying combustible or flammable liquid cargo in bulk.[5]	1. All vessels carrying more than 12 passengers on an international voyage, except yachts. 2. All vessels not over 65 feet in length which carry more than 6 passengers.[7] 3. All other vessels of over 65 feet in length carrying passengers for hire except documented cargo or tank vessels issued a permit to carry not more than 16 persons in addition to the crew.	All vessels carrying freight for hire except those covered by columns 3 and 4.	All vessels except those covered by columns 3, 4, 5, and 7.	None.............	None.
	Seagoing motor vessels of 300 gross tons and over.	All vessels carrying combustible or flammable liquid cargo in bulk.[5]	1. All vessels carrying more than 12 passengers on an international voyage, except yachts. 2. All other vessels, carrying passengers,[7] except: a. Yachts. b. Documented cargo or tank vessels issued a permit to carry not more than 16 persons in addition to the crew.	All vessels except those covered by columns 3 and 4, and those engaged in the fishing, oystering clamming, crabbing, or any other branch of the fishery, kelp, or sponge industry.	All vessels except those covered by columns 3, 4, 5, and 7.	All vessels engaged in oceanographic research.	None.
Sail.........	Vessels not over 700 gross tons.	All vessels carrying combustible or flammable liquid cargo in bulk.	All vessels carrying more than 6 passengers.[7]	Those vessels carrying dangerous cargoes when required by 46 CFR Part 98 or 146.	All vessels carrying 6 or less passengers for hire.[12]	None.............	None.

Table 27–1.—Continued

Method of propulsion	Size or other limitations[1]	Classes of vessels (including motorboats) examined or inspected under various Coast Guard regulations[1]					
		Vessels inspected and certificated under Subchapter D—Tank Vessels[2]	Vessels inspected and certificated under either Subchapter H—Passenger Vessels[2,3,4,5] or Subchapter T—Small Passenger vessels[2,3,4]	Vessels inspected and certificated under Subchapter I—Cargo and Miscellaneous Vessels[2,3]	Vessels subject to provisions of Subchapter C—Uninspected Vessels[2,3,6,7,8]	Vessels subject to provisions of Subchapter U—Oceanographic Vessels[2,3,6,7,9]	Vessels subject to the provisions of Subchapter O—Certain Bulk Dangerous Cargoes[10]
Column 1	Column 2	Column 3	Column 4	Column 5	Column 6	Column 7	Column 8
Sail—Cont..	Vessels over 700 gross tons.	All vessels carrying combustible or flammable liquid cargo in bulk.	All vessels carrying passengers for hire.	Those vessels carrying dangerous cargoes when required by 46 CFR Part 98 or 146.	None	None	None.
Non-self-propelled.	Vessels less than 100 gross tons.	All vessels carrying combustible or liquid cargo in bulk.	All vessels carrying more than 6 passengers.[7]	Those vessels carrying dangerous cargoes when required by 46 CFR Part 146.	All barges carrying passengers except those covered by column 4.	None	All tank barges if carrying certain flammable and combustible liquids and liquefied gases in bulk.
	Vessels 100 gross tons or over	All vessels carrying combustible or flammable liquid cargo in bulk.	All vessels carrying passengers for hire.	All seagoing barges except those covered by columns 3 and 4; and those inland barges carrying dangerous cargoes when required by 46 CFR Part 146.	All barges carrying passengers except those covered by columns 4 and 7.	All seagoing barges engaged in oceanographic research.	All tank barges if carrying certain flammable and combustible liquids and liquefied gases in bulk.

[1] Where length is used in this table it means the length measured from end to end over the deck, excluding sheer. This expression means a straight line measurement of the overall length from the foremost part of the vessel to the aftermost part of the vessel, measured parallel to the centerline.

[2] Subchapters E (Load Lines), F (Marine Engineering), J (Electrical Engineering), and N (Dangerous Cargoes) of this chapter may also be applicable under certain conditions. The provisions of 46 U.S.C. 170 and Subchapter N (Dangerous Cargoes) of this chapter apply whenever explosives or dangerous articles or substances are on board vessels (including motorboats), except when specifically exempted by law.

[3] Public nautical schoolships, other than vessels of the Navy and Coast Guard, shall meet the requirements of Part 167 of Subchapter R (Nautical Schools) of this chapter. Civilian nautical schoolships, as defined by 46 U.S.C. 1331, shall meet the requirements of Subchapter H (Passenger Vessels) and Part 168 of Subchapter R (Nautical Schools) of this chapter.

[4] Subchapter H (Passenger Vessels) of this chapter covers only those vessels of 100 gross tons or more. Subchapter T (Small Passenger Vessels) of this chapter covers only those vessels of less than 100 gross tons.

[5] Vessels covered by Subchapter H (Passenger Vessels) or I (Cargo and Miscellaneous Vessels) of this chapter, where the principal purpose or use of the vessel is not for the carriage of liquid cargo, may be granted a permit to carry a limited amount of flammable or combustible liquid cargo in bulk. The portion of the vessel used for the carriage of the flammable or combustible liquid cargo shall meet the requirements of Subchapter D (Tank Vessels) in addition to the requirements of Subchapter H (Passenger Vessels) or I (Cargo and Miscellaneous Vessels) of this chapter.

[6] Any vessel on an international voyage is subject to the requirements of the International Convention for Safety of Life at Sea, 1960.

[7] The meaning of the term "passenger" is as defined in the Act of May 10, 1956 (Sec. 1, 70 Stat. 151; 46 U.S.C. 300). On oceanographic vessels scientific personnel on board shall not be deemed to be passengers nor seamen, but for calculations of livesaving equipment, etc., shall be counted as persons.

[8] Boilers and machinery are subject to examination on vessels over 40 feet in length.

[9] Under 46 U.S.C. 441 an "oceanographic research vessel" is a vessel "* * * being employed exclusively in instruction in oceanography or limnology, or both, or exclusively in oceanographic research, * * *." Under 46 U.S.C. 443, "an oceanographic research vessel shall not be deemed to be engaged in trade or commerce." If or when an oceanographic vessel engages in trade or commerce, such vessel cannot operate under its certificate of inspection as an oceanographic vessel, but shall be inspected and certificated for the service in which engaged, and the scientific personnel aboard then become persons employed in the business of the vessel.

[10] Bulk dangerous cargoes are cargoes specified in Tables 30.25–5 and 151.01–10(b) of this chapter.

[11] For manned tank barges see § 151.01–10(e) of this chapter.

[12] Lifesaving device requirements of Subpart 25.25 only.

[CGFR 65–50, 30 FR 16650, Dec. 30, 1965, as amended by CGFR 67–83, 33 FR 1104, Jan. 27, 1968; CGFR 70–10, 35 FR 3707, Feb. 25, 1970, CGD 72–172R, 38 FR 8116, Mar. 28, 1973]

mum number of licensed and documented people at different skill levels that are required to operate the vessel. For uninspected vessels, vessel owners and operators must apply the federal manning regulations themselves to be sure that the required numbers and skills of crew members are in accordance with the federal laws.

Personnel Documents

The various licenses, certificates, papers, books, and other documents required of the mariners who operate vessels are varied and complex, perhaps much more so than are the documents required of the vessels themselves. International agreements, as well as federal laws and regulations, all apply to vessel personnel. Some of these standards deal with a vessel's size, some with its route, some with its service, and a few with its propulsion.

Internationally, all commercial and some private vessels on the high seas, of 200 or more gross tons, must be under the control of persons who are deemed competent (licensed) to operate those vessels by the government of the nation whose flag they fly. These standards apply to both U.S. inspected and uninspected vessels of 200 or more gross tons.

All U.S. vessels required by the laws of the United States to be inspected must be manned in accordance with their certificates of inspection. This means that all U.S. steam seagoing motor vessels of 300 gross tons and over (except commercial fishing vessels), steam-propelled vessels, freight and passenger-for-hire vessels of 15 gross tons and over, tank vessels, passenger vessels carrying more than 6 passengers, and certain others, must employ the required number of crew members who have officer or operator licenses and in many cases, merchant mariner documents. All U.S. vessels propelled by steam on inland waters, certain size U.S. vessels engaged in coastwise trade entering U.S. waters from sea, and certain vessels navigating the Great Lakes must be under the control and direction of federally licensed pilots. Note that foreign vessels and U.S. vessels on Register entering U.S. coastal ports are exempt from *federal* pilotage. In turn, they are, in almost every case, required by *state* pilotage laws to take pilots licensed by the states.

Certain other vessels that are usually uninspected are required to have licensed personnel. For example, licensed operators are required on all vessels carrying six or less passengers for hire and on towing vessels over 26 feet in length while engaged in towing.

Merchant Mariners Documents (MMDs) are sometimes called "Z-Cards," because the numbers on them begin with the letter "Z" followed by the person's social security number. MMDs are required of all members of the crew of U.S. commercial vessels 100 gross tons and over (excluding fishing vessels), except those vessels engaged only on river routes. Merchant Marine officers have both a license and an MMD. Unlicensed crew members have MMDs. The MMD lists certain categories of duties on a merchant ship. There are "entry ratings" as well as endorsements for technical positions, including tankerman. The unlicensed ratings other than "entry" require that a candidate present documented experience and pass a written examination. Merchant Marine officer and operator licenses, as well as MMDs, are issued by Coast Guard Regional Examination Centers. Each OCMI, through his designated marine investigating officers, may initiate Suspension and Revocation Proceedings against a person's right to hold a Coast Guard-issued license or document in instances of misconduct, incompetence, negligence or inattention to duty, and violation of statute.

Officer's licenses are required to be posted on inspected U.S. vessels and should be in the possession of licensed operators of uninspected vessels. The terms *licensed officer* and *operator* may be confusing. Generally speaking, and there are exceptions, a licensed officer is a mariner who holds a license issued by his government, which entitles him to serve in a position of responsibility and authority as master, mate, or engineer on board a commercial or private vessel that is registered by that government. Those vessels are usually 200 gross tons or over, but not always. An operator, in the sense of licenses, is a mariner licensed by his government to navigate small craft on particular routes and in specified services. A pilot is a special officer, required by governments to direct and control specified kinds of vessels on inland routes including harbor approaches, who has demonstrated special skills and local knowledge and who has been licensed by a national or state government to provide that specialized service.

U.S. commercial vessels over 1,000 gross tons are usually construed as being those that constitute the U.S. Merchant Marine. Technically, this is not exactly accurate, because there are also smaller commercial vessels that are considered part of our merchant fleet. Nevertheless, using the usual concept of the U.S. Merchant Marine, the following licensed and unlicensed mariners are likely to be part of such a ship's traditional manning requirements.

Licensed Officers

Master. The equivalent of a Coast Guard cutter's commanding officer.

Chief Engineer. The near equivalent of the master except he is not responsible for the overall safety and trade of the vessel. He is totally in charge of the vessel's engineroom and exercises technical overview of the vessel's hull structure.

Chief Mate. Sometimes called the "First Mate." He is the senior deck watchstander and is traditionally in charge of cargo-handling operations. When standing watches at sea, his traditional watch is the "eight to twelve."

First Assistant Engineer. The senior engineering watchstander. When standing watches at sea, his traditional watch is the "eight to twelve." He is also traditionally responsible for maintaining the main propulsion machinery.

Second Mate. The deck officer who traditionally serves as navigator. His traditional watch is the "four to eight."

Second Assistant Engineer. The engineering officer who is traditionally responsible for maintaining the boilers. His traditional watch is the "four to eight."

Third Mate. The deck officer who traditionally is responsible for the ships' boats, deck gear, and anchors. His traditional watch is the "twelve to four."

Third Assistant Engineer. The engineering officer who is traditionally responsible for the auxiliary machinery. His traditional watch is the "twelve to four."

Radio Officers. These officers stand the required radio watches; they also perform a limited amount of electronic maintenance.

Note: Many merchant ships employ additional third mates and third assistant engineers. When carried, these additional officers replace the chief mate and first assistant engineer in watchstanding duties. Cadets are also carried occasionally. All deck officers are also able seamen and all engineering officers are qualified for any unlicensed rating in the engine department.

Unlicensed Personnel

There are many different ratings on board merchant vessels. Each has its own qualifications and job descriptions, not unlike the crews of Coast Guard and Navy vessels. There are several ratings that are required by law to comprise the manning of a U.S. merchant vessel. Out of custom and union contracts, others have evolved. These ratings range from highly technical ratings to minimal level-of-experience "entry" ratings such as ordinary seaman, wiper, and stewards department (food handler). Usually the actual manning level of a U.S. merchant ship is considerably greater than that minimum level required on its Coast Guard Certificate of Inspection. The difference between the two levels is referred to by the Coast Guard as "other persons in the crew." All persons employed to do the business of the vessel are members of the crew, but the master is not considered as "one of the crew" in a traditional sense. At least 65 percent of the deck department, including officers and unlicensed personnel, must be able seamen. All crew members sign a contract with the master before each voyage. Their contract is called the "Shipping Articles."

All vessels that are documented have a person designated as "Master," but this does not mean that that person is required to have a master's license. As on Coast Guard and Navy vessels, the person in charge is called the captain. There is no U.S. license officially termed a "captain license," but frequently operators of passenger-carrying vessels use that term in referring to Coast Guard operators' licenses. The master of a vessel, regardless of his license, works directly for the vessel owner. Sometimes the master is the vessel owner. The master hires his crew, supervises the vessel's business, sees that his vessel complies with laws and regulations, and acts as the vessel owner's direct representative wherever the vessel is located. The master of any vessel is the first person that should be contacted when it is necessary to go on board a vessel. The master may designate a representative to act in his behalf when it is acceptable to the Coast Guard boarding officer or inspector. As a general rule, Coast Guard persons on official business on board a private or commercial vessel should be accompanied by a representative of that vessel.

Having discussed methods of propulsion, size, and vessel and crew documents, let us now proceed to discuss the three general categories of vessels—commercial, private, and public.

Kinds of Commercial Vessels

It would be difficult to list all the specific kinds of commercial vessels in a manual such as this because there are so many. There are also relatively few vessels today that qualify as "class" types, although that was not the case 20 to 30 years ago. There are still a few vessels that bear class distinctions such as the "Mariner" and "Victory" classes of break-bulk cargo vessels, and "T-2" tankers. These older classes are referred to by members of the marine industry on occasion.

Tankers

Technically a "tanker" is any vessel that carries bulk inflammable or combustible liquids as cargo. "Bulk" means over 110 U.S. gallons in a single tank or container. But a tanker is usually thought of as being a self-propelled tank vessel, technically termed a tankship, that hauls petroleum products in tanks that form part of the vessel's hull. "Chemical tankers" haul petro-chemical or other oil-based products, usually carrying more than one product at a time. Chemical tankers are sometimes referred to as being in the "drug store trade." Petroleum tankers are usually thought of as being in one of two kinds of trade—"crude carriers" or "refined oil products." Sometimes refined products and chemicals are carried on the same tanker.

Crude carriers are used in the import-export trade. They haul crude oil from its source to refineries, or to storage areas for transshipment. Types of crude oil differ greatly, sulfur content being one of many distinguishing characteristics. Vessels used in this trade comprise the largest of the world's tanker fleet and bear such categorical type names

Figure 27–2. Keystone Shipping Co.'s *Spirit of Liberty*, a commercially operated tanker under MSC charter, typifies the role of the American Merchant Marine in providing modern logistic support to the military efforts of the United States. Virtually all aspects of Coast Guard marine transportation functions support the continuing rule of U.S. Flag vessels in national defense. (Courtesy Keystone Shipping Co., Philadelphia, PA.)

as Very Large Crude Carrier (VLCC)—one that can lift over 100,000 deadweight tons of oil—or Ultra Large Crude Carrier (ULCC)—one that carries over 200,000 deadweight tons of oil. The very large crude oil tankers are limited by their deep drafts from most U.S. coastal harbors. Smaller crude carriers do frequent U.S. ports, however, particularly U.S. flag tankers engaged in the Alaskan oil trade and other tankers calling at U.S. ports on the East Coast and the Gulf of Mexico.

Refined-oil-product tankers operate in the U.S. coastwise trade, although a few engage in foreign trade as well. Some refined imports are received at U.S. ports in foreign tankers; the SS *Argo Merchant*, which wrecked off Nantucket in 1977, was such a vessel. Generally, tankers that carry refined oil products are smaller than those that import crude oil. Many U.S. flag tankers carrying refined oil products are owned and operated by the oil corporations whose products they haul. The same is true for crude carriers. In addition to the tankers owned by oil corporations, independent tank vessel owners charter (hire out) their vessels for the carriage of crude oil and refined oil products. These charters can be for a single voyage or a certain number of voyages, or they can be for a period of time, some as long as 15 years. Many oil corporations have company unions to which their ships' crews belong. Most independently owned tankers have crew members that are members of maritime trade unions. Independent tanker owners do not necessarily carry only the products of one company, but often hire out different cargo tanks to different firms, which often include large oil corporations that have their own tanker fleets. When different cargoes are carried on one vessel, the integrity of cargo-tank boundaries is very important so that their contents don't mix. Cargo insurers have inspectors to check on the purity of products when they are delivered. If the product is contaminated, the tanker owner must bear the expense of returning the spoiled product to its source. The term "product" is used by tankermen to refer to the liquid contents of their vessel's tanks. Product is classified by grade, with A being the most flammable and E the least combustible. The grade is determined from a number of factors, including vapor pressure and temperature. Products that are flammable or combustible, may also be poisonous. Such cargoes are also classified, and special procedures are specified on safety certificates for their handling, stowage, and gauging.

Chemical tankers operate in much the same manner as refined oil product tankers and are often the same vessels. Tankers hauling chemicals and refined products usually have designated tanks for special kinds of products. Their tank insides are often coated to prevent contamination with the ship's iron hull and to make cleaning them easier. Before a different cargo is put into a tank, the tank must be cleaned to prevent contamination from the previous cargo. Tanker ballast is water that is carried in tanker cargo tanks to counter the excess buoyancy of empty tanks. The water is pumped out before a new load of oil cargo is pumped on board; this is called "deballasting" and is done before the tanker reaches port. If done properly, no marine pollution results. As a general rule, chemical tankers are smaller than oil tankers, because chemical terminals are usually located farther upstream, and maneuvering small ships upstream is easier and requires less water depth.

Chemical tankers and some refined oil tankers have additional safety gear. They also tend to employ electrically driven cargo pumps, called "deep-well pumps." To operate these pumps, chemical tankers need a large electrical source. On the World War II vintage "T–2" tanker, the main propulsion was steam turbo-electric. With a large electrical generating capacity in its stern available in port when the main motor was not in use, these "T–2s" were ready-made for use as chemical tankers. Many "T–2s" have been converted, having new forebodies attached to the old enginerooms, or being jumboized by having a section of new hull added between the old bow and stern sections. At this writing, many "T–2s" are still in service, but their days are numbered as maintenance costs on the old machinery mount.

In addition to the large, oceangoing tanker, there are a number of smaller tankships that the Coast Guardsman may encounter. Many of these are small harbor tankers of the Navy's "YO" design. Some are small coastal tankers that haul refined oil products such as heating oils into small coastal ports and harbors where the water is not deep enough for the larger tankers.

Tank barges are also tank vessels under U.S. law and are governed by many of the same rules and regulations as tankships. Tank barges serve a variety of functions: transporting cargo between ports; lightening cargo from larger tank vessels moored offshore to facilities on shore; serving as floating service stations to fuel oceangoing vessels that are moored—a process known as "bunkering"; and acting as floating storage tanks for waste products. Tank barges are distinguished from tankships in that they are not propelled by their own machinery. Other than that, they trade in the same products and on the same routes. In some cases they are larger in deadweight tons than some

Figure 27–3. A tank barge "bunkering" a dry general cargo freighter. (Courtesy South Carolina State Ports Authority)

self-propelled tankers. A type of tank barge with a "detachable" engineroom and control unit is called an "articulated tug and barge" or "ARTABAR." These are large, usually oceangoing, commercial vessels wherein the tug is specially configured to connect rigidly to the barge to form a composite unit. Some tank barges carry chemical products in sophisticated cargo containers that are temperature- or pressure-controlled, depending upon the product. Some tank barges are manned by a crew, even though the barge is dependent upon a tug or towboat for its navigation. Each time the tank barge handles cargo, a certified tankerman must be in charge of the transfer, just as on a tankship.

Tankers are essentially floating cargo tanks, with a pointed bow fashioned to the forward end of the tank body and an engineroom attached to the stern. The tank vessel is constructed with longitudinal framing similar to military vessels. Fuel tanks are usually aft, and double bottoms are not usually fitted except as dedicated ballast tanks on newer refined and chemical product tankers. Cargo tanks are numbered forward to aft. Oceangoing tankers have transverse bulkheads running the breadth of the ship from the main deck to the ship's hull bottom. Each set of bulkheads represents the boundaries of the numbered tanks. Within those transverse boundaries, fore-and-aft bulkheads are erected, again from the main deck to the ship's hull bottom.

Thus, within each numbered cargo tank division are three smaller tanks, a center tank and one on each side. The side tanks are called "wing tanks," port and starboard as the case may be, and the center tank is appropriately called the "center tank." Tanks are provided access to the main deck by hatches from which ladders extend downward. On top of the hatch cover may be a small opening with a small hatch on it. This is called an "ullage opening." When closed gauging systems are not installed, it is through the ullage opening that the chief mate checks the level of cargo in the tank. The ullage openings are protected by fine mesh screens when cargo transfer is taking place. The screens are to prevent the entrance of a spark into the tank atmosphere. Normally when under way, the ullage openings are closed. Vapor pressure devices called P/V valves also extend upward above deck on piping running from the tops of the cargo tanks. Sometimes these valves and their piping are led up on the tanker's masts, depending upon the grade of cargo. Cargo piping on the deck of the tanker runs from the bottom of the cargo tank to the main deck and along the centerline of the ship. A catwalk may be raised above the main deck to provide easy fore-and-aft access over the maze of cargo piping. Tankers usually have cargo pumprooms. These "rooms" are spaces extending from the main deck downward to the bottom, in which are located the valves that control the flow of product through the main cargo pumps to and from the cargo tanks.

The pilothouse may be located anywhere on a tanker. For many years, it was customary for the ship's bridge and pilothouse to be located amidships. The deck officers' quarters and radio room were located in the same superstructure. The galley, messrooms, and engineers' quarters were in the after deckhouse area, near the stack. The midship house has been omitted on many modern tankers, and the pilothouse has been located atop the after superstructure.

Tank barges and small tankers are laid out on the same principle as the larger tank vessels. Tank barges have empty spaces in their bows, and often in their sterns, called "rake ends." The watertight integrity of rake ends is critical on tank barges because of their usually low operating freeboards.

The Coast Guardsman must never enter any tank space alone, and he must never enter any space, cargo or otherwise, that has not been certified as "safe for men" by a marine chemist on the day of the entry. For safety, escape breathing appliances should be carried whenever possible. Ladders in cargo tanks must not be trusted because of accelerated corrosion in cargo spaces, particularly where the structure has been exposed to air.

Safety considerations are always important to Coast Guardsmen; this is especially so with tank vessels. The tank vessel presents a number of risks. When "gassy," meaning flammable or combustible, vapors are present, the risk of explosion and fire is very real. The explosion of a tanker is not only devastating to itself and its crew but to nearly everything around it. In a port city or restricted waters, the gassy tankship is rightfully considered to be a bomb. In the event of a collision with other vessels, the threat of subsequent fire and explosion endangers both vessels and their crews. A tanker is considered to be "in operation" whenever it is "gassy" even if it is moored or at anchor.

The tank vessel is also a risk to the marine environment. When the product carried in its cargo tank is released into the marine environment, pollution occurs and damage often results from the pollution. Not only can wildlife and marine creatures be threatened by marine pollution, but so also can water supplies, public and private properties, resort economies, commercial and recreational fisheries, and historical sites.

Another risk associated with tank vessels is that which arises from the toxicity of vapors in the cargo tanks. Persons entering those tanks can be exposed to harm in at least three ways: (1) poisonous or toxic vapors within the tank can affect the body's central nervous system when inhaled; (2) absence of oxygen in the tanks can cause death; and (3) cancer-causing chemicals can be absorbed through the skin. Additionally, during ballasting operations when water is pumped into cargo tanks to replace the product pumped ashore, the vapors in the cargo tanks are displaced by water and enter the atmosphere, presenting both toxicity and flammability hazards in the vicinity of the tank vessel. Special attention must be given to this risk, particularly when the air is calm and there is no wind to dissipate the vapors.

When a tank vessel is fully loaded, it is considered to be less of a risk due to an explosion, but, of course, the volume of product on board is greater, thereby increasing the risk of pollution. A source of ignition is necessary in order to cause an explosion on a gassy tank vessel. Marine casualty investigations have found a wide range of ignition sources—including lighted cigarettes, sparks caused by unshielded electric motors, metal tools that are dropped and cause sparks, collisions of vessels that cause frictional heat and sparks, welding and burning on the boundaries of gassy tanks, static electricity, and lightning.

Ballasting by liquid is a normal procedure on board all kinds of vessels. When stores and fuel are loaded on a ship, care is taken to reduce list and obtain the proper trim. Draft marks and the load line provide the ship's officers with the necessary measurements to do this. Also, fuel can be shifted from one tank to another to trim the ship properly. After a ship has used up some of her fuel, the practice on many vessels is to pump sea water into the fuel tanks. With this kind of ballasting, the correct stability values are usually maintained; this practice is employed on most public, private, and commercial vessels. Tank vessels, and particularly tankships, usually fill their cargo tanks with liquid ballast to replace the weight that's lost when cargoes have been transferred off the ship. This is called being "in ballast." Sometimes certain tank spaces are dedicated totally for ballast water, and do not ever carry cargo. Usually, however, ballast water is introduced directly into a cargo tank. The quantity of water added as ballast is carefully calculated so that the hull structure is not overtaxed by the weight of the ballast water. However, even when without ballast and without cargo—in a "light" condition—the hull structure can also be stressed. Varying weights of liquid cargoes, particularly in chemical and refined product tankers, can also cause failure of the ship's structure. When its hull has been improperly loaded, a vessel can break in two, and this has happened on a number of occasions to tank vessels. Most masters of tank vessels today employ small computers that are programmed to the volume capacity of the ships' cargo tanks. By entering the density factors for the cargo carried, be it product or ballast, the master can "load" his ship structure to deadweight tonnage within predetermined safety limits. The ability of a master to load his tank vessel within safe limits, coupled with the variability of a tanker's load line, discussed earlier in this chapter, and the inherent watertight integrity of the cargo tank hull form, all combine to make the worry over tankship freeboard pretty much a thing of the past.

Tank vessels engage in certain operations that are riskier than others. Loading and discharging their cargoes imposes certain risks that have been discussed. Transiting congested or shallow waters poses certain obvious risks arising from potential collisions and groundings. Ballasting can present certain hazards, but perhaps the most dangerous time for a tankship is when it is engaged in the process of tank cleaning. A tank vessel must clean its tanks when it changes the kind of product it carries in the tank to prevent contamination with the next cargo to be carried. The tanker also cleans its tanks so that it can be certified by a marine chemist as being "safe for men, safe for fire," to enable inspection and repair work. The increased use of tank coatings has made the tank cleaning process easier and less time consuming, and also less of a risk. The risk exists because of the presence of flammable vapors and the creation of static electricity during the cleaning process. A tank-cleaning method introduced before World War II called for the introduction of a rotating nozzle into the top of an empty cargo tank through a small plate in the deck above the tank. A stream of sea water mixed with steam was pumped through the nozzle. Also, the hatch on the cargo tank being cleaned was opened, and a tent-like air scoop was erected over the open hatch to ventilate the tank. The hot water from the nozzle loosened the oil product. Cargo tanks that contained product might be empty, but they were full of rich, gaseous residues that collected on the sides of the tank; the residue was washed to the bottom, and the oil and water mixture was pumped overboard as an emulsion. Meanwhile, air was entering the tank through the tank hatch to ventilate the gaseous atmosphere in the tank, because eventually crewmen would enter the tank and clean up the remaining solid residues with brushes, buckets, etc. A dangerous problem arose when the air being introduced into the tank lowered the richness of the vapors and increased the possibility of explosion. During tank cleaning a static charge forms from the turbulence induced by the rapidly rotating head, much like the creation of an electrical charge that discharges as lightning from a thunderhead. Sparks of discharged electricity produced during such tank-cleaning operations are believed to be the cause of many explosions that caused the loss of vessels and their crews. This particular method of tank cleaning has undergone many variations, including the means to prevent the "right" mixture of vapor and oxygen. The inventor of the first rotating heads, a man named Butterworth, lent his name to the process as well ("butterworthing") and to the small round plates that appear in the main deck of a tanker over the cargo tank (butterworth plates). To the credit of the tanker industry, tanker explosions during tank cleanings have diminished in number. The method used by tankers for cleaning tanks, however, is important for Coast Guardsmen to understand when they are tracking mysterious oil spills. Tanker masters prefer to clean their tanks in warm waters, such as the Gulf Stream off the Atlantic Coast, so that they don't have to use as much steam to heat up the sea water used for cleaning, and if possible, will avoid the colder waters for tank cleaning. By understanding the basic operations on board tank vessels, a Coast Guardsman is better able to perform his own mission. The source of a mystery oil spill of tank-washing sludge residue may be detected by tracing the routes of potentially guilty tankers to ship repair yards or to refined product loading points.

For the most part, tank vessel personnel are exceptionally safety conscious and go to great lengths to avoid pollution incidents. They, and their vessels, became the focal points of a lot of misdirected accusations during the upsurge of environmental consciousness during the 1970s. Of particular importance is the fact that U.S. tank vessel owners have taken the lead in the development of safety systems and pollution control devices.

Freighters

The term *cargo* has a different technical definition from the term *freight*. Cargo is the material transported on board a vessel, other than passengers, fuel, and vessel stores. Any vessel can theoretically carry cargo. Freight is the amount charged for the cargo being transported. Freight has also come to mean cargo that is carried for a sum of money; in U.S. vessel inspection laws, it is called "freight for hire." Freight for hire on U.S. vessels is a matter that involves Coast Guard vessel inspection if the vessel measures 15 gross tons or more. Cargo, on the other hand, is regulated if it is hazardous with regard to its stowage, storage, and handling on board ships and at shoreside facilities. The term *dangerous cargo* falls in this hazardous category. A large number of hazardous cargo categories, each with its own specific regulations, are found in Title 49 of the Code of Federal Regulations. Thus, a U.S. vessel might measure less than 15 gross tons and therefore be exempt from vessel inspection, yet still engage in the carriage of hazardous cargo and be subject to federal regulation. When the Coast Guardsman encounters a situation involving the definition of cargo, freight, or hazardous cargo, he or she should consult with the nearest Coast Guard captain of the port, officer in charge of marine inspection, or district legal officer for assistance.

Usually a U.S. vessel that carries freight for hire is of such a size that it is referred to as a "freight carrier" or a "freighter," although its U.S. document would show its service to be simply "freight." Freighters come in an assortment of sizes and purposes. It would not be possible to describe every kind of freighter in a manual such as this.

Cargo ships can be categorized somewhat as being (1) dry general cargo vessels, (2) specialized dry cargo vessels, (3) dry bulk cargo carriers and (4) bulk liquid cargo carriers. Since bulk liquid carriers are almost always engaged in the carriage of flammable or combustible cargoes, they are "tankers" and are recorded for service as such on U.S. vessel documents. And being "tankers," they are not "freighters." Freighters, therefore, include those vessels listed in the first three "dry" cargo categories.

Dry general cargo vessels. This category of vessels includes roll on-roll off (RO/RO), containerships, pallet ships, break-bulk (bulker), refrigerator ships (reefers) and barge carriers. The barge carrier sub-category includes the "Lighter Aboard Ship" or LASH vessels. Dry general cargo vessels, as a category, are somewhat self-descriptive; however, the specific kinds of dry general cargo vessels should be described.

1. Roll on-Roll off. Roll on-roll off (RO/RO) vessels are ships that receive and discharge cargoes that are driven on and off the ships as vehicles. Usually access to a RO/RO is through a large door in the ship's stern. The ramp to the door can be part of the ship or can be part of the shore facility. RO/ROs are different from ferries in that on a ferry, the vehicle itself is the cargo, while on a RO/RO the focus is upon what the vehicle (i.e., truck), which has been driven on board, carries as its cargo. A ferry usually also carries passengers and generally engages in short-run transportation. A RO/RO is not unlike a large military landing ship.

2. Containerships. Containerships have become one of the most numerous types of dry cargo vessels. Containers of standard sizes to fit truck trailer beds are received and discharged from freight ships where they are lifted from and to the truck trailer beds at dockside. Some containerships were designed from the keel up as containerships; others were freighters or tankers that were converted for that kind of cargo. Some freighters can carry both containers and other general cargo. The value of the container is the reduction in necessary handling. Since all of the space inside the container is not always used, the loaded containership transports a lot of air in the container "boxes." Limited visibility from the navigation bridge can be an important safety factor on containerships. Also of critical importance is the stowage of hazardous cargoes that are inaccessible to visual inspection and the potential transport of contraband in containers whose paperwork lists false contents.

Figure 27–4. A roll on/roll-off (RO/RO) ship. (Courtesy South Carolina State Ports Authority)

3. Pallet Ships. Pallet ships are dry general cargo vessels that carry most of their cargoes fitted on pallets. But unlike other vessels that carry palletized cargo, these specific ships load and unload cargo through side doors rather than through their hatches on deck.

4. Refrigerator Ships. Refrigerator ships are those that have been outfitted with refrigerating equipment to preserve a cargo, usually foodstuffs, while the cargo is in transit. The number of "reefer," or refrigerated cargo spaces varies on a given vessel depending upon its

Figure 27–5. A container ship being serviced by a shoreside container crane. (Courtesy South Carolina State Ports Authority)

trade, as does the manner in which a particular cargo is handled. Usually, refrigerator ships haul other general cargo, typically as break-bulk and/or container cargo.

5. Barge Carriers. Barge carriers often are called by the type of barge they carry, be it LASH, BACAT, Seabee, FLASH, etc. Barge carriers are specifically designed to carry, load, and unload barges filled with cargo. Once unloaded, these barges are towed to discharge points ashore where their cargoes are discharged, hence the term *lighter*. This is a particularly effective way to move cargoes into protected ports that may not be able to accommodate full-size vessels at dockside.

6. Specialized Dry Cargo Vessels. In this category are such ships as automobile carriers, lumber ships, and paper ships. What sets these specialized vessels apart is usually their specialized cargo-handling gear and procedures. Similarities of vessel construction with other kinds of dry cargo vessels make further referral to this special kind of freighter unnecessary.

7. Break-Bulk Ships. Break-bulk is a term generally applied to dry general cargo carried as loose packages, boxes, bales, but not on pallets

Figure 27–6. Break bulk cargo being transferred. (Courtesy South Carolina State Ports Authority)

nor in containers. Break-bulk ships are also "boom ships," meaning that their cargo is loaded through hatches into cargo holds by the use of ships' cargo gear, including their booms. For many years, this kind of dry cargo vessel was considered to be the typical freighter. A break-bulk freighter is not limited to break-bulk cargo. Sometimes containers are carried, sometimes bulk dry cargoes such as grain are stowed in cargo holds, and deck loads can include anything that will fit, such as locomotives, military cargo, or portable tanks.

Since a break-bulk ship typifies the usual freighter, a rudimentary nomenclature of a freight vessel is in order. Cargo holds are numbered forward to aft. Cargo hatches are numbered to conform with the holds. A "tonnage hatch" may be located aft. This device is placed on "shelter deck" vessels as a means to exempt part of the cargo space from register tonnage. The tonnage hatch is not considered watertight, and since it breaches the water tightness of what appears to be the main deck, the deck next below it—called the "freeboard deck"—becomes the uppermost watertight deck for the purpose of technical tonnage calculations. Load lines and freeboard are also involved in these calculations. The freeboard deck becomes, technically, the main deck. When the openings above and to adjacent holds have permanent closures, the

Figure 27–7. A modern inland steel barge. (Courtesy American Commercial Barge Lines)

ship is said to have a closed shelter deck, but if one compartment has a temporary closure, the ship has an open shelter deck and is referred to as a "shelter-deck ship" or "shelter-decker." The original purpose of these rules was to allow vessels built to lighter structural standards (or lighter "scantlings") to operate with less cargo tonnage and with greater freeboards. Shelter-deck vessels, are generally those that have bulky, relatively light cargoes that do not require the maximum in freeboard reduction allowances. Dry cargo vessels that do not have open or closed shelter decks are "full scantling" vessels. Full scantling vessels are constructed in accordance with the most demanding structural strength standards of the classification societies.

Freighters, like tankers, are constructed to carry cargo. To maximize internal spaces for cargo stowage, dry cargo vessels are traditionally framed transversely. This type of construction eliminates the huge web of transverse frames found in tankers and in military vessels, both of which are usually framed longitudinally.

Freighters can have their enginerooms and bridges located almost anywhere. Break-bulk ships customarily have both located about midships. Typically, three of the five cargo holds are forward of midships, two are aft. In the conventional freighter, the cargo hold is divided according to whether or not the ship is a shelter-decker or a full scantling. If a shelter-decker, the first deck down below the weather deck is technically the main deck. In the cargo holds, however, it is referred to as the upper 'tween deck. The deck next below is the lower 'tween deck. The bottom part of the hold is called the lower hold. The deck of the lower hold is the "tank top," because conventional dry cargo ships are built with double bottoms. The space between the hull bottoms and the deck in the lower hold is used for fuel and water storage. On a "full scantling ship," the cargo holds are divided into the upper holds and the lower holds.

The cargo hatch extends vertically from the weather deck downward through each of the decks in the cargo hold. Extreme care should be taken around the hatch openings, as there are normally no railings nor coamings below the weather deck around those openings. Hatch boards are placed over the openings, but often become dislodged and damaged with wear. Walking on hatch covers always should be avoided.

Access to cargo holds is usually through access trunks in which permanent vertical ladders are installed. Lighting in cargo holds is usually nonexistent, so except when weather-deck hatches are opened during daylight, portable lights or flashlights must be used. Wooden battens and timber are used on break-bulk vessels to secure cargo from shifting. This material is called dunnage. Under no circumstances should entry be attempted into closed spaces such as double bottoms, anchor-chain lockers, and voids because of the probable absence of sufficient oxygen or the presence of toxic gases. Ladder rungs on all commercial vessels should be regarded suspiciously because of the likely chance that they have been recently damaged and weakened.

Cargo stowed on break-bulk ships is listed in the vessel's cargo manifest. When cargo falls into the category of "hazardous cargo," its stowage and packaging are regulated by Title 49 of the Code of Federal Regulations and/or by published IMCO standards. Coast Guardsmen assigned to COTP units, and surveyors employed by independent cargo associations, such as the National Cargo Bureau, are concerned with a vessel's compliance with cargo stowage and packaging standards.

Dry Bulk Cargo Carriers. Dry bulk cargo is that which is not stowed in containers or packages. Dry bulk includes such cargoes as coal, wheat, phosphates, and ores. Dry bulk carriers also include most of the Great Lakes fleet of bulk ore carriers. Often called "bulkers," dry bulk carriers typically are constructed without cargo hold decks and usually have specially designed cargo hatch systems. The cargo hold may extend the length of the cargo-carrying portion of the ship, or there may be separate cargo holds installed similar to the cargo tanks on tank vessels. Dry bulk carriers may have various ballast tanks to compensate for loss of draft when the ship is "light." The sides and bottoms of cargo holds may be shaped to enable cargo transfer and to enhance vessel stability. Cargo-handling equipment may be located on the bulker, but more often it is located ashore at the ports where cargo is loaded and discharged.

Freighters as a group present their own brand of safety problems. Apart from the hazards presented by their cargoes, which may be regulated under hazardous materials regulations, freighters present risks to longshoremen who are handling cargo, to other vessels and structures in the event of collision, and to the marine environment in case of pollution. Normally, pollution is connected with tankers, but it is a fact that freighters, engaged in deballasting of their fuel tanks, have been the source of a significant number of oil spills. Freighters are allowed to carry a minimum number of passengers without becoming classed as passenger vessels. Many of the passenger accommodations on modern freighters are plush compared with the austere accommodations found on so-called economy cruise ships. Freighters constitute the bulk of the U.S. flag, oceangoing merchant fleet, and Coast Guardsmen should be generally familiar with the way they are constructed and operated.

Passenger Vessels

Passenger vessels fall into three basic categories: oceangoing ships, ferries and excursion boats, and small boats. But when the term *passenger vessel* is used, the oceangoing passenger ship is most often what comes to mind. And since most transoceanic passenger trade on large ocean liners has ceased on a regular basis, most oceangoing ships are now engaged in the cruise trade, where one can enjoy a floating vacation. There are very few U.S.-flag oceangoing passenger vessels of any description still in service; therefore, most of the cruise trade from the U.S. is in foreign flag vessels. Most of these meet the same high standards of safety that are required of U.S. ships; a few older ships still in operation, however, have been allowed concessions because they were in service before the more modern standards went into effect. The Coast Guardsman should recognize that he or she has a long-standing special responsibility for the safety of passengers on passenger ships who, having paid their passage, are generally unaware of the dangers inherent in a marine environment. It was this special federal responsibility for passenger safety that brought about the creation of both the Life Saving Service and the Steamboat Inspection Service, two forerunners of the modern Coast Guard.

Modern oceangoing passenger vessels are designed and constructed to meet specified standards for subdivision stability, structural fire protection, and escape systems. Frequent inspections are supposed to ensure that these safety standards are met and that the design standards are maintained. Passenger vessels intended for transoceanic liner service were designed for speed and reliability; most had a wartime potential as troop carriers. With the decline of the liner service and the rise of vacation cruise operations, coupled with higher energy costs, the earlier criterion for speed in oceangoing ships was dropped. Instead, emphasis has been placed on providing hotel accommodations on a vessel that can be operated economically. No longer can it be assumed that the passenger ship will out-run the freighter.

While the term *passenger vessel* may conjure up an image of an oceangoing cruise ship, far more passenger hours are spent on board ferryboats and excursion craft. These large, inland-water vessels routinely transport tens of thousands of people daily in the U.S. A ferry is a vessel that transports passengers, freight, and vehicles on short

Figure 27–8. Inland passenger ship. (Courtesy *Delta Queen*)

voyages, which are usually over a fixed route, and which also complement a land transportation system. Excursion boats are large vessels
that carry persons on tours of waterways and to waterways attractions.
Both ferries and excursion boats must meet the same kind of rigid
safety standards as U.S. oceangoing passenger ships.

A third category of U.S. passenger vessel is the small passenger
vessel under 100 gross tons. In this category, those that carry seven
or more passengers are fully regulated, while the small passenger
motorboats that carry six or less passengers must meet only minimal
equipment standards. Included in this category are small excursion
boats; charter fishing boats, party fishing (or "head") boats, which
charge passengers by the head as they come on board; and certain
small ferries. These watercraft may be made of steel, aluminum, fiberglass, or wood, and they vary in length and propulsion. They may
operate on oceans or inland waters. Vessels believed engaged in the
passenger trade illegally should be reported to the nearest Coast Guard
OCMI.

Towing Vessels

In describing this type of commercial vessel, it is important to differ-
entiate between a vessel that is designed for the service of towing and
one that is temporarily engaged in towing. The commercial towing
vessel is designed for its service; the occasional towing vessel may be
of any design.

There are a number of types of commercial towing vessels. These
types are similar in that they are designed to move or maneuver other
floating objects. As a result, their characteristics of length, freeboard,
horsepower, and propeller pitch are all oriented toward power and
maneuverability. Several types of towing vessels are common to most
U.S. waters. These include the typical harbor tugs used to maneuver
large ships into and out of their berths; seagoing tugs that perform
ocean salvage work and tow large oceangoing barges; and tow boats or
pushers that push barges on the Western Rivers and intracoastal waterways. Each of these types could be sub-categorized. For example, on
the rivers there are line boats and harbor boats. Harbor tugs are often
configured to handle barges as a full time occupation, as opposed to
maneuvering large oceangoing ships. And seagoing tugs come in a
variety of sizes depending upon the range and endurance expected of
their service.

Once, all tow vessels were steam-propelled; presently, only a handful

Figure 27–9. A traditional docking tug working a freighter to its dock. (Courtesy Marine Contracting & Towing Co., Charleston, SC)

of steam towing vessels remain in the United States. When U.S. tugs were steam vessels, they were inspected by the Coast Guard. When the diesel engine appeared commercially, it was quickly adopted by towing vessels because of its ease of operation, manning, and economy. It was decided that these diesel-powered U.S. towing vessels, by virtue of their relatively small size, did not have to meet the inspection requirements for commercial steam vessels. The term *uninspected towing vessel* has been applied to towing vessels by the Coast Guard for several decades, implying that towing vessels are not subject to safety regulations. That is not true. Operators of towing vessels documented for towing service must be licensed by the Coast Guard; towing vessels must meet minimal life safety, fire equipment, and pollution prevention standards; and towing vessels must comply with federal operating requirements for lights, manning (where applicable), navigation safety, and rules of the road.

Figure 27–10. A "harbor" or "switch" boat—inland waterways tow boat. (Courtesy American Commercial Barge Lines, Jeffersonville, Indiana)

Fishing Vessels

Commercial fishing vessels comprise the most numerous single category of commercial vessels. The term *fishing vessel* generally means a craft of 5 net tons and over. The term *fishing boat* means a watercraft less than 5 net tons. This tonnage for a decked vessel equates to about 30 feet in length. The U.S. commercial fishing vessel is documented for its service. Technically speaking, there are four types of U.S. documented fishing vessels: cod, fishing, oystering, and whaling.

Of course, these are designations used on marine documents in the eighteenth and nineteenth centuries when those four types best represented the U.S. fishing fleet. Today, the types of fisheries range from lobster off Maine to king crab off Alaska. Each fishery has its own peculiar kind of gear, with the result that the vessels used in the different fisheries vary as is necessary to work the particular kind of gear used.

Some of the kinds of commercial fishing vessels likely to be encountered by Coast Guardsmen are:

Figure 27–11. A large ACBL tow on Lower Mississippi. (Courtesy American Commercial Barge Lines, Jeffersonville, Indiana)

Figure 27–12. A Southeast Atlantic shrimp trawler. (Courtesy C.A. Magwood, Mt. Pleasant, South Carolina)

Lobster boats
Gillnetters
Scallopers
Shrimp Trawlers
Langousta boats
Snapper boats
Long-line boats
Oyster boats
Crab boats (Blue crab)
Menhaden seiners
Tuna clippers
King crabbers
Stern trawlers
Eastern and western rigged draggers
Clammers
Seiners

Although this list is not complete, it should indicate to the Coast Guardsman that there is no such thing as a typical fishing vessel.

The operation of small fishing vessels in open waters is subject to risk to both the vessels and their crews. Fishing vessels stand at the head of the list of the number of lives lost on all commercial vessels. Not every fishery has the same risks, so if safety were to be properly analyzed, it would be necessary to deal separately with each fishery. Some fisheries are predominantly "father-son" family-owned businesses. Others, for the most part, are composed of fleets owned by large corporations. Most fishermen, other than those that run family-owned vessels, work for a share of the catch. With no catch, there is no pay; hence, there is always motivation to stay out in search of fish, even in the face of threatening weather. This factor, probably more than any other, accounts for the number of search-and-rescue incidents involving fishing vessels.

Other Commercial Vessels

Other than tankers, freighters, passenger, towing, and fishing vessels, there remain a substantial number of commercial watercraft not categorized. A large number of these other vessels are non-self-propelled, and most of those are unmanned. Barges can carry anything a ship can carry, and some barges carry more than do some ships in the same trade. Dredges that are not self-propelled are considered to be barges by the Coast Guard from the standpoint of safety. Seagoing U.S. barges of 100 gross tons or more are required to be inspected by the Coast Guard, regardless of their service.

Within the category of "other commercial vessels" fall various workboats and supply craft. Whether or not a vessel is required to be inspected is a matter that must be resolved after investigation, and usually on a case-by-case basis. Many vessels that are considered "workboats" might rightfully fall within another commercial category. Questions on this issue should be referred to the cognizant Officer in Charge, Marine Inspection.

Kinds of Private Vessels

We have defined private vessels as being those that are employed, but produce no revenue. In this category fall such craft as pleasure boats, yachts, research vessels, nonfederal training vessels, free ferries, exploration vessels, and certain supply and support vessels. Because a U.S. vessel is a private vessel does not mean that it is exempt from various federal safety and environmental protection standards. Service in passengers or bulk combustible liquids, for example, can bring a private vessel into an "inspected vessel" category. So also can the matter of being propelled by steam. With U.S. vessels under 100 gross tons, the distinction between being a passenger and a passenger for hire is very important. Passengers include everyone except certain individuals in six special circumstances; passengers for hire, on the other hand, are people on board who contribute some "consideration" toward their passage. This consideration can be buying a ticket, or reimbursing expenses, or even being a prospective customer of the vessel owner.

Depending upon its service and the economic circumstances of its operation, a private vessel, then, could be any vessel. For that reason, the term *private vessel*, as opposed to *commercial vessel*, has very little application with regard to Coast Guard enforcement operations. For the most part, when we speak of private vessels, we are thinking of pleasure craft that include millions of state-numbered boats. Again, the fact that a vessel is state-numbered does not mean that the vessel is exempt from federal inspection requirements. As with other private vessels, applicability of federal vessel safety laws to state-numbered boats is a matter of their service and economic circumstances.

A yacht is properly defined as any vessel used for pleasure. In the United States, a yacht may be issued a certificate of documentation if it measures 5 net tons or over. Therefore, there emerged a category of U.S. private craft called documented yachts. There are a number of advantages to having a pleasure boat documented as a yacht. The reason most often given is that such craft can enter and clear foreign customs much more easily than state-numbered U.S. vessels. Another reason is that private marine corporations may obtain preferred mortgages on documented vessels, because those mortgages are recorded on the yacht's certificate of documentation. Even when a vessel moves from state to state, the mortgage is a permanent entity and must be satisfied when the yacht is sold or transferred. Another reason for requesting documentation may be that not every local jurisdiction can gain easy access to yacht ownership records, making the assessment of personal property taxes on yachts much more difficult than on state-numbered boats. Whatever the reason for documenting a yacht, the vessel itself is essentially a private vessel and subject to all the same federal safety regulations as other watercraft.

Pleasure craft and other private vessels operating on U.S. navigable waters are subject to Coast Guard jurisdiction. They are also subject to concurrent state jurisdiction. Public vessels and commercial vessels are usually exempt from state jurisdiction, except for commercial vessels in certain situations where the federal government does not exercise its broad authority to regulate interstate commerce and international trade. Generally speaking, all vessels of the U.S. outside our territorial waters and all U.S. and foreign vessels inside U.S. territorial waters are subject to federal jurisdiction. The exact matter of jurisdiction is one of legal interpretation and requires guidance from persons trained in that field. It is important to note, however, that private vessels are subject to state requirements in instances where commercial and public vessels are not.

While the size of the private vessel is not as important as its service and economic circumstance, tonnage is important insofar as documentation is concerned and the applicability of certain safety statutes dealing with passengers/passengers for-hire. The safety of private vessels, most especially pleasure craft, receives a lion's share of Coast Guard attention. In the boating safety effort—to provide safety education, to ensure reasonably safe boating construction standards, and to enforce safety requirements—the Coast Guard encourages the states to assume a major role. In search and rescue, the Coast Guard will probably always play a major role. In the investigation of boating accidents, to determine if other steps can or should be taken to prevent accidents, the Coast Guard shares a mutual responsibility with the states.

There are three main reasons that pleasure craft get into trouble. One is attempting to use the wrong boat on the wrong water at the wrong time. The second is excessive speed. And the third is substance abuse by the vessel operator.

While commercial vessel people often are placed in a high-risk situation, they are professional sailors and understand the nature of their environment. Even the commercial fisherman who considers staying at sea in the face of gale forecasts weighs the risk on the basis of his experience. But the pleasure boater who has planned an outing for Saturday morning with his friends is likely to attempt, say, a three-man, three-six-pack fishing trip in a 14 foot john boat in an open bay without much regard to the marine weather forecast. The macho element also arises once the expedition is under way, because none of the group want to "chicken out" and head back to the boat ramp, and any likelihood of quitting diminishes as the beer is consumed. Other examples of the wrong boat, on the wrong water, at the wrong time can be cited, but the situation described is all too often the same.

The fastest vessels on the water are usually pleasure craft. They provided the inspiration for the "PT" boats of World War II as well as for the fast crew boats used by the mineral and oil industry. There are few speed limits on inland waters, and those that exist are mostly intended to hold down wake damage. Ski boats epitomize the casual use of hull/engine combinations once limited only to boat racing. The ordinary planing outboard runabout runs at least twice the speed of the fastest displacement hull. Fast boats are fun and almost safe. When driven by experienced, sober boaters, they are at least as safe as automobiles. But when driven on a late weekend afternoon by someone who's been partying all day, they are every bit as dangerous as a car driven at a high rate of speed by a drunk. Boats going fast collide with things and kill and injure people. They collide with other boats, fixed submerged objects, fixed not-submerged objects, the bottom, tree limbs, stumps, and when airborne jumping over a wake, the water itself.

The popular notion that booze goes better in boats has its roots in national advertising campaigns designed to increase alcohol sales. Some boat manufacturers apparently go along with that idea too, as evidenced by their full-color brochures showing a happy group planing along in a deluxe model express cruiser, all sipping on tall and fruited drinks.

There is probably not much considered wrong with the customary consumption of beer and liquor afloat. Social drinking is part of our culture. The problem arises on pleasure craft when the vessel operator loses his or her sense of judgment and memory. It has been reported that the first things forgotten when one is intoxicated are the last things learned. Since holiday party attitudes usually coincide with the trying out of a new toy, the inexperienced person with a new boat and a load on, is the proverbial accident looking for a place to happen.

The safety problems peculiar to private, and particularly pleasure, craft, offer no easy remedies. The Coast Guardsman should be aware, however, that a very large portion of the taxpayers' payment of the Coast Guard's budget goes to the business of preserving the lives of pleasure boaters.

Kinds of Public Vessels

United States public vessels are those that are owned and operated by an agency of the federal government, except those vessels owned and operated by the Maritime Administration. Included in this group are military vessels of the Coast Guard, Navy, Army, and Air Force; Military Sealift Command auxiliary and support vessels that are civilian (civil service) manned; Army Corps of Engineers dredges, survey boats, and other vessels that are civil-service manned; and certain other research and data-gathering ships that are manned by civil service personnel. Some public vessels are inspected by the Coast Guard as the result of interagency agreements. By U.S. law, however, public vessels of the United States are exempt from the inspection provisions of the marine inspection laws.

Various interagency agreements exist that govern casualty investigation procedures when a public vessel is involved. The rules of the road apply to all vessels—commercial, private and public— as do navigation and pollution prevention laws and regulations. The punitive enforcement of these federal standards upon public vessels is usually undertaken by the agency that operates a particular vessel rather than by the Coast Guard.

Since Coast Guard vessels are public vessels, Coast Guardsmen should be aware that their vessels are in a different category from those of the commercial and private sectors. Performance standards for Coast Guard vessels require differing levels of design engineering; military manning requirements have a major impact on habitability, and so on. As a practical matter, however, certain small craft operated as public vessels are identical to their commercial and private counterparts. Off-the-shelf purchases of some electronic and mechanical components, as well as hulls, are common within the Coast Guard and other federal agencies.

Summary

In this chapter, we have briefly touched upon our clientele—both the watercraft and their people. And we have superficially looked at some of the traditional criteria under which other mariners operate. There is no way that a chapter in a manual such as this can equip a Coast Guardsman with all the legal and technical information necessary for detailed interaction with these other sailors. But help and knowledge is available within the Coast Guard for the asking. By using the directives system of the service, and other chapters in this manual, Coast Guard people should be better off for having briefly met these other mariners and their vessels in the pages of this book.

Ribbons of Decorations and Awards

Medal of Honor

Navy Cross

Coast Guard
Distinguished
Service Medal

Silver Star Medal

Legion of Merit

Distinguished
Flying Cross

Coast Guard Medal

Navy and
Marine Corps
Medal

Bronze Star Medal

Meritorious Service
Medal

Air Medal

Joint Service
Commendation
Medal

Coast Guard
Commendation
Medal

Navy
Commendation
Medal

Coast Guard
Achievement Medal

Navy
Achievement Medal

Purple Heart Medal

Combat Action
Ribbon

Presidential Unit
Citation

Coast Guard Unit
Commendation

Navy Unit
Commendation

Coast Guard
Meritorious
Unit Commendation

Navy Meritorious
Unit Commendation

Gold
Lifesaving Medal

Silver
Lifesaving Medal

DOT Outstanding
Achievement Medal

DOT Meritorious
Achievement Medal

DOT Superior
Achievement Medal

Coast Guard
Good Conduct
Medal

Navy
Good Conduct
Medal

Marine Corps
Good Conduct
Medal

Army
Good Conduct
Medal

Air Force
Good Conduct
Medal

Coast Guard Reserve
Meritorious Service
Ribbon

Naval Reserve
Medal

Naval Reserve
Meritorious Service
Medal

Navy Expeditionary
Medal

China Service
Medal

American Defense
Service Medal

American Campaign
Medal

European-African
Middle Eastern
Campaign Medal

Asiatic-Pacific
Campaign Medal

World War II
Victory Medal

Navy Occupation
Service Medal

Medal for
Humane Action

National Defense
Service Medal

Korean
Service Medal

Antarctic
Service Medal

Armed Forces
Expeditionary
Medal

Vietnam
Service Medal

Armed Forces
Reserve Medal

United Nations
Service Medal

United Nations
Medal

Philippine
Presidential Unit
Citation

Republic of Korea
Presidential Unit
Citation

Republic of Vietnam
Gallantry Cross
Unit Citation

Republic of Vietnam
Civil Actions
Unit Citation

Republic of Vietnam
Campaign Ribbon

Coast Guard
Expert Rifleman
Medal

Coast Guard
Expert Pistol
Shot Medal

Coast Guard
Letter of
Commendation

Marine Corps
Expeditionary
Medal

Allied Naval Signal Pennants and Flags and International Alphabet Flags

Pennant	Spoken	Pennant	Spoken	Pennant	Spoken
	PENNANT ONE "WUN"		CODE		SQUAD
	PENNANT TWO "TOO"		BLACK PENNANT		STARBOARD
	PENNANT THREE "THUH-REE"		CORPEN		STATION
	PENNANT FOUR "FO-WER"		DESIG		SUBDIV
	PENNANT FIVE "FI-YIV"		DIV		TURN
	PENNANT SIX "SIX"		EMER-GENCY		FIRST SUB
	PENNANT SEVEN "SEVEN"		FLOT		SECOND SUB
	PENNANT EIGHT "ATE"		FORMA-TION		THIRD SUB
	PENNANT NINE "NINER"		INTER-ROGATIVE		FOURTH SUB
	PENNANT ZERO "ZERO"		NEGAT		PORT
	ANSWER		PREP		SPEED

Flag	Name — Written / Spoken	Flag	Name — Written / Spoken	Flag	Name — Written / Spoken
	A **ALFA** "AL-FA"		**M** **MIKE** "MIKE"		**Y** **YANKEE** "YANG-KEY"
	B **BRAVO** "BRAH-VOH"		**N** **NOVEMBER** "NO-VEM-BER"		**Z** **ZULU** "ZOO-LOO"
	C **CHARLIE** "CHAR-LEE"		**O** **OSCAR** "OSS-CAH"		**ONE - 1** "WUN"
	D **DELTA** "DEL-TAH"		**P** **PAPA** "PAH-PAH"		**TWO - 2** "TOO"
	E **ECHO** "ECK-OH"		**Q** **QUEBEC** "KAY-BECK"		**THREE - 3** "THUH-REE"
	F **FOXTROT** "FOKS-TROT"		**R** **ROMEO** "ROW-ME-OH"		**FOUR - 4** "FO-WER"
	G **GOLF** "GOLF"		**S** **SIERRA** "SEE-AIR-RAH"		**FIVE - 5** "FI-YIV"
	H **HOTEL** "HOH-TEL"		**T** **TANGO** "TANG-GO"		**SIX - 6** "SIX"
	I **INDIA** "IN-DEE-AH"		**U** **UNIFORM** "YOU-NEE-FORM"		**SEVEN - 7** "SEVEN"
	J **JULIETT** "JEW-LEE-ETT"		**V** **VICTOR** "VIK-TAH"		**EIGHT - 8** "ATE"
	K **KILO** "KEY-LOH"		**W** **WHISKEY** "WISS-KEY"		**NINE - 9** "NINER"
	L **LIMA** "LEE-MAH"		**X** **XRAY** "ECKS-RAY"		**ZERO - 0** "ZERO"

UNITED STATES COAST GUARD
BUOYAGE OF THE UNITED STATES
Significance of Shapes, Coloring, Numbering, and Light Characteristics
Symbols shown adjacent to Buoys are those used on Charts to indicate such Aids

LATERAL SYSTEM

PORT SIDE ENTERING FROM SEAWARD	MID-CHANNEL ENTERING FROM SEAWARD	STARBOARD SIDE ENTERING FROM SEAWARD

PORT SIDE
ENTERING FROM SEAWARD

Marks port side of channels and obstructions. To be left to port when passed.
Color: BLACK
Numbering: ODD. (Does not apply to Mississippi River System)
Shape: CAN. (Lighted buoys, sound buoys, and spar buoys, have no shape significance)
Color of Light: WHITE OR GREEN
Light Phase Characteristics: (Does not apply to Mississippi River System)

FLASHING

OCCULTING

QUICK FLASHING

Marking important turns, wrecks, etc., where particular caution is required.

Lighted

Can   Spar

Unlighted Bell

Unlighted Whistle

MID-CHANNEL
ENTERING FROM SEAWARD

Marks Mid-channel
Color: BLACK AND WHITE VERTICAL STRIPES
Numbering: NONE. May be lettered
Shape: NO SHAPE SIGNIFICANCE
Color of Lights: WHITE ONLY
Light Phase Characteristics:

MORSE CODE "A"

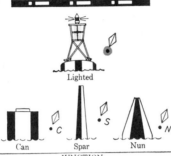
Lighted

Can   Spar   Nun

JUNCTION
ENTERING FROM SEAWARD

Marks junctions and obstructions which may be passed on either side. Preferred channel is indicated by color of top band.
Color: RED AND BLACK HORIZONTAL BANDS
Numbering: NONE. May be lettered
Shape: CAN or NUN ACCORDING TO COLOR OF TOP BAND. (Lighted buoys, sound buoys, and spar buoys have no shape significance)
Color of Lights: WHITE, RED, OR GREEN
Light Phase Characteristics:

INTERRUPTED QUICK FLASHING

Lighted

Where preferred channel is to STARBOARD the topmost band is BLACK	Where preferred channel is to PORT the topmost band is RED

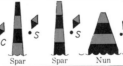
Can Spar Spar Nun

STARBOARD SIDE
ENTERING FROM SEAWARD

Marks starboard side of channels and obstructions. To be left to starboard when passed.
Color: RED
Numbering: EVEN. (Does not apply to Mississippi River System)
Shape: NUN. (Lighted buoys, sound buoys, and spar buoys have no shape significance)
Color of Light: WHITE OR RED
Light Phase Characteristics: (Does not apply to Mississippi River System)

FLASHING

OCCULTING

QUICK FLASHING

Marking important turns, wrecks, etc., where particular caution is required.

Lighted

Spar   Nun

Unlighted Bell

Unlighted Whistle

BUOYS HAVING NO LATERAL SIGNIFICANCE

Color. AS SHOWN: Numbering: NONE. May be lettered. Light Phase Characteristics: Color of Lights: **WHITE**

FIXED	FLASHING	OCCULTING

International Orange
Special Purpose

Quarantine Anchorage

Anchorage

Fish Net

Dredging

APPENDIX D
Channel Markers

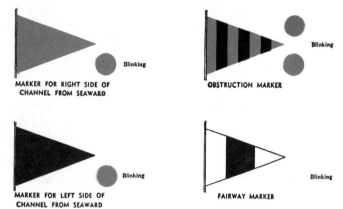

MARKER FOR RIGHT SIDE OF
CHANNEL FROM SEAWARD

Blinking

OBSTRUCTION MARKER

Blinking

MARKER FOR LEFT SIDE OF
CHANNEL FROM SEAWARD

Blinking

FAIRWAY MARKER

Blinking

Storm Warning Signals

DAYTIME SIGNALS

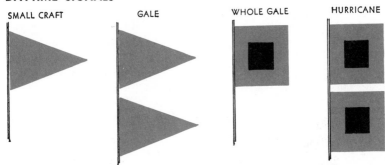

SMALL CRAFT   GALE   WHOLE GALE   HURRICANE

NIGHT SIGNALS

SMALL CRAFT   GALE   WHOLE GALE   HURRICANE

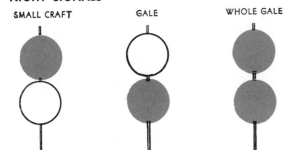

Beaufort Scale

Estimation of the wind's speed and a constant awareness of the state of the sea are important responsibilities of a mariner. Sea state can have a significant influence upon a ship. Course changes, leeway, dead reckoning, engine speeds, and even rudder angles are affected by wind and sea. The photos represent "steady state" sea conditions.

0 Calm 0–1 kts.
Sea like a mirror.

1 Light air 1–3 kts./1/4-ft waves.
Ripples with appearance of scales; no foam crests.

2 Light breeze 4–6 kts./1/2-ft. waves
Small wavelets; crests of glassy appearance, not breaking.

3 Gentle breeze 7–10 kts./2-ft. waves
Large wavelets; crests begin to break; scattered whitecaps.

4 Moderate breeze 11–16 kts./4-ft. waves
Small waves, becoming longer; numerous whitecaps.

5 Fresh breeze 17–21 kts./6-ft. waves
Moderate waves, taking longer form; many whitecaps; some spray.

6 Strong breeze 22–27 kts./10-ft. waves
Larger waves forming; whitecaps everywhere; more spray.

7 Near gale 28–33 kts./14-ft. waves
Sea heaps up; white foam from breaking waves begins to be blown in streaks.

8   Gale 34–40 kts./18 ft. waves
Moderately high waves of greater length; edges of crests begin to break into spindrift; foam is blown into well-marked streaks.

9   Strong gale 41–47 kts./23-ft. waves
High waves; sea beings to roll; dense streaks of foam; spray may reduce visibility.

10   Storm 48–55 kts./29-ft. waves
Very high waves with overhanging crests; sea takes white appearance as foam is blown in very dense streaks; rolling is heavy and visibility reduced.

11   Violent storm 53–63 kts./37-ft. waves
Exceptionally high waves; sea covered with white foam patches; visibility still more reduced.

12   Hurricane 64–71 kts./45-ft. waves
Air filled with foam; sea completely white with driving spray; visibility greatly reduced.

Photos courtesy of the Atmospheric Environment Service of Canada.

Notes on Sources and Suggested Reading Material

The following list of Coast Guard directives was used to prepare this edition. The revised Coast Guard publications numbering system (Commandant Instruction "M" group) has been listed where implemented:

Uniform Regulations	M1020.6
Enlisted Qualifications Manual	M1414.8
Training and Education Manual	M1500.10
Telecommunications Manual	M2000.3
USCG Regulations	M5000.3
Safety Manual	M5100.29
Enlisted Billet Manual	M5320.6B
Military Civil Rights Manual	M5350.11
Operating Facilities of the C. G.	M5440.2A
Register of Cutters	M5441.5A
Security Manual	M5500.11
Nutritional and Dietary Guidelines	M6110.2
Physical Fitness Guidelines	M6110.3
Sound-Powered Telephone Talkers Manual	M9430.1
Reserve and Survival Systems Manual	M10470.10
Marine Safety Manual	M16000.3
Planning and Programming Manual	M16010.1
Boats of the Coast Guard	M16114.1
National SAR Manual	M16130.2

CHRIS	M16465.11
CHRIS Manual No. 2	M16465.12
Hazard Assessment Manual	M16465.13
Aids to Navigation Manual	M16500.1
Personnel Manual	CG–207
Organization and Regulations Manual for Various Cutter Types	CG–260 (series)

Other Coast Guard published material and directives providing reference material include:

1. *On Scene, National Maritime SAR Reviews.*
2. *Surfboats, Rockets and Carronades*, CDR R. F. Bennett USCG, GPO, 1976.
3. *Commandant's Bulletins.*
4. *USCG Navigation Rules* CG–169, May 1, 1977.
5. Portions of the Code of Federal Regulations, Title 33, 46, and 49.

U. S. Navy publications listed below were also used to prepare this edition:

Replenishment at Sea (NWP 38)
Shipboard Procedures (NWP 50 series)
USN Communications Instructions (DNC 27)
Flags, Pennants and Customs (DNC 22)
Naval Ships Technical Manual (NAVPERS 0901–000–0000 series)
Seaman (NAVPERS 10120)
Boatswain's Mate 3 & 2 (NAVPERS 10121)
Quartermaster 3 & 2 (NAVPERS 10149)
Quartermaster 1 & C (NAVPERS 10151)
Gunner's Mate 3 & 2 (NAVPERS 10185A)
Seamanship (NAVPERS 16118 series)

Private publications listed below were also consulted:

Capt. J. V. Noel, Jr., USN (Retired). *The VNR Dictionary of Ships and the Sea*. New York: Van Norstrand Reinhold Company, 1981.
American National Red Cross. *Cardiopulmonary Resuscitation*. ISBN 0–86536–022–7, 1981.

Publications by the Naval Institute Press, Annapolis, Maryland

A Mariner's Guide to the Rules of the Road, 2nd ed. W.H. Tate, 1982.

The Art of Knotting and Splicing, 3rd ed. Cyrus Day, 1970.

The Boat Officer's Handbook. Lt. D.D. Winters, USN, 1981.

Dictionary of Naval Abbreviations. Bill Wedertz, ed., 1977.

Division Officer's Guide, 8th ed. Capt. J.V. Noel, Jr., USN(Ret.), 1982.

Dutton's Navigation and Piloting, 13th ed. E.S. Maloney, 1977.

Eagle Seamanship, 2nd ed. Revised by LCdr. P.M. Regan, USCG, 1979.

Engineering for the OOD. Cdr. D. Felger, USN, 1979.

Farwell's Rules of the Nautical Road, 6th ed. Revised by Cdr. F.E. Bassett, USN, and Cdr. R.A. Smith, RN, 1982.

George Washington's Coast Guard. I.H. King, 1978.

How to Survive on Land and Sea, 5th ed. Smith/Jarvis, 1984.

International Law for Seagoing Officers, 4th ed. B.H. Brittin, 1981.

Marine Navigation 1 and 2, 2nd eds. R.R. Hobbs, 1981.

The Mariner's Pocket Companion. W.E. Tobin III, 1983.

Naval Ceremonies, Customs, and Traditions, 5th ed. VAdm. W.P. Mack, USN(Ret.), and LCdr. R.W. Connell, USN, 1980.

Naval Terms Dictionary, 4th ed. Capt. J.V. Noel, Jr., USN(Ret.), and Capt. E.L. Beach, USN(Ret.), 1978.

Naval Shiphandling, 4th ed. Capt. R.S. Crenshaw, Jr., USN(Ret.), 1975.

Piloting and Dead Reckoning, 2nd ed. Capt. H.H. Shufeldt, USNR(Ret.), and G.D. Dunlap, 1981.

Sail and Power, 3rd ed. R. Henderson, 1979.

Seamanship, 2nd ed. D.O. Dodge and LCdr. S.E. Kyriss, USN, 1980.

Service Etiquette, 3rd ed. Oretha D. Swartz, 1977.

Ships and Aircraft of the U.S. Fleet, 12th ed. N. Polmar, 1981.

U.S. Coast Guard Cutters and Craft of World War II. R.L. Scheina, 1982.

Watch Officer's Guide, 11th ed. Revised by Cdr. K.C. Jacobsen, USN, 1979.

Weather for the Mariner, 3rd ed. RAdm. W.J. Kotsch, USN(Ret.), 1983.

Index

Abandon ship, 358–359, 411–416
Absence indicators, 595
Absence, unauthorized, 51
Academy, Coast Guard, 637
Accidents, 510
Accountability for government
  property, 553–554
Addressing military personnel, 606–8
Administrative and scientific group
  ratings, 624–627
Administrative bills, 354
Advancement in rating, 635–636
Advancement to warrant and
  commissioned grades, 636
Aids to navigation, 23–24, 345–350
Aiguillettes, 129
Aircraft, types of, 583, 587–588
Aircraft markings and designations, 582
Aircraft safety precautions, 510–511
Aircraft signals, 344
Air stations and detachments, 588–589
Alarms, 356
Alaska, operations in, 15
Albatross aircraft, 583
Alcohol abuse, 68
All-hands drills, 356
Allotments, 645
Allowances, 643–645
Alphabet, phonetic, 287
Alphabetical flags, 278
Ammunition, 296–299
Ammunition handling, 511–512
Anchorage Regulations, 22

Anchor lights, 341
Anchors, 222–227
Anchor watch, 152
Animal bites, 477
Armament, 306
Artificial respiration, 466–475
Asbestos suits, 399
Asphyxiation, 477
Attention, position of, 82
Attitude, survival, 436–438
Auxiliary, Coast Guard, 23
Aviation electrician's mate, duties
  of, 623
Aviation electronics technician, duties
  of, 623
Aviation group ratings, 622–624
Aviation machinist's mate, duties
  of, 622
Aviation structural mechanic, duties
  of, 623
Aviation survivalman, duties of, 622
Awards, 135–139

Back float, 442
Back stroke, 446
Bad Conduct Discharge, 650
Bag inspection, 164
Bandages, 477
Barges and gigs, 248
Basic allowance, quarters and
  subsistence, 643
Basic tests, 630
Battle bill, 359

Battle dressing stations, 376
Beach guard, 162
Bearings, navigational, 322–325
Bell signals, engine, 255, 173–174
Bends, in line, 199–222
Benefits, enlisted, 641–643
Billets, shipboard, 39
Biological warfare, 367–368
Black history, 76–77
Bleeding, control of, 477–482
Blisters, treatment of, 482
Blocks and tackle, 221–227
Blue-nose Polar Bear, 614
Boarding inspections, 21–24
Boarding ship, procedure for, 598–599
Boat, vehicle, and passageway
    etiquette, 604–6
Boat crews, 250
Boat equipment, 248–250
Boat hails, 611–612
Boathandling, safety precautions, 255–
    266, 512–513
Boating and drinking, 700–701
Boating safety, 23
Boatkeepers, 250
Boats, types of, 245–248
Boatswain's mate, duties of, 619
Boatswain's mate of the watch, 157–
    158
Boatswain's pipe, use of, 148
Booms, 232–235
Brassards, 129
Breakdown, procedures for, 175
Breakers, 453
Breast insignia, 126, 128
Breast stroke, 446–447
Bridge administration, 20–21
Bridge of ship, 186–188
Bridge watch, 158
Brightwork, 540
Brushes, care of, 547
Buoy boats, 246
Buoy tenders, 578, 581
Buoys, navigational, 345–349
Burial at sea, 615
Burns, treatment of, 482–484
Butterworth, 683

Cadets, Coast Guard, 637–638
Cameras, restrictions on use, 563
Canvas, care of, 541
Capstans, 227

Captain of the Port, 22–23
Captains Inspection, 164
Carbon dioxide extinguishers, 393–395
Cardiac massage, 472–473
Cardiopulmonary Resuscitation,
    467–473
Cargo, defined, 684
Cargo handling, 513–514
Cargo handling rigs, 235–239
Cargo, hazardous, 684
Cargo holds, 193
Casualty agents, 369
Categories of vessels, 659–660
Celestial navigation, 315
Censorship, 289
Ceremonies, military, 110, 591
Certificate of Inspection, 665–672
Chain, anchor, 222, 225
Chain of command, 28
Change of command, 612–613
Channel markers, 345–350
Charthouse, 188
Charts, 311–313
Chemical burns, 483–484
Chemical fire extinguishers, 395
Chemical warfare, 368–371
Chisels, use of, 519–520
Choking, treatment for, 488–489
Christmas lights, 614
Chronometers, 316
Church pennants, 596
Circuit discipline, telephone, 274
Civilian clothing, 129
Civil laws, 53
Civil War, 10–11
Classes of breaking surf, 453–454
Classes of fires, 386–388
Classification societies, 663
Classification tests, 630
Classified matter, 557–558
Cleaning, deck and compartment,
    539–541
Cleanliness, personal, 61–63
Close order drill, 111–116
Closed compartments, safety
    precautions in, 514–515
Clothing allowance, 644
Clothing, care of, 130–133
Clothing, removal in water, 448
Coast Guard, establishment of, 3–9
Coast Guard Academy, 637
Coast Guard Auxiliary, 23

Coast Guard Ensign, 594
Coast Guard Institute, 635
Coast Guard ships, 573–586
Coast Guard stations, 32
Cold injuries, treatment of, 414–415, 476, 485–487
Cold iron watch, 158
Cold water survival, 414–415, 476
Collateral duties, 38
Colored buoys, 347–348
Colors, ceremonies for, 592–599
Combat information center, 189
Commanding officer, duties of, 36
Command pennant, 595–596
Commands, drill, 81–116
Commands, standard, 166–167, 230–231
Commendation Awards, 135–139
Commercial vessels, kinds, 675–698
Commercial vessel safety, 21
Commissioned officers, 121
Commissioning ceremony, 613
Commission pennant, 594
Communications, 269–291
Commuted rations, 644
Compartmentation, 182–186
Compartment cleaners, 162
Compasses, 171, 316–322
Compensatory absence, 656
Compressed air system, 193
Compressed gases, 514–515
Conditions of readiness, 149, 383–385
Constellations, navigational, 329–334
Construction of ships, 117–195
Consumable supplies, 553
Corporal of the guard, 567–570
Correcting compass error, 320–321
Correspondence courses, 635
Courts-martial, 54–57
Crew accommodations, 193
Crossing the Line, 613
Cryptography, 287–288
Currents, 327–328
Currents, surf, 457
Customs, U.S., 165
Customs and ceremony, 591–616
Cutters, current types, 575–582
Cutters, first Coast Guard, 5–6

Daily inspections, 164
Daily routines, 143–147
Damage control, 373–405

Damage controlman, duties of, 620
Damage control markings, 384
Damage control watch, 158
Dangerous Cargo, 684
Dangerous materials, 529
Darken ship, 565
Daymarks, 350
Daytime storm warnings, 350–351
Dead man's float, 442
Dead reckoning, 313
Deadweight tons, 663–664
Deck department, 38
Deck fittings, 223–230
Deck group ratings, 619–620
Decks, names of, 181–182
Decommissioning ceremony, 613
Decontamination, 367, 376
Decorations and awards, 135–139
Departmental duties, 35–43
Department of Transportation, 27
Deposits for safekeeping, 645
Deviation, compass, 318–319
Diet, 63–65
Dipper, constellation of, 331–332
Dipping colors, 594
Discharges, types of, 649–650
Disciplinary system, 48–58
Dishonorable discharge, 650
Displacement tons, 662
Distress signals, 344–345
District organization, 29–30
District units, 31–35
Divine service, 600
Division parades, 154
Divison police petty officer, 163
Documents, personnel, 672–675
Documents, vessel, 664–666
Dog paddle stroke, 444–445
Domestic ice operations, 21
Doors and hatches, 377–381
Dories and dinghies, 247
Dressing ship, 610
Drill commands, 81–87
Drills, emergency, 356
Drowning, first aid for, 466–477
Drugs, 65–69
Dry Bulk Cargo vessels, 690–691
Dry Cargo vessels, 685–690
DUKWs, 247–248
Duties, Coast Guard, 17–24
Duties, watch stander, 151–153
Duty assignments, 647–649

Dysentery, 62

Eagle, training ship, 580–581
Electrical equipment, maintenance of, 515–517, 540–541
Electrical shock, 484
Electrical system, shipboard, 192
Electrician's mate, duties of, 622
Electric tools, 517
Electronic aids to navigation, 23, 314–315
Electronic communications, 283
Electronics technician, duties of, 621
Emergency bills, 357–359
Emergency leave, 656
Emergency procedures, 175
Engineering and hull group ratings, 620–622
Engineering plant, 191
Enginer officer, 38, 43
Engine order telegraph, 173–174
Engineroom watches, 158
Engines, main, 191
Engine signals, powerboat, 255
Enlisted details, 162–163
Enlistments, general, 629
Enlistments, types of, 646–647
Ensign, National, 592–594
Entertainment, 638
Equipage, 553
Equipment, boat and raft, 432
Equipment, types of, 553–554
Equipment aboard ship, 191
Ethnic groups, 75
Etiquette, boat and vehicle, 604–6
Etiquette, service, 552, 604–9
Examinations, advancement in rating, 631–637
Exchange, Coast Guard, 640–641
Executive officer, duties of, 36–37
Explosives, handling of, 511–512
Extension of enlistment, 646
External communications, 277–288
External security, 564–565
Extinguishing agents, fire, 388–398
Eye injuries, 687–688

Facings, drill, 83
Family Separation Allowance, 645
Feeder surf currents, 457
Fiber line, 197–198
Field stripping pistol, 300

Fire control technician, duties of, 620
Fire drill, 361–362
Fire fighting, 385
Fire-fighting equipment, 388–402
Fire-fighting technique, 402–5
Firehose, maintenance of, 541
Firehose, use of, 389–391
Fireman's lift, 503–5
Fire prevention, 385–388, 518
Fires and firefighting, 385–388
First aid, 465–507
First lieutenant, duties of, 38
Fish hooks, 488
Fish stings, 488–490
Fishing boat, 695
Fishing tips, 434
Fishing vessel, 695
Fishing vessels, kinds, 695–697
Flag ceremonies, 592–594, 596–599
Flaghoists, 278, 281
Flags and pennants, 278, 281
Flashing light communications, 278
Foam firefighting equipment, 392–393
Fog signals, 342
Food and water, emergency, 433–436
Foreign duty pay, 644
Foreigners, attitude toward, 78
Fork lifts, 518
Formations, military, 111–116
Fractures, treatment of, 490–492
Freeboard, 663–664
Freight, defined, 684
Freighters, 684–691
Fresh water king, duties of, 163
Fresh water systems, 192
Frostbite, treatment of, 485–486
Fueling, boats, 253
Fueling at sea, 239–241
Fuel oil handling, 518–519
Fuel oil systems, 193

Gas attack, 368–371
Gaskets, 380–381, 541
Gas masks, 370
General courts-martial, 57
General drills, 353–371
General emergency organization, 357
General mess, 164
General muster, 156–157
General orders, 567–570
General prudential rule, 344
General quarters, 361

Golden Dragon, 614
Government property, 553–554
Grooming, personal, 133
Gross tons, 662
Ground tackle, 194–195, 222–227
Group commands, 34–35
Group command watches, 158–159
Guard duty, 567–570
Guard mail petty officer, 163
Gunner's mate, duties of, 620
Guns, parts of, 295
Guns, types of, 294–295
Gun salutes, 608
Gyrocompasses, 321–322

"Hail to the Chief," song, 598
Hammers, use of, 520
Hand lead, use of, 241–243
Handset telephones, 272
Hand tools, use of, 519–520
Harassing agents, 369
Harassment, sexual, 73–74
Harbor tugs, 581
Hazardous duty pay, 644
Headgear, uniform, 120
Headquarters, organization, 29
Headquarters units, 30–31
Headset telephones, 272
Heat exhaustion, treatment of, 493–494
Heaving the lead, 241–243
Heavy weather, safety in, 520
Helicopters, 520, 583, 588
Helmsman, commands to, 166–167
Helmsman, duties of, 159
Hemp line, 198
Hercules aircraft, 583
High endurance cutters, 575
Highline rigs, 236–239
History, Coast Guard, 3–17
Hitches, 208
Hoisting boats, 252–253, 513
Homeward-bound pennant, 614
Homosexuality, 71–72
Honorable discharge, 649–650
Honors, 596, 608–12
Hospital corpsman, duties of, 626
Hot work, 520–521
Hull construction, 178–181
Hull repairs, 381–383
Hurricane warnings, 351
Hygiene, personal, 61–63

Hypothermia, 485

Icebreakers, 578
Ice operations, 21
Ice Patrol, International, 15–16
Identification cards, 653–654
Immersion foot, treatment of, 486–487
Incentive pay, 644
Information and education program, 639–640
Infra-red signals, 278
Injured people, movement of, 503–7
Inland Rules of the Road, 337–345
Insect bites, 494
Insignia, officer and enlisted, 120–125
Inspections, 43–45, 154–156, 163–165, 666–672
Insurance, 642
Intermediate commands, 34–35
Internal communications, 269–277
Internal security, 565–566
International Date Line, 309
International Ice Patrol, 15–16
International Morse Code, 282–283
International Rules of the Road, 337–345
Introductions, personal, 606–7, 609

JA circuits, 273
Jack o' the Dust, duties of, 163
Jellyfish or tuck float, 442
Justice and discipline, 48–51

Keys, custody of, 565–566
Knots and hitches, 208–220

Landing craft, 247
Landing party, 355
Latitude, 309
Launches, 247
Law enforcement, 17–24
LCVPs, 247
Leadership, 47–48, 635
Leadsman, 163, 241–243
Leaving ship, procedures for, 598–599
Legal assistance, 641
Liberty, 153–154, 654–655
Libraries, ship and station, 639
Licensed officer, 673–674
Lifeboats, 245–250, 253, 416–422
Life insurance, 642
Life jackets, 407–11

Life lines, 521–522
Life preservers, 407–11
Life raft, CG Approved, 417–420
Life raft, four man, 420–422
Life raft, Navy MK 5, 417
Life rafts, 416–422
Lifesaving operations, 7–9, 14–17
Lifesaving procedures, 458–461
Light and sound signals, 339–342
Lighthouses, 5
Light Lists, 24
Lights, buoy, 24, 345–350
Lights, distress signal, 429–433
Lights, navigational, 339–341
Lights, shipboard, 150, 522
Lightships, 581
Line, uses aboard ship, 197–208
Linehandlers, commands to, 230–231
Linehandling, 199–202
Lines and rigging, safety precautions, 522
Line-throwing guns, 522
Living quarters, 191, 193
Loadline, 663–664
Locker inspection, 45, 164
Logs, 43
Longitude, 309
Lookouts, duties of, 159–161, 167–169
Loran, 29, 314
Lower deck patrol, 162
Lowering boats, 250–252, 513

Machinery, safety precautions, 523
Machinery technician, duties of, 620–621
Macks, 190
Magazines, 193
Magnetic compasses, 317–321
Mail, 288
Maintenance, general, 539–554
Manholes, 380
Manifest, cargo, or dangerous cargo, 665
Manila line, 198
Manning the rail, 608, 610
Man overboard, 175, 356
Manual for Courts-Martial, 49
Manual of arms, 87–111
Marching commands, 83–87, 113–115
Marijuana use, 67–68
Marine Environmental Protection, 22
Marine inspection, 666–672

Marine Inspection Office, 32
Marine Safety Office, 32
Marine science, 22
Marine science technician, duties of, 624
Marlinspike seamanship, 197–220
Masks, 399–402
Master CPO of the Coast Guard, 626
Masters-at-arm, 57, 158, 163
Material condition of ships, 383–385
Materials handling, 523
MC circuits, 276–277
Medals and awards, 135–139
Medical care, 642
Medium endurance cutters, 575
Meeting, crossing, overtaking situations, 337–345
Mental attitude, 436–438
Merchant Marine, 673
Merchant Mariners documents, 673
Merchant ships, 675
Merchant vessel, 660
Messengers, duties of, 161
Messmen, 164
Mexican War, 10
Military fundamentals, 81–116
Military operations, 22
Mines, 293, 305–6
Minority groups, 75–77
Misconduct, 650, 652
Missions of the Coast Guard, 17–24
Monitoring radiation, 366
Mooring lines, 227–231
Morale, 437, 638
Moral responsibility, 48
Morphine, use of, 494
Morse Code, 282–283
Motorboats, 245–248, 661, 698–701
Motor buoy boats, 246
Motor life boats, 245, 262
Motor surf boats, 246
Motor vehicles, use of, 523–525
Mouth-to-mouth breathing, 466–473
Muster of crew, 154–155

Nancy signal equipment, 278
National anthem, 592
National ensign, salutes to, 592–594
Navigation, science of, 309–334
Navigational aids, 23–24, 345–351
Navigational instruments, 315–316
Navigator, duties of, 38

Navy Classification Tests, 630
NBC defense, 363–371
Net tons, 622
New Year's log, 614
Night vision, 160–161
Non-appropriated funds, 640–641
Non-judicial punishment, 55–56
Notices to Mariners, 24
Nuclear warfare, 363–367
Numbered buoys, 348
Numbering of compartments, 182–186
Numbers, pronunciation of, 286
Numeral flags and pennants, 278, 281
Nylon line, 198, 204–5

Ocean currents, 327–328
Ocean Search and Rescue, 16
Offenses, civil and military, 51–53
Officer Candidate School, 637
Officer in Charge, Marine Inspection, 666–667
Officer of the deck, duties of, 40, 42–43
Officers' country, 151
Oil king, duties of, 163
On-the-job training, 635
Operational bills, 354–356
Operations officer, 37
Operators licenses, 673, 675
Ordnance equipment, 195
Ordnance terminology, 293–299
Organization, Coast Guard, 27–35
Organization, shipboard, 35–45
Orientation, geographical, 334
Orion, constellation of, 331
Outboard motor boats, 247
Overtaking situations, 343
Ownership markings, 133–135
Oxygen breathing apparatus, 398–402

Paint, types of, 544–545
Painting, safety rules for, 525–526
Painting instructions, 542–553
Paintwork, scrubbing, 540
Parades, division, 154
Parceling line, 207
Parts of a ship, 177–182
Passenger vessels, 691–693
Passing honors, 612
Passing the word, 148, 270–271
Patches and shoring, 382–383
Patrol boats, 578

Patrols, security, 162
Pay and allowances, 643–646
Pay grades, duties of, 617–626
Pelorus, 323–324
Pennants, special use, 281, 595–596, 614
Per diem, 604, 645
Personal flotation devices, 407–11
Personal hygiene, 61–72
Personnel assignment, 354
Personnel inspection, 43–45
Personnel protection, 462, 526
Pets, 151
Petty officer training, 631–635
Phone talkers, 161, 272–276
Phonetic alphabet, 286–287
Photo-journalist, duties of, 625
Physical fitness, 61–62
Pilothouse, 187–188
Piloting, 311–313
Pilots, 7, 672
Pistol, .45 automatic, 299–301
Planes, designations of, 582–583, 588
Planets, navigational, 328–329
Plan of the day, 147
Plastics, fire hazard in, 405
Platoon, formation of, 160
Plimsoll mark, 663–664
Plunging breakers, 454–456
Pneumatic tools, 526
Poisonous substances, treatment for, 495–498
Polaris, navigational star, 331
Polar operations, 17
Port and environmental safety, 22
Port security man, duties of, 626
Position angle, 169
Post offices, 641
Power boats, 245–248
Pratique, 165
Precedence of rations, 627
President, honors for, 598, 611
Pressure points, first aid, 478–481
Pre-trial procedure, 54
Prime meridian, 309
Prisoners at large, 153
Prisoners of war, 566
Private vessels, kinds, 698–701
Procedure signs and words, 281–282
Proficiency pay, 644
Projectiles, 296–298
Propulsion methods, 660

Protective clothing and masks, 370–371, 398–402
Prudential rule, 344
Publications, navigational, 24
Public relations, 78
Public vessels, kinds, 701–2
Pumps, firefighting, 388–389, 395–396
Punishment, purpose of, 53–54

Qualifications, ratings, 634
Quarterdeck customs, 599
Quarterdeck watch, 161
Quartermasters, duties of, 619
Quarters, muster and inspection, 154–157

Racial understanding, 75
Radarman, duties of, 619
Radiation hazards, 527–528
Radiation measurements, 366
Radio communications, 283–284
Radioman, duties of, 625
Radioman of the watch, 162
Rafts, life, 416–429
Ranges, 350
Ranks, officer, 121–123
Rates and ratings, 124–126, 617, 627
Rat guards, 231
Rating badges, 126
Records, service, 652–653
Recreation, 638–639
Recreational vessels, 698–701
Recruits, 618
Recruit training, 629–630
Red Cross, American, 640
Red Cross flag, 596
Reenlistments, 646
Regional Examination Center, 673
Relative bearings, 167–169, 322
Relieving the watch, 152
Repair parties, 374–375
Repeats, request for, 276
Reporting objects, 167–169
Requests, special, 654
Rescue and assistance detail, 355
Rescue stations, 8
Reserve, Coast Guard, 657
Respirators, 550
Restricted men, 153
Retirement, 657
Revenue Cutters, 5–6
Revenue Marine, 5

Ribbons, wearing of, 136
Rifle, M16, 301, 306
Rifle salutes, 106
Rigging, 232–241
Rigging, maintenance of, 541
Right of way, rules for, 342–344
Rights of accused, 50
Rip currents, surf, 457
Rope and line, 197–199
Ropemaking, 198–199
Routine aboard ship, 142–147
Rubber life rafts, 416–429
Rudder, operation of, 172–173
Rules of the Road, 337–345
Running lights, 339–341

Sabotage, 564
Safeguarding information, 562–563
Safety at sea, 7–9, 21–24
Safety certificates, 665
Safety devices, 528
Safety precautions, 509–536
Sailing vessels, rules for, 303–4, 343
Saltwater system, 192–193
Salutes, rifle, 106
Salutes to the flag, 592, 596
Saluting situations, 600, 604
Savings, allotments, 645
Schools, Class A, 631–632
Scientific group ratings, 624–626
SCUBA diving, 461, 463
Sculling, 443–444
Seamen, merchant, 672–675
Sea pay, 644
Sea pusses, 457
Search and rescue, 24
Search and rescue equipment, 582–583
Sea watch, 149
Sectors of bearings, 167–169
Security, general, 566–570
Security, external, 564
Security classifications, 559–561
Security clearance, 557–559
Security patrol, 152
Seizing, 207
Self-bailing boats, 246
Semaphore signals, 278–279
Sentry watch, 564, 567–570
Service record, 652–653
Serving of line, 207
Sets, surf, 455

Sextant, 315
Sexual harassment, 73–74
Shark infested waters, 451–453
Ship control, 169–175
Ship control console, 174
Ships, characteristics of, 574–575
Ships, designation symbols for, 573, 575–582
Ships, parts of, 177–182
Ship's bell, 141–142
Ship's Organization Manual, 35
Shipyard security, 566
Shock, treatment of, 499
Shoes, safety, 526
Shops and offices, 194
Shore duty, 648
Shore Patrol, 57–58
Sickbay, uncovering in, 599
Sick leave, 656
Sideboys, 610
Sidestroke, 445–446
Signal bridge, duties of, 158
Signal equipment, 277–278, 281
Signal lights, distress, 429–433
Slatches, 457
Sleeping topside, 529
Small arms, 299–306
Small arms, safe use of, 529
Small boat safety, 255–266
Small craft warnings, 350
Small passenger vessel, 690–691
Smoking, 530
Snake bites, 499–502
Sneak attack, 564
Snorkel diving, 461, 463
Social Security, 641
Solar still, 434–435
SOLAS certificates, 665
Sonar technician, duties of, 619–620
Soundings, 165, 241–243, 311
Sound-powered telephones, 272–276
Sound signals, 341–342
Southern Cross, constellation of, 332
Spanish-American War, 11
Special courts-martial, 56
Special equipment, use of, 531
Special flags and pennants, 278–281
Speed pennant, 596
Spiders and scorpions, bites of, 502–3
Spilling breakers, 453–454
Splices, 205–6
Splinters, removal of, 503

Splints, first aid, 490–493
Sports, 638
Spray painting, 547–550
Sprinkler systems, 396
Squad formations, 111–116
Squawk boxes, 270, 276–277
Stacks, 189
Stadimeter, 313, 316
Stains, removal of, 132–133
Standard commands, 165–167
Standard phraseology, 287
Standard routine, 142–147
Standing lights, 150
Standing rigging, 541
Stars, navigational, 329–334
Steam, smothering systems, 396–397
Steering gear, 194
Steering signals, 341–342
Steering techique, 172–173
Step and march commands, 83–87
Stokes stretcher, 505–7
Storekeeper, duties of, 625
Storerooms, 193
Storm warnings, 350–351
Submarine signals, 344
Subsistence and quarters allowance, 643
Subsistence specialist, duties of, 625–626
Substitute flags, 281
Summary courts-martial, 56
Sun, movement of, 328
Sunstroke, treatment for, 492–493
Superstructure, 186–191
Surfboats, 246, 248
Surf rescue boat, 248
Surf swimming, 453–454
Surging breakers, 456–457
Survival, 407–438
Sweeping and swabbing, 539–540
Swimming and lifesaving, 441–463
Synthetic lines, 198, 204–6, 531

Tackle, 221–222
Tagout procedures, 531
Tankers, commercial, 676–684
Tanks aboard ship, 180
Taps, 148
Tattoos, 69
Teeth, care of, 62–63
Telephone, sound-powered, 272–276
Telephone technician, duties of, 622

Temporary markers, 350
Tenders, buoy, 578, 581
Tests, 630
Tides, 325–326
Time, military, 141–142
Time zones, 289–291, 310–311
Tonnage, 661–664
Top secret classification, 558
Torpedoes, 305
Tourniquets, 480–481
Towing, 231–232, 256–262
Towing vessels, commercial, 693–695
Toxic materials, 531–532
Training, general, 629–637
Training centers, 631–632
Transportation, 645
Trash and garbage, 565
Travel allowance, 645–646
Treading water, 443
True bearings, 322
True course, 311
Tugs, 578–581
Tuition assistance, 641
Tunnel, surf waves, 454
Tunnes, 661

Unauthorized absence, 648
Underwater swimming, 449
Underway replenishment, 235–241
Undesirable discharge, 650
Uniform Code of Military Justice, 49–58
Uniform inspection, 45, 155–156
Uniform of the day, 128
Uniforms, 119, 135
Uninspected vessels, towing, 694
United States Coast Guard, history, 1–17
United States Inspected vessels, 668–701
United States Savings Bonds, 645
Utility boats, 247
Utility boats, forty-one ft., operation of, 262–266

Variation, compass, 318–321
Varnish, 545
Venereal disese, 69–70
Ventilation systems, 192
Ventilators, 541
Vessel lengths, 661
Vessel size measurements, 660
Vessel tonnages, 661–664
Veterans Administration Tuition Assistance, 600, 641
Vietnam, Coast Guard in, 13–14
Visitation and search, 355
Visitors aboard ship, 150–151
Visual aids to navigation, 345–350
Visual communications, 277–281
Volatile fuels, 533–534

War of 1812, 10
Warrant officers, insignia, 121
Watch, quarter and station bill, 39–40, 358–362
Watches, shipboard, 142, 151–152
Watch officers, 153
Water equipment for survival, 433–436
Water king, duties of, 163
Water systems, 192
Watertight integrity, 377–383
Waterways management, 24
Waves, breakers, 453
Weapons, use of, 306
Weekly inspections, 44
Whipping line, 202–3
Winches, 227
Windlasses, 226
Winds and currents, 327–328
Wire rope, 208, 220
Women in the Coast Guard, 72–74
Working aloft, 534
World War I and II, 11–13
Worming, 207

Yacht, 665, 698
Yeoman, duties of, 625

Zone time, 289–291